2nd Edition

Money, Banking and Monetary Policy

Thomas Bishop

MONEY, BANKING
AND MONETARY POLICY
2ND EDITION

ISBN 978-89-97394-60-9 (paperback)

Address 101, Migeun Bldg., 72-3, Migeun-dong, Seodaemun-gu, Seoul, Korea
Tel 82-2-362-4504
Fax 82-2-393-4509
Website www.jiphil.co.kr
ISBN 978-89-97394-60-9 (93320)

MONEY, BANKING
AND MONETARY POLICY
2ND EDITION

발 행 일 2013년 8월 31일
저 자 토마스 비숍
발 행 인 고현희
발 행 처 (주)지필미디어
주 소 서울시 서대문구 미근동 72-3호 미근빌딩 101호
전 화 (02) 362-4504
팩 스 (02) 393-4509
이 메 일 book@jiphil.co.kr
홈페이지 www.jiphil.co.kr
등록번호 제 312-1997-000043호 (1997년 7월 16일)
I S B N 978-89-97394-60-9 (93320)
가 격 33,000원

PREFACE

This textbook examines how money and non-monetary assets function in modern economies, and in particular describes how they evolved and continue to evolve. It next analyzes how markets for monetary and non-monetary assets function theoretically by constructing simple models that represent how interest, yield and return rates on non-monetary assets adjust as market behavior adjusts.

The textbook also covers topics that banks and bank managers are concerned with: traditional deposits and loans, innovative activities, management of financial risk, and regulation.

Finally, the textbook discusses topics that central banks are concerned with: their primary role as lenders of last resort, other roles, the creation of money and credit throughout the financial system, and goals that they try to achieve when trying to stabilize economic behavior.

The textbook was written for undergraduate university students and has problems and applications from the discussion in each chapter, as well as on-line exercises using data from the Bank of Korea, which can be compared to data from the US and other central banks.

CONTENTS

1	An Overview of the Financial System	1
2	Money and the Money Market	15
3	Interest, Yield, Return and Non-Monetary Assets	36
4	Model of the Market for Monetary Assets	58
5	Model of Markets for Non-Monetary Assets	91
6	The Traditional Role of Banks	124
7	Innovative Banking Activities	141
8	Payment Settlement Systems	165
9	Risk Management	200
10	Bank Regulation	236
11	Purpose and Role of Central Banks	262
12	Creation of Credit and Money	291
13	Goals and Targets of Monetary Policy	308
14	Exchange Rates and Foreign Exchange	334

1. An Overview of the Financial System

Preview

What purpose do financial markets and financial institutions serve for society? In this chapter I discuss the role of financial markets and financial institutions and how they make the economy function more efficiently. I also consider various kinds of financial assets and liabilities, financial markets, and financial institutions.

Financial markets and financial intermediaries

When economists talk about goods and services traded in a market, you may imagine cars being bought and sold at a car dealership, or computers being bought and sold at a computer store or hair-cutting services being offered and paid for at a hair salon. But perhaps you never thought of a loan as a good or service that is bought and sold. Yet a loan from a bank to its customer acts as a valuable good, a good that the bank customer is willing to pay for and one that bank is willing to create provided it is compensated. A loan is valuable for a borrower because it allows him to buy goods and services immediately rather than having to wait until he has saved sufficient funds. To pay for this service and to compensate the bank, the bank customer pays interest.

Goods such as loans or services such as loan servicing are bought and sold in financial markets. A **financial market** is a means by which buyers and sellers of financial goods or services make a transaction. A financial market may be a location where buyers and sellers of financial goods and services meet, a network of telephone or computers or another means of conducting a financial transaction.

Buyers and sellers of financial goods and services can directly conduct a financial transaction in a financial market, or use the assistance of another institution or individual, called a **financial intermediary**, to act between them and to coordinate their interests. A financial intermediary may be a bank that accepts funds from savers and lends them to borrowers, so that savers and borrowers do not need to make a direct transaction.

Why are financial markets and financial intermediaries necessary or useful for the economy? Financial markets and financial intermediaries allow savers and lenders to transfer funds to borrowers and spenders, as well as to allow parties to manage and to share risks.

The role of financial markets (direct finance)

Funds transferred through various contracts which we consider below—including loans, deposits, bonds, stocks and other financial contracts—can benefit parties by allowing intertemporal trade of resources between a saver and lender with a surplus of funds or other resources and a borrower and spender with a shortage of funds or other resources. Through voluntary transactions with full and accurate information, the lender/saver usually expects to receive the original amount of saving, called **principal**, and/or additional resources—commonly called *interest*, *yield* or *return*—in the future for lending a given amount of funds today. The borrower/spender is willing to pay this interest, yield or return for being able to spend the funds today.

As long as borrowers/spenders are willing and able to fully honor their promised commitments to repay and other kinds of risk are no larger than expected, then transactions in financial markets and through financial intermediaries can benefit both borrowers/spenders and lenders/savers, for reasons that are similar to why any voluntary transaction with full and accurate information can benefit two parties.

Specifically, many borrowers/spenders, in particular commercial firms, have productive/profitable uses for funds and are willing to borrow to finance investment in their productivity capacity so that they can earn a return on their investment. Furthermore, those who (expect to) increase their productivity/profitability the most should be willing to pay the highest interest, yield or return rate to the savers/lenders. Savers/lenders are compensated with interest, a yield or a return for waiting to spend their funds and for accepting the risk of lending. In this sense, voluntary transactions with full and accurate information in financial markets and through financial intermediaries allow funds to be allocated efficiently, thereby allowing the economy's productive capacity to grow more than it would otherwise. As productive capacity grows, production and income, and therefore economic welfare increase.

For example, when a local government needs funds to build a school, it may need to borrow funds if taxes are not sufficient to cover the costs of building a school. Some citizens may be eager to lend their saved funds as long as they can earn interest, a yield or a return. Both parties could be made better off: the government could quickly finance and build the school for the benefit of educating citizens; savers/lenders could earn interest, yield or return on the funds that they lend to the government. In addition, citizens could have a better school and education.

To the degree that institutions and individuals borrow and spend to finance consumption expenditure, instead of investment expenditure that expands productivity/profitability, such borrowing and spending can allow them to time their purchases better, rather than having to wait until they have sufficient funds to make a purchase. In other words, borrowing to finance current consumption can be sensible if it can make consumption expenditure more stable over time as long as income and revenue are expected to grow. For example, young people are able to buy what they need (say, an expensive education) when they need it through borrowing/spending, rather than having to wait to save enough to finance an expensive purchase. Voluntary transactions with full and accurate information to finance consumption expenditure can also make borrowers/spenders and savers/lenders better off. However, lenders and borrowers can become worse off if either has incomplete or inaccurate information about the willingness and ability to repay, which can occur if too much credit/debt is used to finance consumption expenditure or if the investment expenditure turns out to be less productive/profitable than originally anticipated.

In sum, when financial markets work well, they transfer funds efficiently from savers and lenders to borrowers and spenders, allowing the borrowers and spenders to engage in more investment (or productive) expenditure or more convenient consumption expenditure.

Secondly, financial markets also help institutions and individuals–that is, savers, lenders borrowers and spenders—to share and to reduce risks. Without financial markets, institutions and individuals would have to save all of the funds that they want to spend, being self-reliant, which would be risky if income and saving can decrease unexpectedly. But with financial markets, institutions and individuals can rely on others for sources of funds, effectively allowing others to share in the financing of operations and the risk of operations. In particular, when firms acquire funds from outside savers/lenders, these savers/lenders bear at least some the risk of the firm's operations. They are willing to bear this risk because of the potential to earn interest, yield or return.

In addition, well-functioning financial markets offer many, *diverse* kinds of funds (discussed below), so that borrowers and spenders do not need to rely on one source of funds, which could be risky. For example, because a firm has many sources of funds through diverse financial transactions, this diversity decreases the risk that the firm is unable to acquire funds from a single source. Likewise, savers and lenders do not need to rely on one kind of investment, which could also be risky for them if that investment performs poorly. The strategy of using many diverse kinds of assets and liabilities to avoid poor result that could result from using only a few is called **diversification**. In sum, financial markets reduce risk for borrowers, spenders, savers and lenders because they give them many alternative ways to borrow, spend, save and lend funds.

The role of financial intermediaries (indirect finance)

Financial intermediaries have special roles that can provide additional benefits for savers/lenders and borrowers/spenders, as well as for themselves. When direct finance in financial markets is too time-consuming, risky or otherwise costly; financial intermediaries can reduce the time, effort and cost of trading financial goods and services by specializing in financial transactions. The time, effort and other costs required to make a transaction are called **transaction costs**. Because transaction costs are lowered through financial intermediaries, economic welfare increases for savers/lenders and borrowers/spenders, many of whom would be unwilling or unable to conduct financial transactions directly.

Financial intermediaries try to make a profit by lowering transaction costs and by acting as an intermediary between savers, who transfer or "lend" their funds to the financial intermediary, and borrowers and spenders, who acquire their funds from the financial intermediary. We consider this strategy, called formally called *financial intermediation*, in more detail in chapter 6.

A special kind of transaction cost is called **asymmetric information**, a situation where one party has more information than another, or when full or accurate information is not available to one party but is available to another. For example, savers/lenders may have less information about the ability and the willingness of potential borrowers/spenders to repay a loan, and therefore may be unwilling to lend. A bank or other financial intermediary can study general market conditions and the financial conditions of a potential borrower/spender to acquire more and better information about the ability and willingness of the potential borrower/spender to repay a loan. Formally, this reduces asymmetric information and reduces the risk of making a transaction, thereby allowing the financial intermediary to decide more efficiently if the transaction should be made. We study asymmetric information in greater detail, and specific problems associated with it, in chapter 10.

In addition to the diverse assets traded in financial markets, financial intermediaries also create diverse assets and liabilities—like various loans and deposits—which allow them and their customers to manage the risk of saving/lending and borrowing/spending. For example, banks create various savings and time deposits for their customers and use the funds to invest loans. This is a part of financial intermediation, but having or creating many alternatives allows banks and their customers to manage risk.

Finally, financial intermediaries provide money or cash for their customers who want to spend it on goods and services. Nearly all institutions and individuals need to interact with financial intermediaries to some degree when they want to acquire money to spend on goods and services.

In sum, financial markets and financial intermediaries can contribute to higher investment expenditure on productive assets, to more stable consumption expenditure, to higher income for both savers/lenders and borrower/spenders and to higher production in the economy. Financial intermediaries can also increase economic welfare because they save time and other costs associated with making a transaction, in particular by reducing the costs of asymmetric information; they reduce or diversify the risk of saving/lending; and they provide liquid assets for those want to spend money.

In contrast, when financial markets and financial intermediaries do not function well or do not exist—as is the case in some countries or during some periods—economies are poorer and less efficient because saving, investment in productivity, profit, production, income and consumption expenditure are lower than otherwise, while the risk and costs of making transactions are higher than otherwise.

Figure 1-1 shows that use of one kind of financial market, the stock market, and use of the most popular financial intermediary, banks or depository institutions, is associated with national income earned per person. High income nations have more stock and more bank credit relative to total domestic production and income than middle income nations or poor nations.

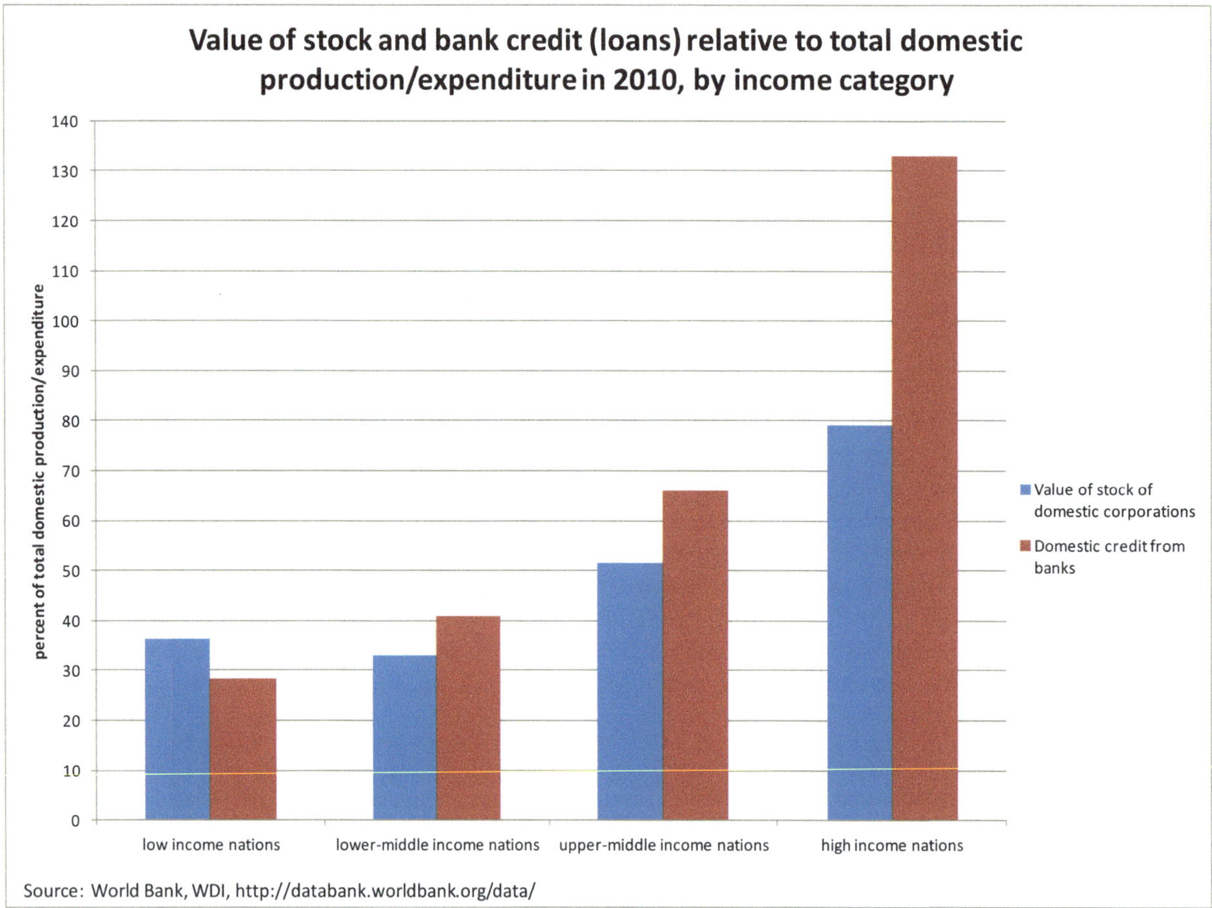

Figure 1-1: Use of financial (stock) markets and financial intermediaries (banks) is associated with the national income.

An introduction to monetary and non-monetary assets

Financial markets and financial intermediaries allow people to exchange monetary and non-monetary assets.

When funds are saved as a financial investment, say in deposits, bonds, loans (for the lender), stocks and so forth, they are called non-monetary assets or *illiquid assets*, which generally earn interest, a yield or a return. When non-monetary assets are bought and sold, they are *securities*, defined below.

When funds are spent on goods and services, they are called monetary assets or *liquid assets*. The common name for both monetary assets and liquid assets is *money* or *cash*. When money is bought and sold, it can be bought and sold *over time*, in which case we usually say that it is borrowed and lent and the price of this money is an interest rate. Money that is borrowed and lent is called **credit** or **leverage**; money that must be repaid after it has been borrowed and lent is called **debt**.

Thus in a financial transaction, borrowers and spenders acquire credit/debt or monetary assets/money to make a transaction; savers and lenders acquire non-monetary assets to earn interest, yield or return.

An introduction to assets and liabilities

After borrowers spend their funds, they are responsible for repaying a loan or another obligation in the future. Their obligation, usually in the form of a legal contract or certificate is called a liability. **Liabilities** are legal obligations to pay for debts, expenses, costs or other financial responsibilities.

After savers lend their funds, they are entitled to receive interest, a yield or a return for their investment. Their entitlement, usually in the form of a legal contract or certificate, is considered an asset. **Assets** are anything with value—because they can earn interest, a yield or a return or because they can be used for some productive purpose or can be consumed—that are legally owned by an individual or institution. Assets may be physical assets (ex., bauxite, computers, buildings) or financial assets (ex., deposits, loans, bonds, stocks).

To specify legal ownership of assets or to specify the legal obligation of liabilities, legal contracts are used to define property rights. Assets generally have legal contracts that give the owner property rights over the assets, and liabilities generally involve legal contracts that give counterparties a legal right to compensation.

Without legally specified property rights that are enforced, buying and selling in financial markets becomes difficult and risky because buyers and/or sellers become uncertain about whether a transaction can be conducted profitably. As a result, financial markets and financial intermediaries function poorly, and economic activity suffers as a result.

A **security** or **financial instrument** is a legal claim on the income from assets, the expenses from liabilities, or other financial commitments that can be traded in financial markets. A security is an asset for the owner of the security, but a liability or other financial commitment for the issuer of the security because it obligates or allows the issuer to compensate the owner.

When securities do not offer easy or quick payments for savers/lenders, they are considered non-monetary or illiquid assets; otherwise they are considered monetary or liquid assets.

A simple model of financial markets and financial intermediaries

Who saves and lends, and who borrows and spends in financial markets? Millions of individuals and institutions throughout the world can buy and sell securities. I classify the individuals and institutions that can save as households, private sector firms (including financial firms that provide financial goods and services and commercial firms that produce and sell goods and services more generally) and public sector institutions, or governments. In many economies, the largest sector of society that saves and lends to other sectors are households. In addition, nearly all financial markets interact at least somewhat with foreign individuals and institutions—foreign households, foreign private sector firms and foreign public sector institutions. Likewise, individuals and institutions that are willing to borrow and spend funds are classified as domestic or foreign households, private sector firms and public sector institutions. In most economies, for any single transaction, private sector firms are the largest borrower/spenders, although governments also borrow significant amounts from time to time.

Figure 1-2 represents how funds and securities can move directly from different kinds of savers/lenders to different kinds of spenders/borrowers. The funds in the form of monetary assets can move directly through financial markets through a direct transaction. With **direct finance**, funds or monetary assets are directly transferred from savers/lenders to borrowers/spenders, in conjunction with a security that is bought by the savers/lenders and borrowers/spenders. This security is an asset for the savers/lenders and a liability or other financial commitment for the borrowers/spenders. The savers/lenders are expected to receive funds in the form of principal and/or interest, a yield or a return in the future; the borrowers/spenders are expected to pay funds in the form of principal and/or interest, a yield or a return in the future. This security can be in the form of a legal contract like a loan, a bond, a stock or a deposit contract which gives the asset owner property rights over the asset and gives a counterparty a legal right to the funds at the present time as well as a legal obligation or other commitment to compensate the asset owner in the future.

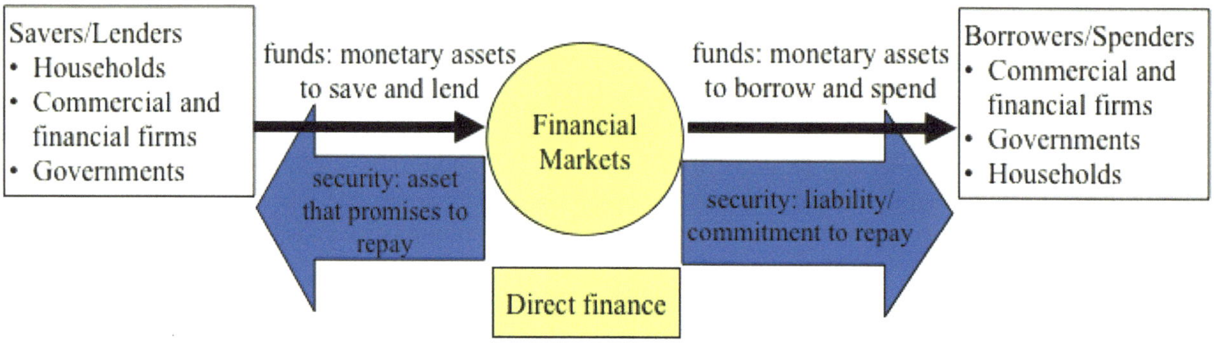

Figure 1-2: Flows of funds in direct finance

Frequently, however, financial transactions between savers/lenders and borrowers/spenders involves a financial intermediary, even if the savers/lenders or borrowers/spenders are financial firms themselves. In this case, the financial intermediary accepts funds from savers and then lends them to borrowers/spenders or invests them in non-monetary assets themselves, which are bought in financial markets.

Figure 1-3 represents how funds can move indirectly from savers/lenders to borrowers/spenders through a financial intermediary or how a financial intermediary can use its funds from its customers to buy non-monetary assets in financial markets. (We discuss types of financial intermediaries in a later section.) With **indirect finance**, spenders/borrowers acquire funds from a financial intermediary, which in turn acquires them from savers/lenders. In the process, the financial intermediary creates a security that acts as a non-monetary asset for the saver/lender and a liability or other commitment for itself. In conjunction or separately from this transaction, the financial intermediary also creates a security that acts as liability or other commitment for the borrower/spender and a non-monetary asset itself. Alternatively, the financial intermediary may buy a security created and sold by a borrower/spender in financial markets. This security again acts as a liability or other commitment for the borrower/spender and an asset for the saver/lender. For example, a bank may buy government bonds, created and sold by the government, with funds from deposits. The government is obligated to pay the bank in the future and the bank has an asset that will pay interest, a yield or a return in the future.

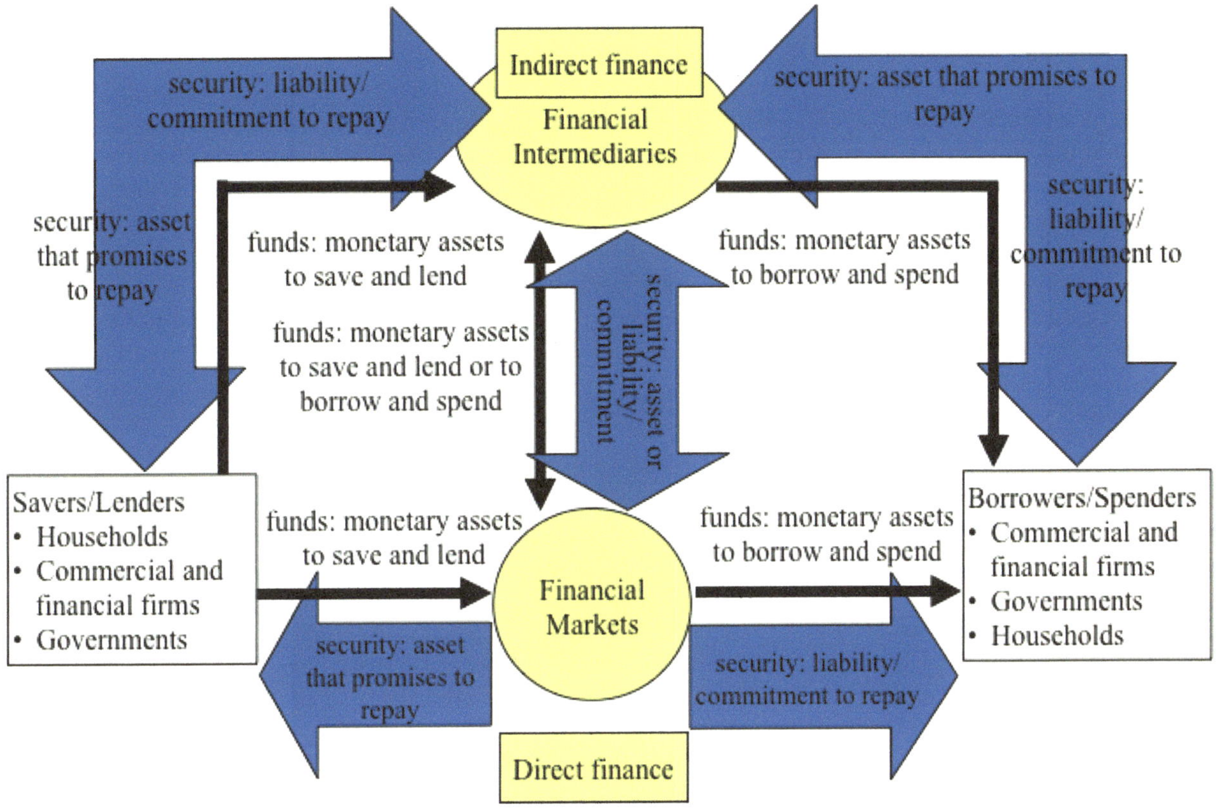

Figure 1-3: Flows of funds in indirect finance and direct finance

Types of assets, liabilities and capital

Saving/lending and borrowing/spending can through various kinds of securities considered to be assets or liabilities. In this section, I define various kinds of assets, liabilities and another kind of commitment called *capital.*

Stocks, equity or (ownership) shares are legal contracts that offer partial ownership and management control of a commercial or financial firm that issues them, called a **corporation**. These assets for the stock/equity/share holders may also make payments, called **dividend payments**, from the profits of the corporation on a regular or irregular basis, payments which are classified as part of the return on the stock, equity or shares.

Direct investment refers to acquiring a substantial amount of ownership and management of a corporation by using funds to acquire a substantial (ex., majority) amount of its shares of stock or productive/physical assets. When investors have little or no control of management and ownership by having relatively few shares of stock of corporation or by investing in loans, bonds or other assets discussed below, the investment is called **portfolio investment**.

Stocks, equity or shares are a way for corporations to acquire and spend funds, although strictly speaking firms do not borrow these funds and they are not obligated to pay any principal, interest, yield or return. Because stocks/equity/shares have no obligation to pay savers/lenders, this kind of investment is considered more risky for savers/lenders than various kinds of credit/debt, which we consider below, which does involve an obligation to pay. However, corporations have an implicit commitment to earn a return for stock holders, otherwise these savers/lenders would be unwilling to lend to the corporation, and sometimes the corporation will make an explicit commitment to pay dividends as long as the firm earns a profit. Because stocks/equity/shares have no obligation to pay, they are not classified as a liability for the corporation but as **capital** paid in by the partial owners (not to be confused with capital gains discussed below). Capital represents funds that are owned by the corporation itself, and therefore they do not need to be repaid to any other institution or individual. The funds may be redistributed among the owners in the form of dividend payments or may be reinvested in productive assets by the corporation's managers. In contrast, liabilities are funds that are owned by other institutions or individuals and therefore must be repaid to them according to various types of contracts between the corporation and these other institutions or individuals. In chapter 6, I show how to account for the value of capital from stocks/equity/shares and other sources, assets, and liabilities together.

In contrast to stocks, equity or shares, debt/credit in the form of **loans** or **bonds** or other contracts is an obligation for the borrower/spender to pay principal and interest, and therefore a liability, but offers no degree of management control and ownership for the saver/lender. Loans and bonds are generally considered safer assets than stocks, although safety depends on the borrower/spender. Loans to and bonds from established governments of wealthy nations are usually considered very safe assets, relative to loans to individuals and unestablished institutions and bonds from unestablished institutions. The ability (and willingness) to pay by these latter institutions and individuals is less certain than the ability (and willingness) to pay of established governments from wealthy countries, which have the ability to earn high tax revenues. Long-term loans and bonds for the borrower/spender are usually for investment expenditure to finance the purchase of productive assets or physical assets or to finance long-term liabilities. Short-term loans and bonds for the borrower/spender are usually for immediate payment purposes, especially if cash on hand or liquid deposits are temporarily unavailable.

Like loans and bonds, **deposits** offer principal and interest payments at the maturity date and/or at various times during the contract's term for the saver/lender; deposit contracts also obligate these payments and therefore are considered a liability for the borrower/spender. Long-term deposits are usually illiquid deposits, whose money is not readily available for the saver unless a fee for early withdraw is paid, and created for long-term investment purposes. Short-term deposits are usually monetary deposits maintained for payment purposes.

Derivative assets and liabilities are financial assets and liabilities whose value is derived from other assets or liabilities. Essentially all assets and liabilities, including stocks, bonds, loans and deposits, are derivative contract whose value is derived from the underlying profitability, productivity, willingness to pay or ability to pay of the institution that issued them. However, the value of derivative assets and liabilities are contractually linked to another asset or liability, called the *underlying asset or liability*, rather than just affected by unspecified market or profitability conditions. We consider specific kinds of derivative assets and liabilities and how they can be used to insure against changes in the value of the underlying asset in chapter 7.

Other assets and liabilities like **trade credits and debits**, are immediate adjustments in monetary deposits for future production or shipments of goods and services. Although trade credits are usually short-term credits and debits, they can be long term as well when they represent a credit (asset) or debit (liability) lasting at least one year.

Besides wanting to earn dividend, interest or other regular payments; owners of stocks, bonds, loan contracts, deposit contracts and other assets may hope to sell these assets at a higher price than the price at which they were purchased. Stocks, loan contracts, bonds, deposit contracts and other assets and liabilities may all be sold by their current owner/holder (exchanged for cash) before they completely pay all forms of income including the principal, or **mature**. (But stocks, equity or shares never mature unless the institution that issued them buys back.) The date at which assets mature is called the **maturity date**, and the time until assets mature is call the **time to maturity**.

Capital gains refer to the gain or profit from the difference between the selling price of an asset (or the value when it matures) and its buying price (or its value when it was created). Capital gains from an asset are considered part of the return on an asset, in addition to any regular payments, like interest payments or dividend payments, that are earned before the asset matures. Capital gains depend on the willingness to buy and the willingness to sell the asset, which in turn depend on (expectations about) the profitability, productivity, willingness to pay and/or ability to pay of the institution or individual that created the security linked to asset, as well as the need for (demand of) cash by the asset owner. When capital gains are negative, they are called *capital losses*.

Types of financial markets

In this section, I classify the markets in which the securities corresponding to assets, liabilities and capital are traded. I classify markets according to the time to maturity, the initial purchase versus secondary and later purchases, and who purchases or sells the securities.

We can divide stocks, loans, bonds, deposits, derivative assets and liabilities and other assets and liabilities into *long-term finance* and *short-term finance*, where the maturity date of assets and liabilities that separates long-term finance from short-term finance is usually set at 1 year. And because stocks never mature unless the corporation that issued them buys them back, stocks are considered long-term assets as well.

The market for short-term assets and liabilities is sometimes called the **money market**, which we consider in chapter 2, because the assets will quickly mature and pay money and liabilities quickly become due and require monetary payments. The market for long-term assets and liabilities is sometimes called the *capital market*, because paying in capital in the form of stocks, equity or shares is usually considered a long-term investment. However, long-term bonds and loans are also often lumped into markets that refer to the capital market. Furthermore, because the term "capital" gets over-used and abused in finance and economics—it is the term from which *capitalism* is derived—I will no longer use capital market in this text.

Because long-term finance allows a long period of time for prices and values of assets to change, the potential for capital gains/losses is large. On the other hand, short-term assets and liabilities usually have small changes in price/values and small capital gains/losses during the short period of time between when they are created and mature.

When most assets and liabilities in modern financial markets are first issued and sold, including those considered in direct finance, they are often bought by financial intermediaries with large amounts money or credit and with special financial arrangements with the institution that issues and sells them. The financial intermediaries are supposed to carefully study market conditions and profitability/productivity conditions of the institution that issues and sells the securities and then offer an initial purchase price that reflects these conditions. This initial offer to purchase the securities by the financial intermediary is called **underwriting**, a term that originally meant that a financial intermediary would write its seal/name under the contractual terms specifying the initial transaction.

The initial, or primary, purchase by the underwriter occurs in what is called the **primary market**. The underwriter may keep the asset or liability for itself, but often chooses to resell it for an expected capital gain in what is called the **secondary market** or **open market**, a market that is legally open to general savers/investors without special financial arrangements or large amounts of money and credit (even if a license is needed to complete a transaction). Stocks, loans, bonds, deposit contracts, derivative assets and liabilities and other assets and liabilities may be bought and sold repeatedly in the secondary or open market before the assets and liabilities mature.

This two-step process of underwriting and selling in the secondary market allows firms to quickly raise funds by going directly to those with large amounts of money or credit (that is, underwriters), rather than trying to sell them to any investor, whose access to money and credit, as well as knowledge about market and profitability conditions, may be limited. Underwriting is typically done by investment banks, which I consider in the next section.

Another way to define markets is when transactions conducted in the markets are completed. **Spot markets** are markets where securities are exchanged for cash immediately or as soon as payments can be settled. In spot markets, securities are simply transferred from the seller to the buyer in exchange for cash; likewise, the ownership of the securities is transferred from the seller to the buyer immediately or very soon.

In **futures markets**, ownership of assets, liabilities or capital happens in the future through a derivative contract/security, which specifies the price, date of exchange and the underlying asset or liability that will be exchanged for cash in the future. By allowing parties to specify these details of a future transaction today, futures markets allow the parties to transfer the risk of a changing (spot) market price for the underlying asset/liability from one party to another. But ownership of the underlying asset or liability is not transferred from the seller to the buyer until a future date or until the buyer requests it.

Types of financial intermediaries

The buying and selling of securities in various financial market usually involves the services of a financial intermediary. These financial intermediaries can be individuals working on behalf of themselves or working as part of a larger financial institution. I consider three types of individual financial intermediaries and several types of institutional financial intermediaries in this section.

Brokers are agents who match buyers of securities or other assets with sellers and who make a profit by charging a fee for this service. Brokers are helpful when asymmetric information exists: for example, when buyers who do not know the needs or characteristics of sellers or sellers who do not know the needs or characteristics of buyers. A common example of a broker is a housing broker.

Dealers are agents who buy and sell securities or other assets themselves, trying to make a profit by buying at a low price and selling at a high price. Dealers generally hold an inventory of the securities or other assets and sell from their inventories. A common example of a dealer is a car dealer.

Those who buy and sell assets (but may or may not have an inventory of assets) are called **traders**. Traders may buy and sell assets for themselves or for someone else (and therefore may act as an individual financial intermediary). Dealers are also traders, but not traders are dealers.

The most popular types of institutional financial intermediaries are **depository institutions**, or banks that create various kinds of deposits, including liquid deposits for payment purposes. With the funds from these deposits, these institutions typically invest in loans, bonds and other forms of debt/credit. (Depository institutions may or may not be allowed to invest in the stock, equity or shares of other institutions, depending on domestic regulations.) Because depository institutions provide financial goods and services to many individuals and small institutions, both savers/lenders and borrowers/spenders, they have special regulations. For example, depository institutions have **reserve requirements**—which require that at least some of the funds in the deposits are held on reserve at the depository institution or at the central bank—and almost always have **deposit insurance**, which insures the funds deposited by customers if the depository institution goes bankrupt. We will consider these regulations and others in detail in chapter 10.

Examples of depository institutions are 1) **commercial banks**, institutions that have traditionally accepted deposits and made loans to commercial firms, 2) **savings banks**, institutions that have traditionally accepted deposits from household savings and made loans to households or small firms, 3) **savings and loan associations**, institutions that have traditionally accepted deposits from household savings and made loans to individuals specifically to finance the purchase of a new house and 4) **credit unions**, non-profit institutions affiliated with a workplace or community that have traditionally accepted deposits from household savings and made loans to households or small firms. In addition, credit unions and some savings banks sell ownership shares to their depositors, thereby giving them partial ownership and management control of the institution.

There can be differences in how each of these depository institutions is regulated; however, many of these regulatory differences have been harmonized over time. Furthermore, the separate markets of each kind of depository institution have merged as regulatory differences have disappeared and as modern computers and telecommunications have allowed each to encroach on the markets of others.

A **bank holding company** is a company that owns or substantially controls one or more banks but does not accept deposits or make loans, but may perform many other services that banks normally provide. In the US, the Board of Governors of the Federal Reserve System regulates and supervises bank holding companies, even if the bank owned by the holding company is under the primary supervision of a different agency (like the Office of the Comptroller of the Currency or the Federal Deposit Insurance Corporation). A **financial holding company** is a bank holding company or other financial institution whose activities conform to the mandates of the Financial Services Modernization Act of 1999 (Gramm-Leach-Bliley Act). Financial holding companies may offer and underwrite insurance, deal and underwrite securities, offer financial and investment advice, engage in merchant banking, issue or sell securitized assets, and engage in other non-banking activities authorized by the Bank Holding Company Act of 1956. Like bank holding companies, financial holding companies are regulated by the Board of Governors of the Federal Reserve System. However, bank holding companies and financial holding companies are not authorized to own or substantially control commercial or other non-financial businesses.

Many other financial intermediaries have similar operations to depository institutions, commonly called "banks", although they are regulated differently. **Finance companies** do not formally accept deposits with deposit insurance and do not have reserve requirements, but acquire funds from savers/lenders by issuing and selling simple, short-term bonds, other forms of debt, or ownership shares. The funds that are acquired by these companies are usually lent to households or firms to finance the purchase cars, homes, office space, commercial real estate and other expensive items.

Mutual funds also do not formally accept deposits with deposit insurance and do not have reserve requirements but acquire funds from savers/lenders by creating deposits without deposit insurance or by selling ownership shares. The funds are then invested in bonds, deposits, stocks or other assets on behalf of the depositors/share holders, depending on the wishes of these savers/lenders. Often the depositors/share holders are given a choice of diverse kinds of bonds, deposits, stocks and other assets, allowing them to engage in diversification. *Money market mutual funds* are mutual funds that allow their depositors/share holders to invest in bonds, deposits and other assets in the money market, with the intention of earning a higher interest or yield than from liquid deposits at depository institutions.

Hedge funds are similar to mutual funds in the sense that they sell ownership shares to savers/lenders and do not formally accept deposits with deposit insurance. However, they are different in the sense that they usually require that each customer buy large amounts of shares or make large deposits, while mutual funds serve those with relatively modest amounts of saving. Secondly, unlike mutual funds, hedge funds often try to insure or *hedge* the risk of investing in assets by investing in another asset or liability, often a derivative asset or liability, whose value is supposed to change in the opposite direction. This strategy can limit losses if they occur, although it can limit gains as well.

Investment banks also do not formally accept deposits with deposit insurance and do not have reserve requirements, but may create other deposits and may sell ownership shares to savers/lenders. In addition, investment banks usually lend to large commercial firms or other financial intermediaries. Investment banks are like traditional commercial banks except they do not have deposit insurance, reserve requirements and other regulations that modern commercial banks face and their customers are usually large (commercial) institutions. Despite formal differences in regulation, there may be only a few practical differences between investment banks, hedge funds, and large commercial banks today, except investment banks are usually larger and better known than hedge funds—which often serve relatively few wealthy customers—and commercial banks—which usually serve many individuals and small firms as well.

Insurance companies insure their customers against various kinds of risk—like car accidents, medical accidents, theft, property damage from fire, earthquakes, floods and other acts of nature, property damage from negligent or abuse, et cetera—by accepting funds, or premiums, from their customers, which are used to pay for the costs of accidents and damage when they occur. In other words, insurance companies accept funds on a regular (ex., monthly or semi-annual) basis and pay for unforeseen events on an irregular basis. Although customers of insurance companies who pay premiums are normally not called savers/lenders, they can be treated as such. And although customers of insurance companies who receive payments for accidents or damage are not called borrowers/spenders, they can be treated as such. In addition, with a large number of customers, the damage and accidents from the unforeseen events, and hence payments, are usually fairly predictable. As a result, any additional funds from premiums that are not immediately spent can be invested in various assets. When the funds are needed to pay for damage and accidents, they must be sold, or *liquidated*.

Pension funds accept funds, or premiums, on a regular basis from workers, which are then accumulated for retirement pensions. Like insurance companies, the rate at which funds are accumulated and paid is usually fairly predictable, since workers usually pay a fixed amount each period and retire at a given age. Pension funds can be *fully funded* pensions, in which each person saves for his own retirement pension during his working lifetime, and then spends those accumulated funds when he eventually retires. Alternatively, pension funds can be *pay as you go* pensions, in which those currently working pay for those who are currently retired, and when those who are currently working eventually retire, a younger generation of workers will pay for them, and so on. With fully funded pensions and to a lesser degree with pay as you go pensions, a pension fund can accumulate saved funds on behalf of its customers and invest them in various assets. When the funds are needed to pay for retirement, they must be liquidated.

Other examples of simple financial institutions include *cashier check shops*, which issue cashier checks for a fee in exchange for cash; *check cashing shops*, which cash checks for a fee; *payday loan shops*, which provide short-term loans (until the next payday) for a fee; *pawn shops*, which convert normally illiquid items like televisions and jewelry into cash for a fee; *currency exchange shops*, which exchange currency for a fee; and *microcredit organizations*, which provide small loans to small communities for a fee.

Summary

This chapter introduces basic concepts related to finance. A financial market is a means by which buyers and sellers of financial goods or services, classified as either savers/lenders or borrowers/spenders, make a transaction. Transactions can occur directly between savers/lenders and borrowers/spenders or indirectly with the assistance of a financial intermediary, an individual or institution that assists the parties make the transactions. Savers/lenders benefit from financial transactions because they are able to earn income called interest, yield or return. Borrowers/spenders also benefit from these transactions, even though they must pay the interest, yield or return, because they can acquire funds to spend, either for their own investment expenditure on productive or financial assets or for consumption expenditures. Financial intermediaries can benefit savers/lenders and/or borrowers/spenders because they can reduce transaction costs, in particular the costs of asymmetric information, reduce or diversify the risk of saving, and provide liquid assets for spenders.

Types of financial assets, liabilities and capital, which are associated with a security, include stocks (or equity or shares), bonds, loans, deposits, derivative assets and liabilities, and trade credits and debits. Types of financial markets include those for short-term assets and liabilities, called the money market, and long-term assets and liabilities; primary markets, where underwriting occurs, and secondary markets, which are open to general savers/lenders; off-exchange markets, which have dealers, and exchange markers, which have brokers and traders. Types of financial intermediaries include brokers, and possibly traders, depository institutions, finance companies, mutual funds, hedge funds, investment banks, insurance companies and pension funds.

Problems and Applications

Short answer problems

1. What distinguishes depository institutions from other kinds of financial intermediaries?

2. What distinguishes mutual funds from hedge funds?

3. What are 4 benefits or services that financial intermediaries provide?

4. How does stock, equity or shares differ from bonds and loans?

5. How do liabilities differ from capital?

6. How do dealers differ from brokers?

7. What are names for the income that savers/lenders earn and borrowers/spenders pay?

8. How do derivative assets and liabilities differ from "regular" assets and liabilities?

9. How do investment banks formally differ from commercial banks?

10. Describe the traditional difference among the 4 kinds of depository institutions.

11. What are two regulations that depository institutions face but other financial intermediaries do not?

12. What is the common name for the market where short-term assets and liabilities are traded? What is the name for the market where derivative assets and liabilities are traded? What is the name for the market where underwriting occurs?

13. How do spot markets differ from futures markets?

14. How does the primary market differ from the secondary market?

15. Can a saver earn capital gains on a bond? If so, how?

16. When is the ownership of assets, liabilities or capital transferred in spot markets? When is the ownership of assets, liabilities or capital transferred in futures markets? What occurs at the present time for transactions in futures markets?

17. Who could be classified as savers/lenders and borrowers/spenders for insurance companies and for pension funds?

18. Distinguish between pay-as-you-go pensions and fully funded pensions. If the government begins a pension plan for its citizens, in which case should national saving rise more, and why? Alternatively, if the government begins a pension plan for its citizens, in which case should consumption expenditure be higher, and why?

Internet applications

1. Go to http://databank.worldbank.org/data/ to find data on GDP per capita (constant 2000 US$), domestic credit provided by banking sector (% of GDP) and market capitalization of listed companies (% of GDP) for your country for all available years. Make a graph of this data with the GDP per capita data on one axis and the two other variables on a second axis. Do you see a positive correlation between GDP per capita on one hand and the financial variables on the other hand?

2. Money and the Money Market

Preview

In this chapter, you will learn a precise definition of money that economists use. You may find that this definition differs from your everyday conception of money, and you may be surprised to find that money is not the same as wealth or income. This chapter will also describe three functions that money serves in an economy, as well as different assets that have functioned as money throughout history. We will also learn about the concept of liquidity, a characteristic of money. Finally, we will discover that various assets can function as money in today's economy and learn why the aggregate amount of these assets has been adjusted by monetary policy makers to affect economic production.

Definition of money

Money is any asset that is generally accepted to pay for goods and services or to repay debt. In other words, money is an asset used to conduct a transaction. A common name for money is *cash*. Various assets can be considered as money or cash and can be used to conduct a transaction. For example, paper bills, the funds in a checking deposit, the funds available through a debit card may all be used to buy goods and services or to repay debt.

Note that this definition of money may differ from your everyday conception of money. When people say that someone "has a lot of money", they usually mean he has a lot of wealth. **Wealth** is a stock of assets, only some of which may be used to conduct a transaction. For example, the value of someone's home is included in his stock of wealth but not in the amount of money that he has, since a home generally can not be used to pay for goods and services or to repay debt. When people say that someone "earns a lot of money", they usually mean that he earns a high income. **Income** or **revenue** represents the amount of earnings in a given time period, some of which may be in the form of money. In other words, income or revenue is something that people *earn*, by providing a valuable good or service or by investing in assets wisely, or is *transferred* from one party to another as a gift or entitlement. **Return** represents income or revenue that an asset (instead of an individual or firm) will earn in a given time period, in the form of interest, a yield, dividends, capital gains or another form of earnings. Return is usually expressed as a annualized rate or percent to make it convenient to compare the earnings of various assets. Income or revenue could be in the form of money for the recipient, or not. For example, paychecks provided to individuals and institutions for providing a valuable good or service usually need to be processed by a bank before they can be spent on goods and services or used to repay debt, so strictly speaking paychecks are not money until they have been "cashed" or processed. Finally, money is not necessarily the same as currency, although currency is usually an asset included in the definition of money. **Currency** refers to the amount of paper bills (also formally called notes) and coins circulating in the economy, but other assets may also be defined as money.

The relationship between wealth, money and currency may be represented as Figure 2-1.

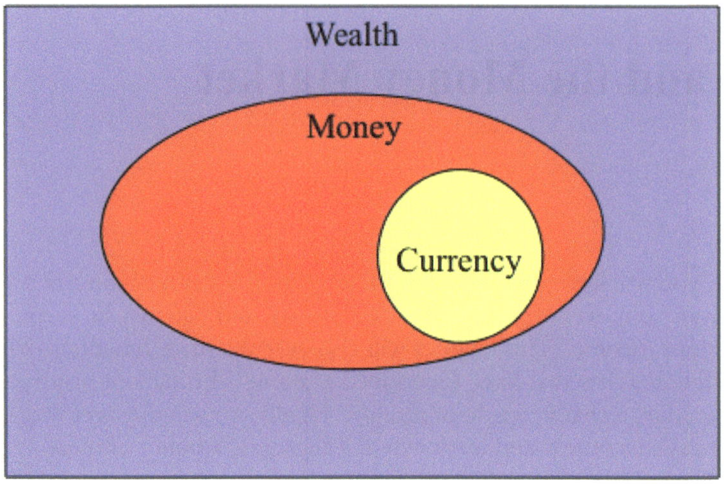

Figure 2-1: How money is related to wealth and currency

Wealth, money and currency are each a measure of a stock of assets, with a value that is measured at a point in time. In contrast, income and revenue (including a return) represents a flow of earnings over a period of time. A person may earn an income or revenue during a week, month or year. Figure 2-2 represents money (or more broadly, wealth, or more narrowly, currency) measured at a point in time and income or revenue earned over a period of time.

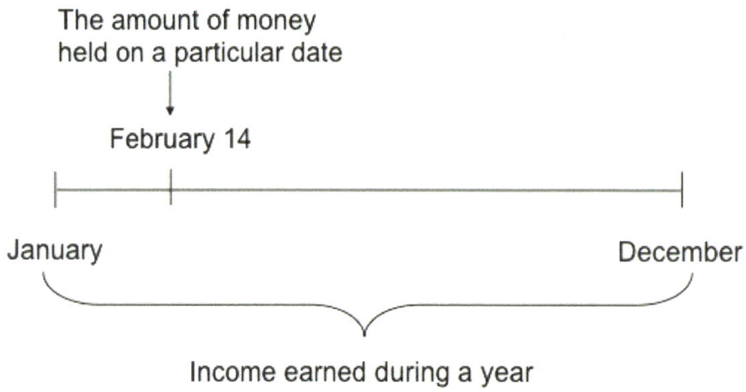

Figure 2-2: The timing of income or revenue and monetary measurements

Functions of money

For an asset to be used as money, it must do three things. As the definition of money indicates, money must first be something that is generally exchanged for goods and services and generally used for the repayment of debt. In other words, money must act as a **medium of exchange** or a **means of payment**.

Why is it useful to have money function as a medium of exchange? Money in paper, electronic or another form reduces transaction costs; it allows us to exchange the money for the goods and services that we desire easily. Imagine if an economy did not have money, as in some points in history or in some remote regions that are disconnected from larger economies. Suppose a butcher in this imaginary economy needed to buy new shoes. Not only would the butcher have to find a shoemaker, but he would also have to find one that would want something that the butcher could provide, say cuts of lamb. This situation of needing to find a counterparty to satisfy a person's wants and needs, and for this person to satisfy the counterparty's wants is called the **double coincidence of wants.**

Transactions between people could occur in an economy without money, but they would be very cumbersome and costly. Trading one good or service for another, without the use of money, is called **barter.** With barter, people need to spend time and other resources to search for others to trade with—a waste of resources. To use our previous example, suppose that the butcher searches for several days and finds a shoemaker that would like cuts of lamb, but only lamb chops. If the butcher wanted to conduct a transaction with the finicky shoemaker, the butcher might have to throw out some of his cuts of meat if they are undesirable. The lost time and any lost meat would be costs for the butcher when conducting the transaction with the shoemaker. Economists call the time, effort and other costs required to buy or sell **transaction costs.**

A medium of exchange reduces transaction costs between a buyer and seller by providing a readily acceptable means of payment for goods and services. If a butcher wants to buy shoes, he need not search for a carnivorous shoemaker and need not transact with one who only wants lamb chops. Instead, a butcher only needs to find a shoemaker and pay for the shoes using money. The shoemaker can then buy lamb, pork, fish, lentils, chickpeas or any good or service that he desires. In an economy with money, transactions are conducted more efficiently, transaction costs are reduced, and people no longer face the double coincidence of wants.

A second function of money is that it acts as a **store of value**, something that maintains value or purchasing power over time. Because money stores or maintains value, people are willing to save it for the future sometimes rather than spend it as a medium of exchange today. Lamb chops would not be a good store of value because without a very good freezer, they would not maintain their value over time. And during some periods of history, currency has substantially lost its value as the prices of goods and services rapidly increased. During these periods, the purchasing power of currency decreased rapidly, and currency no longer served as a good store of value. As a result, people desired to hold other assets that maintained value or purchasing power, and buyers and sellers often relied on other assets to conduct transactions.

In chapter 1, we learned that an asset is property that has value, so that assets in general are considered to be stores of value. Since money is one type of asset, it is therefore considered a store of value.

To describe the third function of money, imagine again how an economy would function without it. The prices or value of goods and services would have to be quoted in terms of other goods and services if money did not exist. For example, the price of a pair of shoes could be 5 lamb chops. Or, the price of an apple could be quoted as 2 oranges, 1/2 grapefruit, 30 grapes, 1/4 pineapple, and so on. If consumers wanted to buy an apple in an economy with no money, they would have to think about countless different prices, quoted in terms of countless other goods and services. Moreover, comparisons of the value of goods and services would be difficult without money. An apple could be worth 2 oranges, which could be worth 1/2 of a lamb chop, which could be worth 1/3 of a pork chop. But with many goods and services in an economy, it would soon become burdensome to determine the value of each good or service relative to the value of others.

Money eliminates the need to quote prices of goods and services in terms of other goods and services. It greatly simplifies transactions and comparisons of value because only a single price unit exists for all goods and services. Money functions as a **unit of value** or a **unit of account**; it is the unit to measure prices or to account for the value of all goods and services. For example, when people in today's economies ask how much apples or all other goods cost or what they are worth, the answer is stated in units of money: dollars in the US, yen in Japan, euros in Germany, won in Korea, and so forth.

What is credit?

Credit refers to funds that are borrowed and can be spent today but must be repaid in the future plus interest—with money. Like money, credit can also be paper or electronic, but it is increasingly electronic in today's world. A means to use electronic credit for many people is a *credit card*: the bank extends credit to its customer, who repays the debt in the future. A means to use electronic money for many people is a *debit card*: it debits money from a monetary deposit.

Because credit refers to the ability to spend today, it is also sometimes called **leverage** in finance or accounting to refer to this ability or power. Credit is also called **debt**, which refers to the obligation to repay.

To review, money refers to an *asset* that can be spent today or saved for the future. Credit, leverage and debt refer to funds that can be spent today but are a *liability* that must be repaid in the future.

What is liquidity and illiquidity?

Liquidity refers to the ease in which money or credit can be acquired to pay for goods and services or debt. Alternatively, the condition of having access to money or credit (to pay for goods and services or debt) is called *liquidity*; and the condition of not having access to money or credit is called *illiquidity*. The term "liquid" refers to the gold, silver or copper which were often melted into coins in the past, which we will consider in the next section.

Money is a liquid asset because it can easily be used to pay for goods and services or debt—that is, without substantial transaction costs. Non-monetary assets are more or less liquid depending on the time and other transaction costs necessary to convert them to money. But relative to money, non-monetary assets are *illiquid* assets because they require more time or other transaction costs to pay for goods and services or debt than money itself.

Examples of liquid assets are the monetary assets that we mentioned previously: currency, checking deposits and debit card deposits. Most vendors readily accept (links to) one or more of these assets: paper bills and coins, paper checks and plastic debit cards. In contrast, a house is an example of an illiquid asset. To acquire funds from a house to pay for something, a house must be sold, a process which involves a substantial amount of time, effort, fees and perhaps even discounts.

Individuals and institutions decide how much of their wealth they want to hold as liquid assets often by comparing benefits and costs. Although monetary assets or liquid assets are convenient to pay for things, it is costly to hold them because they earn little or no interest, yield or return. On the other hand, non-monetary assets or illiquid assets are usually able to earn a high interest, yield or return rate, even though they are inconvenient for conducting transactions. However, sometimes illiquid assets earn a *negative* return rate so liquid assets are considered safer than illiquid assets. So monetary assets or liquid assets are primarily used for transaction purposes and for safety, while non-monetary assets or illiquid assets are used for investment purposes.

Economists often simplify their analysis of how people decide to allocate their wealth among different assets by separating assets into only two categories: liquid assets and illiquid assets. But the liquidity of assets is really a matter of degree. A greater degree of liquidity represents an easier and less costly means to pay for goods and services or debt. Figure 2-3 shows that various assets can be classified according to their liquidity, with more liquid assets near the center of the figure. But because there is no clear boundary between "liquid" and "illiquid" assets, the figure uses dashed lines to represent indeterminate boundaries between different types of assets and places some assets on both sides of a particular boundary. Liquid assets like currency, checking deposits and debit card deposits almost always require very little time, effort, fees or discounting when their owners want to pay for goods and services or debt. Some deposits are fairly liquid but can not be immediately used to make a transaction. Likewise, very short-term bonds and short-term trades of bonds for money, called *repurchase agreements*, allow individuals and institutions to have quick but not immediate access to money. We will consider fairly liquid assets that individuals and institutions use as substitutes for money, called *M2* and *money market assets*, below. Less liquid assets include long-term bonds, real estate, deposits set aside for retirement, art and even used goods, which usually require a substantial amount of time, effort, fees or discounting when their owners want to sell them to acquire funds to pay for goods and services or debt.

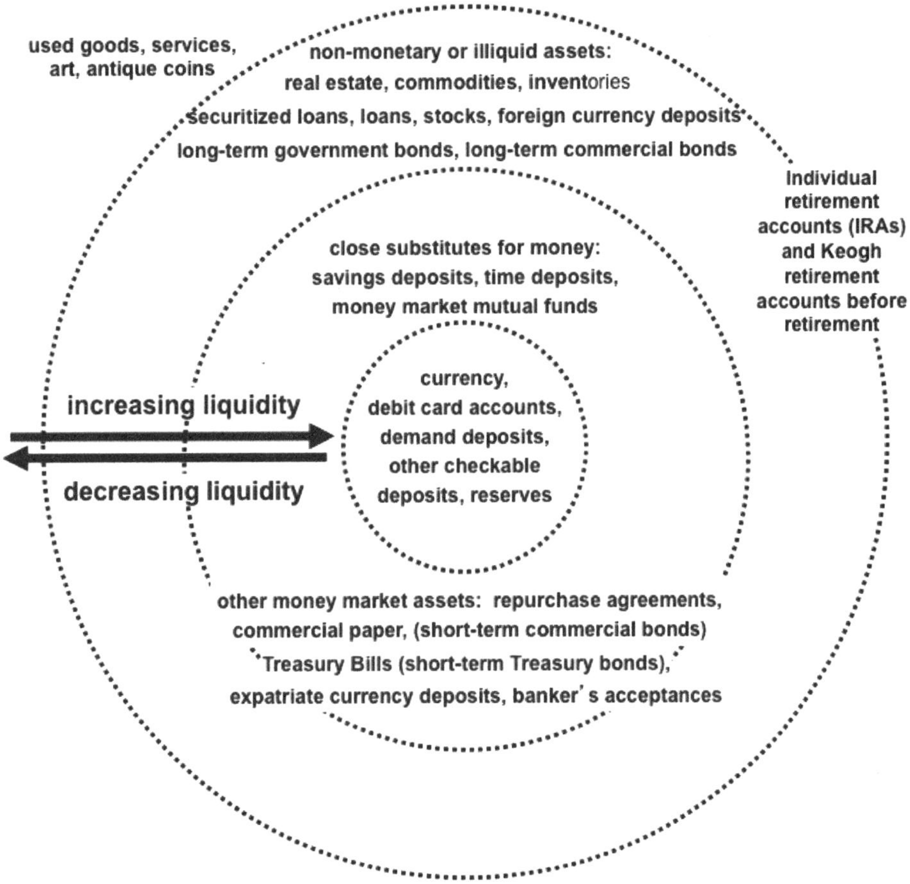

Figure 2-3: The degree of liquidity varies among assets

Types of money today and in the past

Almost all societies today use some form of money, but this was not always the case. Before money existed, **barter**—trading one good or service for another—was how people got the goods and services that they wanted. The simple case using lamb chops and shoes described earlier is an example of barter. Barter still exists today for informal transactions, but it is not the primary means to conduct transactions in today's economies.

Commodity money. As described in Box 1, various commodities such as livestock, grains, cocoa beans, copper, bronze, silver or gold have been used in history to serve as money. Commodities that act as money are called **commodity money**.

Box 1: Brother, can you spare a cowrie shell? A brief history of money

The use of money has a long history. After the beginning of agriculture, from about 9000-6000 BC, human societies began to use domesticated livestock and quantities of grain as money.[1] Livestock and grains acted as mediums of exchange, units of account and stores of value (for as long as the livestock remained alive and grains did not spoil). Cattle, sheep, camels, wheat and other crops were used as money to avoid the transaction costs and double coincidence of wants that barter involves.

Humans have also used shells, metals and ornaments as money. In about 2500 BC, silver, gold and copper pieces weighed to standard amounts were used in Egypt as money.[2] At about the same time, standard weights of silver were used in Mesopotamia for transactions.[3] In about 1200 BC, cowrie shells, the shells of a mollusk in the Pacific and Indian Oceans, were used in China.[4] At about 700 BC, metal coins with impressions or seals were used in Lydia, a region of Western Turkey.[5] Lydia's idea of coining metals spread to Persia, Greece, Macedonia and other nearby regions. Copper, bronze, silver and gold were all used to make coins.

In about 600 BC, replicas of small bronze knives and spades were used in China, and bronze coins and bronze ornaments in the shape of cowrie shells were used a century later.[6] Some Chinese coins had holes in them so that they could be linked as a chain. Square pieces of decorated leather made from deer skin were also used in China in 118 BC.[7]

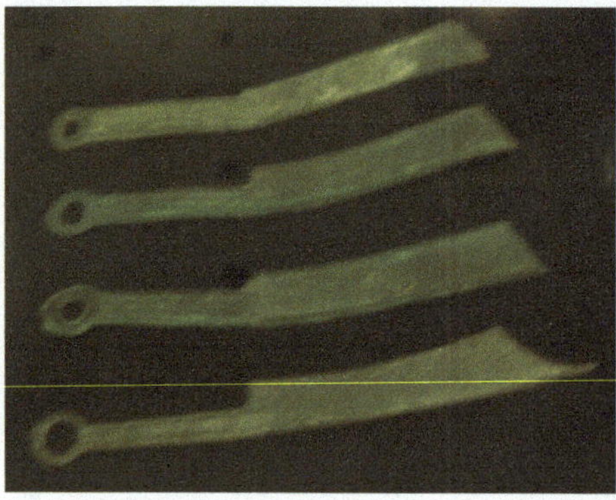

[1] NOVA, Public Broadcasting System: http://ww.pbs.org/wgbh/nova/moolah/history.html

[2] Federal Reserve Bank of Minneapolis: http://minneapolisfed.org/econed/curric/history.cfm

[3] Jonathan Williams, editor, Money: A History, St. Martin's Press, 1997, chapter 1.

[4] Ibid., chapter 6.

[5] Federal Reserve Bank of Minneapolis: http://minneapolisfed.org/econed/curric/history.cfm

[6] Jonathan Williams, editor, Money: A History, St. Martin's Press, 1997, chapter 6.

[7] NOVA, Public Broadcasting System: http://ww.pbs.org/wgbh/nova/moolah/history.html

Figure 2-4: Chinese money in the form of small knives and with square holes, the latter from AD 990-994

And in 806 AD, paper notes imprinted with the seals of the emperor—which could be exchanged for bronze, iron and other types of coins—were first issued in China.[8] With paper notes, people could conduct transactions without transporting heavy and low-value iron coins, and paper notes were useful to conduct inter-regional trade because some regions banned the export of bronze.[9] But as the quantity of paper notes in circulation increased, their value fell and prices of goods and services denominated in paper money rose. Contributing to this problem, many regional governments and local banks were free to issue their own notes and coins until the twentieth century.

Before 1500, the Mayans started to use cocoa beans, fabric and precious stones as money.[10] Although perishable and therefore not a good store of value, cocoa beans were small and divisible. Historical records show that 10 beans were traded for a rabbit and 100 beans were traded for a slave.[11] The Aztecs also used cocoa beans as money and were doing so when the Spaniards arrived in Mexico in the early 1500s.

Paper money began to be used in Sweden after 1661, when a bank in Stockholm issued paper notes backed by the value of large copper plates, created because of the stable value of copper relative to the increasingly abundant silver and gold imported from the Americas. The copper plates were deposited at the bank and not used directly in transactions because they were too large and heavy.[12]

Accounts accessed through checks also acted as money. In fact, the use of checks started in the late 1200s in Italy, preceding the use of paper currency in Europe.[13] Early checks were written instructions to transfer funds from the account of the note writer to the note bearer. Historically, accounts were denominated in units of commodities such as grains, silver or gold. For the wealthy, these accounts were maintained at banks, which could specialize in securing and accounting for the wealth. Instead of going to banks to complete a transaction, bank patrons wrote notes instructing their banks to give a specified amount to the person carrying the note. The authenticity of the note was supposedly provided by a signature or a seal of the bank patron.

By the 1700s, this note-writing system had been used in several countries in Europe. But because counterfeiting of the written notes was a problem, English banks in the 1700s began to issue standardized notes with serial numbers to track or "check" their authenticity.[14]

Representative money and a commodity standard. Many economies used commodity money in the form of gold, silver, or copper, but transporting these metals and verifying their purity was time consuming and costly. As a result, governments and private banks, which acted as authorities or specialists for weighing and verifying the purity of precious metals, began to issue paper or tokens to represent their value. Because people believed that the paper and tokens could be redeemed for precious metal, they accepted them when conducting a transaction. Thus, a new form of money evolved, called representative money. **Representative money** is money in the form of paper or tokens with the promise that they can be readily exchanged for gold, silver, copper or other commodities that are intrinsically valuable. (Gold, silver and copper can be used to

[8] Ibid.: http://ww.pbs.org/wgbh/nova/moolah/history.html

[9] Jonathan Williams, editor, Money: A History, St. Martin's Press, 1997, chapter 6.

[10] Piedad Peniche Rivero, UNESCO: http://findarticles.com/p/articles/mi_m1310/is_1990_Jan/ai_8560999

[11] Oveido y Valdes F. Historia General y Natural de las Indias, 1535, quoted in Erowid E, Erowid F. "The Origins of Chocolate." Erowid Extracts. Nov 2004; 7:4-8.

[12] The American Numismatic Society and the Federal Reserve Bank of New York: http://www.amnumsoc.org/exhibits/DrachmasDoubloonsDollars/

[13] Jonathan Williams, editor, Money: A History, St. Martin's Press, 1997, chapter 7.

[14] Pearson Education, Inc.: http://www.infoplease.com/ipa/A0001522.html

produce many valuable goods, although their "intrinsic" value may be questionable when they are used as representations of social status.)

A monetary system that uses representative money is called a **commodity standard**, since money represents standardized amounts of a commodity whose purity can be verified by an accepted authority. Two examples of a commodity standard system are a gold standard and silver standard, both of which existed during various periods in the 19th and 20th centuries in several countries. Figure 2-5 shows one form of representative money from the US that could be redeemed for a certain amount of silver during the 19th century.

Figure 2-5: An example of representative money: a silver certificate issued in 1886 that could be redeemed for $5 worth of silver

A monetary system that uses commodity money has prices of goods and services that are quoted in terms of the commodity itself. For example, the price of shoes under a monetary system that uses gold as commodity money would be expressed in terms of a certain amount of gold. In other words, gold would be the unit of account (as well as a medium of exchange and a store of value). In contrast, a monetary system that uses a commodity standard has prices quoted in terms of the representative money. For example, the price of shoes under a gold standard would be expressed in terms of dollars or another currency that represents a standard amount of gold. Dollars or another currency, not gold, would be the unit of account (as well as a medium of exchange and a store of value).

Under a commodity standard, the quantity of gold, silver or other precious metals that was reserved for the exchange of representative money was called *bullion*. Bullion and precious metal coins in circulation acted as the *monetary base*, the most basic form of money from which other forms of money were derived. The monetary base under a commodity standard allowed other forms of money—representative money—to be issued, and a larger monetary base allowed more representative money to be issued. In today's economies, the monetary base is composed of currency in circulation and accounts denominated in currency, called *reserves*, that are owned by banks. As we study in chapter 12, today's monetary base allows other forms of money, such as checking deposits, to be issued by banks.

Fiat money. Most economies today no longer use commodity money or representative money. They use instead **fiat money**, money in the form of tokens or paper without a promise by banks or governments to exchange the money for a valuable commodity. The value of currency today is backed only by the legal decree, or fiat, of central banks and the confidence that others in society will value it.

All US currency in circulation today is fiat money. The US Treasury stopped redeeming the value of silver certificates in silver coins in 1963 and in silver bullion in 1968. (For domestic citizens, the US Treasury had stopped redeeming the value of gold certificates in gold coins and gold bullion in 1934. For foreign citizens, the Federal Reserve System had stopped redeeming the value of US dollars in gold bullion in 1968.)

By 1970, silver coins were no longer minted, and old silver coins were gradually removed from circulation and replaced with coins made of a copper-nickel alloy.[15] These new coins have only a token value. Traditionally made of mostly copper, US pennies since 1982 have been made almost entirely of zinc, a less valuable commodity than copper.[16]

Fiat money in other countries includes polymer currency, or "plastic" currency, which is circulated in Australia, New Zealand and Romania. Polymer currency is about twice as expensive to print as paper currency, but it lasts about four times as long. Even so, polymer currency still has only a token value.

Although fiat money circulates in the US today, this was not always the case. In the 19th century, private banks in the US legally issued their own forms of representative money, which were called "bank notes". In fact, there were several types of bank notes and US currencies in circulation in the 19th century, and the West Coast used primarily a gold standard or gold commodity money while the East Coast relied mostly on bank notes. The US government issued fiat money called "greenbacks" to finance the Civil War and "continentals" to finance the Revolutionary War. Only one type of US currency circulates today, and it is issued under the authority of the Federal Reserve System, the central bank of the US. Bills or "notes" that you carry have printed on them "Federal Reserve Note".

Nonetheless, private banks continue to issue money today in the form of **checkable deposits**—deposits accessed through paper checks—and electronic deposits. The value of these deposits is measured in currency and can be exchanged one for one with currency. We now study how these deposits are used as money.

Checkable deposits. Checkable deposits include traditional checking deposits and other deposits that work like checking deposits. They may be accessed with paper checks, which are formal, written instructions to transfer money from the checkable deposit to another account. Because checks are generally accepted to pay for goods and services or to repay debt, the value in checkable deposits is usually included as a monetary asset.

As with money in general and representative money in particular, the development of the checkable deposits has increased economic efficiency by reducing transaction costs. For large purchases, it is not necessary to carry large amounts of currency or commodity money. (See Box 1 for a description of the historical development of checks.) By using checks, people and their banks can also avoid the time, effort and cost of moving large amounts of currency or commodity money from one account to another when a transaction is made between customers of different banks.

(Paper) fiat currency and checks are somewhat different, but on closer inspection can seem similar as well. Fiat currency is issued only by the central bank of a country, whereas checks are issued by (many) private banks in a country. However, electronic money (and credit) may be issued by both the central bank and private banks by creating electronic accounts that accept or receive payments. We discuss the creation of credit and money in chapter 12, and discuss electronic money in the next section. And counterfeiting of currency and checks, both in paper and electronic form, can sometimes be problems. Paper currency may be more liquid than paper checks, because nearly everyone accepts paper currency but not everyone might accept a paper check. However, in an increasingly electronic and online world, electronic checking deposits and transfers might be more readily acceptable than paper money. And of course, the denomination of paper check can be any amount, whereas paper currency has pre-determined amounts. An important difference

---

[15] The Federal Reserve Bank of Minneapolis: http://minneapolisfed.org/econed/curric/history.cfm

[16] US Mint: http://www.usmint.gov/about_the_mint/fun_facts/index.cfm?action=fun_facts2

between paper currency and checks and electronic checking deposits today is that the use of paper currency is generally anonymous for a third party, where as the processing of checks/checking deposits might not be.

Processing of paper checks still involves some transaction costs, and to reduce the time to process checks and the costs of physically moving paper checks from one bank to another, banks and many vendors now process checks electronically through a system called the *automated clearing house* (ACH). Under this system, a paper check can be digitally scanned and sent to the proper financial institutions via the routing number and account number listed on the check. This scanning may be done by banks themselves or by vendors when a transaction is conducted. The time to process checks is reduced substantially; paper checks do not even need to be shipped to different financial intermediaries in many cases. And the time and shipping costs for processing paper checks can be substantial, since the number of checks processed in the US was almost 50 billion in 2000.[17] The ACH system also includes the electronic processing, or "direct deposit", of payroll or government benefit checks. Many payroll and government benefit checks are processed electronically to reduce transaction costs.

In addition, the ACH system allows immediate crediting and debiting, which allow a buyer and a seller to more easily trust each other when making a transaction. Without ACH, a paper check may need a few days to be fully processed, during which a seller is not completely certain about a buyer's ability or willingness to pay. This lack of trust or lack of information about the willingness or ability of parties to conduct a transaction is another form of transaction cost, since people have to wait or spend resources to acquire information. As a result, a seller may be unwilling to conduct a transaction by check or may charge a fee to the buyer if the buyer does not have sufficient funds. With ACH, a seller can immediately determine the ability of the buyer to pay, and therefore is more willing to conduct a transaction via check. Buyers and sellers can both benefit from increased information that ACH can provide since a transaction can be more easily conducted.

The ACH system is an example of a more general system called the *electronic transfers of funds*, which the banking sector increasingly uses to settle payments as computer technology and telecommunications becomes more advanced and more widespread. Individuals and institutions increasingly rely on electronic instructions to transfer funds from one account to another when they want to conduct a transaction. For example, payments can be settled via the Internet, rather than writing a check and sending the piece of paper via mail. On-line banking also allows bank customers to transfer funds between accounts. Finally, automated teller machines (ATMs) allow electronic withdrawals, deposits and transfers from accounts. As with ACH, the purpose of electronic transfers of funds is to reduce the time and cost needed to conduct transactions.

Electronic money. Electronic transfers of funds include a wide variety of activities, and it is involved in a new definition of money called electronic money. **Electronic money** is a deposit of funds that is accessed electronically through a computer, a card or other device to pay for goods and services or debt. For example, you can use a personal computer to create an electronic deposit, such as a PayPal account, to purchase goods via the Internet. In addition to computers connected to the Internet, several types of cards that can access a liquid deposit electronically, including debit cards and smart cards, are also classified as electronic money. Box 2 describes these cards in detail. Technology even exists for consumers to make purchases through mobile phones embedded with a computer chip.

Credit cards accounts, however, are not classified as electronic money, even though many people use credit cards to conduct transactions electronically. Use of a credit card is classified as a (short-term) loan, and credit cards are not linked to a deposit of funds that the user owns. During a transaction involving a credit

[17] Chicago district Federal Reserve Bank: http://www.chicagofed.org/publications/economicperspectives/2002/3qepart3.pdf

card, the credit card issuer (a financial intermediary) pays for the good or service until the credit card user pays for the debt with money from another account, such as a checking deposit. Nonetheless, the practice of extending credit through credit cards and other means affects the amount of money that circulates in an economy, as we will see in chapter 12, as well as total expenditure, production and employment.

Figure 2-6 shows the relationship between currency, electronic money, checkable deposits (which may be accessed electronically or through paper checks) and credit cards. The boundary between checkable deposits and electronic money is not a clear one today because paper checks are increasingly being processed electronically by banks, by vendors or by both. Soon there may be little difference between a paper check and a paper receipt from a transaction using electronic money.

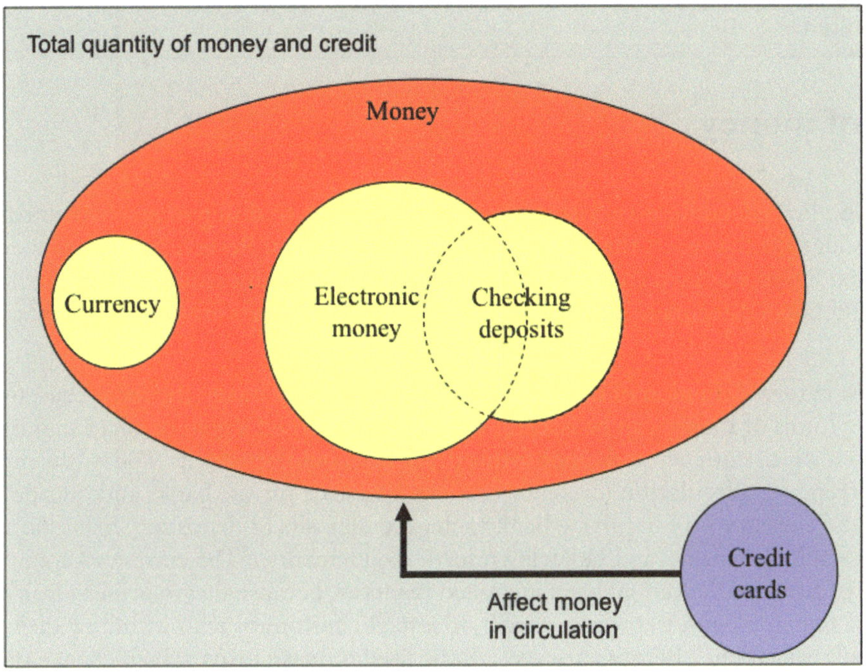

Figure 2-6: How money is related to currency, electronic money, checking accounts and credit cards

Box 2: Paper or plastic? Cards used to access electronic money or for credit

People increasing use various kinds of plastic cards instead of (paper) currency to purchase goods and services.

Debit cards are cards that are linked to a checking, saving or other deposit, from which the value is debited during a transaction. Debit cards may be used with many vendors and automated teller machines because they are issued through the assistance of a major bank, such as Visa or MasterCard. Debit cards that are linked to checking deposits are sometimes called check cards. The most modern cards use an embedded computer chip to debit funds from the deposit, although older technologies rely on only a magnetically coded strip on the back of the card.

Stored value cards are not linked to a bank deposit but have a monetary value that is electronically stored on them and debited as purchases are made. After this value is depleted, they may be recharged with value or thrown away. Like debit cards, stored value cards use computer chips and/or magnetic strips to store an account's value and other financial information. And like debit cards, stored value cards may be used widely, or they may be limited to specific uses like paying for public transportation or paying for laundry services in automatic machines. Government programs that provide aid to the poor, such as Temporary Assistance to Needy Families and the Food Stamp Program, now frequently use stored valued cards (or debit cards). Stored valued cards may also be issued in lieu of a paycheck for employees to reduce the cost of replacing lost or stolen checks, eliminate check processing fees, and may allow an employer to manage its cash flow better because a check with the total value of wages earned is not cashed at one time. And because a stored value card is not linked to a bank deposit, it is anonymous (like currency)—unlike a debit card, which has the name of the deposit holder on it.

Credit cards are unlike debit cards and stored valued cards in that they do not access a deposit of funds, although they usually access a pre-determined amount of credit. As the name suggests, credit cards are form of credit and debt, in which the credit card issuer pays for goods and services for a temporary time, and the credit card user is expected to repay the loan eventually plus interest. Therefore, credit cards are not classified as money, although they and other forms of credit/debt certainly affect the amount of expenditure in the economy and the quantity of money. Like debit cards and stored value cards, credit cards can use computer chips in addition to magnetic strips to record financial information.

Measures of money

In the US, the Federal Reserve System measures the values of different assets defined as money. We have already considered a few assets that act as money, but the Federal Reserve System includes several more. In fact, the Federal Reserve System and most central banks define and measure a few categories of monetary assets: narrow and broad categories. These categories of monetary assets are called "monetary aggregates".

The most narrow definition of money is called the **monetary base**: the most basic form of money from which other forms of money can be issued. When countries used a gold or silver standard, these metals were the base from which currency and other forms of money could be issued. Today, the monetary base is composed of **currency in circulation** (currency circulating outside private banks and outside the Federal Reserve Banks) and currency kept in private bank vaults and deposits of depository institutions at the central bank (used from settling payments and satisfying reserve requirements). The currency kept in bank vaults and the deposits of banks at the central bank are called **reserves**, because they represent cash on reserve that the banks can use to make loans, to process checks, to issue to customers who withdraw their funds or to perform other daily operations. Because reserves can be used to make loans, which change the amount of money that individuals and institutions can spend and deposit, they and currency in circulation (which can be easily deposited in banks to become reserves) are called the monetary base, or sometimes **M0**.

A slightly less narrow definition of money includes the most liquid assets that were traditionally the only assets used in transactions: currency in circulation, traveler's checks and checkable deposits. Checkable deposits are also called **transaction deposits** because they are deposits that can be readily used to make a transaction. Traditional checking deposits are called **demand deposits** because the funds in the deposits are accessible on demand when the owner writes a check. Demand deposits in the US are currently not allowed to pay interest by law, although today other checkable deposits do pay interest. The Federal Reserve System calls this definition of money **M1**. M1 has traditionally been larger than M0, although recently the amount of reserves has increased so much that M0 is now larger than M1.

A broader definition of money includes M1 as well as other assets that are less liquid since they usually require a little time or a fee before funds are made available for transactions: savings deposits, small denomination (less than $100,000) time deposits and retail (those not associated with financial intermediaries) deposits at money market mutual funds. Time deposits are funds that must be deposited at a financial intermediary for a given amount of time, unless a fee is paid for early withdrawal. The common name for a time deposit is a *certificate of deposit*, or CD, since a certificate is issued to the saver that specifies the length of time needed to hold the money, the interest that will be earned and other details. Recall from the previous chapter that money market mutual funds are financial intermediaries that invest in short-term securities traded in the money market. Deposits made at these institutions by their (retail) customers can function as a savings deposit and even a checking deposit from which a limited number of checks can be written. The Federal Reserve System calls the intermediate definition of money **M2**.

Table 1 and Figure 2-7 show the values of M1 and M2, as well as their components. Table 1 also shows the values of M1 and M2 relative to the total value of final goods and services bought and sold (GDP). The value of M2 was more than $8.8 trillion, which was about 57% of the value of the total value of final goods and services bought and sold. Note also that all of M1 is part of M2, as shown in Figure 2-7, but only part of M0 (currency in circulation) is part of M1.

Table 1: Measures of US monetary aggregates, July 2012

Category of monetary assets	Value in billions of $	Value as a fraction of the total value of final goods and services bought and sold in the domestic economy (GDP)
M0 or monetary base	2648.9	17.0%
Currency in circulation	1051.2	
Reserves	1583.8	
M1	1832.2	14.8%
Currency in circulation	1051.2	
Traveler's checks	4.0	
Demand (checking) deposits	825.0	
Other checkable deposits	426.6	
M2 (includes M1)	8816.4	56.5%
Savings deposits	6344.9	
Time deposits less than $100,000	689.3	
Retail deposits at money market mutual funds	633.0	

Source: Federal Reserve System: http://www.federalreserve.gov/econresdata/statisticsdata.htm

Bureau of Economic Analysis, http://www.bea.gov/national/index.htm#gdp

Note: Individual figures may not exactly sum to total figures due to rounding; gross domestic product is nominal, annualized income for the fourth quarter 2010.

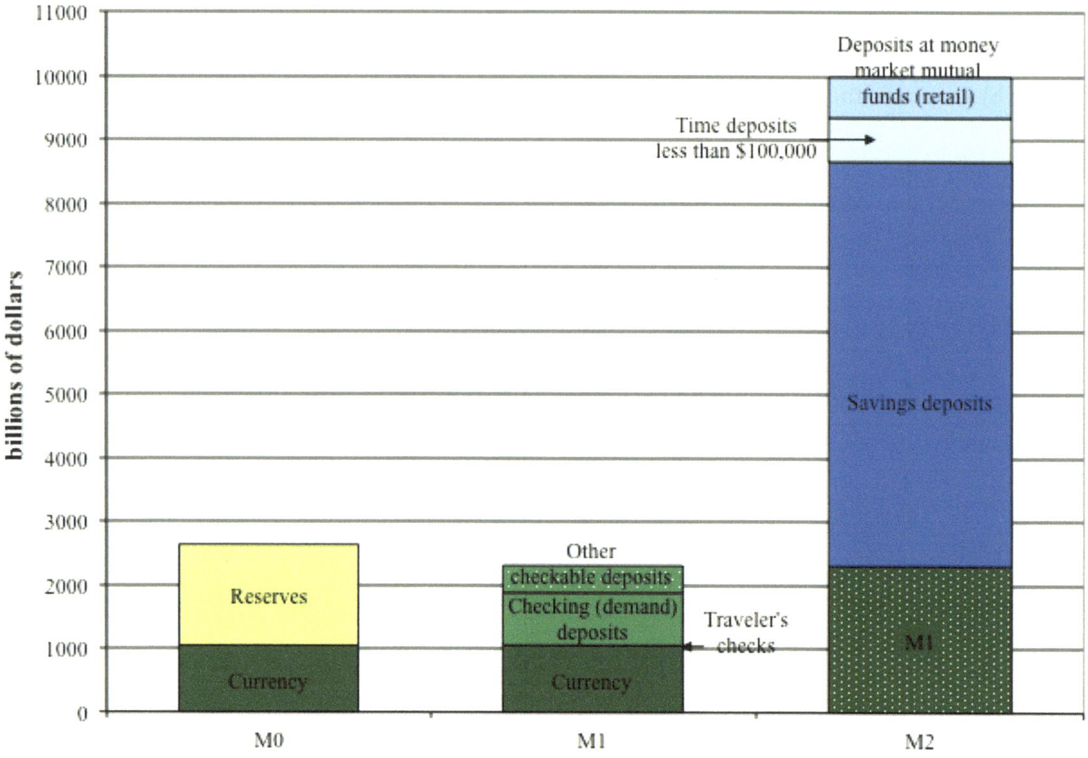

Source: Federal Reserve System, http://www.federalreserve.gov/econresdata/statisticsdata.htm

Figure 2-7: Measures of US monetary aggregates, July 2012

Figure 2-8 shows the growth rates of monetary aggregates from 1960-2012, and displays three trends in the growth of money. First, growth in all three monetary aggregates was positive in most years; the quantity of money used in transactions has grown over time as production of goods and services and prices of those goods and services have grown over time. Secondly, the growth rates of the monetary aggregates have differed substantially in many years, and changes in the growth rate of one monetary aggregate often did not correspond to changes in the growth rate of other monetary aggregates. Thirdly, growth in M1 has become more volatile since 1980, and the growth of M0 was especially volatile since 2008. This first fact was partly due to technological innovations, regulatory changes and increasing competition in financial markets that affected how banks and individuals maintained and accessed M1 accounts, as well as a change in the policy of Federal Reserve System. Since 1982, the Federal Reserve System has no longer set a targeted growth rate of M1 when determining monetary policy, but has let it fluctuate according to the wishes of banks and the public who hold M1 assets. The volatility of M0 since 2008 has been largely due to the efforts of the central bank to increase the amount of reserves among banks and to increase lending and spending among bank customers.

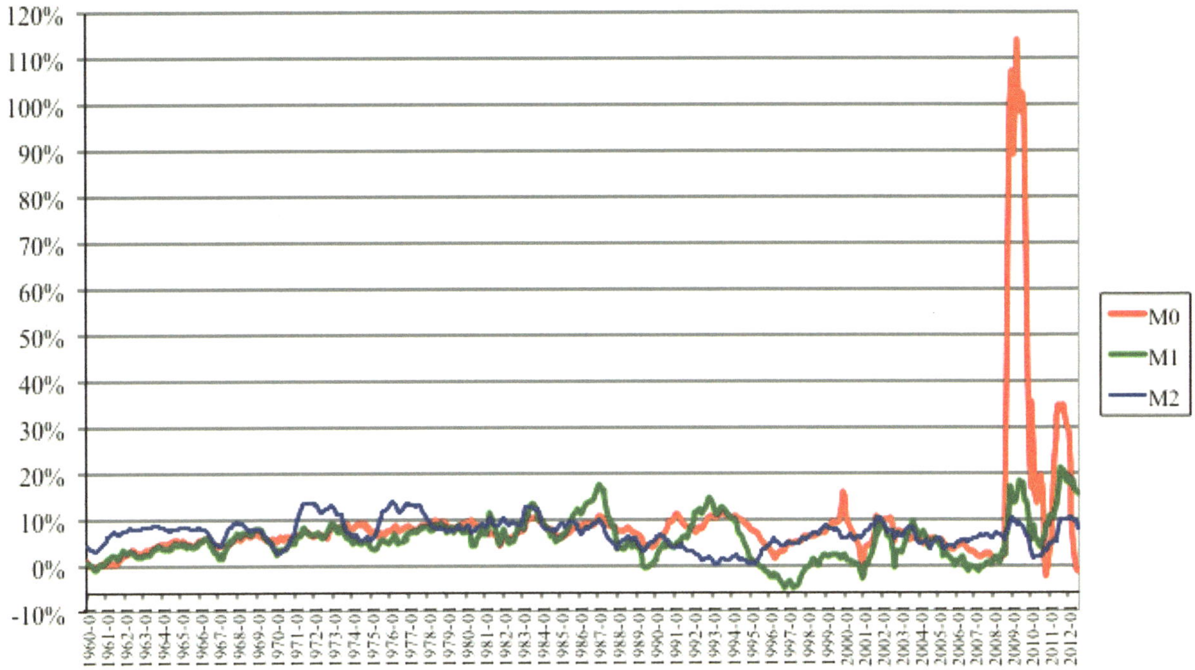

Source: Federal Reserve System, http://www.federalreserve.gov/econresdata/statisticsdata.htm

Figure 2-8: Annual growth rates of monetary aggregates, 1960-2012

Money market securities

The definition of M2 includes deposits at mutual funds used to purchase securities in the money market, the set of markets where short-term liquid assets are bought and sold. In addition to these deposits, money market securities in general can be considered a substitute for money for institutions and individuals because they pay off very quickly or can be easily sold to acquire money. In other words, while most of the value of securities in the money market is not counted in the official definition of monetary aggregates, they act as substitutes for money for many individuals and institutions.[18]

Individuals and institutions use money market securities to temporarily "store" their funds when goods and services or debts need to be paid for in the near future. That is, those that will need money to pay for expenditures in the near future can make a quick investment in the money market for a modest interest/yield/return rate. Alternatively, those who have a temporary shortage of money because desired expenditures exceed current income or revenue can temporarily borrow money in the money market. Individuals and institutions can hold monetary assets or money market securities to insure that expenditures can occur independently of revenue and income. Holding monetary assets is convenient and protects against unforeseen decreases in revenue or income and unexpected expenses, but involves a cost in the form of foregone interest. Money market securities are only slight less liquid than the monetary assets in M1 because

[18] In fact, an old definition of an monetary aggregate, M3, explicitly included three money market securities— repurchase agreements, time deposits larger than $100,000 and expatriate dollar deposits—which we describe below.

they can be quickly and easily sold, but they pay a slightly higher interest rate. On the other hand, money market securities, like money itself, do not generally earn high rates of interest compared to less liquid assets.

Let's consider the securities that are part of the money market and how they act as substitutes for money.

Reserves. As we learn in later chapters, banks need to maintain a certain amount of liquid funds "on reserve" in their vaults to satisfy requirements of the Federal Reserve System and to satisfy their customers. These liquid funds are officially called *reserves* or sometimes called "federal funds", and are considered part of today's monetary base or M0. If reserves become too low, banks can borrow these funds from another bank (or the Federal Reserve System) and pay back the loan the next day or in a few days as other funds flow in. Although reserves are included in the money market, they are considered money for banks to make transactions to settle payments and to make loans. We discuss the payment settlement systems and the lending process in later chapters.

Repurchase agreements. Repurchase agreements are short-term, temporary exchanges of money for non-monetary securities—usually short-term government bonds—that are usually completed within two weeks and often within 24 hours. Repurchase agreements occur between two institutions, say a firm and a bank, a borrower/spender and a saver/lender. Under the agreement, suppose that a firm purchases non-monetary securities from a bank for a short period of time, after which the bank would repurchase the securities from the firm. This transaction would allow the bank to borrow and spend money temporarily and would allow the firm to save and to make a temporary loan to earn a little interest, yield or return. In other words, repurchase agreements give borrowers/spenders temporary access to money (so that expenses can be paid) and act as a temporary investment for lenders/savers that allows them to earn a little interest, yield or return. Alternatively, we can say that the repurchase agreements act as a substitute for money for the saver/lender, because they pay off quickly and can be easily sold (transferred) to another party for money. (For an institution that lends money and acquires a non-monetary security, like the firm described above, the transaction is called a *reverse* repurchase agreement.)

Commercial paper. Commercial paper is a form of simple, short-term debt of commercial firms, commercial banks and other financial intermediaries, which is usually paid off in a few days or a few months. These securities are also considered a substitute for money for those who hold them because they pay off quickly and can be easily sold in the money market for money.

Negotiable time deposits. Retail time deposits that are less than $100,000 are considered part of M2, and larger time deposits and time deposits of financial institutions can also considered substitutes for money in the money market when they can be sold (exchanged for cash). A time deposit which is negotiable is one that can be sold (exchanged for cash) to another institution (after the buyer and seller "negotiate" an amount of cash). The seller of the deposit acquires cash immediately (usually at a discount relative to the value of the deposit), whereas the buyer acquires the security (certificate) for the funds in the deposit plus interest that can eventually be acquired. Thus, because these deposits can be easily issued and sold in the money market, they are considered a substitute for money. Also, negotiable time deposits usually pay off from one month to six months, so the depositor will soon have access to money regardless of whether a sale of the security occurs.

Expatriate currency deposits. Dollars deposited outside of the US are called expatriate dollar deposits or "eurodollar" deposits. Despite its common use, the name eurodollars is misleading and confusing because some expatriate dollars are deposited in non-European countries and because they are not necessarily related to the euro that circulates in many European Union countries. This author therefore uses the name "expatriate dollar deposits" to refer to deposits of dollars held outside the US. In general, currency deposited outside the country where it was issued is called expatriate currency deposits. Expatriate currency deposits are often negotiable time deposits but are sometimes more liquid funds. They can be easily sold in the money market or spent outright, so they act as a substitute for money.

Banker's acceptances. A banker's acceptance refers a bank's acceptance or guarantee of the payment of the notes, commercial paper or other forms of short-term debt issued by the bank's customers. The bank requires a deposit of funds, plus fees, to guarantee the future payment. In other words, if the bank customers are unable or unwilling to pay for the debt, the bank uses the funds deposited by its customers to pay the counterparty, which hold the banker's acceptance contract (security). Banker's acceptances are often used when one party is not certain that the other (the bank's customer) will pay fully on time. Parties may not trust each other enough to make a transaction directly, but they are willing to make a transaction indirectly through a financial intermediary that accepts a deposit of funds for payment and creates a banker's acceptance contract.

If the counterparty or anyone who holds the banker's acceptance needs cash before the payment is due, it can sell the security for a discounted amount of cash today, analogous to negotiable time deposits. The buyer of the banker's acceptance security has a claim on the deposited funds, which it can redeem when the contract matures (with its implied interest payment).

Government bills. Government bills are forms of simple, short-term debt of the government, analogous to commercial paper from the private sector. This simple debt, which we will study in more detail in the next chapter, has a single payment when the debt matures, which is usually from one to six months. Because these securities can easily be sold for money and because they will pay off within one to six months, they are considered a substitute for money for those who hold them. Government bills are usually called *treasury bills* because the government's treasury or finance department issues them.

Although government bills can be considered a substitute for money because they pay money relatively quickly and can be sold easily, they can also be classified as a non-monetary asset, which we will do in later chapters, because they usually can not be immediately used to pay for goods and services and debt. As shown in Figure 2-3, there is no precise distinction between liquid assets and illiquid assets, and the definition of monetary assets can vary depending on which assets we want to consider as substitutes for money.

Figure 2-9 represents transactions in the money market between two parties, *bank 1* and *bank 2*. *Bank 1* originally owns the money market security, which then it sells to *bank 2* for cash. The price that they negotiate for the security determines the amount of money that *bank 1* receives today and the amount of money that *bank 2* will receive in terms of principal plus interest, yield or return in the short-term future.

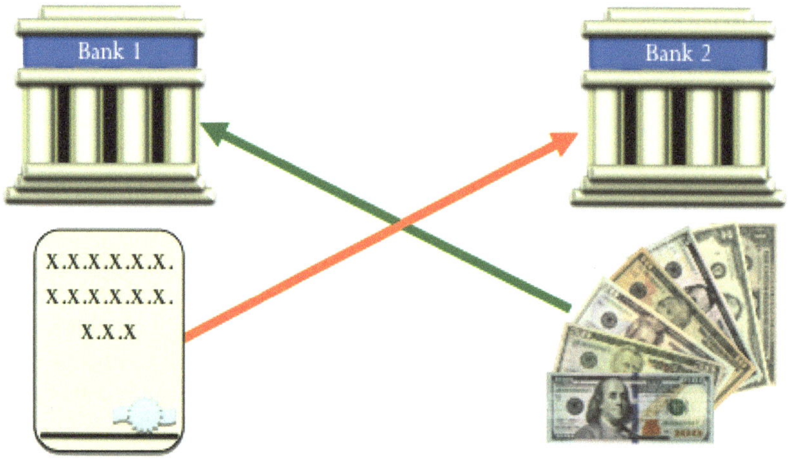

Price of contract determines the amount of money to be exchanged and the interest/yield rate of the asset for *bank 2*.

- reserves loan contract
- repurchase agreement
- negotiable time deposit contract (owned by *bank 1*)
- expatriate currency deposit contract (owned by *bank 1*)
- banker's acceptance (owned by *bank 1* and written by another bank)
- commercial paper
- treasury bill

Figure 2-9: A representation of a transaction in the money market between *bank 1* and *bank 2*.

In the cases of a negotiable time deposit, an expatriate currency deposit or a banker's acceptance, suppose that *bank 1* originally deposited money in another bank, say *bank 3* (which is not represented in the figure above), and *bank 3* issued a time deposit contract, an expatriate currency deposit contract or a banker's acceptance contract to *bank 1* at that time. During the money market transaction, *bank 1* now negotiates a price to sell the contract to *bank 2*, which will pay for the contract today but receive the principal plus interest in the future from *bank 3*.

Velocity of money and monetary policy

Money represents assets that can be used to conduct transactions, and it should therefore be closely tied to the value of goods and services produced and sold in transactions. The ratio of the value of production to the value of the money in circulation is called the **velocity** of money. Velocity indicates how frequently an average dollar circulates in the economy and how often an average dollar is used to finance the production of goods and services. The value of velocity is determined by many factors, such as preferences and customs of holding monetary assets versus non-monetary assets, automatic teller machines, electronic transfers of funds, credit cards, regulations, and expectations about the economy. Regardless of its value, a stable velocity indicates that an increase in the quantity of money will lead to a predictable increase in the value of goods and services produced.

During the 1980s the Federal Reserve System targeted growth in M2 to influence the growth of the economy due to the relative stability of M2 velocity. (We will study how the Federal Reserve System influences growth rates of monetary aggregates in later chapters.) Given an increase in M2, the Federal

Reserve System was able to predict with some degree of confidence the increase in the amount of production. But partly because of technological innovations and increasing competition in financial markets, velocity of M1 become less stable in the 1980s and the velocity of M2 became less stable in the 1990s, so that targets of M1 and M2 growth became unreliable guides to how expenditure and production would respond. Figure 2-10 shows the velocity of M1 and M2, using the nominal measure of expenditure on (final) goods and services (GDP) to represent how money is spent.

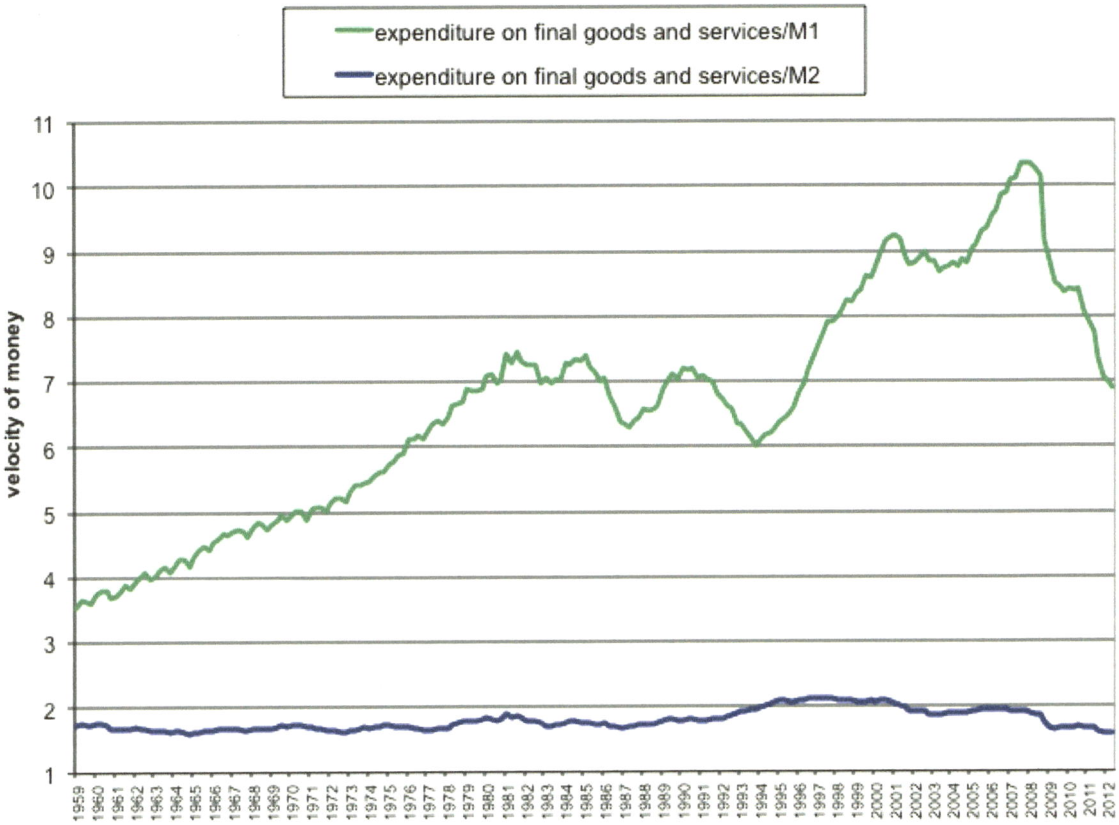

Figure 2-10: The velocity of money: the value of final goods and services bought and sold (GDP) relative to the quantity of money (M1 or M2)

Additional reasons for not setting targeted growth rates for monetary aggregates are that they are hard to measure accurately and quickly and that they are subject to revisions and seasonal adjustments. As a result, conducting monetary policy by adjusting the monetary aggregates is difficult even when the velocity of money is stable. Today, the Federal Reserve System focuses on adjusting a particular interest rate, called the federal funds rate, as discussed in chapter 11.

Summary

In this chapter we have defined precisely what money is and what it does. Money is any asset that is generally accepted to pay for goods and services or to repay debt, and money functions as a medium of exchange, a unit of account and a store of value. Money allows an economy to function more efficiently by lowering transaction costs. It eliminates the problem of the double coincidence of wants and the need to quote the price of a good or service in terms of other goods and services, problems which occur under a barter system. Like money, credit, debt and leverage refer to funds that can be used to buy goods and services; but unlike money, credit, debt and leverage must be repaid in the future. They are liabilities instead of assets. Many items have acted as money in history, but today most economies use fiat money, something that has value only because people believe it has value. Currency and checks have been major innovations in history and electronic money has been a major innovation in the last generation because they have further reduced transaction costs.

The Federal Reserve System defines two categories of assets, called monetary aggregates, that can be used as money or close substitutes for money. The narrow measure, M1, includes the most liquid assets; the broader measure, M2, includes liquid assets as well as less liquid assets. Growth rates of monetary aggregates can affect the growth rate of economic production, but the Federal Reserve System has not set well-defined growth rates for monetary aggregates in recent years because the relationship between the value of production and the value of money, called velocity, has become unstable and less predictable. Also, accurate and quick measurements of monetary aggregates is difficult, making monetary policy based on targeted growth rates of monetary aggregates difficult.

Although the Federal Reserve System officially defines groups of assets that function as money or close substitutes for money, other assets traded in the money market can also be considered as substitutes for money. Many institutions hold the short-term liquid securities traded in the money market in order to keep their funds readily available when they might need to pay for goods and service or debts in the near future.

Problems and Applications

Short answer problems

1. What are the differences among wealth, money, currency, income and return?

2. When does currency not have a store of value? During this time, what asset would have a store of value?

3. Which asset is more liquid: time deposits or savings deposits? Why? Which asset is more liquid: paintings or debt card deposits? Why?

4. What were some early forms of commodity money?

5. What are reserves? In which monetary aggregate are reserves included?

6. What are the components of M0, M1 and M2? Which monetary aggregate is the largest?

7. What is the difference between a debit card and a credit card? What is the difference between a debit card and a stored value card? Which card(s) is/are considered a form of (electronic) money? Which card(s) is/are considered a form of (electronic) debt?

8. What is the public sector (government) equivalent to commercial paper issued by private commercial firms and commercial banks?

9. How are negotiable time deposits and banker's acceptances similar? How are they different?

10. What determines the interest or yield rate of a (non-monetary) contract exchanged in the money market, like a negotiable time deposit (contract) or a commercial paper (contract), as well as the amount of money exchanged between the buyer and the seller of the contract?

11. What asset/liability bought and sold in the money market is considered part of the monetary base?

12. Describe one way in which checks are similar to currency. Describe one way in which they are different.

13. Consider Figure 2-10. Why do you think the velocity of M1, and to a lesser degree the velocity of M2, decreased during 2008-2009 in the US? (Hint: what do you think happened to GDP and the quantity of money during this time?)

Internet applications

1. Go to http://ecos.bok.or.kr/ and duplicate Table 1 for Korea using the latest available data.

2. Go to http://ecos.bok.or.kr/ and plot total reserves in Korea from 2004 to the latest quarter. What happened at the end of 2006? (Hint: search for information about required reserves.)

3. Go to http://ecos.bok.or.kr/ and create a figure analogous to Figure 2-8 using Korean data: plot the growth rates M0, M1 and M2 in Korea from the earliest available quarter to the latest quarter.

4. Go to http://ecos.bok.or.kr/ to find data on Korea's the nominal (monetary) value of national income (from domestic production) and the quantity of money. Calculate the velocity of money using M1 and M2 from 1970 to the latest quarter, analogous to Figure 2-10.

5. How is the interest or yield rate of a (non-monetary) contract in the money market, like a negotiable time deposit (contract) or a commercial paper (contract), determined in the money market—between the buyer of the contract and the seller of the contract?

6. Do an Internet search to find out when representative money was last used in your country. What commodity or commodities was/were used to back the value of the representative money?

7. Do an Internet search to find out when fiat money was first used in your country.

3. Interest, Yield, Return and Non-Monetary Assets

Preview

This chapter first considers how to value funds that become available at different times by using the concept of present value. We then define a way to calculate interest rates on assets in general and yields on bonds in particular when savers/lenders hold them until they completely pay off in the future. We also calculate measures of interest, yield or return rates when investors buy assets or hold them only for a short time. Finally, we consider how to adjust interest, yield or return rates for inflation in order to determine the inflation-adjusted rates that savers/lenders earn and borrowers/spenders pay.

The role of interest

What role does interest play in the economy? Interest is the price that a borrower pays for the use of someone else's funds and the price that a spender implicitly pays for spending money instead of saving it. A borrower/spender is willing to pay interest because credit or money allows him to buy goods and services at the present time, thereby avoiding having to wait to make a purchase after saving. A borrower promises to repay the principal (the original amount of money) and interest of a loan, whereas a spender simply forgoes interest after spending the original amount of money.

Interest is also the compensation that a lender/saver receives for giving up the ability to use funds, as well as for accepting the risk that the value of the funds will fall as the prices of goods and services rise during the lending/saving period. When a loan is made to a borrower, interest also compensates the lender for the risk that a borrower will not repay the funds fully or on time as promised and for the transaction costs (time and other resources) to complete a transaction with an external party.

In sum, interest represents a cost for a borrower/spender, either an explicit or implicit cost, but a form of income or earnings for a lender/saver. A borrower/spender is willing to pay this cost in order to have the benefit of using funds at the present time. A lender/saver is willing to give up the use of funds because he expects to earn interest in the future.

Present value

When money is not spent today, but saved or lent, how much interest should be earned? Alternatively, if money will be acquired in the future, after it is saved or lent, what will be its value *in the future* and what is its value *in the present*? Money at different times is valued differently, and the value of money over time is related to interest. Let use some simple examples to think about the value of money over time and interest.

Imagine that you have saved $1000 and want to lend or invest your funds. You could invest in a time deposit and earn interest, say at a 5% annual rate. At the end of one year, you would earn an interest payment and receive the original principal. You would receive

$$\$1050 = \$1000 + \$50 = \$1000 + \$1000(5\%) = \$1000(1+i)$$

where the \$1000 represents the principal, the \$50 represents the interest payment and i represents the interest rate (of 5%). By rearranging the previous equation, we can write

$$\$1000 = \frac{\$1050}{(1+i)} \tag{1}$$

The \$1050 amount represents future funds from the time deposit and the *future value* of those funds that you would have in one year if you invest; it represents the value of the interest payment and principal that will be available one year in the future.

The \$1000 represents the value of your investment today. Economists call this amount the present value of future funds from the time deposit. **Present value** represents the value of future funds as if they were available at the present time. Equation (1) states that the value of the \$1000 presently available is equivalent to the value of the \$1050 available one year from now, when the interest rate is 5%.

The value of funds that are available at different times is represented in the following figure:

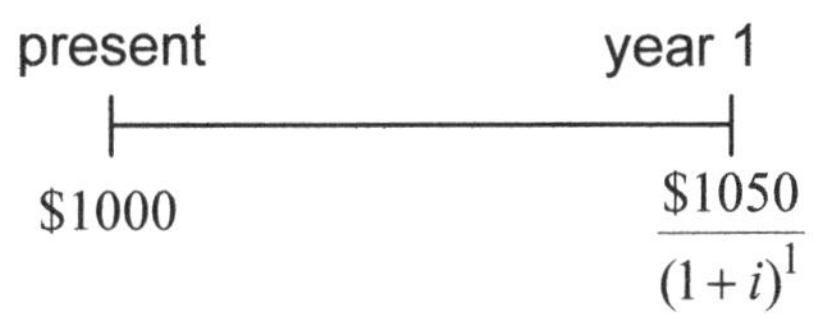

To determine the present value, the future value is *discounted* (that is, divided) by a function of the interest rate and the number of periods until the future funds become available. In other words, \$1050 that will be received one year in the future is not really worth \$1050 today when the interest rate is 5%. Why should a given amount of funds available in the future be considered less valuable than the same amount of funds available in the present? Future funds should be worth less than funds today because choices are limited when savers/lenders must wait for funds. In particular, savers/lenders can not yet use the future funds elsewhere to earn interest, nor can they spend the future funds until they become available. And as the waiting time increases, we should expect that the value of the future funds falls. Alternatively, when funds are available today, people have more choices: they may lend or invest the funds in many kinds of assets to earn interest or they may spend the funds (and avoid having to borrow and pay interest).

The concept of present value allows us to precisely compare the value of funds that become available at different times. Future funds should be valued less than the same amount of funds available in the present, but how much less? The calculations for the one-year time deposit state that \$1000 of today's funds should be worth exactly \$1050 available one year from now, when the interest rate is 5%. Alternatively, we say that the \$1050 which will be available one year from now should be worth exactly \$1000 in today's funds, when the interest rate is 5%.

Now suppose that you consider investing in a two-year time deposit with a constant annual interest rate i equal to 5%. If you invested for only one year, you would earn \$1050, but if you invested for a second year you would earn \$1050(1 + i) = \$1102.50. This amount is expressed as

$$\$1102.50 = \$1050(1+i) = \$1000(1+i)(1+i) = \$1000(1+i)^2$$

and

$$\$1000 = \frac{\$1102.50}{(1+i)^2}$$

The future value of funds from the two-year investment is \$1102.50, and the present value of these future funds is \$1000. According to present value calculations, savers/lenders should treat \$1102.50 that will be available in two years as equivalent to \$1000 that is available today, when the interest rate is 5%. The value of funds that are available at different times is represented in the following figure:

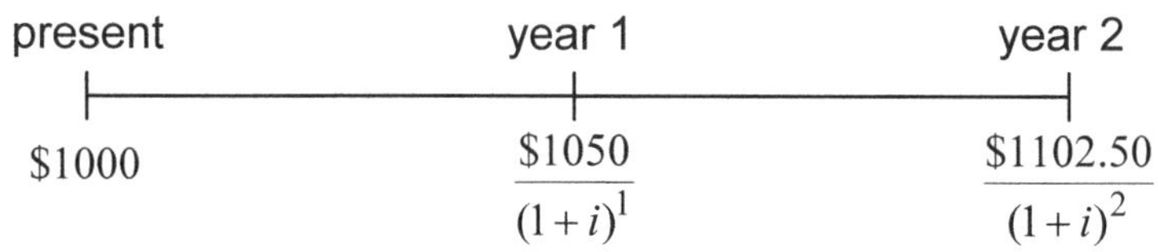

If you invest in a three-year time deposit with a constant annual interest rate i equal to 5%, you would earn \$1102.50(1 + i) = \$1157.63, which is expressed as

$$\$1157.63 = \$1102.50(1+i) = \$1000(1+i)(1+i)(1+i) = \$1000(1+i)^3$$

and

$$\$1000 = \frac{\$1157.63}{(1+i)^3} \qquad \textbf{(2)}$$

The future value of funds from the three-year investment is \$1157.63, and the present value of these future funds is \$1000. According to present value calculations, savers/lenders should treat \$1157.63 that will be available in three years as equivalent to \$1000 that is available today, when the interest rate is 5%. The value of funds that are available at different times is represented in the following figure:

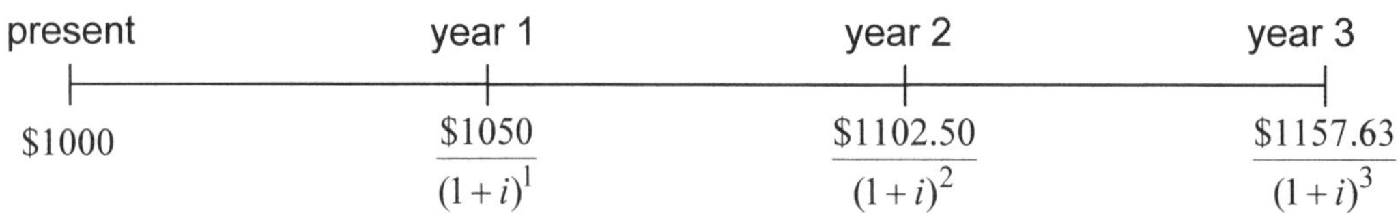

By using the preceding logic, we can calculate the present value of future funds that become available in any period. The present value of future funds equals the future value of those funds discounted by a function of the interest rate and the number of periods until the funds become available. This function represents the interest that can not be earned each period by investing in other assets or the interest that must be paid each period when it is necessary to borrow due to the fact that future funds are not yet available.

For any interest rate *i* and any *n* periods until future funds become available, we represent present value of those funds as

$$\text{present value} = \frac{\text{future value}}{(1+i)^n}$$

(3)

We apply our concept of present value to calculate the values and to predict the prices of assets, such as bonds, that promise to pay funds in the future. But before doing so, we must take a brief detour to introduce how bonds work.

An introduction to bonds

Bonds are formal debt contracts that obligate the bond issuer to pay a specified amount at a given date. Bonds work like loans, where the bond issuer is the borrower/spender and the bond buyer is the lender/saver, who gives up his funds when the bond is bought. The funds that the bond issuer receives from the bond buyer act as the principal of the loan; the funds that the bond buyer receives from the bond issuer at a future date act as the repayment of the principal plus interest.

Some bonds offer small, periodic payments before the bond matures, called **coupon payments**, also to represent interest payments on debt. At one time, bonds were issued with coupons attached to them, so that the owner of the bond clipped and mailed them to the bond issuer to receive a specified periodic payment. Today, it is no longer necessary to clip and mail small pieces of paper to receive these periodic payments from a bond, but these periodic payments are still called coupon payments and bonds with coupon payments are still called **coupon bonds**. All bonds offer a large, single payment when the bond matures, called the face value payment, or simply the **face value**, because its value is printed on the face of the bond. Figure 3-1 shows an example of an old coupon bond issued in 1944 by a mining company in the Congo with a face value of 500 francs.

Figure 3-1: An example of an old coupon bond (with coupons attached on the side) issued by the Kilo-Moto mining company in 1944.

Coupon bonds have a rate to represent value of coupon payments earned each period divided by the face value of a bond. This rate is called the **coupon rate.** We write

$$\text{coupon rate} = \frac{\text{coupon payments}}{\text{face value}} \equiv \frac{C}{F}$$

The coupon rate does not change over the life of the coupon bond because the coupon payments and the face value do not change after the bond has been issued. In particular, the coupon rate does not depend on the bond's price, which changes frequently over the life of the bond. Although some authors define the coupon rate to be a coupon bond's interest rate, we define a bond's interest rate below by relying on the bond's price because the earnings (rate) of a bond does depend significantly on market prices that savers/lenders pay.

Figure 3-2 shows a more modern example of a bond from the Stauffer Chemical Company with an annualized coupon rate of 4.5 %, a face value of $10000 and a maturity date of April 1, 1991 (and an issue date of August 18, 1975). This bond offered two coupon payments per year, with a total value of approximately 4.5% x $10000 = $450.

Figure 3-2: An example of a coupon bond from the Stauffer Chemical Company that was due in 1991.

Not all bonds offer coupon payments. Some bonds offer to repay only the face value at the maturity date, with no periodic payments between the issue date and the maturity date, even though they look very similar to today's coupon bonds. Such bonds are called **zero coupon bonds** or **discount bonds**. As we will see in the following sections, the earnings or interest income of these bonds depends on the relationship between the price that is paid by the buyer of the bond and the face value payment that the buyer eventually receives. Of course, when the buyer pays a low price relative to the face value that will be received in the future, his earnings and interest income will be high. When the buyer pays a high price relative to the face value that will be received in the future, his earnings and interest income will be low.

The earnings or interest income from either a coupon bond or a zero coupon bond is frequently called the **yield**, or as a percent, the *yield rate.* In the following sections, I discuss different ways to calculate the yield rate of both coupon bonds and zero coupon bonds. The first way can be applied to both kinds of bonds, while the second is applied only to coupon bonds and the third is applied only to zero coupon, or discount, bonds.[19]

But first I show how to calculate the present value of payments from both coupon and discount bonds, and thus to represent market values and prices of these bonds.

[19] Caution: the yield or yield rate is sometimes confused with the coupon rate. I define yield rates in three ways below, all of which are different from the coupon rate.

Using present value to predict the prices of bonds and other assets

To relate the previous introduction of bonds to present value, first suppose that you are able to invest in a coupon bond and that the bond promises to pay its face value of $1000 on its maturity date in three years, plus $100 coupon payments at the end of the first, second and third years. We would represent the timing of the initial investment and the repayment of the bond using the following diagram:

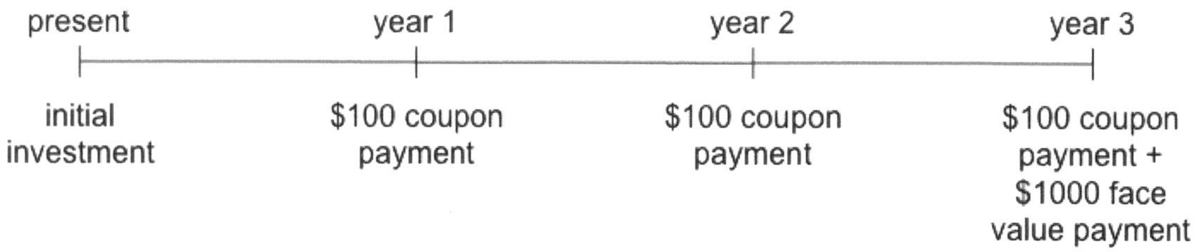

If you invest in the coupon bond that promises to pay its face value of $1000 on its maturity date in three years, plus $100 coupon payments at the end of the first, second and third years, how much should you pay for such a bond?

Present value gives us a methodical way of calculating the value or price of a bond. To calculate the present value of the coupon bond, suppose first that the interest rate for similar alternative assets, like for time deposits, is 5%. Next, we should determine the future value of funds and when they become available. The future value of funds available in one year is $100; the future value of funds in two years is $100; the future value of funds available in three years is $100 + $1000. Finally, we discount the future value of the funds according to when they become available, and then add all of the discounted values together to determine the present value of all funds from the bond. Using equation (3), we calculate that

$$\text{present value} = \frac{\$100}{(1+i)^1} + \frac{\$100}{(1+i)^2} + \frac{\$100}{(1+i)^3} + \frac{\$1000}{(1+i)^3}$$

If the interest rate is 5% for alternative assets with similar risk, liquidity and other characteristics, then

$$\text{present value} = \frac{\$100}{(1+.05)^1} + \frac{\$100}{(1+.05)^2} + \frac{\$100}{(1+.05)^3} + \frac{\$1000}{(1+.05)^3}$$

$$= \$95.24 + \$90.70 + \$86.38 + \$863.84 = \$1136.16 \tag{4}$$

You and millions of other savers in bond markets (assuming everyone can buy the bond and the same alternative investments) should value the bond at its present value since present value accounts for interest that is not earned in similar alternative assets that you could buy. In other words, the market price of the bond that you pay should be its present value:

price = present value = discounted future value

Present value helps us make investment decisions. If you were interested in buying bonds, you could find the price you would have to pay in bond markets. If the bond's market price were below its present value, then you should buy the bond because you would value the bond more than what it costs in the market. In this case the yield that you could get from the bond would be greater than the earnings or interest income that you could get from similar alternative assets. If its market price is above its present value, then you should not buy it because you would value the bond less than what it costs in the market. In this case the yield that you could get from the bond would be less than the earnings or interest income that you could get from similar alternative assets.

Next, suppose that you are considering to invest in a discount bond that promises to pay $1000 at its maturity date in one year. We would represent the timing of the initial investment and the repayment of the bond using the following diagram:

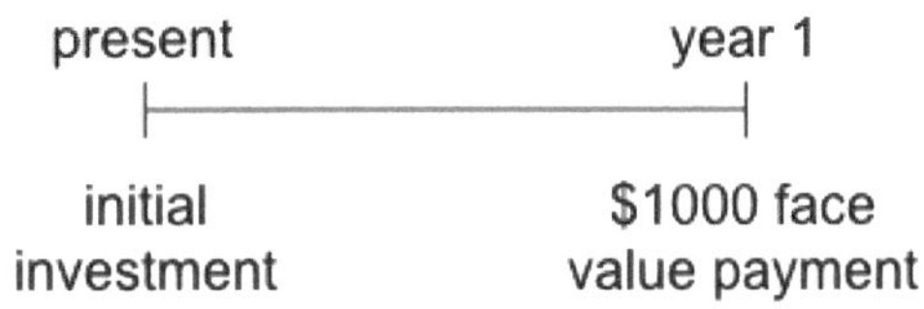

When the interest rate is 5% for similar alternative assets, we calculate that

$$\text{present value} = \frac{\$1000}{(1+.05)^1} = \$952.38$$

Therefore, you should buy this bond if the price is $952.38 or less. In this case, its yield would be at least as great as the earnings or interest income from alternative assets. Otherwise, you should invest in similar alternative assets and earn an interest rate of 5%.

Yield to maturity

The prices of bonds are easily determined through bond markets, but we may have to consider a lot of interest rates on alternative assets in order to calculate present value, and perhaps to account for possible differences in risk, liquidity and other characteristics among the assets. Instead of considering interest rates on alternative assets, we can calculate a yield rate or an interest rate on an asset by using only characteristics of the asset itself. In particular, we can consider the price of an asset, the future value of funds from the asset and the dates on which those funds become available in order to determine the interest or yield that would be earned if we held the asset until its maturity date. This rate, called the **yield to maturity**, acts as an asset's own yield rate or interest rate, even if the only payment from the asset arrives at the maturity date.

Suppose that you are considering to invest in a discount bond that promises to pay $1000 at its maturity date in one year. The bond's price would be determined by bond markets, and suppose the bond currently has a market price of $960. Because you would pay only $960 for a $1000 face value bond, the bond would yield a $40 payment that acts interest for waiting one year to receive the face value payment. We can express this yield or interest payment as a rate: a rate called the yield to maturity.

To calculate the bond's yield to maturity, we set the bond's price equal to the present value of all future funds paid from the bond:

price = present value = discounted future value

In this example,

$$\$960 = \frac{\$1000}{(1+ytm)^1} \tag{5}$$

where *ytm* represents the bond's yield to maturity, or its interest rate. We can solve for *ytm* to determine that the bond's yield to maturity is 4.2%.

Now let's suppose again that you are considering to invest in the coupon bond that promises to pay a $1000 face value on its maturity date in three years, plus $100 coupon payments at the end of the first, second and third years. Suppose that the bond has a market price of $1100.

To determine the bond's yield to maturity, we equate the bond's price with the present value of its future funds:

$$\$1100 = \frac{\$100}{(1+ytm)^1} + \frac{\$100}{(1+ytm)^2} + \frac{\$100}{(1+ytm)^3} + \frac{\$1000}{(1+ytm)^3}$$

With a financial calculator, you could determine that the bond's yield to maturity is 6.24%.[20] At a yield (interest) rate of 6.24%, the bond's price equals the present value of the future funds from the bond.

In this case, the coupon bond has a higher yield to maturity than the interest rate of 5% on the three-year time deposit described by equation (2). If the bond were similar to the time deposit in ways other than the interest rate, in particular similar in terms of risk and liquidity, then the bond would be a more attractive asset, so that you and millions of other savers/lenders should move funds from the time deposits to the bond market, eventually causing prices and rates to adjust until the yield/interest rates on the two assets converge.

Alternatively, notice also that the market price of $1100 for the coupon bond is lower than the $1136.16 present value that we calculated when a similar alternative asset had a 5% interest rate, as shown in equation (4). Since the bond's present value is higher than its market price, the bond should be a good investment for you: you value the bond more than what the bond costs in the market, and the yield of the bond is higher than the earnings or interest income from similar alternative assets. The bond's price should therefore rise as you and other savers/lenders become more willing to buy these kinds of bonds, which would then decrease the yield to maturity for new buyers until it is no longer greater than interest rates on similar alternative assets.

---

[20] On-line financial calculators are located at http://www.investopedia.com/calculator/AOYTM.aspx and http://www.moneychimp.com/calculator/bond_yield_calculator.htm

In general, by calculating the yield to maturity, we can compare the bond's yield to the earning potential of other types of assets.

The relationship between prices of assets and yields to maturity

If a coupon bond that promises to pay a $1000 face value on its maturity date in three years, plus $100 coupon payments at the end of the first, second and third years had market price of $1136.16, then we could calculate the yield to maturity by setting the bond's price equal to its present value:

$$\$1136.16 = \text{present value} = \frac{\$100}{(1+.05)^1} + \frac{\$100}{(1+.05)^2} + \frac{\$100}{(1+.05)^3} + \frac{\$1000}{(1+.05)^3}$$

which is the same result as in equation (4). Now suppose that the price of the bond falls to $1106.92. What will happen to the yield to maturity? With a lower price, savers/lenders need to pay less to buy the bond, so that its yield rate would increase. In fact, we see that the yield to maturity will rise to 6% since

$$\$1106.92 = \text{present value} = \frac{\$100}{(1+.06)^1} + \frac{\$100}{(1+.06)^2} + \frac{\$100}{(1+.06)^3} + \frac{\$1000}{(1+.06)^3}$$

Alternatively, let's suppose that interest rates on similar alternative assets rise from 5% to 6%. What will happen to the price of bonds? If interest rates on similar alternative assets are 5%, then

$$\text{price} = \text{present value} = \frac{\$100}{(1+.05)^1} + \frac{\$100}{(1+.05)^2} + \frac{\$100}{(1+.05)^3} + \frac{\$1000}{(1+.05)^3}$$

$$\text{price} = \text{present value} = \$95.24 + \$90.70 + \$86.38 + \$863.84 = \$1136.16$$

If interest rates on similar alternative assets rise to 6%, then the price of bonds will fall as some savers/lenders sell their bonds and move use their funds to buy the alternative assets. Specifically,

$$\text{price} = \text{present value} = \frac{\$100}{(1+.06)^1} + \frac{\$100}{(1+.06)^2} + \frac{\$100}{(1+.06)^3} + \frac{\$1000}{(1+.06)^3}$$

$$\text{price} = \text{present value} = \$94.34 + \$89.00 + \$83.96 + \$839.62 = \$1106.92$$

In general, as interest rates on alternative assets increase, saving/lending in bonds looks less attractive because bonds offer a fixed face value payment and fixed coupon payments (if any), so that bonds do not become more profitable as other investments become more profitable. To attract investors, issuers of bonds would need to offer high yields to maturity to match high interest rates on other assets. Alternatively, issuers and sellers of bonds would need to lower their price of bonds to attract savers/lenders. At a lower purchase price, but with the same fixed future payments, bonds become more attractive assets. On the other hand, as interest rates on similar alternative assets decrease, saving/lending in bonds looks more attractive because bonds offer fixed payments that do not decline as other assets become less profitable. In this case, issuers and sellers of bonds can offer low yields to maturity or can ask for high prices and still attract investors.

Figure 3-3 compares investments in deposits at banks and bonds. If interest rates on bank deposits increase then money tends to flow to banks after people sell bonds to acquire cash. As people sell bonds, their prices tend to decline, which increases their yield rate for new buyers. (However, this would decrease the rate of return of bonds, as discussed below.) Alternatively, if interest rates on bank deposits decrease, then money tends to be withdrawn from bank deposits and invested in bonds. As people buy bonds, their prices tend to rise, which decrease their yield rate for new buyers. (However, this would increase the rate of return of bonds, as discussed below.)

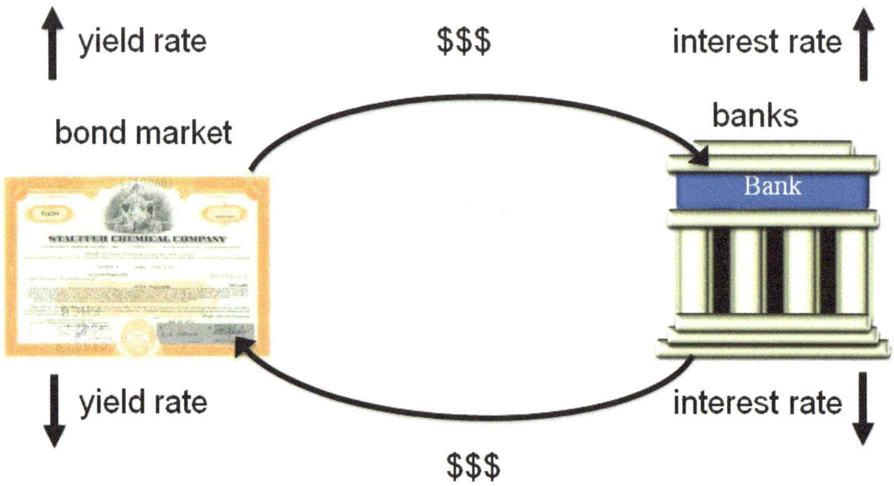

Figure 3-3: If interest rates rise on bank deposits, money tends to flow from bond markets to banks, thereby decreasing the prices of bonds and increasing their yield rates.

If interest rates fall on bank deposits, money tends to flow from bank deposits to bond markets, thereby increasing the prices of bonds and decreasing their yield rates.

We have discovered two relationships. Firstly, yields to maturity on bonds and interest rates on similar alternative assets move together: there is a direct relationship between yields to maturity (interest rates on bonds) and interest rates on other assets.

Secondly, yields to maturity and prices of bonds are inversely related. As yields to maturity and interest rates rise, the present value of a bond's future payments decreases because we discount those future payments more. A fall in the present value of future payments will cause a fall in the market price of bonds when many buyers and sellers in bond markets value bonds according to their present values. Alternatively, as the prices of bonds fall, savers/lenders need to pay less to receive a given face value payment and coupon payments, so that the yield to maturity should rise. Conversely, as the prices of bonds rise, investors need to pay more to receive a given face value payment and coupon payments, so that the yield to maturity should fall.

Putting these two relationships together, we conclude that when interest rates in general and yields to maturity in particular rise, prices of bonds fall.

Furthermore, the inverse relationship between interest rates and prices of bonds is more pronounced as the maturity date of the bonds increases. Why? Long-term bonds offer fixed payments far into the future, and the present value—and hence the market value or price—of these future payments changes substantially when interest rates on similar alternative assets change. For example, if interest rates on similar alternative assets rise, then a saver/lender will forgo an attractive investment opportunity for a long period of time if he invests his funds in a long-term bond. In this case, few investors would be willing to buy long-term bonds offering fixed future payments. The willingness to buy long-term bonds would decrease substantially and the willingness to sell long-term bonds would increase substantially, and the price of long-term bonds would fall substantially as a result. The risk of bonds changing their market value due to changes in interest rates is called **interest rate risk**.

Let's look at an example that shows the interest rate risk of long term bonds. Suppose that we can invest in a $1000 face value discount bonds with different maturities—30 years, 10 years, 5 years, 3 years and 1 year. What is the risk that the market value of the bonds falls if interest rates rise from 5% to 6%? Using equation (3), we calculate the present value of the bonds as interest rates change, and then predict that the market prices of those bonds equal their present values. Table 2 shows the results of the calculations.

Table 2: Changes in predicted prices of $1000 face value discount bonds with different maturity dates when interest rates on similar alternative assets rise from 5% to 6%.

Years to maturity	Predicted price at a 5% interest rate	Predicted price at a 6% interest rate	Change in predicted price
1	$952.38	$943.40	-$8.98
3	$863.84	$839.62	-$24.22
5	$783.53	$747.26	-$36.27
10	$613.91	$558.39	-$55.52
30	$231.38	$174.11	-$57.27

We see from Table 2 that interest rate risk is more substantial for long-term bonds than for short-term bonds because by investing in bonds for a long period of time, savers/lenders run a greater risk of not profiting from similar alternative assets if their interest rates rise. A small change in interest rates causes substantial changes in the price of long-term bonds, whereas the effect on the price of short-term bonds is less substantial. This greater interest rate risk on long-term bonds causes greater volatility in the prices of long-term bonds. In Table 2 the price of the 30 year bond changes by -$57.27, while the price of the 1 year bond changes by a relatively small -$8.98. And then if interest rates fell from 6% to 5%, the changes in the prices of bonds would be +$57.27 for the 30 year bond and +$8.98 for the 1 year bond.

Yield to maturity is one way to measure the earnings from an asset, but its calculation assumes that the asset is held until the maturity date. How could we represent the gains from owning or acquiring an asset if a saver/lender does not want to hold an asset until its maturity date? We develop three alternative ways to measure earnings for a saver/lender that do not rely on the assumption that he holds the asset until its maturity date: current yield, discount yield and rate of return.

Current yield

The **current yield** represents an asset's current interest rate or current earnings rate: it equals an asset's (interest) payments in the current period divided by the asset's current price.

$$\text{current yield} = \frac{\text{payments in the current period}}{\text{current price}}$$

The current yield of a coupon bond considers the coupon payments that are paid in the current period:

$$\text{current yield of a coupon bond} = \frac{\text{coupon payments in the current period}}{\text{current price}} \equiv \frac{C}{P_t}$$

where C is equal to the amount of coupon payments in the current period t and P_t is the price of the coupon bond in the current period t.

Because only current payments are considered when calculating the current yield, no discounting is necessary. The current yield is relatively easy to calculate, and it may be used as an approximation to the yield to maturity as the current price of a bond approaches its face value and as the maturity date increases. But as Box 1 shows, when the maturity date is short or when price differs widely from the face value, the current yield and the yield to maturity differ significantly. Nonetheless, because changes in price are associated with inverse changes for both the yield to maturity and the current yield, the current yield changes in the same direction as the yield to maturity.

Discount yield

An alternative measure to the yield to maturity for discount bonds represents the yield for savers/lenders when they buy a discount bond at a low price. Discount bonds are bought at a discount, meaning that the market price paid by investors is less than the face value of the bond. The discount for a bond equals its face value minus the market price and represents the amount of "interest" earned. How large is this discount relative to the face value of the bond? The **discount yield** represents the yield of buying a bond at a discount at an annualized rate. It is calculated by dividing the discount by the face value of the bond, and then expressing this rate in annualized terms:

$$\begin{aligned}\text{discount yield} &= \frac{\text{discount}}{\text{face value}}\, x\, \frac{360\text{ days}}{\text{days to maturity}} \\ &\equiv \frac{F - P_t}{F}\, x\, \frac{360\text{ days}}{\text{days to maturity}}\end{aligned} \tag{6}$$

where F represent the face value of the bond, P_t represents the current price of the bond in period t and discount = $F - P_t$. The second term in equation (6) represents a factor that expresses the first term at an annualized rate. Banks typically use 360 days to calculate annualized short-term interest rates, so we use "360 days" in the numerator of the second term. In the denominator of the second term, we put the number of days until the discount bond matures. For example, if the maturity date of a discount bond is in 90 days, the second term in the equation would equal 4. This factor of 4 would multiply the first term to express it at an annualized rate.

The discount yield is frequently used for short-term discount bonds—discount bonds that mature in 1 year or less. The discount yield is relatively easy to calculate, and it may be used as an approximation to the yield to maturity. Also, because changes in price are associated with inverse changes for both the yield to maturity and the discount yield, the discount yield changes in the same direction as the yield to maturity.

Box 1: Interest rates on government bonds

Governments issue bonds to finance many projects, from building roads and schools to paying for retiree benefits. At the national level, the US Treasury issues several types of bonds, some of which we consider below. In addition, US government and government sponsored agencies issue bonds to help finance or insure mortgages. These agencies are the Federal National Mortgage Association ("Fannie Mae"), the Federal Home Loan Mortgage Corporation ("Freddie Mac") and the Government National Mortgage Association ("Ginnie Mae"). State, municipal, county and other local governments also frequently issue bonds to finance various projects.

US Treasury securities have special names, only some of which use the term "bonds", even though all are considered "bonds" in a general sense. Data for two of these securities, called US Treasury Bonds and Notes, are listed in Table 3. US Treasury Bonds are coupon bonds with maturity dates of 10 years or more, while US Treasury Notes are coupon bonds with maturity dates from 2 to 10 years. The annualized coupon rate indicates how much the bond owner receives as a coupon payment, which is paid every six months. For example, if the face value of one of these securities is $10000, an annualized coupon rate of 2% indicates that (2% x $10000)/2 = $100 is paid every six months until the maturity date. The maturity dates for the securities listed in the table range from the current month to 30 years later. The bid price is the price that buyers "bid" or quote, and the asked price is the price that sellers "ask for" or quote. The asked yield is the yield to maturity based on calculations using the asked price. The current yield (C/P_t) can be calculated by taking the coupon rate (C/F) times the face value (F) divided by the price (P_t). Note that the current yield differs substantially from the yield to maturity when the price deviates from the face value or when the maturity date is soon.

Table 3 also lists data for indexed securities, represented with an i after the maturity date. These securities, called Treasury Inflation-Protected Securities, offer coupon and face value payments that are increased at a rate to match the inflation rate. As a result, the prices are higher and the yields to maturity are lower for these securities than for non-indexed securities. Treasury Inflation-Protected Securities are discussed further below.

Table 3: US Treasury Bonds and Notes

Coupon rate	Maturity date	Bid price: price that buyers bid	Asked price: price that sellers ask for	Change in asked price	Asked yield: yield to maturity based on asked price	Current yield
1.625	Feb 06 n	99:29	99:30	....	3.72	1.63
1.500	Mar 06 n	99:22	99:23	+1	4.33	1.50
2.250	Apr 06 n	99:18	99:19	+1	4.45	2.26
2.000	May 06 n	99:13	99:14	+1	4.50	2.01
3.375	Jan 07 i	101:19	101:20	+2	1.49	3.32
3.125	Jan 07 n	98:11	98:12	....	4.82	3.18
3.625	Jan 10 n	96:09	96:10	-1	4.67	3.76
4.250	Jan 10 i	108:28	108:29	+7	1.86	3.90
9.250	Feb 16	136:20	136:21	-1	4.61	6.77
7.250	May 16	121:02	121:03	-1	4.62	5.99
5.375	Feb 31	112:20	112:21	-6	4.52	4.77

3.375	Apr 32 i	131:30	131:31	+16	1.83	2.56
4.500	Feb 36	99:20	99:21	-7	4.52	4.52

Footnotes:

Numbers after the colons in bid and asked prices represent 32nds; 101:01 means 101 1/32.

Change is in 32nds of asked price.

The actual prices of the securities depend on the face value. For example, if the face value equals \$10000, 101:01 means 101 x \$100 + 1/32 x \$100 = \$10100 + \$3.125 = \$10103.125. If the face value equals \$1000, 101:01 means 101 x \$10 + 1/32 x \$10 = \$1010 + \$0.3125 = \$1010.3125.

i represents inflation-indexed US Treasury Bond or Note.

n represents a US Treasury Note.

Source: Wall Street Journal, 24 February 2006, and author's calculations

Table 4 shows a sample of data for US Treasury Bills, discount bonds with maturity dates of one year or less. The longest term US Treasury Bill listed in the table matured about 6 months (180 days) from the posted date. The bid and asked prices are quoted in terms of the discount yield, so that 4.24 represents a price that is discounted 4.24% below the face value at an annualized rate.

Note that longer-term Bills have a slightly higher discount yield; their prices are discounted slightly more than those for shorter-term Bills. Also note that the discount yield (based on either the asked or bid price) always is slightly lower than the yield to maturity. To see why, we could calculate the yield to maturity for a 360 day discount bond as $ytm = (F - P_t)/P_t$, and compare our result to equation (6). Note that equation (6) has F in the denominator, which is larger than the price of a discount bond, implying that the discount yield should be lower than the yield to maturity on a discount bond.

Table 4: US Treasury Bills

Maturity	Days to maturity	Bid: discount yield based on bid price	Asked: discount yield based on asked price	Change in discount yield based on asked price	Asked yield: yield to maturity based on asked price
Mar 02 06	5	4.24	4.24	+0.05	4.30
Mar 30 06	33	4.30	4.28	+0.08	4.36
May 25 06	89	4.49	4.48	+0.01	4.59
Aug 24 06	180	4.55	4.55	....	4.72

Source: Wall Street Journal, 24 February 2006

Rate of return

The yield to maturity assumes that investors hold their assets until their maturity date, but of course, savers sometimes sell their assets before the assets mature. How much does an investor gain by reselling an asset? Recall that capital gains can be calculated for bonds, loans, deposits, stocks or any other asset by comparing the purchase price (or initial value) of the asset with its selling price (or value at maturity). The **rate of return** accounts for capital gains or capital losses, as well as any other income like that from coupon payments and dividend payments, and any expenses that were paid while owning the asset.

Rates of return are often used for stocks and other assets like houses or commodities that do not mature. Figure 3-4 shows an example of 100 shares of common stock in the New York, Chicago and St.

Louis Railroad Company that was issued in 1957 and does not mature as long as the company remains in business. (However, the company issuing the stock can repurchase it later or can convert it to bonds or other securities that do mature.) In chapter 6, I distinguish between *common stock* and another type of stock called *preferred stock*.

Figure 3-4: 100 shares of common stock in The New York, Chicago, and St. Louis Railroad Company issued in 1957.

One can also calculate rates of return for assets that mature. Suppose that you bought a bond for \$1100, but then resold it the next year for \$1150 instead of holding it until its maturity date. And suppose that during the year in which you owned the bond you received \$100 in coupon payments. The total amount that you earned from your investment would be the \$100 in coupon payments plus the difference between the resale price and the purchase price: \$1150 - \$1100 = \$50. In other words, your return would be \$100 + \$50 = \$150.

To calculate the rate of return for the bond, we express the return in terms of a percent, or *rate*, by dividing the total earnings by the original purchase price. The rate of return on your bond would be

$$\text{rate of return} = \frac{\$100}{\$1100} + \frac{\$1150 - \$1100}{\$1100} = 9.1\% + 4.5\% = 13.6\%$$

In general, the rate of return is represented by

$$\text{rate of return} = \frac{\text{net payments to the owner}}{\text{purchase price}} + \frac{\text{resale price - purchase price}}{\text{purchase price}}$$

To shorten this equation, let's use some notation. Let P_t represent the price of an asset during the period in which you bought the asset. Let P_{t+1} represent the resale price one period after period t. Let NPO represent net payments (income minus expenses) that the owner of an asset acquires, like coupon payments from bonds or dividend payments from stock. A one-period rate of return for the asset is expressed as

$$rr = \frac{NPO}{P_t} + \frac{P_{t+1}\text{-}P_t}{P_t} \tag{7}$$

where rr represents the rate of return. The second term in equation (7) represents the rate of capital gains (or capital losses).

If an asset is not resold, then there is no capital gain and the rate of return on an asset equals its interest rate or yield rate. For example, consider a one-year time deposit that offers a 5% interest rate. A \$1000 initial deposit is considered the "purchase price" of the asset, P_t. The net payments to the owner of the time deposit would be \$50 in interest payments. The rate of return of the time deposit would simply be NPO/P_t = \$50/\$1000 = 5% because there is no capital gain. For a second example, consider a one year discount bond with a face value of \$1000, and suppose a saver/lender buys this bond for \$960 and holds it until it matures. The net payment would be \$1000 – \$960 = \$40, and the rate of return would be \$40/\$960 = 4.2% since there is no capital gain. The yield to maturity on this discount bond is also 4.2%, as we verified in equation (5). Eager students are encouraged to try to calculate the rate of return on a coupon bond that is held until its maturity date and to compare that rate of return with the yield to maturity, or interest rate, on the bond.

Rates of return are used to calculate the earnings

We can express the rate of return at an annualized rate when the asset is held for less than one year or more than one year. Box 2 shows how to calculate an annualized percentage yield for assets and an annualized percentage rate for debt.

Box 2: Calculating an annualized percentage yield (APY) an annualized percentage rate (APR)

Suppose that you buy a \$1000 face value discount bond for \$982, and the bond has a maturity date of 91 days. With an investment period of 91 days, we would calculate the yield to maturity as

$$\$982 = \frac{\$1000}{1 + ytm}$$

$$1 + ytm = \frac{\$1000}{\$982} = 1.0183$$

$$ytm = 0.0183 = 1.83\%$$

The value of 1.83% represents the yield to maturity and the interest rate earned during an investment period of 91 days. And since there is no reselling of the asset, the rate of return equals the yield to maturity. To compare yield rates and rates of return on different assets with different investment periods, investors usually standardize rates by expressing them in annualized form. An annualized yield rate or rate of return that savers/lenders earn is called the **annualized percentage yield** (APY). To calculate the annual percentage yield, we adjust the non-annual yield rate or rate of return by a function of the number of investment periods in a year:

$$1+APY=(1+ytm)^{\text{number of investment periods in a year}}$$

We calculate the number of investment periods in a year by dividing the number of days in a year by the number of days in the investment period.

$$1+APY=(1+ytm)^{\text{days in a year / days in investment period}}$$

For example, if a year has 365 days and if 91 days is the time period during which the investment occurs, then the number of investment periods in a year is 365/91 = 4.01. (However, sometimes there are only 360 days in a year when a yield is earned, due to holidays or other factors.) The 1.83% yield rate during a period of 91 days has an APY of

$$1+APY=(1+0.0183)^{365/91}=1.0754$$
$$APY=0.0754=7.54\%$$

Sometimes lenders express interest rates on loans with different maturity dates as annualized interest rates. An annualized interest rate that borrowers pay is called the **annualized percentage rate** (APR), which is just another name for the APY for the saver/lender. For example, if you have a credit card that charges a 0.03764% daily interest rate, then your APR on daily credit card balances would be

$$1+APR=(1+i)^{\text{number of borrowing periods in a year}}$$
$$1+APR=(1+i)^{\text{days in a year/days in a loan period}}$$
$$1+APR=(1+0.0003764)^{365\text{ days/1 day}}=1.1472$$
$$APR=0.1472=14.72\%$$

But when calculating the APR and APY, lenders usually include other costs for borrowers, like loan processing fees, which make the calculations more complicated. When borrowing through a bank, be sure to know how the APR is calculated and which costs it represents.

Real interest rates

When savers/lenders earn interest on their assets, how much can they eventually buy with their earnings when they receive their interest, yield or return? The amount of goods and services that savers/lenders can buy after their investment pays off depends on how much the prices of goods and services have changed during the investment period.

Suppose that a potential saver considers investing \$1000 in a one year time deposit, and the time deposit will earn \$50 in interest payments. If he saves, he would earn a \$50/\$1000 = 5% **nominal interest rate**, a rate that accounts only for the monetary (or nominal) value of interest. Nominal interest rates are the interest rates that you usually find posted at banks, in financial markets and in newspapers. (See Box 1.)

To determine how much additional purchasing power our saver is expected to earn if he invested in the time deposit, we must adjust nominal interest rates for the inflation that is expected to occur during the investment period. The **real interest rate** is the nominal interest rate adjusted for expected inflation; it measures the expected purchasing power of interest earned by savers/lenders, as well as the purchasing power of interest forgone by borrowers/spenders. For example, if the inflation rate is expected to be 2% during the investment period, then the real interest rate for our potential saver would be 5% – 2% = 3%. Our saver could expect to buy 3% more goods and services at the end of the investment period. In general, the relationship between real interest rates and nominal interest rates is shown in the following equation:

$$1 + r = \frac{1 + i}{1 + \pi^e}$$

or more simply

$$r = i - \pi^e \tag{8}$$

where r represents the real interest rate, i represents the nominal interest rate and π^e represents the inflation rate that is expected to occur during the investment period. When inflation is expected to be positive, real interest rates are less than nominal interest rates.

We could change our perspective and consider real interest rates for a potential borrower. Suppose that an institution or individual considers borrowing a loan of $1000 with a nominal interest of 8%. If such an institution borrows, it would pay $80 = (8%)$1000 in interest at the end of the loan. Suppose further that the inflation rate is expected to be 2% during the borrowing period and that the income, revenue or wages of the potential borrower are expected to rise to match this expected inflation rate. (For the average wage earner, wages do rise over a long period to match higher prices earned by sellers of final goods and services. And higher prices of final goods and services can contribute to higher incomes and revenues for the sellers.) When the monetary value of the potential borrower's income, revenue or wages are expected to rise by 2%, say from $1000 to $1020, the real cost of borrowing would be $80 – $20. After adjusting for inflation, the borrower would pay a 8% – 2% = 6% interest rate using the inflation-adjusted income, revenue or wages that it earns.

How do we determine what savers and borrowers expect about inflation? Since 1997, buyers and sellers in bond markets have provided their own answers by buying and selling bonds offered by the US Treasury Department, which are called Treasury Inflation Protected Securities (TIPS). These bonds, or securities, are designed to remove the risk that inflation will result in a low real interest rate by having coupon and face value payments adjusted for inflation. If inflation is expected to be high, savers/lenders can expect coupon payments and face value payments to be adjusted upwards, so that the purchasing power of earnings from the bonds remains constant. In effect, the inflation-adjusted yield rate, or real interest rate, on these bonds remains constant once the bonds have been purchased.

By comparing the inflation-adjusted yield to maturity on TIPS with the nominal yield to maturity on standard Treasury securities, we can determine what investors in bond markets expect about inflation. We treat yield rates and interest rates as the same in this case, since the yield to maturity is a bond's own interest rate, and use equation (8) to determine expected inflation.

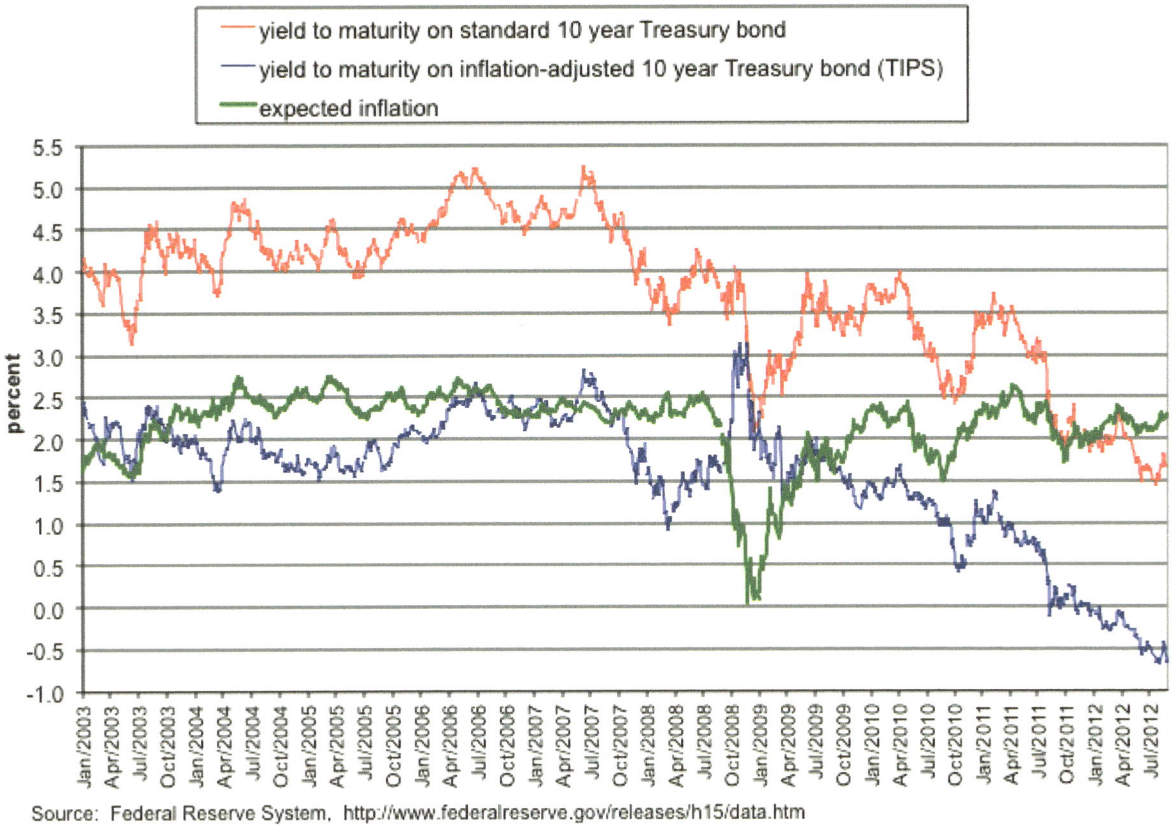

Figure 3-5: Nominal interest rates, real interest rates and expected inflation in the US, 2003.01-2012.08

Figure 3-5 compares the yield to maturity on a standard 10-year security from the US Treasury and the yield to maturity on a 10-year TIPS. The nominal yield to maturity, or interest rate, on the standard security was between 2% and 5% during 2003-2011. The inflation-adjusted yield to maturity, or real interest rate, on the TIPS was between 2.5% and 0.5% during most of this period, except during late 2008 and early 2009. By subtracting the real interest rate from the nominal interest rate and by using equation (8), we can determine what buyers and sellers in bond markets expect about future inflation during the period in which the bonds are held. During 2003-2012, savers/lenders in bond markets expected future inflation to be between 1.5% and 3% per year during the following decade or however long they expected to hold the bonds, except during late 2008 and early 2009. Interestingly, during late 2008 and early 2009 when a financial crisis erupted in the US, people buying and selling Treasury bonds expected the inflation rate to be near zero, when in fact it was near zero and even negative during several months. During 2012, when large amount of cash were available to invest in government bonds and expectations about inflation increased about 2%, the TIPS became so attractive that their prices exceeded the face value of their payments so that their yield rates became negative.

Summary

In this chapter we have considered different ways to calculate interest, yield and return rates. We first considered how to calculate the present value of an asset by realizing that funds which become available at different times are valued differently. Funds available at the present time are considered to be more valuable than the same amount of funds available in the future because currently available funds can be saved to earn interest or they can be spent to avoid borrowing and paying interest. To reflect this fact in present value calculations, funds that become available in the future are discounted by a function of the interest rate and the number of periods until they become available. In other words, present value represents the value of future funds as if they were available at the present time. Once we have understood present value, we can calculate the yield to maturity on an asset by setting the price of the asset equal to the present value of future funds paid until the maturity date and by using the yield to maturity as the interest rate that discounts the value of future funds. The yield to maturity represents the interest rate that would be earned on an asset if it were held until the asset's maturity date.

Savers do not always hold an asset until its maturity date, and so may desire other ways to measure earnings from an asset. Current yield represents current payments from an asset divided by the asset's current price and represents an asset's current interest rate. Discount yield represents the discount from buying a bond relative to the bond's face value, with an adjustment to express this yield at an annualized rate. The rate of return measures the earnings rate from the net payments to an asset owner plus the rate of capital gains that an investor earns when he resells the asset.

Real interest rates are inflation-adjusted interest rates, and they measure the real earnings rate for investors and the real cost of borrowing for debtors. They represent the additional goods and services that a saver/lender is expected to be able to afford after an investment and the additional goods and services that a borrower/spender is expected to forgo after paying back a loan or spending money. Real interest rates are calculated by subtracting the expected inflation rate from the nominal interest rate.

Problems and Applications

Short answer problems

1. Why are future funds considered less valuable than funds available in the present?

2. Name three reasons for why interest is used to compensate savers/lenders.

3. Calculate the yield to maturity of a 2 year discount bond with a face value of $10,000 and a price of $9570.

4. Calculate the yield to maturity of a 2 year coupon bond with a face value of $10,000 with four $100 coupon payments, one every 6 months (1/2 year), and a price of $10,200.

5. Calculate the discount yield of a 6 month (180 day) discount bond with a face value of $10,000 and a price of $9950.

6. Calculate the current yield of a $10,000 face value coupon bond with a coupon rate 2% and a price of $10,500.

7. How does the yield to maturity differ from a rate of return? When are the two the same?

8. Why do long term bonds have more interest rate risk than short term bonds?

9. How does the yield to maturity differ from the current yield and discount yield? In what way are they the same?

10. Calculate the real interest rate when the expected inflation rate is 5% and the nominal interest rate or yield rate is 4%. In this case, would you rather be a saver/lender or a borrower/spender whose income, revenue and wages rise to match the expected inflation rate.

Internet applications

1. Go to http://ecos.bok.or.kr/ and plot yield rates (yields to maturity) on 1 year Treasury bonds, 10 year Treasury bonds and 3 year corporate bonds rated BBB- from 2000 to the latest month.
   a. Between 1 year Treasury bonds and 10 year Treasury bonds, which bond generally has the higher yield rates? Why do you think this is true?
   b. Between 10 year Treasury bonds and 3 year corporate bonds rated BBB-, which bond generally has the higher yield rates? Why do you think this is true?

2. Go to http://ecos.bok.or.kr/ and plot yield rates (yields to maturity) on 91-day Bank of Korea bonds ("Monetary stabilization bonds"), 364-day Bank of Korea bonds, and 2-year Bank of Korea bonds from 2006 to the latest month.

   a. Which bond has the highest average yield rate? Why do you think this is true?
   b. In chapter 9 we consider how to calculate the standard deviation to measure risk or volatility. Try to calculate the standard deviation in a spread sheet for the 91-day, 264-day and 2-year bonds. Which bond has the highest standard deviation of the yield rates, or the most volatile yield rates?
   c. Is your result measuring the volatility of yield rates with the predictions in Table 2?

3. Go to http://ecos.bok.or.kr/ and plot yield rates (yields to maturity) on 1-year Treasury (Ministry of Finance) bonds, 3-year Treasury bonds, 5-year Treasury bonds, 10-year Treasury bonds and 20-year Treasury bonds from 2006 to the latest month.

   a. Which bond has the highest average yield rate? Why do you think this is true?
   b. In chapter 9 we consider how to calculate the standard deviation to measure risk or volatility. Try to calculate the standard deviation in a spreadsheet for the yield rate of each bond. Which yield rate has the highest standard deviation, or the most volatile yield rates, from 2006?
   c. Is your result measuring the volatility of yield rates with the predictions in Table 2?
   d. Worries of a financial crisis occurred in late 2008 that made prices of short-term government bonds increase and their yield rates decrease substantially. After these worries subsidized in January 2009, which yield rate had the highest standard deviation? Is your result more consistent with the predictions in Table 2?

4. Go to http://ecos.bok.or.kr/ and plot yield rates (yields to maturity) on 1 year Treasury bonds and the inflation rate using the consumer price index from 2000 to the latest month. If the inflation rate using the consumer price index can be considered the expected inflation rate for savers/lenders, calculate the real yield/interest rate for these bonds.

4. Model of the Market for Monetary Assets

This chapter describes theories by several economists to explain why individuals and institutions are willing to hold monetary assets. I consider theories by Irving Fisher, Alfred Marshall, A.C. Pigou, John Maynard Keynes, William Baumol, James Tobin and Milton Friedman. After considering these theoretical reasons for holding monetary assets, I construct a model to represent the willingness to hold monetary assets, as well as the quantity of money and credit available from the central bank and financial intermediaries. With this model of the market for monetary assets, or money market, we can consider how changes in the willingness to hold monetary assets and the quantity of money and credit are predicted to change interest, yield and return rates on non-monetary assets.

The demand of monetary assets

A relationship or function that describes how prices of a good or service are related to the quantity of the good or service that people are willing to buy at those prices is called the **demand** of the good or service. The demand of good or service represents the willingness to buy the good or service at each possible price, when other factors like quality, expected quality, expected future price, status associated with holding the good, service or asset, available information, and so on remain constant.

We can consider monetary assets to be a good or service that is necessary to pay for other goods or services or to repay debt with a price, value or cost in terms of the prices of goods or services that are purchased or in terms of the interest, yield or return that could have been earned by buying and holding non-monetary assets. The theories in this chapter can be used to relate the value of money either to the prices of goods and services or to interest/yield/return rates on non-monetary assets.

Thus, a **theory of the demand of monetary assets** explains and predicts why individuals and institutions are willing to hold a given quantity of monetary assets given various measures of the price, value, cost or risk of holding money, as well as other factors like the rate at which monetary assets are used and the amount of goods and services purchased. I consider several theories; the first is the oldest theory, called the quantity theory of money.

Quantity theory of money

The quantity theory of money is a theory of how the total quantity of monetary assets (and possibly credit too) that circulates in the economy is related to the total expenditure on goods and services produced in the economy. The theory can also tell us a simple demand function for monetary assets because the amount of monetary assets that individuals and institutions want to hold is related to the prices of goods and services produced, sold and bought in the economy, as well as the amount of goods and services.

Irving Fisher in *The Purchasing Power of Money*, published in 1911, examined the link between the total quantity of monetary assets (the money supply), represented as M, and the total expenditure on goods and services produced, sold and bought in the economy, represented as $P \times Y$, where P represents the average prices of goods and services and Y represents the aggregate amount of goods and services produced, sold and bought. ($P \times Y$ also represents the nominal value of goods and services produced in the economy and the nominal income earned by selling those goods and services.)

A *level of average prices* is an index, or number, that averages the prices of goods and services by using quantities of the goods and services to weight the importance of the prices in total expenditure. Two commonly used price indices are the *Consumer Price Index*, or CPI, which averages the prices that a typical consumer must pay,[21] and the *Implicit Price Deflator* or *GDP Deflator*, which averages the prices of all final goods and services produced within the domestic economy.[22] Changes in these price indices therefore represent changes in the level of average prices of goods and services. In practice, we could use one of these indices to represent P and use the measure of gross domestic production, or *GDP*, adjusted for price changes to represent Y, or simply use the nominal value of gross domestic production to represent $P \times Y$. Homework questions below also ask to download an actual measure of the total quantity of monetary assets M.

Mr. Fisher related total expenditure on final goods and services to the total quantity of monetary assets through a ratio and called this ratio the **velocity of money**, V:

$$V = \frac{P \times Y}{M} \tag{9}$$

By rearranging, we obtain what Mr. Fisher called the **equation of exchange**:

$$M \times V = P \times Y \tag{10}$$

This equation says that the amount of money spent times the rate at which it is spent (exchanged for goods and services) matches the amount of goods and services bought and sold times the level of average prices of those goods and services.

Mr. Fisher argued that the velocity of money is determined by how individuals and institutions conduct transactions. For example, if many use short-term credit through charge accounts, letters of credit and credit cards to conduct transactions, less money is required to conduct transactions at any point in time so that M falls relative to $P \times Y$ and the velocity of the remaining money in circulation increases. Mr. Fisher believed that institutions, social norms and technology affect velocity only slowly over time, and he predicted that velocity would be roughly constant in the short run.

From the equation of exchange, we can form the **quantity theory of money**, which states that nominal expenditure is determined by the quantity of money if the velocity of money is constant. For example, suppose that the velocity of an average dollar is 5 times per year, total nominal expenditure (GDP) is \$5 trillion and the quantity of money in circulation is \$1 trillion. If the quantity of money in circulation doubles to \$2 trillion, the quantity theory of money predicts that nominal expenditure on goods and services will double to \$10 trillion when the rate at which money is spent remains constant. Nominal expenditure on goods and services would increase because prices of goods and services increase, the production and sale of goods and services increase, or both.

Even when the velocity of money (or more generally, the demand of monetary assets) is not constant, we can still use the quantity theory of money to predict how nominal expenditure on goods and services is

[21] See http://www.bls.gov/cpi/home.htm for a description.

[22] See http://www.bea.gov/bea/dn/nipaweb/nipa_underlying/NIPAHelp.htm for a description.

affected. For example, if the velocity of money and the willingness to spend money decreases (and when the quantity of money is constant), then nominal expenditure (prices and/or goods and services produced and sold) should also decrease.

Mr. Fisher and other economists during his time generally claimed that prices adjusted to market conditions, and that the quantity of goods and services produced was determined primarily by the productive capacity of the economy. In particular, they claimed that producers would continue to produce at full capacity (which is determined by available factors of production like the number of workers, technology, machinery, transportation infrastructure, communications infrastructure and so on) over time as prices either quickly increase when shortages temporarily develop or quickly decrease when surpluses temporarily develop. As a result, Mr. Fisher predicted through the quantity theory of money that if the quantity of money in circulation doubles, then the level of average prices of goods and services would double because productive capacity would not be able to increase but prices would quickly increase as expenditure increased from the additional money. Thus, the quantity theory of money provides a simple explanation for why prices change: changes in the level of average prices are caused by changes in the quantity of money when the quantity of goods and services produced and the velocity of money remain constant.

Because the quantity theory of money tells us how much money individuals and institutions hold for a given level of aggregate expenditure, it can be used to represent a demand function for monetary assets. Rewrite the equation of exchange as

$$M = \frac{1}{V} \times P \times Y$$

When institutions and individuals hold the correct amount of monetary assets to pay for goods and services relative to non-monetary assets for investment purposes, then the quantity of monetary assets that individuals and institutions want to hold also equals the quantity of monetary assets supplied by the central bank (which can be used to buy goods and services or non-monetary assets). In this case, we write $M = M^d$ where M^d represents the quantity of monetary assets that individuals and institutions are willing to hold. Accordingly,

$$M^d = \frac{1}{V} \times P \times Y \tag{11}$$

Thus, Mr. Fisher claimed through this equation that the velocity of money (which was believed to be stable in the short run) and total expenditure on goods and services determined the quantity of monetary assets that individuals and institutions wanted to hold. Mr. Fisher argued that individuals and institutions want to hold monetary assets only to buy goods and services after they already purchased the correct amount of non-monetary assets.

(When Mr. Fisher was developing the demand function from the quantity theory of money, Alfred Marshall and A.C. Pigou and their colleagues derived as similar demand function based on the willingness to hold money as a medium of exchange and as a store of wealth.)

Changes in velocity

The claim that total expenditure is determined solely by the quantity of monetary assets rests on the assumption that velocity of money is constant. However, this assumption is nowhere near true. Even in the short run, velocity fluctuates substantially, especially during times of market turmoil, like in 1915 when Mr.

Fisher's writing was popularized and war in Europe shut down many financial markets. More recently, the velocity of money declined sharply in the US during the 2008-2009 financial crisis, as individuals and institutions hoarded cash in response to the increased risk of holding non-monetary assets and the decreased liquidity of these assets. The risk of holding non-monetary assets, the liquidity of non-monetary assets and expectations about these factors can change the willingness to hold and to spend money, especially in the short run. We formally model how the risk of non-monetary assets and liquidity of non-monetary assets affects the willingness to hold money later in this chapter.

In general, velocity usually falls or at least has a lower growth rate during economic contractions as individuals and institutions want to hold more monetary assets and spend them less frequently as a precaution against lower income and/or higher expenses. Economists say that velocity is *pro-cyclical*; it tends to change in tandem with changes in economic activity, or what is called the business cycle.

Furthermore, velocity in the long run can also become unstable, as technology, institutions and social norms change. After 1982, the velocity of the M1 measure of money in the US was more volatile than in the previous decades because of changes in technology and financial regulations. And even though the velocity of the M2 measure of money was relatively stable compared to M1 velocity, it was far from constant. It also changes especially in the 1990s as further technological changes, like electronic and internet banking, became more widespread.

During the Depression from 1929-1933, it was apparent that the rate at which people were spending money slowed significantly as individuals and institutions hoarded cash and stopped spending so freely. Economists thus began to search for other factors besides the overall level of production, income and expenditure that might explain the demand of monetary assets and changes in velocity. John Maynard Keynes developed another theory, called the liquidity preference theory, which tried to explain both.

Liquidity preference theory

John Maynard Keynes in *The General Theory of Employment, Interest, and Money*, published in 1936, examined the link between nominal interest/yield rates on one hand and the willingness to hold monetary, or liquid, assets on the other hand and developed a theory called the **liquidity preference theory**. His theory recognized that people hold money to make transactions, but also as a precaution against unknown expenses and changes in income, and to speculate about the rate of return on bonds and other non-monetary assets. I describe each of these factors in turn.

Irving Fisher and his colleagues argued that individuals and institutions hold money to conduct transactions, and Mr. Keynes agreed with this belief. And like earlier economists, Mr. Keynes modeled the *transactions motive* behind the demand of monetary assets to be proportional to total expenditure.

In addition, Mr. Keynes believed that individuals and institutions hold monetary assets as a precaution against unexpected expenses and changes in income or revenue. But Mr. Keynes argued that the amount of monetary assets that people want to hold as a precaution is primarily determined by the total expenses, income, revenue and expenditure that they plan to do in the future and these values are proportional to current expenses, income, revenue and expenditure. He therefore argued that the *precautionary motive* behind the demand of monetary assets is also proportional to total expenditure.

The departure that Mr. Keynes made from earlier theories is that he claimed that individuals and institutions want to hold monetary assets as a store of wealth, *and* that this motive for holding monetary assets depends not only on income but on the interest rates, the yield rates and rates of return that people expect to earn on non-monetary assets. Mr. Keynes called this motive the *speculative motive* behind the demand of monetary assets because individuals and institutions purportedly speculate about prices and rates of return on non-monetary assets and adjust their holdings of non-monetary assets, especially bonds and loans, accordingly. Box 1 gives some quotes from Mr. Keynes' 1936 text.

Box 1: John Maynard Keynes in "The General Theory of Employment, Interest and Money"

[An individual must decide] in *what form* he will hold the command over future consumption which he has reserved, whether out of his current income or from previous savings. Does he want to hold it in the form of immediate, liquid command (i.e. in money or its equivalent? Or is he prepared to part with immediate command for a specified or indefinite period, leaving it to future market conditions to determine on what terms he can, if necessary, convert deferred command over specific goods into immediate command over goods in general? In other words, what is the degree of his *liquidity-preference*—where an individual's liquidity-preference is given by a schedule of the amounts of his resources, valued in terms of money or of wage-units, which he will wish to retain in the form of money in different sets of circumstances.

...

...let us...consider why such a thing as liquidity-preference exists. In this connection we can usefully employ the ancient distinction between the use of money for the transaction of current business and its use as a store of wealth. As regards the first of these two uses, it is obvious that up to a point it is worthwhile to sacrifice a certain amount of interest for the convenience of liquidity. But, given that the rate of interest is never negative, why should anyone prefer to hold his wealth in a form which yields little or no interest to holding it in a form which yields interest (assuming, of course, at this stage, that the risk of default is the same in respect of a bank balance as of a bond)?

...

[because of] the existence of *uncertainty* as to the future of the rate of interest, i.e. as to the complex of rates of interest for varying maturities which will rule at future dates. [At this point, what Mr. Keynes calls uncertain rates of interest, I call uncertain rates of return.]

...

There is, moreover, a further ground for liquidity-preference which results from the existence of uncertainty as to the further of the rate of interest, provided that there is an organised market for dealing in debts. For different people will estimate the prospects differently and anyone who differs from the predominant opinion as expressed in market quotation may have a good reason for keeping liquid resources in order to profit, if he is right, from its turning out in due course that [various future rates of interest] were in a mistaken relationship to one another.

...

The three divisions of liquidity-preference which we have distinguished above may be defined as depending on (i) the transactions-motive, i.e. the need of cash for the current transaction of personal and business exchanges; (ii) the precautionary-motive, i.e. the desire for security as to the future cash equivalent of a certain proportion of total resources; and (iii) the speculative-motive, i.e. the object of securing profit from knowing better than the market what the future will bring forth...in the absence of an organised market, liquidity-preference due to the precautionary-motive would be greatly increased; whereas the existence of an organised market give an opportunity for wide fluctuations in liquidity-preference due to the speculative-motive.

It may illustrate the argument to point out that, if the liquidity-preference due to the transaction-motive and the precautionary-motive are assumed to absorb a quantity of cash which is not very sensitive to changes in the rate of interest as such and apart from its reactions on the level of income, so that the total quantity of money, less this quantity, is available for satisfying liquidity-preferences due to the speculative-motive, the rate of interest and the price of bonds have to be fixed at the level at which the desire on the part of certain individuals to hold cash (because at that level they feel "bearish" of the future of bonds) is exactly equal to the amount of cash available for the speculative-motive.

Mr. Keynes assumed in 1936 that the expected rates of return on monetary assets was zero, although today there are some types of checkable deposits that pay very low rates of interest, and many assets in the money market will pay slightly higher interest, yield or return rates. Nonetheless, interest rates on checkable deposits and in the money market are usually less than the usual interest, yield or return rates on non-monetary assets. Despite the low interest, yield or return rates on monetary assets, sometimes, as was the case during Mr. Keynes' time, non-monetary assets are expected to have low or even negative return rates as their prices are expected to fall. During these times, the willingness to hold monetary assets increases due to their perceived safety. And even if nominal interest and yield rates on non-monetary assets can not decrease below zero, a situation often called a "liquidity trap" because of the claim that individuals and institutions have no incentive to further increase their liquidity, expected rates of return on non-monetary assets can become negative, so that individuals and institutions will want to increase the amount of monetary assets that they hold by selling the non-monetary assets.

During these times, a few other fairly safe assets, like short-term government bills or very short-term loans to established institutions, can have high prices/values and thus low yield rates and interest rates. But most non-monetary assets like long-term bonds, long-term loans, long-term deposits and stocks are considered risky or illiquid or otherwise undesirable. Thus, the willingness to hold them decreases, their prices/values decrease, and their yield and interest rates increase. (Although Mr. Keynes did not explicitly consider non-monetary assets like stocks or houses, rates of return on long-term bonds tend to change with rates of return on other non-monetary assets as people sell one asset to buy another.)

Formally, Mr. Keynes argued that if prices of long-term bonds or other risky/illiquid non-monetary assets are expected to fall, then individuals and institutions who have already purchased the bonds at a high price could expect their return rates to be low or negative if they want to sell them in the future. In this case, Mr. Keynes claimed that individuals and institutions would be more willing to sell the bonds and other non-monetary assets as quickly as possible (at highly discounted prices) and hold monetary assets in anticipation of their falling prices and low/negative return rates. (But it is unclear why people would not want to hold other non-monetary assets for which they expect a positive or even rising rate of return, unless no non-monetary assets are expected to have a positive rate of return.) Thus, Mr. Keynes argued that the quantity of monetary assets that individuals and institutions are willing to hold is high when prices of bonds and other non-monetary assets are expected to fall. In this case, return rates are expected to be low (and possibly become negative) and their yield rates or interest rates are currently low (but expected to rise). In other words, current interest rates, yield rates and expected (future) return rates are all low, even though interest/yield rates and return rates (determined by changes in prices) are expected to change in opposite directions.

Likewise, Mr. Keynes argued that if the prices of non-monetary assets are low and expected to rise, then their return rates are expected to be high and their yield rates or interest rates are currently high (but expected to fall). In other words, current interest rates, yield rates and expected (future) return rates are all high, even though interest/yield rates and return rates are expected to change in opposite directions. In this case, Mr. Keynes claimed that individuals and institutions would be more willing to buy non-monetary assets today by spending their money in anticipation of their rising prices. Thus, Mr. Keynes argued that the quantity of monetary assets that individuals and institutions are willing to hold is low when prices of bonds and other non-monetary assets are expected to rise, when return rates are expected to be high and when yield rates or interest rates are currently high (but expected to fall).

In addition to bonds, Mr. Keynes also considered loans from banks and other financial intermediaries to be a common non-monetary asset for saving/lending. So if current interest rates are high when other factors like risk remain steady, then the reserves at banks are costly to hold, so that the quantity of reserves (monetary assets) that banks and other financial intermediaries are willing to hold will be low as they lend to customers. If current interest rates are low when other factors like risk remain steady, then banks and other financial intermediaries are less willing to lend and more willing to hold more reserves to be sure of always having enough cash to settle payments and to satisfy customers.

When Mr. Keynes, like other economists, argued that money is used for transactions (and not as a store of value), he postulated that individuals and institutions want to hold a certain amount based on its purchasing power. In other words, people should want to maintain a *real* quantity of money, given the (expected) interest, yield and return rates on non-monetary assets and given (expected) expenditure, expenses, income and revenue.

Keynes summarized his arguments about the transactions, precautionary and speculative motives for holding a real quantity of monetary assets by defining a demand function for real monetary assets:

$$\left(\frac{M}{P}\right)^d = f_0(i, Y)$$

where P represents the level of average prices of goods and services, and $(M/P)^d$ represents the demand function for holding a real quantity of monetary assets. i represents the (average) interest rate, yield rate and expected return rate on non-monetary assets (and in particular, on bonds or loans), whose changes are related to expected changes in prices of assets, Y represents both the level of real expenditure and expenses by individuals and institutions and the level of real income and revenue for individuals and institutions, and f_0 is a general function that shows a negative relationship between i and the real quantity of monetary assets that individuals and institutions are willing to hold and a positive relationship between Y and the real quantity of monetary assets that individuals and institutions are willing to hold.

Alternatively, we can say that the nominal quantity of monetary assets that individuals and institutions are willing to hold depends positively on the level of average prices of goods and services, positively on (real) expenditure, expenses income and revenue (and positively on nominal expenditure, expenses, income and revenue), negatively on nominal interest rates, yield rates, expected return rates and expected changes in the prices of assets:

$$M^d = f_1(i, P \times Y)$$

where f_1 shows a negative relationship between nominal interest, yield and expected return rates, i, and the nominal quantity of monetary assets that individuals and institutions are willing to hold and a positive relationship between nominal expenditure, expenses, income and revenue, $P \times Y$, and the nominal quantity of monetary assets that individuals and institutions are willing to hold. Essentially, this function says that we want to hold a certain quantity of money depending on the willingness to hold non-monetary assets (which depends on their interest/yield/expected return rates and expected price changes) and the willingness to buy goods and services (which depends on their prices and the amount of production and income earned from production).

In a special case, this nominal money demand function can be rewritten as

$$M^d = P \times L(i, Y) \tag{12}$$

where L represents a special function that specifies the willingness to hold a real quantity of monetary, or liquid, assets. This special function again represents a negative relationship between i and the quantity of monetary assets that individuals and institutions are willing to hold, adjusted for the prices of goods and services, and a positive relationship between Y and the quantity of monetary assets that individuals and institutions are willing to hold, adjusted for the prices of goods and services.

In this special case, we can compare the demand of nominal monetary assets with the quantity of money that circulates in the economy and the velocity of money. Recall that the velocity of money is defined as $(P \times Y)/M$, which equals $(P \times Y)/M^d$ when institutions and individuals hold the "correct" amount of monetary assets relative to non-monetary assets (when financial markets are in equilibrium), so that $M = M^d$. When $M^d = P \times L(i, Y)$, this implies

$$V = \frac{P \times Y}{M^d} = \frac{Y}{L(i, Y)} \tag{13}$$

Like equation (12), equation (13) predicts when interest rates, yield rates and expected return rates are high (and the prices of non-monetary assets are expected to rise), the quantity of real monetary assets that individuals and institutions are willing to hold is low as they use more monetary assets to purchase more non-monetary assets. So, the remaining monetary assets used to buy final goods and services must circulate at a faster rate (at a higher velocity). But equation (13) makes an ambiguous prediction about the effect of real expenditure and income on the velocity of money. For example, if real expenditure and income fall, both the numerator and the denominator in (13) will decrease, so it is unclear whether this result can explain the apparent pro-cyclical movements in velocity. However, because nominal interest, yield and expected return rates also tend to be pro-cyclical, the effect of i only would predict a pro-cyclical movement in velocity.

Regardless, the result from equation (13) leads to the claim that the velocity of money is not constant, even in the short run. Furthermore, because the demand of monetary assets depends on the expected prices and expected return rates of non-monetary assets, the velocity of money depends on people's expectations. In particular, when individuals and institutions expect or speculate that prices and return rates on non-monetary assets will fall (and interest rates and yield rates will rise), and in the extreme will become negative, the demand of monetary assets is predicted to increase as individuals and institutions hold cash instead of spending, which causes the velocity of money to decrease.

As a result, Mr. Keynes' model also implies that changes in velocity, not just changes in the quantity of money, can affect aggregate expenditure, production, income and prices.

Baumol-Tobin theory of the demand of monetary assets

William Baumol and James Tobin independently developed demand functions for monetary assets, which also predict that the quantity of monetary assets that individuals and institutions want to hold for transactions is sensitive to interest rates on non-monetary assets, but for reasons slightly different from the reasons in Mr. Keynes' theory.[23] While Mr. Keynes focused on the speculation about the rates of return on non-monetary assets, Mr. Baumol and Mr. Tobin focused on the transaction costs of selling and buying non-monetary assets (that is, their illiquidity).

The basic idea of the Baumol-Tobin models can be explained using an example. Both models assume that individuals and institutions received income and revenue infrequently but needed to spend money frequently (daily). Suppose that Big State University (BSU) receives tuition revenue of $10000 at the beginning of each semester but needs to pay for expenses at a constant rate each day. If the university holds

[23] William J. Baumol, (1952), "The Transaction Demand for Cash: An Inventory Theoretic Approach", *Quarterly Journal of Economics*, 66, 545-552. James Tobin, (1956), "The Interest Elasticity of the Transaction Demand for Cash", *Review of Economics and Statistics*, 38, 241-247.

$10000 in cash and it spends all of the $10000 by the end of each semester, its cash flow could be represented in the following diagram:

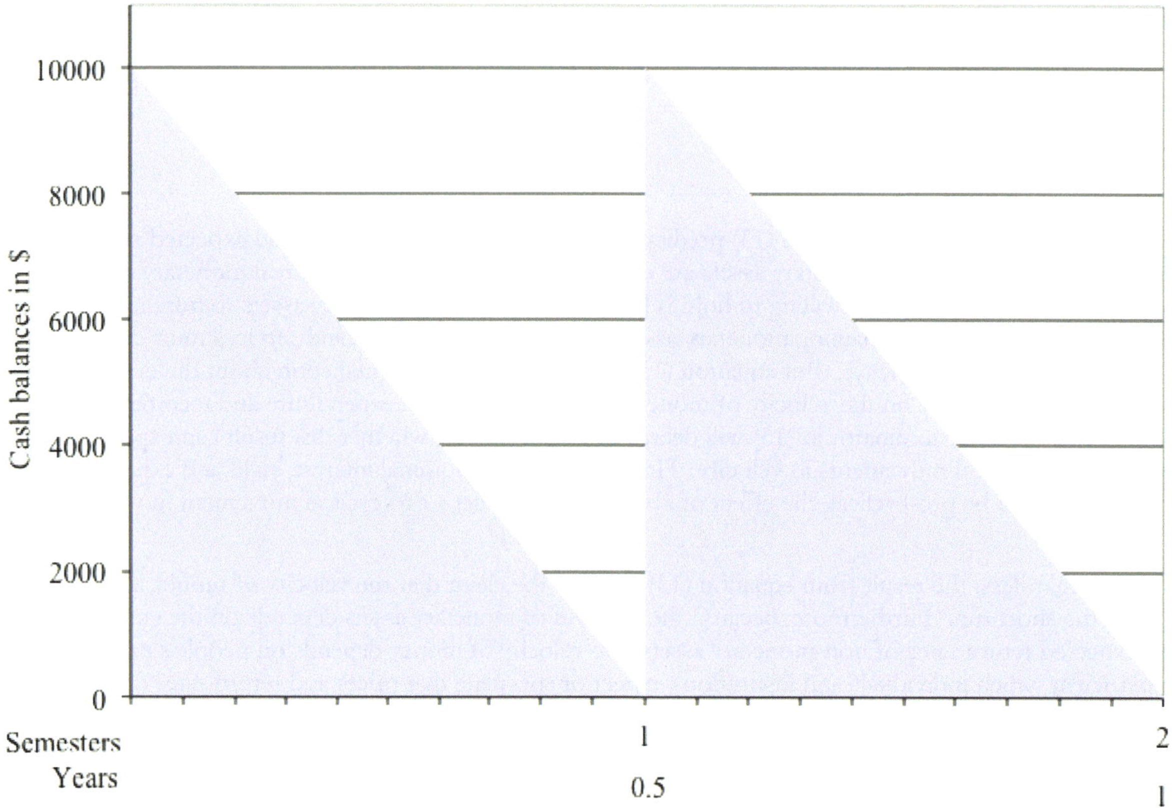

Figure 4-1: When income or revenue is received infrequently but spent frequently, and all of income or revenue is held as cash, cash balances steadily decline to zero, until more income or revenue is received.

When BSU holds all of its tuition revenue as cash plans to spend all of its revenue each semester, we can say that BSU maintains $5000 in its cash accounts during the year on average. If this pattern continues throughout the year and there are two semesters continue throughout the year, then total expenditure, expenses, income and revenue for BSU will be $20000/year, and the velocity of money (the average rate at which money is used in transactions) will be $V = P \times Y/M$ = $20000/year/$5000 = 4 times/year.

Suppose that instead of holding such large cash balances, BSU tries to earn interest income by buying some bonds and holding less money. At the beginning of each semester, suppose BSU holds $5000 in cash and saves/lends the rest of tuition revenue in the bond market. As shown in Figure 4-2, BSU will deplete its cash balances in the middle of the semester, and will need to sell its bonds to replenish its cash balances.

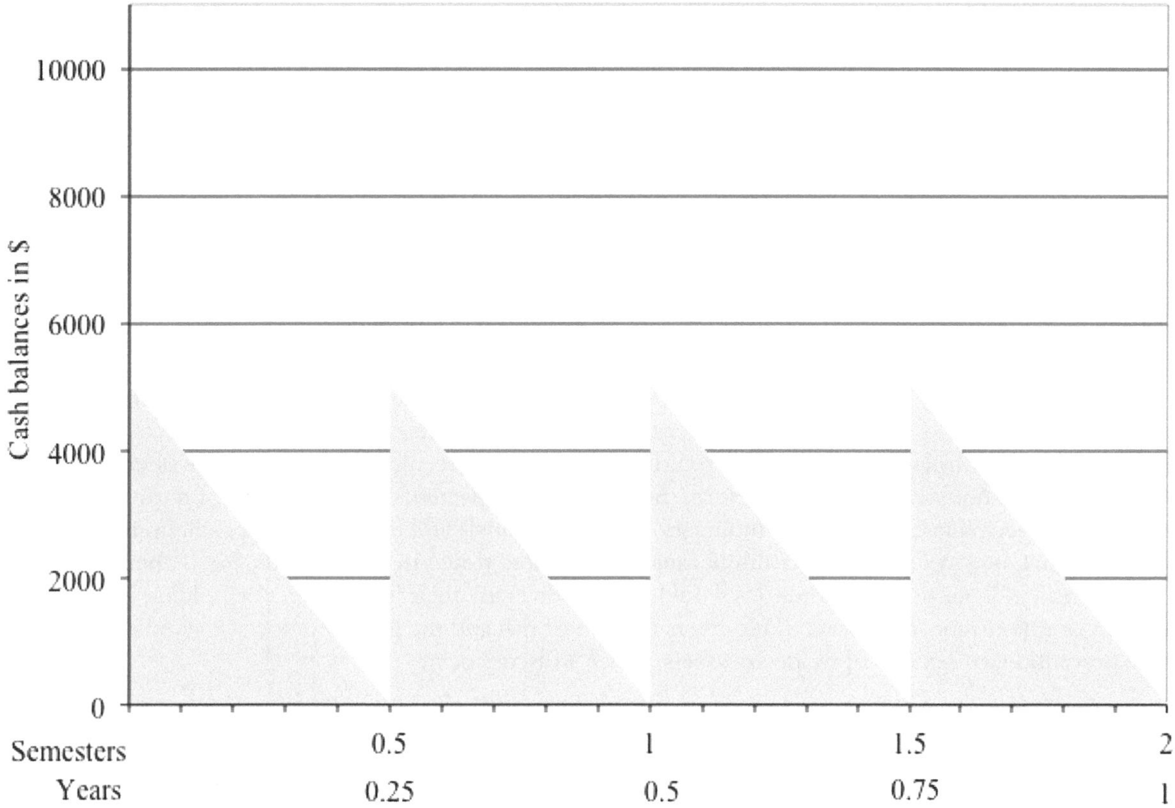

Figure 4-2: When half of income or revenue is used to purchase bonds and the remaining value is held as cash balances, cash balances steadily decrease to zero in the middle of the semester, at which time bonds are sold to acquire cash balances that will last to the end of the semester.

By holding lower cash balances, the velocity of the remaining money in circulation will increase. BSU maintains average cash balances of ($5000 + $0 + $5000 + $0 + $5000 + $0 + $5000 + $0)/8 = $2500 during the year, and expenditure per year is $20000, so that velocity of money becomes $20000/year/$2500 = 8 times/year.

By holding lower cash balances, BSU will earn 1/2 x $5000 x *i* interest income per year, where *i* represents the yield rate on bonds. And if BSU holds even lower average cash balances and buys and sells more bonds, it can earn more interest income. But when buying and holding bonds, BSU incurs two types of transaction costs. Buying and selling bonds, unlike cashing a check, usually involves an explicit fee, paid to a broker, dealer or trader. Secondly, BSU will have to hire someone to spend time to organize the accounts and transactions. As the cash balances decrease and holdings of bonds increase at BSU, both of these costs will increase.

Also, as the cash balances decrease and holdings of bonds increase at BSU, the Baumol-Tobin models predict that the velocity of the remaining money in circulation will increase.

Like Mr. Keynes' model, the Baumol-Tobin models predict that interest rates on non-monetary assets are inversely related to quantity of monetary assets that individuals and institutions want to hold. This prediction follows from the idea that holding monetary assets has an opportunity cost—the interest, yield or return that can not be earned on non-monetary assets. This cost should be compared with the benefit of holding money—the reduction of transaction costs or simply the convenience of paying for expenses when needed. (Because the Baumol-Tobin models focus on deposits, and not bonds, loans or other non-monetary assets, they ignore another benefit of holding money—avoiding the risk of a negative return rate, which Mr. Keynes focused on.) Furthermore, as the quantity demanded of monetary assets changes due to changes in interest rates, the models also predict that the velocity of money will change. In particular, as interest rates on non-monetary assets rise and the quantity demanded of monetary assets decreases, the velocity of the remaining money in circulation increases.

But Baumol-Tobin models predict a subtly different relationship between interest rates and rates of return on non-monetary assets and the quantity demanded of monetary assets than Mr. Keynes' model. Mr. Tobin argued that individuals and institutions care about the risk of investing in assets, as well as their expected rates of return. Like most economists, Mr. Tobin assumed that most people are *risk averse*: they want to avoid more risky assets when they offer the same expected rate of return as a safe asset. Monetary assets have a near constant nominal rate of return of about zero percent, but non-monetary assets can have substantial fluctuations in their rates of return. So even if the expected, or average, rate of return on bonds exceeds the expected rate of return on monetary assets, individuals and institutions may still prefer to hold some monetary assets as a store of wealth because they are less risky. In other words, Mr. Tobin argued that to reduce risk, individuals and institutions would want to diversify their investments by holding both monetary and non-monetary assets. This diversification of risk and the goal to reduce or avoid risk is related to the precautionary demand of monetary assets, which I discuss next.

Precautionary demand of monetary assets

In his liquidity preference theory, Mr. Keynes assumed that the precautionary motive to hold monetary assets is proportional to current expenditure, expenses, income and revenue. However, this need not be true. The **precautionary demand of monetary assets** recognizes that the precautionary motive need not be proportional to current expenditure expenses, income and revenue; more importantly, this motive can change over time as the uncertainty or expectations about future expenditure, expenses, income, revenue, interest rates and rates of return change.

In particular, during financial crises or economic contractions, as uncertainty about future expenditure, expenses, income or revenue increases, the precautionary demand of monetary assets increases because the benefit/safety of holding money for possible future transactions increases relative to the opportunity cost of foregone interest.

Like Mr. Tobin's model, the precautionary demand of monetary assets recognizes that most individuals and perhaps even some institutions behave as if they were risk averse. But this theory goes a little further in recognizing that this risk aversion can vary over time as macroeconomic conditions and expectations change. Expanding the notation from Mr. Keynes model, I write

$$M^d = P \times L(\gamma_t, i, Y)$$

where γ_t represents risk aversion that can change over time (t), depending on macroeconomic or financial market conditions. Therefore, the demand of monetary assets is supposed to depend positively on one's own risk aversion and more broadly on financial market/macroeconomic conditions that can vary over time (represented by γ_t), positively on expenditure (represented by P and Y) and negatively on interest/yield/expected return rates and expected prices of non-monetary assets (represented by i), which also depend on financial market/macroeconomic conditions.

The theory of long-run expected income

Milton Friedman developed a demand function for monetary assets that discounted the importance of (short-term changes in) interest rates, yield rates and return rates on non-monetary assets and considered income or revenue that is expected to be earned over the long run (which, of course, will be used for expenditure and expenses), as well as the prices of goods and services, as the primary determinants of money demand.[24]

Mr. Friedman argued that the demand of monetary assets is determined by the factors that determine the demand of any asset: total resources (wealth) for investment and the expected rate of return on monetary assets relative to other assets. Like Mr. Keynes (and by extension Mr. Tobin and Mr. Baumol), Mr. Friedman proposed that individuals and institutions want to hold monetary assets based on their purchasing power and that

$$\left(\frac{M}{P}\right)^d = \frac{M^d}{P}$$

But unlike Mr. Keynes, Mr. Tobin and Mr. Baumol, Mr. Friedman argued that interest rates or return rates on monetary assets was not constant and it should be compared to rates on non-monetary assets when trying to represent or measure the demand of monetary assets. And even though Mr. Friedman explicitly considers the effect of return rates on the demand of monetary assets, the predictions from his demand function are more similar to those from Mr. Fisher's demand function, which considered only (current) income from production, the prices of goods and services and the velocity of money. Mr. Friedman's demand function is represented as:

$$\left(\frac{M}{P}\right)^d = \frac{M^d}{P} = f_2(Y_p, r_b - r_m, r_s - r_m, r_c - r_m)$$

where Y_p represents total expected resources over time (wealth), or "permanent income" that an individual or institution expects to earn in the indefinite future. r_b represents the expected rate of return on bonds, r_s represents the expected rate of return on stocks, r_c represents the expected rates of return on commodity contracts or on goods and services and r_m represents the expected rate of return on monetary assets.

Somewhat similar to Mr. Keynes, Mr. Friedman argued that the demand of monetary assets depends on the expected rates of return on non-monetary assets *relative to* the expected rate of return on monetary assets, but unlike Mr. Keynes, Mr. Friedman argued that the expected rate of return on monetary assets was not zero and not constant. Although holding currency pays a zero percent nominal interest rate, Mr. Friedman argued that banks can make holding monetary assets more attractive by providing better services and even paying interest if they are allowed to. (Banks in the US were prohibited from paying interest on demand deposits according to a 1933 law.) Today, many checkable deposits pay a positive, although small, rate of interest. And even though demand deposits in the US still pay a zero rate of interest, banks can encourage their customers to hold more of these assets by providing more valuable services and benefits when opening and maintaining such accounts—like giving gifts and rewards, linking the account to a debit card so that payments can be made electronically, providing automatic bill payment or bill payment through the internet, providing cancelled checks as receipts and summary statements of transactions, providing financial records for tax purposes, and so on. Moreover, money market assets are still very liquid and

[24] Milton Friedman, (1956), "The Quantity Theory of Money: A Restatement" *Studies in the Quantity Theory of Money*, Milton Friedman, editor, (Chicago: University of Chicago Press), 3-21.

generally pay higher interest, yield or return rates than checkable deposits. For example, a US business that does foreign transactions can create expatriate currency deposits, whose interest payments are not limited by US law. And many individuals and institutions invest in money market mutual funds, which can substitute for a savings or checking account and pays a rate of interest comparable to the yield rate on US Treasury Bills.

Mr. Friedman also argued that the rates of return on non-monetary assets and the rate of return on and benefits from monetary assets move together. This argument is a little harder to justify, since rates of return on long-term bonds, securitized loans, stocks and commodities do not always track each other closely, especially in the short run, although one can argue that interest rates on some short-term, liquid assets, like US Treasury Bills, do track rates on long-term bonds and securitized loans in the long run. One can also argue that when interest rates on loans rise (fall), banks are willing to offer higher (lower) rates of return and benefits on their deposits, which serve as forms of money or close substitutes for money for bank customers.

In any case, Mr. Friedman argued that if relative rates of return do not change substantially because the rates of return and benefits on monetary assets move with the rates of return on non-monetary assets, then the relative rates of return should not substantially affect the demand of monetary assets. In other words, even though changes in a single interest, yield or return rate will change the incentives for holding money relative to other assets, changes in these rates are predicted to occur together so that the incentives for holding money relative to other assets do not change much. In the extreme, the demand of monetary assets depends only on available resources during the indefinite future, or "permanent income":

$$\left(\frac{M}{P}\right)^d = \frac{M^d}{P} = f_2(Y_p)$$

Permanent income, measured as average income or revenue over time, is less volatile than current income because transitory fluctuations of current income occur around the average. In particular, during an economic expansion, income rises and for many individuals and institutions, and current income rises above its long-run average. According to Mr. Friedman's theory, this implies that the demand of monetary assets (for spending) does not rise as much as current income because individuals and institutions would tend to save and invest more in non-monetary assets during an economic expansion. On the other hand, we should borrow during economic contractions, so that the demand of monetary assets (for spending) does not fall as much as income.

This prediction further implies that the demand of monetary assets is relatively stable, since it depends primarily on "permanent income" and the level of average prices, both of which do not change much in the short run.

According to the equilibrium specification of velocity that Mr. Keynes used, the velocity of money is predicted to be:

$$V = \frac{Y}{f_2(Y_p)}$$

This specification of velocity can predict that the velocity of money will be somewhat procyclical, since current income earned from producing goods and services and current expenditure on goods and services—represented by Y—will increase more than Y_p and can increase more than $f_2(Y_p)$ during an economic expansion and will decrease more than Y_p and can decrease more than $f_2(Y_p)$ during an economic contraction.

Mr. Friedman's theory further assumes that individuals and institutions treat commodities or sellable goods and monetary assets as substitutes: when people buy and hold more commodities or sellable goods, they hold fewer monetary assets (as a store of wealth); and when people buy and hold fewer commodities or sellable goods, they hold more monetary assets (as a store of wealth). This assumption implies that changes in the quantity of money have a direct effect on aggregate expenditure, and changes in aggregate expenditure have a direct effect on the quantity of money.

Empirical evidence on the demand of monetary assets

In earlier sections, I considered some theories which predicted that the demand of monetary assets is sensitive to interest, yield and return rates and some which did not. The evidence supports the theories that the willingness to hold monetary assets is sensitive to interest, yield and return rates on non-monetary assets, as I show in a later section.

However, Mr. Friedman's theory can be recognized as valuable because it does recognize the fact that individuals and institutions may consider expected long-term trends in expenditure, expenses, income and revenue when making decisions about how much in monetary assets to hold, especially when holding the assets is done for investment purposes. In addition, Mr. Friedman recognizes that monetary assets do have non-zero, non-constant interest rates or rates of return. And finally, Mr. Friedman's theory explicitly considers the effect of the rates of return on non-monetary assets other than bonds.

Mr. Irving's theory is valuable because it explicitly recognizes velocity and can show how velocity is related to the willingness to hold money. It also explicitly shows how the quantity of money is related to prices and the production of goods and services, which we will consider in later chapters.

As noted in an earlier section, evidence strongly supports that the velocity of money is not constant and has become even less stable over time. Because of the inverse relationship between the rate at which monetary assets are spent (velocity) and the willingness to hold monetary assets (demand), we can also say that the demand of monetary assets is not constant and has become less stable over time. After financial innovations in the past few decades, the types of assets that could be used as money or credit expanded greatly, and the stability of the demand of monetary assets declined. As a result, the usefulness of having the central bank target a quantity of money to meet the demand of monetary assets and to achieve a targeted level of aggregate expenditure has also declined. As we discuss in chapter 13, central banks now frequently target interest rates on reserves instead.

A model of the market for monetary assets

Given the theories about why individuals and institutions are willing to hold monetary assets, I now develop a model that considers the willingness to hold monetary assets, in addition to the supply (or quantity supplied) of money and credit from the central bank and from financial intermediaries. In some texts, this model is called the liquidity preference model, because it was developed by Mr. Keynes, even though it can incorporate many elements from the theories about the willingness to hold monetary assets. The model represents behavior in the money market, where institutions and individuals buy and sell short-term liquid assets, as well as behavior of those who hold or issue monetary assets in general. Furthermore, the model partially reflects behavior in the market for non-monetary assets as well, an in particular, the interest, yield and return rates on non-monetary assets.

The model groups all assets (that is, wealth) into either of two categories: monetary (or liquid) assets, which are safe assets that are convenient to conduct transactions, and non-monetary (or illiquid) assets, which generally earn higher interest/yield/return rates than monetary assets but are less safe (in terms of risk, liquidity and other characteristics) and can not be readily used to conduct transactions.

The model assumes that monetary assets earn an insignificant amount of interest, but they are desirable because they can be easily used to buy goods and services. On the other hand, non-monetary assets are not useful to conduct transactions, but they do earn an interest, yield or return for savers/lenders. Like Mr. Keynes' model, the model of the money market represents the various nominal interest rates/yield/expected return rates on non-monetary assets as an average value *i*.

The willingness to hold (or quantity demanded of) all assets must equal the willingness to hold monetary assets plus the willingness to hold non-monetary assets, and the total available quantity (or quantity supplied) of all assets must equal the total available quantity of monetary assets plus the total available of non-monetary assets. Because available assets must be owned/held by someone, I write

$$Q_d(\text{non-monetary}) + Q_d(\text{monetary}) = Q_s(\text{non-monetary}) + Q_s(\text{monetary})$$

where Q_d(non-monetary) is the quantity demanded of (willingness to hold) non-monetary assets
Q_d(monetary) is the quantity demanded of (willingness to hold) monetary assets
Q_s(non-monetary) is the quantity supplied of non-monetary assets
Q_s(monetary) is the quantity supplied of monetary assets

We can rewrite this condition as

$$Q_d(\text{non-monetary}) - Q_s(\text{non-monetary}) = Q_s(\text{monetary}) - Q_d(\text{monetary}) \quad \textbf{(14)}$$

Using both sides of this equation, we can make several observations. If institutions and individuals are holding the correct amount of monetary assets relative to non-monetary assets, then the quantity demanded of monetary assets equals the quantity supplied of monetary assets (which can be used to buy goods, services or non-monetary assets), so that Q_s(monetary) – Q_d(monetary) = 0, or Q_d(monetary) = Q_s(monetary), a condition called *equilibrium* for the money market, expressed earlier as $M^d = M$. In this case, the model implies that individuals and institutions also hold the correct amount of non-monetary assets: Q_d(non-monetary) = Q_s(non-monetary).

The model presents an argument for why this equilibrium condition tends to occur in the market for monetary assets (and by implication in the markets for non-monetary assets), but before discussing this argument, I first construct functions that represent the willingness to hold monetary assets and the quantity of money and credit available.

The demand of monetary assets, revisited

The various interest/yield/expected return rates from investing in non-monetary assets represent the opportunity cost of holding monetary assets either in the form of currency, reserves, transaction deposits or close substitutes for money including the various money market assets that we considered in chapter 2.

Borrowing Mr. Keynes' idea, the model predicts that as interest/yield/expected return rates rise (and as asset prices are expected to rise), the opportunity cost of holding monetary assets rises, so monetary assets become less desirable: formally, the quantity demanded of monetary assets falls. Instead, the demand of non-monetary assets like (illiquid) bonds, (illiquid) loans, (illiquid) deposits and stocks increase, which I will consider formally in the next chapter. On the other hand, as interest/yield/ expected return rates fall (and possibly become negative in real terms or even nominal terms), the opportunity cost of holding monetary assets falls, so monetary assets become more desirable assets because of their convenience and safety: the quantity demanded of monetary assets therefore rise. Especially when the return rates are expected to become negative, people say that "cash is king". More generally, monetary assets are good to hold as a precaution against unexpected expenses or an unforeseen drop in revenue.

The demand of monetary assets is a relationship between interest/yield/expected return rates on non-monetary assets—the opportunity cost or "price" of holding monetary assets—and the quantity of monetary assets that institutions and individuals are willing to hold (the quantity demanded). Figure 4-3 shows a demand curve for monetary assets, which represents this inverse relationship, with the average of interest/yield/expected return rates represented on the vertical axis and the quantity of monetary assets that institutions and individuals are willing to hold represented on the horizontal axis. The curve shows that that as the average interest/yield/expected return rate falls (rises), the quantity demanded of monetary assets rises (falls).

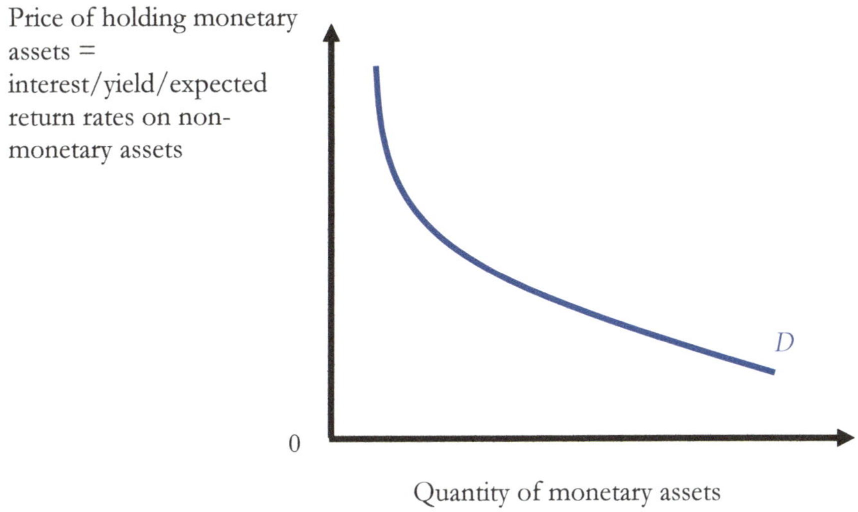

Figure 4-3: The demand curve for monetary assets shows an inverse relationship between the interest/yield/expected return rates on non-monetary assets and the quantity of monetary assets that institutions and individuals are willing to hold.

In fact, we do see an inverse relationship between the quantity of monetary assets and the price of holding monetary assets—the yield rate on one kind of bond—when other factors are held constant.[25] Figure 4-4 relates the yield rate on bonds to the quantity of monetary assets for each year during the last decade.[26] In

[25] This bond is actually a short-term Treasury Bill, which I classified as a money market asset. However, relative to M2, it can be considered an illiquid or non-monetary asset. Eager students are invited to graph the relationship using yields from longer-term and more illiquid bonds.

[26] We divide the quantity of monetary assets by the value of goods and services, or gross domestic production, because we want to ignore the effects that changing national income and prices have on the quantity demanded of monetary assets. Higher total production

years when the yield rate was high, the quantity of monetary assets held by institutions and individuals was low. In years when the yield rate was low, the quantity of monetary assets held by institutions and individuals was high.

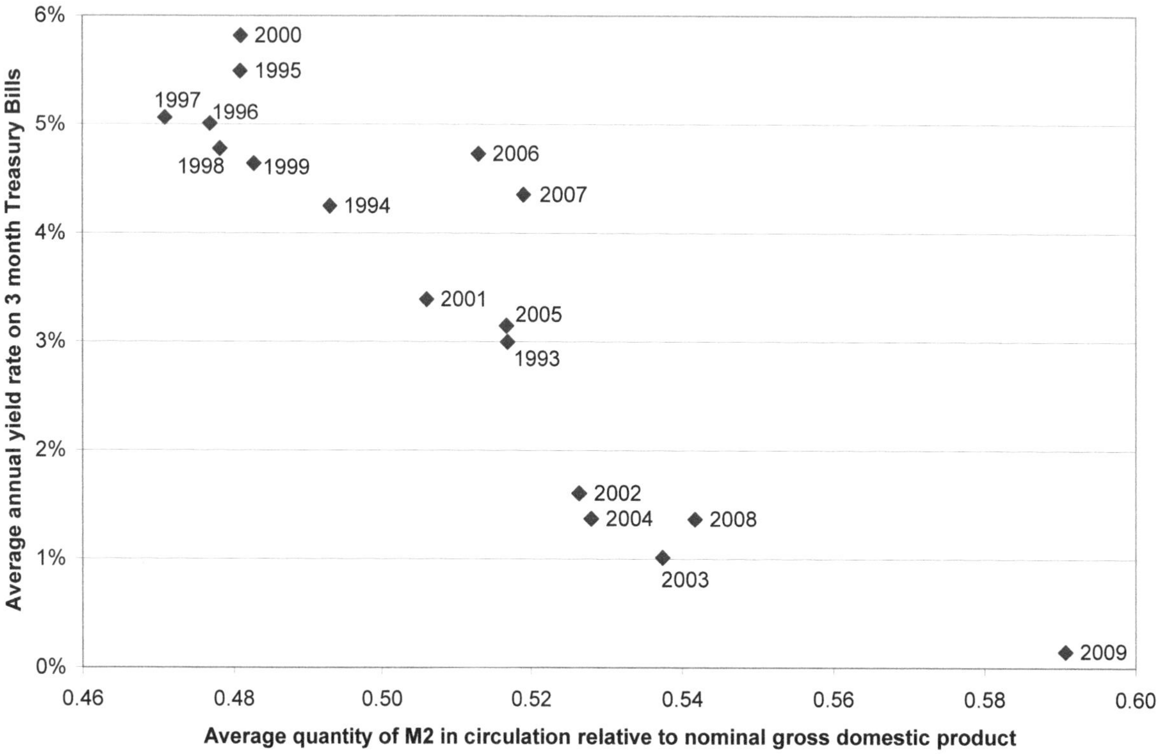

Source: Board of Governors of the Federal Reserve System, http://www.federalreserve.gov/releases/
Bureau of Economic Analysis, http://www.bea.gov/bea/dn/home/gdp.htm

Figure 4-4: An inverse relationship between the yield rates and the quantity of monetary assets exists: the quantity of money (M2) relative to yield rates on US Treasury Bills, 1993-2009.

The supply of monetary assets

In reality, financial intermediaries and even their customers can significantly influence the quantity of money and credit, as we will see in chapter 12. But to keep the model simple, we will assume for now that the actions of the central bank primarily determine how much money circulates in the economy. Furthermore, we will assume that the central bank adjusts the quantity supplied of monetary assets after considering the inflation rate and the unemployment rate (its two most important targets), not the nominal interest/yield/expected return rates on non-monetary assets. Although changes in the inflation rate, the unemployment rate and the quantity of money and credit can be associated with changes in certain

---

in the domestic economy means that national income earned from producing goods and services increases and/or prices of the goods and services sold increase. We will see in a following section that higher national income and higher prices change the demand of monetary assets. But to ignore these changes in the graph, we normalize (divide) the quantity of monetary assets by gross domestic production.

interest/yield/expected return rates, it is not clear how they are associated with an average rate, and we will assume here that they are independent of the average rate for simplicity.[27]

The supply of monetary assets is a relationship between the interest/yield/expected return rates on non-monetary assets and the quantity supplied of monetary assets. Figure 4-5 shows a supply curve for monetary assets, which represents an independent relationship between the average interest/yield/expected return rate on non-monetary assets and the quantity supplied of money by assumption: at a high or low interest/yield/expected return rate the central bank and financial intermediaries are predicted to supply the same quantity of monetary assets for the economy when other factors like the inflation rate and the unemployment rate remain constant.

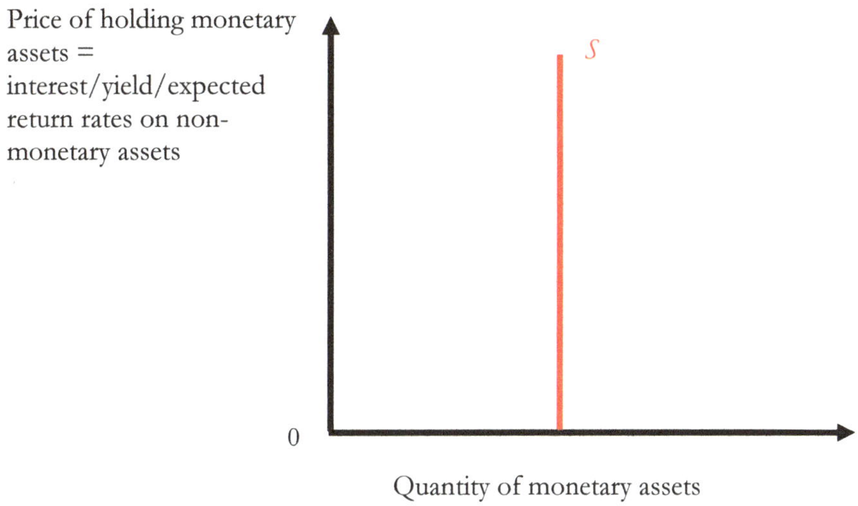

Figure 4-5: The supply curve for monetary assets shows an independent relationship between the interest/yield/expected return rates on non-monetary assets and the quantity of monetary assets supplied by the central bank and financial intermediaries.

Equilibrium in the model of the market for monetary assets

Equilibrium in economics refers to a condition where there is no incentive or tendency for buyers and sellers, or in this case the holders of money and the providers of money, to change their behavior. Alternatively, in equilibrium there are no shortages or surpluses of monetary assets, and the quantity that institutions and individuals want to hold matches the quantity that is supplied by the central bank and financial intermediaries. As a result, individuals and institutions who want to hold monetary assets given interest/yield/expected return rates are able to do so, and they do not have an incentive or tendency to buy or sell non-monetary assets or otherwise change their behavior.

---

[27] In particular, expected return rates on many non-monetary assets may increase as the quantity of money and credit supplied by the central bank and private financial intermediaries increases. In addition, as loan interest rates increase, banks should be more willing to increase the quantity of money and credit by lending more. Based on these two arguments, we should have a positive relationship between interest/yield/expected return rates and the quantity of money (and credit) rather than an independent relationship.

Equilibrium is a theoretical construct, not an actual condition in the money market since behavior is always changing in response to other changes. Nonetheless, we can say that institutions and individuals tend to behave in a way that is consistent with the idea of equilibrium.

If the money market is not in equilibrium, there is a tendency for it to gravitate towards equilibrium through adjustments in people's behavior and through corresponding adjustments in interest/yield/expected return rates. If the quantity of monetary assets supplied exceeds the willingness to hold monetary assets (quantity demanded), a surplus of monetary assets would exist (and a corresponding shortage of non-monetary assets.) Formally, the reason for this surplus is that interest/yield/expected return rates on non-monetary assets are very attractive. (That is, prices of non-monetary assets are expected to rise.)

When a surplus of money exists, holders of monetary assets and non-monetary assets have an incentive to adjust their behavior, thereby allowing interest, yield and expected return rates to fall. With a surplus of money, banks will charge lower interest rates on their loans and will offer lower interest rates on their deposits. Likewise, bank customers will be more willing to borrow and use money as interest rates are lowered, and they will be more willing to withdraw money from interest-bearing deposits when those deposits offer only low interest rates. With a surplus of money, bond investors will be willing to accept lower yields and to pay higher prices to get the bonds that they desire (decreasing the expected rate of return); bond issuers and sellers will be able to offer lower yields and will be able to afford to ask for higher prices for the bonds that they issue and sell. A higher price of bonds and a lower yield give individuals and institutions a greater incentive to sell bonds and hold money.

As for expected return rates and expected prices of non-monetary assets, the model assumes that there is an objectively "correct" value/price and the actual price will rise only to this correct value/price. In the process, the expected return rate decreases. However, when assets can be bought and sold before maturity, higher prices of non-monetary assets can lead to *higher* expected return rates *if* buyers and sellers of the assets expect that higher prices today will lead to higher prices in the future. In other words, with a surplus of money, the demand and prices of non-monetary assets increase, which *may* lead people to expect that prices will continue to increase indefinitely so that we can earn higher expected return rates through capital gains. (We discuss this speculation about indefinitely rising prices of non-monetary assets in greater detail in chapter 14).

When interest, yield and expected return rates on non-monetary assets decrease, institutions and individuals become willing to hold more monetary assets than otherwise because of their convenience and safety. These adjustments are represented in Figure 4-6, where the interest/yield/expected return rate of 10% would tend to fall and the surplus of 6000 – 1000 units of money would tend to shrink as individuals and institutions become more willing to hold monetary assets.

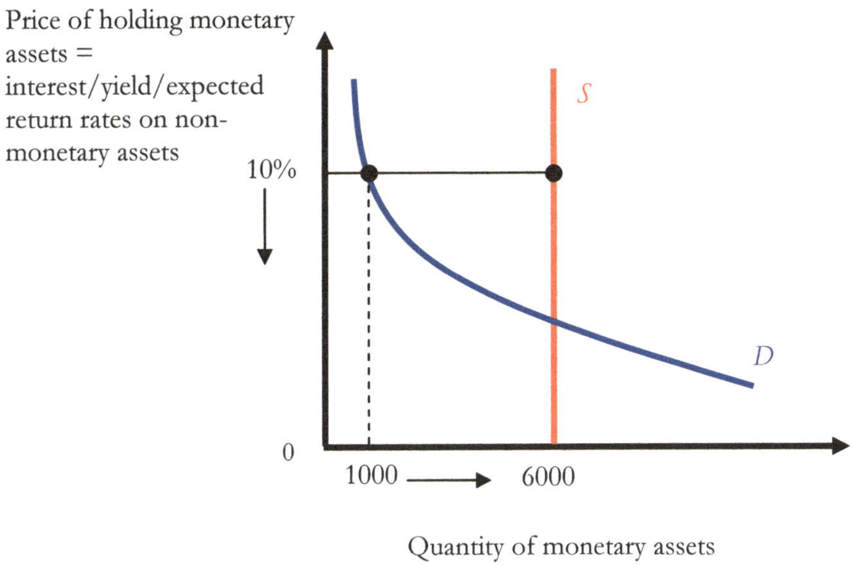

Figure 4-6: When a surplus of monetary assets exists, the interest/yield/expected return rate tends to fall, thereby decreasing the surplus as individuals and institutions become more willing to hold monetary assets.

The incentive for holders of money and bonds to adjust their behavior and the tendency for the interest/yield/expected return rate to fall exist until the surplus of money is reduced to zero. When there is no surplus of monetary assets, individuals and institutions are satisfied with the amount of cash they hold for transactions purposes and with the amount of non-monetary assets they hold for investment purposes. As a result, the quantity supplied of monetary assets equals the quantity demanded of monetary assets, and there is no tendency for interest, yield and expected return rates to fall further.

If the willingness to hold monetary assets (quantity demanded) exceeds the quantity of monetary assets supplied, a shortage of monetary assets would exist (and a corresponding surplus of non-monetary assets.) Formally, the reason for this shortage is that interest/yield/expected return rates on non-monetary assets are very unattractive. (That is, prices of non-monetary assets are expected to fall.)

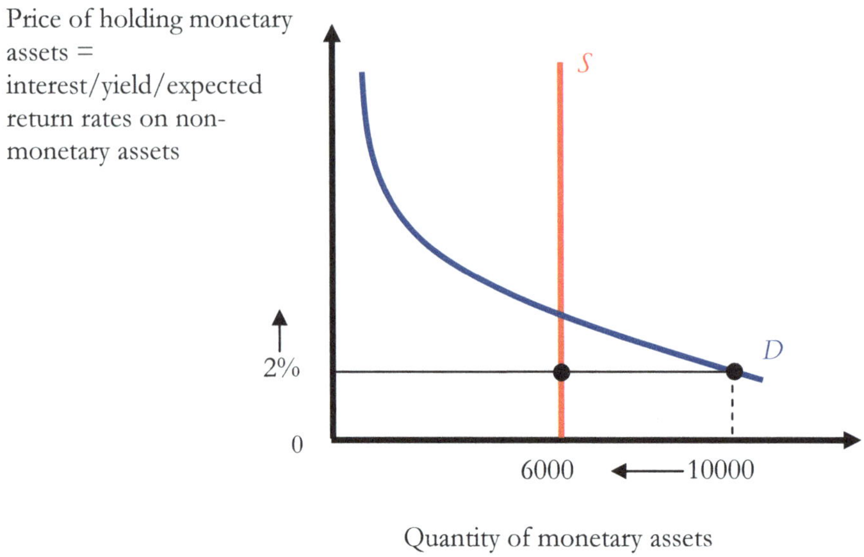

Figure 4-7: When a shortage of monetary assets exists, the interest/yield/expected return rate tends to rise, thereby decreasing the shortage as individuals and institutions become more willing to hold non-monetary assets.

When a shortage of money exists, holders of monetary assets and non-monetary assets have an incentive to adjust their behavior, thereby allowing interest, yield and expected return rates to rise. With a shortage of money, banks will charge higher interest rates on the money that they do lend and will offer higher interest rates on their deposits to attract more money from depositors. Likewise, bank customers will be more willing to save and less willing to borrow and use money as interest rates are raised, and they will be less willing to withdraw and use money from interest-bearing deposits when those deposits offer higher interest rates. With a shortage of money and a surplus of bonds, bond investors can ask for higher yields and lower prices on bonds when they buy bonds and give up their scarce money (increasing the expected rate of return); bond issuers and sellers must offer higher yields and accept lower prices for the bonds that they issue and sell. A lower price of bonds and a higher yield give individuals and institutions a greater incentive to buy bonds and hold less money.

Expected return rates can increase if actual prices fall but an objectively "correct" value/price remains fixed. On the other hand, when assets can be bought and sold before maturity, lower prices of non-monetary assets can lead to *lower* expected return rates *if* buyers and sellers of the assets expect that lower prices today will lead to lower prices in the future. In other words, with a lower quantity of money and credit, the demand and prices of non-monetary assets decrease, which *may* lead people to expect that prices will continue to decrease indefinitely so that we face lower expected return rates through lower capital gains or capital losses.

When interest, yield and expected return rates on non-monetary assets increase, institutions and individuals become willing to hold fewer monetary assets than otherwise because of the higher opportunity cost of holding money. These adjustments are represented in Figure 4-7, where the interest/yield/expected return rate of 2% would tend to rise and the shortage of 10000 – 6000 would tend to shrink as individuals and institutions become less willing to hold monetary assets.

The incentive for holders of money and bonds to adjust their behavior and the tendency for the interest/yield/expected return rate to rise exist until the shortage of money is reduced to zero. When there is no shortage, people are satisfied with the amount of monetary assets that they hold for transactions purposes and with the amount of non-monetary assets they that hold for investment purposes. As a result, the quantity supplied of monetary assets equals the quantity demanded of monetary assets, and there is no tendency for interest, yield and return rates to rise further.

Exogenous changes in the demand of monetary assets

In the model of the money market, the interest/yield/expected return rate and the quantity of monetary assets (and implicitly, the quantity of non-monetary assets) are endogenous variables, and other factors not explicitly represented are treated as *exogenous variables*, variables outside of the model. But these other variables can also affect interest, yield and expected return rates on non-monetary assets and the quantity of monetary assets that institutions and individuals hold. We first consider the variables that affect the demand of monetary assets, and then consider what affects the supply of monetary assets.

Risk and pessimism. Greater risk of holding bonds, loans, stocks and other non-monetary assets imply that monetary assets are more desirable to hold as precaution against the risk of earning a negative rate of return. In particular, when institutions and individuals expect to earn a negative rate of return on (have pessimistic expectations about) non-monetary assets, they often want to sell these assets quickly and hold cash instead (which generally earns a nominal rate of return close to 0%). Formally, the demand of monetary assets rises when the willingness to hold non-monetary assets falls due to higher risk or more pessimistic expectations.

We represent an increase in the demand of monetary assets by shifting the demand curve for monetary assets right, as shown in Figure 4-8. A shift of the demand curve right means that the quantity of monetary assets that people are willing to hold increases at each interest/yield/expected return rate on non-monetary assets. After demand initially increases, institutions and individuals are predicted to adjust their behavior by selling non-monetary assets and making fewer loans from cash on reserve, which tends to decrease the prices/values of non-monetary assets and increase their interest and yield rates. Figure 4-8 represents this by moving from i_1 to i_2 for a given quantity of monetary assets supplied Q_1.

For a fixed quantity of money (and credit), why in fact should an increase in demand of monetary assets be associated with an increase in interest rates and yield rates? An increase in the willingness to hold monetary assets (but not to spend them) reduces the liquid funds available for transaction purposes and decreases the velocity of money. Because of a greater willingness to hold money (reserves), banks charge higher interest rates for any reserves that are lent and offer higher interest rates on money deposited by their customers. Banks would also charge higher interest rates for loans that they deem more risky. Institutions and individuals in the bond market are likewise willing to offer higher yields and ask for lower prices for bonds that they want to sell for cash. Bond savers/lenders would also bid lower prices and require higher yield rates for bonds that they deem more risky. Alternatively, we can say that an increase in the demand of monetary assets results in a *decrease* in the demand of non-monetary assets like bonds and loans. And a decrease in the demand of bonds and loans leads to a decrease in their prices/values and an increase in their interest rates or yield rates. These higher interest rates and yield rates are intended to compensate for the higher risk that non-monetary assets are expected to have.

As for expected return rates, however, they could increase or decrease depending on whether pessimism about higher risks continues over time or quickly abates. If it quickly abates then lower prices of non-monetary assets could increase expected return rates for new buyers if prices are subsequently expected to rise or if payments from the assets are expected to be made in full. However, if pessimism continues, usually due to a belief that the value of the assets is truly lower because payment are expected not to be made in full, then rates of return could fall.

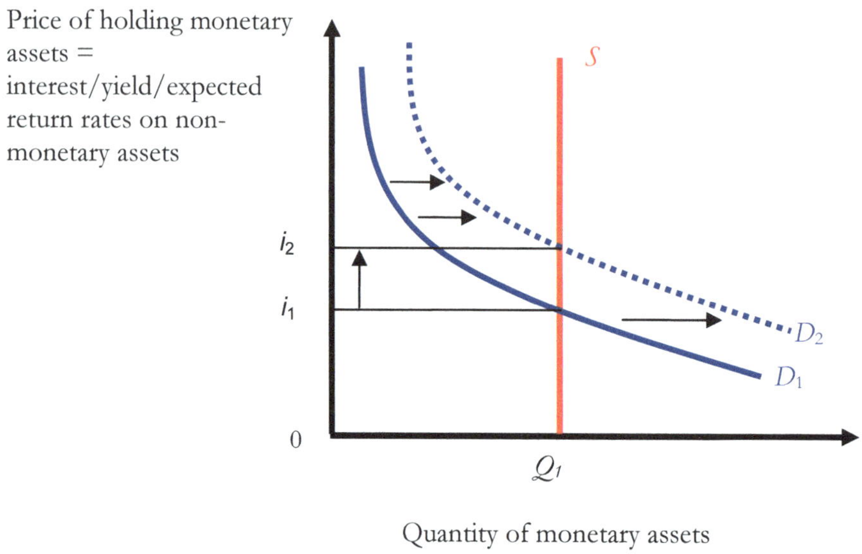

Figure 4-8: An increase in the demand of monetary assets, from D_1 to D_2, is predicted to increase the interest/yield/expected return rate on non-monetary assets.

In practice, however, central banks in modern economies often increases the quantity of money and credit to match the increase in the demand of monetary assets due to increased risk and pessimism, so that interest/yield/expected return rates on (at least some) non-monetary assets do not need to increase. In the next section, I represent an increase in the quantity of monetary assets supplied by the central bank and its effect on interest/yield/expected return rates.

Lower risk of and pessimism about holding non-monetary assets imply that monetary assets are less desirable to hold because bonds, loans, stocks and other non-monetary assets generally earn a higher rate of return. In particular, when institutions and individuals expect to earn a positive rate of return, they want to buy some of these assets instead of holding cash (which generally earns a nominal rate of return close to 0%). Formally, the demand of monetary assets falls when the willingness to hold non-monetary assets rises due to lower risk or more optimistic expectations.

We represent a decrease in the demand of monetary assets by shifting the demand curve for monetary assets left, as shown in Figure 4-9. A shift of the demand curve left means that the quantity of monetary assets that people are willing to hold decreases at each interest/yield/expected return rate on non-monetary assets. After demand initially decreases, institutions and individuals are predicted to adjust their behavior by buying non-monetary assets and making more loans from cash on reserve, which tends to increase prices/values of non-monetary assets and decrease their interest and yield rates. Figure 4-9 represents this by moving from i_1 to i_2 for a given quantity of monetary assets supplied Q_1.

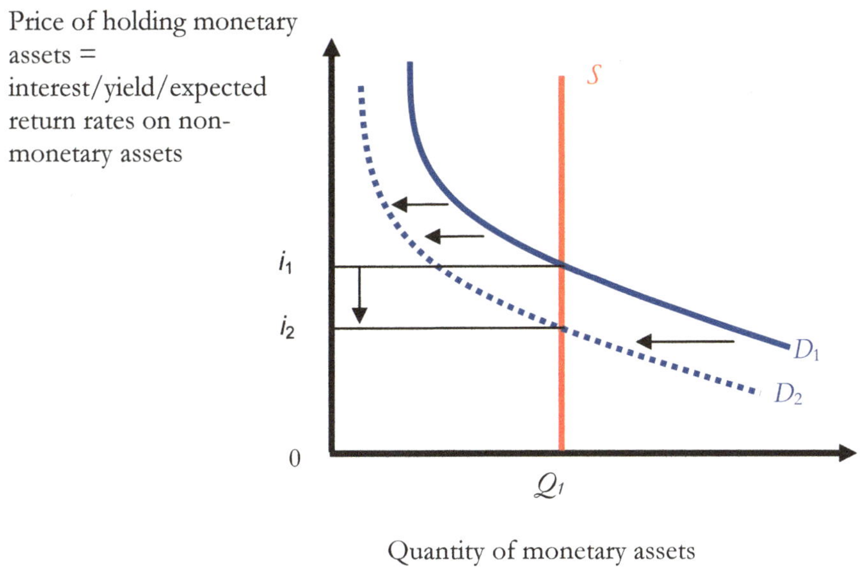

Figure 4-9: A decrease in the demand of monetary assets, from D_1 to D_2, is predicted to decrease the interest/yield/expected return rate on non-monetary assets.

Again, consider the common effects that changes in the demand of monetary assets have on interest/yield/expected return rates. Given a fixed amount of money from the central bank, a decrease in the willingness to hold monetary assets at each interest rate increases the willingness to buy non-monetary assets like bonds and loans or to lend money directly. With a lower willingness to hold cash (reserves), banks tend to charge lower interest rates to give their customers a greater incentive to borrow, and they will also tend to offer lower interest rates on funds deposited by their customers. Institutions and individuals in the bond market are likewise willing to offer lower yield and ask for higher prices for any bonds that they could sell for cash. Bond savers/lenders would also bid higher prices and require lower yield rates for bonds that they deem less risky. Banks would also charge lower interest rates for loans that they deem less risky. Alternatively, we can say that a decrease in the demand of monetary assets results in an *increase* in the demand of non-monetary assets like bonds and loans. And an increase in the demand of bonds and loans leads to an increase in their prices/values and a decrease in their interest rates or yield rates.

Expected return rates could increase or decrease depending on whether optimism about lower risks continues over time or quickly abates.

Liquidity. Lower liquidity of bonds, loans, stocks and other non-monetary assets (possibly due to the risk of and pessimism about rates of return by potential buyers) implies that monetary assets are more desirable to hold to pay for future expenses. Formally, the demand of monetary assets rises when the ability to sell non-monetary assets or otherwise convert them into liquid funds decreases because of the safety of having cash on hand to pay for expenses when they are due. After the initial increase in the demand of monetary assets, we predict an increase in interest/yield/expected return rates, as Figure 4-8 shows.

When the liquidity of non-monetary assets rises, say due to the willingness of the central bank or the government to buy non-monetary assets or because of a technological innovation that makes the non-monetary assets easier to sell, we predict that people will want to hold fewer monetary assets at each interest/yield/expected return rate because cash can be more easily obtained when needed by selling the non-monetary assets. Formally, the demand of monetary assets decreases. After the initial decrease in the demand of monetary assets, we predict a decrease in interest/yield/expected return rates, as Figure 4-9 shows.

Prices of goods and services. As the level of average prices rises, a given quantity of money will not be able to purchase as many goods and services, so that institutions and individuals need to have more monetary assets on hand at each interest/yield/expected return rate to buy the goods and services that they need. Formally, the demand of monetary assets will increase. After the initial increase in the demand of monetary assets, we predict an increase in nominal interest/yield/ expected return rates should rise, as Figure 4-8 shows.

Higher prices of goods and services in modern economies are often a result of a higher quantity of money and credit, as Mr. Fisher's quantity theory of money predicts. For now, we abstract from the cause of changes in prices of goods and services and focus only on the relationship between the level of average prices of goods and services and interest, yield and expected return rates on non-monetary assets. In the next section, we consider the relationship between the quantity of money and credit and the interest, yield and expected return rates on non-monetary assets. In the next chapter, we consider relationship among all three: the quantity of money and credit, the prices of goods and services, and the interest, yield and expected return rates on non-monetary assets.

Higher prices are predicted to lead to higher nominal interest/yield/expected return rates as the demand of monetary assets increases when other factors remain constant. Banks will need to charge higher interest rates on their loans when the prices that they pay are higher and if they are faced with a cash shortage because their customers need to hold and withdraw more cash; bank customers will require higher interest rates on illiquid deposits if they are going to be enticed to save their cash at banks instead of spending it or holding it in liquid deposits. (However, interest rates on liquid deposits could decrease.) Bond savers/lenders will require higher yield rates (and lower bond prices) if they are going to be enticed to buy bonds that pay less valuable money; bond issuers will accept lower bond prices and offer higher yield rates if their revenues increase due to higher prices and when they are more desperate to acquire cash.

In cases when the price level falls,[28] the model predicts a fall in the demand of monetary assets when other factors remain constant: a smaller quantity of money is necessary to purchase the goods and services that people need. After the initial decrease in the demand of monetary assets, we predict a decrease in nominal interest, yield and expected return rates, as Figure 4-9 shows. In fact, many interest, yield and return rates on non-monetary assets were very low in Japan and the US in the 2000s when prices of goods and services were falling.

Expected inflation. The inflation rate is the rate of change in the level of average prices. Changes in the expected inflation rate can also affect the willingness to hold monetary assets, but in ways that are different than a change in the level of prices. In reality, changes in the expected inflation rate occur with changes in the level of average prices, but in the model we separate their effects to understand both clearly.

I previously said that higher prices causes institutions and individuals to hold more monetary assets to pay for more expensive items, but a higher expected inflation rate gives institutions and individuals an incentive to hold *fewer* monetary assets because the (store of) value of the monetary assets is eroded due to the higher inflation. Instead of holding so many monetary assets, institutions and individuals may choose to buy

[28] The level of average prices fell in the US during most years from 1873-1896 and during the early 1930s, as well as during a few other years. It has also fallen in Japan during some years in the late 1990s and the 2000s, and in the US during some months in 2008 and 2009.

more non-monetary assets like commodities, real estate and stocks, whose prices tend to rise with the level of average prices. Formally, higher expected inflation decreases the demand of monetary assets (and increases the demand of some non-monetary assets) because institutions and individuals want to avoid losing purchasing power. After the initial decrease in demand, we predict lower real interest, yield and expected return rates, although nominal rates are predicted to increase, according to the previous chapter.

Box 2 discusses a case of higher expected inflation and of lower expected liquidity of one type of non-monetary assets, US Treasury Notes (a type of government bond). A very significant buyer of the bonds, the US central bank, was expected to stop buying them due to a change in monetary policy. As a result, many tried to sell their bonds quickly and their prices decreased and their yield rates increased. But while the article discusses sellers of these bonds acquiring alternative assets like commodities, it does not consider savers holding more monetary assets because of the fear that inflation will erode the value of monetary assets, as well as the fixed monetary payments from bonds. Thus, while decreased liquidity of non-monetary assets should increase the demand of monetary assets *if other factors remain constant*, the change in expected inflation may offset this predicted effect. In addition, the article discusses default risk on these bonds, which should also increase the demand of monetary assets *if other factors remain constant*, but again, expected inflation increases at the same time.

Box 2: Inflation risk and nominal yield rates on US Treasury Notes and Bonds

In early February 2011, nominal yield rates on 10-year Treasury Notes, a type of coupon bond from the US Treasury with a medium term maturity date, surpassed 3.5%. Likewise, those on 30-year Treasury Bonds surpassed 4.7%.

These rates jumped to their highest levels in almost a year, due to perceptions of more robust production from firms that issue stock, buy commodities, borrow from banks, issue their own debt or issue titles to other alternative assets. In other words, as many alternative assets to US government bonds are now expected to have increasing prices and returns, these alternative assets have become more attractive. Hence, the prices of the US government bonds have fallen and their yields (for new buyers) have risen.

Furthermore, the increases in the yield rates on Treasury Notes and Bonds has recently accelerated, reflecting a worry that inflation in the prices of goods and services may also increase as expenditure and production increase. Inflation is bad for bondholders, at least those who hold standard Treasury Notes and Bonds, because it erodes the value of their fixed payments. This worry has caused many to sell their government bonds, thereby further pushing the prices of the bonds lower and their yield rates higher.

Prices of medium-term Treasury Notes—which have been the main focus of "Quantative Easing 2", a monetary policy of the Federal Reserve System meant to encourage lending and spending by buying these bonds—have decreased the most, indicating that investors are giving up hope that the central bank will continue this policy when it expires in June.

Yield rates on government bonds have also risen because of concerns about the ability of the US to pay back its borrowing in the future, especially after the US Treasury has announced plans to sell an additional $72 billion of new notes and bonds this year.

Source: Wall Street Journal, "Bond Market Flashes Inflation Warning", 7 February 2011.

On the other hand, lower expected inflation increases the demand of monetary assets because money is convenient and safe. After the initial increase in demand, we predict higher real interest, yield and expected return rates, although nominal rates are predicted to decrease, according to the previous chapter.

Production, income and expenditure. As the production of goods and services expands and income earned from this production increases, institutions and individuals can also afford to buy more goods and services or to spend more. To spend more, they will generally want to hold a higher quantity of monetary assets (unless the velocity of money increases, which I consider next). Formally, the demand of monetary assets increases, and after this initial increase, interest, yield and expected return rates are predicted to increase, as shown in Figure 4-8.

However, this logic assumes that the quantity of money and credit (from the central bank and private sector financial intermediaries) will remain fixed as the demand of monetary assets increases due to a change in income and expenditure. But as with higher prices of goods and services, higher income and expenditure are usually associated with a greater quantity of money and credit in modern economies. As a result, when *real* (inflation-adjusted) income and expenditure increase, the quantity of money and credit also increases due to central bank policies, so that real interest, yield and expected return rates tend to remain relatively stable over time.

On the other hand, as the production of goods and services decreases and income earned from this production decreases (i.e., during an economic contraction), institutions and individuals can afford to buy fewer goods and services or to spend less. To spend less, they will generally want to hold a lower quantity of monetary assets. Formally, the demand of monetary assets decreases, and after this initial decrease interest, yield and expected return rates are predicted to decrease, as shown in Figure 4-9.

Velocity. Recall that the velocity of money is determined by many factors, such as preferences and customs of holding monetary assets versus non-monetary assets, automatic teller machines, electronic transfers of funds, credit cards and other forms of credit, regulations, and expectations about the economy.

If one of these factors allows people to hold lower cash balances and if the quantity of monetary assets is reduced accordingly as people save/lend more non-monetary assets, the remaining monetary assets would circulate more quickly. Formally, the demand of monetary assets would decrease when an exogenous factor allows more saving/lending and the velocity of the remaining monetary assets to increase. After this initial decrease in demand, interest, yield, expected return rates are predicted to decrease, as shown in Figure 4-9.

In cases when the velocity of money decreases, say due to widespread credit card fraud that makes people use credit cards less or a distrust of electronic transfer of funds and likewise makes us want to hold higher money balances, the demand of monetary assets would increase, and as people sell more non-monetary assets and each unit of money in circulation would be used at a slower rate. After this initial increase in demand, interest, yield and expected return rates are predicted increase, as shown in Figure 4-8.

Table 5 summarizes the discussion about exogenous variables that influence the demand of monetary assets. The table lists the predicted effects when exogenous variables increase, but the predicted effects when exogenous variables decrease are exactly the opposite. Note that a change in demand results in a change in the equilibrium interest and yield rates that is always in the same direction. Because changes in expected return rates can be ambiguous, they are shown only in the next table. Eager students are encouraged to draw a model of money market and to show the effects of a decrease in each exogenous variable.

Table 5: Variables that influence the demand of monetary assets

Exogenous variable	Change in exogenous variable	Change in demand	Change in equilibrium interest/ yield rates
Risk of and pessimism about holding non-monetary assets	Increase	Increase	Increase
Liquidity of non-monetary assets	Increase	Decrease	Decrease
Prices of goods and services	Increase	Increase	Increase
Expected inflation of the prices of goods and services	Increase	Decrease	Decrease
Income and expenditure	Increase	Increase	Increase
Velocity	Increase	Decrease	Decrease

Exogenous changes in the supply of monetary assets

When thinking about exogenous variables that affect the supply of monetary assets, we have only to consider the actions of the central bank since we ignored other factors that could affect the quantity of money (and credit) in circulation. However, actions by private financial intermediaries that affect the quantity of money and credit could easily be incorporated into the model, and the main predictions below would not change substantially.

Central bank transactions. If the central bank decides to distribute a greater quantity of money throughout the economy, based on changes in the inflation rate or the unemployment rate, then we would represent this action by increasing the quantity supplied of monetary assets at each interest/yield/expected return rate. More concisely, the supply of monetary assets would increase, represented by shifting the supply curve for monetary assets right, as shown in Figure 4-10. After the supply of monetary assets initially increases, institutions and individuals are predicted to adjust their behavior by buying more non-monetary assets and making more loans, which tends to increase the price of non-monetary assets and decrease their interest/yield/expected return rates. Figure 4-10 represents this by moving from i_1 to i_2 for a given demand of monetary assets. The quantity supplied and quantity demanded of monetary assets increase from Q_1 to Q_2.

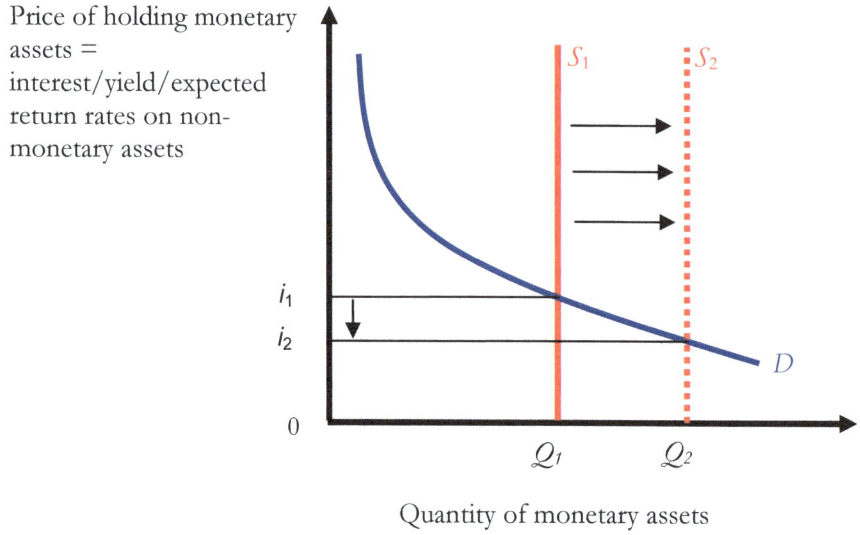

Figure 4-10: An increase in the supply of monetary assets, from S_1 to S_2, is predicted to decrease the interest/yield/expected return rate on non-monetary assets.

Why in fact should an increase in the supply of monetary assets be associated with a decrease in nominal interest/yield and expected return rates? When the supply of monetary assets increases, banks have more liquid funds to lend to their customers and to buy other non-monetary assets. To give an incentive to bank customers to borrow more when liquid funds are plentiful, banks would tend to lower interest rates on their loans. And with more liquid funds from the central bank, private banks would need fewer funds deposited by their customers, so deposit interest rates would also tend to fall. In addition, an increase in the supply of monetary assets results in an increase in the demand of non-monetary assets like bonds, since more funds are available to purchase them, so prices/values of these assets would tend to increase and their yield rates would tend to decrease.

Expected return rates would also decrease when expected future payments from the assets remain fixed. Higher purchase prices at the present time but the same amount of future payments imply a lower return rate. But when assets can be sold before maturity, higher prices of non-monetary assets can lead to *higher* expected return rates *if* buyers and sellers of the assets expect that higher (buying) prices today will lead to higher (selling) prices in the future. In other words, with a higher quantity of money and credit, the demand and prices of non-monetary assets increase, which *may* lead people to expect that asset prices will continue to increase indefinitely so that we can earn higher expected return rates through capital gains.

If the central bank decides to distribute a lower quantity of money (we will discuss how it can do this in the next chapter), the quantity supplied of monetary assets would decrease at each interest/yield/expected return rate in the model. More concisely, the supply of monetary assets would decrease, represented by shifting the supply curve for monetary assets left, as shown in Figure 4-11. After the supply of monetary assets initially decreases, institutions and individuals are predicted to adjust their behavior by selling more non-monetary assets and making fewer loans, which tends to decrease the price of non-monetary assets and increase their interest/yield/expected return rates. Figure 4-11 represents this by moving from i_1 to i_2 for a given demand of monetary assets. The quantity supplied and quantity demanded of monetary assets decrease from Q_1 to Q_2.

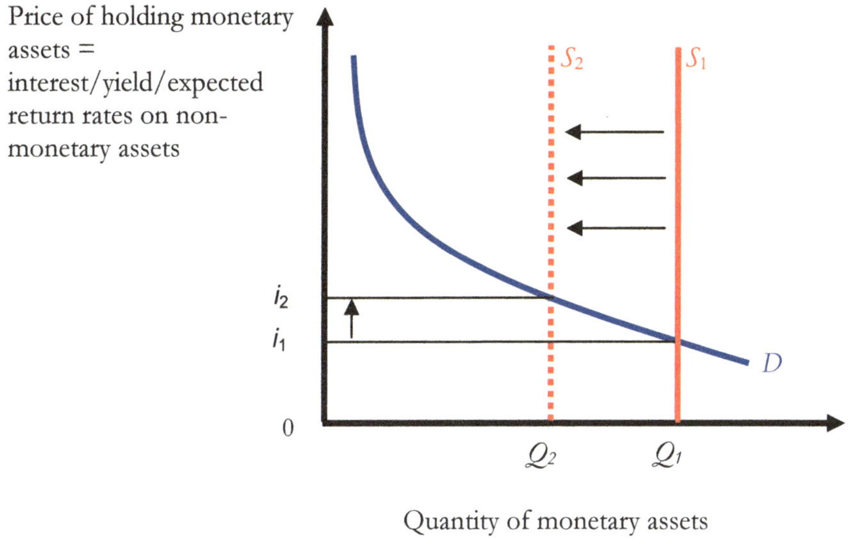

Figure 4-11: A decrease in the supply of monetary assets, from S_1 to S_2, is predicted to increase the interest/yield/expected return rate on non-monetary assets.

When the supply of monetary assets decreases, banks have fewer liquid funds to lend to their customers and to buy other non-monetary assets. Banks would therefore tend to raise interest rates on any scarce funds used for loans and would tend to offer higher interest rates on deposits to attract more funds from customers. In addition, a decrease in the supply of monetary assets results in a decrease in the demand of non-monetary assets like bonds, since fewer funds are available to purchase them, so prices/values of these assets would tend to decrease and their yield rates would tend to increase.

Expected return rates would also increase when the expected future payments from the assets remain fixed. Lower purchase prices at the present time but the same amount of future payments imply a higher return rate. But when assets can be sold before maturity, lower prices of non-monetary assets can lead to *lower* expected return rates *if* buyers and sellers of the assets expect that lower (buying) prices today will lead to lower (selling) prices in the future. In other words, with a lower quantity of money and credit, the demand and prices of non-monetary assets decrease, which *may* lead people to expect that asset prices will continue to decrease indefinitely so that we will earn lower expected return rates through lower capital gains or capital losses.

Table 6 summarizes the discussion about the exogenous variable that influences the supply of monetary assets. Note that a change in supply results in a change in the equilibrium interest and return rates that is always in the opposite direction.

Table 6: Variables that influence the supply of monetary assets

Exogenous variable	Change in exogenous variable	Change in supply	Change in equilibrium interest/yield rate	Change in expected return rate
Central bank transactions	Distribute more money	Increase	Decrease	Decrease when expected future payments remain

	and credit			fixed; can increase otherwise.
Central bank transactions	Distribute less money and credit	Decrease	Increase	Increase when expected future payments remain fixed; can decrease otherwise

Summary

The demand of monetary assets represents the willingness to hold a quantity of monetary assets given a price, value, cost or risk of holding monetary assets. The quantity theory of money can be used to represent this demand by comparing the quantity of money that individuals want to hold to the average price of goods and services (which also represent the value of money), the rate at which money is spent (velocity of money) and the amount of goods and services produced, sold and bought. However, this theory assumes that the velocity of money is constant, which is not true, especially in the short run.

The liquidity preference theory developed by Mr. Keynes and modified by Mr. Baumol and Mr. Tobin considers the role of interest, yield and/or expected return rates and rates of return on non-monetary assets, which represents an opportunity cost of holding monetary assets. These theories predict that when the interest, yield and expected return rates are low, individuals and institutions want to hold more monetary assets and fewer non-monetary assets than otherwise.

The precautionary demand of monetary assets explicitly considers how changes in uncertainty about future expenditure, expenses, income, revenue, interest rates, yield rates and return rates affect the willingness to hold monetary assets. In particular, individuals and institutions want to hold monetary assets as a precaution against income and revenue that may be lower than expected, expenditure and expenses that may be higher than expected, and negative rates of return on non-monetary assets.

Mr. Friedman's theory argues how individuals and institutions may consider long-run changes in expenditure, expenses, income and revenue when making decisions about how much in monetary assets to hold. Mr. Friedman also argued that monetary assets have non-zero, non-constant interest rates or return rates that can be compared to the interest rates, yield rates and return rates of many non-monetary assets.

The model of the market for monetary assets, or money market, incorporates elements of the theories of the demand of monetary assets and constructs a demand function of monetary assets which states that the willingness to hold monetary assets is inversely related to the interest/yield/expected return rates on non-monetary assets. In addition, the model predicts that the willingness to hold monetary assets is 1) directly related to the risk and pessimism of investing in non-monetary assets, 2) inversely related to the liquidity of non-monetary assets, 3) directly related to the prices of goods and services, 4) inversely related to the expected inflation rate of the prices of goods and services, 5) directly related to real production, income and expenditure on goods and services and 6) inversely related to the velocity of money. Changes in these variables, for a fixed quantity of money and credit, are predicted to influence the interest/yield/expected return rates on non-monetary assets after the willingness to hold monetary assets changes.

The quantity of money (and credit) is significantly influenced by the central bank, and the quantity of money and credit supplied from the central bank can also significantly influence the interest/yield/expected return rates on non-monetary assets because the quantity of money influences the demand of non-monetary assets and their prices. In particular, with more money and credit from the central bank, the demand and prices of non-monetary assets increase, which will decrease interest and yield rates for non-monetary assets. Expected return rates will also decrease for non-monetary assets that are not sold before maturity, but expected return rates may otherwise increase because they depend on the expected prices of the non-monetary assets in the future, which can increase if current prices are increasing. With less money and credit, the demand and prices of non-monetary assets decrease and we predict the opposite trends for interest/yield/expected return rates.

Problems and Applications

Short answer problems

1. Name ways to represent the value, price, cost or benefit of holding money.

2. Explain how the velocity of money is inversely related to the willingness to hold money as a store of value or a store of wealth.

3. Explain how the willingness to hold money as a store of value or a store of wealth is inversely related to the (expected) interest, yield or return rates on non-monetary assets.

4. If banks have a "surplus" of monetary assets (possibly due to central bank policy), what are they predicted to do, and how should interest and yield rates on non-monetary assets (deposits, loans, bonds,…) change?

5. If banks have a "shortage" of monetary assets (possibly due to central bank policy), what are they predicted to do, and how should interest and yield rates on non-monetary assets (deposits, loans, bonds,…) change?

6. How did Mr. Keynes' theory of money demand differ from the previous theory about the demand of monetary assets? Besides spending on goods and services, what else did his theory predict that individuals and institutions use money for and spend money on?

7. How does the precautionary demand of monetary assets differ from Mr. Keynes precautionary motive for holding monetary assets?

8. Of Mr. Keynes 3 motives for holding money—the transaction motive, the precautionary motive and the speculative motive—which one is most consistent with Mr. Friedman's theory about permanent income and money demand? Which one is most consistent with Mr. Fisher's theory about the quantity theory of money and money demand?

9. Although the central bank substantially influences the quantity of money and credit available for the economy, how might private financial institutions influence the quantity of money and credit. (Hint: think about which institutions issue credit cards and most loans.) How might the role of private financial institutions in the creation of money and credit be influenced by interest, yield and expected return rates (including those on loans, bonds and other forms of credit).

10. Both the level of average prices of goods and services and its expected inflation rate are predicted to influence the willingness to hold money. How are their predicted effects different?

11. If the central bank increases the quantity of money and credit, explain how expected return rates on non-monetary assets could decrease; explain also how they could increase.

12. If risk of or pessimism about non-monetary assets increases, explain how expected return rates on non-monetary assets could decrease; explain also how they could increase.

Internet applications

1. Go to http://ecos.bok.or.kr/ to find data for Korea's the nominal (monetary) value of national income (from domestic production) and the quantity of money. Calculate the velocity of money using M1 and M2 from 1970 to the latest quarter. How did the velocity of money change during the financial crisis of 1997-1998. Why do you suppose this occurred?

2. Go to http://ecos.bok.or.kr/ to download data for M2 or "broad money", gross domestic production or expenditure (at current prices), and interest rates on 180-day time deposits, or certificates of deposits (CDs), for all available years. Create a graph with annual averages of interest rates on the vertical axis and annual averages of M2/GDP on the horizontal axis, analogous to Figure 4-4. Do you see an inverse relationship between interest rates and the quantity of money in circulation relative to gross expenditure? If not, are there other factors that could vary over time that could affect the quantity of monetary assets that are held by institutions and individuals?

3. Go to http://ecos.bok.or.kr/ to download data for M2 or "broad money", gross domestic production or expenditure (at current prices), and yield rates on 5-year Treasury bonds for all available years. Create a graph with annual averages of yield rates on the vertical axis and annual averages of M2/GDP on the horizontal axis, analogous to Figure 4-4. Do you see an inverse relationship between yield rates and the quantity of money in circulation relative to gross expenditure? If not, are there other factors that could vary over time that could affect the quantity of monetary assets that are held by institutions and individuals?

5. Model of Markets for Non-Monetary Assets

In this chapter we construct a model of bonds to help us understand how interest, yield and return rates for non-monetary assets in general change over time. The model focuses specifically on the willingness to buy and the willingness to sell bonds; however, the logic and discussion can be applied to other non-monetary assets as well, and sometimes even to monetary assets, which we considered in the previous chapter. And as we learned in the previous chapter, the willingness to buy and the willingness to sell assets affects the price of those assets and their interest rates, yield rates and return rates. The model is constructed to show how. The construction of the model of the market for non-monetary assets differs from the construction of the model of the market for monetary assets from the previous chapter, although the underlying logic remains essentially the same. And even though this chapter focuses on non-monetary assets, the appendix shows how monetary assets are related to interest rates and return rates.

A model of bond markets

Like most models in economics, the model of bond markets has a demand function and a supply function. A demand function of bonds, or more simply the demand of bonds, represents the willingness to buy or acquire bonds at each price. The supply function of bonds, or more simply the supply of bonds, represents the willingness to sell or issue bonds at each price. Let's construct each of these functions from intuitive arguments.

Demand of bonds

The quantity of bonds that savers are willing to buy *at a given price* (for example, $950) is called the **quantity demanded** of bonds. A relationship or function that describes the quantity of bonds that savers are willing to buy *at each price* (for example, $950, $951, $952,...) *when other factors remain constant* is called the **demand** of bonds. The demand of bonds is a relationship between the quantity demanded of bonds and bond prices (and yield rates).

To construct the demand of bonds, we ask: how does the quantity demanded of bonds change when only the price of bonds and their yield rate change? A higher price of bonds requires that buyers give up more of their funds to bond sellers, so that the quantity of bonds that savers are willing to buy should fall as the price rises and other factors like expected future prices and quality remain constant. A lower yield rate results in a lower earnings rate for bonds, so that the quantity of bonds that savers are willing to buy should fall as the yield rate falls and other factors remain constant. Alternatively, we expect a lower price and a higher yield rate to have the opposite effect: the quantity of bonds that savers are willing to buy would increase when other factors are constant.

We summarize the relationship between the quantity demanded of bonds on one hand and the prices of bonds and yield rates on the other hand by drawing a **demand curve** for bonds, a graph showing the demand of bonds. Figure 5-1 shows a typical demand curve for bonds, which is labeled *D*. When price is on a vertical axis and the quantity of bonds is on the horizontal axis, a demand curve is downward sloping to represent the inverse relationship between price and quantity demanded of bonds.

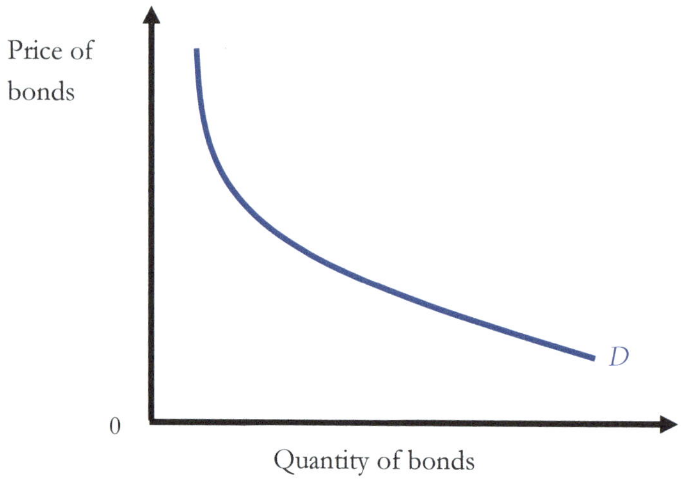

Figure 5-1: The demand curve for bonds shows the inverse relationship between the price of bonds and the quantity demanded of bonds.

To account for the relationship between the yield rate and the quantity demanded of bonds, we need to draw another axis. Because price and the yield to maturity are inversely related, we draw the axis for the yield rate as an inverted vertical axis, where 0 is at the top of the graph and higher interest rates are represented by moving down the inverted axis. The quantity demanded of bonds increases as the yield rate increases, and we represent this direct relationship in Figure 5-2.

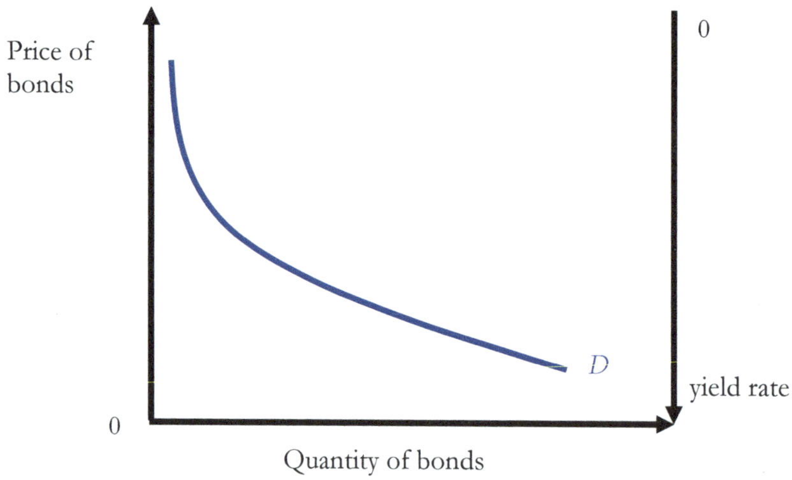

Figure 5-2: The demand curve for bonds shows the inverse relationship between the price of bonds and the quantity demanded of bonds and the direct relationship between the yield rate and the quantity demanded of bonds.

The "when other factors remain constant" phrase is crucial because the price of an asset like a bond (or any product) changes due to many other things that can change as well, like quality (or risk), expected quality, liquidity of the asset and the expected future price. In particular, it is often hard to disentangle price movements from expected future price movements because we may associate current price movements with expected future price movement. For example, if the current price of an asset declines, we might expect that the future price to decline (based on what we might think other market participants think) so that we would want to buy less of the asset instead of more. And if the price of an asset rises, we may expect that the future price to rise, so that we would want to buy more of the asset instead of less. The conflation of changes in current price and expected future price, expected quality and other factors can make the law of demand (and the law of supply and idea of equilibrium, discussed below) seem less descriptive of actual behavior in asset markets. However, as long as we are careful in stating that other factors are supposed to remain constant, the law of demand can help us understand actual market behavior of individuals and institutions in many cases.

Supply of bonds

The quantity of bonds that sellers (including borrowers/spenders) are willing to sell *at a given price* is called the **quantity supplied** of bonds. A relationship or function that shows the quantity of bonds that sellers are willing to sell *at each price* when other factors remain is called the **supply** of bonds. The supply of bonds is a relationship between the quantity supplied of bonds and their prices (and interest rates).

To construct the supply of bonds, we ask: how does the quantity supplied of bonds change when only the price of bonds and their yield rate change? A higher price of bonds allows sellers of bonds to receive more funds from bond buyers, so that the quantity of bonds that sellers are willing to sell should rise as the price rises and other factors like expected future prices remain constant. A lower yield rate results in a lower cost of borrowing for bond issuers and a lower earnings rate for bond holders, so that the quantity of bonds that bond issuers and holders are willing to sell should rise as the yield rate falls and other factors remain constant. Alternatively, we expect a lower price and a higher yield rate to have the opposite effect: the quantity of bonds that bond issuers and holders are willing to sell would decrease when other factors are constant.

We summarize the relationship between the quantity supplied of bonds on one hand and the price of bonds and the yield rate of bonds on the other hand by drawing a **supply curve** for bonds, a graph showing the supply of bonds. Figure 5-3 shows a typical supply curve for bonds, which is labeled *S*. When the price of bonds is on a vertical axis and the quantity of bonds is on the horizontal axis, a supply curve is upward sloping to represent the direct relationship between the price and quantity supplied of bonds. When the yield rate is on an inverted vertical axis and the quantity of bonds is on the horizontal axis, a supply curve is upward sloping to represent the inverse relationship between the yield rate and the quantity supplied of bonds.

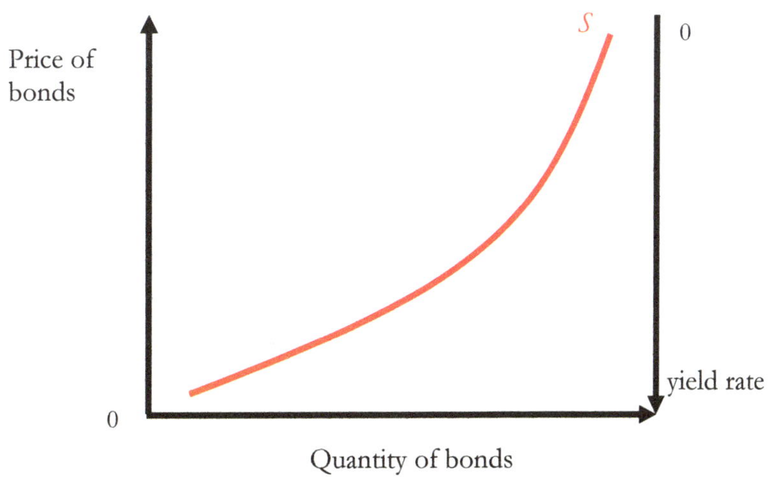

Figure 5-3: The supply of bonds shows the direct relationship between the price of bonds and the quantity supplied of bonds and the inverse relationship between the yield rate and the quantity supplied of bonds.

Equilibrium in the model of bond markets

As we learned in the last chapter, **equilibrium** in economics is a condition where there is no incentive or tendency for buyers and sellers to change their behavior. In particular, there is no incentive or tendency to change buying (bid) prices or selling (ask) prices or no incentive or tendency to buy or sell more or fewer bonds. Alternatively, in equilibrium there are no shortages or surpluses of the asset and the quantity that people want to buy matches the quantity that people want to sell.

Equilibrium is a theoretical construct, not an actual condition in bond markets since behavior and prices always changing in response to other changes. Nonetheless, we can say that buyers and sellers tend to behave in a way that is consistent with the idea of equilibrium.[29]

If the bond market is not in equilibrium, there is a tendency for it to gravitate towards equilibrium through adjustments in people's behavior and through corresponding adjustments in prices and yield rates. If the willingness to sell (quantity supplied) exceeds the willingness to buy (quantity demanded), a surplus of bonds would exist. Figure 5-4 shows that at a price of 990, the quantity supplied equals 1200 while the quantity demanded equals 100. A surplus of 1200 – 100 = 1100 bonds exists.

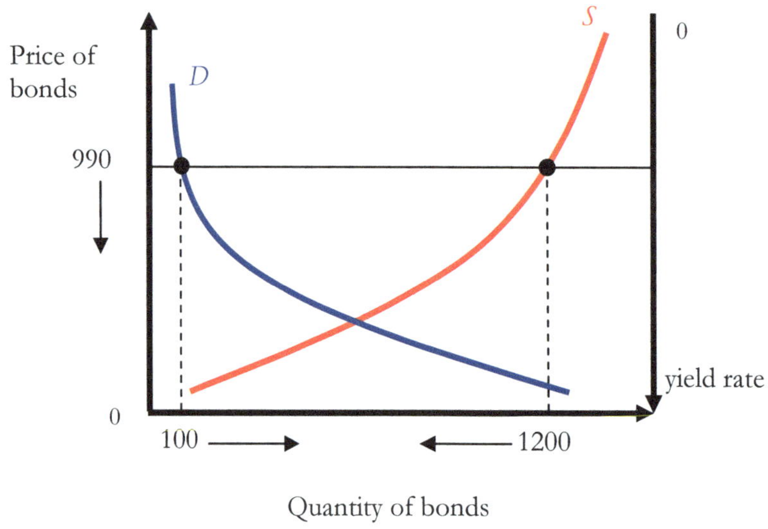

Figure 5-4: When a surplus of bonds exists, the price tends to fall, thereby decreasing the shortage.

When a surplus exists, buyers and sellers have an incentive to adjust their behavior, thereby allowing the price to fall. Because some sellers of bonds are not able to sell everything that they want to sell, they have an incentive to set or accept a lower price, thereby attracting more buyers and reducing the surplus.

[29] Nonetheless, in order for a stable or equilibrium condition to be valid, expected future prices should not changes when current prices change. However, if expected future prices change in the same (or opposite) direction when current prices change, the concept of equilibrium becomes invalid.

Furthermore, if potential buyers of bonds believe that sellers can not sell everything that they want to sell, they have an incentive to bid a lower price. Thus, the price of 990 in Figure 5-4 would tend to fall and the surplus of 1100 would tend to shrink.

The incentive for buyers and sellers to adjust their behavior and the tendency for the price to fall exist until the surplus is reduced to zero. When there is no surplus, sellers can sell all that they want to sell, buyers want to buy everything that sellers want to sell, and there is no tendency for the price to fall further.

If the willingness to buy (quantity demanded) exceeds the willingness to sell (quantity supplied), a shortage of bonds would exist. Figure 5-5 shows that at a price of 900 the quantity demanded equals 1000, while the quantity supplied equals 300. A shortage of 1000 – 300 = 700 bonds exists.

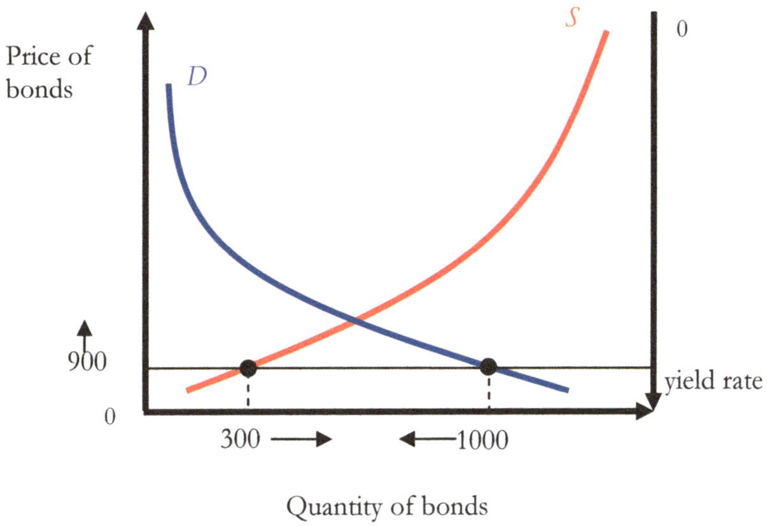

Figure 5-5: When a shortage of bonds exists, the price tends to rise, thereby decreasing the shortage.

When a shortage exists, buyers and sellers have an incentive to adjust their behavior, thereby allowing the price to rise. Because some buyers of bonds are not able to buy all that they want to buy, they have an incentive to bid a higher price to ensure that they can attract a seller. At a higher price, potential sellers are enticed to sell their bonds and fewer savers decide to buy bonds, thereby reducing the shortage. Furthermore, if sellers of bonds believe that buyers can not buy all that they want to buy, sellers have an incentive to ask for or set a higher price. Thus, the price of 900 in Figure 5-5 would tend to rise and the shortage of 700 would tend to shrink.

The incentive for buyers and sellers to adjust their behavior and the tendency for the price to rise exists until the shortage is reduced to zero. When there is no shortage, buyers can buy everything that they want to buy, sellers want to sell everything that they want to sell and there is no tendency for the price to rise further.

Changes in demand in the model of bond markets

Equilibrium is a condition towards which markets tend to gravitate, but changes in the prices and yield rates occur frequently: in fact they can change by the minute or even by the second. What causes these changes and how do buyers and sellers respond?

We use the bond market model to make predictions about how yield rates change when variables outside of the model, called *exogenous* variables, change. The price of bonds, the yield rates, the quantity demanded and the quantity supplied are called *endogenous* variables because their values are predicted within the model.[30] Exogenous variables are those other than the endogenous variables, and changes in exogenous variables change the willingness to buy bonds at each price and yield rate—the demand of bonds—and the willingness to sell bonds at each price and yield rate—the supply of bonds.

I list several exogenous factors that affect the demand of bonds and supply of bonds and how buyers and sellers of bonds react to these changes by changing the amount that they are willing to buy and sell and the prices/yields of these bonds. First, we consider factors that affect demand:

Saving. By definition, wealth is a stock of assets accumulated over time, and the quantity of these assets depends on income or revenue and expenditure. **Saving** is the difference between current income or revenue and current expenditure in a given time period, and represents the *change* in wealth.[31] Wealth will increase when saving is positive (when income or revenue exceeds expenditure) and decrease when saving is negative (when income or revenue is less than expenditure).

As wealth accumulates through saving and shrinks through negative saving, or what economists call *dissaving*. Retirees typically engage in dissaving and deplete their wealth as expenditure exceeds income.

As institutions and individuals, both domestic and foreign, save/lend more in bond markets, the willingness to buy (demand of) bonds increases. We represent an increase in the demand of bonds by shifting the demand curve for bonds right, as shown in Figure 5-6. A shift of the demand curve right means that the quantity of bonds that people are willing to buy increases at each price (and yield rate) and/or the price that they are willing to pay increases at each quantity (and the yield that they are willing to accept decreases at each quantity). When demand increases, we then predict that price rises from P_1 to P_2 and the yield rate falls from y_1 to y_2 until buyers can buy all that they want at the given price, a quantity represented as Q_2 in the figure.

[30] Endogenous comes from Greek roots endo– and –genes, meaning generated or born from within. Exogenous comes from Greek roots exo– and –genes, meaning generated or born from outside.

[31] Some people use "savings" to mean wealth, as in the accumulated effect of past saving. This text uses wealth to mean a stock of assets that have accumulated over time through past saving.

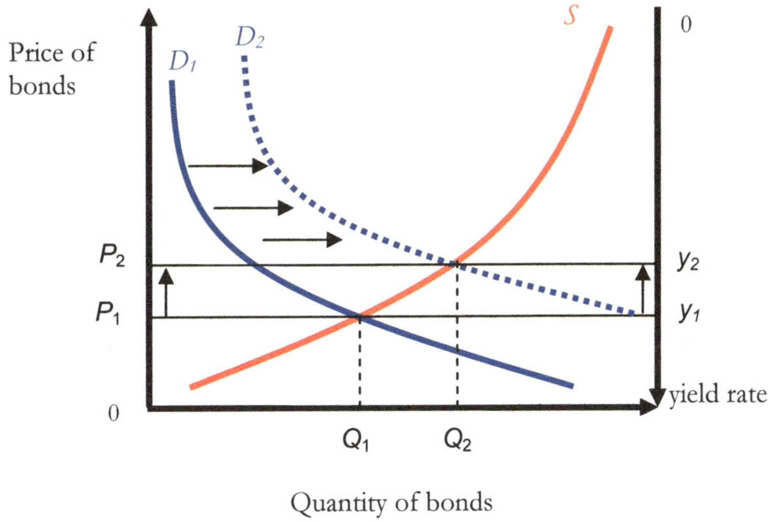

Figure 5-6: An increase in the demand of bonds, from D_1 to D_2, increases the price and decreases the yield rate.

We need to distinguish between an initial change in demand (or supply), represented by a shift in the demand curve (or supply curve), and the subsequent change in the price of bonds, the yield rate, the quantity demanded and the quantity supplied of bonds. The initial shift of the curve is caused by a change in an exogenous variable, such as wealth. The subsequent changes in the endogenous variables represent the tendency of markets to achieve equilibrium after it has been subject to this outside change. Changes in exogenous variables are caused by changes in outside factors, and changes in endogenous variables are caused by the *tendency of buyers and sellers to change their behavior* in response to the exogenous change. Distinguishing between exogenous changes and subsequent endogenous changes will help us understand better how to make predictions about prices, yield rates and quantities bought and sold.

When we consider an initial change in demand (or supply) caused by a change in an exogenous variable, we implicitly hold other factors constant. In reality, there may be many factors that change simultaneously, and to use the model to make predictions with many changes we would need to account for these changes one by one. But to keep the analysis here as simple as possible, we usually consider only one exogenous change at a time. When we account for only one exogenous change, say an increase in saving, we say "when other factors remain constant". To be thorough, we should explicitly state this phrase when considering each exogenous change, but I usually drop the phrase in the rest of the chapter for brevity.

As people reduce their wealth by spending more than they earn in income or revenue, the willingness to buy bonds at each price decreases. In other words, the demand of bonds decreases as wealth decreases.

We represent a decrease in the demand of bonds by shifting the demand curve left, as shown in Figure 5-7. A shift of the demand curve left means that the quantity of bonds that people are willing to buy decreases at each price (and yield rate) and/or the price that they are willing to pay decreases at each quantity (and the yield that they are willing to accept increases at each quantity). When demand decreases, we then predict that price falls from P_1 to P_2 and the yield rate rises from y_1 to y_2 until sellers can sell all that they want at the given price, a quantity represented as Q_2 in the figure.

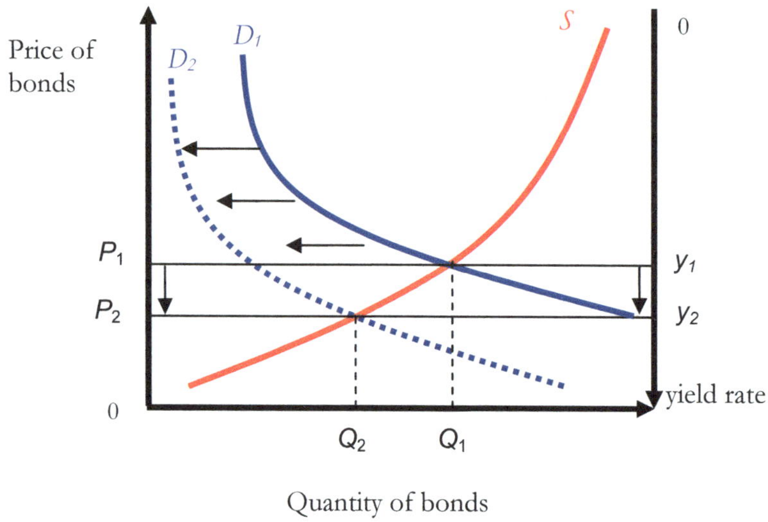

Figure 5-7: A decrease in the demand of bonds, from D_1 to D_2, decreases the price and increases the yield rate.

Expected interest rates and rates of return on alternative assets. Changes in interest rates on alternative assets affect the yield rate because people treat bonds and alternative assets as substitutes in their portfolio of assets.

If yield rates on alternative assets are expected to rise, the demand of bonds decreases. We then predict that the price of bonds decreases and the yield rate increases (so that the yield rate moves with expected interest rates on alternative assets). Refer to Figure 5-7 again to see the predicted effects of a decrease in demand. On the other hand, if interest rates on alternative assets are expected to fall, the demand of bonds increases. We then predict that the price of bonds increases and the yield rate decreases (so that the yield rate moves with expected interest rates on alternative assets). Refer to Figure 5-6 again to see the effects of an increase in demand.

Changes in expected rates of return on alternative assets have the same effect as changes in expected interest rates on alternative assets. For example, if resale prices of stocks or houses are expected to rise, then the expected rate of return on these assets rises. The demand of these assets likewise rises, and the demand of bonds falls when other factors like saving and wealth remain constant. As a result, the price of bonds falls and the yield rate rises.

The previous example compared different assets, but we could also compare a single asset at different times. In essence, using funds to buy bonds in the future is different from using them to buy bonds today, so that future bonds can be thought of as an alternative asset to today's bonds. How does what people expect about future bonds affect today's bonds?

When savers expect the price of future bonds to fall and their yield rates to rise, the expected rate of return on today's bonds held will therefore fall: those who continue to hold bonds in the future will be able to sell them for less, which decreases the expected rate of return on today's bonds. As a result, bonds today are viewed as less attractive investments, and the willingness to buy bonds today will decrease. (However, the yield to maturity of today's bonds after they have been purchased will remain the same.) A decrease in demand of bonds today will lead to a decrease in the price on *today's* bonds and an increase in the yield rate on *today's* bonds. Thus, when people expect the prices of bonds to fall, they actually do fall.

Alternatively, when savers expect the price of future bonds to rise and their yield rates to fall, the expected rate of return on today's bonds held will therefore rise: those who hold bonds in the future will be able to sell them for more, which increases the expected rate of return on today's bonds. As a result, bonds today are viewed as more attractive investments, and the willingness to buy bonds today will increase. An increase in demand today will lead to an increase in *today's* price and a decrease in *today's* yield rate. Thus, when people expect the prices of bonds to rise, they actually do rise.

Expected inflation in the prices of goods and services. Because most bonds pay a fixed nominal amount, changes in expected inflation in the prices of goods and services affect the expected real yield rate and real rate of return on bonds. Higher expected inflation results in lower expected real yield rates and rates of return on bonds at given nominal yield rates because the purchasing power of the fixed nominal income from bonds falls.

When expected inflation increases, the demand of bonds falls, while the demand of alternative assets whose real rate of return does not fall increases. For example, alternative assets could include houses and commodities, since these assets generally maintain their values and real rates of return as expected inflation increases. When increased expected inflation causes the demand of bonds to fall, the price of bonds that pay a fixed nominal amount falls and the nominal yield rate on such bonds rises, as shown in Figure 5-7.

When expected inflation decreases, the demand of bonds that pay a fixed nominal amount increases, while the demand of alternative assets whose real rate of return does not fall decreases. As a result, the price of bonds that pay a fixed nominal amount rises and the nominal yield rate on such bonds falls, as shown in Figure 5-6.

Taxes. When considering changes in expected interest rates and rates of return, either in a real sense or a nominal sense, we should also distinguish between pre-tax measures and after-tax measures. After-tax interest rates, yield rates and rates of return determine saving behavior and demand of assets, since after-tax income earned from assets is what people care about.

To measure the after-tax interest rate, yield rate or rate of return, we adjust the pre-tax interest rate, yield rate or rate of return by first measuring the tax rate on income earned from assets. Let rr represent the pre-tax rate of return on assets and let t represent the tax rate on income earned by those assets. For example, t could be 20%, indicating that 20% of income earned from assets would be paid in taxes. To calculate the after-tax rate, we need to consider how much income earned from assets is left after paying taxes: if t percent of asset income is paid as taxes, then $(1 - t)$ percent of asset income is left after paying taxes. The after-tax rate of return would therefore be $(1 - t)rr$. For example, if the pre-tax rate of return is 3% and the tax rate is 20%, then the after-tax rate of return is (1 – 20%)3% = 2.4%. (Note that 20% = 0.20 and 3% = 0.03 and 2.4% = 0.024.)

Because taxes on income earned from assets affect the after-tax interest rate, yield rate or rate of return, they will therefore affect the willingness to buy assets. When other factors remain constant, higher taxes on bond yields will generally decrease the demand of bonds, while increasing the demand of alternative assets. When other factors remain constant, lower taxes on bond yields will increase the after-tax rate of return on bonds and therefore make them more desirable assets: the willingness to buy bonds at each price and at each yield rate will increase. After the increase in demand, we predict that the price of bonds will increase and the yield rate will decrease, as Figure 5-6 shows.

Figure 5-6 also shows that the quantity of bonds bought and sold rises: lower taxes on bond yields are predicted to increase saving in bonds and investment in production processes financed through bonds. Although we should expect purchases of alternative assets to fall somewhat as taxes on bonds decrease, total saving and investment in the economy would generally increase as taxes on assets in general decrease. Proponents of lower taxes on the interest, yield or return from saving thus argue that such a policy change would promote saving and investment in production processes, leading to higher economic growth.

On the other hand, higher taxes on bond yields will decrease the after-tax rate of return on bonds and therefore make them less desirable assets. Higher taxes on bond yields will therefore decrease the demand of bonds, which decreases the price of bonds and increases the yield rate, as Figure 5-7 shows.

Risk. **Risk** measures the uncertainty about the rate of return on an asset. Risk affects the willingness to buy assets at each price, since savers/lenders generally care about not only an asset's expected rate of return but also the degree of uncertainty about the actual rate of return.

When savers/lenders prefer a safe asset with a given rate of return to a risky asset that pays the same rate of return on average, they are said to be **risk averse**. Risk averse savers/lenders would rather buy a safe asset with a certain rate of return than a risky asset which is expected to pay the same rate of return, but which may pay a rate higher or lower than expected. In fact, most savers/lenders behave as if they were risk averse because they choose to buy safe assets instead of risky assets with the same expected rate of return. (Box 1 considers how *you* might respond when facing financial risk.)

Box 1: Are you risk averse?

Economists determine if people are risk averse by examining how they behave when faced with comparable risky and safe options. For example, suppose that you have the chance to gain $100 with a 50% probability and the chance to lose $100 with a 50% probability. If you took this gamble many times, you could expect to break even on average: one-half of the time you would lose $100 and the other half of the time you would gain $100, and the gains and loses would balance each other on average. On the other hand, a safe option for you would simply be not to take the gamble—nothing would be gained and nothing would be lost.

Most people most of the time would not accept a gamble with an equal probability of a gain and a loss when the amount of the potential gain equals the amount of the potential loss. Would you? Research suggests that most people will accept a gamble with equal probability of a gain and a loss only when the amount of potential gain is at least 2 times the amount of the potential loss.[32] For example, most people would need to have a potential gain of at least $200 in order to choose a gamble with a 50% chance of that gain and a 50% chance of a $100 loss. How large would the potential gain have to be for you to take a gamble if there were a 50% chance of winning that gain and a 50% chance of losing $100? If you need more than $100 of potential winnings to be willing to take the gamble, you are risk averse. If you need just $100 of potential winnings to be willing to take the gamble, you are risk neutral. If you need less than $100 of potential winnings to take the gamble, you are risk seeking: you welcome a gamble that will lose money on average. Because most people are risk averse, they need to be compensated with a larger potential gain relative to the potential loss in order to take a financial risk.

[32] Tversy, Amany and Daniel Kahneman, (1992), Advances in Prospect Theory: Cumulative Representation of Uncertainty, *Journal of Risk and Uncertainty*, 5(4).

We also see that most savers/lenders need to be compensated with higher average rates of return in order to be willing to buy risky assets instead of safe assets. Stocks, equities or shares are more risky assets but have higher average rates of returns over time compared to the yield rates or return rates of long-term bonds and short-term bonds. In some years, the rate of return on stocks is negative by a large amount, while long-term bonds perform modestly. But in other years the rate of return on stocks is large and positive, while bonds continue to perform modestly. The annual real rate of return of US common stocks was 9.63% on average between 1926 and 1999, but annual real rates of return on long-term government bonds was only 5.30% on average during that time.[33] However, in the following decade the difference was smaller, since the rate of return of US common stocks was lower on average. To compensate for the risk of holding stock, a higher average rate of return over time is required by savers in order to be willing to hold significant amounts of stock.

The difference between the expected rate of return on a risky asset and that on a safe asset is called the **risk premium** on the risky asset. In the case of stock or equity, the risk premium is also called the *equity premium*. If long-term bonds are considered a safe asset, we would calculate the equity premium as 9.63% – 5.30% = 4.33%. Risk premiums can also be calculated with bonds. Government treasury/finance department bonds, at least those from wealthy countries, are considered to be safe assets. But bonds from private commercial firms, especially those that are not well established, are considered to be more risky assets and likewise generally have lower prices and higher yield rates than corresponding government bonds. The difference between the yield rates between the two bonds can be called the risk premium for the more risky commercial firm bonds; it is also sometimes called the **spread**.

The most safe asset is money or cash, which generally has a rate of return at or near 0%. As a result, monetary assets are not desirable to hold when bonds, stocks, loans, (non-monetary) deposits and other non-monetary assets have relatively high expected interest, yield, or return rates. Contrarily, when non-monetary assets have negative expected rates of return or are otherwise too risky to hold, monetary assets are desirable to hold: "cash is king". Formally, when the demand of non-monetary assets increases (decreases), the demand of monetary assets decreases (increases) when other factors like the total amount of wealth remain constant.

Because savers are generally risk averse, the demand for an asset falls if the risk of buying that asset is perceived to rise when other factors like the rate of return and the total amount of wealth remain constant. Moreover, as an asset is perceived to become more risky, the demand for alternative (safe) assets rises when other factors remain constant. If the risk of buying an asset is perceived to fall, then the demand for the asset will rise and the demand of alternative assets will fall when savers are risk averse and other factors remain constant.

There are various kinds of risk that non-monetary assets in general and bonds in particular face. I already mentioned **interest rate risk** in chapter 3, the risk of an asset's value changing when interest rates on similar alternative assets change. Long-term bonds face this risk more than short-term bonds, and when this risk increases the demand of long-term bonds decreases, while the demand of alternative assets (perhaps short-term bonds) would increase. Conversely, when interest rate risk decreases, the demand of bonds subject to this risk increases and the demand of alternative assets decreases when other factors remain constant.

[33] Center for Research in Security Prices, Graduate School of Business, University of Chicago. Ibbotson Associates, 2000. Quoted in Ravi Jagannathan, Ellen R. McGrattan and Anna Scherbina, (2000), The Declining US Equity Premium, Federal Reserve Bank of Minneapolis Quarterly Review, 24, 4.

Interest rate risk applies not only to changes to interest rates on alternative assets like deposits and loans, but also to rates of return on alternative assets like stocks, commodities and real estate. If rates of return on alternative assets (are expected to) increase or become more stable, bonds become relatively less attractive assets and the demand of bonds decreases. As a result, the price of bonds decreases and the yield rate increases. The lower price and higher yield rate would benefit new buyers, and the yield rates/rates of return would adjust in the same direction. (However, the lower price would not benefit holders of existing bonds if they wanted to sell the bonds before the maturity date, since the rate of return on these bonds would decrease.) If rates of return on alternative assets (are expected to) decrease or become more unstable, the demand of bonds increases. As a result, the price of bonds increases and the yield rate decreases. The higher price and lower yield rate would not benefit new buyers, and the yield rates/rates of return would adjust in the same direction. (However, the higher price would benefit holders of existing bonds if they wanted to sell the bonds before maturity, since the rate of return on these bonds would increase.) Thus, instability in prices, yield rates and rates of return on bonds can be caused by changes in the rates of return on alternative assets, as well as interest rates on alternative assets. As a result, the phrase *interest rate risk* can be generalized to **interest/return rate risk**.

Another type of risk that results in uncertain rates of return for bonds and other forms of credit/debt is default risk. **Default risk** is the risk that a bond issuer or another borrower will be unable or unwilling to repay—the risk that the borrower will default on the credit/debt. More generally, the risk that the borrower will default on debt or become delinquent in paying the credit/debt is called **credit risk**. We discuss credit risk and interest/return risk in more detail in chapter 9, when we discuss loans and other assets for banks.

When default risk of a bond is perceived to be greater, say due to unfavorable information about economic conditions or because a borrower develops a bad reputation from not paying back previous debts, the demand of the bond falls (and the demand of alternative assets rises) for risk averse savers/lenders. This leads to a fall in the price of the bond and a rise in the yield rate on the bond. When favorable information about economic conditions becomes available or a borrower develops a good reputation from paying back previous debts, default risk decreases and bonds and other forms of debt become more attractive assets for risk averse savers. The bond market changes in the opposite direction: higher demand of bonds (and lower demand of alternative assets), a higher price of the bond and a lower yield rate on the bond.

A third type of risk that results in uncertain real rates of return is **inflation risk**, the risk that inflation will erode the purchasing power of income earned from an asset. For example, most bonds pay a fixed amount regardless of inflation. If inflation is higher than expected, the purchasing power of income from such bonds would be lower than expected. When inflation risk is perceived to be greater, say due to uncertain economic policies or conditions, the demand of bonds which pay fixed nominal amounts decreases while the demand of alternative assets like houses and commodities whose prices tend to increase as well increases when other factors remain constant. The decrease in demand of bonds leads to a decrease in bond prices and an increase in bond yield rates. But if inflation risk falls as economic policies or conditions become more stable, then the bond market changes in the opposite direction: higher demand of bonds, higher prices of bonds and lower yield rates.

As you might have already guessed, *changes in* default risk and inflation risk are causes of interest rate risk, since changes in default risk and inflation risk cause the demand of bonds and other assets with interest rates to fluctuate, which in turn causes yield rates and prices (market values) of bonds to fluctuate.

Greater political and economic uncertainty can lead to greater interest rate risk in general, and can lead to changes in default risk and inflation risk specifically. When savers perceive a change in default risk or inflation risk due to a change in political or economic conditions, the demand of bonds changes, leading to a change in prices and yield rates. Box 1 describes a case of unstable yield rates in Argentina caused by changes in the default risk and inflation risk of Argentinean bonds during the financial crisis of the early 2000s.

Box 2: Interest rate risk, default risk and inflation risk in Argentina

During the 1990s and early 2000s, the Argentinean government issued many bonds, so that its outstanding debt rose substantially. But from 1999-2002, a recession limited tax revenues and increased government expenditures, which reduced the ability of the government to repay its growing debt. As a result, the risk of default began to rise, and the demand of Argentinean bonds began to fall by mid-2000, decreasing the prices of bonds and increasing yield rates. Financial assistance in January and August 2001 from the International Monetary Fund, an international organization that helps countries with financial problems, temporarily allowed the government to repay part of its debt, reducing the default risk temporarily. The government was also able to extend debt payments in June 2001, which also reduced default risk for a brief time. But ultimately, the government defaulted on its debt in December 2001, and it shut down bond markets for several weeks thereafter. It re-opened bond markets in early 2002, but demand, prices and yield rates of bonds continued to fluctuate as the government started negotiations with creditors about partial repayments, causing uncertainty about the degree of default. Adding to the amount of bonds in default, some large private sector companies also defaulted on their bonds.

The graph below shows interest rates on 30-day loans between banks, which moved with the yield rates since banks used their funds to invest in bonds or to invest in loans made to other banks. During 2001-2002, default risk was high as savers expected the government and firms to default to some degree on their debts, which caused the demand of bonds to fall and interest rates to rise. Also during this time, changes in default risk made the interest rates fluctuate wildly: interest rate risk was high. But interest rates had stabilized by 2003 to levels similar to those before the default, as the economy recovered and as the government started to repay part of its old debt. This gave savers more confidence about buying newly issued bonds, and default risk on new bonds has remained relatively low and steady as the economy has grown rapidly during 2003-2006. Because default risk has remained steady, interest rate risk has not been high since 2003.

Finally, inflation risk was a concern during 2001-2002 due to an expected rise in the price of imports. Bond holders who were paid in pesos feared that the value of their pesos would be reduced as the price of imports rose. Their fears were well-founded as the peso became less valuable relative to foreign currencies in 2002; the peso could buy fewer imports so that imports became more expensive. Nonetheless, the prices of domestic goods and services remained relatively stable, so inflation risk was not as detrimental as it could have been.

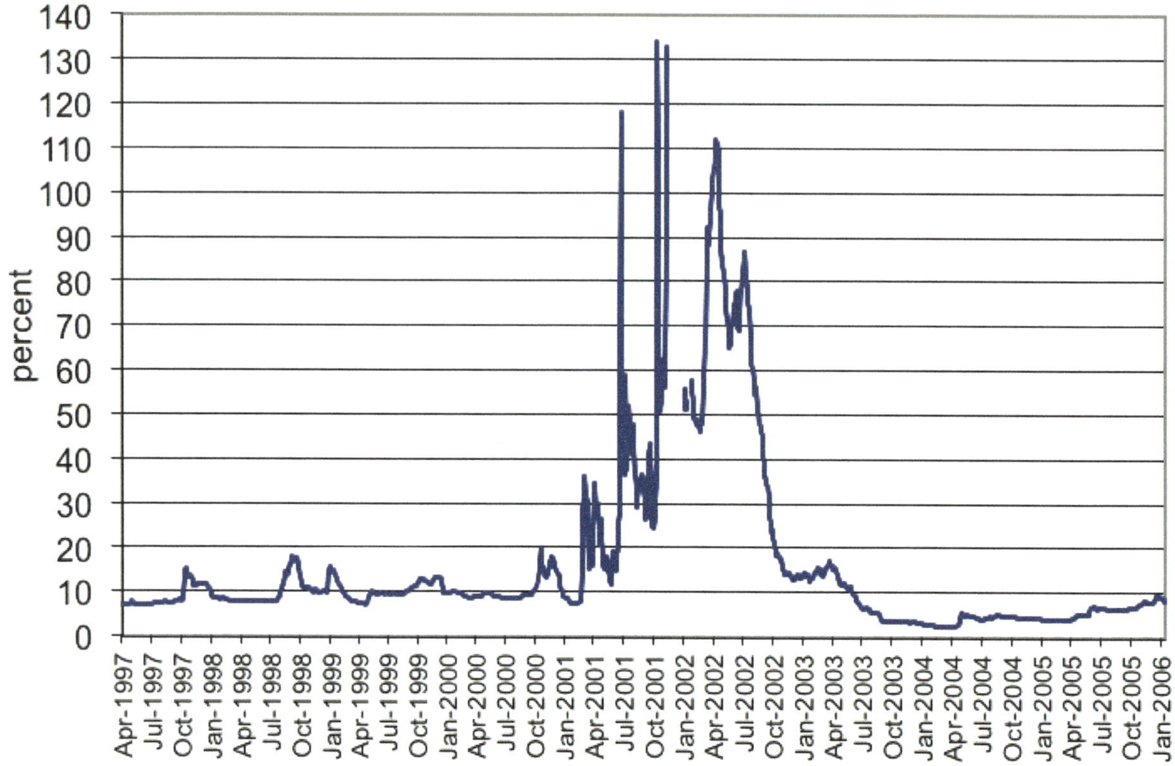

Source: Central Bank of Argentina, http://www.bcra.gov.ar/index_i.htm

Figure 5-8: Changes in the default risk and inflation risk of Argentinean bonds made interest rates (on 30 day inter-bank loans) unstable in 2001 and 2002.

Liquidity. As we discuss in the chapter on monetary assets and the money market, liquidity measures the ease of converting an asset into funds that can be used to pay for goods and services or debt. When an asset is liquid, owners of the asset can acquire funds to pay for goods and services or debt without substantial transaction costs. Holding liquid assets is beneficial when investors might need to pay for goods and services or debt quickly. For example, holding liquid assets would be beneficial as a precaution against unexpected expenses or an unforeseen fall in income. When other factors remain constant, a liquid asset is therefore more desirable than an illiquid asset.

But when comparing liquid and illiquid assets, other factors like interest, yield and return rates are often *not* constant. Just as risk averse savers who hold risky assets need to be compensated with a higher expected rate of return relative to that of safe assets, savers who hold illiquid assets need to be compensated with a higher expected rate of return relative to that of liquid assets. For example, short-term bonds can generally be sold easily without substantial fees or waiting time because these bonds will soon mature and pay money anyway. Long-term bonds, especially those issued by small institutions, usually have fewer willing buyers, so substantial time and brokers fees may be needed if holders want to sell them for cash. Long-term bonds, however, generally offer higher yields (have lower prices) than short-term bonds. Savers must therefore weigh the benefits of liquidity against the lower interest, yield or return rates that liquid assets offer.

How easily or cheaply assets can be used to acquire funds to pay for goods and services or debt may vary from time to time, as the number of willing buyers for the assets changes. Moreover, savers may not know with certainty if they will need to acquire liquid funds in the future to pay for goods and services or debt. **Liquidity risk** is the risk that a saver will need to convert an asset to liquid funds by paying higher than expected transaction costs like brokers' fees and penalties for early withdrawal of funds and by receiving lower than expected prices (or higher than expected discounted prices).

An improvement in technology, a decrease in regulation or a decrease in transaction costs could make bonds easier to buy and sell, thereby making bonds a more liquid asset. If bonds become more liquid assets through such changes, they become more attractive assets since people could sell them more easily if necessary. Formally, the liquidity risk of holding bonds decreases and the demand of bonds therefore increases, which increases the price of bonds and decreases the yield rate.

If bonds become less liquid assets, say due to an increase in regulation or transaction costs, they become less attractive assets and the demand of bonds would fall. The price of bonds would decrease and the yield rate would increase.

Furthermore, if other assets like stocks, loans, houses or commodities become more liquid assets, the demand of bonds would decrease. The price of bonds would decrease and the yield rate would increase. If other assets become less liquid, the demand of bonds would increase, increasing the price of bonds and decreasing the yield rate.

Costs of processing information. A special type of transaction cost is the cost of processing information about an asset. Savers must think about and process information about an asset when they decide if the asset would be a worthwhile purchase for their portfolios. When savers consider an asset to buy for their portfolios, they need to determine if it will offer a sufficient rate of return and an acceptable level of risk. Thus, the time, mental effort and other resources spent in the decision making process represent the cost of processing information.

For some assets, like government bonds and stocks of large corporations and bonds, information is readily available in financial newspapers and on websites. As a result, the cost of processing information for these assets is relatively low. But when less well known companies issue stocks or bonds, savers must spend a substantial amount of resources to collect and analyze information about the potential rate of return and the level of risk before deciding whether to buy these assets. For a fee, financial specialists acquire and analyze financial information for those who do not have the time or expertise to do the research. This fee is another example of the costs of processing information.

If information about bond markets becomes more accessible, say due to an improvement in technology, deciding whether to buy bonds or keep them in a portfolio becomes less costly or burdensome. Bonds could therefore become more attractive assets, and the demand of bonds could likewise increase.

On the other hand, if the cost of processing information increases, say due to a new regulation that no longer requires firms to publish financial information, bonds could become less attractive assets and the demand of bonds could fall.

Furthermore, if information about other assets like stocks becomes less or more costly to acquire and interpret, demand of bonds could change as well.

Because the costs of processing information can be substantial, people sometimes use reputation as a sign, or *signal*, for reliable information. Some assets are issued by institutions with a reputation for offering substantial and safe rates of return. If savers rely on this reputation, the cost of processing information would be low for these assets. But assets issued by institutions that are not well known require extensive research to determine if they would offer a sufficient rate of return and an acceptable level of risk.

As an institution becomes established and earns a reputation for offering reliable yield rates (such as the government of a wealthy country), the cost of processing information about its assets may fall. If so, the demand of its assets increases and the demand of alternative assets decreases when other factors remain constant. But if the reputation of an institution suffers because some information suggests that it is in poor financial health, savers may need to spend more time and other resources to determine the expected yield or return rate and the level of risk from buying the institution's assets. If so, the demand of the institution's assets will decrease and the demand of alternative assets would increase when other factors remain constant.

Central bank transactions. Central banks in modern economies heavily influence bond markets, usually the secondary market for government bonds, as we will learn in detail in chapter 11. Central banks are only one type of actor in bond markets, but their actions have important effects.

Formally, when the central bank buys bonds, the demand of bonds increases, since this large institution is willing to buy additional bonds at each price. If other factors like expected rates of return and expected inflation remain constant, the price of bonds therefore increases and the yield rate therefore decreases.

Table 7 summarizes the discussion about exogenous variables that influence the demand of bonds. The table lists the predicted effects when exogenous variables increase, but the predicted effects when exogenous variables decrease are exactly the opposite. Note that a change in demand results in a change in the equilibrium price of bonds that is always in the same direction and a change in the equilibrium yield rate that is always in the opposite direction. Eager students are encouraged to reconsider the effects of changes in the risk, liquidity and costs of processing information on assets that are alternatives to bonds.

Table 7: Variables that influence the demand of bonds

Exogenous variable	Change in exogenous variable	Change in demand	Change in equilibrium price of bonds	Change in equilibrium yield rate
Saving/Wealth	Increase	Increase	Increase	Decrease
Expected interest rates and rates of return on alternative assets	Increase	Decrease	Decrease	Increase
Expected inflation of the prices of goods and services	Increase	Decrease	Decrease	Increase
Taxes on income (yields) from bonds	Increase	Decrease	Decrease	Increase
Risk of holding bonds	Increase	Decrease	Decrease	Increase
Liquidity of bonds	Increase	Increase	Increase	Decrease
Costs of processing	Increase	Decrease	Decrease	Increase

information about bonds				
Central bank transactions	Purchase bonds	Increase	Increase	Decrease

Changes in interest/return rates associated with changes in the demand of bonds

As yield rates on bonds change, how are interest rates on loans and deposits and (expected) return rates on alternative assets predicted to change? Alternatively, as the demand of bond changes, changing the price and yield of bonds, how are interest rates on loans and deposits and (expected) return rates on other assets predicted to change?

To answer these questions, we consider how the demand of bonds affects the demand and supply of monetary assets and the demand and supply of alternative non-monetary assets. Consider Figure 5-9, which represents wealth as monetary assets and various kinds of non-monetary assets.

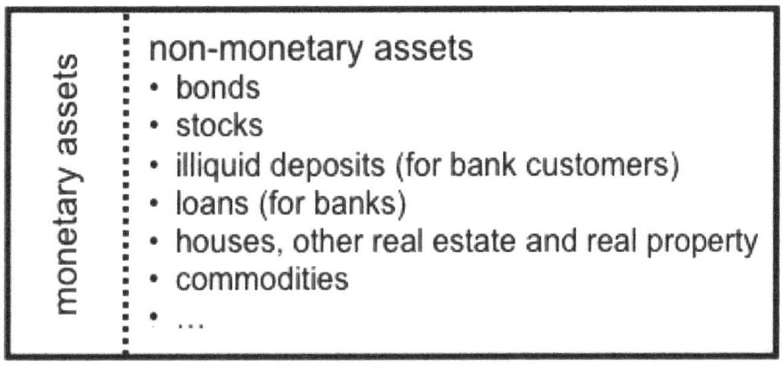

Figure 5-9: A representation of different kinds of wealth

Changing the demand of bonds can thus change the demand and supply of monetary assets and/or the demand and supply of alternative non-monetary assets. In particular, if the willingness to buy and to hold bonds increases, the price of bonds increases and yield rates decrease.

If these changes are associated with a decrease in the willingness to hold money, then interest rates on deposits and loans are predicted to decrease: when bank customers desire less money (and more bonds at the same time), they can deposit more money in illiquid deposits, putting downward pressure on illiquid deposit interest rates. When banks desire less money as reserves (and more bonds at the same time), they can lend more at lower interest rates.

If an increase in the demand and price of bonds and a decrease in yield rates are associated with an increase in the supply of money from the central bank (because the central bank buys bonds in exchange for cash), then interest rates on deposits and loans are also predicted to decrease: a greater quantity of money acquired by bank customers implies more illiquid deposits at lower interest rates, and a greater quantity of money acquired by banks implies more loans at lower interest rates.

If an increase in the demand and price of bonds and a decrease in yield rates are associated with a decrease in the willingness to buy alternative non-monetary assets like stocks and real estate or an increase in the willingness to sell these assets, then the prices and return rates of these alternative assets are also predicted to decrease. Like stocks and real estate, loans and illiquid deposits can be bought and sold too, so their prices would decrease and their return rates would decrease as banks and bank customers buy less and sell more of these assets. And to the degree that banks compete with bond markets, they must decrease interest rates on loans and can decrease interest rates on deposits as yield rates decrease. However, *expected* return rates for new buyers of these alternative non-monetary assets may increase if low prices of these alternative assets imply that prices are expected to increase, instead of to decrease further, in the future.

Changes in supply in the model of bond markets

Now let's consider exogenous variables that influence the supply of bonds. Since firms and governments are the major institutions that issue bonds, we consider factors that affect their behavior, in addition to the behavior of bond sellers in general.

Expected rates of return on productive assets. Firms need to decide how much they should borrow to spend on projects that will expand future production. That decision depends on the expected profitability or the expected rate of return on productive assets, assets that are used to produce other goods and services. Formally, the expected rates of return on productive assets (for borrowers/ spenders) influence the willingness to issue and sell bonds, whereas the expected rates of return on financial assets (for savers/lenders) like stocks, loans, deposits and so on influence the willingness to buy bonds, as I discussed in the last section. Of course, the expected rates of return on productive assets are often highly correlated with the expected rates of return on financial assets, but it is easier to model them separately.

As the expected rate of return of productive assets increases, the willingness to issue and sell new bonds to finance these investments increases at each price of bonds. More concisely, the supply of bonds increases.

We represent an increase in the supply of bonds by shifting the supply curve for bonds right, as shown in Figure 5-10. A shift of the supply curve right means that the quantity of bonds that institutions and individuals are willing to sell increases at each price (and yield rate) and/or the price that they are willing to accept decreases at each quantity (and the yield that they are willing to pay increases at each quantity). When supply increases, we then predict that price falls from P_1 to P_2 and the yield rate rises from y_1 to y_2 until sellers can sell all that they want at the given price, a quantity represented as Q_2 in the figure.

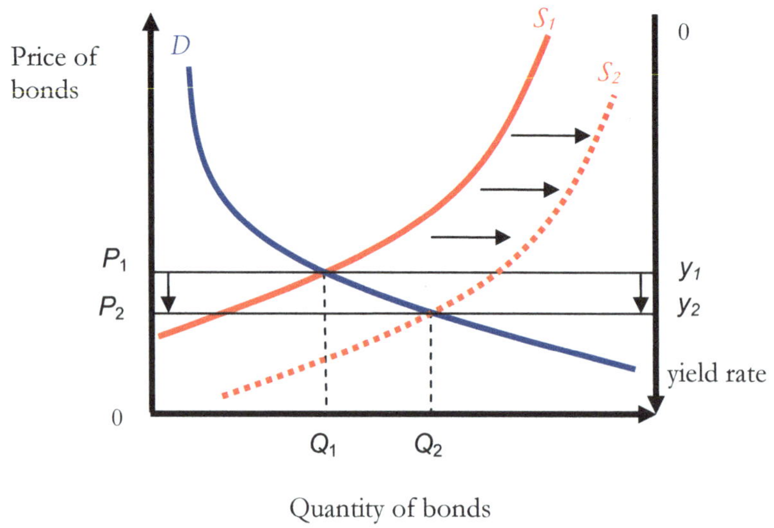

Figure 5-10: An increase in the supply of bonds, from S_1 to S_2, decreases the price and increases the yield rate.

Conversely, as the expected rate of return on productive assets decreases, the willingness to issue and sell new bonds decreases at each price of bonds. In other words, the supply of bonds decreases.

We represent a decrease in the supply of bonds by shifting the supply curve for bonds left, as shown in Figure 5-11. A shift of the supply curve left means that the quantity of bonds that institutions and individuals are willing to sell decreases at each price (and yield rate) and/or the price that they are willing to accept increases at each quantity (and the yield that they are willing to pay decreases at each quantity). When supply decreases, we then predict that price rises from P_1 to P_2 and the yield rate falls from y_1 to y_2 until buyers can buy all that they want at the given price, a quantity represented as Q_2 in the figure.

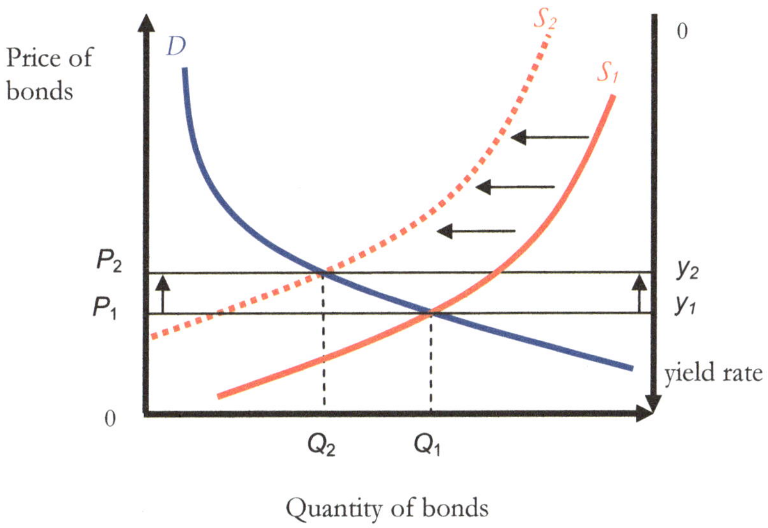

Figure 5-11: A decrease in the supply of bonds, from S_1 to S_2, increases the price and decreases the yield rate.

Expected income and revenue. Income and revenue are related to the return on productive assets, which is essentially another name for the profitability of production. But we might want to consider income and revenue from selling goods and services (a function of the demand of goods and services), which do not include the cost of production, separately from return because income and revenue are used to repay debt (from bonds), which may be more important than other payments that can be deferred. In other words, income and revenue affect the real cost of borrowing and therefore the willingness to issue bonds. When expected incomes and revenues increase, the real cost of borrowing falls for a given nominal yield rate. In contrast, when expected incomes and revenue are revised downward, the real cost of borrowing increases at each nominal yield rate because revenues and incomes are not expected to grow as fast or are even expected to fall. Therefore, bonds are expected to be repaid with more scarce income or revenue.

More formally, when expected income and revenue increase, the supply of bonds that pay fixed nominal amounts increases because real interest rates/yield rates decrease. Therefore, the price of bonds falls and the nominal yield rate rises, as shown in Figure 5-10. Conversely, when expected income and revenue decrease, the supply of bonds that pay fixed nominal amounts decreases because the real yield rate increases. Therefore, the price of bonds rises and the nominal yield rate falls, as shown in Figure 5-11.

Government borrowing. Of course, governments are major players in bond markets because they frequently issue bonds to finance various kinds of expenditure. More government borrowing is represented as an increase in the supply of bonds, which decreases the prices of bonds and increases the yield rate.[34] Conversely, less government borrowing is represented as a decrease in the supply of bonds, which increases the price of bonds and decreases the yield rate.

Agencies of the national, state or local governments that oversee government expenditures and do budget accounting are often called *finance* or *treasury* departments. These departments are responsible for issuing and selling new government bonds to finance borrowing (as well as paying off bonds that have matured). Finance departments should be distinguished from the central bank, a national bank or banking system that regulates private banks and the amount of money that circulates in the economy.

Central bank transactions. To regulate the amount of money that circulates in an economy, central banks frequently buy and sell bonds that were previously issued by finance departments in the secondary or open market. The central bank of the US, the Federal Reserve System, does not issue bonds, but rather acts as a very important buyer and seller of existing bonds that have been issued by the Treasury Department, which is considered to be the finance department of the US government.

In the model of bond markets, selling bonds by the central bank increases the supply of bonds, since one important institution in bond markets is willing to sell additional bonds at each price. If other factors like expected rates of return and expected inflation remain constant, the price of bonds decreases and the yield rate increases when the central bank sells bonds.

Table 8 summarizes the discussion about exogenous variables that influence the supply of bonds. The table lists the predicted effects when exogenous variables increase, but the predicted effects when exogenous variables decrease is exactly the opposite. Note that a change in supply results in a change in the equilibrium price of bonds that is always in the opposite direction and a change in the equilibrium yield rate that is always in the same direction.

Table 8: Variables that influence the supply of bonds

Exogenous variable	Change in exogenous variable	Change in supply	Change in equilibrium price of bonds	Change in equilibrium yield rate
Expected rate of return on productive assets	Increase	Increase	Decrease	Increase
Expected income and revenue	Increase	Increase	Decrease	Increase
Government borrowing	Increase	Increase	Decrease	Increase
Central bank transactions	Sell bonds	Increase	Decrease	Increase

[34] Governments also can borrow loans from private banks, but nearly all governments of large countries borrow at least somewhat in bond markets.

Changes in interest/return rates associated with changes in the supply of bonds

As the supply of bond changes, changing the price and yield of bonds, how are interest rates on loans and deposits and (expected) return rates on other assets predicted to change?

Changing the supply of bonds can change the demand and supply of monetary assets and/or the demand and supply of alternative non-monetary assets. In particular, if the willingness to issue and to sell bonds increases, the price of bonds decreases and yield rates increase.

If these changes are associated with a increase in the willingness to hold money, then interest rates on deposits and loans are predicted to increase: when bank customers desire more money (and sell more bonds at the same time), they can deposit less money in illiquid deposits, putting upward pressure on illiquid deposit interest rates. When banks desire more money as reserves, they lend less at higher interest rates.

If an increase in the supply of bonds is associated with an decrease in the supply of money from the central bank (because the central bank sells bonds in exchange for cash), then interest rates on deposits and loans are also predicted to increase: a lower quantity of money held by bank customers implies fewer illiquid deposits at higher interest rates, and a lower quantity of money held by banks implies fewer loans at higher interest rates.

If an increase in the supply of bonds is associated with a increase in the willingness to buy alternative non-monetary assets like stocks and real estate or a decrease in the willingness to sell these assets, then the prices and return rates of these alternative assets are also predicted to increase. Like stocks and real estate, the prices and return rates for loans and illiquid deposits would increase as banks and bank customers buy more and sell fewer of these assets. And to the degree that banks compete with bond markets, they can decrease interest rates on loans and must increase interest rates on deposits as yield rates increase. However, *expected* return rates for new buyers of these alternative non-monetary assets may decrease if high prices of these alternative assets imply that prices are expected to decrease, instead of to increase further, in the future.

Changes in supply and demand in the model of bond markets

We learned that an increase in expected income and revenue increases the supply of bonds, since the real yield rate falls at each nominal yield rate, and an increase in expected inflation decreases the demand of bonds for the same reason. Note that the change in prices caused by a change in the willingness to buy goods and services affects a change in income and revenue in the same way. In other words, (expected) inflation in the prices of goods and services can be directly related to the (expected) change in income and revenue from selling goods and services when the willingness to buy goods and services changes. (When prices change due to an initial change in the cost of production, rather than an initial change in expenditure and subsequent change in production, income and revenue (and profit) should not increase and may even decrease.)

In particular, when prices of goods and services, income and revenue are all expected to increase due to an increase in the demand of goods and services, we predict that nominal yield rates increase because of an increase in the supply of bonds (due to the increase in expected income and revenue) and a decrease in the demand of bonds (due to the increase in expected prices of goods and services). Figure 5-12 shows the effects of an increase in supply and a decrease in demand, leading to an increase in yield rates from y_1 to y_2 (and a decrease in the price of bonds from P_1 to P_2).

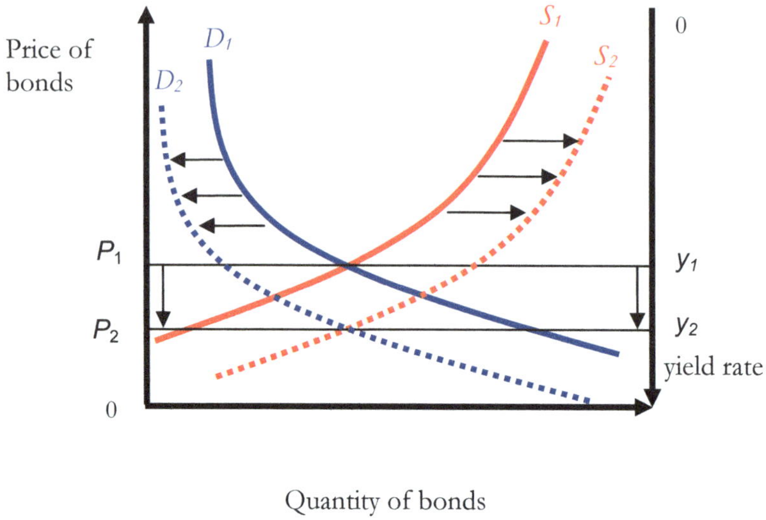

Figure 5-12: An increase in expected inflation of the prices of goods and services, income and revenue increases the supply of bonds, from S_1 to S_2, and decreases the demand of bonds, from D_1 to D_2, resulting in a decrease in the price of bonds and an increase in the yield rate.

If we use the actual inflation rate as a simple approximation for expected inflation and expected changes in income and revenue, we find that nominal yield rates track the inflation rate fairly closely over time (regardless of whether the inflation in the prices of goods and services was caused by an initial increase in demand (expenditure) or an initial increase in the cost of production). Figure 5-13 shows that in recent periods of high inflation, nominal yield rates were also high; in periods of low inflation, nominal yield rates were also low. Figure 5-13 also suggests that the expected real yield rate has been relatively stable during recent decades.

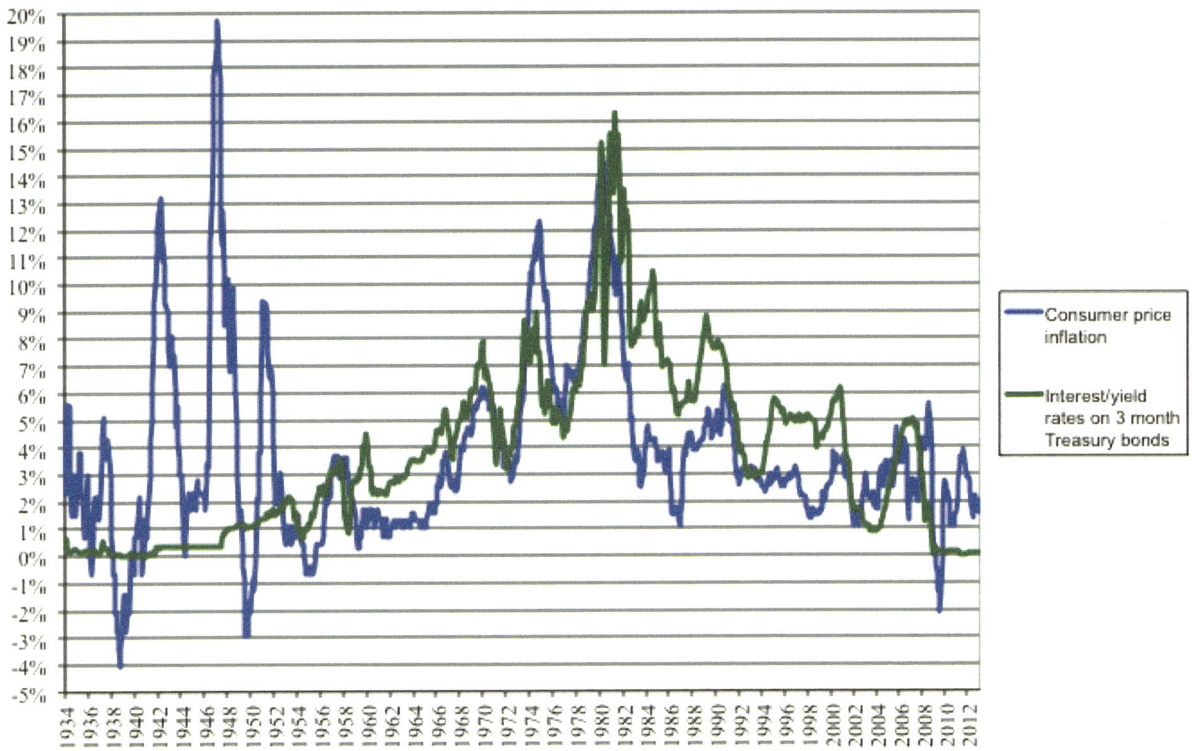

Source: Board of Governerors of the Federal Reserve System, http://www.federalreserve.gov/releases/h15/data.htm/
Bureau of Labor Statistics, http://www.bls.gov/cpi/home.htm

Figure 5-13: Nominal yield rates generally track the inflation rate over time, indicating that real yield rates are relatively stable over time.

Summary

In this chapter we have constructed a model of the bond market that helps us think about how interest, yield and return rates on non-monetary assets change when the economy is subject to various changes. This model considers how changes in the following affect the willingness to buy bonds at each price and yield rate: saving, expected interest and return rates on alternative assets (including bonds in the future), expected inflation in the prices of goods and services, taxes on bond yields, the risk of holding bonds, the liquidity of bonds, the costs of processing information about bonds and central bank transactions. The model also considers how changes in the expected rate of return on productive assets, expected income and revenue, government borrowing and central bank transactions affect the willingness to sell bonds at each price and yield rate.

Appendix

Changes in the price level and in expected inflation

There are subtle differences between a change in the level of average prices and a change in expected inflation. A change in the level of average prices at the present time does not imply that the prices will continue to change in the future—it does not imply that continued inflation will occur over time. The level of average prices may change today, but thereafter stop changing so that inflation would not occur in the future. By comparison, a change in expected inflation implies that prices are expected to continue to change at a certain rate in the future. Also, a change in expected inflation represents a change in what people think about the *future* rate of change in the level of average prices, whereas a change in the level of average prices represents a change that *has already occurred.*

Consider a level of average prices that is stable until the beginning of 2010, but then unexpectedly starts to rise. Thereafter, suppose people expect it to continue to rise at the same rate until the beginning of 2011. At that time, suppose that prices become stable again so that the expected inflation rate reverts to 0%. Figure 5-14 shows that the price level at the beginning of 2011, 150, would be higher than the price level at the beginning of 2010, 100. The (expected) rate of inflation is represented as the slope of the line that measures the level of average prices; a positive slope represents a positive (expected) rate of inflation. (For eager students: what is the (expected) rate of inflation from January 2010 to January 2011?)

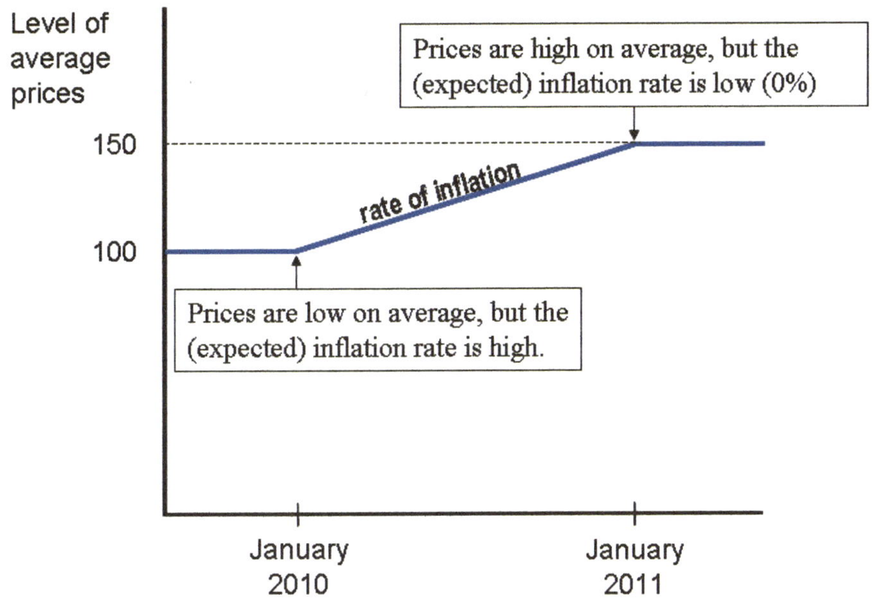

Figure 5-14: The relationship between the level of average prices and (expected) inflation.

If we were to represent the change in the level of average prices in the model of the market for monetary assets, we would increase the demand curve for monetary assets after prices have changed, that is, in January 2011. If we were to represent the change in expected inflation in the model of the market for monetary assets and in the model of the bond market, we would change the demand functions and the supply function when people change their expectations about how prices will change *in the future*. Expectations about how prices will change in the future could change in January 2010 or another time.

People can be forward looking about changes in future prices, thereby adjusting their behavior (that is, their demand and supply of monetary assets and non-monetary assets) today. Alternatively, people may adapt their behavior to what has already happened, thereby slowly changing their behavior (that is, their demand and supply of monetary assets and non-monetary assets).

Relationships between interest/yield rates and the quantity of money

We learned from the model of bond markets that the central bank can buy bonds, increasing the demand of bonds and decreasing the yield rate. When the central bank buys bonds from institutions and individuals, they receive money from the central bank, so that the quantity of money in circulation increases. Thus, we predict that when the yield rate decreases the quantity of money in circulation increases—a result consistent with the model of the money market, which also predicts that banks will lower interest rates on loans and deposits. When other factors are held constant, Figure 5-15 describes the relationship between the quantity of money in circulation and interest rates/yield rates when the central bank buys (increases the demand of) bonds.

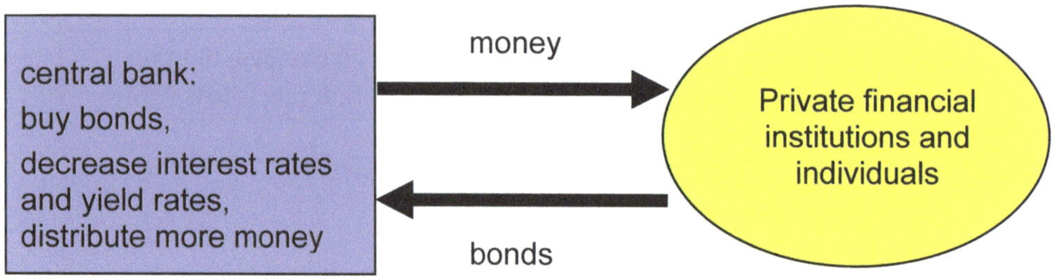

Figure 5-15: When the central bank buys bonds from the public, interest rates decrease and the quantity of money in circulation (held by the public) increases.

Alternatively, when the central bank sells bonds, the supply of bonds increases and the yield rate increases. When the central bank sells bonds to institutions and individuals, they must pay money to the central bank, which then puts the money in its vaults and takes it out of circulation. Thus, when the yield rate increases, the quantity of money in circulation decreases—another result consistent with the model of the money market, which also predicts that banks will raise interest rates on loans and deposits.[35] When other factors are held constant, Figure 5-16 describes the relationship between the quantity of money in circulation and interest rates/yield rates when the central bank sells (increases the supply of) bonds.

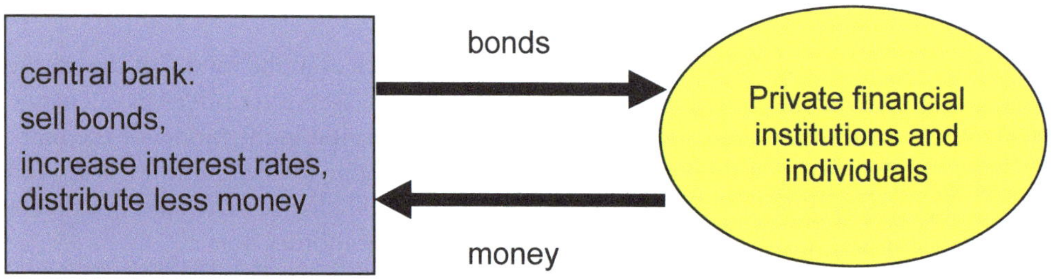

Figure 5-16: When the central bank sells bonds to the public, yield rates increase and the quantity of money in circulation (held by the public) decreases.

Thus, in this case, both the model of bond markets and the model of the market for monetary assets predict a negative relationship between the quantity of money in circulation and interest rates/yield rates, and both models assume that when the central bank conducts transactions other factors remain constant. In particular, the models assume that the level of average prices and expected inflation will remain constant.

But the level of average prices and expected inflation may not remain constant when the quantity of money in circulation changes. When people acquire more money, they are willing to buy more goods and services at given prices: the demand of goods and services increases. With increased demand of goods and services, producers tend to raise prices of goods and services when their inventories fall, leading to an increase in the level of average prices and inflation. Furthermore, people may foresee this outcome before it actually happens; they may expect changes in prices given an expected change in the policy goals of the central bank. If so, they may adjust prices of goods and services, the demand and supply of non-monetary assets, the demand of monetary assets, yield rates, and interest rates on loans and deposits today in anticipation of the expected increases in the prices of goods and services. In fact, there is a positive relationship between growth in the quantity of money in circulation and inflation or expected inflation over

[35] More accurately, the rate of growth of the quantity of money decreases when yield rates increase since other factors rarely remain constant. Various measures of the quantity of monetary assets only occasionally decrease when yield rates increase, since the quantity of monetary assets usually grows at least a little as the economy and the level of average prices grow.

time. Figure 5-17 shows that the level of average prices has risen in tandem with the quantity of money in circulation.

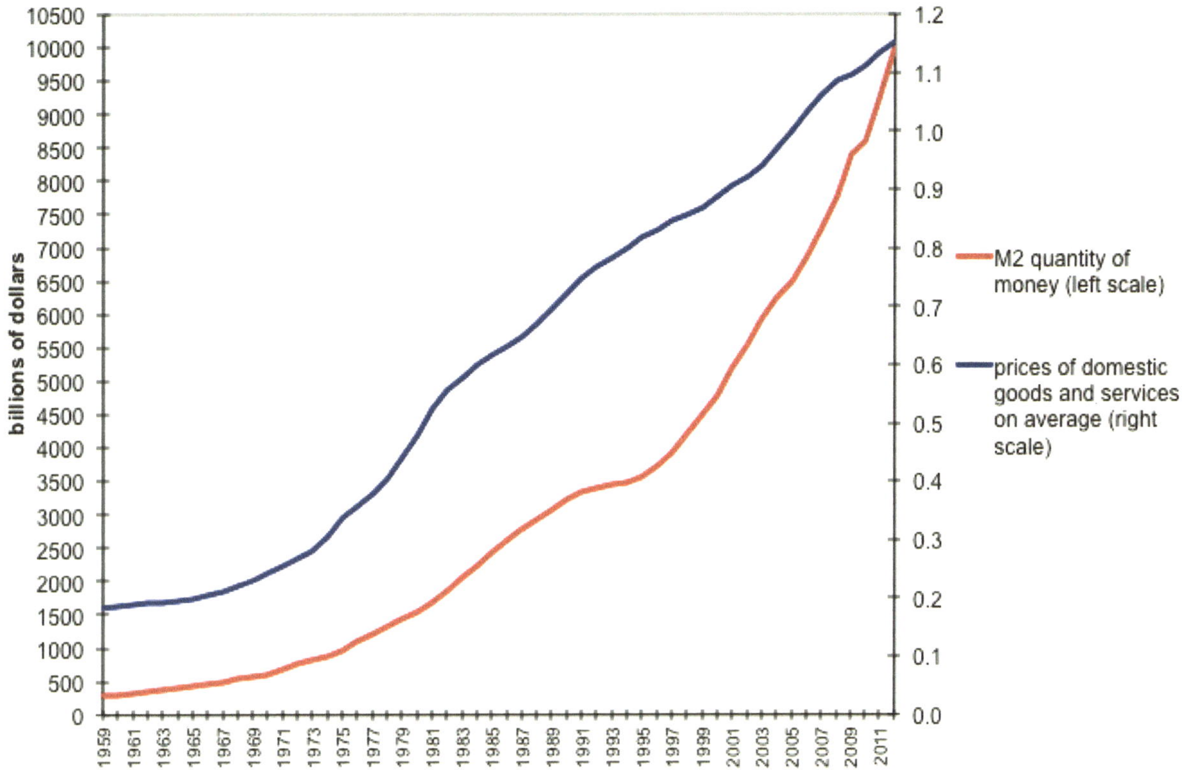

Source: Board of Governors of the Federal Reserve System, http://www.federalreserve.gov/releases/ Bureau of Economic Analysis, http://www.bea.gov/bea/dn/home/gdp.htm

Figure 5-17: The price level has risen with the quantity of money from 1959-2012.

How would this relationship affect nominal interest rates? In chapter 3, we learned that higher expected inflation (and, by extension, actual inflation) leads to higher nominal interest rates if real interest rates are constant. If people expect an increase in the inflation rate because of an increase in the growth of the quantity of money, then nominal interest rates will *increase* when other factors remain constant, a prediction that is generally consistent with Figure 5-13. In this scenario, we predict a positive relationship between the growth rate in the money supply and nominal interest rates over time.[36] Furthermore, when expected inflation increases, the model of bond markets predicts an increase in nominal interest rates, when real interest rates and other factors remain constant. On the other hand, the model of the market for monetary assets predicts a decrease in real interest rates when nominal interest rates are constant. When the level of average prices increases, the model of the market for monetary assets then predicts an increase in nominal interest rates.

Thus, we have opposing predictions:

- Nominal and real interest rates are predicted to fall when the quantity of money increases but the level of average prices of goods and services and expectations about inflation remain constant. This prediction is called the **liquidity effect**.

[36] In the long run, real interest rates are determined by real factors in the economy, such as the amount of resources saved and borrowed, as well as policies that affect saving and borrowing, such as taxes, government borrowing and regulation that manage risk. If these factors are stable, then real interest rates will remain stable in the long run.

- Real interest rates are predicted to fall when expected inflation increases but when the level of average prices of goods and services and nominal interest rates remain constant. This prediction is called the **purchasing power effect**.
- Nominal interest rates are predicted to rise when the inflation rate of the prices of goods and services is expected to increase but when real interest rates remain constant. This prediction is called the **Fisher effect**, named after Irving Fisher, who first documented the relationship between nominal interest rates and the inflation rate.
- When actual inflation results and the level of average prices rises, nominal interest rates are also predicted to rise when real interest rates remain constant. This prediction is called the **price level effect**.

Note how each predicted effect requires that we hold certain variables constant. The liquidity effect assumes that we hold the prices of goods and services or expectations about inflation constant, while the Fisher/price level effects do not. The purchasing power effect assumes that we hold the level of average prices constant but not expectations about inflation. Also, the Fisher effect and purchasing power effect are both related in the sense that both assume that expected inflation increases, but the former assumes that real interest rates remain constant, while the latter assumes that nominal interest rates remain constant.

I discussed why the liquidity effect, the purchasing power effect and the price level effect should occur in the last chapter. The liquidity effect was predicted by an increase in the supply of monetary assets; the purchasing power effect was predicted by a decrease in the demand of monetary assets; the price level effect was predicted by an increase in the demand of monetary assets.

As for the Fisher effect, the logic is related to the price level effect. Institutions and individuals will tend to raise nominal interest rates on loans and deposits to require higher yield rates to account for higher expected costs. In other words, as prices of goods and services are expected to increase, institutions and individuals want to be compensated with higher nominal interest rates and yield rates in order to keep the expected real return rate constant. Likewise, if wages, incomes and revenues are expected to increase with inflation (which is generally true when inflation is caused by an increase in the quantity of money and the willingness to buy), borrowers will be able to pay back loans and bonds with more plentiful money, and they will not need low interest rates as an incentive to borrow more.

Do the liquidity/purchasing power effects or the Fisher/price level effects dominate when the quantity of money increases? As the prices of goods and services (including wages, the price of labor services) increase or are expected to increase, perhaps because of an increase in the quantity of money, the liquidity effect is predicted to disappear and the other three effects are predicted to emerge, and the Fisher/price level effects are predicted to counteract the other two effects. So ultimately, the answer depends on how people expect inflation to change in response to a change in monetary policy and how they adjust prices accordingly and whether they increase interest/yield rates and increase the demand of monetary assets to a larger degree than they decrease the demand of monetary assets. Changes in expectations about prices can be slow or fast, depending on how people think and in particular depending on what people think about monetary policy.[37] If people are slow to adjust their expectations about inflation and therefore slow to adjust prices, then the relationship between the quantity of money and interest rates should be explained by the liquidity effect. But

[37] See Monnet, Cyrill and Warren E. Weber, (2001), "Money and Interest Rates," *Federal Reserve Bank of Minneapolis Quarterly Review*, (25), 4. The authors find evidence of the Fisher/price level effects especially in the "long run" when expectations and prices have a sufficient time to adjust and find evidence of the liquidity effect especially in the "short run" when they do not. They also predict interest rates given people's expectations about changes in the quantity of money in circulation. With expected changes in the quantity of money, (expected) inflation and prices adjust quickly so that the Fisher/price level effects dominate. With unexpected changes in the quantity of money, (expected) inflation and prices do not have sufficient time to fully adjust so that the liquidity effect dominates.

if people are quick to adjust their expectations and therefore quick to adjust prices, then the relationship between the quantity of money and interest rates should be explained by the Fisher, price level and purchasing power effects.

Looking at data suggests that both the liquidity and purchasing power effects and the Fisher/price level effects are important, depending on the time frame involved. Figure 5-18 suggests that the relationship between the M2 quantity of money and short-term yield rates on US Treasury Bills is represented by the liquidity effect during short time spans, from a few months to a few years. But over longer time periods, the Fisher/price level effects seem better at explaining the relationship between interest rates and the quantity of money. From 1982-1993, the growth rate of M2 decreased on average, as did yield rates. From about 1994-2000 the growth rate of M2 increased on average, as did yield rates. Figure 5-19 suggests that the relationship between the M1 quantity of money and yield rates is also represented by the liquidity effect during short time spans. But over longer time periods the Fisher/price level effects are not apparent, possibly because of the technological and regulatory changes that occurred during the last few decades. We study some regulatory changes in later chapters.

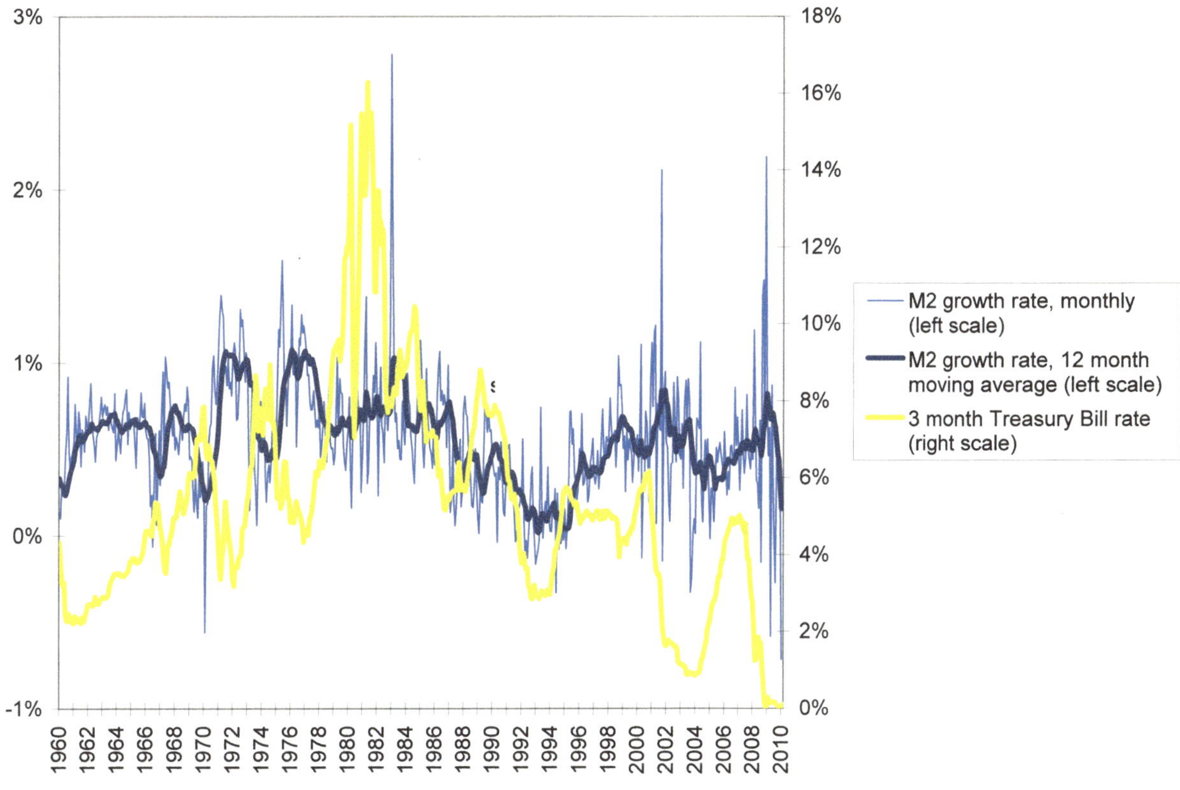

Source: http://www.federalreserve.gov/releases/h3/hist/h3hist1.txt

Figure 5-18: Growth in M2 relative to nominal yield rates, 1960-2010.

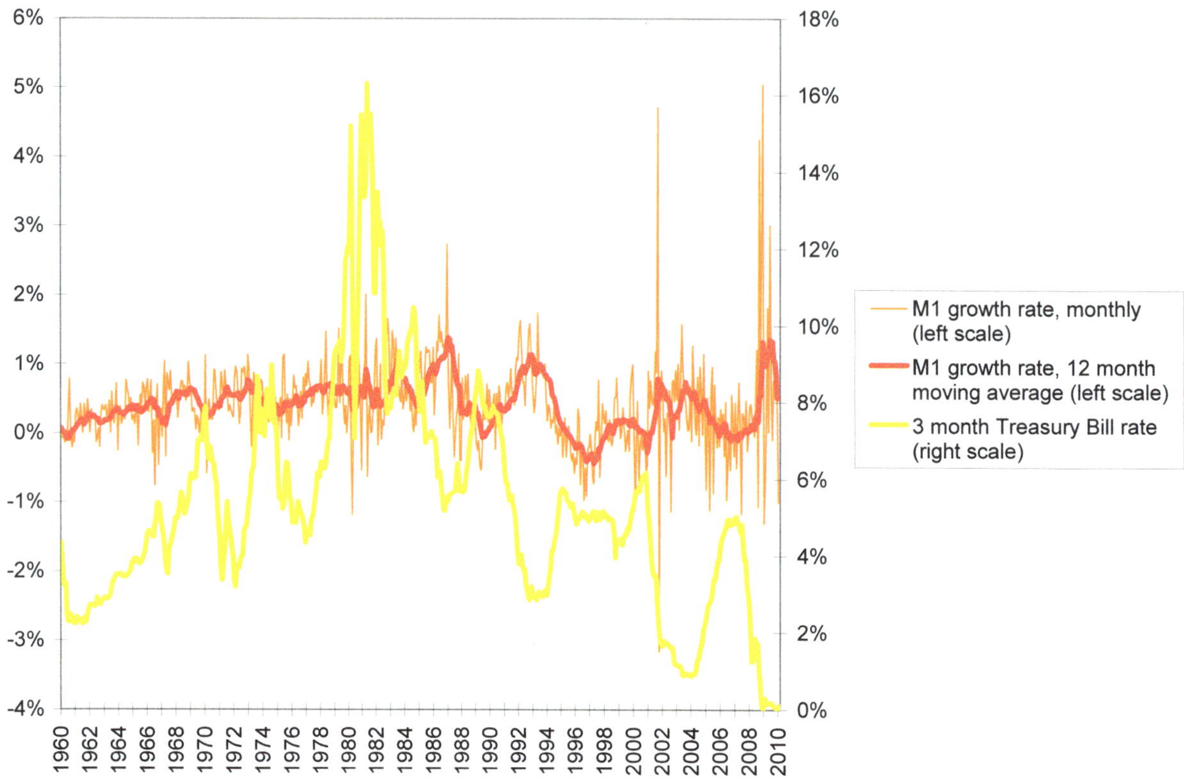

Source: http://www.federalreserve.gov/releases/h3/hist/h3hist1.txt

Figure 5-19: Growth in M1 relative to nominal yield rates, 1960-2010.

Problems and Applications

Short answer problems

1. If an economy produces and spends more, so that the expected rate of return on productive assets increases, and also saves more because it earns more income from production, then what is predicted to happen to yield rates on bonds? What is predicted to happen to the quantity of bonds that are issued bought and sold?

2. If stocks are expected to have higher return rates, then what is predicted to happen to the yield rate on bonds?

3. If bonds in the future are expected to have a higher price, because the central bank or government is expected to start a buying program for them to increase the quantity of money and expenditure, then what is predicted to happen to the yield rate on bonds *today*?

4. If bonds are expected to have greater liquidity, because the central bank or government is expected to start a buying program for them to increase the quantity of money and expenditure, then what is predicted to happen to the yield rate on bonds today?

5. If *securitized loans*, packages of loans that are created as a new security and sold to savers (like bonds), are expected to have greater liquidity, because the central bank or government is expected to start a buying program for them to increase the quantity of money and expenditure, then what is predicted to happen to the yield rate on bonds today?

6. If the inflation rate of the prices of goods and services is expected to increase, then what is predicted to happen to the yield rate on bonds? Go back to the previous chapter to consider the predicted effect of an increase in the expected inflation rate and the level of average prices of goods and services in the model of the market for monetary assets.

    a. Is the prediction about expected inflation from the model of the market for monetary assets consistent with the prediction about expected inflation from the model of the bond market? Why or why not?
    b. Is the prediction about the level of average prices from the model of the market for monetary assets consistent with the prediction about expected inflation from the model of the bond market? Why or why not?

7. If the government decides to spend more on goods and services by borrowing more in the bond market, in what way is this good for savers/lenders? In what way is this bad for borrowers/spenders in the private sector?

8. If the risk of bonds increases, what is predicted to happen to the yield rate on bonds? Go back to the previous chapter to consider the predicted effect of an increase in risk and pessimism about non-monetary assets in the model of the market for monetary assets. Is the prediction about the risk of bonds in the model of the bond market consistent with the prediction about risk of and pessimism about non-monetary assets in the model of the market for monetary assets? Why or why not?

9. If the central bank sells more bonds, what is predicted to happen to the yield rate on bonds? If the central bank sells more bonds, it requires money as payment and effectively takes it out of circulation. Go back to the previous chapter to consider the predicted effect of a decrease in the quantity of money and credit from the central bank. Is the prediction about the central bank selling bonds in the model of the bond market consistent with the prediction about the central bank distributing less money and credit in the model of the market for monetary assets? Why or why not?

10. If income, revenue and the prices of goods and services are expected to increase because expenditure is expected to increase, then what is predicted to happen to the yield rate on bonds? If the expected increase in expenditure occurs because the central bank buys bonds from individuals and private institutions and gives them more money in return, then what is predicted to happen to the yield rate on bonds? Are you answers consistent? Why or why not?

Internet applications

1. Go to http://ecos.bok.or.kr/ to download data for M2 or "broad money" and interest rates on 180 day time deposits, or certificates of deposits (CDs), for all available years. Create a graph with interest

rates, monthly changes in the M2 quantity of money and a 12 month moving average of monthly changes, analogous to Figure 5-18. Do you see evidence of the liquidity/purchasing power effects and/or Fisher/price level effects? For which time periods?

2. Go to http://ecos.bok.or.kr/ to download data for M2 or "broad money" and yield rates on 5 year Treasury bonds for all available years. Create a graph with yield rates, monthly changes in the M2 quantity of money and a 12 month moving average of monthly changes, analogous to Figure 5-18. Do you see evidence of the liquidity/purchasing power effects and/or Fisher/price level effects? For which time periods?

3. Go to http://ecos.bok.or.kr/ to download data for M1 or "narrow money" and interest rates on 180 day time deposits, or certificates of deposits (CDs), for all available years. Create a graph with interest rates, monthly changes in the M1 quantity of money and a 12 month moving average of monthly changes, analogous to Figure 5-19. Do you see evidence of the liquidity/purchasing power effects and/or Fisher/price level effects? For which time periods?

4. Go to http://ecos.bok.or.kr/ to download data for M1 or "broad money" and yield rates on 5 year Treasury bonds for all available years. Create a graph with yield rates, monthly changes in the M1 quantity of money and a 12 month moving average of monthly changes, analogous to Figure 5-19. Do you see evidence of the liquidity/purchasing power effects and/or Fisher/price level effects? For which time periods?

5. Go to http://ecos.bok.or.kr/ to download data for consumer price inflation and interest rates on 180 day time deposits, or certificates of deposits (CDs), for all available years.

    a. Create a graph with the inflation rate and interest rates, analogous to Figure 5-13. Do nominal interest rates track the inflation rate over time?
    b. Try to calculate the correlation coefficient for these two variables using a software program. (A correlation coefficient of 1 means that the two variables move perfectly in tandem; a correlation coefficient of 0 means that the two variables do not move together at all.)
    c. Calculate real interest rates using actual inflation for expected inflation, then calculate the standard deviation of real interest rates using a software program. (The standard deviation represents how much on average a value deviates from its average.) Next calculate the standard deviation of nominal interest rates. Which measure of interest rates has a greater standard deviation?

6. Go to http://ecos.bok.or.kr/ to download data for consumer price inflation and yield rates on 5 year Treasury bonds for all available years.
    a. Create a graph with the inflation rate and yield rates, analogous to Figure 5-13. Do nominal yield rates track the inflation rate over time?
    b. Try to calculate the correlation coefficient for these two variables using a software program. (A correlation coefficient of 1 means that the two variables move perfectly in tandem; a correlation coefficient of 0 means that the two variables do not move together at all.)
    c. Calculate real yield rates using actual inflation for expected inflation, then calculate the standard deviation of real yield rates using a software program. (The standard deviation represents how much on average a value deviates from its average.) Next calculate the standard deviation of nominal yield rates. Which measure of yield rates has a greater standard deviation?

7. Go to http://ecos.bok.or.kr/ to download data for interest rates on 180 day time deposits and yield rates on 6 month Treasury bonds for all available years. Create a figure analogous to Figure 5-8 for

these deposits and bonds from 1995-2005. Did both rates generally increase from 1997-1998? Which increased more? Why do you suppose that one variable increased more than the other?

8. Try to find data for interest rates on 180 day time deposits and yield rates on 6 month Treasury bonds for Greece during the last decade. Create a figure analogous to Figure 5-8 for these deposits and bonds. Did both rates generally increase from 2009-2010? Which increased more? Why do you suppose that one variable increased more than the other?

9. Go to http://ecos.bok.or.kr/ to download data for M2 or "broad money" and the implicit price (gross domestic production) deflator for all available years. Create a graph with two vertical axes displaying how both of these variables have changed over time, analogous to Figure 5-17. Do you see a direct relationship between the quantity of money and the prices of (final) goods and services produced in the domestic economy? If not, are there other factors that could explain how the prices of (final) goods and services produced in the domestic economy could vary over time?

6. The Traditional Role of Banks

Preview

Banks traditionally act as intermediaries between savers and borrowers. And by acting as an intermediary, banks transform the assets of savers into their own by creating loans with the saved funds, but they are then liable for repaying the savers who deposits their funds at the bank. Banks record the value of their assets and liabilities on a balance sheet, as well as the difference between the value of assets and the value of liabilities, called capital. In addition, banks are the institutions that traditionally provide money and credit to individuals and institutions that want to spend. In this chapter, we formally represent the traditional intermediary roles of banks and examine the assets, liabilities and capital that are recorded on the balance sheets of banks.

The traditional role of banks: financial intermediation

Banks traditionally offer checking, savings and other deposits to individuals and institutions that want to save. Savers deposit their funds at banks and expect an interest payment in return. But during the time when funds are deposited at banks, banks will lend a large portion of them to borrowers. Thus, the traditional role of banks is to move funds between savers and borrowers—that is, to act as an intermediary between them—while trying to earn income from their loans and pay for their deposits when they are due. This practice is formally called **financial intermediation**, as we first learned in chapter 1. Figure 6-1 represents the financial intermediation of banks, which create deposit accounts for savers and loan contract for borrowers in the process.

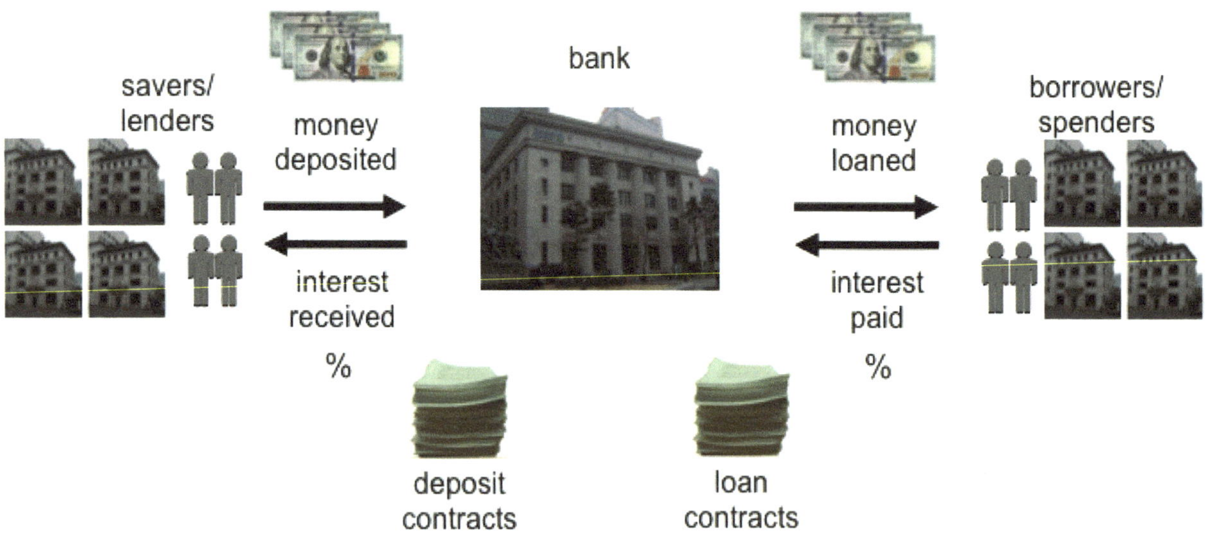

Figure 6-1: Financial intermediation between savers/lenders and borrowers/spenders.

We also learned in chapter 1 that bank customers—both savers and borrowers—can benefit from this financial intermediation: savers can earn interest on their deposits and borrowers can have access to credit when they need it or want it. In this section, we create a simple model of financial intermediation that allows us to better understand the behavior and interests of savers, borrowers and the financial intermediaries (that is, banks).

One can represent the intermediary role of banks with simple logic that relates the amount of saved and borrowed funds to the interest rates on deposits and loans. The amount of funds that borrowers are willing to borrow should be inversely related to the interest rates on loans: as interest rates on loans increase, bank customers should be willing to take out fewer loans and smaller loans; as interest rates on loans decrease, bank customers should be willing to take out more loans and larger loans. Figure 6-2 represents this inverse relationship between the quantity of funds that individuals and institutions want to borrow and the interest rates on loans with a downward-sloping graph of a demand function for loans, D_{loans}, with the amount of funds that bank customers want to borrow as a function of the interest rates on loans. The (graph of the) demand function for loans is more simply called the demand of loans.

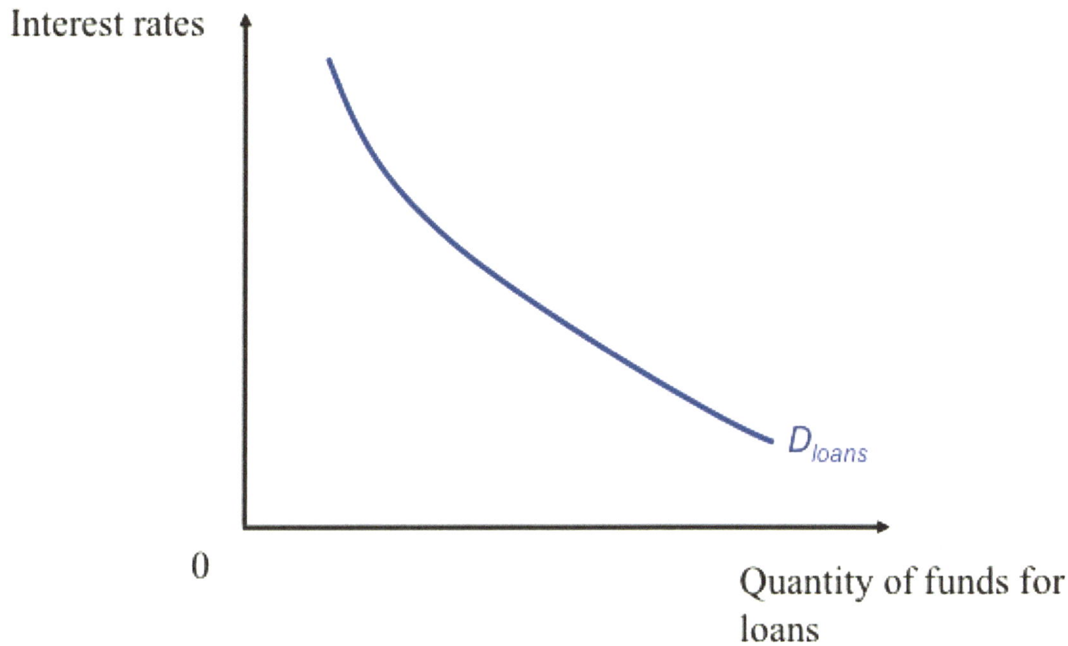

Figure 6-2: The demand of loans shows an inverse relationship between the quantity of funds that bank customers want to borrow and interest rates on loans.

The amount of funds that banks are willing to lend should be directly related to the interest rate that they can charge on their loans: as interest rates on loans increase, banks should be willing to lend more loans and larger loans; as interest rates on loans decrease, banks should be willing to lend fewer loans and smaller loans (and hold cash or find alternative investments). Likewise, the amount of funds that depositors are willing to save should also be directly related to the interest rates they can earn on their deposits. As interest rates on deposits increase, bank customers should be willing to deposit more funds. As interest rates on deposits decrease, bank customers should be willing to deposit fewer funds (and hold cash or find alternative investments). Figure 6-3 represents the direct relationship between the quantity of funds that banks want to lend and the interest rates on loans with upward-sloping graph of supply function for loans, S_{loans}, with the quantity of funds that banks want to lend as a function of the interest rates on loans. It also represents the direct relationship between the quantity of funds that bank customers want to deposit and the interest rates on deposits with an upward-sloping graph of a supply function for deposits, $S_{deposits}$, with the quantity of funds that bank customers want to deposit as a function of the interest rates on deposits. The (graph of the) supply function for loans is more simply called the supply of loans, and (the graph of the) the supply function for deposits is more simply called the supply of deposits.

Figure 6-3 also shows that the graph of the supply of loans is above the graph of the supply of deposits. Why should this be the case? In order to make a profit, banks generally must charge a higher interest rate on the funds that they lend to their customers who borrow than the interest rate that they pay to their customers who deposit funds.

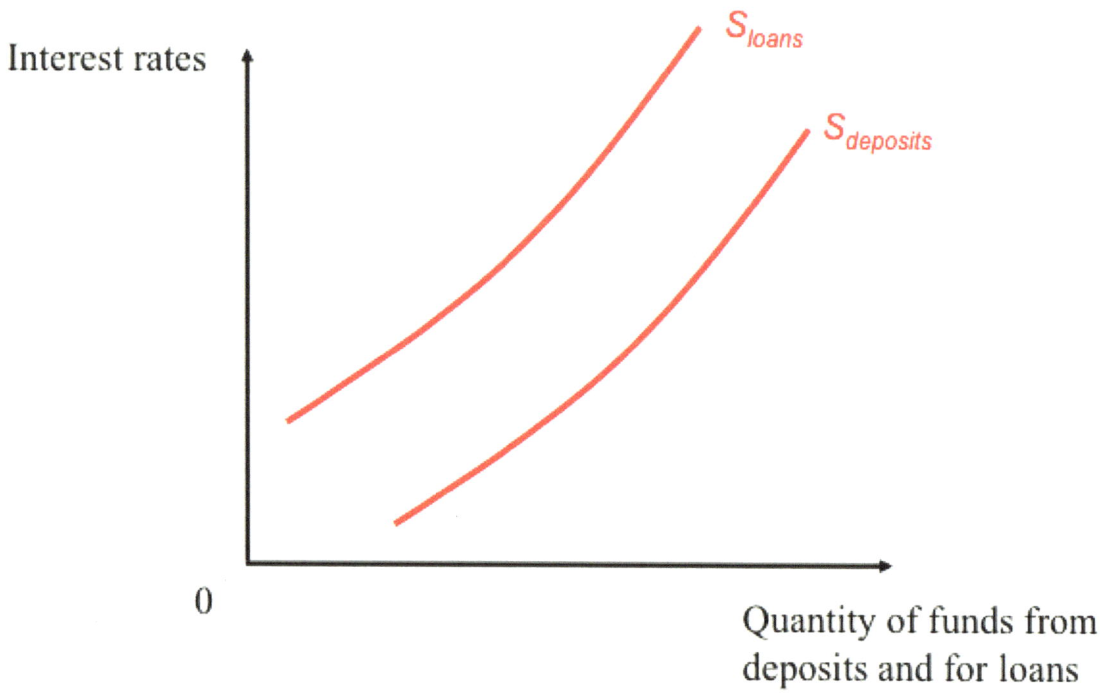

Figure 6-3: The supply of loans shows a direct relationship between the quantity of funds that banks want to lend and the interest rate on loans. The supply of deposits shows a direct relationship between the quantity of funds that bank customers want to deposit and the interest rate on deposits. Because banks generally charge a higher interest rate on loans than they pay on deposits, the supply of loans lies above the supply of deposits.

Figure 6-4 shows the supply of deposits from those who want to save and the demand of loans from those who want to borrow, after I rename the supply function for deposits as a supply function for saved funds. I rename the supply function because individuals and institutions that save funds could transact directly with individuals and institutions that want to borrow funds. In this case, there would be a tendency for the interest rate that savers earn and the interest rate that borrowers pay to adjust so that there are no shortages or surpluses of loanable funds. For if there were a surplus of loanable funds, interest rates that savers earn and borrowers pay would tend to fall; if there were a shortage of loanable funds, interest rates that savers earn and borrowers pay would tend to rise. The figure represents the interest rate that would eliminate shortages and surpluses of loanable funds if savers and borrowers could transact directly with each other, without the intermediation of banks, as i^*. At i^*, the quantity supplied of funds from savers or "depositors" would match the quantity demanded of funds for borrowers. These quantities are represented as Q_{direct} in the figure because savers and borrowers directly transact with each other. When savers and borrower can bypass banks, the supply of loans from banks becomes irrelevant.

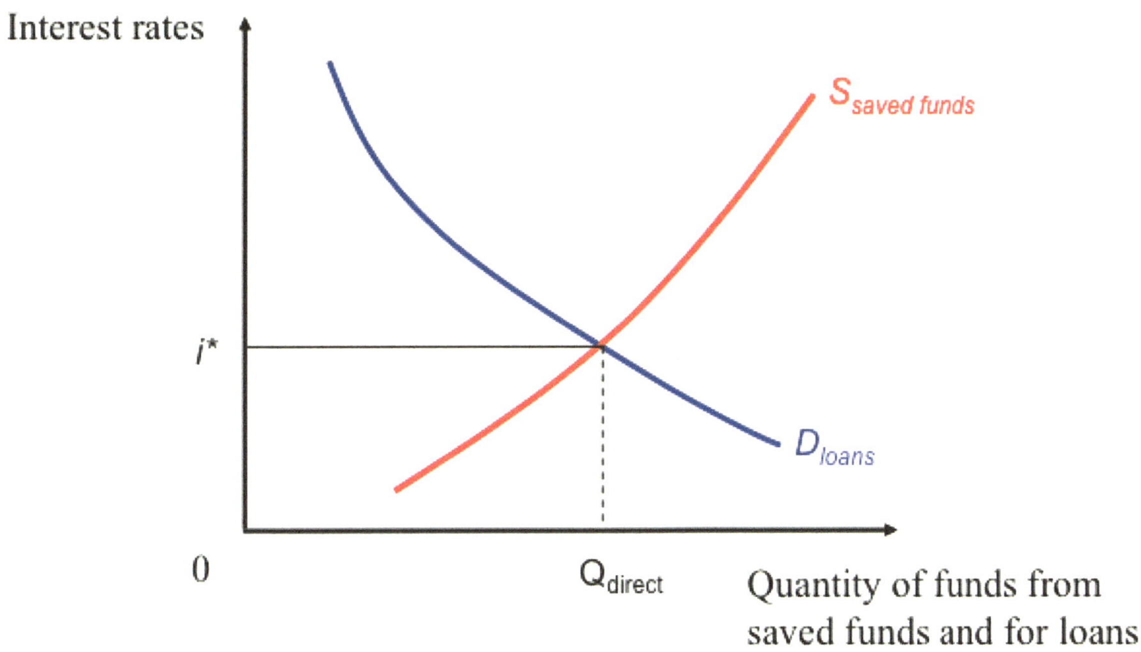

Figure 6-4: If savers and borrowers can directly transact with each other, the quantity of funds saved, lent and borrowed would be Q_{direct} when interest rates adjust to i^* to eliminate shortages and surpluses of loanable funds. When savers and borrowers can bypass banks, the supply of loans from banks becomes irrelevant.

Sometimes direct transactions between savers and borrowers are possible, for example, through markets of commercial paper. In such cases, the interest rate paid by borrowers may be lower than the interest rate that banks charge on loans, especially when a good credit rating of the borrower allows lenders to know quickly which borrowers are credit worthy. Likewise, the interest rate earned by savers may be higher than the interest rate that banks offer on deposits. Direct transactions between savers and borrowers should be most likely when the costs of searching for counterparties are low (such as when credit ratings are easily available), verifying and monitoring their actions is easy (such as when borrowers have widely published financial information and news) and enforcing the terms of the transaction is easy (such as when loan contracts like commercial paper are simple and standardized).

However, savers and borrowers often can not directly transact with each other because of prohibitive costs of searching for counterparties, verifying and monitoring their actions and enforcing the terms of the transaction. In such cases, a bank can act as an intermediary between savers and borrowers because banks may be able to more easily find the parties to the transaction, verify and monitor their actions and enforce the terms of the transactions. To cover the transaction costs and to earn compensation for its intermediation, a bank will charge a high interest rate for borrowers and offer a low interest rate to savers. In Figure 6-5, the high interest rate on loans is represented by i_L and the lower interest rate on deposits is represented by i_D. The difference, or **margin**, $i_L - i_D$ should be sufficient for the bank to cover transaction costs and to earn a respectable rate of return for the bank's investors, where the rate of return deemed "respectable" is determined by the amount of competition. Due to the high interest rate charged on loans by the bank, borrowers will want to borrow less than would be the case *if* borrowers and savers could directly make a transaction at a lower interest rate. And due to the low interest rate offered on deposits by the bank, savers will want to save less than would be the case *if* savers and borrowers could directly make a transaction at a higher interest rate. The lower amount of funds borrowed and saved with the bank acting as an intermediary is represented by the $Q_{intermediary}$, which is lower than Q_{direct}, the quantity of funds borrowed and saved if borrowers and savers could directly transact with each other.

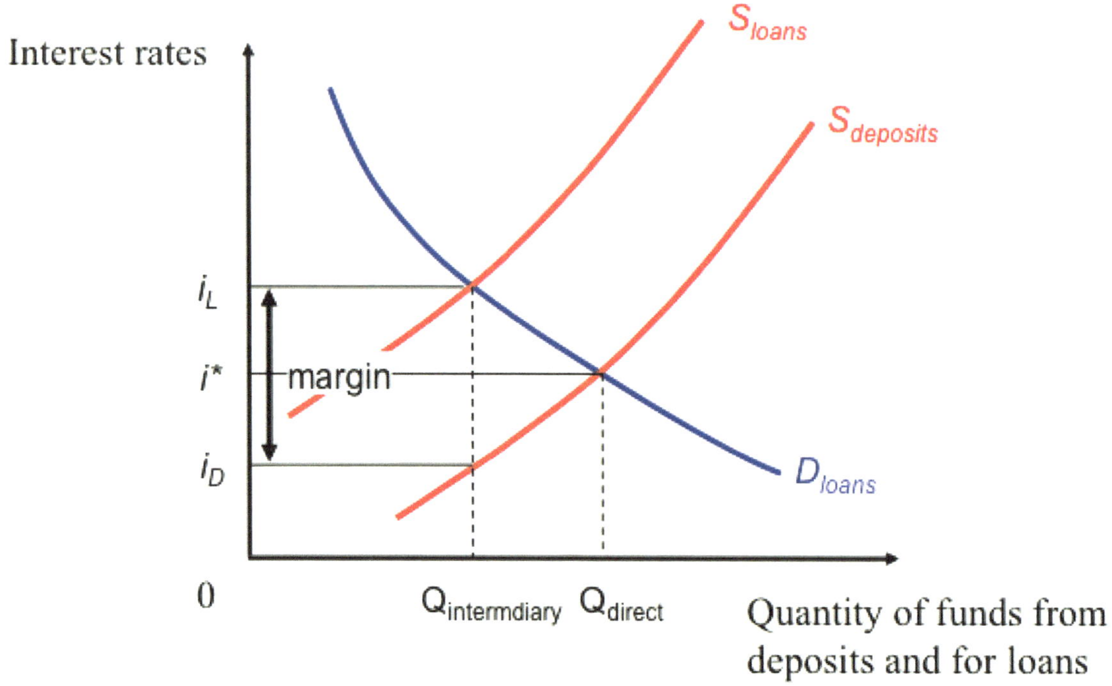

Figure 6-5: When banks act as intermediaries, they cover their costs and earn a rate of return by charging a high interest rate on loans ($i_L > i^*$) and offer a low interest rate on deposits ($i_D < i^*$), so that fewer funds are saved and borrowed ($Q_{intermediary}$), compared to the case if savers and borrowers could directly transact with each other (Q_{direct}).

Asymmetric information is the primary reason why financial intermediaries are necessary to conduct financial transactions and why margins exist. Unlike the average saver, banks and other financial intermediaries are willing and able to spend time and resources to acquire the necessary information—to reduce asymmetric information—so that loans or other forms of credit can be extended with the high expected profit. As I discuss in chapter 9, financial intermediaries can analyze the risk of lending by gathering information about the financial health of these potential customers and analyzing it in a number of ways.

In addition, once credit through a financial intermediary is extended, asymmetric information for other counterparties can be reduced as well. Stiglitz and Weiss (1988) showed that bank loans can convey signals about the creditworthiness of the borrower, which could help it raise further funding through direct or further indirect transactions. In other words, because one bank is willing to trust the borrower with a loan, and the bank supposedly has been able to reduce asymmetric information through its own research, then other potential counterparties are willing to trust the borrower in additional transactions.

More generally, banks can lower transaction costs by efficiently collecting funds from many depositors and issuing funds to many borrowers. Alternatively, after collecting funds from thousands of small deposits, banks can buy large denomination bonds that effectively allow them to make large loans, effectively allowing a transaction between thousands of savers and a single institution. In other words, banks can lower transaction costs by operating on a large scale. If a large number of transactions is more efficient than a small number of transactions, the market or the firm is said to experience **economies of scale**. For example, offering the same type of loan contract to thousands of home buyers can be more efficient than lending to just a few home buyers.

Banks can lower transaction costs by offering a wide variety of services and products. To serve the interest of many depositors or borrowers, banks usually offer a range of deposits and loans, which differ in terms of interest rates, maturity and other characteristics, depending on the needs and desires of customers. If offering a wide scope of services and products is more efficient than offering a limited number of services and products, the market or firm is said to experience **economies of scope**. In this case, customers could efficiently save in a variety of assets offered by a single bank, rather than through various financial markets or different financial intermediaries.

Through financial intermediation, banks are said *to transform* assets from savers to their own when they use the funds from savers to make loans. The loans become the banks' own assets because they are expected to earn income over time, which can be used to repay depositors (plus interest) and to earn a rate of return for the banks' capital (equity) investors. Moreover, by investing in a diverse group of assets, banks, depositors and capital investors can reduce the loss that might arise from investing in a single asset and can enjoy a higher average rate of return over time.

Other traditional roles of banks: liquidity and diversification

Besides acting as an intermediary between savers and borrowers, another traditional role of banks is to provide money or cash to customers, both to borrowers when they take out loans and to depositors when they withdraw their funds.

But depositors and borrowers have different needs for liquid assets. Borrowers generally want to spend all funds available to them immediately, while depositors generally are willing to wait to spend some of their funds (otherwise their deposit balances would be reduced to zero). On the other hand, depositors can withdraw their funds quickly while borrowers generally repay their loans slowly, and depositors might withdraw their funds more quickly (or less quickly) than anticipated and borrowers might repay their loans less quickly (or more quickly) than anticipated. As a result, banks must manage the flow of their liquid assets carefully to try to avoid shortages or large surpluses of cash. Banks need to have enough cash on reserve to pay depositors when income from loans is not sufficient, or else need to be able to borrow from other banks or the central bank when deposit withdrawals are higher than expected and/or income payments from loans are lower than expected. We will discuss borrowing from other banks or the central bank in chapter 11.

Even though banks need to have sufficient cash on reserve to provide money to depositors, they do not keep all of funds deposited at banks as cash on reserve, since they use some funds to make loans. Edgeworth (1888) was one of the first to identify that banks generally hold less than 100% of deposits as cash on reserve and earn a return by investing in loans, securities or other assets. In other words, only a fraction of funds from deposits is generally held on reserve, while the remainder is invested interest-bearing assets. This type of banking is called **fractional reserve banking**, which we consider in detail in chapter 12.

By lending a large fraction of deposited funds and by providing liquidity to customers, banks have a significant effect on the amount of money that circulates in the economy, and by extension, the demand of goods and services. In particular, when a bank makes a loan to its customers, it provides additional money to individuals and institutions that spend the money on goods and services. As the amount of funds that are lent and borrowed increases, the amount of money circulating in the economy increases, and the demand of goods and services increases. We further discuss the effect that banks have on the quantity of money in chapter 12.

Other traditional services that banks offer include safety deposit boxes, brokering and management of trusts and other assets of customers. For these services, banks charge fees, the principal source of non-interest income.

Thus, the primary good or service that asset of banks offer to their customers continues to be loans and deposits, although other kinds of assets, like reserves and bonds, and other kinds of liabilities help banks and their customers diversify the risk of saving, lending or borrowing. In the next section, we examine the various assets and liabilities of US banks that are recorded on a balance sheet. Also, in the next chapter, we consider various non-traditional assets and liabilities that are intended to reduce risk for banks and their customers.

The traditional balance sheet of banks

A balance sheet is the traditional way of recording the financial status of an institution to give bank managers and investors an idea about how well the institution is performing financially. Although other financial activities not recorded on the balance sheet may affect bank profits (which we consider in the next chapter), the assets, liabilities and capital recorded on the balance sheet are traditionally the most influential on bank profits.

Assets of banks

Assets of banks are items with value that are legally owned by the bank. Assets have value for a bank because they will generate income for the bank in the future or because they could be sold to generate income for the bank. Banks use their available funds to acquire or purchase assets so that they can earn interest, yield, return or other forms of income.

In chapter 2 we defined a liquid asset as one that can be used to pay for goods and services or debt without substantial transaction costs. In this chapter, we extend the definition of a liquid asset as one that can be used to pay for goods and services, debt or any *liability* without substantial costs.

The most liquid assets for banks are **cash assets**, which include reserves, a bank's deposits at other banks and cash that is in the process of being transferred to the bank. As suggested in the previous section, **reserves** are liquid assets that banks. Reserves include currency held in the bank's vault, as well as banks' deposits at the central bank. These deposits can be used to settle transactions, in particular check processing transactions, between the central bank and the private sector banks. Some reserves are required by central bank; they are called *required reserves.* But banks may want to hold reserves in additional to the amount required by the central bank to satisfy customer demands or to settle large transactions between the central bank and themselves. Reserves in excess of what is required by central bank are called *excess reserves.*

Like banks' deposits at the central bank, banks' deposits held at other private banks are included in cash assets. But unlike banks' deposits at the central bank, banks' deposits held at other private banks are not included in reserves.

When banks process checks, they typically pay the bearer of the check immediately and then begin to process the check so that it can be reimbursed for the funds that they have paid. After the bearer has cashed a check but before the check is fully processed, banks add an asset called **cash items in the process of collection** to their balance sheet to account for the income that they expect to receive soon from the check processing, as soon as payments can be settled.

Other assets for banks include securities, which are often government bonds or bonds from agencies that have explicit or implicit support of the national government. These securities may be short-term or long-term, and may be liquid or illiquid assets depending on the ease in which they could be sold. Banks may or may not hold bonds from private institutions, stocks or other securities, depending on whether regulations allow banks to purchase such assets. While bonds, especially government bonds, are viewed as relatively safe assets for banks, stocks and other securities may be viewed as too risky by regulators and thus prohibited. Government bonds, at least those from large economies, are considered safe assets because the governments can usually raise taxes or print money to make bond payments. And bonds in general are considered safer than stocks and real estate because their values fluctuate less, they legally promise to pay interest and principal on specified dates, and their promised payments are made first if bankruptcy actually occurs.

Loans are typically the largest group of assets for banks, which may or may not be in the form of securities. (Recall that a security is a legal claim on the income from assets, the expenses from liabilities, or other financial commitments that can be traded in financial markets.) There are many types of loans: home loans, other real estate loans, car loans, business loans and other loans, and some financial institutions specialize in issuing a particular kind of loan. Some depository institutions have traditionally specialized in home loans, while others have specialized in commercial business loans. But these days, many banks offer a variety of loans, as competition between the different types of traditional depository institutions has increased.

An important difference among the many kinds of loans is whether they require collateral or not. **Collateral** is an asset that can be seized by the lender (and usually sold for cash) if the borrower is unable or unwilling to repay the loan on time. Those loans with collateral are called *collateralized loans*, *asset backed loans* or sometimes even *secured loans* (which, confusingly, is not the same as securities or securitized loans—loans that are bought and sold as a security—which we consider in the next chapter). Those loans without collateral are called *uncollateralized loans* or *unsecured loans.* Credit card loans are usually uncollateralized loans, while home loans and other real estate loans are not.

A **mortgage loan** is a loan secured by real property, like a home or other real estate, by pledging that property as collateral for the loan. The value of loans on the balance sheet accounts for the expected value of interest payments, the expected repayment of the principal and payment of any fees.

Liabilities of banks

Liabilities of banks are items for which the bank is responsible for paying in the future. In the meantime, liabilities act as sources of funds for banks. For example, time deposits are liabilities for banks because banks are responsible for paying for the owner of the deposit when the deposit matures in the future. But in the meantime, the funds that are deposited are a source of funds that the bank can use to invest in assets.

The primary types of liabilities for commercial banks include checking deposits and other checkable deposits, savings deposits, time deposits and borrowed funds. Formally, checking deposits and other checkable deposits are often called **transaction deposits**, because these deposits can be directly used to pay for goods and services or debt in a transaction. Savings deposits and time deposits are called **non-transaction deposits** because these deposits could not traditionally be used directly to make a transaction, although cash can be acquired by either selling the deposit to another party or by withdrawing the money after making a simple transaction at the bank or waiting for a time deposit to mature. However, these days many savings deposits are linked electronically to debit cards and ATMs, so practical differences between savings deposits and checking deposits are becoming blurred.

Borrowed funds are funds that banks borrow from other institutions, and the funds are considered a liability for banks because banks are legally obligated to pay back the funds. Borrowed funds should be distinguished from loans that a bank makes: When a bank acquires borrowed funds, it is the borrower and another institution is the lender. When a bank makes a loan, it is the lender and another institution or individual is the borrower.

The tables below show the assets, liabilities and capital (discussed below) and some off-balance sheet items of US commercial banks in 2012 in dollars and as a fraction of the total. Loans are the largest category of assets, but government securities are also a significant fraction of all assets. Cash assets, including vault cash and reserves, and interbank loans are a relatively minor part of all assets; nonetheless, these assets are important for the day-to-day operations of banks.

Table 9: Assets and liabilities of commercial banks in the US in seasonally adjusted $billions, June 2012

Assets		Liabilities + Capital	
Total credit to the non-banking sector	9689.5	Deposits	8709.7
Securities bought from the non-banking sector	2606.6	Large time deposits	1467.5
Treasury and national government agency securities	1806.7	Other deposits	7242.2
Asset (mortgage) backed securities	1331.8	Borrowed funds	1555.8
Non-asset backed securities	474.9	Borrowed funds from banks in the US	133.0
Private sector securities	799.9	Borrowed funds from others	1422.8
Asset (mortgage) backed securities	131.7	Special trading liabilities (including for short positions)	303.7
Non-asset backed securities	668.2	Derivatives with a negative fair value††	261.8
Loans and leases to the non-banking sector	7082.9	Other special trading liabilities	41.9
Commercial loans, non-real estate	1434.5	Net due to related foreign offices	257.0
Real estate loans	3518.2	Other liabilities (including subordinated debt and net deferred tax liabilities)	470.3
Open-ended (revolving) home equity loans	538.2	Total liabilities	11296.4
Closed-end residential loans	1564.8		
Commercial real estate loans	1415.2		
Consumer loans	1110.9		
Credit cards and other revolving credit	604.6		
Other consumer loans (including for cars, mobile homes, education, medical bills)	506.3		
Other loans and leases	1019.2		
Reserves and reverse repurchase agreements	295.0		

(including to brokers and dealers)			
All other loans and leases (including loans to foreign institutions and non-bank financial institutions)	724.2		
Allowance for loan and lease losses (corresponding to general loss reserves)	-162.4		
Interbank loans	117.6		
Reserves and reverse repurchase agreements	104.7		
Other loans to commercial banks, not secured by real estate	12.9		
Cash assets†	1792.6		
Special trading assets (excluding most securities)	333.9		
Derivatives with a positive fair value††	307.6		
Other special trading assets	26.3		
Other assets (including fixed assets and intangible assets)	1155.3		
Total assets	12926.4	Net worth (assets minus liabilities)	1630.0
†includes vault cash, cash items in process of collection, balances due from depository institutions, and reserve deposits held at Federal Reserve Banks. ††fair value determined by Financial Accounting Standards Board, FIN 39			
Source: Federal Reserve System, www.federalreserve.gov/releases/h8/current/			

Table 10: Selected off-balance sheet items for commercial banks in the US in seasonally adjusted $billions, June 2012

Selected off-balance sheet items	
Difference between fair value and historical cost for securities classified as available-for-sale under FASB Statement 115	33.2
Securitized loans (the outstanding principal of these loans securitized and sold plus securitizing fees)	919.5
Securitized consumer loans	19.5
Securitized credit cards and other revolving plans	10.8
Other securitized consumer loans	8.7
Securitized real estate loans	900.0
Source: Federal Reserve System, www.federalreserve.gov/releases/h8/current/	

Table 11: Assets and liabilities of commercial banks in the US as a fraction of totals, June 2012

Assets		Liabilities + Capital	
Total credit to the non-banking sector	75.0%	Deposits	77.1%
Securities bought from the non-banking sector	20.2%	Large time deposits	13.0%
Treasury and national government agency securities	14.0%	Other deposits	64.1%
Asset (mortgage) backed securities	10.3%	Borrowed funds	13.8%
Non-asset backed securities	3.7%	Borrowed funds from banks in the US	1.2%
Private sector securities	6.2%	Borrowed funds from others	12.6%
Asset (mortgage) backed securities	1.0%	Special trading liabilities (including for short positions)	2.7%
Non-asset backed securities	5.2%	Derivatives with a negative fair value††	2.3%
Loans and leases to the non-banking sector	54.8%	Other special trading liabilities	0.4%
Commercial loans, non-real estate	11.1%	Net due to related foreign offices	2.3%
Real estate loans	27.2%	Other liabilities (including subordinated debt	4.2%

		and net deferred tax liabilities)	
Open-ended (revolving) home equity loans	4.2%	Total liabilities	100.0%
Closed-end residential loans	12.1%		
Commercial real estate loans	10.9%		
Consumer loans	8.6%		
Credit cards and other revolving credit	4.7%		
Other consumer loans (including for cars, mobile homes, education, medical bills)	3.9%		
Other loans and leases	7.9%		
Reserves and reverse repurchase agreements (including to brokers and dealers)	2.3%		
All other loans and leases (including loans to foreign institutions and non-bank financial institutions)	5.6%		
Allowance for loan and lease losses (corresponding to general loss reserves)	-1.3%		
Interbank loans	0.9%		
Reserves and reverse repurchase agreements	0.8%		
Other loans to commercial banks, not secured by real estate	0.1%		
Cash assets†	13.9%		
Special trading assets (excluding most securities)	2.6%		
Derivatives with a positive fair value††	2.4%		
Other special trading assets	0.2%		
Other assets (including fixed assets and intangible assets)	8.9%		
Total assets	100.0%	Net worth (assets minus liabilities)	12.6%
†includes vault cash, cash items in process of collection, balances due from depository institutions, and reserve deposits held at Federal Reserve Banks. ††fair value determined by Financial Accounting Standards Board, FIN 39			
Source: Federal Reserve System, www.federalreserve.gov/releases/h8/current/			

Table 12: Selected off-balance sheet items for commercial banks in the US as a fraction of total assets, June 2012

Selected off-balance sheet items	
Difference between fair value and historical cost for securities classified as available-for-sale under FASB Statement 115	0.3%
Securitized loans (the outstanding principal of these loans securitized and sold plus securitizing fees)	7.1%
Securitized consumer loans	0.2%
Securitized credit cards and other revolving plans	0.1%
Other securitized consumer loans	0.1%
Securitized real estate loans	7.0%
Source: Federal Reserve System, www.federalreserve.gov/releases/h8/current/	

Capital

Like any corporation, stocks, equity or shares are a way for banks to acquire and spend funds. The value of these and similar funds represent the profitability or net value of the bank for the investors. In this sense, capital can be calculated as the value of its assets minus the value of its liabilities. It also represents the value of funds available to absorb losses from an unexpected increase in the value of liabilities or an unexpected decrease in the value of assets. These funds are intended to be available to protect the bank's creditors and owners from losses.

capital = net value of an institution = value of assets – value of liabilities or
capital = funds to protect against a decrease in value of assets or an increase in value of liabilities

Accountants and economists debate about which types of funds should be included as capital. According to some, the value of capital should be the accounting value of assets minus the accounting value of liabilities, perhaps with adjustments for items like derivative contracts (to be discussed in the next chapter) whose value is not traditionally recorded on the balance sheet. However, accounting issues make this definition undesirable sometimes. This calculation must determine how to calculate depreciation of assets over time and **goodwill**, the difference between a market value (or liquidation value) of a company and the book value of its assets and liabilities, if the company were to be sold or liquidated. Goodwill can be negative, especially if liquidation costs are substantial, so that the market value of a bank could be less than the value of its capital if liquidation value were ignored.

According to others, the value of capital should be the value of retained earnings plus the market value of stock (and similar securities discussed below), which represents the bank's immediate profitability and the market's assessment of the bank's value. However, because a bank's stock price may fluctuate wildly without a fundamental change in its business prospects, this definition of capital may also be undesirable.

Economists and accountants specify different types of funds that can be considered capital. The most important, called **tier 1 capital** is composed of funds from or the values of common stock (equity or shares), preferred stock (equity or shares) and retained earnings. (Like common stock holders, preferred stock holders are considered partial owners of the company but do not have voting rights and are paid before common stock holders.) Capital funds that are paid by stock, equity or shares holders are often called **capital paid in** by the partial owners.

We can consider tier 1 capital to be funds that are paid in by investors or retained funds from earnings. Other funds can function like the capital funds paid in by investors or those that are retained "on reserve". These funds, which are considered to be less reliable in the event of unexpected losses, called **tier 2 capital**.

There are two types of tier 2 capital that function essentially like the capital paid in of tier 1 capital; these are funds paid in by investors of hybrid securities and subordinated debt. **Hybrid securities** are those that have characteristics of both debt and common stock; **subordinated debt** is debt paid after regular forms of debt during normal business operations and during bankruptcy. These securities can be considered similar to stock, equity or shares and similar to debt at the same time. Thus, while the funds are not part of tier 1 capital, they are part of a second definition of capital, tier 2 capital. However, some accounting standards require subordinated debt to be recorded as a liability, as Table 9 and Table 11 indicate.

There are three types of tier 2 capital that function like retained earnings held "on reserve". These exclude regular reserves, which are consider an asset, but include other funds maintained or retained "on reserve", usually for the purposes of paying for liabilities when income from assets is unexpectedly low. **Undisclosed reserves** are reserves or other liquid assets recorded off the balance sheet for various payment purposes that the bank does not want to disclose to its share holders or to the public. But these reserves can be used for payment purposes, and their value is recorded on the balance sheet as tier 2 capital. Adjustments to the book value of assets according to changing market conditions are called **revaluation reserves**. In particular, physical assets or stock of another company can be revalued as market conditions that make the assets either more or less desirable. If these assets become more valuable, assets and revaluation reserves can both increase; if they become less valuable, assets and revaluation reserves can both decrease. **General loss reserves** or **provisions for general losses** are adjustments to the book value of assets and capital for losses in the value of assets that are expected to occur in the future but are unrecognized or unrealized today. Reserves can be set aside as capital and even though the current market value of assets remains high and no losses have yet occurred; capital can remain high until losses in the value of assets actually occur.

Table 13 relates the different types of tier 1 capital to the different types of tier 2 capital.

Table 13: Types of capital

Tier 1	Tier 2
Retained earnings	**Tier 2 capital similar to retained earnings**
	a. undisclosed reserves
	b. revaluation reserves: adjustments in the book value of assets/capital
	c. general loss reserves: adjustments in the book value of assets/capital
Capital paid in	**Tier 2 capital similar to capital paid in**
a. funds from common stock, equity or shares	a. funds from hybrid securities
b. funds from preferred stock, equity or shares	b. funds from subordinated debt

Sources of funds or financing

After discussing the types of liabilities and capital, we can consider how banks and other corporations can raise funds to finance investment in assets. In particular, we can distinguish between short term financing versus long term financing and debt/credit/leverage financing versus capital financing.

Borrowed funds (loans from other banks) are called debt or credit. They may also be called **leverage** because they allow the borrower to acquire more funds for investing in assets. From a broader perspective, however, all liabilities (deposits + borrowed funds) may be called debt, credit or leverage, since funds from all of these sources must be repaid in the future and at the same time allow banks to invest in assets in the meantime.

Short term financing is classified as *short term debt/credit/ leverage*. This kind of financing is necessary when reserves (cash assets), income from assets and funds from capital are insufficient to pay for other liabilities. Most banks rely somewhat on short term financing to manage their cash flows. But a large amount of short term debt may indicate that the bank can not acquire other types of financing and may go bankrupt or become "insolvent" in the near future.

Long term debt/credit/leverage is borrowed for long term investments, such as for long term bonds or stock in (joint ventures with) other companies. Creditors are generally willing to lend long term debt/credit/leverage if they believe that borrower is a viable institution in the long term. Even so, long term debt generally has higher interest rates than short term debt because when other factors are equal long term debt involves more waiting and risk. If lenders are unwilling to accept the risk of default or other kinds of non-payment over the long term, they may be wiling to lend only short term debt/credit/leverage or nothing at all.

Capital financing is also considered to be long term financing because capital funds are ultimately acquired from issuing stock/equity/shares (hopefully) for the long term. It consists partially of *retained earnings*, which depend on profitability and productivity of the corporation. Financing through retained earnings is also called **internal finance** because the funds are saved within the institution. Other sources of finance, with the possible exception of capital paid in, are called **external finance** because the funds come from outside of the institution. Internal finance is considered to be less risky than external finance, especially debt financing, because the bank has already saved what it will spend.

The other part of capital financing comes from *capital paid in*, as well as some elements of *tier 2 capital*. As discussed in the previous section, capital paid in comes from stock/equity/share investors, and some securities classified as tier 2 capital are similar to stock/equity/shares. The willingness to invest through capital determines the value of capital paid in and similar forms of capital that the corporation can raise, as well as the value of the stock/equity/shares and similar securities in the secondary market. The willingness to invest in a corporation's capital depends on the corporation's (expected) profitability, productivity, retained earnings and dividend payments.

Management of assets and liabilities

As the simple model showing the margin between the interest rates on loans and deposits suggested, managing assets and liabilities to retain high earnings and profit basically involves acquiring funds from deposits and other liabilities at a low expected cost (interest rate) and investing the funds in loans and other assets at a high expected return (interest rate). Competition between banks, however, will tend to increase the interest rates on liabilities and decrease the interest rates on assets, so that margins, earnings and profit are squeezed.

In addition to trying to create the largest margin possible, banks must also try to manage the risk of having assets that unexpectedly pay low income or liabilities that unexpectedly have high expenses. I discuss several techniques of risk management in chapter 9, but the most basic form of risk management involves managing capital prudently.

Management of capital

Regulators regulate the amount of tier 1 and tier 2 capital to be confident that the funds are sufficient to protect against a decrease in the value of assets or an increase in the value of liabilities. A bank without a sufficient amount of capital to absorb an unexpected decrease in the income from assets or an unexpected increase in the expenses from liabilities is called **insolvent** and is usually punished or even closed by regulators.

However, a bank may also be forced to close due to a lack of liquidity (that is, cash) to pay for liabilities when they are due, even if the value of all assets exceeds the value of all liabilities by a sufficient amount, or if the value of stock, retained earnings and other forms of capital meet regulatory standards. We discuss insolvency and illiquidity from the perspective of central banks and other regulators in chapter 10.

If banks currently have a low amount of capital (but are not yet insolvent), they can acquire more by selling new equity (stock) to share holders or by retaining more earnings (profits), principally by reducing dividend payments to share holders or by not investing the earnings in new assets. Likewise, existing assets can be sold for cash and maintained as retained earnings, undisclosed reserves or even general loss reserves. Alternatively, revaluation of assets can increase the value of assets and capital, but this may simply involve an accounting trick if the value of assets has not "fundamentally" changed.

When banks try to manage the value of their capital, they must keep sufficient capital to satisfy regulators and to avoid insolvency, but they do not want to maintain too much capital because the funds from capital generally earn little or no interest or return. In other words, funds from capital that are not invested in assets imply that current and future earnings may be lower than otherwise. In sum, banks face a tradeoff between maintaining a high amount of capital for safety and trying to earn a high return on funds paid in by partial owners and others.

Summary

The traditional role of banks is to act as an intermediary between savers and borrowers—to transform the assets of savers into their own by providing loans to borrowers and then acquiring the liabilities of repaying depositors when the funds are due. This process is formally called financial intermediation. Profitable financial intermediation basically involves trying to acquire funds from depositors, other creditors and those who pay in capital at a low cost and using those funds to invest in assets that can earn a high interest, yield or return. In addition, banks are traditionally responsible for providing their customers—principally, borrowers and depositors—the cash or liquid assets that they need to pay for goods and services and for managing risk through diversification for themselves and their customers.

Banks account for these and other assets and liabilities, as well as capital, on a balance sheet. The most common assets for banks are various kinds of loans, which may or may not have collateral that can be sold in the event of default. In addition, government bonds and other securities are also important assets. The most common liabilities for banks are various kinds of deposits, either transaction deposits or non-transaction deposits. In addition, borrowed funds are also important liabilities. Capital represents the net value of a bank, which can be interpreted to mean either the value of its assets minus the value of its liabilities or the value of various kinds of funds paid in by the bank's partial owners plus the value of retained earnings. Banks need capital to protect themselves against an unexpected fall in the value of assets or an unexpected rise in the value of liabilities, but they do not want to maintain too much capital because these funds do not earn a high rate of interest or return.

Problems and Applications

<u>Short answer problems</u>

1. If the interest rate margin is positive, can it serve as a profitable financial intermediary between depositors and borrowers? Explain.

2. If the interest rate margin is very large, are transaction costs between savers and borrowers/spenders significant? Explain.

3. As transaction costs, including asymmetric information, between savers/lenders and borrowers/spenders decrease, will financial intermediation by banks and bank profits increase or decrease? Explain.

4. How can economies of scale increase efficiency and profits for banks?

5. Before a check that has been deposited by a bank customer has settled between banks, how is its value accounted for on a bank's balance sheet?

6. If a bank borrows money from another bank and uses the money to lend to one of its important customers, how will assets and liabilities be affected?

7. What is a mortgage loan? Is it considered a collateralized loan or uncollateralized loan? Why?

8. How does tier 1 capital differ from tier 2 capital? If partial owners of a bank pay in capital by buying stock, equity or shares of the bank, are the funds included in tier 1 capital or tier 2 capital?

9. Which of the following are classified as internal finance or external finance, and why: retained earnings, capital paid in, long-term bonds, short-term loans?

10. Which is generally considered the most stable form of finance, and why: retained earnings, capital paid in, long-term bonds, short-term loans?

11. Which could be considered the least stable form of finance, and why: retained earnings, capital paid in, long-term bonds, short-term loans?

12. If a bank expects general or unspecified losses to occur in the future because of worsening economic conditions, but specific losses have not yet occurred today, how might it adjust this fact on the balance sheet?

13. Explain the difference between illiquidity and insolvency.

14. If bank customers deposit their funds in transaction or non-transaction deposits, do banks keep all of the money on reserve as cash assets? If not, how are most of the funds used?

Internet applications

1. Go to http://ecos.bok.or.kr/ to find data for Korea's depository institutions, under the "Depository Corporations Survey". Create a balance sheet, analogous to Table 11, which lists the assets, liabilities and capital of domestic depository institutions as a percent of all assets or all liabilities and capital for the latest month. Which asset is the largest asset on the balance sheet? Which liability is the largest liability on the balance sheet? How much capital (net worth) is available as a percent of the total value of assets?

2. Go to http://ecos.bok.or.kr/ to find data for interest rates on newly extended deposits and newly extended loans from the earliest available month to the latest available month. Graph the two interest rates over time and calculate the average interest rate margin during this time.

Bibliography

Stiglitz, J.E. and A. Weiss, (1988), "Banks as Social Accountants and Screening Devices for the Allocation of Credit", Working Paper 2710, Washington: National Bureau of Economic Research.

Edgeworth, F.Y., (1888), "The Mathematical Theory of Banking", Journal of the Royal Statistical Society, 51, 113-127.

7. Innovative Banking Activities

Preview

In addition to the traditional activities of acting as an intermediary between savers and borrowers and providing liquidity, banks today can offer a wide variety of financial services and products: mutual fund investments, money market mutual fund deposit accounts, insurance, real estate brokering and other real estate services, pension fund management, and stock brokering. Banks also engage in activities that can affect their income and expenses, but whose value is not yet fully realized and depends on other assets and liabilities, whose values may change with market conditions.

Derivative contracts

An increasing number of banks have at least a few **derivative contracts**, contracts whose value is derived from an *underlying* asset (like a stock, bond, loan, deposit, commodity or currency) or liability (like a deposit or borrowed funds). The owner of the contract has a claim to buy or sell this underlying asset or liability in the future at a price that is specified today. In other words, the owner of the contract has a claim to buy or sell the underlying asset, and the counterparty is obligated to meet the terms of the contract when or if the owner decides to buy or sell the underlying asset or liability. Some derivative contracts have been around for centuries, although they have been less important for banks than providing liquidity and acting as an intermediary between savers and borrowers. Recently, however, derivative contract have become more important for some banks and other financial institutions, especially large ones.

Figure 7-1 represents how a derivative contract works and how it may be linked to various underlying assets or liabilities like the value of a bond or other security, wheat, copper, silver, natural gas, electricity or money.

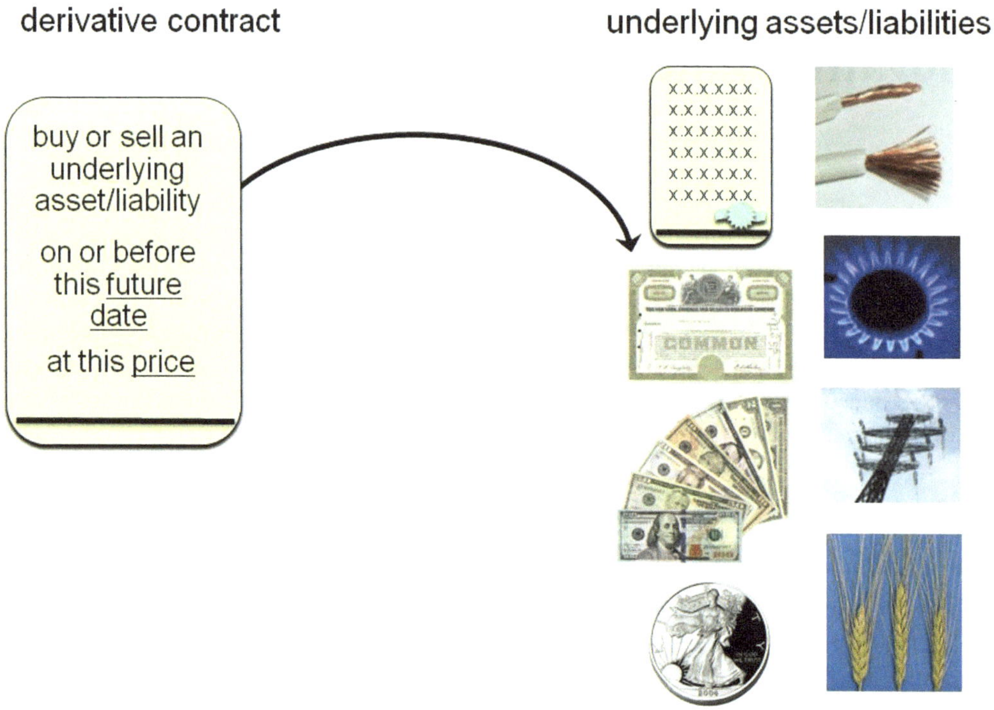

Figure 7-1: The value of a derivative contract is derived from the value of an underlying asset or liability, like a bond, stock, money, silver, copper, natural gas, electricity or wheat. The contract allows the owner to buy or sell an underlying asset or liability at a future date at a price that is specified today.

Because the value of the underlying asset or liability changes, the value of the derivative contract can change. Furthermore, the values of the derivative contract and the underlying asset or liability are contingent on some event in the future, like a potential request to borrow more funds in the future or a potential default on a loan in the future.

Because the values of the derivative contracts are only contingent and have not yet been realized, their values have traditionally been recorded *off the balance sheet* and not shown to capital investors, depositors, other creditors and/or the public. Only when the contingent value becomes an actual asset or liability (for example, when the underlying asset or liability is actually bought or sold) or otherwise affects the value of assets or liabilities is the value of the recorded on the traditional balance sheet. However, in the interest of giving capital investors, depositors, other creditors and the public more information about the financial activities of banks, regulators may now require that the value of the derivative contracts be recorded on the balance sheet.

As further discussed below, the value of a derivative contract recorded on or off the balance sheet depends on the contractual price, or **exercise price**, or **strike price**, to buy or sell the underlying asset or liability relative to its market price. It also may depend on the date in the future when the underlying asset or liability is bought and sold, or **settlement date**. More broadly, the value of a derivative contract can be represented as 1) a **notional value**—the value of the underlying asset or liability bought or sold at the strike price, 2) the current market value of the derivative contract—the value of the contract if it were currently sold to someone else, 3) the current market value of the underlying asset/liability (which is usually the same as the market value of the derivative contract) or 4) another measure of value.

Derivative contracts and risk

By setting a price to buy or sell an underlying asset today for a delivery that is completed in the future, derivative contracts, or *derivatives*, allow a risk about the transaction to be transferred from one party to another. For example, a farmer and a miller could sign a derivative contract to buy and sell wheat in the future at a price and amount that are specified today. Both parties reduce a risk in this transaction: for the farmer, the risk of selling at a low price is reduced and for the miller, the risk of buying at a high price is reduced. Thus, derivatives can be used to insure against the risk that the value of the underlying asset will change unexpectedly. In effect, parties "lock in" the price of the underlying asset or liability today and then the purchase or sale of the underlying asset or liability is transferred at a future date.

In addition, the miller reduces the risk that he will not be able to buy the wheat, and the farmer reduces the risk that he will not be able to sell the wheat.

But from broader perspective, we can say that the farmer and the miller both reduce a risk and acquire a risk when they sign the futures contract. And in general, one party can use derivative assets to reduce a risk, while the other party can use them to acquire that risk, betting that the first party will be wrong or overly cautious. The farmer reduces the risk that the price of wheat will fall below the price specified in the contract and acquires the risk that the price of wheat will rise above the price specified in the contract (thereby losing additional income that he could have earned). The miller acquires the risk that the price of wheat will fall below the price specified in the contract (thereby paying more in the future than he otherwise would) and reduces the risk that the price of wheat will rise above the price specified in the contract. In this sense, one party is the insurer (risk taker) for one type of risk, and the counterparty is the insurer (risk taker) for another type of risk.

As for the uncertainty about the amount of wheat, we can also view the parties as both reducing a risk and acquiring a risk. The miller reduces the risk that he will be unable to acquire wheat in the future, but acquires the risk that he is obligated to buy the wheat from the farmer when he does not need it or if he could have bought it from another party at more favorable terms. The farmer reduces the risk that he will be unable to sell wheat in the future, but acquires the risk that he is obligated to sell the wheat when he does not have it or when he could have sold it to another party at more favorable terms.

In general, the other side of insurance is risk taking, and if one party insures a risk with a derivative contract, another party must be willing to take that risk. In fact, some individuals and institutions will enter into a derivative contract to speculate on the value of the underlying asset or liability, betting that the party seeking insurance will be wrong about the future value of the underlying asset or liability.

A particular case of insuring, or *hedging*, by using derivative contracts occurs when an individual or institution buys an asset (like a commodity, a bond that has coupon payments, a stock that pays dividends, and so on) and promises to sell it in the future at the strike price. This allows the buyer of the asset and the owner of the derivative contract to hold asset temporarily, thereby earning income or a return from the asset while reducing the risk that the selling price will change unexpectedly.

A particular case of acquiring risk by using derivative contracts occurs when individuals and institutions speculate that the market price of an underlying asset will fall below the strike price, so that they can take advantage of arbitrage by buying at the market price and selling at the strike price. Likewise, other parties can speculate that the market price of the underlying asset will rise above the strike price, so that they can take advantage of arbitrage by buying at the strike price and selling at the market price.

In general, a derivative contract can allow one to sell an underlying asset in the future, a transaction that is called *going short* or *short selling* the underlying asset. The counterparty in the transaction will agree to buy the underlying asset in the future, a transaction that is called *going long* or *long buying* the underlying asset. And in general, the value of the derivative contract depends on or is derived from the value or market price of the underlying asset. In particular, a derivative contract that allows one to go short will rise in value as the market price of the underlying asset decreases below the strike price. And a derivative contract that allows one to go long will rise in value as the market price of the underlying asset increases above strike price.

Types of derivative contracts

Common derivative contracts include forward contracts, futures contracts, option contracts and swap contracts. The basic properties of these 4 general types of derivative contracts are briefly described in Table 14 and more fully described in the pages below.

Table 14: Types of derivatives

Transaction	Standardized contracts issued and insured by a clearing house that can easily be bought and sold after being issued	Specialized contracts created by the buyer and seller themselves in the over the counter market that are less liquid and more risky
Buying or selling an underlying asset/liability at a specified price on a future date	Futures contracts	Forward contracts
A right, but not an obligation, to buy or sell an underlying asset/liability at a specified price on or before future date	Option contracts	Option contracts
The exchange of cash based on the value of underlying assets or liabilities on a future date		Swap contracts

Forward contracts

Forward contracts, or *forwards*, are contracts to buy or sell an underlying asset/liability on future date at a price that is specified today and are customized to suit the needs of each party. The individuals and institutions that buy and sell the underlying assets and liabilities are the ones who design forward contracts, possibly with the assistance of a dealer, to meet their specifications.

In general, *over the counter* contracts, like forward contracts and swap contracts considered later, are those specially made for a particular transaction and traded directly between two parties.

We have already considered one type of a forward contract in an earlier chapter. Recall that a **banker's acceptance** refers a bank's acceptance or guarantee of the payment for notes, commercial paper or other forms of short-term debt issued by the bank's customers. The bank requires a deposit of funds, plus fees, to guarantee the future payment. In other words, if the bank customers are unable or unwilling to pay for the debt, the bank uses the funds deposited by its customers to pay the counterparty, which holds the banker's acceptance (derivative) contract. The value of the contract depends on or is derived from the amount of funds deposited and the value of the underlying credit/debt contract, which are considered the underlying assets or liabilities. More broadly, the value of the derivative contract, the deposit of funds and the debt/credit contract depend on the willingness and ability of the bank's customer to repay. A banker's acceptance can create additional liabilities for the bank contingent on the event that the bank customer that issued the debt defaults on its obligation to pay and if the deposited funds are not sufficient to pay for the debt.

Similar to a banker's acceptance, a **letter of credit** is a letter issued by a bank on behalf of a buyer of goods or services that guarantees payment to the seller of the goods or services. A letter of credit reassures the seller of the goods or services that he will be paid, so that the buyer and the seller can more easily make a transaction. Like the banker's acceptance, the bank will require a deposit of funds, plus fees, to guarantee the future payment. The value of the contract depends on the amount of funds deposited, which is considered the underlying asset/liability, as well as the willingness and ability of the bank's customer to pay for the goods or services. A letter of credit can create additional liabilities for the bank contingent on the event that the bank customer that issued the debt defaults on its obligation to pay and if the deposited funds are not sufficient to pay for the debt. Because of their similarities, many use banker's acceptance and letter of credit interchangeably.

Figure 7-2 represents how a banker's acceptance or a letter of credit works between two parties. In the case of a banker's acceptance, the two parties are a borrower and a lender (of money); in the case of a letter of credit, the two parties are a buyer and a seller (of a good or service, like a car). Other than that difference, the two types of derivative contract work essentially in the same manner.

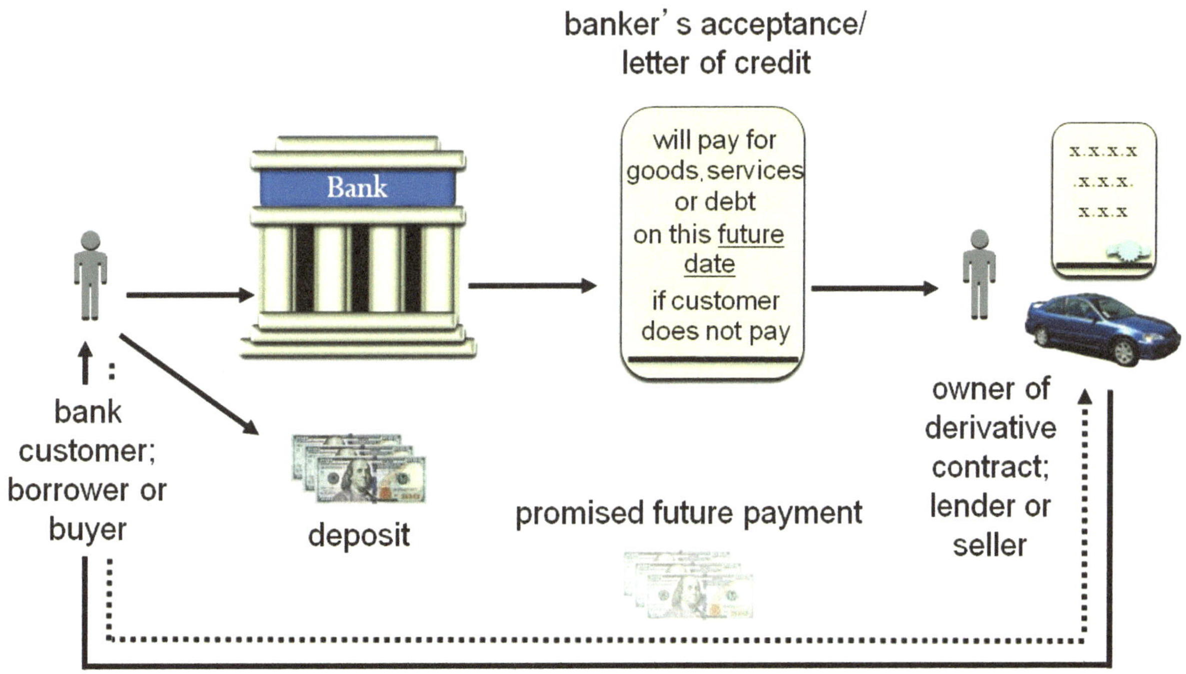

Figure 7-2: With a banker's acceptance and a letter of credit, a bank accepts the risk of non-payment on behalf of its customer but requires a deposit of funds to take this risk.

Another type of a forward contract in which money is the underlying asset or liability is a **loan commitment**. This is a commitment to provide an amount credit to a customer, who may or may not borrow the entire amount that the bank has made available. An open-ended loan commitment is a revolving line of credit, whereby if a portion of the loan is extended and then paid off, the principal repayment increases the credit line and the potential assets of the bank to its original amount. A close-ended loan commitment is an initial extension of a given amount of credit that does not increase to its original amount after repayments are made. **Overdraft credit** is a type of loan commitment, whereby a bank will pay for a transaction made by its customer even though the customer has insufficient funds in his account. In effect, the customer receives short-term credit from the bank and then must pay for the transaction in the future plus a fee that acts as interest. A loan commitment creates assets for the bank contingent on the event that customers borrow funds; it also creates a need to have reserves to loan if customers borrow. Banks record the notional amounts of loan commitments off the balance sheet, even if customers never fully utilize the notional amount, and record only the actual amount of credit issued on the balance sheet.

In the over the counter market, each party can design the contract according to its wishes, but this may also be a drawback. Because the quantity of the underlying asset/liability and the settlement date may vary freely, it may be difficult to find a counterparty who wants that quantity and date. And even if a counterparty is found to sign a contract today, one party may later want to end or "to unwind" its obligation. When it is difficult to find counterparties to sign specific contracts and difficult to sell existing contracts so as to unwind an obligation to buy or sell the underlying asset/liability, the market and the contract itself are called *illiquid*.

Another problem with forward contracts is the risk of default, either from the buyer or seller of the underlying asset/liability. That is, one of the parties who promised to buy or sell in the contract might decide not to buy or not to sell the underlying asset/liability according to the terms of the derivative contract. Because both parties are subject to the risk of default, both parties are subject to **counterparty risk**, the risk that a counterparty might not fulfill its obligations in a transaction.

Over the counter contracts traditionally do not require *margin payments*, payments based on the margin or difference between the contract price of the underlying asset/liability and its market price, to insure the risk of default and counterparty risk. But governing boards that oversee transactions in today's over the counter markets have started to require margin payments by one or both parties to limit counterparty risk. In other words, some forward contracts are starting to function like futures contracts because of the traditional limitations of forward contracts.

Futures contracts

Like forward contracts, **futures contracts** are agreements to buy or sell an underlying asset/liability on future date at a price that is specified today. But unlike forward contracts, futures contracts are standardized and insured by third parties, called *clearing houses*, to reduce illiquidity and the risk of default. Futures contracts are standardized with respect to the quantity of the underlying asset/liability (for example, US$100,000 of Treasury bonds) and the settlement date (for example, at the end of every quarter).

Clearing houses are financial intermediaries that write and insure futures contracts and act as a counterparty to each party buying or selling the underlying asset/liability. In effect, there are two separate transactions with a futures contract: one involving the buyer of the underlying asset/liability with the clearing house and the other involving the seller of the underlying asset/liability with the clearing house. A clearing house issues a contract to a party who will deliver (sell) the underlying asset to the clearing house as specified by the contract in return for cash. The clearing house will issue a corresponding contract to another party who will deliver (sell) cash to the clearing house as specified by the contract in return for the underlying asset. On the settlement date, the clearing house then delivers the cash or the underlying asset to the party to whom it is due. Figure 7-3 represents transactions with a clearing house that issues futures contracts to a buyer and a seller of an underlying asset/liability, and compares these transactions with a transaction involving a forward contract.

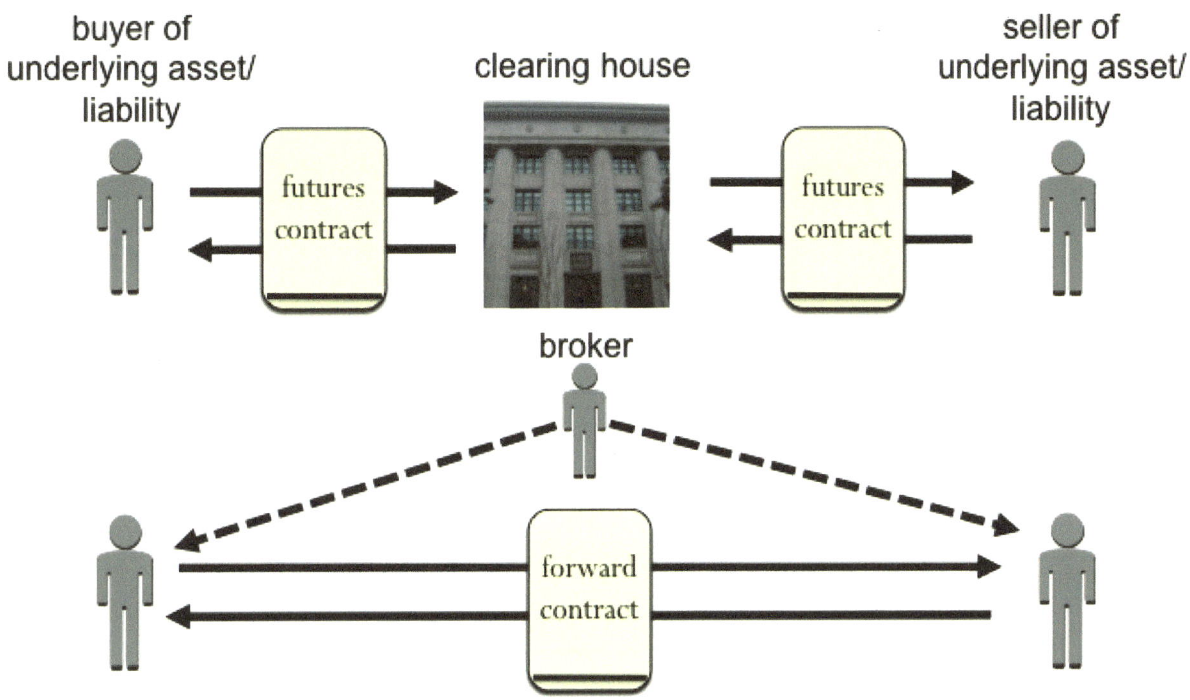

Figure 7-3: A representation of transactions involving futures contracts and forward contracts.

Clearing houses operate at major exchanges, like the London International Financial and Futures Exchange, the Chicago Board of Options Exchange, the Chicago Mercantile Exchange, the Philadelphia Board of Trade, the Sydney Futures Exchange and the Singapore Monetary Exchange. They can make a profit by charging a fee for each transaction, and by acting as a "market maker", an individual or institution that facilitates transactions by standardizing them and/or insuring them.

Because futures contracts are standardized and insured by clearing houses they can be more easily sold to a third party, thereby reducing the amount of illiquidity that plagues forward contracts.

To insure the terms of the futures contract, the clearing house requires *margin payments* in a **margin account**, a deposit of insurance payments which depend on the difference between the value of the contract and the market value of the underlying asset/liability. The margin account effectively acts as collateral against counterparty risk. The clearing house will allow a party to unwind or to cancel the contract, if it forfeits the margin payments, and then use the money to compensate the counterparty. The clearing house will also often pay interest on the funds deposited in the margin account until the contract is settled or is canceled to compensate parties for forgoing the use of their cash.

Margin accounts are adjusted according to the market price of the underlying asset/liability relative to the exercise price, a process called **marking to market**. Clearing houses require an *initial* margin payment to sign a futures contract, as well as *maintenance* or *variation* margin payments as the contract is marked to market daily. Margin payments depend on the difference, or margin, between the spot market price of the underlying asset/liability and the exercise price, as shown in Figure 7-4.

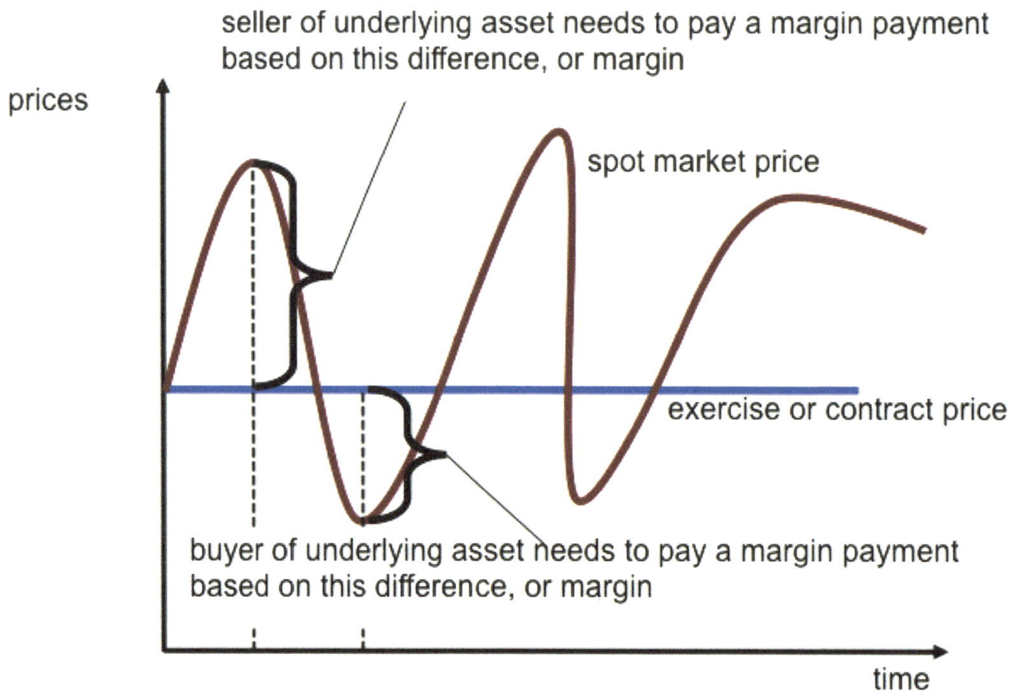

Figure 7-4: Marking to market involves comparing the margin between the exercise (contract) price of the underlying asset and the market price. According to this margin, the clearing house adjusts the initial and maintenance margin payments.

Option contracts

An option contract gives the owner the option, but not the obligation, of buying or selling an underlying asset/liability on or before a future date at a price that is specified today. But if the owner exercises this option, the counter party has the obligation of carrying out the transaction. Because an option contract gives the owner more freedom about buying or selling the contract in the future, it must pay an additional amount, or **premium**, to the counterparty or clearing house relative to the amount charged for a forward contract or a futures contract. Option contracts may be standardized and issued by clearing houses, or they may be created by the buyer and the seller of the underlying asset/liability and customized according to their needs.

Issuers/sellers of option contracts speculate that the price of the underlying asset/liability will not be volatile or change in an unfavorable way. Buyers/holders of option contracts insure the risk that the price of the underlying asset/liability will be volatile or change in an unfavorable way. Issuers/sellers therefore accept **market value risk**, the risk that a changing market value of the underlying asset/liability will change its income or expenses. In return, they receive the premium as compensation. Buyers/holders accept *default risk* because the issuer could default on its obligation to sell or to buy the underlying asset/liability if the holder exercises its right. Buyers/holders or a clearing house may collect margin payments as collateral against this risk.

European options specify that the owner of the contract has the option of exercising the contract on a specified date called the maturity date of the contract. In other words, the settlement date may only be on the maturity date. American options allow the owner the option of exercising the contract from a specified date until the maturity date. In other words, the settlement date may occur from the specified date (usually the date on which the contract is signed) until the maturity date. Despite their names, both American and European options may be traded in Europe, the US and elsewhere.

A **call option** gives the owner of the contract the option of *buying* an underlying asset/liability on or before a specified future date at a price specified today. The owner of a call option contract will exercise the option if the market price of the underlying asset exceeds the exercise price, allowing him to buy at a low price, assuming that the future market price of the underlying asset is not expected to be even higher. In this case, the call option is said to be *in the money*. If the exercise price exceeds the market price, the call option is said to be *out of the money*, and of course the call option should not be exercised.

A **put option** gives the owner of the contract the option of *selling* an underlying asset/liability on or before a specified future date at a price specified today. The owner of a put option contract will exercise the option if the market price of the asset falls below the exercise price, allowing him to sell at a high price, assuming that the future market price of the underlying asset is not expected to be even lower. A put option is in the money if the market price of the underlying asset falls below the exercise price; it is out of the money if the market price of the underlying asset rises above the exercise price.

The issuer of a call option contract is exposed to losses if the market price of the underlying asset rises above the exercise price. Likewise, the issuer of a put option contract is exposed to losses if the market price of the underlying asset falls below the exercise price. In general, although option contracts are intended to decrease the market value risk for the owner of the contract, they will increase this risk for the issuer of the contract. The premium is intended to compensate the issuer for accepting this risk.

Factors that influence the value (and premium) of option contracts include market value risk, that is, the risk of buying or selling the underlying asset/liability. As the market value risk increases, usually measured by the standard deviation of the market price from its average (see chapter 9), the value and the premium of an option contract increases.

Secondly, the time to maturity or *expiration* also affects the value of an option contract, and in a non-linear way. With many days left before the maturity date, the change in value should be small when other factors are constant. But with just a few days left before maturity date, the change in value for a contract that is in the money will decrease at a faster rate, and rapidly approach zero as the maturity date approaches. The loss in value as time progresses towards the maturity date is called **time decay**.

Thirdly, the difference between the exercise price and the market price of the underlying asset/liability affects the value of the option contract. As the difference increases, the value of the option contract increases. In particular, as the market price increases above the exercise price, the value of a call option contract increases, and as the market price falls below the exercise price, the value of a put option contract increases.

In sum, one can represent the value of option contracts and the premium paid for option contracts as a positive function of

$$[V, T, \max\{P_m - P_e, 0\}] \text{ for a call option}$$

$$[V, T, \max\{P_e - P_m, 0\}] \text{ for a put option}$$

where V represents the volatility of the price of the underlying asset/liability or market value risk, T represents the time to maturity, P_m represents the market price/rate and P_e represents the exercise price.

Other kinds of option contracts include **average price option contracts**, or *Asian options*, which use the average market price/rate during the life of the contract as the exercise price at the settlement date.

A **cap option contract** limits payments for a buyer/borrower by having the issuer of the contract pay the extra amount above the exercise price/rate, if a variable market price/interest rate rises above the exercise price/rate (*the cap*). A **floor option contract** protects the revenue for a seller/lender by having the issuer of the contract pay extra revenue, if a variable market price/interest rate falls below the exercise price/rate (*the floor*). A **collar position** is a position where an individual or institution buys a cap option contract and issues a floor option contract simultaneously (or vice versa).

A **straddle position** combines a call option contract with a put option contract with the same exercise price/rate. For a holder, this reduces market value risk for large potential changes (increases *and* decreases) in the market price/rate, although it will magnify market value risk for moderate potential changes in the market price/rate because the holder must pay two premiums for the two contracts. For an issuer, this reduces market value risk for moderate potential changes in the market price/rate because it earns two premiums for the two contracts, although it will magnify market value risk for large potential changes (increases *and* decreases) in the market price/rate.

A **strangle position** combines a call option contract with a put option contract, but unlike with a straddle position, the exercise price of the call option contract is not the same as the exercise rate of the put option contract. However, the effects of a strangle position are similar to those of a straddle position for both the holder and the issuer.

Option contracts can also be combined with swaps, discussed below, to give parties the option of swapping cash flows on or before a specified date. A contract that combines an option and a swap is called a swap option.

Swap contracts

Swap contracts give the parties the right or the option to swap cash (flows) from underlying assets or liabilities on a specified future date(s), contingent on the value of (and therefore the income or expenses from) the underlying assets or liabilities. Like forward contracts, swaps are non-standardized contracts between two parities that expose both to counterparty risk unless margin payments are collected beforehand.

The logic of swap contracts is represented by Figure 7-5, which shows that one type of cash (dollars) is swapped for another type of cash (euros).

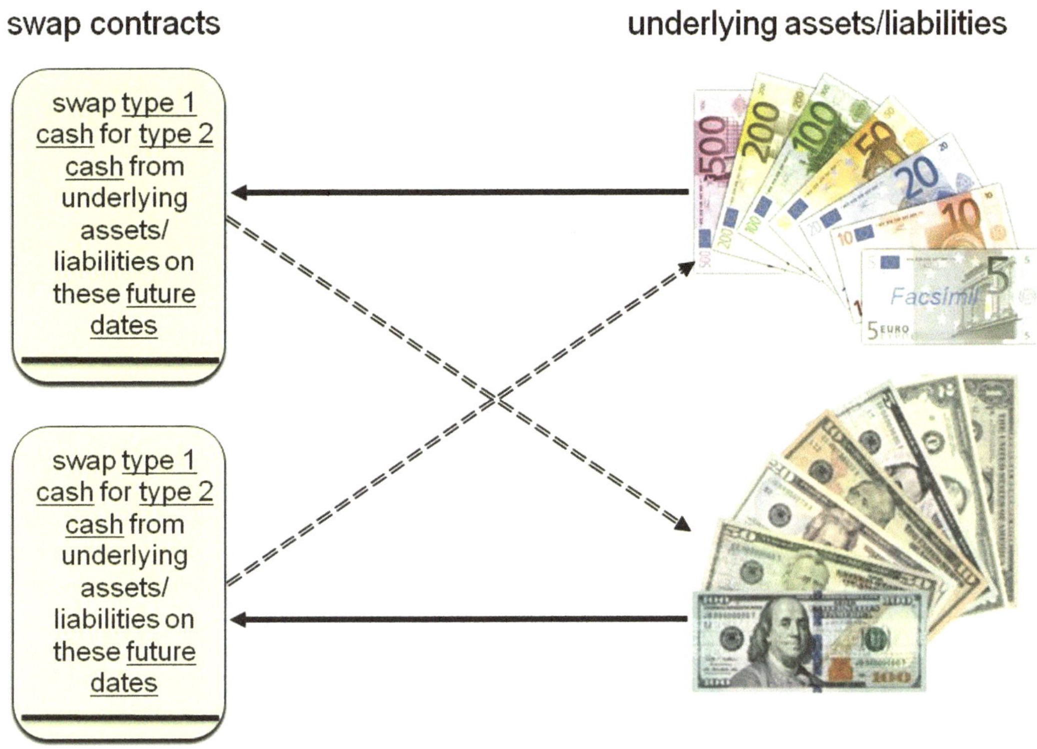

Figure 7-5: Swap contracts involve swapping cash flows from one underlying asset/liability for another.

A **currency swap contract** involves an exchange of payments denominated in different currencies. Figure 7-5 represents the basic idea of a currency swap contract. The need for currency swaps arises because one party may want debt or income denominated in a particular currency but it is costly to issue debt or acquire income in that currency. For example, a US firm building a subsidiary firm in Germany might be able to easily issue US dollar denominated bonds but not euro denominated bonds because it is not well known outside the US. A German company that sells many products to US customers may want to have dollar denominated debt, but can not do so for similar reasons. Each firm could issue bonds in its home currency, then swap the principal and interest payments.

Table 15 shows another example of a currency swap contract: a contract signed by *bank 1* and *bank 2* which involves the swapping of Australian dollars (A$) and Canadian dollars (C$) for 5 years (2005-2009). The contract specifies that *bank 2* would receive C$500,000 and *bank 1* would receive A$490,000, every year during the life of the contract. Therefore, the contract exchange rate, or exercise exchange rate, is A$490,000/ C$500,000 = A$0.9800/C$.

During the life of the contract, the market A$/C$ exchange rate changes due to demand and supply conditions, and these changes could favor one party or the other in the swap contract. Table 15 shows that the market exchange rate increases in 2005, indicating that the C$ appreciates and *bank 2* has a more valuable currency than it did when the contract was signed. The table shows that the value of C$ in A$ increases to A$527,850, so that the payment to *bank 1* has a lower value than the payment to *bank 2* (from *bank 1*) by A$37,850. Similarly, if the C$ continues to appreciate in 2006 and 2007, the value of payments to *bank 2* will continue to increase, as shown in the table. On the other hand, if the C$ depreciates and the A$ appreciates in 2008 and 2009, then the value of the payments to *bank 2* will decrease and the value of the payments to *bank 1* will increase, as shown in the table.

Table 15: an example of currency swap between *bank 1* and *bank 2* with A$ and C$

Date	A$/C$ exchange rate	Payments to *bank 1* in A$	Payments to *bank 2* in C$	Payments to *bank 2* valued in A$	Net value of payments to *bank 1* - payments to *bank 2* in A$
contract date	0.9800				
2005	1.0557	490000	500000	527850	-37850
2006	1.0672	490000	500000	533600	-43600
2007	1.0752	490000	500000	537600	-47600
2008	0.9762	490000	500000	488100	1900
2009	0.8957	490000	500000	447850	42150

Currency swaps can be structured as **parallel loans**, contracts that allow lending in one currency and borrowing in another currency between two parties at the same time. The swap of the principal is usually based on the spot market exchange rate, whereas the interest payments/rates are based on exchange rates determined by the *forward exchange rate*, a rate determined by forward contracts with currency dealers. This kind of currency swap can be useful to avoid capital controls and other limits on the amount of foreign exchange. More generally, parallel loans can reduce transaction costs by combining lending and borrowing in a single transaction, rather than doing each transaction separately.

Figure 7-6 shows a three-period currency swap between *bank 1* and *bank 2* with yen (¥) and Australian dollars (A$) structured as a parallel loan. The ¥ loan has a principal of ¥65,000,000 and an interest rate of 2%. The A$ loan has a principal of A$1,000,000 and an interest rate of 5%. The interest rate on the A$ loan may be higher because the value of the A$ is expected to depreciate relative to the ¥ during periods 1, 2 and 3 according to the forward exchange rate, so that *bank 2* requires a corresponding higher interest payment.

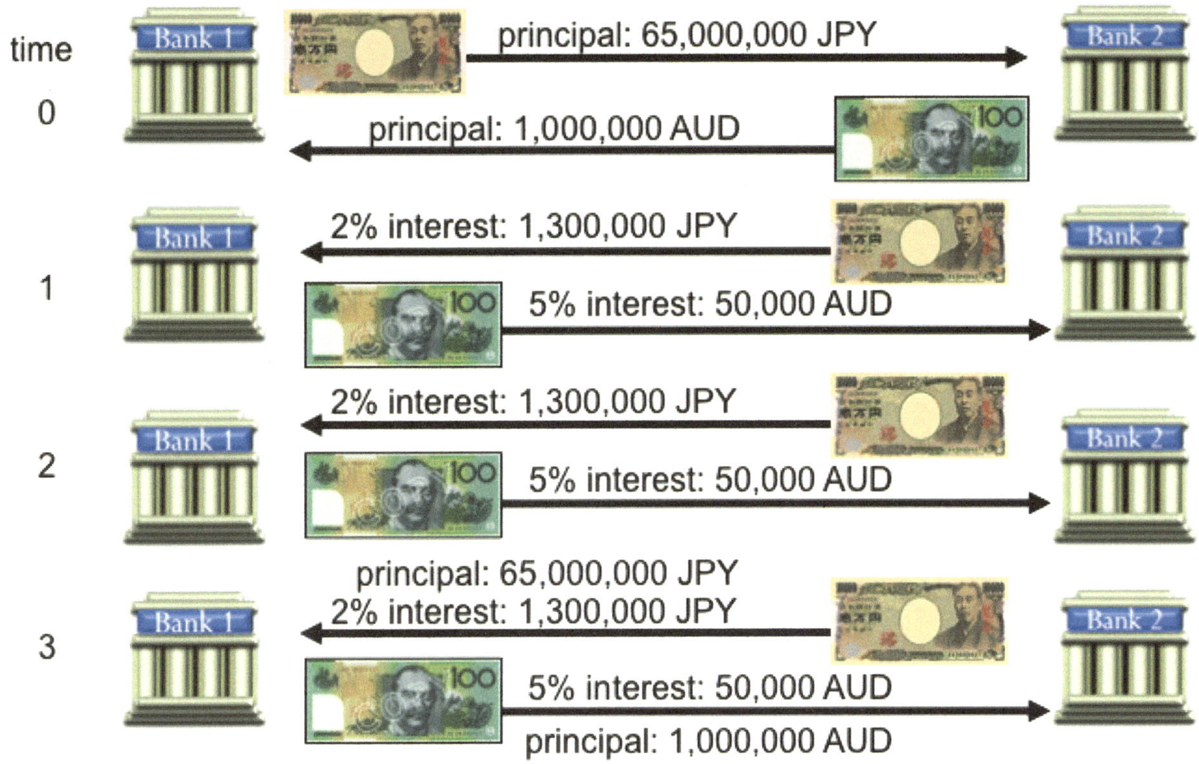

Figure 7-6: A three-period currency swap with ¥ and A$ structured as a parallel loan between *bank 1* and *bank 2*. The ¥ loan has a principal of ¥65,000,000 and an interest rate of 2%; the A$ loan has a principal of A$1,000,000 and an interest rate of 5%.

Sometimes a currency swap contract uses payments only in one currency, but the payments are adjusted according to the value of another currency. A single currency, currency *x*, acts as the currency in which payments are made over time; while an amount of another currency, currency *y*, acts as **notional principal**, a nominal amount that is not exchanged but used only to calculate payments. For example in Table 15, *bank 1* and *bank 2* could both make payments in A$: the payment of *bank 1* would be A$490,000 during each year, and the payment of *bank 2* would be the market value of C$500,000 in terms of A$ during each year. That is, the payment of *bank 1* would be A$490,000 during each year; payments of *bank 2* would be A$527,850 in 2005, A$533,600 in 2006, A$537,600 in 2007, and so forth. The notional principal would be C$500 000, while both banks make payments in A$. *Bank 1* would have a fixed payment in A$, while *bank 2*'s payment in A$ would vary depending on the spot market A$/C$ exchange rate.

When individuals or institutions use notional principal or more generally use a single currency in a swap contract, they often use *net payments* instead of gross payments, depending on whether the spot market price/rate increases above or decreases below the exercise price/rate. In the example with *bank 1* and *bank 2* shown in Table 15, *bank 1* would make a net payment to *bank 2* of A$37,850, A$43,600 and A$47,600 during the first three years of the life of the contract, as shown in the last column of the table. During the last two years of the life of the contract, *bank 2* would make a net payment to *bank 1* of AS$1,900 and A$42,150.

Swap contracts with notional principal involve payments in the same currency, which depend on a fixed exercise price/rate relative to a variable market price/rate. This idea was extended to credit/debt contracts denominated in the same currency, whose payments depend on different kinds of interest rates, like a fixed interest rate and a variable interest rate. *Interest rate swap contracts* were thus created.

A **basic interest rate swap contract** involves swapping one fixed interest payment and one variable interest payment in the same currency on specified future dates, with notional principal or actual principal from credit/debt contracts, which act as the underlying assets/liabilities. For example, a fixed interest payment could involve fixed coupon payments from a coupon bond or note, and a variable interest payment could involve a payment on a variable interest rate loan from a bank. Like currency swap contracts with notional principal, a basic interest rate swap contract has one fixed payment and one variable payment, which depend on variable (credit) market conditions relative to a fixed exercise price/rate.

If notional principal is used with an interest rate swap contract, the principal on the underlying liabilities or assets are not swapped, and both parties will still make or will still receive their own principal payment. However, parties can also decide to swap the actual principal on credit/debt contracts.

A basic interest rate swap contract can be useful when institutions can get one form of credit/debt (for example, bank loans, coupon bonds, notes, discount bonds or commercial paper) on favorable terms, but desire another type of credit/debt. They could benefit by borrowing in the first form of credit/debt and then swapping the interest payments with another party to make the terms of the credit/debt even more favorable.

Suppose *bank 1* and *bank 2* both want to borrow for investment purposes. *Bank 1* can issue bonds or commercial paper at a given price, after which the interest rate will remain at 10%. *Bank 2* can also issue bonds/paper, but because of a lower credit rating it must accept a lower price, so that its interest rate from bonds/paper will be 12.5%. For both *bank 1* and *bank 2*, the interest rates on the bonds/paper will remain fixed after they are issued and the borrowed money is received (but the yield and return can vary for saver/lender because the resale price can vary). Next, suppose these banks can also borrow from another bank, *bank 3*, and pay a variable rate based on the London inter-bank offer rate (LIBOR), a lending/borrowing interest rate that London banks charge each other and change everyday according to market conditions. Suppose that *bank 1* can borrow from *bank 3* at 0.5% more than LIBOR, and *bank 2* can borrow from *bank 3* at 1.0% more than LIBOR due to *bank 2*'s lower credit rating. In sum, *bank 1* can issue bonds at a lower rate and borrow in the inter-bank market at a lower rate, compared to *bank 2*.

Finally, suppose *bank 1* desires to have liabilities with a variable interest rate because most of its assets have variable interest rates, and *bank 2* desires to have liabilities with a fixed interest rate because most of its assets have fixed interest rates.

Under these conditions, *bank 1* and *bank 2* could design a contract to swap interest payments in a way that is mutually beneficial. In particular, *bank 1* could borrow at a fixed rate of 10% but pay a variable interest rate equal to the LIBOR rate (less than LIBOR + 0.5%). *Bank 2* could borrow at a variable rate of LIBOR + 1.0% but pay a fixed rate of 11% (less than 12.5%). In this way, both parties could acquire the kind of interest expenses from liabilities that match their income from assets, but would pay less interest than if they would borrow directly at that kind of interest. Table 16 and Figure 7-7 summarize how the interest rate swap contract would benefit both banks:

Table 16: A basic interest rate swap with an unspecified (notional) principal

	Fixed interest rate from bills/paper	Variable interest rate from *bank 3*	Interest paid with a swap contract	Interest rate saved with swap contract
Bank 1 wants a variable interest rate payment but can	10.0%	LIBOR + 0.5%	**LIBOR**	0.5%

borrow relatively cheaply at a fixed rate.				
Bank 2 wants a fixed interest rate payment but can borrow relatively cheaply at a variable rate.	12.5%	**LIBOR** + 1.0%	10.0% + 1.0%	1.5%
Note: LIBOR = London interbank offer rate, a variable interest rate for interbank lending and borrowing from London banks.				

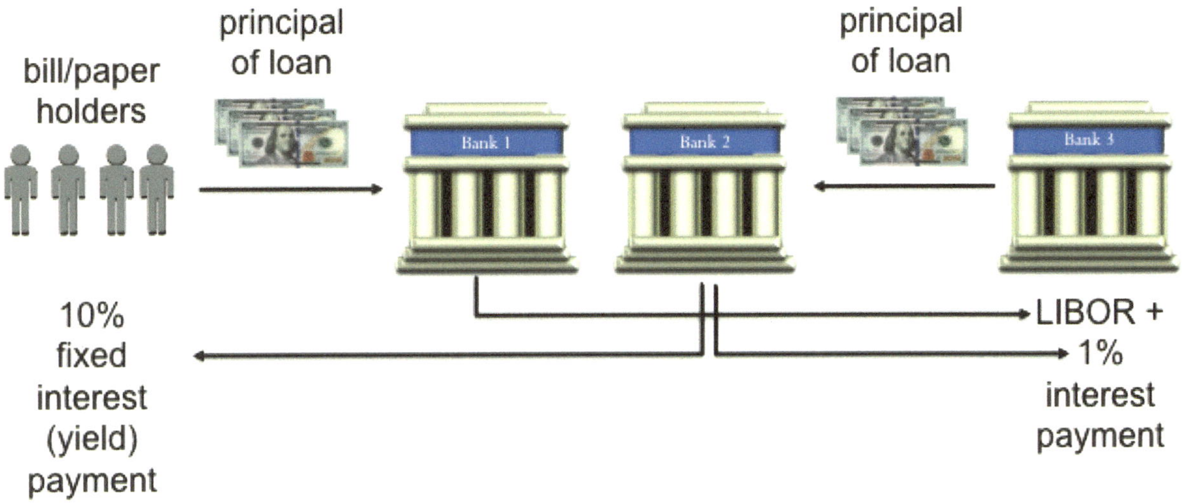

Figure 7-7: A basic interest rate swap with an unspecified (notional) principal

A **variable interest rate swap contract** involves the two parties swapping interest payments based on separate variable interest rates. Because banks often link their deposit interest rates on one market interest rate and their loan interest rates on another market interest rate, and the two market interest rates may change relatively over time, banks may expose themselves to interest rate risk, and in particular, margin risk. A variable interest rate swap can allow a bank to swap variable interest payments so that the margin between the interest rates on loans and the interest rates on deposits remain more stable over time, so that profits remain more stable over time.

A combination of a currency swap and a basic interest rate swap is called a **cross-currency interest rate swap**: a swap of fixed rate cash flows in one currency and variable rate cash flows in another currency.

Foreign exchange swap contracts are contracts to exchange currencies at one date (ex., today) and then reverse the trade at a later date at the forward exchange rate. Foreign exchange swaps are effectively (reverse) repurchase agreements, where a dealer/trader (purchases) sells an asset while agreeing to (resell) repurchase it at a later date. Foreign exchange swaps allow a party to have access to foreign currency for a temporary time, as needed. Figure 7-8 represents the idea of a foreign exchange swap.

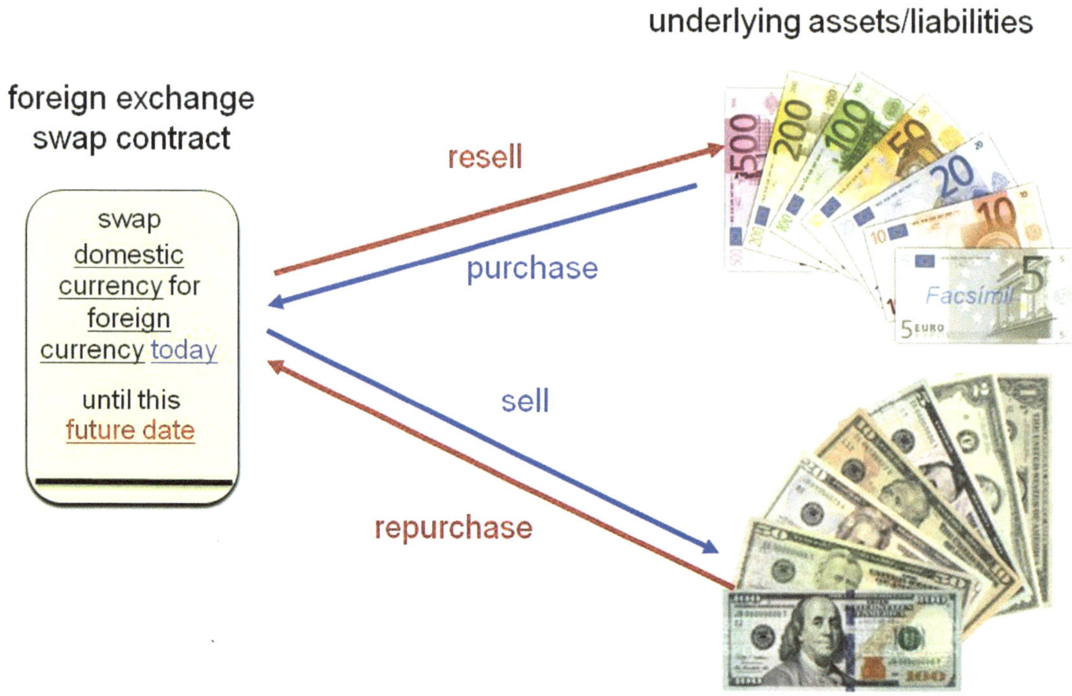

Figure 7-8: A representation of a foreign exchange swap.

Credit default swaps are designed to separate default risk from market value risk on a form of credit that serves as an underlying asset. In other words, one party bears the risk of unexpected movements in the value of the asset, usually the institution that created or **originated** the asset, and another institution (such as an insurance company) or even other individuals bear the risk of default. The party that passes the default risk to the party that bears this risk pays a fee, or *premium* (different from that on an option contract) to the party that bears the risk. In the event of a default, the insurer pays the party that issued the credit for all or part of the losses, as represented by Figure 7-9 below.

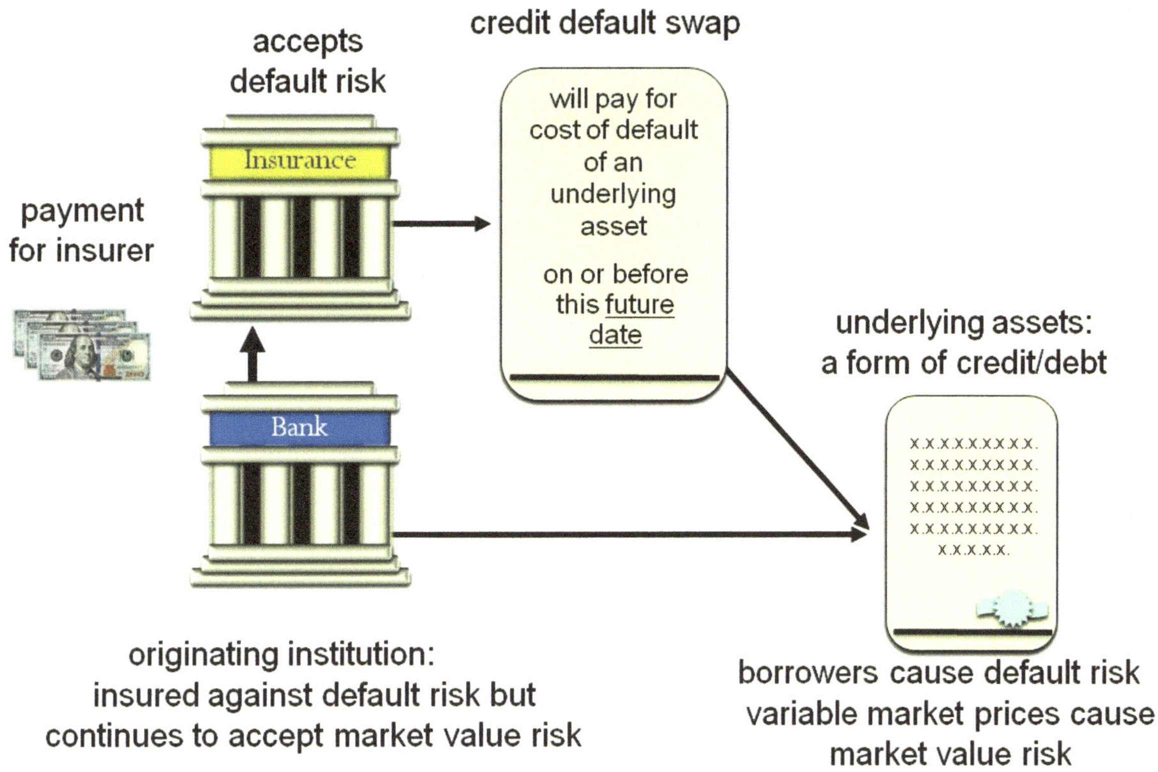

Figure 7-9: A representation of a credit default swap.

Despite the name, a credit default swap is really just a form of insurance, but we can say that the insurance company and the originating institution swap cash for the risk of default. The originating institution pays the insurance company cash in the form of a premium, and the insurance company pays the originating institution cash in the form of an insurance payment in the event that default occurs.

However, these contracts need to specify explicitly the conditions in which default occurs. Legal definitions of default vary across countries. In some European countries, when a borrower encounters payment restructures debt (for example, extending the time to repay or reducing interest payments) but continues to promise to repay, this event is usually not legally considered default so that the insurer would not obligated to pay for the default. In the US, however, such restructuring under Chapter 11 is legally considered default.

The market for credit default swaps has grown rapidly in the US and elsewhere during the last two decades. Because the notional value of credit default swaps are usually recorded off the balance sheet, regulators are becoming concerned that credit risk is spread to more institutions and individuals, leading to the possibility of contagion, rather than reducing risk through diversification.

A **total return swap** allows parties to swap both default risk and market value risk for cash. In other words, the return from an asset will not change due to default or due to changes in its market price or interest rate in exchange for a premium paid to the insurer. Suppose that *bank 1* lends money to a borrower, and the borrower becomes *delinquent* (late) in repaying the credit/debt contract but has not actually defaulted. If the credit/debt contract were a marketable contract, then it would have a lower market value, often represented by a lower credit rating. (In the next section, I discuss how banks make their credit/debt contracts (loans) into securities that can be sold in credit/debt markets.) Alternatively, broader market conditions could decrease the demand of or increase the supply of similar credit/debt contracts, decreasing the market value of all of these contracts. In either case, if *bank 1* has made a total return swap with an insurer, then the insurer would compensate *bank 1* for the loss in market value if *bank 1* tries to sell the contract to another party, even if default has not occurred. If default does occur, then the insurer would also compensate *bank 1* for the loss from default.

Securitization

Recall that a **security** is an asset that can be bought and sold in financial markets. Assets that are not normally bought and sold in financial markets, like home loans, automobile loans and credit card loans, can be turned into a security by creating a derivative contract whose value is based on payments from these underlying assets. This process of creating a derivative security that can be more easily bought and sold in financial markets than the underlying asset itself is called **securitization**. I discuss two types of securities that are created through securitization: asset backed securities and collateralized debt obligations. These securities are generally forward contracts or futures contracts, and the underlying asset/liability are the specified payments that will be received/must be paid in the future.

Asset backed securities. An **asset backed security** (ABS) is a security whose value and income payments are derived from and collateralized (or "backed") by a specified portfolio or "pool" of underlying assets. The pool of assets is typically a large group of small denomination and illiquid loans or other credit/debt contracts that are unable to be sold individually. Pooling the assets allows them to be sold to general investors, and allows the risk of investing in the underlying assets to be diversified because each security will represent a fraction of the total value of the diverse pool of underlying assets. The pools of underlying assets can include regular payments from credit cards, auto loans and mortgage loans or esoteric cash flows from aircraft leases, royalty payments and movie revenues.

Figure 7-10 represents the basic function of securitization and an ABS.

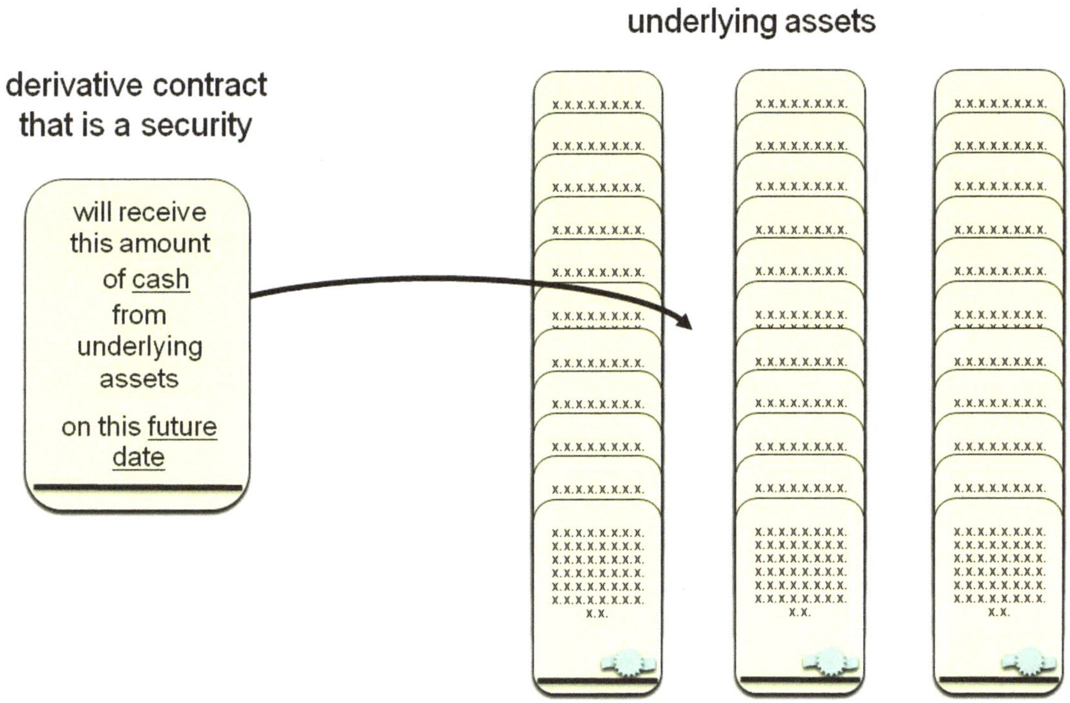

Figure 7-10: A representation of securitization in general and an asset backed security in particular.

Often an institution that is separate from the originating institution, called a *special purpose entity*, is organized to handle the securitization of ABSs. The special purpose entity, which creates and sells the securities, uses the proceeds of the sale to pay back the bank that originated the underlying loans or other credit/debt contracts. The special purpose entity is responsible for "bundling" the underlying assets into a pool that will fit desires and needs of investors who might want to buy the securities, for managing credit risk—often by transferring it to an insurance company after paying a premium—and for distributing payments from the securities.

If the credit risk of the underlying assets is transferred to another institution through a credit default swap or simply accepted by the investors, the originating bank removes the value of the underlying assets from its balance sheet as it receives cash from the sale of the ABSs. Because the credit risk is transferred to another party, this transaction can improve the bank's credit rating and reduce the amount of capital that it needs to protect itself against risk. (Capital requirements to protect against risk are discussed in chapter 6). The ABSs themselves receive a credit rating according to the assets (expected income) and liabilities (expected expenses) of the special purpose entity, and this rating could be higher than if the originating bank issued the ABSs by itself. A higher credit rating for the ABSs could allow the special purpose entity to pay a lower interest/yield rate and charge a higher price for the ABSs than if the originating bank issued the ABSs by itself.

Thus, one incentive for banks to securitize assets like ABSs is to remove risky assets from their balance sheet by having another institution or individuals assume the credit risk. Another incentive is that the banks can receive cash today when they sell the ABSs rather than having to wait for the loans or other credit/debt contracts to mature. This allows banks to invest more quickly in new loans or other assets and possibly have a lower capital requirement. Obay (2000) found no evidence that banks securitize their safest assets and found that those banks which securitize assets have significantly lower risk-based capital ratios.

The interest and principal payments from the underlying credit/debt contracts can be made to the special purpose entity or the originating bank. This institution may then pass these payments directly to the owners of the ABSs, after subtracting administrative and other fees. In this case, the securities are called **pass through ABSs**. Alternatively, the payments may be adjusted or "structured" for the market value (risk) of the pool of underlying credit/debt contracts and the ABSs. For example, if the market value of the underlying credit/debt contracts decreases due to poor economic conditions, then the payments from **structured ABSs** are adjusted downward to account for this lower economic value. Because structured ABSs make the owners bear at least some of market value risk (and credit risk), they generally offer a higher yield rate than pass through ABSs.

Figure 7-11 below represents the relationships among the originating bank, a special purpose entity, savers/lenders who invest in ABSs and borrowers/spenders who borrow through underlying credit/debit (loan) contracts.

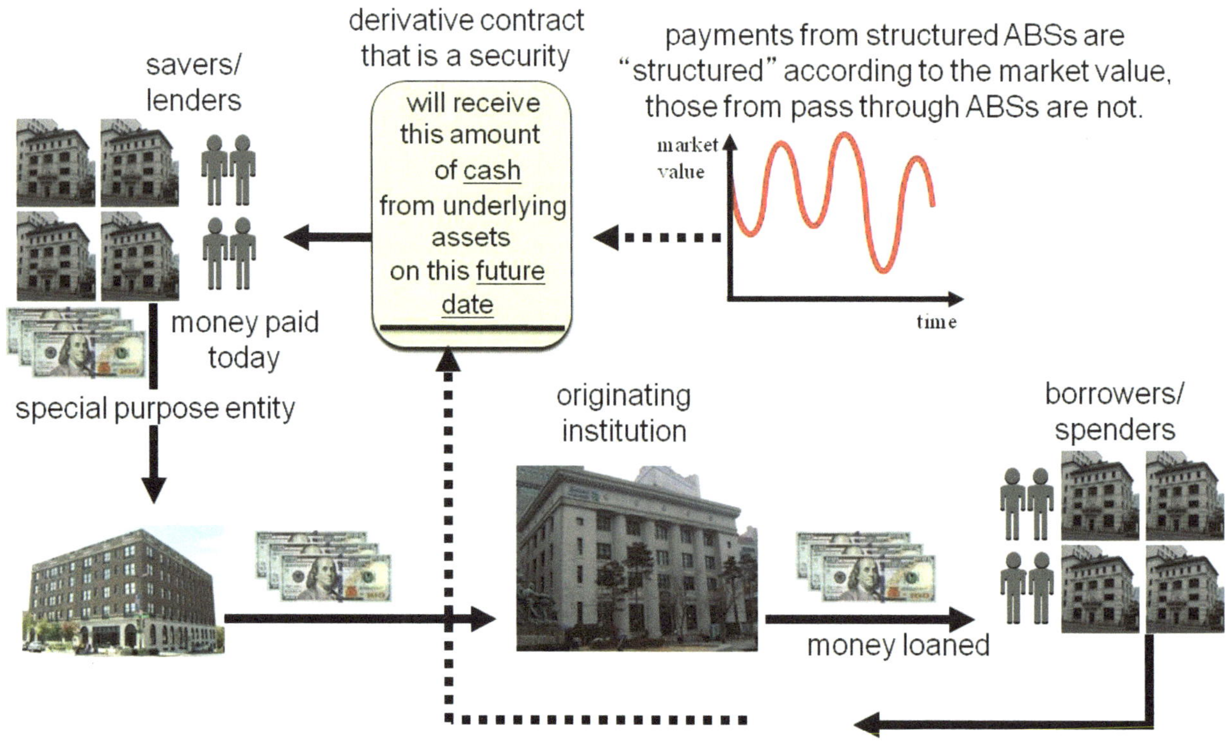

Figure 7-11: A representation of the role of the originating institution, a special purpose entity, savers/lenders and borrowers/spenders in the securitization process.

Collateralized debt obligations. A collateralized debt obligation (CDO) has different meanings in finance. It can mean a derivative contract whose underlying asset is an asset backed security itself instead of a "regular" underlying assets like loan contracts, bonds or other credit/debt contracts directly linked to the borrower's ability and willingness to pay. A CDO in this sense is effectively a derivative asset with two layers of underlying assets.

Figure 7-12 represents the function of CDOs when they use asset backed securities as underlying assets.

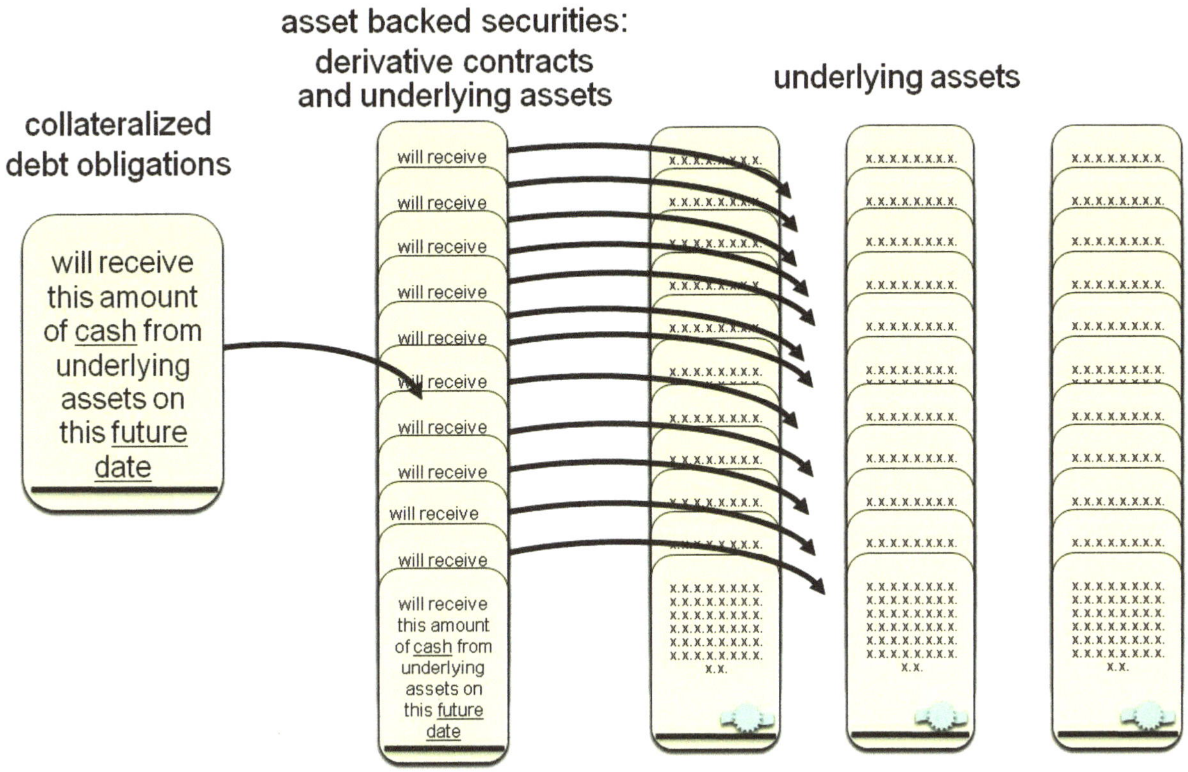

Figure 7-12: Collateralized debt obligations that use asset backed securities as underlying assets.

Alternatively, some people define a CDO as an asset backed security (with underlying assets like loan contracts) that assigns a class, or **tranche**, to the underlying assets according to their credit risk (and possibly market risk as well). Underlying assets in a higher risk tranche are associated with a higher risk CDO, which naturally has a lower price and a higher yield than alternative CDOs. But when some of the underlying credit/debt contracts unexpectedly default or otherwise lose value, the CDOs associated with the high risk tranche are the first to stop their principal and/or interest payments. In other words, the CDOs associated with the lowest risk tranche are the first to receive their principal and interest payments, when defaults (or prepayments) are larger than expected. The CDOs associated with the highest risk tranche will not pay principal or interest until CDOs associated with all of the other tranches have been paid.

CDOs associated with tranches give investors a greater range of risk and return choices than regular asset backed securities. If an investor is willing to risk unexpectedly large default and unexpectedly large prepayments (thereby sacrificing interest income), he can purchase a CDO associated with a high risk tranche for a low price and receive a large yield if actual payments equal what was expected.

Figure 7-13 represents the function of CDOs when they use risk based tranches.

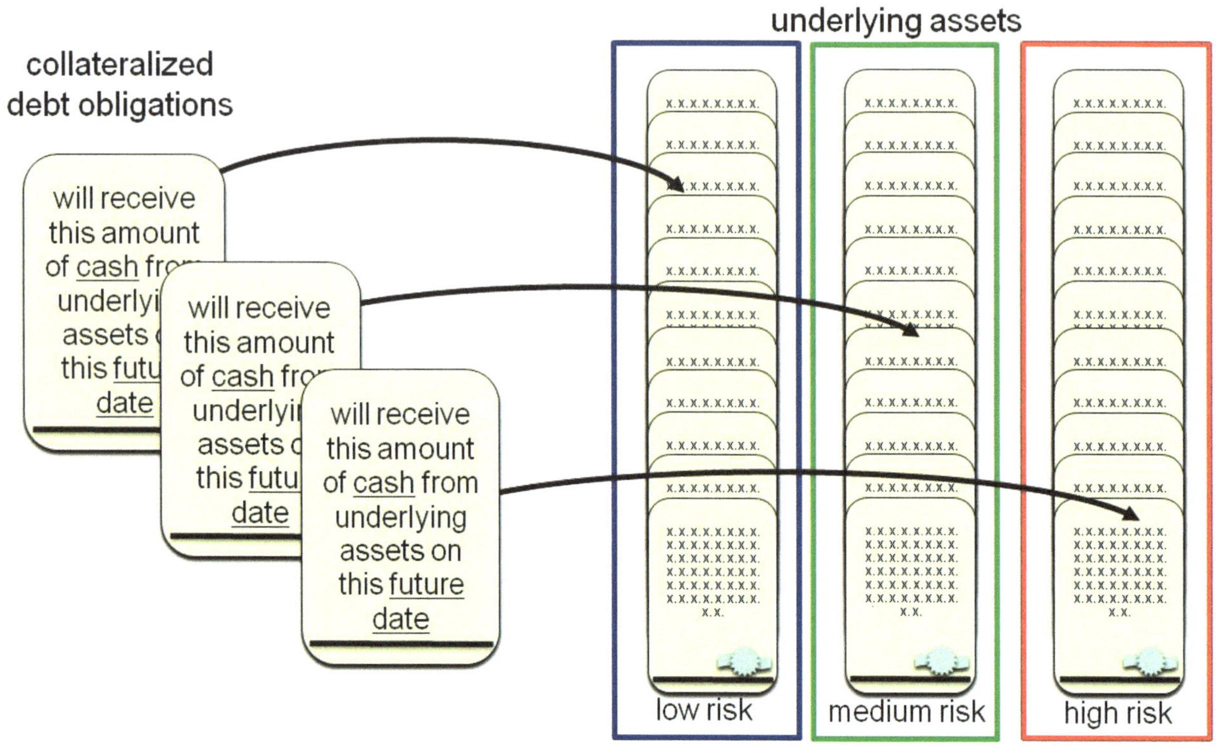

Figure 7-13: Collateralized debt obligations that use tranches to separate the underlying assets into different risk groups.

Like ABSs, CDOs enable the originating bank of the underlying assets to pass credit risk to another institution or to individual investors and receive cash in return, thereby allowing it to reinvest in new loans or other assets more quickly than if it did not securitize the underlying assets.

Government sponsored enterprises and securitization

ABS and CDO markets are larger in the US than in other countries primarily because US government sponsored enterprises—Fannie Mae, Freddie Mac and Ginnie Mae—securitize mortgage loans (typically housing loans) after purchasing them from many individual banks. Because these agencies do not pay state or local income taxes and are exempt from Securities and Exchange Commission fees and disclosure requirements, they can issue ABSs and CDOs more cheaply and with a higher return rate for investors—both domestic and foreign investors. And many depository institutions and other financial institutions are willing to invest in these securities because they are considered relatively safe assets according to risked-based capital requirements under the Basel Accords, so that these institutions are allowed to use more of their capital for investment purposes. In addition, Fannie Mae and Freddie Mac buy and keep some mortgage loans themselves, although they restrict the size of the loans that they are willing to accept. As a result, these institutions receive some income from the sale of ABSs and CDOs, but because they keep a pool of mortgage loans for themselves, they are also exposed to some default risk and market value risk.

The national government established the Federal National Mortgage Association (Fannie Mae) in 1938 to encourage home ownership by buying mortgage loans from savings and loan associations. Like today, buying the mortgage loans provided cash immediately to the savings and loan associations, which could then start lending more rather than having to wait for existing loans to pay off. In addition, buying the mortgage loans allowed taxpayers to insure the default risk of loans made by the savings and loan associations so that the savings and loan associations would be willing to make more mortgage loans than otherwise.

In 1968, the organization was separated into two parts: Fannie Mae and Ginnie Mae. Fannie Mae was given a charter to become a private corporation to continue to buy mortgage loans, but without an explicit insurance from the US government against default risk (and market value risk). The risk was borne by the originating institution or was passed to an insurer if the originating institution paid it a premium. Ginnie Mae became a publicly financed institution to insure the default risk and market value risk of securities backed by certain mortgages made to government employees and veterans. In 1970, the Federal Home Loan Mortgage Corporation (Freddie Mac) was created to provide competition for the newly private Fannie Mae and to further increase the availability of funds to finance mortgage loans and home ownership.

Although Fannie Mae and Freddie Mac are private corporations, their charters require that the mortgage loans that they purchase must be for residential property and may not exceed certain limits that are currently $801,950-$1,202,925 for a 4-unit home depending on its location. Fannie Mae and Freddie Mac are prohibited from originating loans—they must buy them from depository institutions, so as to provide these institutions with more funds to originate more loans.

After 1970, Fannie Mae, Freddie Mac and Ginnie Mae began to issue asset (mortgage loan) backed securities to sell to individuals and institutions. These securities have become their principal liability, worth nearly $3 trillion, and these three government-sponsored institutions now finance or guarantee nearly half of all outstanding mortgages in the US.

The widespread use of asset back securities from Fannie Mae, Freddie Mac and Ginne Mae has encouraged depository institutions and other financial institutions to securitize other assets—like commercial real estate loans; mobile home loans; car loans; credit card receivables and receivables from computers, appliances, furniture and other durable goods.

Summary

Besides the traditional role of acting as an intermediary between savers and borrowers and providing liquidity to customers, banks may pursue various activities whose effects are recorded off the balance sheet. These include offering letters of credit, banker's acceptances, loan commitments and derivative contracts.

Derivative contracts are those whose value is derived from underlying assets and include futures contracts, forward contracts, option contracts and swaps. Futures and forward contracts involve buying or selling an underlying asset in the future at a price specified today. An option contract gives one the option of buying or selling an underlying asset in the future at a price specified today. And a swap involves the exchange of cash based on the value of underlying assets or liabilities on a future date.

Two other derivative contracts are asset backed securities and collateralized debt obligations, whose value is derived from a portfolio of typically small denomination and illiquid loans and other bank assets. ABSs and CDOs can allow banks to sell their assets for cash and reduce their capital requirements, further allowing them to make investments in new loans or other assets. CDOs differ from ABSs in that they are classified according to various degrees of credit and market value risk. The popularity of ABSs and CDOs in the US has been increased because government sponsored organizations are very active in their markets.

Problems and Applications

Short answer problems

1. How does the notional value differ from the market value of a derivative contract?

2. Describe how a derivative contract can hedge or insure one risk for a party in a transaction. Describe how the same transaction can increase another risk for the same party.

3. Describe how a derivative contract can hedge or insure risk for a party in a transaction. Describe how the same transaction can increase risk for another party in the transaction.

4. How do derivative contracts that are issued by clearing houses differ from derivative contracts that are issued in the over the counter market?

5. How does a futures contract differ from a forward contract?

6. How does a futures contract differ from an option contract?

7. What is a basic interest rate swap? What is a credit default swap? What is a parallel loan? Are they considered over the counter contracts or contracts issued by a clearing house?

8. What is the underlying asset for an asset backed security? What are the possible underlying assets for a collateralized debt obligation?

9. Describe how the tranches of collateralized debt obligations can appeal to a diverse group of investors with different preferences about risk and return.

10. How does a pass through asset backed security differ from a structured asset backed security?

Internet applications

1. Go to http://ecos.bok.or.kr/ under the Balance of Payments/Trade/FX link to find data for the total value of derivative assets and the total value of derivative liabilities from the earliest available period to the latest available period. Create a graph for both series of data.

Bibliography

Obay, L. (2000), *Financial Innovation in the Banking Industry: The Case of Asset Securitization*, Garland Publishing, London.

8. Payment Settlement Systems

Preview

In this chapter, I describe the various means or systems that allow banks and bank customers to transfer funds and to settle payments. **Payment settlement systems** are systems that process, clear or settle various payments, including those by paper checks and electronic transfers of funds.

We can divide these payment settlement systems into those that are used by bank customers and sometimes banks themselves to settle payments, called retail payment settlement systems, and those that are used primarily by banks to settle payments, called inter-bank or wholesale payment settlement systems. However, this distinction is somewhat arbitrary because banks are sometimes customers of other banks. For example, systems or networks that are normally used between bank customers and between a bank customer and a bank—such as the Interbank Remittance System, ATM networks, Cash Management Service (CMS) System and Electronic Banking System—can also be inter-bank systems. And the BOK Wire is normally used for inter-bank or wholesale transfers of funds, but can also be used for retail transfers by some bank customers. We discuss the details of each of these systems in the sections below.

Many innovations have been created during the past generation. I discuss some of these innovations, and in particular, innovations with electronic versions of currency and bills, called *electronic money* and *electronic bills*, as well as innovations in security, risk management, settling payments via the internet and presenting bills for payment electronically or via the internet.

Retail payment settlement systems

Retail payment settlement systems are separated into currency and non-currency systems, including check settlement systems and various systems/networks to electronically transfer funds. In Korea, nearly all of the non-currency systems are operated by or overseen by the Korea Financial Telecommunications and Clearings Institute (KFTC).

Currency payments. The most basic form of payment settlement is with paper currency and coins, which are issued solely by the Bank of Korea (BOK) in Korea. Currency is widely used as a payment system, although its share in total payment settlements has been declining since the 1990s due to increasing use of electronic forms of payments. Nonetheless, the total value of currency transactions has grown over time, partly due to inflation, so the BOK started to issue the 50000 won notes in 2009 to facilitate larger transactions. The BOK currently issues paper currency in denominations of 1000 won, 5000 won, 10000 won and 50000 won.

Due to counterfeiting, central banks have had to introduce increasingly sophisticated designs and printing techniques for their fiat currency. For example, the 50000 note has holograms (appearing as a gold circle and a silver strip) that show different images depending on the angle from which the currency is viewed. The 10000 won note and 5000 won note also have holograms, but in different forms. In addition, plastic or other special film is woven into the paper, which can be viewed by the human eye and/or read by electronic readers. Color-shifting ink and watermarks are also easily recognizable for the human eye but difficult for counterfeiters to reproduce.

Retail payment settlement systems/networks. Nearly all of the non-currency retail payment settlement systems or networks in Korea are owned and operated by the Korea Financial Telecommunications and Clearings Institute (KFTC), a non-profit organization jointly owned by member banks. All domestic banks (depository institutions) are either general or associate members of the KFTC, and the Bank of Korea is also a general member. The KFTC also allows special participants—such the post office, non-bank credit institutions, foreign banks and financial insurance corporations—to settle payments through its payment settlement systems. At the end of 2009, there were 11 general members, 10 associate members and 43 special participants using the KFTC retail payment settlement systems.

The KFTC operates the following retail payment settlement systems:

- Check and bill clearing system
- Giro network
- Cash Management System (CMS)
- Interbank Remittance System
- ATM networks
- Electronic Banking System
- Electronic Funds Transfer at the Point of Sale (EFTPOS) system
- Networks of electronic mediums of exchange
- Business-to-Business E-commerce Payment System
- Business-to-Consumer E-commerce Payment System
- Bankline System

I discuss these systems in the sections below except for the last system, which receives only a brief mention in this paragraph due to its limited use and due to the fact that the Electronic Banking System has similar functions but is more popular. The Bankline System connects the computer networks of regional banks to allow their bank customers to access banking services through their bank branches. The Electronic Banking System uses the internet to allow banks and bank customers to do similar operations and this System has largely replaced the Bankline System.

To settle payments using one of these systems, the KFTC will calculate the net multilateral obligation of each member of a system throughout the business day. It then notifies the members and the BOK of the obligation, and the BOK will then settle the payments of each member at prearranged times from members' accounts through the BOK Wire. The BOK Wire is an inter-bank/wholesale payment settlement system, which we consider after various retail payment settlement systems.

Each member of a retail payment settlement system must pay a one-time membership fee, as well as annual fees to the KFTC. The membership fee depends on the member's investment in the system's infrastructure, such as computer networks and security devices. The annual fees depend on the cost of maintaining and operating the system. Each member will then determine how much of these fees and other costs to pass on to their customers using the retail payment settlement system.

I next discuss the details of 7 retail payment settlement systems operated by the KFTC. I later discuss the details of 3 electronic payment settlement systems when I discuss innovation more generally.

Checks and bills (of exchange). In Korea, checks and bills are mainly used by businesses. Individuals may also issue checks and bills, but they rarely do so in Korea, and instead rely more on currency, credit cards, debit cards or other means of payment.

Checks are payments orders redeemable from bank, while a bill (or more formally called a *bill of exchange*) is a payment order redeemable from any institution or individual.[38] Also, payments from checks are usually redeemed and settled *on demand*, but the issuer of a bill is usually entitled to three days before the payment is made. Similarly, when a bill can not be settled due to lack of funds, the recipient must notify the issuer to make the latter liable. But the issuer of a check is automatically liable if it can not be redeemed and settled (on demand).

Checks include *cashier's checks* (issued by a bank cashier or teller), in which the bank secures settlement by making the issuer deposit funds into a separate account before the check is issued. These checks can be blank and issued in any amount, but are often issued in standard amounts of 100,000 won, 500,000 won and 1,000,000 won. Recipients can cash or deposit the checks at ATMs.

Bills can be *promissory notes*—notes or certificates by which the issuer promises to pay a certain amount to the recipient. Promissory notes are used mainly in commercial transactions or as a form of credit between financial institutions. For example, promissory notes are often issued by a corporation's finance department to pay for goods or services on short-term credit.

Similar to currency payments, the share of payments by (paper) checks and bills have become less important since about 2000, as electronic funds transfers and (other) electronic payments become more popular. Figure 8-1 shows that the total volume and value of checks and bills has declined recently, partly due to the fact that checks and bills were traditionally issued on paper.

[38] However, the Bank of Korea calls a check that is issued by a corporation similar to a (bank) cashier's check a corporate "check" instead of a corporate bill of exchange.

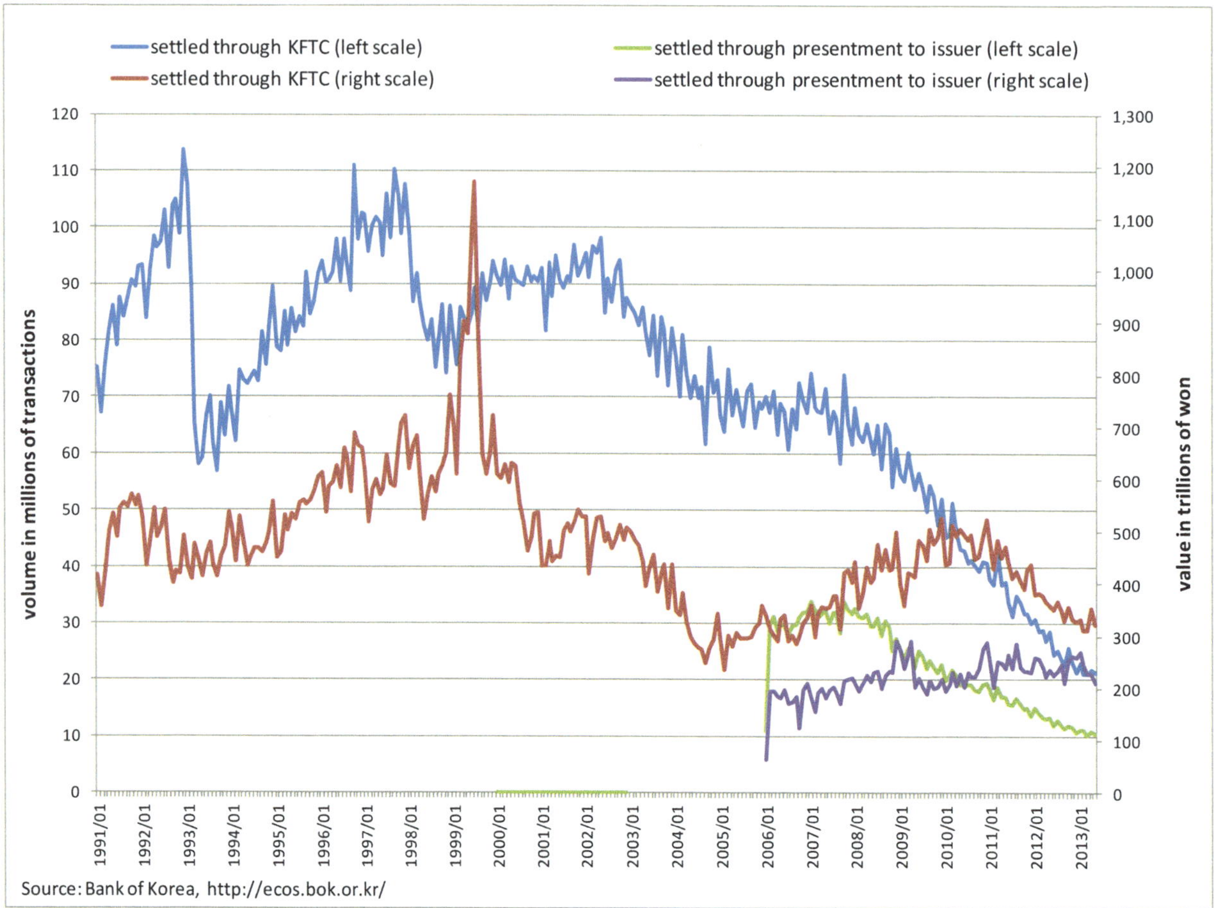

Figure 8-1: Volume and value of checks and bills settled through the KFTC and presentment to issuer in Korea, 1991.01-2103.05

However, checks and bills are now all settled electronically, even those originally issued on paper. Since November 2010, all paper checks and bills in Korea have been settled through the KFTC after scanning or "truncating" them. The payee's bank scans the check using an electronic scanner and sends the information to the KFTC.

After receiving electronic information from a check on day *T*, the KFTC calculates the *net* (credit – debit) *multilateral* (for multiple parties involved) obligation of each bank and sends the information to the BOK for final settlement on day *T*+1 at 11:00. With sufficient funds to pay for the check, the payee's account is credited after 14:20 on the same day.

But when a payer (check issuer) has insufficient funds to cash the check or bill, the payer's bank must notify the payee's bank no later than 14:00 on day *T*+1. The payee's bank does not credit the funds to the payee's account until the payer deposits sufficient money in his account. If the issuer of the check fails to deposit the necessary amount in his account by the end of business hours on day *T*+1, the check is dishonored. It may be re-settled on the next day if the check issuer has deposited funds by then.

Checks and bills can also be settled through presentment to the issuer. **Presentment** refers to presenting or submitting a check or bill for payment settlement, before the actual settlement. In other words, it refers simply to the process by which a payee (payer) presents a bill to the payer (payee). When banks or other payees present a check or bill to the issuer, they can settle payments directly among themselves through an inter-bank transfer without the KFTC. Most inter-bank transfers occur through the BOK Wire, which we discuss in a later section. Figure 8-1 distinguishes between the checks settled through presentment to the issuer and those settled via the KFTC.

Giro network and Cash Management System (CMS). The Giro network and Cash Management System (CMS) are two systems that are used for transfers of funds. They are especially convenient for large volumes of regular payments—such as payments for wages and salaries, credit cards, insurance, pensions or other payments from wages and salaries. Both individuals and institutions use the Giro system, but mostly firms or businesses use the CMS because it allows bank customers with several bank accounts in more than one bank to send and receive transfers in a systematic way.

The Giro network allows payers to transfer funds to recipients with a bank account anywhere in the country. The bills to transfer funds can be paper-based or electronic, although institutions and individuals increasingly use electronic bills.

The internet Giro network, in which electronic bills are presented and paid via the internet, was set up in March 2000. Payees request a (debit) transfer by sending payment details to the KFTC, which notifies the payers via the internet. Then the payer initiates the payment via the internet, and the transfer is completed electronically. The internet service can save printing and mailing costs, as well as time because payers do not need to visit bank branches or ATMs.

Transfers of funds via the Giro network and the CMS can be credit transfers or debit transfers, both of which are transmitted via the KFTC and settled via accounts at the BOK. In a *credit* transfer, the payer or the payer's bank (or more generally, the payer's "payment service provider") originates the electronic instructions and sends the instructions and the funds to the payee, whose account is credited. Credit transfers include direct deposit of wages, government transfer payments and business payments to wholesale vendors. Figure 8-2 represents a credit transfer via the KFTC and the BOK.

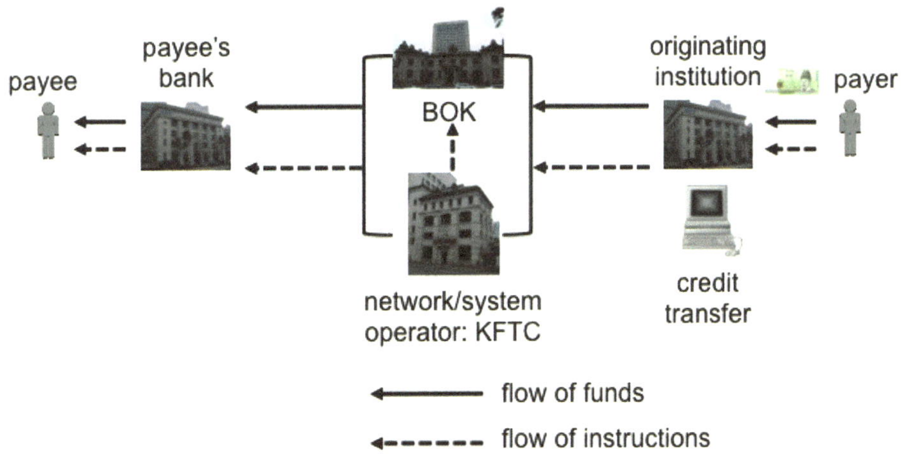

Figure 8-2: A credit transfer via the Bank of Korea and the KFTC.

In a *debit* transfer, the payee or the payee's bank originates the electronic instructions and sends the instructions to the payer, whose account at the BOK is debited by the KFTC, after which money flows to the payee. In a debit transfer, the payer and its bank give advanced authorization for the payee and its bank to debit/deduct funds from the payer's account. Debit transfers include payments for checks that are electronically processed, loan payments, insurance payments and other payments that consumers approve to be automatically debited from their accounts. In addition, individuals and institutions can make tax payments to the national government using a debit transfer. (They can receive tax refunds/reimbursement from the national government using a credit transfer.) Figure 8-3 represents a debit transfer via the KFTC and the BOK.

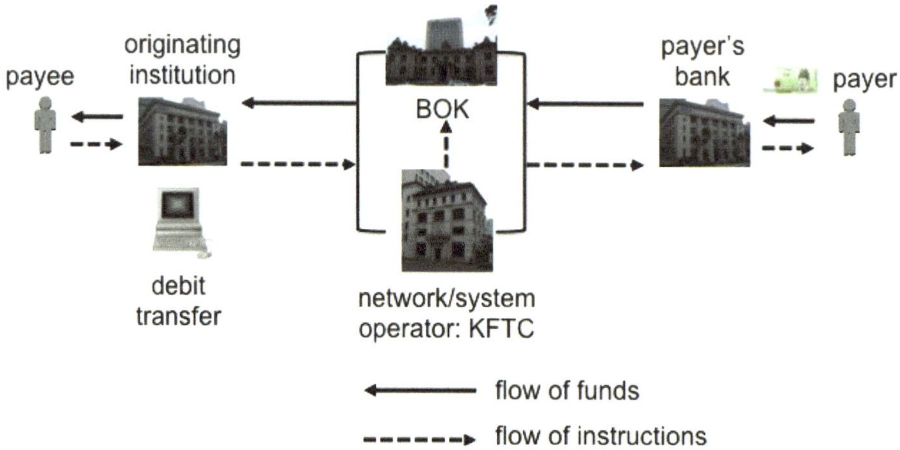

Figure 8-3: A debit transfer via the Bank of Korea and the KFTC.

The KFTC uses different procedures to settle transfers via the Giro network and CMS, depending on whether the bill requests a credit transfer or a debit transfer. Giro bills for a credit transfer can be paper or electronic, but all Giro bills requesting debit transfers are processed electronically. And all bills in the CMS, requesting debit *or* credit transfers, are processed electronically.

When a payer's bank delivers instructions for a credit transfer from a paper or electronic Giro bill to the KFTC on day *T*, the KFTC calculates the net multilateral obligation of members and sends instructions to payee's bank on day *T*+1 and to the BOK by 10:00 on day *T*+2. The BOK then settles the net multilateral obligations at 11:00 on day *T*+2, allowing the payee's bank and the payee to receive the funds.

A credit transfer via the CMS is similar to an electronic credit transfer via the Giro network.

When a payee's bank delivers instructions for a debit transfer from an electronic Giro bill to the KFTC on day *T*, the KFTC notifies the payer's bank on the same day. The payer's bank withdraws the funds from the payer's account on day *T*+1 and transmits the funds and the information to the KFTC on day *T*+2. The KFTC calculates the net multilateral obligations of members in the network and then sends the information to the BOK on day *T*+4. The BOK settles the payments on that day, allowing the payee's bank and the payee to receive the funds.

A debit transfer via the CMS is similar to an electronic debit transfer via the Giro network, except that settlement via accounts at the BOK occurs more quickly than with Giro transfers. When a payee's bank delivers instructions for a debit transfer from a CMS bill to the KFTC on day *T*, the KFTC notifies the payer's bank on the same day, as with a Giro debit transfer. The payer's bank withdraws the funds from the payer's account on day *T*+1 and transmits the funds and the information to the KFTC on day *T*+2. The KFTC calculates the net multilateral obligations and then sends the information to the BOK on day *T*+2.

The BOK settles the payments on that day, allowing the payee's bank and the payee to receive the funds on that day, which is 2 days more quickly than with a Giro debit transfer.

Figure 8-4 shows that the volume and value of Giro debit transfers have increased rapidly during the last two decades and that the volume of Giro paper credit transfers has declined during the last decade. The volume of Giro electronic credit transfers has grown somewhat during the last decade, although it has declined slightly during the last few years. Figure 8-5 shows that the value of all kinds of Giro transfers has increased during the last two decades; the value of Giro debit transfers has increased the most rapidly.

Figure 8-6 shows that CMS debit transfers are larger in volume and value than CMS credit transfers, and that the volume and value of CMS credit transfers have decline sharply recently.

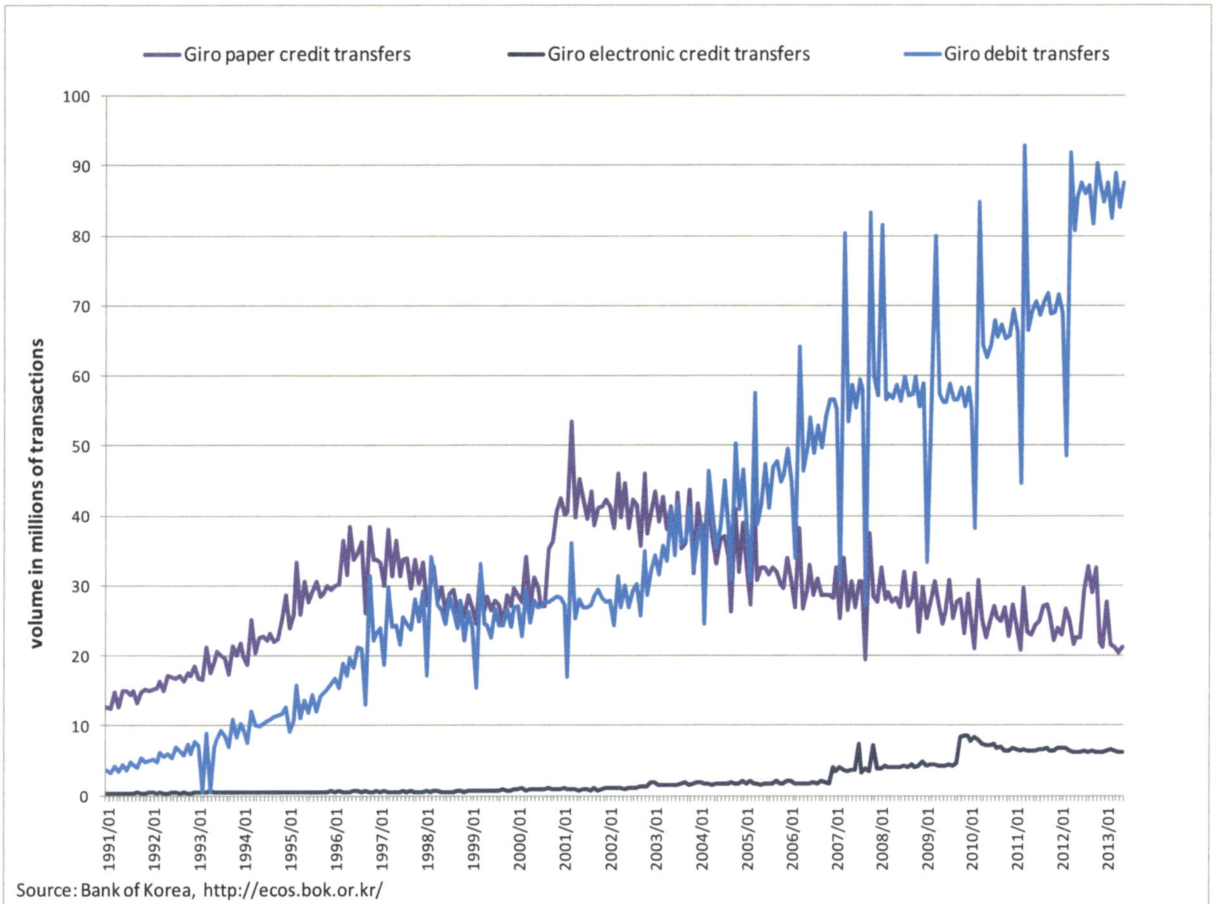

Figure 8-4: Volume of Giro credit and debit transfers in Korea, 1991.01-2103.05

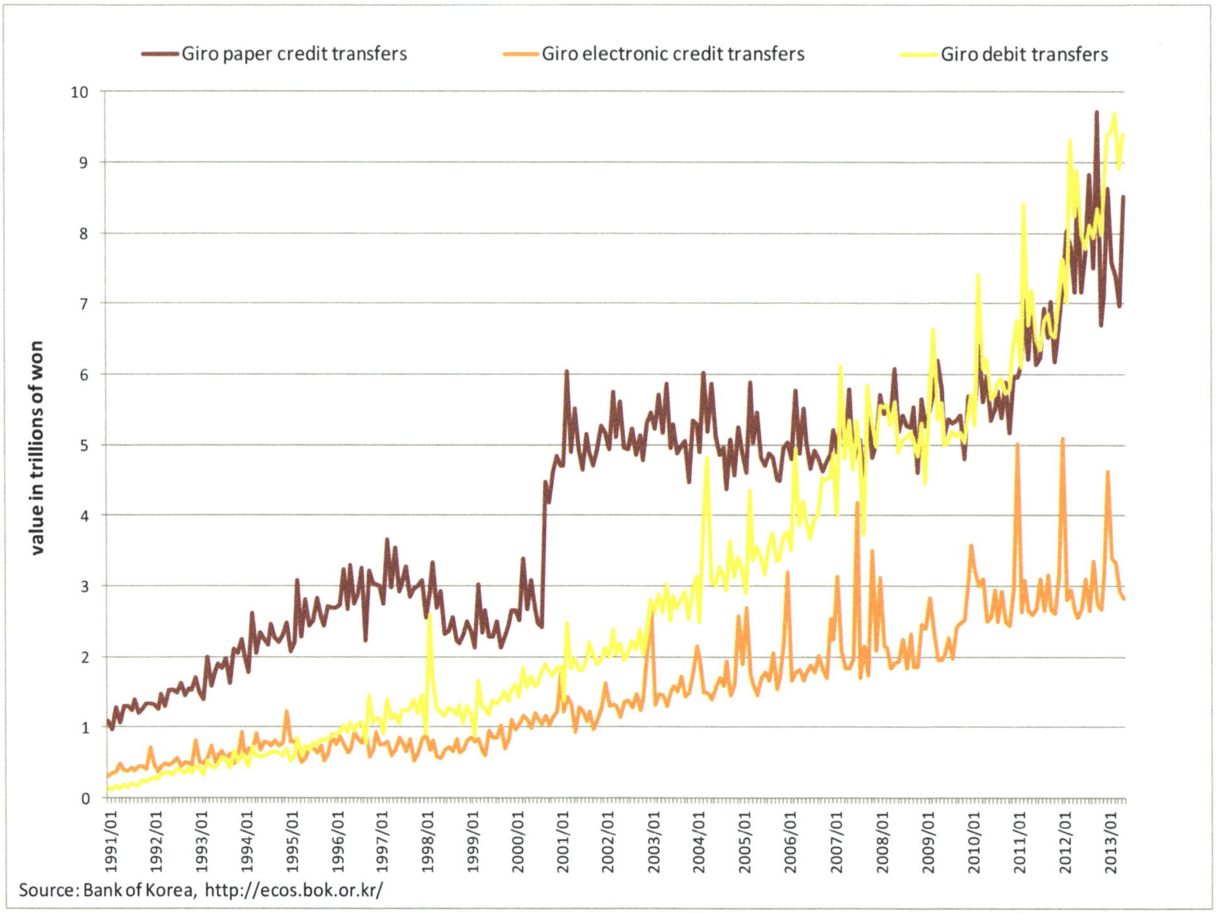

Figure 8-5: Value of Giro credit and debit transfers in Korea, 1991.01-2103.05

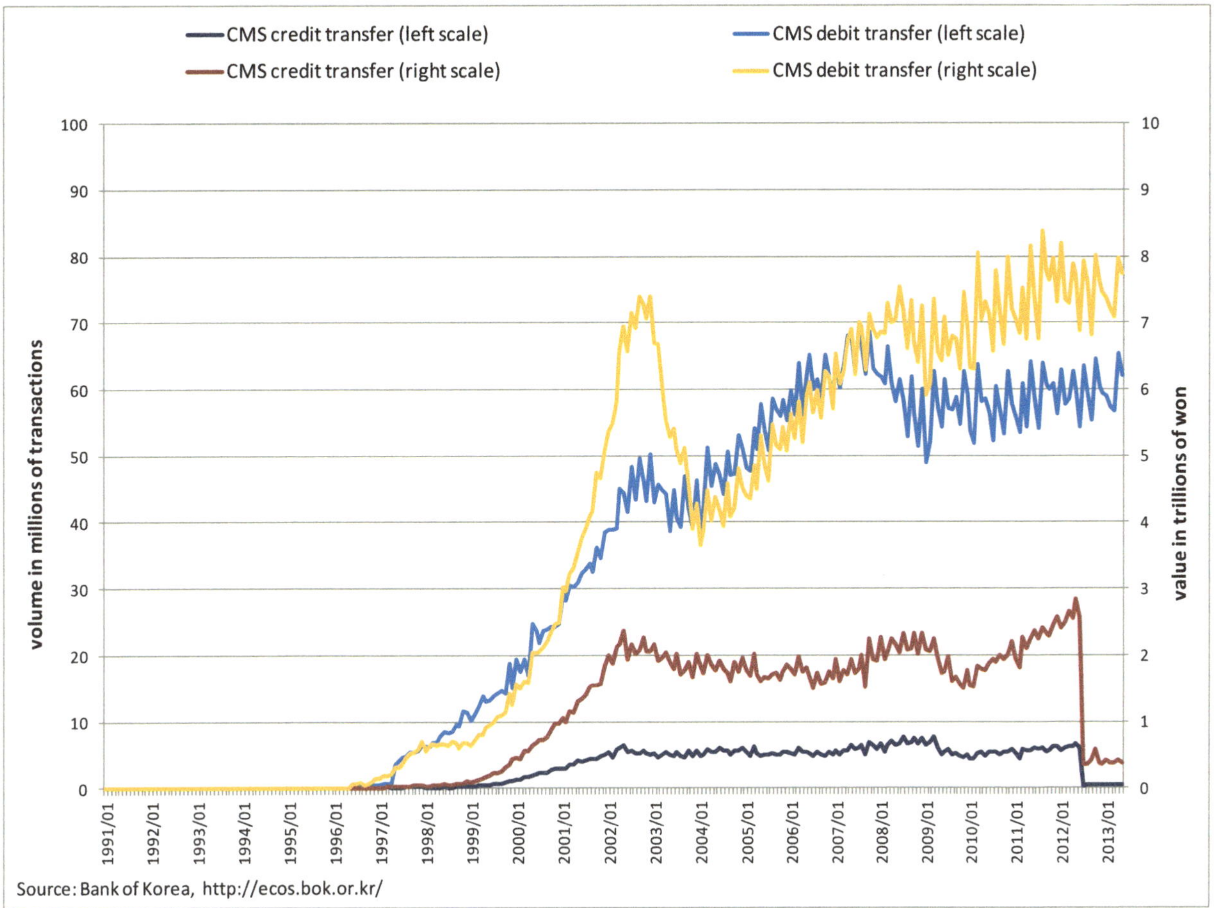

Figure 8-6: Volume and value of CMS credit and debit transfers in Korea, 1991.01-2103.05

The Interbank Remittance System, the Electronic Banking System and ATM networks. In contrast to the Giro network and the CMS, the Interbank Remittance System, the Electronic Banking System and ATM networks are primarily used for transfers of irregular payments. These systems accept electronic credit transfers only, in which the payer initiates the transfer electronically.

Unlike the Giro network and the CMS, the Interbank Remittance System does not require that the payee or payer have a bank account. The payer can transfer funds from a bank teller, after the payer pays the bank teller with cash or through another payment system, up to 100 million won. Once the payer has transferred the funds via the system, the recipient can immediately acquire the funds through another bank teller's window.

More specifically, after a payer submits a transfer through a bank teller on day *T*, the bank sends the instructions to the KFTC, which then sends the instructions to the payee's bank. As soon as it receives these instructions, the payee's bank allows the payee to withdraw funds in cash. The KFTC then calculates the net multilateral obligations on the following business day (*T*+1) and sends the information to the BOK, which settles the payments on the same day.

The Electronic Banking System uses the internet, mobile phones or traditional telephones to transfer funds. It is part of internet banking, which we consider later. Because of transactions on the internet, Electronic Banking System has grown rapidly during the last decade.

When a payer uses the Electronic Banking System on day *T*, the information is sent to the KFTC via the internet or telephone networks, which then transmits the information to the payee's bank. As soon as the payee's bank receives the information, it credits the payee's account. The KFTC then calculates the net multilateral obligations on the following business day (*T*+1) and sends the information to the BOK, which settles the payments on the same day.

Credit transfers can also be initiated through ATM networks, even if the ATMs are operated by different banks or companies. However, because of the risk involved with ATM withdrawals especially from customers of different banks or companies, banks may set withdrawal and transfer limits for individual customers, up to the maximum values determined by the Financial Services Commission.

When a payer initiates a credit transfer through an ATM on day *T*, the KFTC and the payee's bank are notified through the ATM network. As soon as the payee's bank receives the information, it credits the payee's account. The KFTC then calculates the net multilateral obligations on the following business day (*T*+1) and sends the information to the BOK, which settles the payments on the same day.

When a customer tries to withdraw cash through an ATM of another bank on day *T*, the transaction details are quickly sent to the KFTC and to his bank electronically. The customer's bank verifies the transaction details and if valid, the customer's bank sends verification to the bank operating the ATM. This allows the customer to withdraw cash almost immediately. As with the Interbank Remittance System and the Electronic Banking System, KFTC then calculates the net multilateral obligations on the following business day (*T*+1) and sends the information to the BOK, which settles the payments on the same day.

When a customer tries to withdraw cash through his bank's ATM, the transaction details are processed within the bank's internal (electronic) accounting system: debiting the customer's deposit and debiting the reserves (cash) of the bank at the same time. The KFTC and the BOK are not directly involved in this kind of payment.

Figure 8-7 shows the volume and value of transfers made through the Interbank Remittance System, the Electronic Banking System and the ATM network. The Electronic Banking System has grown most rapidly in volume and in value, as banks and other financial institutions increasingly rely on internet transfers. Transactions via ATM networks have also grown, but not as rapidly. Use of the Interbank Remittance System has declined.

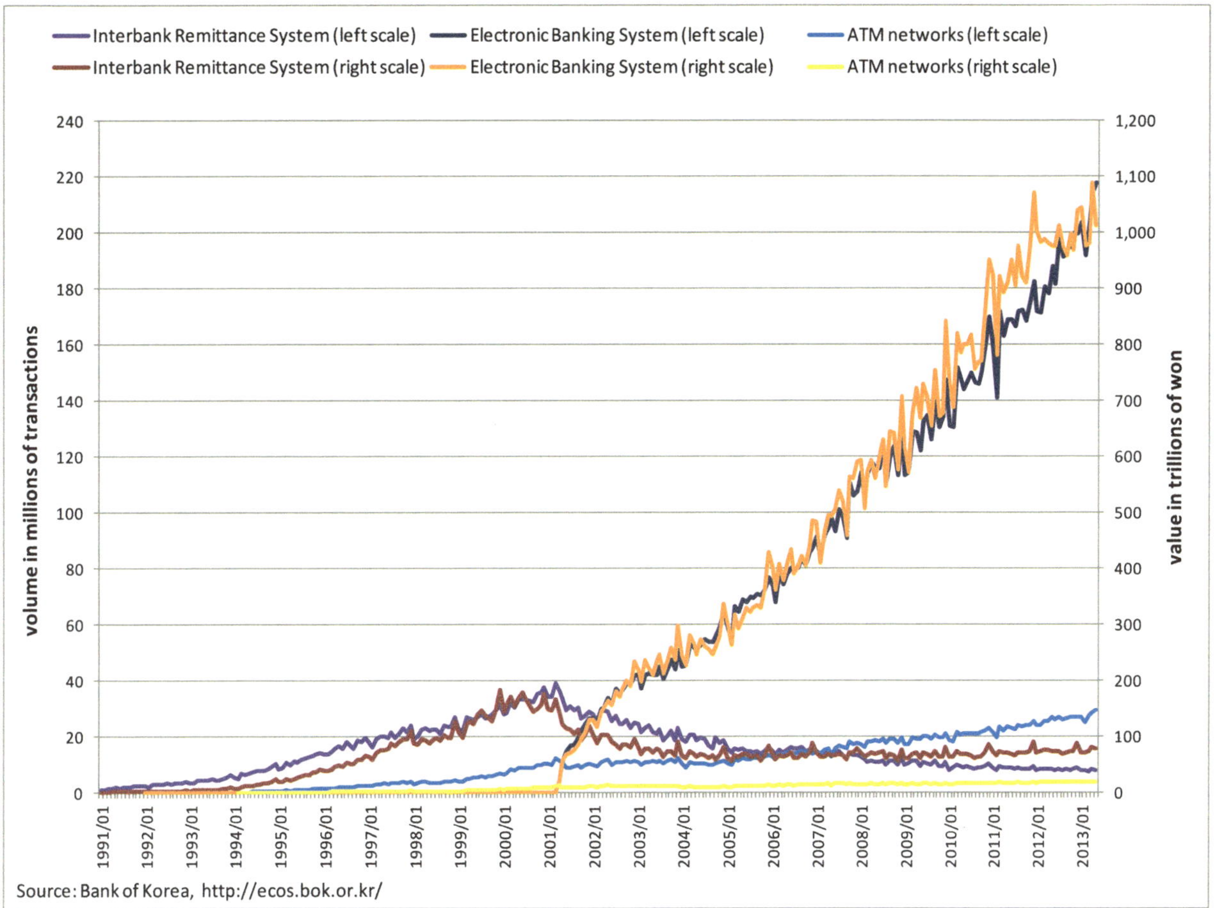

Figure 8-7: Volume and value of transfers using the Interbank Remittance System, the Electronic Banking System and the ATM networks in Korea, 1991.01-2013.05

Credit card and debit card networks. Separate from the payment settlement systems owned and operated by the KFTC, credit card banks and other private financial institutions own and operate several card payment systems that can read credit cards, debit cards and prepaid cards. However, these financial institutions use the KFTC to help settle payments between banks in the networks.

Credit cards are the most widely used card in Korea. There are 11 domestic credit card brands are currently issued by banks and specialized credit card companies, which frequently use foreign brands like Visa and MasterCard to make them more popular. These 11 banks and credit card companies form a network called the BC Card network to settle payments between cardholders and merchants. In addition, five solely foreign brands are sometimes accepted in this network depending on the merchants.

When a cardholder (buyer) uses a credit card from one 11 domestic BC Card members for a transaction, the network sends the information electronically to the card issuer for approval. If the transaction is approved, the payee (seller) will then send the transaction information to its bank, which will request an inter-bank payment from the card issuer. The card issuer will then send the funds to the payee's bank in one to two days, directly if it is a bank or indirectly (through a bank) if it is a non-bank credit card company. In addition, the card issuer will bill the cardholder and request payment from the cardholder in approximately 30 days. At that time, the cardholder can pay fully to avoid interest charges or may only partially pay if he wants to pay interest later.

Card issuers charge sometimes users annual membership fees and always charge merchants who accept credit cards transaction fees. The average merchant transaction fee was 2.2% of the transaction in 2009. There are no inter-bank, or *interchange*, fees because all credit card transactions are cleared through the KFTC and the BOK regardless of which bank issued a credit card.

Debit cards are the second most widely used card in Korea. In the past, debit cards were in the past used mainly by people who were ineligible for credit cards, since they provided fewer rewards than credit cards. Recently, however, they have become more popular as a way to restrict impulse spending and debt. There are two kinds of debit cards in Korea: debit cards that authorize a transaction via the cardholder's signature and debit cards that authorize a transaction via a cardholder's personal identification number (PIN).[39]

Signature-based debit cards are issued by credit card companies and use the more extensive networks shared with credit cards. As a result of the more extensive networks, signature-based debit cards are more popular than PIN-based debit cards. Each day, this network calculates the net multilateral obligation of members and settles payments in one to two days. In effect, debit card transactions using a signature and a credit card network are like credit card transactions that are automatically paid in one to two days. As with credit card transactions, members of the network may need to provide collateral to decrease credit risk.

Alternatively, local banks issue PIN-based debit cards, and their payments are settled via a separate network called the electronic funds transfer at the point of sale (EFTPOS) network. PIN-based debit cards are not widely used in Korea partly because local banks have not built national networks and the cards can only be used when the EFTPOS network operates from 08:00 to 23:00. In contrast to credit card and signature-based debit card networks, PIN-based debit card networks can settle transactions almost immediately through inter-bank transfers, so credit risk is less of a concern.

Prepaid cards are not widely used in Korea. Credit card issuers issue the few prepaid cards in Korea, which are usually used at gasoline stations, department stores and at a few other retailers that have access to credit card networks.

Figure 8-8 shows the volume and value of transactions by credit cards, signature-based debit cards, PIN-based debit cards and prepaid cards in Korea. Credit card transactions are the most popular, and signature-based debit card transactions are also growing in volume and value.

[39] To distinguish the two kinds of cards, banks in Korea often call signature-based debit cards "check" cards, because funds are debited from a checking deposit after signing a transaction receipt (in a way similar to a writing a check).

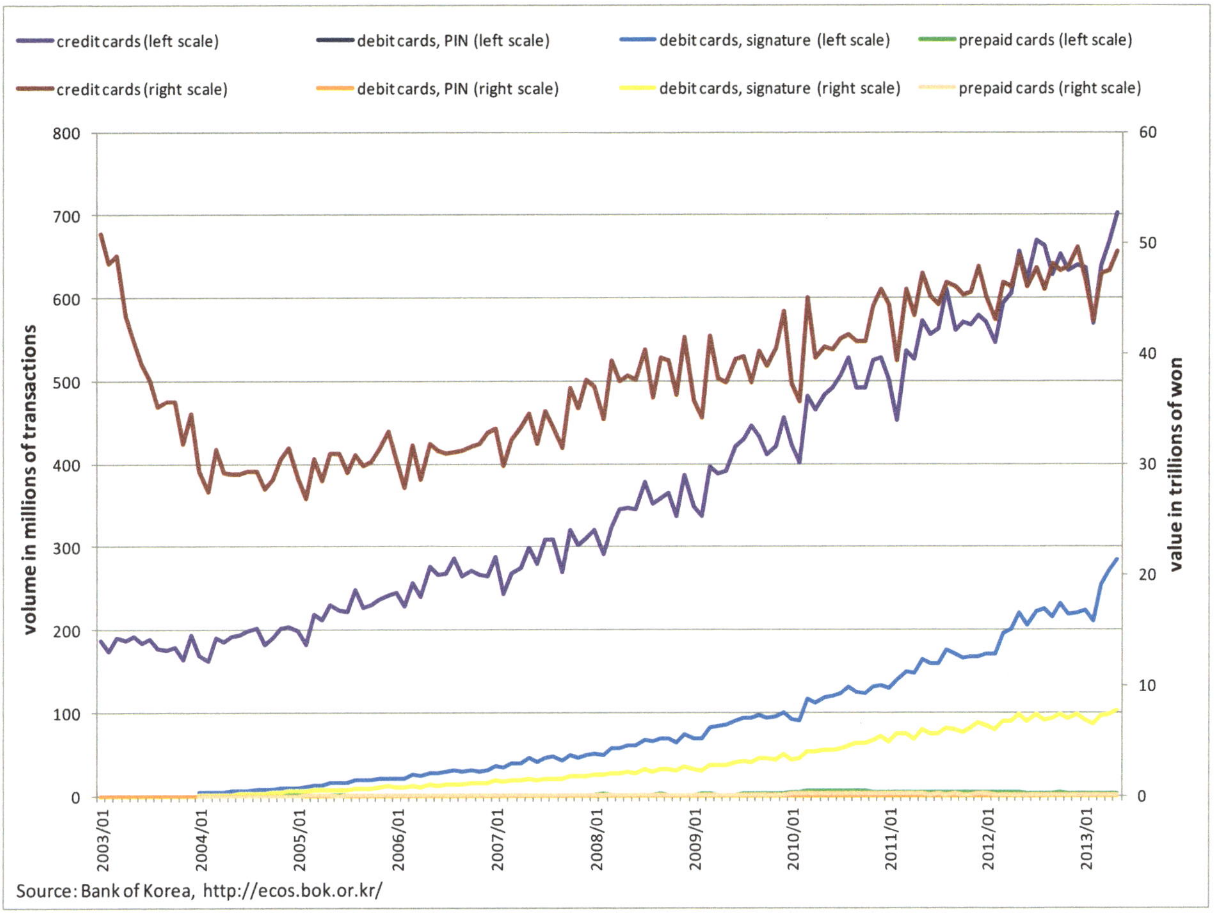

Figure 8-8: Volume and value of transactions by credit, debit or prepaid cards in Korea, 2003.01-2103.05

Foreign exchange settlement systems. Financial institutions in Korea, including foreign bank branches, can transfer foreign exchange funds in up to 20 currencies through the systems privately owned and operated by several domestic banks. KEB, Kookmin Bank and Shinhan Bank are three examples of Korean banks that operate their own foreign exchange settlement systems. These systems typically transfer relatively small values of retail foreign exchange and corresponding domestic currency funds. In contrast, we consider wholesale market transactions in the next section, which are typically large value transfers (US $1 million or more). But like the wholesale market transactions, these private systems are able to transfer funds immediately.

Domestic banks operate their foreign currency payment settlement systems typically from 09:00 to 17:00. In other words, it might not be possible to buy and to sell foreign exchange in Korea through these networks when traders and dealers in foreign countries are operating.

To use these systems, the payer and the payer's bank sends foreign exchange to the operator of the foreign exchange settlement system and requests that it transfer the funds to the payee and the payee's bank. For the transaction to be accepted, both the payer's bank and the payee's bank must have accounts with the operator (settlement bank). If the payer's bank balance in foreign currency is insufficient, the settlement bank might provide limited intra-day credit in foreign currency to limit credit risk for its system. Such credit would be repaid by a correspondent bank in a foreign country acting on behalf of the payer's bank (which is also usually in a foreign country).

To the degree that they offer intra-day credit, settlement banks are exposed to credit risk and liquidity risk themselves. For credit in some currencies, settlement banks are unable to confirm until the following business day whether intra-day credit has been repaid by an overseas correspondent bank. To mitigate these risks, settlement banks limit intra-day credit according to the borrower's credit rating, frequency of transactions in the settlement bank's system and the quantity of assets.

Risk management in retail payment settlement systems. Credit risk, liquidity risk and settlement risk can be problems in any payment settlement system where one bank or the operator of the system credits the payee's account without having yet received the funds from the payer's bank. This can occur in retail foreign exchange settlement systems, the Interbank Remittance System, the Electronic Banking System and ATM networks. For the last three systems, the payee's bank immediately credits funds to the payees' accounts and the corresponding inter-bank obligations are settled on the following business day. And because the payee's bank has obligations to other banks, systemic risk also occurs. More generally, liquidity risk and settlement risk can occur in any system when the payee is expecting that the payment will be settled on time, but it is not because of a lack of funds from the payer. When the payee is a bank itself, systemic risk again occurs.

To limit these risks, the Bank of Korea requires 1) net debit limits for some systems, 2) collateral for all systems and 3) loss-sharing agreements by members of each system. It also requires that 4) members who are non-bank credit institutions (those without required reserves) in each system use a correspondent bank (with required reserves) that guarantees the payments for the non-bank institution. I discuss each of these requirements in more detail:

A **net debit limit** is a limit on member's maximum net obligation (debit amount). If a member's net obligation exceeds this limit in a given system, it is not allowed to send additional payment orders through that system until its net obligation is reduced below the limit. The Interbank Remittance System, the Electronic Banking System and the ATM network all use net debit limits. Perhaps surprisingly, members of these systems set their own limits, but the BOK uses this self-imposed limit to calculate the required collateral, which we consider next.

Each retail payment settlement system requires *collateral* from members. If a member defaults on a particular transaction or goes bankrupt in general, the BOK can sell the collateral to settle outstanding transactions. Acceptable collateral includes Korean government bonds, bonds guaranteed by the government and central bank bonds (called Monetary Stabilization Bonds). For systems that use a net debit limit, the required collateral equals 30% of this limit. For systems that do not use a net debit limit, the required collateral equals 30% of the daily average of the net payments during the previous 6 months. The BOK also watches the daily market values of the collateral, and if these values decrease, members are required to provide more collateral to meet the 30% targets.

In the event of a default, if the collateral is not sufficient to settle the defaulting member's payments, all other members in the system must collectively pay for the loss so that outstanding payments can be settled. This agreement is called **loss sharing**. The fraction of the loss that each of the other members must pay for depends on their own required collateral. Once payment orders from the defaulted member have been settled, the defaulted member is obligated to repay the other members with interest at a rate determined in the loss sharing agreement.

When non-bank credit institutions and financial investment institutions are allowed to use retail payment settlement systems, the values of their net obligations are usually similar to regular banks of similar size.[40] However, non-bank credit institutions and financial investment institutions are not required to submit reserves to the BOK and therefore have a higher risk of not having sufficient funds in the current accounts that the BOK uses to settle payments in retail payment settlement systems. Because of this higher risk, the BOK requires non-bank credit institutions and financial investment institutions to use a correspondent bank that guarantees their obligations in a retail payment settlement system.

Inter-bank (wholesale) payment settlement systems

BOK Wire. The Bank of Korea (BOK) settles payments on behalf of private financial institutions and government financial institutions by using a payment settlement system called the BOK Wire. Private financial institutions and government financial institutions submit payment orders to the BOK Wire, which settles them depending on the type of payment order. Government financial institutions that are members of the BOK Wire include including the KFTC and the Ministry of Strategy and Finance. Private financial institutions that are members of BOK Wire include banks, the Korea Securities Depository and Continuous Linked Settlement (CLS), an international institution that uses the BOK Wire for foreign exchange transactions. At the end of 2009, there were 129 members of BOK Wire, 53 banks and 76 non-bank institutions. In June 2010, the BOK opened the BOK Wire to other institutions if they could find a member to act as an intermediary. To use the BOK Wire, members must maintain accounts with the BOK and dedicate at least six people within the institution to processing the transactions. Members must also maintain an average of at least 50 transactions per month.

The BOK Wire is divided into two sub-systems, and members sometimes can choose the system that is more convenient depending on their available liquidity. The first sub-system is the traditional system that settles many payments as soon as they are submitted ("in real time") by a single party and on a gross basis. This system is called the *real time gross settlement (RTGS) system.* Secondly, the BOK started another payment settlement system in 2009 that can settle payments by using bilateral or multilateral offsetting (calculating net values), and these transactions are not necessarily settled immediately. But these transactions are settled quickly, often in 30 minutes or less, as soon as counterparties have submitted their payment orders. This second system is called the *hybrid (payment settlement) system*, because it can use offsetting bilateral settlement, offsetting multilateral settlement, as well as the traditional real time gross settlement (without offsetting).

To settle payments using these two systems, members of the BOK Wire hold two accounts for payment settlement. One is a *current account* for RTGS system; the second is a *deposit account* for a hybrid payment settlement system. When submitting payment orders, members classify them either for the RTGS system using their current account or for the hybrid system using their deposit account.

The BOK Wire settles the payments from retail payment settlement systems, including those calculated by the KFTC and credit/debt card banks. The BOK Wire also allows members to transfer funds between themselves, including for inter-bank loans, to transfer funds to a third party, to trade and to repurchase government securities, to issue and to redeem government securities, and to transfer foreign exchange.

[40] Non-bank credit institutions are savings banks and credit unions or federations of them. Financial investment institutions trade or broker financial securities or provide another financial investment activity according to the Financial Investment Services and Capital Markets Act of 2009.

Since November 1999, the BOK has allowed Korea Securities Depository to use the BOK Wire to simultaneously transfer, or *to deliver*, securities and the corresponding cash payment on behalf of its customers. The Korea Securities Depository calls this simultaneous transfer a *delivery versus payment* (DVP) service. Simultaneously transferring securities and payment for these securities is supposed to eliminate the settlement risk for these transactions. However, we will learn that because DVP transactions are settled within the hybrid system, they are not strictly "simultaneous" but can involve a delay of about 30 minutes or less.

Since 2004, the BOK has allowed an international financial institution called Continuous Linked Settlement (CLS) to use BOK Wire, which the company links to RTGS systems in other major countries.[41] CLS uses its current account to receive or to discharge funds in foreign currency or domestic currency on behalf of its customers. At the end of 2009, 14 domestic banks and 11 foreign bank branches in Korea used the services of CLS for real time transfers of foreign exchange. But the 11 foreign banks branches indirectly use CLS through 3 of the 14 domestic banks that use the CLS's services via the BOK Wire. The CLS accepts payment orders denominated in 17 foreign currencies.

Because the Continuous Linked Settlement company has "continuous links" to RTGS systems in other countries, it can simultaneously transfer foreign exchange and domestic currency (won), a service that it calls *payment versus payment* (PVP) service. Simultaneously transferring foreign exchange and a corresponding payment in domestic currency is supposed to eliminate the settlement risk for these transactions.

However, because foreign RTGS are not always open during the business hours of the BOK Wire, many PVP transfers are not always strictly "simultaneous". The settlement for payments involving currencies from countries in the Asia-Pacific region is simultaneous and occurs at 14:00-17:00 Korean Standard Time, which is 07:00-10:00 Central European Time and 00:00-03:00 Eastern Standard Time.

When payment orders are sent to/from foreign countries through the BOK Wire, CLS must convert these orders from/to the electronic format of the BOK Wire, which is not the same as the electronic format of foreign RTGS systems. Foreign currency payment orders from foreign countries use an electronic format from the Society for Worldwide Interbank Financial Telecommunication (SWIFT), but this format is not compatible the BOK Wire's network.

The BOK also uses the BOK Wire to conduct normal monetary policy: to allow institutions to apply for discount loans, to transfer funds from these loans and repurchases of government securities, and to purchase and to sell government securities outright.

On behalf of the Ministry of Strategy and Finance, the BOK also collects taxes, fines and other duties from members and issues (sells) new government securities through the BOK Wire.

Figure 8-9 shows the BOK Wire separated into two subsystems, one using a current account and the other using a deposit account, and what kinds of payments these accounts are used to settle. Funds transfers for retail payment settlement systems, issuing and redeeming government securities, BOK loans, foreign exchange transactions with the CLS use the real time gross payment system. Payments for general funds transfers, short-term inter-bank loans, transfers of securities via the Korea Securities Depository (DVP transactions) and repurchasing of existing government securities use the hybrid system.

---

[41] According to US law, CLS is regulated as an Edge Act corporation.

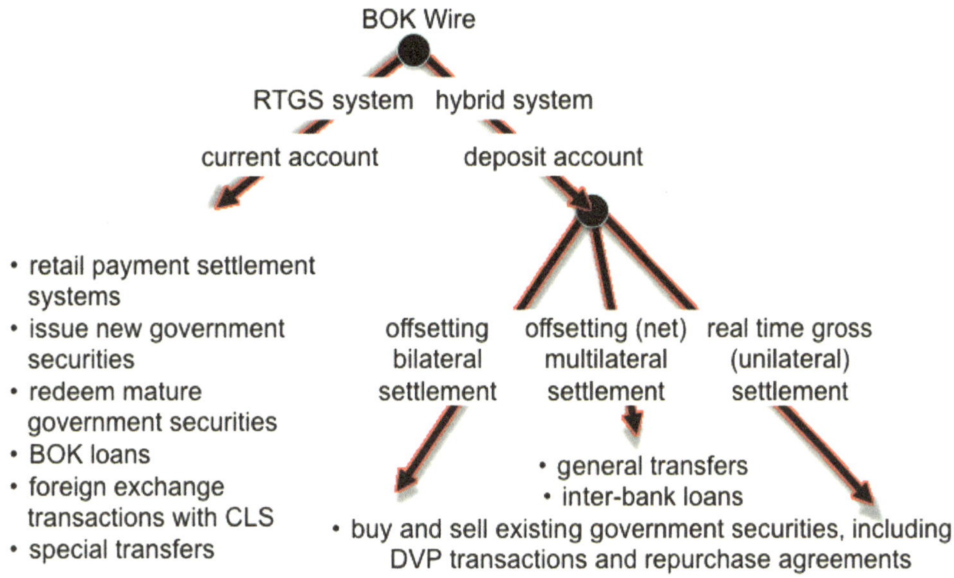

Figure 8-9: The BOK Wire is divided into the real time gross settlement (RTGS) system and a hybrid payment settlement system that uses offsetting bilateral transactions, offsetting multilateral transactions or real time gross (unilateral) settlement to settle various payments.

The operating hours of BOK Wire are 9:00–17:30 from Monday to Friday. The BOK may extend these hours temporarily if deemed necessary.

Even though the RTGS system is called a "real time" (an immediate) payment settlement system, some payments are settled only at designed times during the day. The BOK Wire settles net multilateral obligations from retail payment systems at 11:00, with the exception of check clearing houses outside of Seoul, whose payments are settled at 14:00. Repayments of loans to the BOK are settled at 11:05, 14:05 or 16:05 for overnight loans, morning loans and afternoon loans, respectively. Payments to and from the Ministry of Strategy and Finance are settled at 14:00.

Otherwise, payment orders using the real time gross settlement system are settled as soon as they are submitted through the payer's current account, as long as the account has a sufficient balance. The RTGS system processes payment orders using a bypass first in, first out (FIFO) rule; that is, the system attempts to settle the first payment order in a queue, but when the balance or other conditions for settlement are unsatisfied, that order is bypassed and the system attempts to settle the next order. When the conditions to settle the payment are unsatisfied, the payment order is sent to the end of the queue and not processed until sufficient funds are deposited in the current account or other necessary conditions are satisfied. Alternatively, a member can reclassify the payment order for settlement in the hybrid system with the hope that offsetting (net) settlement conditions will be satisfied.

The hybrid system allows members to conserve cash by processing orders only after their values have been offset (netted) by orders from counterparties. This offsetting can be bilateral or multilateral, and the time necessary to calculate the net values also implies that cash balances do not need to be sufficient to clear a transaction at every instant. The BOK launched this hybrid system in 2009 because the increasing volume of RTGS payment orders meant that members needed and increasing amount of cash to be sure to clear these transactions at any time when their institution or counterparties submitted payment orders. The bilateral or multilateral offsetting resulted in lower amounts of cash needed to settle payments throughout the business day.

When a member submits a payment order to the hybrid system, the hybrid system tries to match the payment order with a corresponding order from the counterparty from a short queue. If there are two orders to match and both parties have sufficient funds in their deposit accounts to settle the orders and neither party exceeds the net debit limit (see above), then the system simultaneously and bilaterally settles the two orders. Legally, the system settles both orders on a gross basis, but because the orders are matched (bilaterally) and settled simultaneously, then the payment settlement practically occurs on a net basis for both parties.

If the hybrid system can not initially match two payment orders or if there are not sufficient funds in the deposit account for either payment order or if either order exceeds the net debit limit, the system sends the order or orders to a second queue and begins to calculate the net multilateral obligations of all members in this queue. After 30 minutes of calculating and waiting, the system then proceeds to settle these net multilateral obligations for all members in the queue. If a member does not have sufficient funds in its deposit account to settle payment orders in this queue or if an order exceeds the net debit limit; the order is resubmitted to the queue, and the system tries to settle the payment order after 30 more minutes when it has recalculated the net multilateral obligations. Figure 8-10 represents the possible ways to settle a normal payment order in the hybrid system, depending on whether conditions to settle the payment order are satisfied or not.

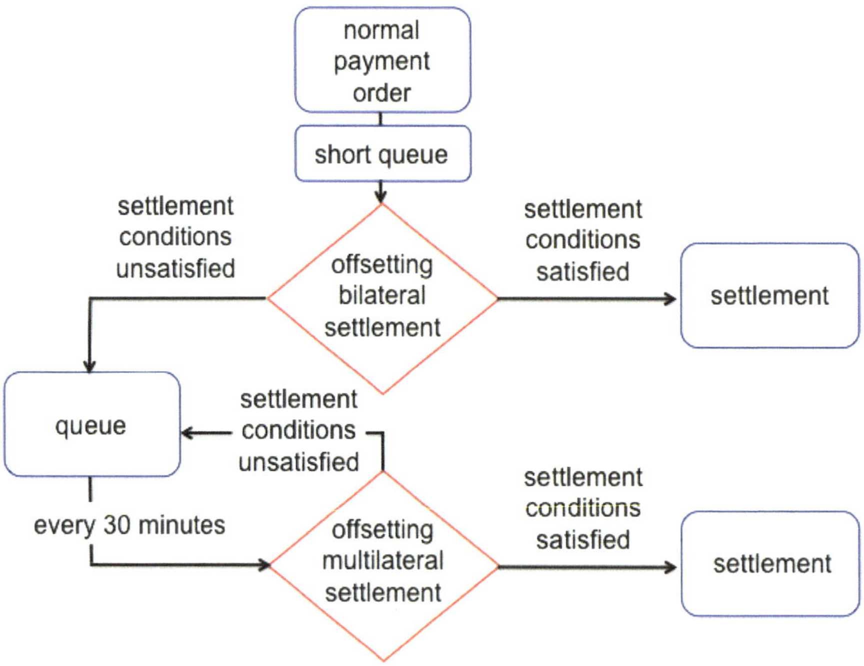

Figure 8-10: The hybrid system first tries to settle a normal payment order through bilateral offsetting. But if it fails, it then tries to settle it through multilateral offsetting every 30 minutes.

The hybrid system uses a first in, first out rule except that it distinguishes between "normal" payment orders and "urgent" payment orders. Members classify payment orders as "normal" or "urgent" when submitting them to the hybrid system. The hybrid system moves the urgent payment orders to the front of the queue and tries to settle them first using real time gross (unilateral) settlement. In other words, the system does not attempt to offset urgent payment orders. After the system attempts to settle urgent payment orders, it then proceeds to try to settle the normal payment orders, using a first in, first out rule, as shown in Figure 8-10.

While normal payment orders are queued in the hybrid system, members can adjust the priority of the payment order from "normal" to "urgent" to speed up settlement. Likewise, all payment orders in the RTGS system are considered to be urgent and processed in a bypass first in, first out rule. Figure 8-11 represents payment settlement for urgent payment orders in the hybrid system and the payment orders in the RTGS settlement, both of which use the bypass first in, first out rule without any offsetting.

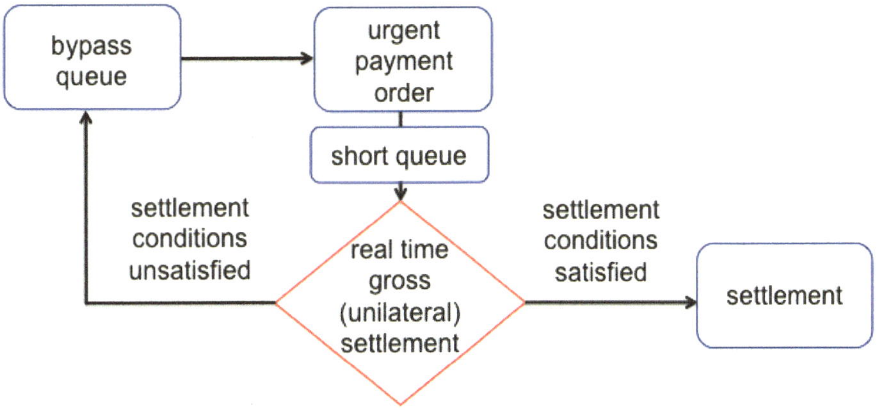

Figure 8-11: Payment settlement for urgent payment orders in the hybrid system and payment orders in the RTGS settlement both use the bypass first in, first out rule without any offsetting.

At 17:05, all payment orders in the hybrid system are reclassified as "urgent" payment orders, and settlement should occur before the close of business at 17:30.

Next, let's consider the volume and value of the various kinds of payments through the BOK Wire. Figure 8-12 shows the volume and value of real time gross settlement transfers and payments that are settled by the KFTC after it calculates net multilateral obligations from retail payment settlement systems (which are also settled by the RTGS system). The volume and value of RTGS payments generally are both larger and have grown more quickly than KFTC settlements.

Figure 8-13 shows kinds of transfers that occur through the RTGS system involving the government or central bank: transfers to and from the Ministry of Strategy and Finance (treasury department), transfers for BOK loans, and transfers for BOK repurchases of government bonds. These actions largely deal with fiscal or monetary policy to influence economic activity in the private sector. For example, the value of transfers for BOK loans was especially large in early 1998 and in 2009 due to weak economic conditions in the private sector.

Figure 8-14 shows transactions that involve short-term inter-bank loans (now settled through the hybrid system) or general transfers of cash, or *call funds*, through the RTGS system. Because general transfers are now generally handled through the hybrid system, which normally relies on offsetting, the volume and value of RTGS transfers of cash has now dropped to near zero. (No data on general cash transfers through the hybrid system are yet available.) The volume and value of inter-bank loans have risen, especially after 2009 when the hybrid system became operational.

Figure 8-15 shows transactions that involve buying and selling existing securities: general transfers of funds to buy or sell securities and transactions via the Korea Securities Depository called DVP transactions. DVP transactions are now both larger in volume and value and growing more quickly than transactions involving general transfers of funds for securities. Both general transfers and DVP transactions now occur through the hybrid system.

Figure 8-16 shows transactions that involve foreign exchange: transactions through the CLS and general transfers of funds for foreign exchange. General transfers of funds for foreign exchange remain larger than CLS transactions in terms of volume and value.

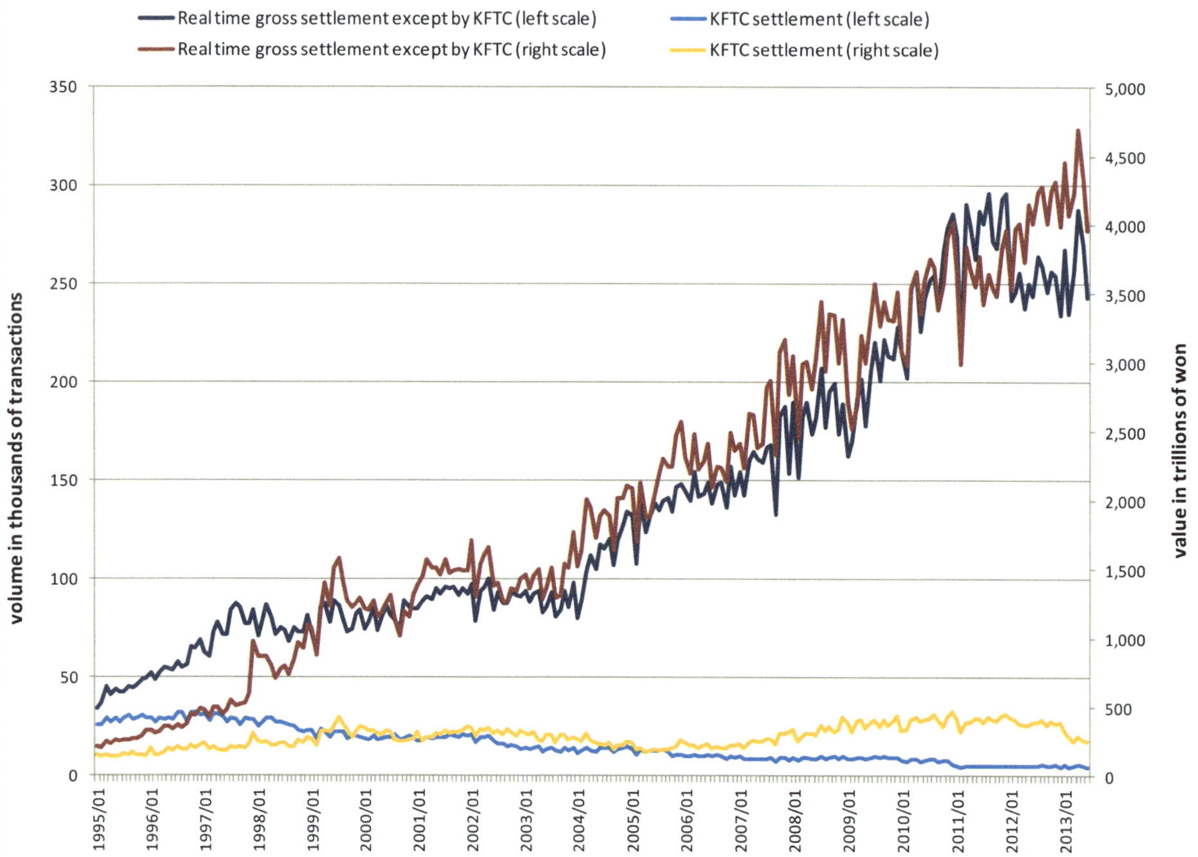

Source: Bank of Korea, http://ecos.bok.or.kr/

Figure 8-12: Volume and value of real time gross settlement transactions and net (offsetting) settlement transactions through the BOK Wire, 1995.01-2013.06

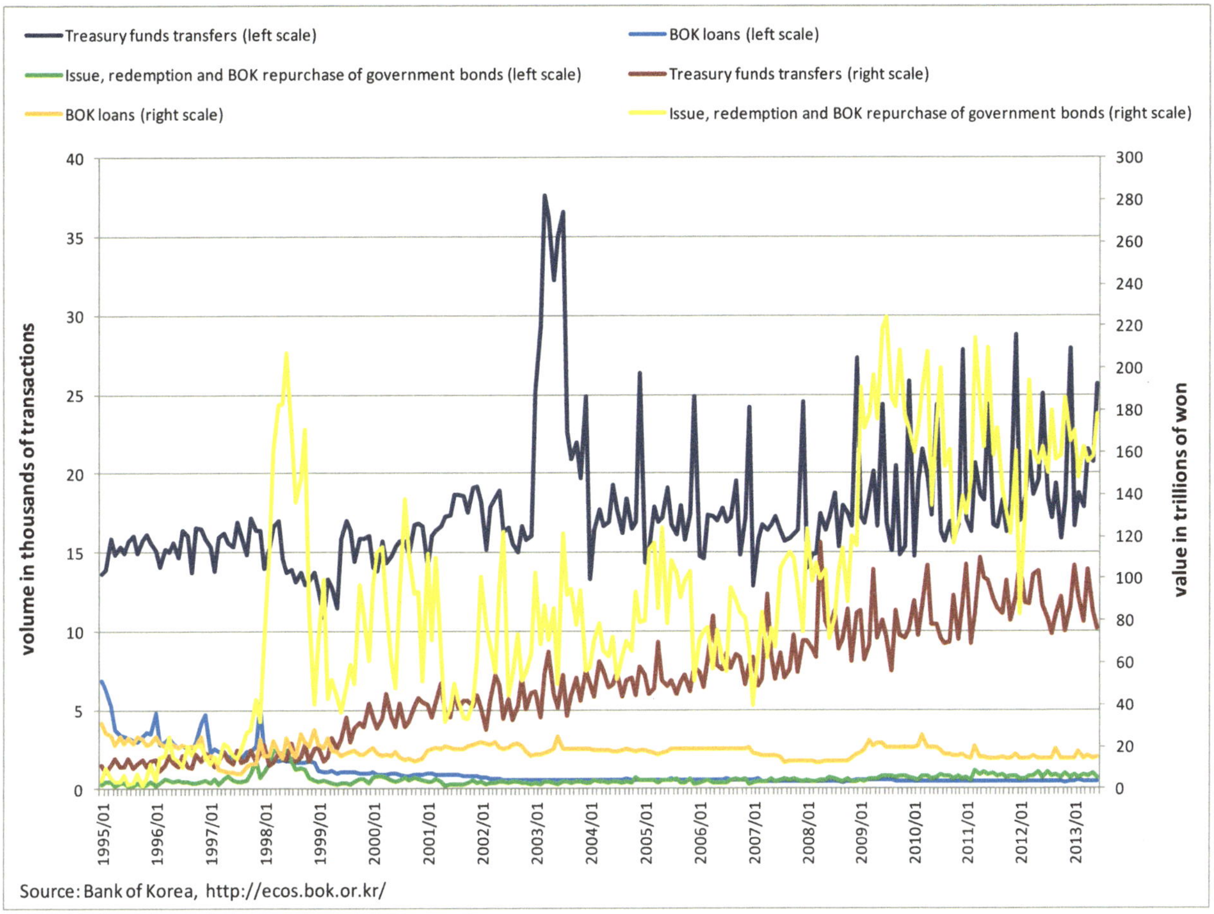

Figure 8-13: Volume and value of Treasury (Ministry of Strategy and Finance) transfers, BOK loans and BOK repurchases of government bonds through the BOK Wire, 1995.01-2013.06

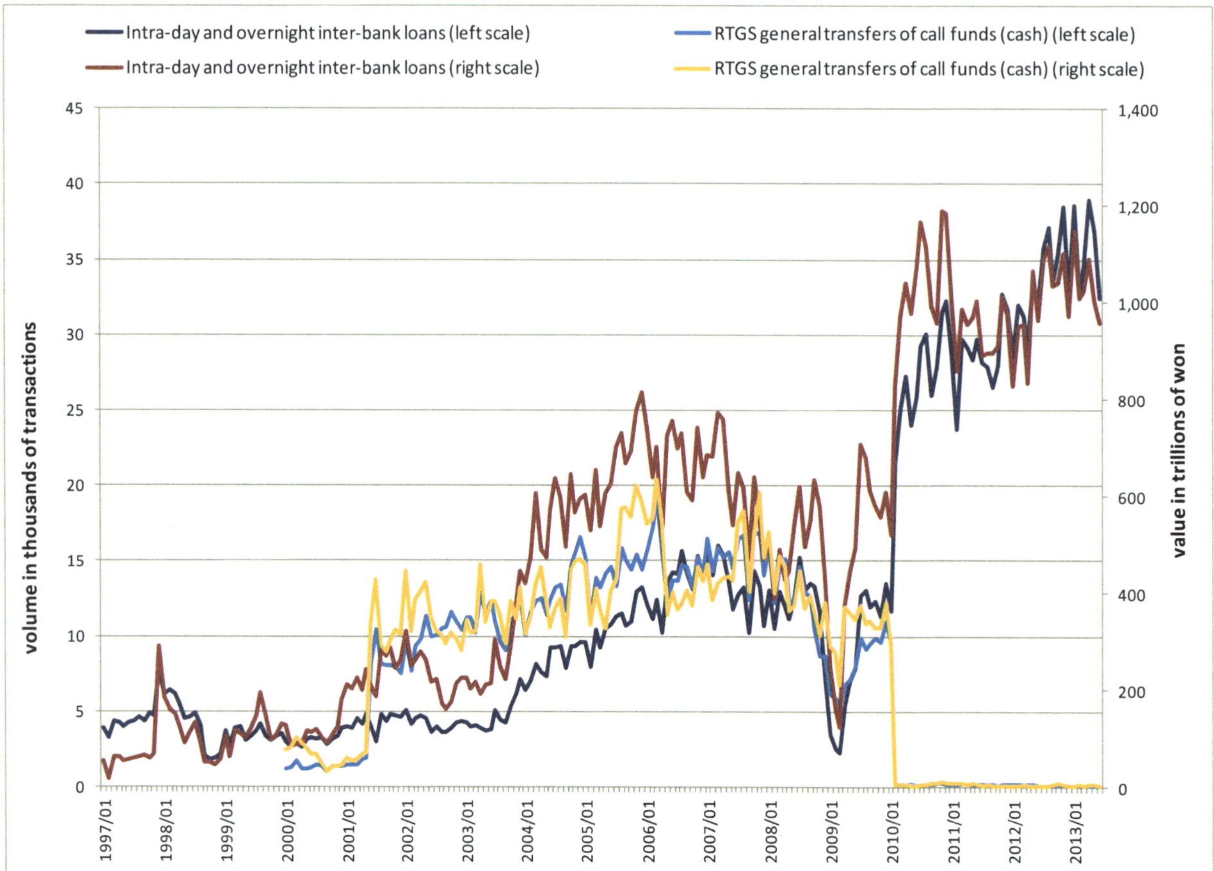

Source: Bank of Korea, http://ecos.bok.or.kr/

Figure 8-14: Volume and value of transactions involving short-term inter-bank loans (now through the hybrid system) and general transfers of call funds through the RTGS system, 1997.01-2013.06

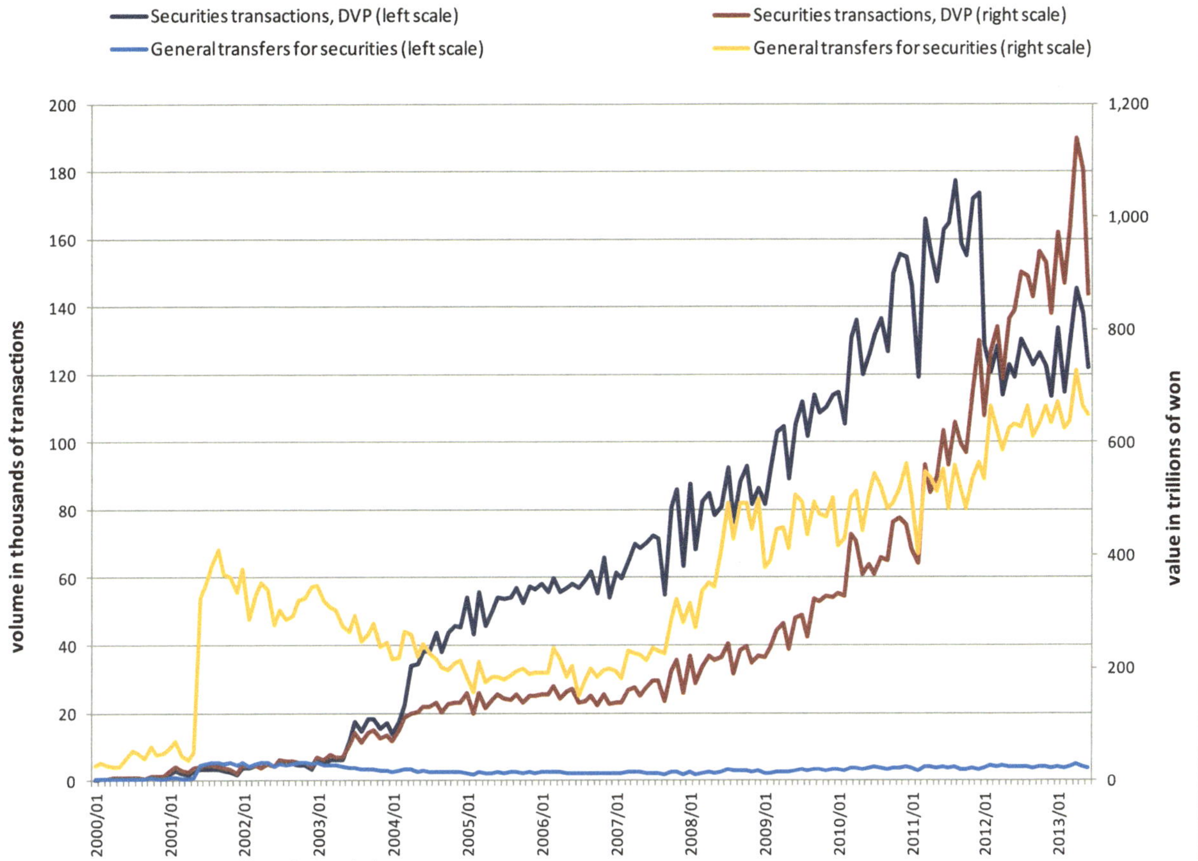

Source: Bank of Korea, http://ecos.bok.or.kr/

Figure 8-15: Volume and value of transactions involving the buying and selling of securities, either DVP transactions or general transactions, 2000.01-2013.06

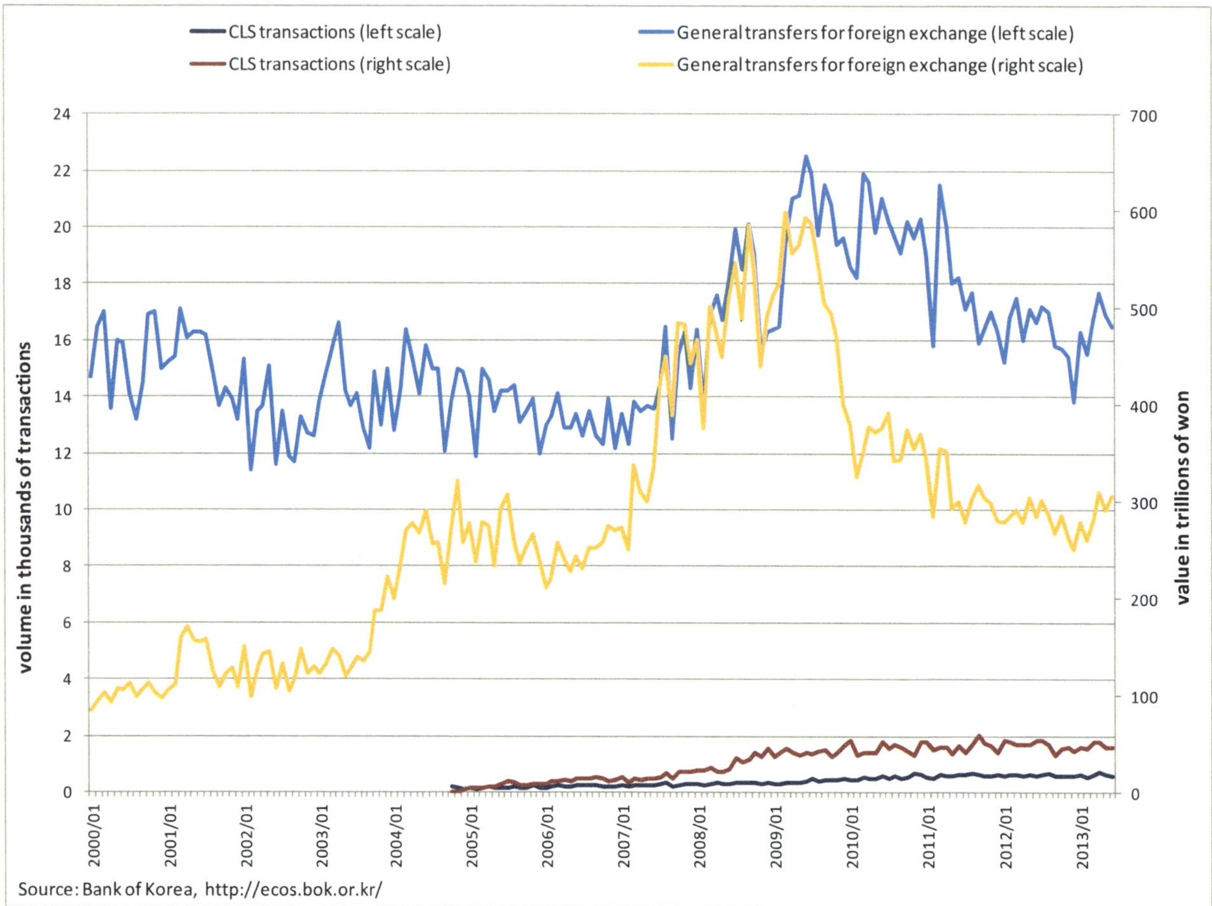

Figure 8-16: Volume and value of foreign exchange transfers through the BOK Wire, 2000.01-2013.06

To use the BOK Wire, the BOK charges members a monthly fixed fee of 100,000 won and transaction fees that vary according to when members submit the payment order. In particular, the BOK charges a transaction fee of 150 won for payment orders entered before 16:00 and a transaction fee of 500 won for payment orders submitted from 16:00-17:30. This encourages members to submit their payments early and discourages them from rushing to submit them at the end of the business day. If the BOK extends payment settlement after 17:30, transaction fees are 4000 won. The BOK charges 800 won for cancelled payment orders during the business day and 4000 won for cancelled payment orders after 17:30.

Other inter-bank payment settlement systems. Some savings banks and credit unions in Korea have formed federations that operate their own payment settlement systems for members in the federation. The Korea Federation of Savings Banks, the Korea Federation of Community Credit Cooperatives and the National Credit Union Federation of Korea have payment settlement systems that settle payments on a net multilateral basis for members through member accounts. Payment settlement between federation members and non-members occur through one of the retail payment settlement systems via the KFTC and BOK Wire, with the federation acting on behalf of each member. In such a transaction, after the KFTC has credited or debited the federation's account via the BOK Wire, the federation then credits or debits the account of the member accordingly.

Risk management in the BOK Wire and by the BOK. To reduce the credit risk, settlement risk, liquidity risk and systemic risk; the BOK Wire settles payments immediately or very quickly. In addition, the settlement is final (irreversible), even in the event of bankruptcy. The Debtor Rehabilitation and Bankruptcy Act of 2006 stipulates that bankruptcy procedures shall not affect settled BOK Wire transactions.

To reduce credit risk, settlement risk, liquidity risk and systemic risk further; the BOK allows intra-day overdrafts to members that are subject to the BOK's reserve requirement (that is, to depository banks). The credit can be in the form of intra-day overdrafts or overnight loans called "liquidity adjustment loans". Because these loans can help members continue payments to other members in the payment settlement system, they also reduce systemic risk. For overdrafts that exceed 25% of the value of the borrower's stock or equity, the BOK charges an interest rate equal to the three-year treasury yield rate minus the private market overnight inter-bank interest rate.

Also, the hybrid payment settlement system was created partly to reduce liquidity risk. Because the hybrid system effectively uses net payments and might not settle the payments immediately, liquidity requirements of members are not as strict at any point in time during the business day. Because liquidity requirements have been reduced, liquidity risk and settlement risk have been reduced for other members in the system, thereby reducing systemic risk.

In addition to providing credit to limit risk, the BOK also oversees and regulates retail payment settlement systems to enforce prudent financial practices. For example, it requires the settlement banks that operate foreign exchange settlement systems to periodically submit data and to notify it of major changes in the system. The BOK also monitors the settlement bank's own risk management practices, such as limits on intra-day credit to its customers.

To manage risk more generally, the BOK also agrees to share information about payment settlement systems with multiple government institutions: the Ministry of Strategy and Finance, the Financial Services Commission, the Financial Supervisory Service and the Korea Deposit Insurance Corporation.

In addition, the BOK researches how to innovate payment settlement systems in terms of efficiency and risk management. I consider various innovations in payment settlement systems in the next section.

Innovations in payment settlement systems

In general, innovations in payment settlement systems can occur among payment *devices*—for example, cards, computers, telephones, or paper—or among payment *channels*—for example, point-of-sale terminals, ATMs, internet, mobile services. Both devices and channels involve issues of efficiency and security, and innovations generally try to make devices and channels more efficient, more secure or less risky.

The major innovation in payment settlement systems during the last decade has been the increasing use of electronic devices and channels and a relative decrease in the use of paper currency and paper checks. In particular, we discussed scanning paper checks and processing them electronically to make payment settlement more efficient.

In addition, we discussed various anti-counterfeiting (security) measures that the Bank of Korea has implemented for paper currency.

In this section, I discuss extending the use of currency and other mediums of exchange from paper to an electronic form, and then consider presenting bills electronically and settling payments through the internet to make transactions more convenient and more efficient. I also consider innovations in security and the management of credit risk.

Electronic mediums of exchange. Like money more generally, currency itself can be used in an electronic form. **Electronic money** or *e-money* is defined as any electronic media to store and to transfer funds in a way that allows the funds to be *fully and quickly* converted into (electronic or paper) cash *on demand* from the issuers, as well as a means of payment for goods and services more generally. Common media to store and to transfer funds are a card, a hard drive, a USB drive, a mobile phone and a computer server. Electronic money can be credited on this device by using funds from an electronic deposit at a bank, often repeatedly. Electronic money can be debited by scanning a card, USB drive or hard drive through direct contact or with **near field communication** (NFC), which allows a reader to scan the value on a device through weak radio waves at a distance of about 1-10 cm.

One example of electronic money in Korea is the K-Cash card, which is issued by Korean banks, including two credit card banks. Money can be credited or debited electronically at these banks, at ATMs in the K-Cash network or on the internet. Korea Financial Telecommunication and Clearings Institute settles payments from the K-Cash card through a separate network called the K-Cash network. K-Cash is largely used for public transportation today, but wider usage has not yet materialized.

Another example of electronic money in Korea is T-money, which is also largely used for public transportation, but also has limited used in taxis and in some private retail stores. T-money can be credited and debited electronically at participating banks, retail stores and kiosks. The T-money system was started in 2004 and is operated by by Korea Smart Card Co., a joint venture between the Seoul municipal government, LG CNS and the Credit Card Union.

Electronic prepayments and **electronic bills** use similar electronic media and devices as electronic money, but they permit the issuer a given amount of time to convert the funds to cash and to convert them at a discount. Also, according to the Electronic Financial Transactions Act, electronic prepayment instruments and electronic bills need to be accepted in only two business sectors, whereas electronic money must be accepted in at least five business sectors.

Electronic prepayments generally use either an integrated circuit (IC) card as a device or a computer network as a device and a channel. Those using an IC card are used mostly for public transport, and those using a computer network are used mostly for internet transactions. The latter device and channel store funds in and transfer funds through a computer network server; funds are accessed via a computer terminal.

Electronic bills, or *e-bills*, are simply bills of exchange in electronic form. The bill is issued, redeemed, endorsed and repaid online or through another computer network; the bill's information is stored on a computer server and can be accessed online. To increase efficiency, corporations that are audited by external companies have been required to use electronic bills instead of traditional paper bills of exchange since November 2009. According to the Act on External Audit of Stock Companies, a company with more than 10 billion won in assets or a corporation listed on the Korea Exchange must have an external auditor.

As a practical matter, consumers generally use electronic money and electronic prepayment (IC) cards, while financial institutions generally use electronic bills. Also, because transactions with electronic money and electronic prepayments usually involve some fees at the present and in the future, the distinction between electronic money and electronic prepayments can be arbitrary.

Banks, non-bank credit institutions and credit card companies may issue electronic money, electronic prepayments and electronic bills without the approval of the Financial Services Commission; other institutions first need approval.

Because stored value cards today use a computer chip or another electronic storage device, they are classified as one form of electronic money or as an electronic prepayment card. Most stored valued cards now use *EMV chips*, which contain an integrated circuit that stores information and provides security. The organization that developed a network for these IC cards was made of representatives of Europay, MasterCard and Visa (EMV), and was joined by JCB (formerly Japan Credit Bureau) in 2004 and American Express in 2009. The EMV organization developed standards for cards of both direct contact scanners and NFC scanners, called International Standardization Organization (ISO)/International Electrotechnical Commission (IEC) 7816 and ISO/IEC 14443 respectively. These standards are promulgated so that the cards can be easily used and widely accepted in many countries.

While various kinds of electronic money were launched in the late 1990s and early 2000s, many failed to acquire widespread and lasting use. In the US, Visa launched one stored valued card which could have funds credited to it at most ATMs. The card was supposed to reduce the burdens of cash management, especially management of coins and currency for small purchases, among both consumers and retailers. It was supposed to be especially convenient when consumers made frequent, small purchases from parking meters, vending machines and other unmanned points of sale.

However, consumers were reluctant to use this card because funds could not be reimbursed if the card was lost and because once money was credited to the cards it did not earn interest like some bank deposits. Retailers were also unwilling to adopt/accept the cards because they were responsible for installing a separate electronic reader to make transactions. Finally both standard debit cards and credit cards were widely available, and the new stored value cards offered no clear benefits relative to these alternatives.

Thus, while debit cards and credit cards are widely used in many countries, electronic money and electronic prepayment cards have only limited uses, such as for bus/subway fare, purchases on the internet and purchases from some vending machines. Figure 8-17 shows that while the number (volume) and value of new devices of E-money issued in Korea has risen, consumer transactions involving E-money have declined in terms of number of transactions (volume) and value. Figure 8-19 also shows that transactions involving E-money that are settled by the KFTC (after it calculates net obligations among issuers) has also declined in terms of volume and value.

In contrast, financial institutions have issued more electronic bills with a larger total value during the past few years, as shown in Figure 8-18.[42] After an initial increase a few years ago, the amount of trading of existing bills (for cash) has remained steady in terms of volume and value. When comparing Figure 8-17 and Figure 8-18, note also that the value of transactions for electronic bills is 1000 times larger than the value of transactions for electronic money, while the volume of transactions for electronic bills 100 times smaller. This indicates that financial institutions trade a relatively small amount of large denomination electronic bills compared to (largely consumer) transactions involving electronic money.

[42] The Bank of Korea has no data or has made no distinction for electronic prepayments.

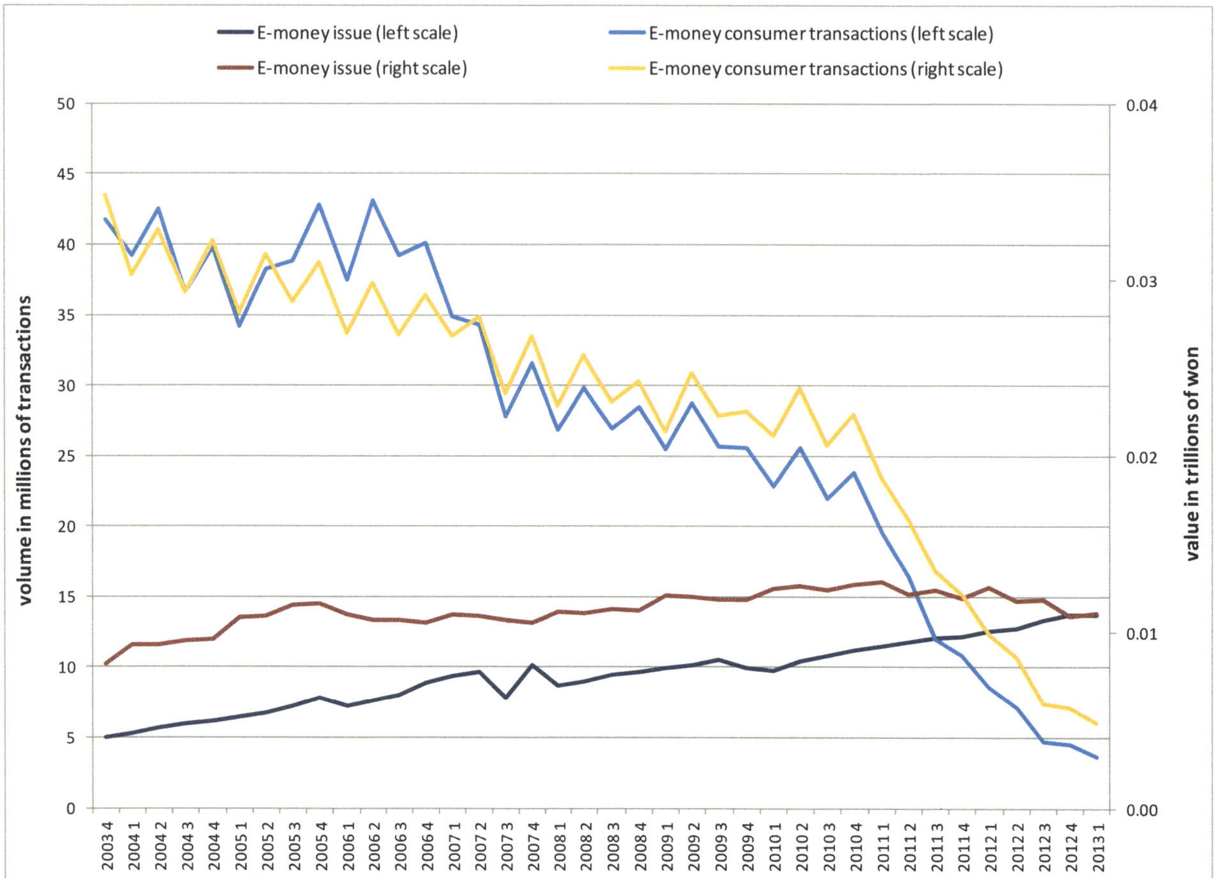

Source: Bank of Korea, http://ecos.bok.or.kr/

Figure 8-17: Volume and value of (issuing) devices with E-money and of consumer transactions involving E-money, 2003.4-2013.1

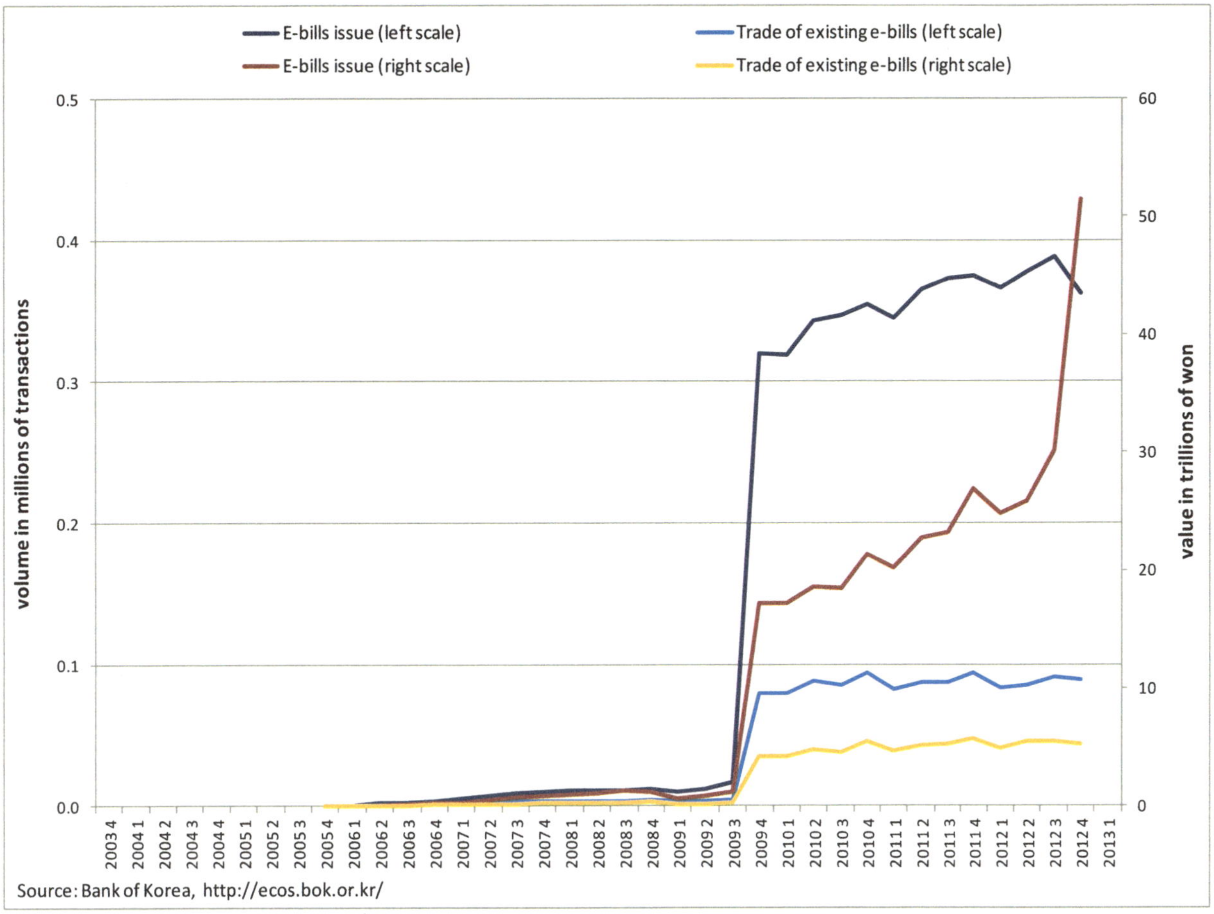

Figure 8-18: Volume and value of (issuing) devices with electronic bills and of trades involving existing electronic bills, 2003.4-2013.1

Why have electronic bills grown in popularity, while electronic money has not? In general, both the payer and the payee must accept an innovation in payment settlement systems for it to be widely adopted. And for social conventions like payment settlement systems, regulation can also play a key factor in making the payer or the payee accept an innovative payment settlement system: large companies are now required by law to use electronic bills to increase the efficiency of auditing. Also, innovative systems will also face competition from established payment settlement systems, such as standard debit cards and credit cards. And the more established the standard systems are, the more difficult it will be for innovative payment systems to compete because of economies of scale and positive network externalities that exist for the established social conventions. Either the payer or the payee will not want to switch to an innovative system unless the innovation offers very large benefits or very low costs that obviate the economies of scale and positive network externalities of established systems. In other words, incremental innovations will be ignored because transition costs of the new technology are too large relative to the benefits.

However, electronic money has been adopted in cities where a large number of transactions can occur within a small geographical network and for specialized uses like public transportation, largely replacing paper tickets. For example, the Octopus Card in Hong Kong was started in 1997, followed by the SmarTrip card in Washington DC in 1999, the Suica card in Tokyo in 2001, the EZ-link card in Singapore in 2001, the Oyster Card in London in 2003 and the OV-Chipkaart in Rotterdam in 2006. The lack of competition in a transport system and the government regulation of the public transportation system can force consumers to quickly adopt electronic money, but the specialized used that prevents competition can later hinder wider adoption in a larger geographic market.

To promote wider adoption, a few of these public transportation cards have evolved from a single purpose into a multi-purpose payment system, a general form of electronic money. For the transport companies and retailers operating in and around stations, multi-purpose payment cards can increase revenues and possibly lower transaction costs because of positive network externalities and economies of scale.

But making a stored value card a multi-purpose payment system is not risk or cost free. A transportation company may need to improve technical/security standards for itself or for consumers when the card is used outside a closed system. A stored value card with insufficient security and safety, whether real or perceived, could prevent consumers or retailers from refusing to use and to accept it. A transport company may also be subject to broader regulation and supervision when consumers outside of the public transport system use its stored valued card. Instead of developing a multipurpose stored value card primarily for public transportation, Washington DC and New Jersey are now considering using general purpose credit cards and debit cards in their public transportation systems.

Other payment devices and channels. One payment settlement system that can be considered both a device and a channel is the *UbiTouch* system, a Universal Subscriber Identity Module (USIM) chip installed on mobile phones with the readers installed on ATMs. This system allows bank customers to use ATMs in the system (channel) regardless of underlying bank affiliation of the ATM. In other words, the UbiTouch system can extend an ATM network, granting access to more customers to the ATM. In addition, bank customers can also transfer funds and check account information via mobile phones without visiting ATMs.

The BOK is negotiating to link Korea's ATM networks with the ATM networks in several other countries. These international links would allow cardholders to withdraw cash in a foreign country more easily and at a lower cost. Currently, foreign cardholders in Korea and Korean cardholders in foreign countries can use only VISA, MasterCard or other global ATM card companies. The BOK hopes to allow cardholders to withdraw cash with cards not affiliated with a global ATM card company and to lower transaction fees in all cases.

Electronic presentment. As with payment and settlement, banks and other billers are increasingly relying on electronic presentment, the act of presenting a bill before funds are actually paid and settled.

In the early 1990s, more than 60% of bills (invoices) in Saudi Arabia were settled in person at bank branches, mainly with paper currency. To make this payment settlement more efficient, the Saudi Arabian Monetary Agency (SAMA) in 2004 established an electronic presentment and payment settlement system, known as SADAD, which provides a uniform interface between billers, their customers and banks. In particular, billers can upload their invoices to the system, and customers can access and settle them through point-of-sale devices, ATMs, the internet, telephones banking, bank branches and, in some cases, mobile devices. By 2010, more than 91% of all invoices in Saudi Arabia were settled with SADAD.

Internet payment settlement systems and transactions. E-commerce Payment Systems facilitate and settle internet transactions either between businesses (firms) or between firms and consumers. For non-financial institutions and consumers, these systems correspond to or are an extension of the Electronic Banking System used by financial institutions and their customers.

As retail and wholesale transactions via the internet have grown, the reliance on E-commerce payment systems to settle payments has grown. Like financial institutions that use the Electronic Banking System, businesses have become more willing to settle transactions among themselves and with their customers by using the internet. In contrast, consumers have become less willing to use E-money, which can involve transactions using computer systems like the internet or using cards. Figure 8-19 shows that the volume of payments settled by E-commerce Payment Systems has grown steadily while the volume of transactions involving E-money that are settled by the KFTC has declined.

As a service for customers, most banks today offer internet banking, which customers seem to increasing want and use for basic transactions like funds transfers and inquiries. Figure 8-20 shows that the number (volume) of inquiries and funds transfers has grown steadily during the past decade. The total value of funds transfers has also grown rapidly.

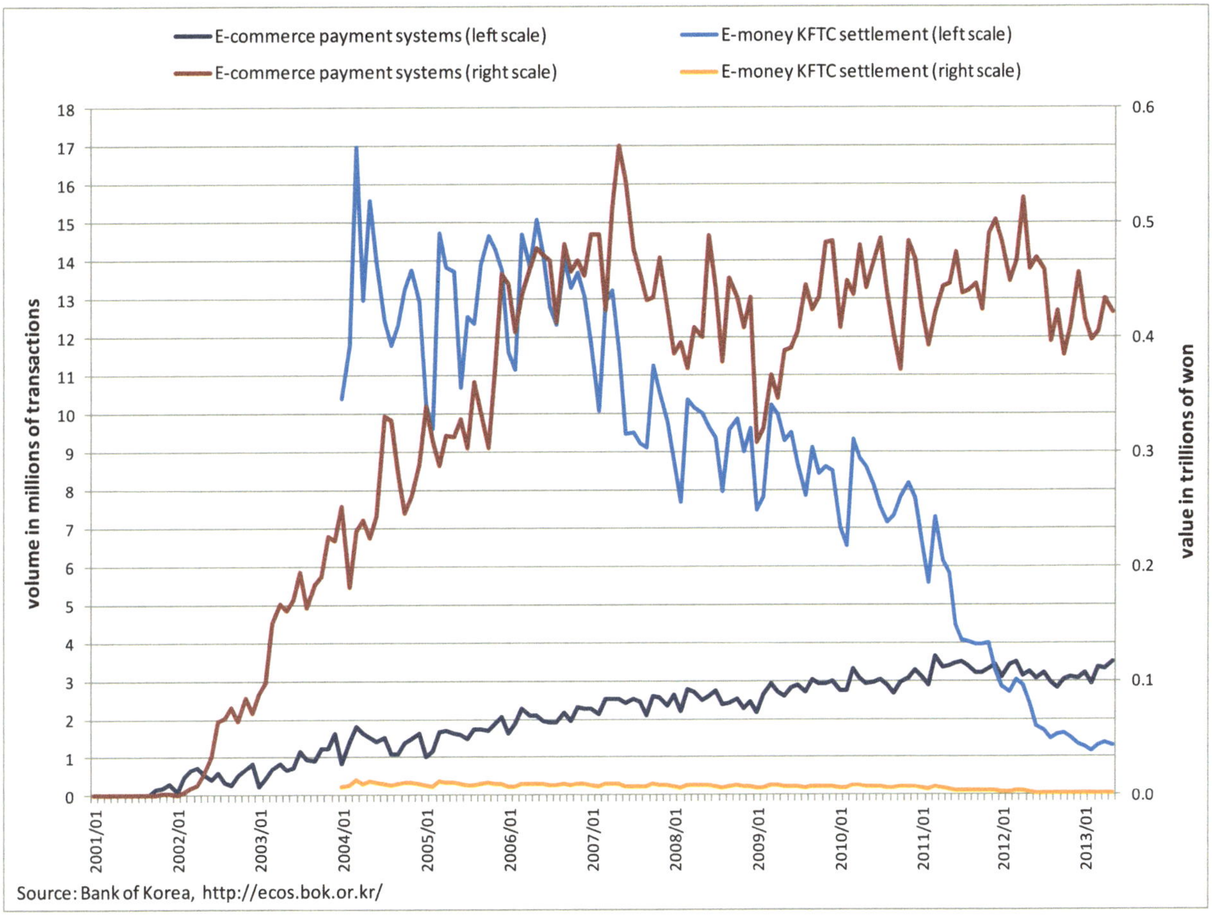

Figure 8-19: Volume and value of E-commerce payments and E-money transactions settled by the KFTC, 2001.1-2013.05

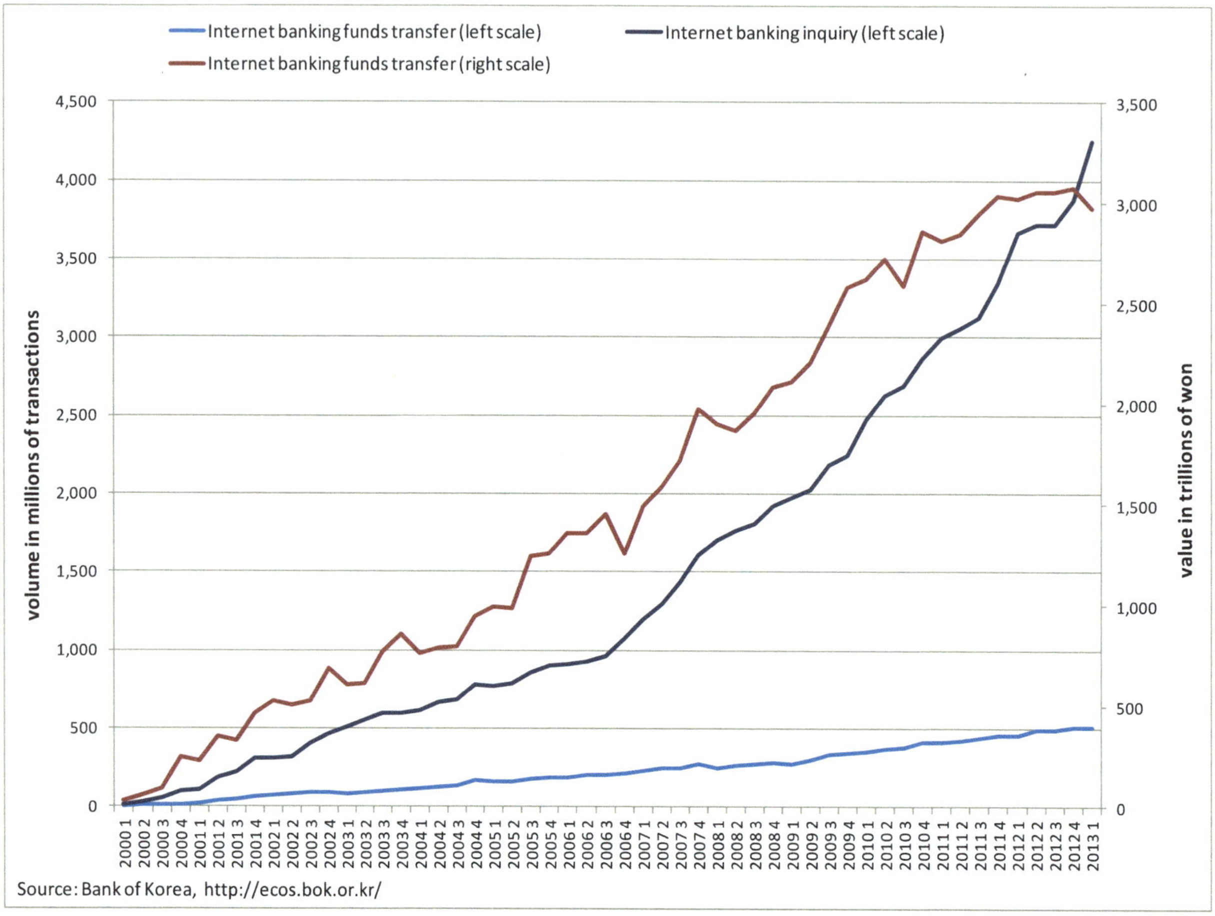

Figure 8-20: Volume and value of funds transfers and number (volume) of inquiries made through internet banking, 2000.1-2013.1

Security and risk management. Transactions via the internet involve transferring data via an open network and storing data on a hard drive, server or other device. To maintain security when transferring or storing data, banks have developed temporary passwords (often random numbers) that can be sent to a mobile phone, a computer or another device. Certificates using passwords or PINs are also used to validate the identity of the device performing the transaction.

The KFTC supports joint electronic operations with financial institutions and helps operate and electronic certification system called *yessign* with financial institutions. Financial institutions issue electronic certificates through the yessign system to certify internet transactions and to prevent electronic fraud. Yessign has grown rapidly in scale and scope since it was launched in December 2000, as electronic transactions on the internet or via mobile networks have also grow rapidly since then. See http://www.yessign.or.kr/.

Innovations can also reduce credit risk, such as faster or more secure ways to provide collateral or more effective guarantees to make due payments. Some financial companies provide escrow services for one or both parties in transactions via the internet to ensure either or both the payment and delivery of a good or service. Companies can also guarantee refunds or provide insurance services for internet transactions if payment or delivery of a good or service is not completed as promised.

Summary

Retail payment settlement systems include currency as well as a range of payment settlement systems and networks operated by the Korea Financial and Telecommunications and Clearing Institute (KFTC).

The check clearing system now settles all paper checks and bills electronically by scanning them and converting the data to electronic form. However, the value and volume of checks and bills has declined as individuals and institutions increasingly use other (electronic) payment settlement systems.

The Giro network and the Cash Management System allow individuals and institutions to transfer funds on a regular basis, either by having the payer initiate the transaction to credit the payee's account (a credit transfer) or by having the payee initiate the transaction to debit the payer's account (a debit transfer).

The Interbank Remittance System, the Electronic Banking System and ATM networks allow transfers of cash on an irregular basis through a credit transfer. The Interbank Remittance System does not require that the payer and the payee have bank accounts. The Electronic Banking System relies on the internet and telephone systems to transfer funds. ATM networks allow withdrawals of currency.

Domestic banks and other financial institutions operate credit card networks, debit card networks and foreign exchange networks. Credit cards are the most popularly used card in Korea. Signature-based credit cards use the same network as credit cards; PIN-based credit cards use a separate network called the electronic transfer of funds at the point of sale (ETFPOS) network.

The BOK Wire is the primary inter-bank payment settlement system. It settles payments from the retail payment settlement systems (via the KFTC), as well as general inter-bank funds transfers, transfers to non-banks, repurchases and trades of government securities, issuance and redemption of government securities, and transfers of foreign exchange. It is divided into a real time gross settlement system that settles payments immediately and on a gross (and unilateral) basis and a hybrid system that uses real time gross (unilateral) settlement, offsetting bilateral settlement or offsetting multilateral settlement. The real time gross settlement system is the traditional payment settlement method of BOK Wire; the hybrid system was developed recently to help financial institutions save cash by allowing offsetting (netting) for normal payment orders.

These systems have been updated and innovated in the past generation and increasingly rely on electronic transfer of funds. In addition, consumers can use an electronic form of currency, called electronic money, but its use has heretofore been limited to specialized cases like public transportation. Banks and other institutions can use electronic bills of exchange. Both consumers and firms can use the internet for presentment of bills and to settle payments so that transactions become more efficient. Other innovations involve security measures, especially for internet transactions, faster or more effective ways to provide collateral or escrow services, and more efficient presentment of bills.

Problems and Applications

Short answer problems

1. How does a check differ from a bill of exchange?

2. How does a credit transfer differ from a debit transfer?

3. In check clearing/settlement, what is presentment? Besides through presentment, what are other ways in which checks might be cleared or settled?

4. How does the Giro network differ from Cash Management System? Through which kind of network/system is a debit transfer settled more quickly?

5. How do banks or the operators manage risk in the Interbank Remittance System, the Electronic Banking Network and the ATM networks, especially since payments to bank customers are made before inter-bank payments are settled?

6. In retail payment settlement systems, what is loss sharing? How much collateral do members need to have?

7. How does a signature-based debit card differ from a PIN-based debit card? Which uses credit card networks to settle payments? Which one is more popular and why?

8. In the BOK Wire, what is the difference between the RTGS system and the hybrid (payment settlement) system? What is the difference between the current account and the deposit account? What is the difference between a "normal" payment order and an "urgent" payment order?

9. In the BOK Wire, what is delivery versus payment (DVP)? What is payment versus payment (PVP)? What is the purported advantage of DVP and PVP, even if these transactions are not strictly settled "immediately"?

10. How does the BOK reduce credit risk, settlement risk, liquidity risk and systemic risk in the BOK Wire?

11. What is the difference between electronic money and electronic prepayments? How might this difference be arbitrary?

12. In regard to electronic money, what is an EMV chip? What is near field communication (NFC)?

13. Where or in what case is electronic money most frequently used? What are factors that prevent consumers or retailers from adopting electronic money?

14. What are two innovations that have helped reduce credit risk for internet transactions?

Internet applications

1. Go to http://ecos.bok.or.kr/ to find data for average daily volume (number) and value of cleared checks in Korea from the earliest available month to the latest available month. Create a graph for both series of data. When was the average volume the largest? When was the average value the largest?

2. Go to http://ecos.bok.or.kr/ to find data for the volume (number) and value of the ratio of dishonored checks (including electronic settlement) from the earliest available month to the latest

available month. Create a graph for both series of data. When was the average volume the largest? When was the average value the largest?

3. Go to http://ecos.bok.or.kr/ to find data for the total value and volume of credit card transactions from the earliest available month to the latest available month. Create a graph for both series of data. Which has grown more steadily over time: the value of credit transactions or the volume of credit transactions?

4. Go to http://ecos.bok.or.kr/ to find data for the total volume of (real time) gross settlement and the total volume of transactions via the BOK Wire from the earliest available month to the latest available month. Calculate the fraction of the total volume of transactions that are due to real time gross settlement transactions and create a graph for this fraction. When was this fraction the largest?

5. Go to http://ecos.bok.or.kr/ to find data for the total value of (real time) gross settlement and the total value of transactions via the BOK Wire from the earliest available month to the latest available month. Calculate the fraction of the total value of transactions that are due to real time gross settlement transactions and create a graph for this fraction. When was this fraction the largest?

6. Go to http://ecos.bok.or.kr/ to find data for the total volume of the various types of credit transfers and debit transfers from the earliest available month to the latest available month. Create a graph for the volume of all of these kinds of transfers. Which kinds of transfers are currently the 3 largest in volume?

7. Go to http://ecos.bok.or.kr/ to find data for the total value of the various types of credit transfers and debit transfers from the earliest available month to the latest available month. Create a graph for the value of all of these kinds of transfers. Which kinds of transfers are currently the 3 largest in value?

9. Risk Management

Preview

In finance and in other realms of life, we always face some kinds of risks and unknown situations. Taking some risks and managing them well is not only necessary but can be beneficial and profitable. Most successful people become successful because they took some risks and managed them well over time, although there are always a few "lucky" people who can succeed without thinking about managing risk. (And there are always a few "unlucky" people who fail despite trying to manage risk.) "Luck"—a good outcome that resulted without thoughts or actions about risk management—can be beneficial, but no one is always lucky.

This chapter first describes theoretical concepts that can help us manage risks and how to decide when facing the unknown. Among unknown situations, we can distinguish between "risky" situations and "uncertain" situations, although this distinction is ultimately arbitrary. I then consider various ways to measure risk, and logical steps involved in estimating, predicting and forecasting unknown situations like the future. It then describes several types of risks that banks and other financial institutions are exposed to and methods in which they can manage these risks. I discuss liquidity risk, credit risk, settlement risk, market value risk and capital risk. Finally, I discuss strategies in managing risk and uncertainty: hedging, insurance, diversification.

How much do we know about the unknown?

There are many kinds of unknown situations, and some are more problematic than others. For example, it is very difficult to say what will happen to the whole economy during the next 10 years because macroeconomic behavior will depend on so many unknown factors, many of which each individual and possibly everyone is unaware of at the present time. It is also unknown who will win in your next favorite sports game. But we can probably make better guesses about these games than about the macroeconomy during the next decade. There will be fewer unknown factors and fewer unforeseeable outcomes that affect the sports match than affect the whole economy. For most sports games there are relatively few potential outcomes (for example, win, lose or tie), whereas there are so many outcomes and variables within the macroeconomy that it would be impossible to list them completely: growth rates of production of goods and services, growth rates of prices of goods and services, growth rates of prices or returns of all assets, employment rates or unemployment rates…

Different unknown situations can be distinguished by how much we do not know or how much that we (think that we) do know. **Uncertainty** can refer to a case where potential outcomes are unknown (a case of "unknown unknowns") or to a case where probabilities about potential outcomes are unknown. For example, in the second case of uncertainty, we may know that we will win or lose a game according to well defined and well enforced rules, but not the probability of winning and losing because we have no information about the specific rules of the game (just that they are defined and enforced), our opponents, or past games. In the first case, we may not even know how to play or how to satisfy the rules, if or how the rules are enforced, if we can be barred from the game for not complying with the rules, if we can win, how we can win, if we can lose, how we can lose, if we can tie, et cetera.

Risk usually refers to a case where we define what we think are all possible outcomes ("known unknowns") *and* define what we think are their probabilities. For example, we may think that the only potential outcomes of a sports game are winning or losing, and the probability of winning is 55% and the probability of losing is 45%.

Through practice and experience (and by learning through mistakes), a case uncertainty can evolve into a case of risk because we can learn more about what potential outcomes are possible and how likely they are. We can manage cases of risk better than cases of uncertainty, as long as what we think we know about risk is true. On the other hand, the first type of uncertainty is the most unmanageable, because we can not even think about all possibilities.

But the distinctions between the two kinds of uncertainty and risk are ultimately unclear and arbitrary. A case of what we believe is risk could really be a case of uncertainty when we fail to consider a potential outcome and/or fail to represent its probability accurately, which we might finally realize after the potential outcome becomes reality. In other words, we are never certain how accurately we know all of the potential outcomes and their probabilities. So, a case of risk can change into a case of uncertainty, and as I mentioned earlier, a case of uncertainty can evolve or transform into a case of risk through practice and experience.

Whatever the type of unknown situation that we face, we can set criteria to try to manage the situation. I discuss decision criteria for uncertain situations first. I then consider how to measure risk before considering decision criteria for risky situations. And then I consider a decision criterion that can be used for either an uncertain situation or a risky situation.

Decision criteria under uncertainty

In the first case of uncertainty, there may be *some* potential outcomes that are known, so that not all potential outcomes are "unknown unknowns". In the second kind of uncertainty, (some) potential outcomes are known, but their probabilities are not. In either of these cases, decision makers might be able to find a way to reduce or to limit losses based on the limited knowledge that they have.

In cases of uncertainty, we may be able to use insurance to limit losses from bad potential outcomes that are known or unknown, and essentially let an insurance company plan for the uncertain outcomes (which it may know more about through experience). But an insurance company will not insure uncertain potential outcomes unless it knows something about the magnitude of the potential outcomes and their probabilities—in brief, unless the uncertain situation for potential customers is a risky situation for itself.

When an uncertain situation is uninsurable, a decision maker could plan an exit from the situation if a financial loss of a certain magnitude actually occurs. For example, if financial losses from an investment could exceed $1000, then we can decide beforehand that we should exit the market by selling the remaining value of the asset (if any) and try to find better alternatives if such a loss occurs.

Finally, if we can not leave an uncertain situation but must continue to face the uncertainty even if losses occur, then there may be little to do but recognize the situation that we are in.

Measures of risk

To consider decision criteria under a risky situation and to measure risk, we first need to define or represent the risky situation: to identify potential outcomes and to quantify them, as well as to quantify the probabilities of these potential outcomes. To identify/quantify potential outcomes and their probabilities, we typically examine past data or think about past experiences, and then consider unknown situations in the present or in the future by extrapolating based on these recollections. In essence, our definition of risk and our conceptions of the unknown are determined by what we already know or what we believe that we know based on our past experiences and observations. (But because experiences, observations, beliefs and perceptions vary from individual to individual, our measures of risk and our tolerance of risk will vary.)

To quantify potential outcomes, we could use monetary values or index values relative to an arbitrarily chosen reference point. Given quantities from potential outcomes, we can calculate the average or expected value, dispersion or deviation from that average value, frequencies of the outcomes and a probability distribution—a mathematical representation of frequencies of individual outcomes, their average value, their deviation and other measures of risk.

Expected value is the probability-weighted average value from the range of potential outcomes. When known outcomes are related to risky situations, the average value of the known outcomes is often related to (or conflated with) the *expected* value of future data, even though we can expect many different things about the future. When probabilities are defined mathematically or through frequencies (discussed below), we can use them to calculate a value that we expect in the future or in another unknown situation but has not yet been observed in past data. Or when using only past data (when all probabilities of all known outcomes equal 1), we calculate the expected value as simply the average value.

Expected or average value is not really a measure of risk, but it can be used as a decision criterion for a risky situation, and it is used in measures of risk like the standard deviation, variance, covariance and correlation.

Standard deviation. A common measure of risk is the dispersion or deviation around an average of expected value of observations. The **standard deviation** measures how much a value is likely to deviate from the expected or average value during a period of time on average. The standard deviation from set of n actual or potential observations that are used to calculate that average or expected value $\bar{x}$ is defined as

$$\sqrt{\frac{\sum_{i=1}^{n}(x_i - \bar{x})^2}{n}} \tag{15}$$

where $x_i - \bar{x}$ represents the deviation of observation x_i from the average or expected value $\bar{x}$. The standard deviation weights all deviations equally, and in particular, squares all deviations so that positive and negative deviations are treated equally. (We could weight different deviations with different probabilities or frequencies, which is what some decision criteria discussed below do.) After adding all of the squared values of the deviations, we divide by the number of observations n to determine the average squared deviation from the expected or average value. We then take the square root of the average squared deviation to express the deviation in the same units as the expected or average value. Figure 9-1 illustrates the concept of the standard deviation:

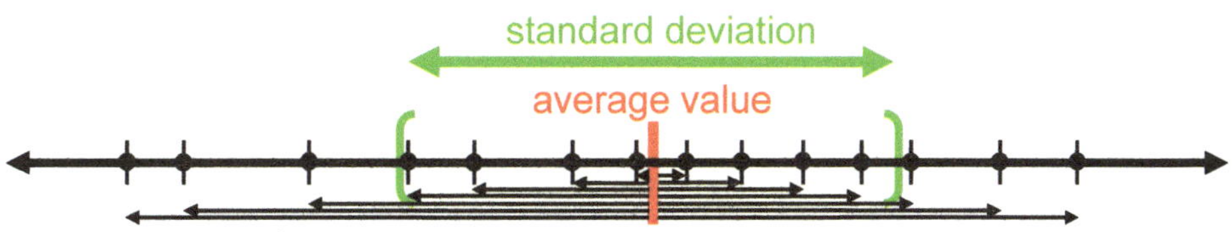

Figure 9-1: A representation of deviations from an average value and the standard deviation

However, a problem with the standard deviation and other measures of risk is that they use known values from *past* events to represent risk, which represents uncertainty about future outcomes or outcomes events that are unknown. If future outcomes will evolve like past outcomes and if currently unknown outcomes are like known outcomes, this should generally present no problems and the standard deviation will be helpful in managing risky outcomes.

Other measures of risk are based on the standard deviation and/or expected value.

Variance, covariance and correlation. The **variance** of a variable is simply the squared value of the standard deviation:

$$\frac{\sum_{i=1}^{n}(x_i - \bar{x})^2}{n} = \frac{\sum_{i=1}^{n}(x_i - \bar{x})(x_i - \bar{x})}{n}$$

Variance may be used instead of the standard deviation to represent dispersion of potential outcomes, but the order of magnitude of variance is two times that of the expected value and the standard deviation.

Once we understand how to calculate the variance of one variable, it is easy to calculate the *covariance* of two variables. **Covariance** represents how two variables vary around their average values concurrently; it is the average product of the deviation of the two variables from their average values. For variables *x* and *y* and *n* observations of these variables, covariance is calculated by:

$$\frac{\sum_{i=1}^{n}(x_i - \bar{x})(y_i - \bar{y})}{n}$$

Covariance has the same order of magnitude as the variance, and to reduce that magnitude to that of the expected value and the standard deviation we could use the square root operator, or more commonly, divide by the standard deviations of the variables. **Correlation** uses the later calculation; it is the covariance of two variables normalized by the product of their standard deviations:

$$\frac{\sum_{i=1}^{n}\frac{(x_i - \bar{x})(y_i - \bar{y})}{n}}{std\ dev\ x \times std\ dev\ y}$$

where *std dev x* represents the standard deviation for variable *x* defined by equation (15) and *std dev y* represents the standard deviation for variable *y*, also defined by equation (15).

Instead of the relying on the dispersion of potential outcomes to represent risk, **frequency** uses the number of times each outcome occurs out of a total number of outcomes. For example, if an outcome has occurred 55/1000 times during the past, then the frequency is 55/1000 or 5.5%. Frequency of past outcomes is used to represent probability of future outcomes, regardless of where that outcome lies relative to an expected or average value.

As with standard deviation and other measures of dispersion, if future events will be like those from the past, then frequency can be an accurate measure of risk. In particular, the frequency calculated from observed data can accurately represent the probability of the same or similar outcome will occur again in the future. For example, if an event has occurred 55/1000 times during the past, we can say that the probability of that event in the future will be 5.5%.

We can combine measures of probability with measures of dispersion in a probability distribution.

Probability distribution. A **probability distribution** is a mathematical function that represents a distribution or range of potential outcomes and their probabilities, both of which are usually consistent with past data. We can use past data to calculate a distribution or range of outcomes and their frequencies, and the probability distribution is designed mathematically "to fit" this distribution of outcomes, their frequencies and other properties of the data. In general, measures of dispersion and measures of probability calculated from past data and from a probability distribution should be similar.

Some risky situations can be represented by a *Gaussian distribution* (named after Carl Friedrich Gauss who developed it in 1809), which is often called a *normal distribution*, because "normal" outcomes lie close to the average or expected value and "abnormal" outcomes become increasingly rare. In other words, the distribution assumes that the most frequent events will be "normal" events—those close to the average or expected value and that "abnormal" outcomes or large deviations away from the average or expected value will occur with vanishing small probability. Probabilities of outcomes can change according to changes in their dispersion, and vice versa.

Because of its complexity, I do not show the mathematical function for a Gaussian distribution, but you can find this function on many statistical webpages or in many textbooks.

Gaussian distributions are accurate when outcomes cluster around an average value and have a stable, or standard, deviation from the average value. The speed of cars on a highway, the weights of people, the heights of people, air pressure at a given location, temperature at a given location, rainfall at a given location all tend to vary by a well defined amount from an average value across time and across people.

A "standard" Gaussian distribution also assumes that the median (or middle) value equals the mean (or average) value along a continuum of values and that the (small) probability of large negative deviations from these values equals the (small) probability of large positive deviations. For many physical variables like weight and height in a population, this is largely true.

However, values are sometimes *skewed to the left*, meaning that the mean lies to the left of the median on a continuum of values because a few infrequent outcomes, or *outliers*, at the left end of the distribution decrease the mean below the median. Alternatively, distributions can be *skewed to the right* when the mean lies to the right of the median on a continuum of values because a few outliers at the right end of the distribution increase the mean above the median. Figure 9-2 shows a distribution that is skewed to the left, and Figure 9-3 shows a distribution that is skewed to the right.

Figure 9-2: A distribution that is skewed to the left because a few outliers to the left decrease the mean below the median

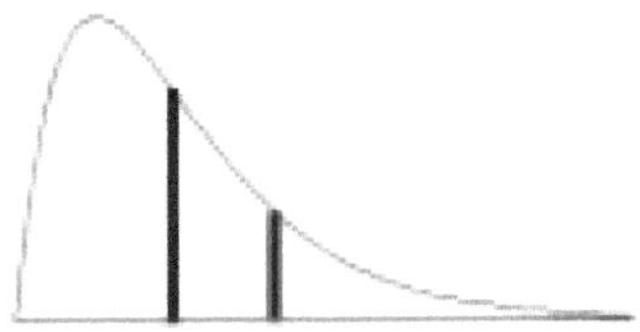

Figure 9-3: A distribution that is skewed to the right because a few outliers to the right increase the mean above the median

Other outcomes do not cluster around an average value and do not have a stable deviation from the average. Instead, due to rare "structural" or revolutionary changes that shift the average and the standard deviation of the whole distribution, the average and the standard deviation vary over time depending on when the large changes occur. Other distributions may have a stable average and standard deviation, but these measures provide little meaning about the true dispersion or distribution of outcomes. For example, although we can calculate the average value of cities around the world, most people live in mega-cities of 1 million or more, while a vast number of small villages and towns outnumber the very large cities.

In these cases, a power law (power function) may more accurately describe the distribution of potential outcomes than a Gaussian distribution. A variable *x* is distributed according to a power law if the distribution of its values can be accurately described by the function:

$$p(x) = c \cdot x^{-\alpha}$$

where $p(x)$ represents the probability (or frequency) of given values of x, and c and α are constants.

Because this probability (density) function is not defined when $x = 0$, it is useful and accurate to describe the distribution of outcomes for values at least as great as a minimum value: $x \geq x_{min} > 0$. In other words, a distribution of outcomes that are mostly close to zero would not be accurately described a power law, but perhaps a Gaussian distribution could perhaps do a more accurate job.

We can specify the constant c by integrating the probability density function from ∞ to x_{min} and then differencing the integrals.

$$\int_{x_{min}}^{\infty} p(x)dx = \int_{x_{min}}^{\infty} c\, x^{-\alpha} dx$$

$$= 1 - \frac{-c}{-\alpha+1} x_{min}^{-\alpha+1} = 0$$

$$\Rightarrow c = (\alpha - 1)x_{min}^{\alpha-1}$$

Thus,

$$p(x) = (\alpha - 1)x_{min}^{\alpha-1} \cdot x^{-\alpha}$$

Figure 9-4 shows a graph of a power law, which uses the distribution of (potential) outcomes on the horizontal axis and their probabilities or frequencies on the vertical axis. By construction, outcomes with large magnitudes are improbable or infrequent; on the other hand, small outcomes are very probable or very frequent. A graph of a power law looks like a distribution that is skewed to the right because of a few outliers at the right end of the distribution. However, the mean of a power law distribution is not well defined when the magnitude of the outcomes can increase forever with a non-zero probability.

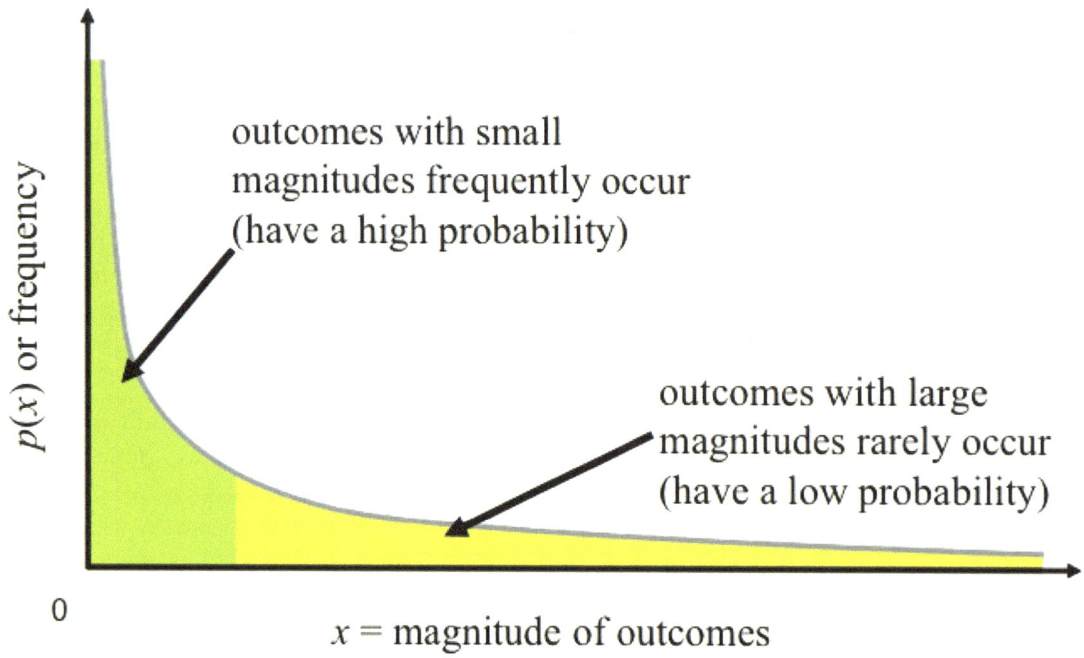

Figure 9-4: A power law distribution

Because the magnitudes of the outcomes are all supposed to be positive, transforming the power law using the natural logarithm function can allow us to manipulate the power law more easily:

$$\ln(p(x)) = (\alpha - 1)\ln((\alpha - 1)x_{min}) - \alpha \ln(x)$$

which is a linear function that can be easily graphed. Thus, a straightforward way to look for a power law distribution of x is to graph the logarithm of outcomes, $\ln(x)$ with the logarithm of their frequencies or probabilities, $\ln(p(x))$. A linear slope (equal to $-\alpha$) and intercept (equal to $(\alpha-1)\ln((\alpha-1)x_{min})$) suggests a power law distribution.

Alternatively, $-\alpha$ and a constant (intercept) can be estimated through linear least squares regression.

Unfortunately, these simple methods can commonly hide or neglect systemic errors, so using them does not definitely show when data are distributed according to a power law. With a finite number of observations, it is possible that a non-power law distribution will appear to look like a power law distribution because of what statisticians call sampling or observations error—errors that result from a sampling a limited number of unrepresentative observations. In addition, with a finite number of observations, it is possible that a power law distribution will not appear to look like a power law distribution because of this error. And we should be especially circumspect when trying to look for a power law distribution with a small number of observations. In essence, what statisticians call sampling or observational error occurs when our representation of risk is inaccurate and our unknown situation should really be considered a case of uncertainty.

There are many other probability functions that we could study, and all of them can be accurate depending on how outcomes are or will be distributed and depending on their probabilities. On the other hand, a probability function is useful only if it is an accurate representation of the unknown, and any specification of risk is useful only if we can accurately identify all potential outcomes and their probabilities. When probability distribution or other specification of risk is inaccurate, it may be misleading and worse than useless.

Decision criteria under risk

Using measures in the previous section, we can define different criteria to help us choose among risky outcomes.

Expected value and expected utility. One criterion is to maximize *expected wealth* or the expected value of wealth from the distribution of potential outcomes, assuming that the magnitudes of potential outcomes are represented by monetary values. Or when relying on past data, expected wealth is simply the average wealth. Under this criterion, the best risky opportunity is the one with the highest probability-weighted average wealth from past data or from data that are supposed to represent the probabilities and the distribution of potential outcomes.

A similar, but more difficult, criterion is to maximize the *expected utility of wealth*. Originally devised by von Neumann and Morgenstern in their book *The Theory of Games and Economic Behavior* (1944), a **utility function** is a mathematical function that indexes or ranks the desirability (or utility) of outcomes. That is, a utility function maps preferences about (uncertain) outcomes to an indexed scale. For example, if an individual prefers outcome A to outcome B, then a utility function is supposed to represent how much the individual prefers A to B or at least represent the mathematical inequality $u(\text{A}) > u(\text{B})$, where $u(.)$ is a defined or undefined utility function.

Most people most of the time seem to dislike a loss more than they like a proportional gain. In other words, we have a desire to avoid risk and uncertainty is called or **risk aversion**, and a utility function can be constructed to reflect this preference. In effect, a utility function is a mathematical way to weight potential negative outcomes more heavily than corresponding potential positive outcomes, when in fact this is how we feel. A utility function does not change the probability of potential outcomes but changes the weights of the potential outcomes based on our feelings and preferences by using an index based on an arbitrary reference point (rather than the monetary values that expected wealth uses).

Also, we can say that a risk averter is willing to pay for insurance to avoid the risk of some exposure. A utility function is a mathematical way to quantify the weights that a risk averter places on losses relative to gains and to quantify the amount that the risk averter is willing to pay to acquire insurance.

Given the index from a utility function, von Neumann and Morgenstern argued that rational decision makers should try to maximize the value of this index when they choose among various certain outcomes or potential outcomes. They also showed that preferences among potential outcomes can be ranked by calculating the probability-weighted average utility level among all of potential outcomes, which they called the **expected utility (level)**. Thus, to choose a project or action, we could choose the one with the highest probability-weighted average utility of wealth after we define a utility function that is supposed to reflect how we feel about potential changes in our wealth.

Related to the amount that risk averters are willing to pay for insurance is the certainty equivalent value. The **certainty equivalent value** represents an amount of cash whose value is certain and which exactly corresponds to the value of the expected value of a risky prospect. In other words, if a decision maker could trade a risky prospect for a certain amount of money, the certainty equivalent value would make him indifferent before and after the trade. And if a decision maker would prefer to resolve unknown outcomes, he would be willing to pay to insure against the risky prospect and the remaining cash after the insurance payment would be called the certainty equivalent value.

Figure 9-5 represents a utility function that indexes welfare or satisfaction for a decision maker who is risk averse and would be willing to pay for insurance, as a function of wealth. It shows that losses of a certain magnitude (10000 won) and a 0.5 probability are disliked more than gains of the same magnitude and probability are liked. Secondly, it also shows that the welfare of a current (certain) level of wealth is greater than the welfare of the expected value of wealth with the risky prospect. Thirdly, it shows that a decision maker is willing to pay the cost of insurance to avoid risk, thereby keeping a risk-free value of wealth called the certainty equivalent value. Because the insurance is costly, the decision maker's welfare is lower than what it would be without risk. The diagram implies that insurance companies in a competitive market would reduce their economic profits to zero, so that the welfare of the expected value with risk is the same as the welfare of the certainty equivalent value without risk.

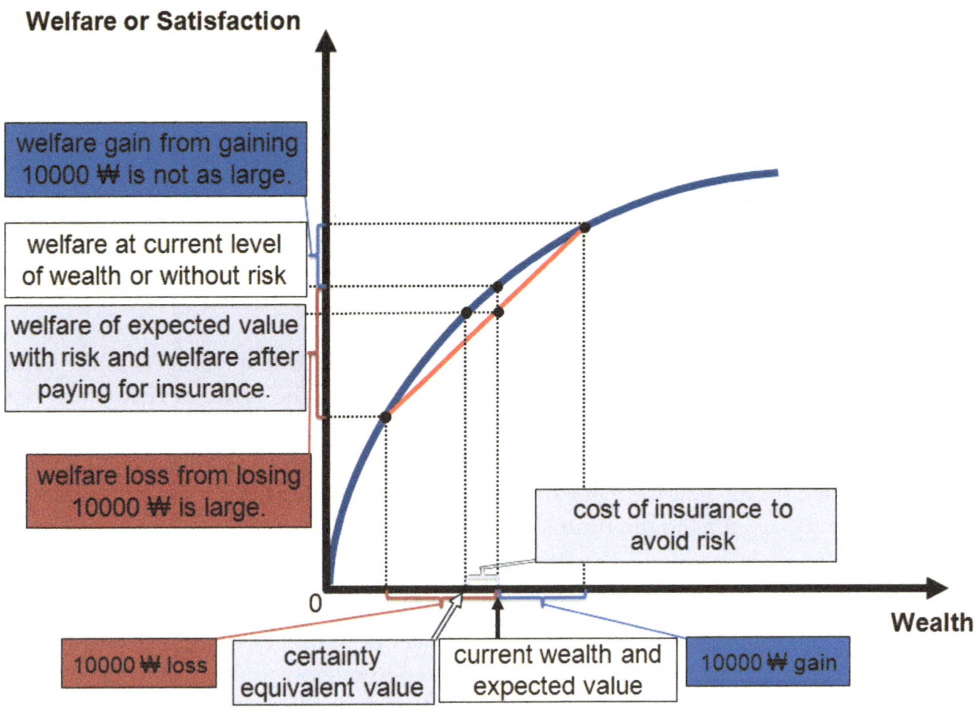

Figure 9-5: A utility function that represents expected value, certainty equivalent value and risk aversion.

However, a utility function is only a mathematical convenience and does not always correspond to actual valuation of gains and losses. In particular, we might sometimes seek risk—like when we skydive, smoke tobacco and gamble at casinos—rather than try to avoid risk. So we must be careful when applying such a function to represent risk and a decision criterion objectively because the function is unknown to an objective observer (and some argue that a function may unknown or at least inconsistent for an individual). A utility function can mislead and can add more uncertainty about a situation that is unknown rather than to clarify the situation.

Dispersion. Dispersion or **deviation** represents how much a variable can deviate from an average or expected value. It is often measured by standard deviation or variance.

As we learned in the previous section, standard deviation and variance weight dispersion or deviation according to their probabilities, which are 1 in the case of outcomes that have already occurred. However, other measures of dispersion or deviation can place more weight on negative deviations than on positive deviations from the average or expected value. In the extreme, we might put all weight on the largest negative deviation and no weight on more positive deviations.

Whatever calculation of dispersion that we use, we usually want to pursue the action with the lowest value, since we usually want to avoid unnecessary risks in finance.

We can also use expected wealth (or expected utility of wealth) with the standard deviation to form a decision criterion. We can calculate a deviation-adjusted expected value of wealth by the difference between or ratio of the expected wealth and the standard deviation:

$$E(w) - \sigma(w) \qquad \text{or} \qquad E(w)/\sigma(w)$$

where E(w) represents the expected wealth and σ(w) represents the standard deviation of wealth from various options that we could choose.

The reason for adjusting expected wealth for deviation is because the two are directly related: a high expected return on assets (which increases wealth) is often associated with higher deviation or risk. Therefore, savers usually face a trade off between return and risk.

Value at risk. Unlike the standard deviation and the decision criteria based on it, the value at risk considers only negative deviations from an expected or average value. The **value at risk** (VaR) represents the maximum acceptable *loss* on the current or expected value at a certain probability (usually 1% or 5%) during a given time period (usually in days, weeks or months). For example, the VaR could be $46 million at a 1% probability each day, which means that the value of assets is not expected to decrease by more than $46 million 99 days out of every 100 days in the future.

The VaR does not distinguish between potential values that are larger in magnitude than the maximum acceptable loss, or larger in magnitude than this lower bound. For example, if the VaR = $46 million with a 1% probability per day, then losses greater than $46 million could occur 1% of the time. However, these excessive losses could range from $46,000,001 to $46 billion or more.

There are three ways of calculating the VaR. The first two we have already considered: using past data and using a probability distribution. The third way is called Monte Carlo simulation.

Using past data to find a distribution of values and its worst case scenarios assumes that potential future values will have similarly bad scenarios to the same degree. Past data is shown in Figure 9-6 for the S&P 500 stock index. The figure shows that there were more than 5000 days out of the past 12625 days when the daily return was between 0% and 1% and about 800 days (5% of the past 12625 days) when the daily return was -1.493% or less. Thus, the VaR in this case can be expressed as a loss of -1.493% each day with a 5% probability, if we assume that future potential values will be distributed like past values shown in the historical figure. Alternatively, we can claim that an investment in the S&P 500 index should lose no more than 1.493% of its value per day with a 95% probability.

If we are unwilling to take this risk, then perhaps we should invest in safer asset, diversify our assets or buy insurance—strategies that we consider in a later section. If we are prepared to take this risk, we should still prepare a strategy to follow if a loss larger than the VaR occurs—such as selling the assets or using insurance.

We could also choose the VaR to be a loss of -2.61% each day with a 1% probability. Such a loss occurred in 1% of the last 12625 days, and if we assume that future potential values will be distributed like past values, then we can claim that an investment in the S&P 500 index should lose no more than -2.61% of its value in 99 out of the next 100 days.

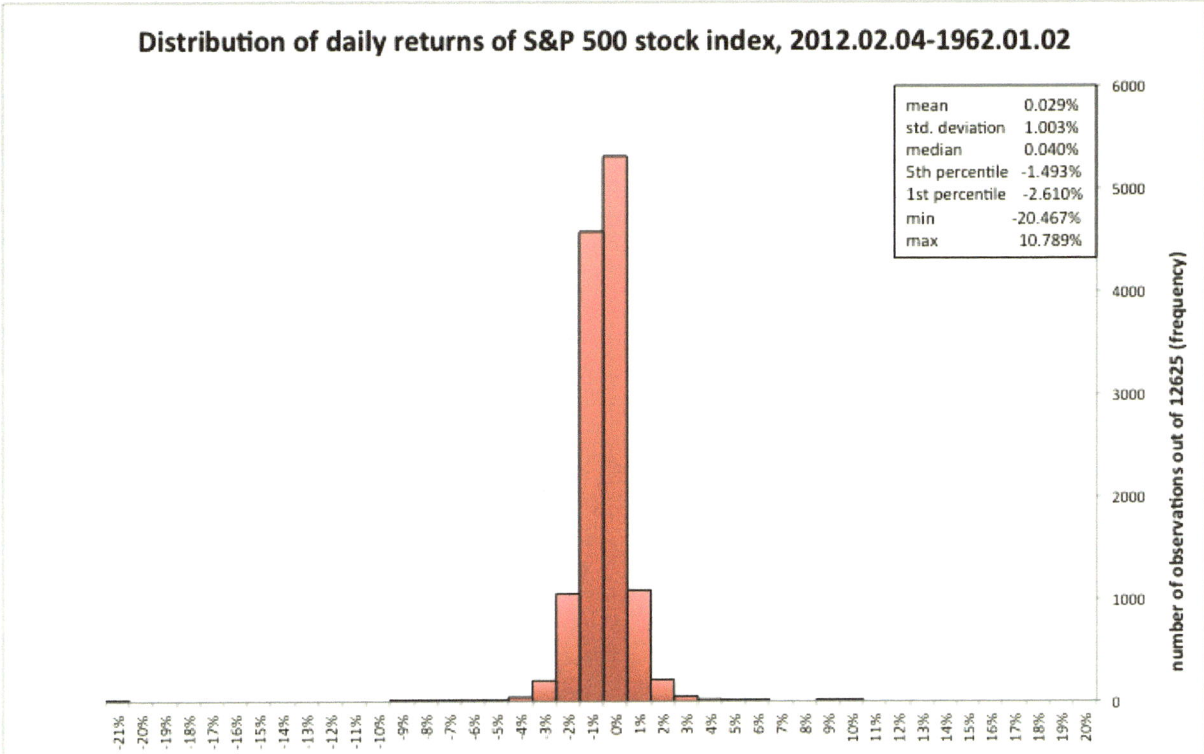

Figure 9-6: Using past data to calculate the VaR for the S&P 500 index

Using a probability distribution (like the normal distribution) assumes that future potential values can be represented by this distribution, given average values and a standard deviation calculated from past data. Figure 9-7 plots the normal distribution with the average or mean and the standard deviation from the past data of the S&P 500 daily returns, in conjunction with the past data itself.

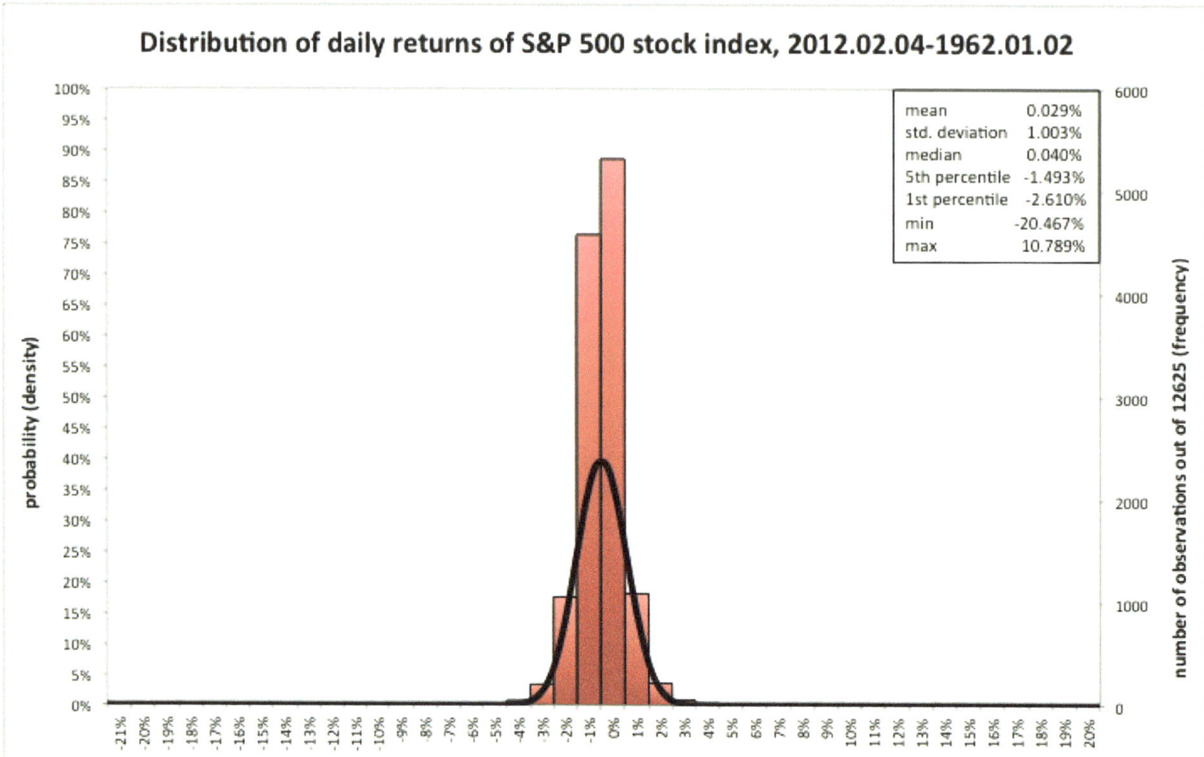

Figure 9-7: Using a probability (normal) distribution to calculate the VaR for the S&P 500 index

The principal difference between using only past data and a probability distribution is that the former calculates probabilities of potential values based only from the range of past data, while the latter calculates probabilities from the probability distribution itself, even though past data are used to measure the mean and standard deviation and perhaps other parameters of the distribution. The two methods generate similar results, but the results are not exactly the same. For example, using frequencies from past data only would imply that potential outcomes near the mean of 0.029% would be more frequent in the future than using probabilities from the probability function. Both methods, however, assume that potential events in the future will resemble events that have occurred in the past.

The probabilities of potential values in the future represented by a normal distribution can be used to calculate the VaR. According to the mathematical function that defines the normal distribution, the VaR at a 5% probability from a normal distribution is calculated as *mean* – 1.645 x *standard deviation*. In Figure 9-7, the mean of the historical data is 0.029% and the standard deviation is 1.003%, so that the VaR is 0.029% – 1.645 x 1.003% = -1.621%, which is slightly larger in magnitude than the -1.493% value representing the 5th percentile from the historical data. If potential future values can be represented by a normal distribution (versus past data), we can say that there is a 5% probability that the S&P 500 index will lose -1.621% or more of its value on any day in the future.

The VaR from a normal distribution can also be calculated from at the 1% probability. We use the formula *mean* – 2.58 x *standard deviation* to calculate this larger VaR: 0.029% – 2.58 x 1.003% = -2.559%. If potential future values can be represented by a normal distribution, we can say that there is 1% probability that the S&P 500 index will lose -2.559% or more of its value on any day in the future.

The third method of representing the VaR is through a Monte Carlo simulation, a method which simulates "random" values on a computer after defining a domain of potential values and their probabilities. For example, a Monte Carlo simulation can specify that random values are represented by a normal distribution with a mean and a standard deviation calculated from past data. After the domain and their probabilities have been specified, a computer would simulate a finite number of random values, which could then represent potential future values. However, other domain values and probabilities can be used depending on one's beliefs about potential values in the future. In particular, the Monte Carlo simulation allows one to make assumptions that can differ from past trends or a specified probability distribution.

Because of the ability to make assumptions that can represent a wide array of possibilities and potential values, Monte Carlo simulation may be used in **stress testing**, simulated tests about how well an institution's investments or balance sheet may perform during periods of financial stress. In particular, stress testing with Monte Carlo simulation (or other methods) allows banks to consider losses larger than the VaR calculated using past data or a probability distribution partially based on past data. In stress testing, various unfavorable scenarios are identified which could cause extreme losses—such as shortages in liquid assets, capital or collateral obligations—and then are represented by Monte Carlo simulation to guess how well the bank could perform under periods of financial stress.

Shortcomings of the VaR include the assumption that potential future values can be approximated either by past values, a probability distribution or a simulation based on the assumption that one can foresee and correctly model bad events and their effects. Instead of using quantifications and numbers, determined by patterns and data entry from the past, some prefer to rely on subjective beliefs about the uncertain future. Furthermore, a mathematical model can appear to estimate, predict and forecast risk well, but in conditions of risk, uncertainty or financial stress, we may forget our mathematical predictions and decision criteria and instead rely on intuition, emotion or instinct.

Secondly, VaR models often assume that market values of assets and liabilities are not only normally distributed but *uncorrelated* or *independent*, meaning that changes in the value of one asset or liability on the balance sheet are not associated with changes in the value of another asset or liability on the balance sheet. But often the values of many assets and liabilities on the balance sheet change together, as industry-wide or economy-wide changes affect different kinds of assets and liabilities in the same manner.

Furthermore, if most institutions use the same assumptions with the VaR, an industry-wide crisis can result as losses at one bank cause losses at other financial institutions. These correlated losses across institutions are called *contagion*, which in turn is often caused by widespread *panic*. Both contagion and panic can be caused by widespread fears about the quality and accuracy of company financial statements or rumors about various kinds of risks that financial institutions face. For example, after the Russian government defaulted on its debt in 1998, losses at many financial institutions exceeded their VaR, and a herd of individuals and institutions panicked by trying to sell their depreciated Russian bonds and related assets, further decreasing the market value of these assets and increasing the value of safe assets like cash, leading to higher default rates and shortages of liquid assets at many institutions. This case illustrates that assumptions behind the VaR calculations may be valid under normal conditions, but will break down during a crisis, when losses larger than the VaR occur at many institutions. In particular, while there may be little correlation between asset prices in periods of stability, the market value of most assets (except those of the safest assets) tends to decrease during a crisis, so that any benefits from diversification that exist during normal times will disappear.

Figure 9-8 shows that percent changes in, or volatility of, daily return rates of the S&P stock index are not uncorrelated or independent over time, but in fact large changes appear to be concentrated during some periods, especially in the mid-1970s, late 1987, the late 1990s, the early 2000s and the late 2000s. And during these times; financial stress, financial crises, panic or contagion of one type or another occurred, and people quickly sold and bought stocks, causing the return rates to fluctuate wildly. In particular, part of the cause of the volatility in 1998 can be blamed on the crisis in Russia at the time.

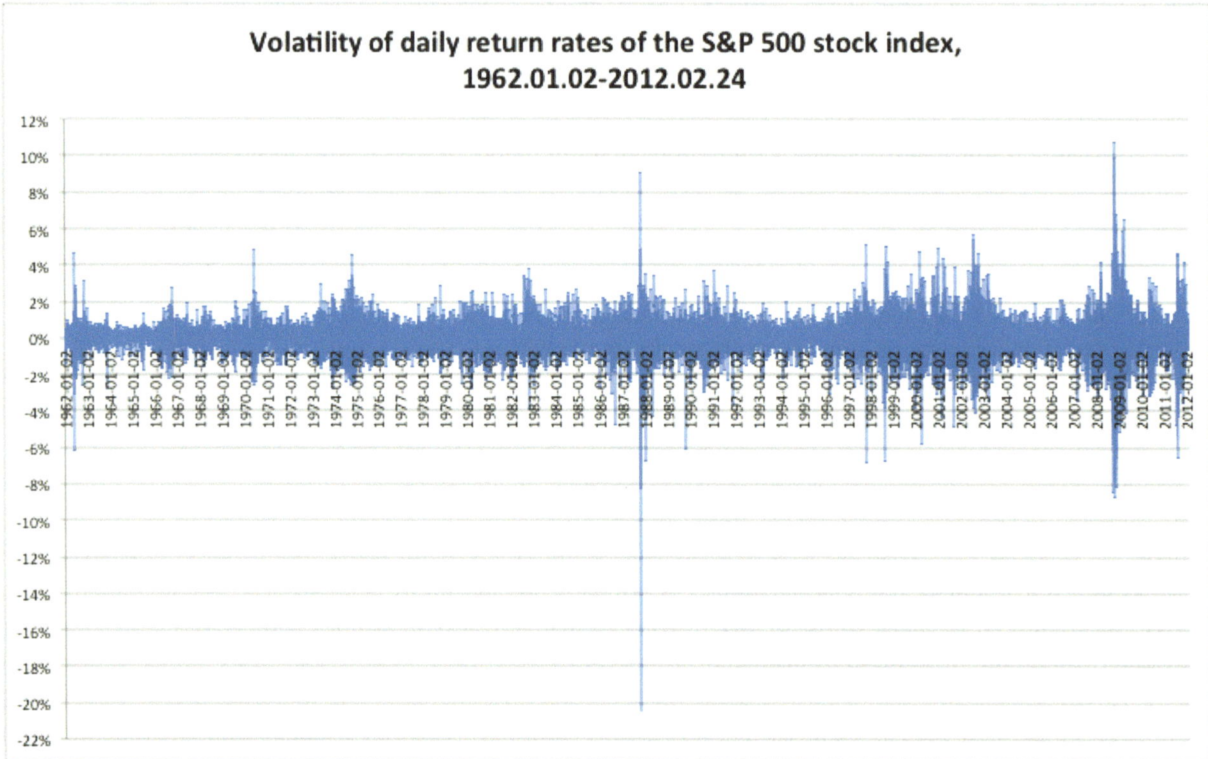

Figure 9-8: Volatility of return rates of the S&P 500 stock index is generally less than +/-3%, but periods of higher volatility were concentrated during some periods.

Figure 9-8 also shows that the most frequent daily returns were small in magnitude, less than +/-3%, and that large changes were infrequent. These types of outcome suggest that a power law could describe the distribution of returns.

A decision criterion under risk or uncertainty

One criterion for deciding under risk or uncertainty is called hypothesis testing: we form a hypothesis about the unknown state of the world and the test that hypothesis by collecting and analyzing data. We first form an initial hypothesis, or **null hypothesis**, about the unknown situation. For example, a doctor could form a null hypothesis about the unknown health situation of a patient: the patient has a disease. Then after collecting and analyzing available data, the doctor must decide whether *to reject* or *not to reject* this hypothesis. For example, based on analyzing a test result, the doctor will reject or not reject the hypothesis that the patient has a disease. If we are confident about the accuracy of available data and its analysis, then we reject the hypothesis if the analysis of the data is not consistent with the hypothesis, or otherwise we do not reject the hypothesis. I represent hypothesis testing in Figure 9-9. If we are not confident, then we simply can rely on the null hypothesis, not rejecting our original way of thinking.

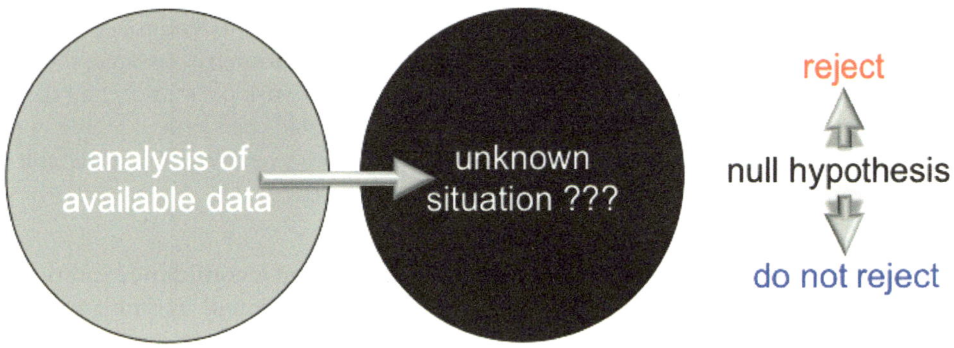

Figure 9-9: A representation of hypothesis testing.

But we can make errors in our hypothesis testing. A **type I error** represents the chance that the null hypothesis is rejected based on the analysis and available data when in fact it is true. In this case, the analysis or available data is inaccurate, unrealistic or misleading because it leads us to reject our initial hypothesis about the unknown state of the world, but in fact we should not have done so. A **type II error** represents the chance that the null hypothesis is not rejected based on the analysis and available data when in fact it is false. In this case, the estimate is inaccurate, unrealistic or misleading because it leads us not to reject our initial hypothesis about the unknown state of the world, but in fact we should have done so. Figure 9-10 represents type I and type II errors when testing a hypothesis about an unknown situation.

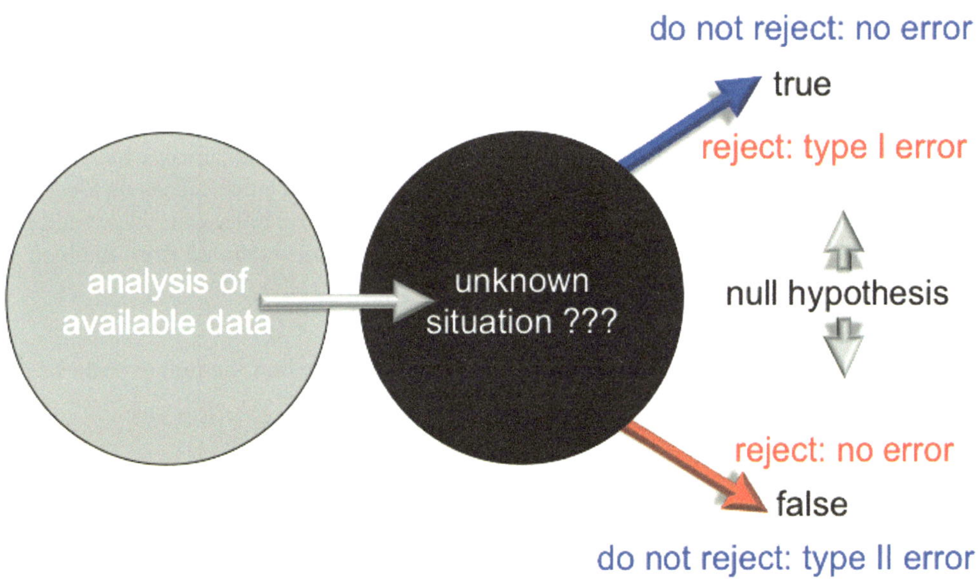

Figure 9-10: A representation of type I errors and type II errors.

Hypothesis testing can occur in finance if a bank decides whether to lend to a customer after analyzing the credit worthiness of a potential borrower from available data (I discuss how in the section on credit risk below). In this case, a null hypothesis could be that a borrower would repay on time if the bank lends to it, and the bank managers must decide whether to reject this hypothesis or not based on the analysis of the available data. A type I error in this case represents the risk of rejecting the hypothesis that a potential borrower would repay on time when in fact it is true. The bank would refuse to lend to a potential customer because the bank erroneously believes that the potential customer would not repay on time, thereby missing a profitable lending opportunity. A type II error in this case represents the risk of not rejecting the hypothesis that a borrower will repay on time when in fact it is false. The bank would then lend to a borrower because the bank erroneously believes that the borrower will repay on time, thereby suffering from default or delinquency.

Part of the analysis of available data may involve the estimation of a **confidence interval** around an estimate from available data. A confidence interval represents an interval around an estimate that makes a decision maker confident to a certain degree that the "true" value that could be obtained from completely accurate, realistic and infinite data will lie within this interval around the estimate obtained from somewhat inaccurate, unrealistic and finite data.

Similarly, a level of confidence represents how confident we are that an estimate can "accurately" predict the outcome of an unknown situation, where accurately is defined to be within the confidence interval. For example, at a 99% level of confidence, we can say that the estimate will predict an outcome lying within the confidence interval 99 times out of 100.

To test a (null) hypothesis, we compare estimated values and their confidence intervals to a **critical value**, a value below (or above) which estimated values are no longer acceptable. A critical value can represent the lower bound of a confidence interval, the lowest acceptable estimated value and/or the maximum acceptable risk. We reject the hypothesis if the estimate or the bounds of the confidence interval are below and/or above a critical value.

The relative risk of type I and type II errors depends on the critical value. The probability of a type I error increases when a higher critical value causes the decision maker to reject the null hypothesis more frequently. For example, if the null hypothesis is that a borrower will/would repay on time, more borrowers who would have repaid on time are excluded from the loan applicants as the critical value increases. On the other hand, the probability of a type II error decreases when a higher critical value causes the decision maker not to reject the null hypothesis. For example, if the null hypothesis is that a borrower will/would repay on time, more borrowers who would not have fully repaid the loan on time are excluded from the loan applicants as the critical value approaches increases.

How type I errors and type II errors depend on the critical value when the null hypothesis is that a borrower will repay on time is represented in Figure 9-11:

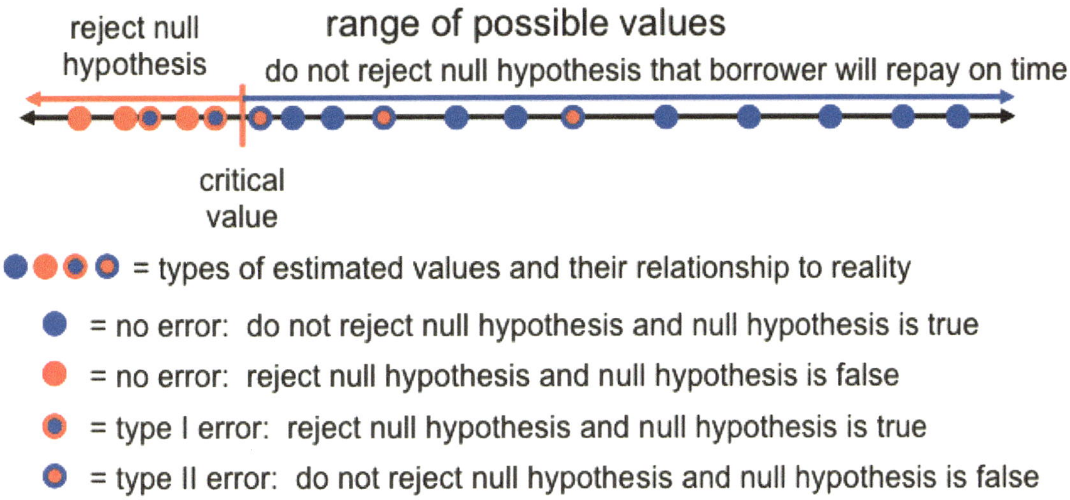

Figure 9-11: A representation of type I errors, type II errors and their relationship to the critical value.

In general, the relative risk of type I and type II errors is expressed as:

$$\text{Relative risk} = \frac{\text{risk of type I error}}{\text{risk of type II error}}$$

I next describe several types of risk and related problems that financial institutions could face, and discuss how these risks can be represented or measured using the standard deviation, a probability distribution, a confidence interval and a critical value.

Liquidity risk

Liquidity refers to the ability to convert an asset to cash. **Liquidity risk** is the risk of having a suboptimal amount of cash to pay for liabilities when they are due or to invest in new assets. Of course, liquidity risk can be caused by a lack of cash, but it can also be caused by an inability to borrow. Liquidity risk can also result from unexpected defaults on loans or other unexpected losses in income from assets. I discuss *default risk* and unexpected losses in income below. Finally, off-balance sheet activities, such as loan commitments or other contingent credit, can cause liquidity risk. If loan commitments are unexpectedly used, or used more than was originally anticipated, then a bank must be sure that it has sufficient cash.

Recall that reserves are the amount of money or cash that banks have in their vaults and deposited at the central bank. In the US, the Federal Reserve System requires that banks hold an amount of reserves relative to the value of their transaction deposits in order to facilitate transactions and payment settlement. In addition, banks may also want to hold excess reserves to satisfy customer needs and to better manage liquidity risk. Banks can reduce its liquidity risk by maintaining large balances of reserves, but the cost of this strategy is a lower expected rate of return on assets, since reserves earn little or no interest. Maintaining large balances of reserves has a cost, an opportunity cost, and managing liquidity risk involves minimizing this opportunity cost as well as minimizing the cost of having an insufficient amount of reserves. In other words, banks must keep sufficient cash to satisfy regulators and customers, but they do not want to maintain too many reserves because they earn little or no interest or return.

Adjusting assets and liabilities so that the maturity of liabilities (when expenses are due) better matches the maturity of assets (when income will be paid) can also reduce liquidity risk. But as we learned in chapter 6, banks traditionally pay low interest rates to savers for their deposits and charge high interest rates to borrowers for loans. The primary reason that deposits have low interest rates is that they are typically liquid liabilities for banks, meaning that banks must pay their customers cash in a short period of time. The primary reason that loans have high interest rates is that they are illiquid assets for banks, meaning that banks must wait a long time to receive all of the interest and principal payments. As a result, it would be costly to match the maturity of assets and liabilities by making liabilities less liquid and/or making assets more liquid. Nonetheless, some maturity matching occurs when the cost of selling assets for cash or the cost of borrowing is high, so that banks will want to keep some cash on hand (reserves), a very liquid asset, to pay for liquid liabilities.

The most common strategy to reduce liquidity risk is to ensure that banks have access to short-term loans in the money market when income from assets is lower than expected, when expenses from liabilities are higher than expected or when an unexpected opportunity to invest in new assets arises. Banks typically borrow from and lend to each other in the money market (or more specifically, the market for reserves), as those with a temporary surplus of reserves lend to those with a temporary shortage of reserves, at an interest rate called the federal funds rate in the US and the London interbank offer rate in the UK. Alternatively, banks can borrow from the central bank, which typically requires some collateral and then discounts its value to determine the amount of cash to provide for the loan.

A more costly strategy to manage interest rate risk involves banks selling or sacrificing investments to acquire reserves. Banks can sell securities or other assets and give up the interest or rate of return that those assets earn, which is typically more than the interest rate that they would pay for short-term loans in the money market. In addition, selling assets may involve substantial transaction costs. Banks can also reduce the amount of new loans that they were planning to make and give up the interest that those new loans would have earned. And in some cases, banks can “call on” callable loans, loans in which the borrower must repay the principal earlier than scheduled if the lender asks for early repayment. In sum, if a bank has insufficient reserves and is unable to borrow cash, it must try to liquidate less liquid assets, possibly at a steep discount.

Of course, an important goal of central banks is to act as a lender of last resort and to reduce liquidity risk. But central banks usually have a policy to lend only to illiquid banks, not insolvent ones in order to limit imprudent lending in the future. Furthermore, the distinction between illiquidity and insolvency is often not clear in practice, since both illiquidity and insolvency can be caused by an unexpected rise in expenses from liabilities, an unexpected fall in income from assets and an inability to acquire funds. Moreover, when these unexpected events occur, capital and reserves serve essentially the same purpose. Thus, central banks can not totally eliminate "liquidity risk" in this sense.

In sum, each of the strategies of managing liquidity risk—maintaining cash balances, borrowing from other banks, borrowing from the central bank, selling securities or other assets or reducing the amount of interest-bearing loans—involves a cost, and bank managers must determine which of these strategies is the least costly.

Credit risk

Credit risk has traditionally been the largest risk for banks because the traditional business of banks has been to extend credit to borrowers. **Credit risk** is the risk that a borrower would or will renege on the terms of credit by defaulting or being delinquent. When credit risk refers to risk of default, it is usually called **default risk.** But more generally, credit also includes the risk of delinquency, that is, being tardy on meeting the interest or principal payments so that the lender can not acquire the income from a loan, bond or other form of credit when it is expected. I discuss eight ways to minimize credit risk: loan pricing, limiting credit, monitoring, using collateral and other means.

Loan pricing. The price of a loan or other forms of credit refers to the price that a borrower pays to receive the credit and the price that the lender receives to issue the credit. This price can be divided into different parts to represent different costs that banks must bear:

$$\text{price} = i_{oc} + p + f$$

where i_{oc} represents the (opportunity) cost for the lender of acquiring and using the funds for the credit, such as a market interest rate at which funds are borrowed or could have been saved, p represents a risk premium to compensate for credit risk and other risks that the lender must bear, f represents fees and other costs for processing the transaction.

p and i_{oc} are usually positively related because as market interest rates rise, interest rates charged on variable rate loans also rise, which will increase the difficulty of repaying the loan and the probability of default. Also, as the market interest rate rises, fewer prudent customers will decide to borrow, leaving a larger pool of potential risky borrowers for the lender (a problem called *adverse selection*), which would increase the average default rate and therefore the risk premium. Collateral can lower the risk and cost of default, and therefore lower the risk premium (and limit the problem of adverse selection). The sum of i_{oc} and p represents the total interest rate on a loan.

Non-interest fees f can compensate for any transaction costs necessary to issue the loan and any other costs not covered by the market interest rate and risk premium, such as administration costs or losses from other assets. Banks may lower the explicit interest rate on a loan and raise fees if borrowers focus on the easy to recognize interest rate and do not carefully calculate the cost of fees.

While the (opportunity) cost of acquiring funds, i_{oc}, is generally easy to calculate, in general loan pricing is more of an art than a science because there is no precise formula for determining the right value of the risk premium and the right mix of fees and interest charges. Experience and observation of past data can help determine an accurate value of the risk premium, but the strategy of relying on past experiences and observations assumes that the future will be like the past. I discuss in the next section how banks look at an applicant's financial data to determine if he is suitable for a loan, and if the bank decides to lend, to help determine how much credit is appropriate and the risk premium p.

Credit limits. Credit may be limited both in the size of loans that are issued and in the number of individuals and institutions who can borrow.

Limiting the size of loans limits credit risk when a higher amount of credit gives the borrower an incentive to spend money less carefully or to overspend so that the ability to repay the full amount decreases. Limiting the size of loans reduces the hazard that the borrower will spend the funds or otherwise behave carelessly. Formally, economists say that limiting the size of loans reduces the problem called *moral hazard*, one type of credit risk.

Limiting the number of individuals and institutions who can borrow reduces the number of adverse applicants who would be unable or unwilling to repay the credit in the pool of potential borrowers. Formally, economists say that limiting the number of individuals and institutions who can borrow reduces the problem called *adverse selection*, another type of credit risk.

To limit the number of individuals and institutions who can borrow, a lender must first *screen* or separate potential borrowers to try to determine which would be unwilling or unable to repay a loan from those who are willing and able. To screen potential borrowers, lenders collect information about the loan applicant's credit history, the leverage ratio: how much the loan applicant has already borrowed relative to his wealth, the stability of earnings, total wealth, employment history, history as a bank customer and the length of time at a certain address. In addition, a lender will consider whether collateral will be required, whether macroeconomic changes can affect the applicant's ability to repay and the frequency of default or delinquency in the past.

This financial information can be summarized through a **credit score**, a weighted average of the financial information. A credit score for individual or institution i at time t, y_{it}, can be calculated as a linear function of relevant financial information:

$$y_{it} = \sum_i \alpha_i X_{it}$$

where X_{it} represents a vector of variables indicating or measuring default, delinquency, leverage ratio, wealth, et cetera for individual i at time t. a_i represents a vector of weights for each variable associated with individual or institution i. Alternatively, we can write

$$P(y_{it+1}|X_{it}) = f(\sum_i \alpha_i X_{it})$$

where $P(y_{it+1} \mid X_{it})$ represents the probability of a borrower i being in default at time t+1 given values of financial information for individual i at time t, and $f(.)$ represents a function. We can calculate the probabilities using frequencies in past data or a probability distribution, given a distribution of credit scores from financial information for individual i at time t.

Credit scores, or more accurately the probability of default, can also be calculated as a non-linear function through a *logit function* (probability distribution):

$$P(y_{it+1} \mid X_{it}) = [e^{\alpha_i X_{it}}]/[1 + e^{\alpha_i X_{it}}]$$

This kind of function may be better than a linear function when the probability of default or delinquency changes exponentially for at least some values of X_{it}.

The credit scores estimated both linearly and non-linearly can be compared to critical values. The critical value would represent a value below which credit would be denied, and above which credit can be given. Of course, the estimated value can be inaccurate, leading to either a type I error or type II error, as discussed previously.

To calculate a level of confidence, the bank could examine how accurate past credit scores were in predicting default or delinquency. For example, the bank could determine that of past borrowers with a credit score of 700, 97% of these borrowers actually repaid fully and on time. On the other hand, 3% actually defaulted or were delinquent. If past customers and credit scores are similar to present customers and credit scores, then the bank could say that a potential customer with an estimated score of 700 will have a 97%

probability of repaying on time in the future. Alternatively, the bank could say that of 100 potential customers with a score of 700, 97 would repay on time in the future, while 3 would not.

In general, credit scores are only as accurate as the analysis and past data that are used to predict future behavior. However, future defaults may be unrelated to analysis of past outcomes if the "structure" of the economy changes.

Another problem of basic credit scores with a critical value is that they impose a binary outcome: the potential borrower is predicted to default or not. But in fact, a range of outcomes is possible, from a delinquency in interest payments to non-payment of interest, to default on both interest and principal payments, to renegotiation of the terms of the loan contract. These other outcomes could be included in a multi-dimensional model, but the degree of complexity and of potential errors would increase exponentially.

Thirdly, given that basic models consider only binary outcomes, they ignore the fact that the amount of credit risk is determined not only by whether or not default or delinquency occurs, but also the amount of loss if default or delinquency occurs. The amount of the loss is determined by the amount of credit outstanding at the time of default or delinquency, the presence or absence of collateral (discussed below) and whether other parties share the credit risk through derivative or insurance contracts (discussed below).

Finally, these models typically assume that the probability of one borrower defaulting is independent of the probability of another borrower defaulting, but consistently sloppy lending practices or a macroeconomic contraction can cause credit risk among individuals and institutions to be correlated. A lender may want to consider *aggregate credit risk*, the risk that the value of loans from a pool of applicants will decrease together, which can be measured and managed through the risk adjusted return on capital and the value at risk methods that are discussed in a later section.

In addition to limiting the amount of credit, banks also generally mange credit risk by increasing the price of credit, or the interest rate. In particular, credit scores can be used to set a credit limit and a risk premium for borrowers. However, as the interest rate (risk premium) rises, the risk of default may also rise because the loan becomes more expensive. So there is a limit to how much banks can compensate for credit risk by charging a high risk premium.

Monitoring. Even after credit has been extended, a lender may want *to monitor* the activities of the borrower to limit credit risk or to compensate for additional credit risk. For example, a lender may want to monitor the financial status of borrower to examine the ability to repay the loan. If the ability to repay the loan has decreased because the borrower has acquired more debt from other sources, the lender could ask for (more) collateral or require higher interest payments to limit its potential losses. However, like charging excessive risk premia, this strategy can be counter-productive because it can raise the risk of default. Monitoring by the lender reduces the hazard that the borrower will engage in risky or careless behavior.

Collateral is an asset that can be seized by the lender in the event of default, and sold for cash to compensate for the loss. Requiring collateral can reduce the number of adverse applicants in the pool of potential borrowers because adverse applicants are not willing or able to provide collateral. Requiring collateral can also reduce the hazard that borrowers will engage in risky or careless behavior, such as not repaying on time, because they are not willing to lose the collateral.

However, if the value of collateral is negatively correlated with the ability of the borrower to repay, the collateral is less useful in limiting credit risk. For example, the value of houses decreased substantially in

Britain and Japan in the 1990s and in the US in the late 2000s as income and the willingness to buy houses decreased together. In many cases, homeowners saw the value of their house decrease below the value of the outstanding debt, a situation called **negative equity**, at the same time that their incomes were falling. Negative equity made more borrowers unwilling to repay and falling income made more borrowers unable to repay. As a result, some banks tried to accommodate distressed borrowers by reducing interest payments, reducing the principal or extending the time to repay rather than foreclose. Although renegotiating the terms of the loan was costly, losses would have been higher if the houses with negative equity were repossessed and sold.

In general, when the market value of the collateral decreases, the value of the collateral is said to experience a loss called a *haircut*. In this situation, banks often require that institutional borrowers make an extra payment, called a **margin payment**, based on the difference or margin between the value of the collateral and the value of the outstanding debt. This extra payment is added to the value of the collateral to increase the total value to the original value of the collateral.

Collateral is often an illiquid asset like a home, an automobile, an office or inventory goods. However, sometimes banks require liquid assets as collateral. **Compensating balances** are balances of liquid funds that borrowers are required to deposit with the lender that can be seized in the event of default.

In sum, to limit credit risk banks will try to accurately price loans, screen adverse applicants, limit credit, monitor borrowers and require collateral. Formally, the kinds of credit risk that banks try to limit through these practices are called adverse selection and moral hazard, which are represented in Figure 9-12.

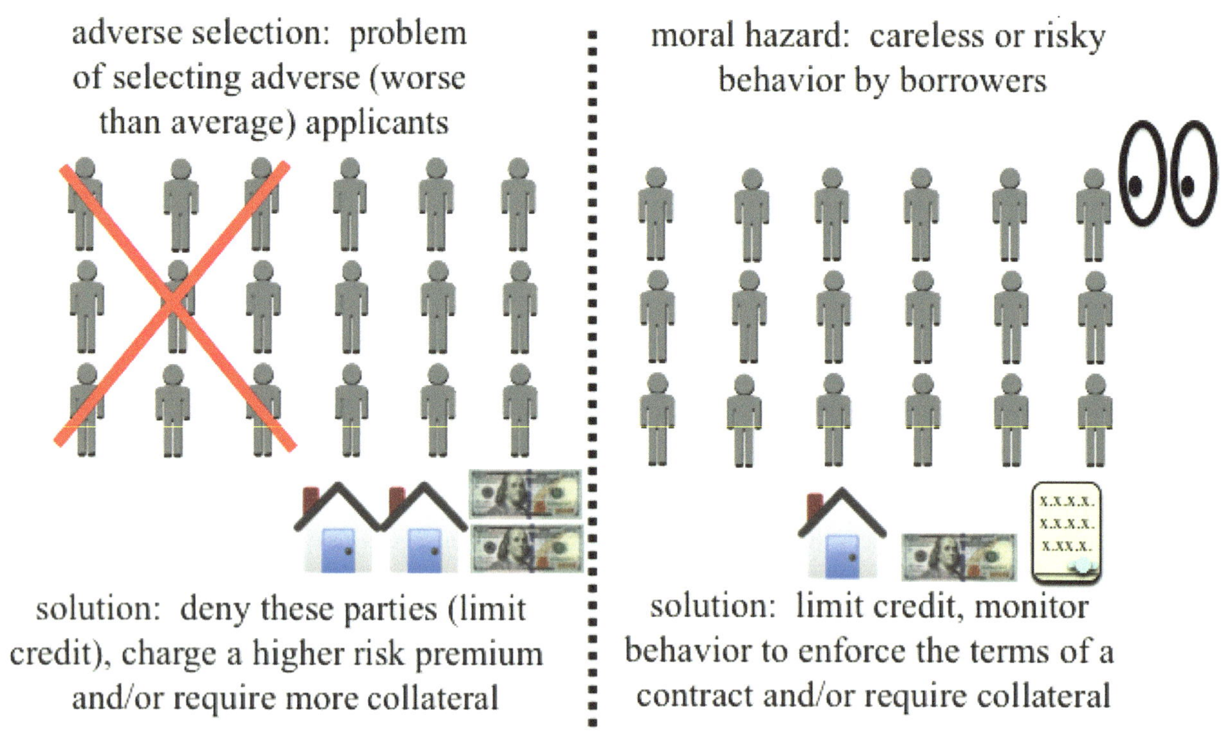

Figure 9-12: A representation of adverse selection and moral hazard for banks and the policies that they use to try to limit these credit risks.

Settlement risk

Like credit risk, settlement risk is also a form of **counterparty risk**, the risk that a counterparty might not fulfill its obligations in a transaction. **Settlement risk** is the risk that a counterparty will renege on the terms of a transaction after a party has settled its part of a transaction but before it has received the cash settlement or other reimbursement that it is due from the counterparty. Settlement risk can also include liquidity risk if a bank is not able to pay for expenses before the contract is settled.

Settlement risk is primarily a concern in inter-bank markets and payment settlement systems, especially when large payments are involved. Problems with one bank settling its payments can quickly cause other banks to be unable to meet their obligations, causing systemic risk. Making net payments is one way to reduce (systemic) settlement risk because of the lower amounts of cash used in transactions. Yet even with net payments, settlement risk in the inter-bank markets and payment settlement systems can be substantial because of the interdependence of banks. Central banks and regulatory bodies further try to limit settlement risk through voluntary agreements to limit bilateral and multilateral credit exposures and penalties for sending payments late in the day, after it is too late for the payments settlements operator to send them to the counterparty on that day.

However, central banks, clearing houses and other operators of the payment settlement systems have begun to rely more on real time gross settlement instead of net payments at the end of the day principally because electronic payment systems can allow real time payments in large denominations. The real time payments can reduce settlement risk because payments are immediately settled, but gross payments makes exposure to settlement risk larger if the payments fail to be made.

Market value risk

Market value risk or **market risk** refers to the risk of the market value of assets or liabilities unexpectedly changing. Market value risk is caused by market prices, interest and/or yield rates unexpectedly changing the income from assets and the expenses from liabilities. Separately, the risk of market prices unexpectedly changing and affecting the value of assets and liabilities is called *price risk*. The risk of market interest rates unexpectedly changing and affecting the value of assets and liabilities is called *interest rate risk*. One kind of interest rate risk that occurs as market interest rate change is called, margin risk. **Margin risk** is the risk that the margin, or difference, between two interest rates, say those on deposits and those on loans, will change unexpectedly.

Market value risk is important for marketable assets like bonds securitized loans and negotiable deposits for savers. It is also important for marketable liabilities like bonds and borrowed funds with variable interest/yield rates for borrowers.

Operational risk

Operational risk refers to risk associated with operations other than lending, borrowing, and investing in securities—such as fraud, non-compliance of safety and employment laws, lawsuits from flaws in a service, and accidents.

Types of operational risk involving accidents include 1) the breakdown of computer systems that process financial transactions. Many banks have a duplicate computer system which is backed up in real time in a secret location should anything go wrong with the main computer system. In addition, banks insure against fire or other catastrophes that threaten computer systems or other records. 2) unintentional errors made by employees resulting in losses.

Capital risk

Capital risk refers to the risk of not having the correct amount of capital when the values of assets or the values of liabilities unexpectedly change. This risk can result from liquidity risk, credit risk, settlement risk, market risk and/or operational risk. Recall that capital can be calculated as the difference between the value of assets and the value of liabilities or can be defined by the types of funds saved or retained (and kept "on reserve") and the type of funds that are paid in (to) the bank by the bank's investors/partial owners.

Banks with capital that is too low may violate domestic regulations and thereby be penalized and may have difficulty raising additional capital from investors. The Basel Accords, international agreements for accounting and capital standards, recommend that capital to relative risk-weighted assets and off-balance sheet activities be 8% for depository institutions, and most national governments of major economies adopt these recommendations when regulating banks and other financial institutions.

On the other hand, when capital is above its target ratio, which could lead to an inefficient use of resources if the capital is not reinvested to contribute to future profits. Capital is generally maintained as liquid funds that earn little or no return.

In addition to the measures of risk that we discussed earlier, capital risk can be measured by gap analysis, duration analysis or the risk-adjusted return on capital, which are discussed next.

Gap analysis is a simple way to determine when capital may be needed in the future by measuring the gap or difference between the values of assets and liabilities with various maturities. By examining possible negative gaps between the value of assets and the value of liabilities according to various maturity dates, an institution can better plan to adjust assets, liabilities or capital.

A simple example of gap analysis is shown in Table 17. Table 17 shows that the value of assets with a maturity between 3 and 6 months is less than the value of liabilities with the same maturity, which means that income from assets at that time will be insufficient to pay for the expenses from liabilities. As a result, the financial institution should plan to have cash on reserve, to be able to sell other assets for cash, to borrow, or to use capital to meet these obligations. In other words, there will be a decrease of capital in 3-6 months according to the accounting definition of capital, even if presently there is a sufficient amount of capital. A similar situation exists for maturities of 6-12 months and 2-5 years, although for maturities of 1-2 years and more than 5 years, the income from maturing assets is expected to be more than sufficient to meet the liabilities at those times.

By examining possible negative gaps between the book (or accounting) value of assets and the book value of liabilities according to various maturity dates, a bank can better plan to adjust assets, liabilities or capital on its balance sheet (and off its balance sheet) so that it does not face a shortage of capital when it faces a relative shortage of income from assets.

Table 17: Example of gap analysis with assets and liabilities of various maturities

	Maturity					
	overnight- 3 months	>3-6 months	>6-12 months	>1-2 years	>2-5 years	>5 years
Assets						
Inter-bank loans	$5					
3-month securities	$5					
2-year securities				$20		
Loans						$30
Liabilities						
Borrowed funds	-$5					
Deposits		-$10	-$20		-$15	-$10
Gap	$5	-$10	-$20	$20	-$15	$20

Most banks have positive incremental gaps for long maturities and negative incremental gaps for shorter maturities because they make large volumes of long-term loans and accept large volumes of short-term rate deposits. As a result, banks typically need to have sufficient cash on reserve to pay for short-term liabilities, have access to money markets to borrow or to sell short-term assets, or otherwise to have sufficient capital.

Duration analysis. A more complicated way of determining when capital may be needed in the future is *duration analysis.* Similar to gap analysis, duration analysis considers a difference or "gap" between the value of assets and the value of liabilities by maturity date. But unlike gap analysis, which only considers the book value of assets and liabilities, duration analysis considers the present value of assets and liabilities. By considering the present value of assets and liabilities that a bank could maintain on its balance sheet (or off its balance sheet), duration analysis considers how changes in market interest, yield or return rates of alternative assets or liabilities could affect the book value of assets, liabilities and capital. In effect, duration analysis considers market risk to represent capital risk. Moreover, while gap analysis considers the maturity date of assets and liabilities for various maturity dates, duration analysis considers the maturity date of all assets and liabilities *on average.*

Duration represents when, on average, assets will generate income or liabilities will require a payment; or more precisely, duration measures the weighted average maturity date of payments from assets or for liabilities. Duration can be calculated, as shown below, by considering how the present value of cash payments that will be received from assets or will be due from liabilities change as interest, yield or return rates on alternative assets change.

But before calculating duration, consider a few simple examples to understand the concept of a average maturity date. Suppose a bank has a six-month time deposit, and uses the funds to issue a loan with a maturity of six months, but with part of the loan repaid each month. Because some income from the loan is repaid before the maturity date, the duration of the loan will be less than its maturity date. For the time deposit, the duration is identical to the maturity date if depositors are paid all principal and interest at the end of six months. Alternatively, if the deposit were a savings deposit, from which funds could be withdrawn immediately, the duration would be much shorter on average when bank customers would typically withdraw at least some funds before the end of six months and the remaining funds at the end of six months. A bank could calculate the expected duration of a savings deposit based on past withdrawals by customers.

To calculate duration, I represent the present value of income from assets or expenses from liabilities over time as

$$PV = \sum_t C_t (1+i)^{-t}$$

where *PV* is the present value of (cash) payments that will be received or due in the future, C_t is the amount of (cash) payments received or due at time *t*, and *i* is the relevant saving or borrowing market interest, yield or return rate for alternative assets and liabilities.

Duration is the weighted average maturity date (time) of payments from an asset or for a liability, where the weights are the present value of the (cash) payments received or due at each time:

$$duration \equiv \frac{\sum_t t \cdot C_t (1+i)^{-t}}{PV}$$

(16)

Calculus can show that a linear approximation of the change in the present value of assets or liabilities with respect to a change in interest rates equals

$$dPV / di = \sum_t -t \cdot C_t (1+i)^{-t-1}$$

so that the percentage change in the present value of fixed income assets or fixed expense liabilities with respect to a percentage change in interest rates can be expressed as

$$(dPV / di)/(PV /(1+i)) = \frac{\sum_t -t \cdot C_t (1+i)^{-t}}{PV}$$

(17)

which equals the negative value of duration. In words, Equation (17) represents the risk that the present value of assets that will pay income at given times in the future and liabilities that will require payment at given times in the future will change when interest, yield or return rates on alternative assets and liabilities change.

Duration analysis relies on present value of all assets or liabilities, and it assumes (see equation (17)) a linear relationship between interest, yield or return rates and present value. But because equation (16) is a convex function when the time period exceeds 1, duration analysis is most useful to approximate the change in the present value of assets and liabilities for small changes in interest, yield or return rates.

Duration analysis is used to represent how the (present) value of capital will change as interest, yield or return rates on alternative assets change and as the present value of assets and of liabilities (for all maturities) change. Using the accounting definition of capital and equation (17), one can write:

$$\%\Delta capital = \%\Delta assets - \%\Delta liabilities$$

$$\frac{\%\Delta capital}{\%\Delta i} = \frac{\%\Delta assets}{\%\Delta i} - \frac{\%\Delta liabilities}{\%\Delta i}$$

$$\frac{\%\Delta capital}{\%\Delta i} = -D_A + D_L$$

(18)

where D_A represents the duration of assets of all maturities—the weighted average time of when income from all assets will be paid. D_L represents the duration of liabilities of all maturities—the weighted average of time of when expenses from liabilities will be due. $\%\Delta i$ represents the percent change in interest, yield or return rates on alternative assets or liabilities that the institution could acquire for its balance sheet. When determining how much the present value of today's capital will change as market rates change, this kind of calculation more heavily discounts the importance of income and expenses far in the future (with a long maturity) relative to income and expenses that will arrive soon.

For example, suppose that $D_A = 4$ years and $D_L = 2$ years, indicating that the institution has more long-term assets than long-term liabilities and fewer short-term assets than short-term liabilities, as most banks do. If (average) interest, yield or return rates on alternative assets or liabilities are expected to rise from 5% to 5.5%, then $\%\Delta i = 10\%$. Because of these higher interest, yield or return rates, the present value of assets on the balance sheet is predicted to decrease, according to equation (17), as alternative assets become more attractive. In addition, the value of investing available capital increase as interest, yield and return rates increase. The present value of liabilities on the balance sheet will also decrease (become relatively less expensive), as alternative liabilities with the higher interest or yield rates make these alternative liabilities less attractive and current liabilities relatively more attractive. But when the duration of assets is longer than the duration of liabilities, the decrease in the present value of assets will be greater than the decrease in the present value of liabilities, and the (present) value of available capital will decrease. In this simple example, the (present) value of capital changes by $(-4 + 2) \times 10\% = -20\%$. Therefore, a bank may want to use (20% of) its capital or to sell existing assets and invest in the more profitable alternative assets.

However, if interest or yield rates increase due to an increase in risk or a decrease in liquidity, then a bank may want to increase the (present) value of capital to compensate for the higher risk and lower liquidity rather than to invest in new assets. Therefore, duration analysis does not unambiguously predict the optimal change in (or level of) capital because it can not predict how much risk, liquidity and other factors change when interest, yield or return rates change.

Risk adjusted return on capital. The **risk adjusted return on capital** (RAROC) considers the average income from assets and the average expenses from liabilities, as well as their deviation, relative to value of capital for a specified time period:

$$\text{RAROC} = \textit{average net return}/(\textit{standard deviation of net return}/\textit{capital})$$

where *average net return* = average income from assets – average expenses from liabilities during a specified period.

The average net return is calculated from a specified amount of past data (for example for the last 10 years) and is usually intended to represent the *expected* net return during a specified future period (for example, during the next year). Likewise, the standard deviation is calculated from this past data and is intended to represent the average deviation from the expected value during the future. Capital, as usual, represents the funds available to pay for unexpected losses from assets and unexpected expenses from liabilities.

Mathematically, the RAROC can also be expressed more clearly as

$$\text{RAROC} = (\textit{average net return}/\textit{standard deviation of net return}) \times \textit{capital}$$

This second formula shows what capital can be expected to earn (on average) if it is invested in new assets. It also shows what stock/equity/share holders have earned on average from their investments in the bank after accounting for deviations (variations) in their return rates.

According to either formula, if average net returns decrease (assets have lower income and/or liabilities have higher expenses) or if the standard deviation of net returns increase (net returns become more risky over time), then capital should be increased rather than invested in new assets to keep the RAROC constant.

Strategies to manage risk and uncertainty

Banks can manage liquidity, credit, settlement, market value, operational and capital risk through various strategies: buying insurance, using derivative contracts, diversifying assets and liabilities, specializing in certain assets and liabilities, otherwise adjusting their assets, liabilities or capital.

Insurance. Insurance allows society to spread risk, uncertainty and responsibility of losses among many people. For example, fire insurance protects individual home owners, and the risk of fire is shared by the many people who are share holders of an insurance company, as represented by Figure 9-13.

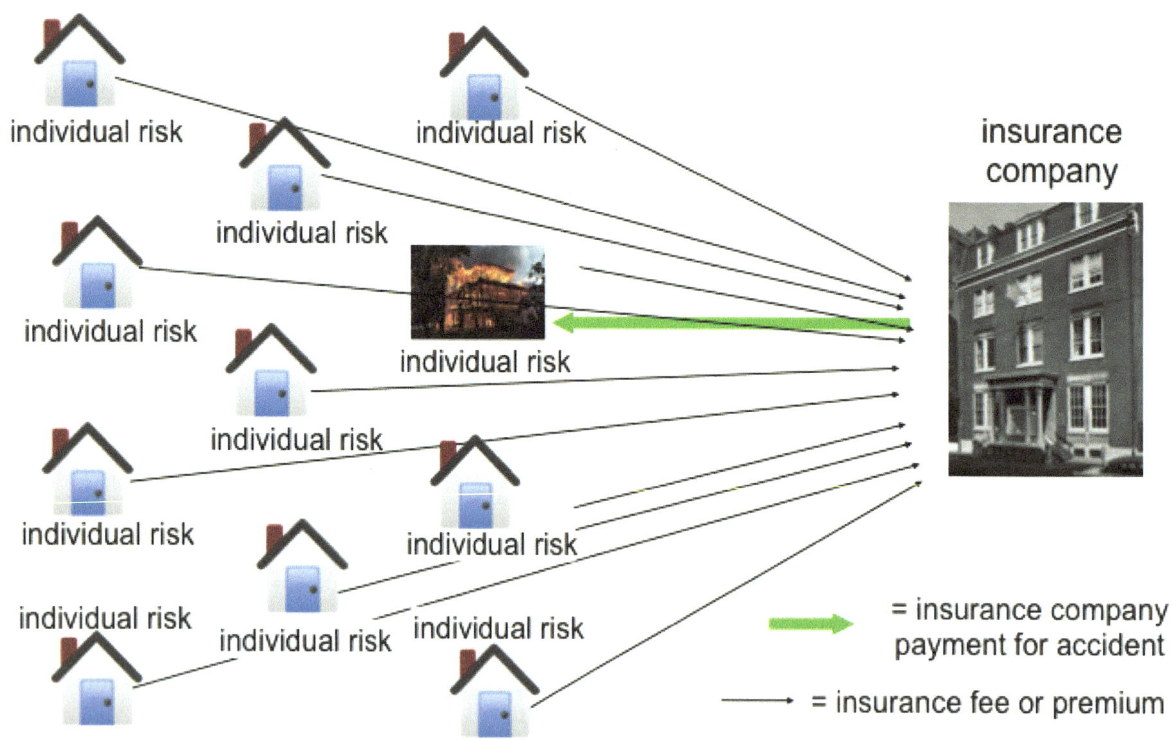

Figure 9-13: A representation of insurance.

Financial insurance also exists: banks can insure against default of their loans by paying a premium to a financial insurance company. In the event of the default, the insurance company will compensate the bank for all or part of the loss, according to the insurance contract.

Insurance contracts require a person facing a risk to pay a fee, or **premium**, in return for the insurance company accepting all or part of the risk.

Derivative assets and liabilities. Forward contracts, futures contracts, swap contracts and options contracts discussed in the previous chapter can also function as insurance contracts. These contracts can decrease some risks for some parties by allowing them to buy or to sell an underlying asset/liability at a price that is set today instead of a market price that will vary over time. However, recall also that setting the price of a contract today can cause the parties to increase other risks as well, because the contract obligates them to make a transaction or to pay a fee. In addition, derivative contracts require counterparties that function as insurers and that must acquire more risk if the first party hopes to insure or decrease risk.

Diversification and specialization. Diversification refers to managing risk by accepting small, unrelated risks together rather than a single large risk, by reducing exposure in a single asset or liability. In other words, diversification is a strategy to reduce risk by acquiring a diverse group, or portfolio, of assets (or liabilities) whose values are not positively correlated.

Insurance is a type of diversification, and diversification is a type of self-insurance. An insurance company tries to cover (reduce) risk by having many diverse customers. A bank can try to cover (reduce) risk by having many diverse assets and liabilities.

With diversification, a relatively small loss in wealth may occur, but the cost of this loss will be limited because exposure is limited and the loss can be covered by other assets/liabilities when they do not have a bad outcome.

A loss for all customers or all assets/liabilities is unlikely to occur at the same time when individual risks are unrelated. **Idiosyncratic risk** is a risk that is unrelated to other types of risk. For example, a risk of fire at one home is usually unrelated to the risk of fire at nearly all other homes. Likewise, a person who invests in a single company is usually undertaking a fair amount of idiosyncratic risk, because factors that affect the profitability of the firm are usually specific to that firm: revenue and expenses from individual products, research potential, lawsuits against firm, strikes by the firm's workers and conditions that affect the firm's cost of inputs.

By buying a diverse group of assets, an owner of a portfolio could avoid large drops in the value of the portfolio caused by idiosyncratic risk of a single asset. Even if one asset in the portfolio had a rate of return that was lower than expected due to changes in idiosyncratic factors, other assets would not be affected by these factors and would perform relatively well.

Thus, diversification reduces idiosyncratic risk, although it can not reduce all risk because sometimes risks of assets and liabilities are correlated. For example, when we considered the VaR in an earlier section, we considered the possibility of losses that are correlated over time and correlated across markets (contagion). Thus, VaR is not guaranteed to measure risk accurately, and diversification is not guaranteed to manage risk completely.

Table 18 demonstrates how diversification could work to limit risk of losses in assets. Suppose that you have 1,000,000 **원** to invest in asset *A* or asset *A* and 9 other assets, labeled *B-J*. In the latter case, suppose you divide you investment equally among all assets. Suppose next that a large (20%) loss occurs on your investment in asset *A* but the return rates of the other assets are not correlated and do not change to the same degree. If you had invested all of your money in asset *A*, you would lose 200,000 **원**, but if you limit your investment in asset *A* to only 100,000 **원**, you would lose a relatively small amount 20,000 **원** from asset *A*. Furthermore, if you had invested in 10 diverse assets, the losses from other assets will also be limited, and in many cases will be smaller loses or even gains. Therefore, the total losses could be smaller than a -20% return that would occur if you had invested only in asset *A*.

Table 18: An example of diversification

A 1,000,000 **원** – 200,000 **원**	*A* 100,000 **원** – 20,000 **원**
	B 100,000 **원** – 30,000 **원**
	C 100,000 **원** – 5,000 **원**
	D 100,000 **원** – 1,000 **원**
	E 100,000 **원** – 0 **원**
	F 100,000 **원** – 0 **원**
	G 100,000 **원** – 0 **원**
	H 100,000 **원** + 1,000 **원**
	I 100,000 **원** + 5,000 **원**
	J 100,000 **원** + 10,000 **원**

Banks can define the degree of diversification through a **concentration limit**: a limit on the amount of exposure in a particular asset or liability relative total value of assets or liabilities. In the example above, the concentration (limit) was 10% in each asset.

In contrast to diversification, *specialization* in particular assets or liabilities can increase the knowledge of particular credit markets and borrowers, thereby limiting credit risk, market risk or capital risk. More knowledge through specialization can limit the adverse applicants in the pool of potential borrowers and limit the hazard that borrowers will engage in risky or careless behavior, such as not repaying on time, the risk of market prices or interest rates changing unfavorably and the risk that the amount of capital will be suboptimal.

Bank managers and officers must decide to what degree they want to specialize and to what degree they want to diversify.

Holding safe assets and capital. People can also reduce risk by holding safe assets, like domestic cash, short-term bonds or liquid deposits. These assets generally offer only a low interest, yield or return rate, but this rate is fairly stable regardless of economic conditions.

Capital, like domestic cash, is also very safe but has a low (zero) interest or return rate.
As I discussed in the section on capital risk, capital is held specifically to protect against an unexpected fall in the value of assets and an unexpected rise in the value of liabilities.

On the other hand, risky assets include stock and real estate, whose prices and returns depend on unpredictable expectations and economic conditions. Stocks and real estate generally have a high return rate only if expenditure and production expand. On average, expenditure and production have expanded and these assets generally offer higher return rates than safe assets or capital. But during financial crises, these assets can have negative return rates and thus perform poorly relative to safe assets and capital.

Summary and Conclusion

In this chapter we examined various ways to measure risk: standard deviation, variance, covariance, correlation, frequency, probability distributions and the value at risk.

Next we considered hypothesis testing about the unknown or uncertain state of the (future) world, and possible errors that we could make after we reject or not reject our hypothesis about the unknown or uncertain state of affairs, according to estimates, predictions or forecasts from data that is presently available.

We also considered liquidity risk, credit risk, settlement risk, market value risk, operational risk, capital risk and ways to measure and manage these risks. To manage liquidity risk, bank managers must measure the opportunity cost of holding liquid assets (cash) with the explicit interest cost of acquiring liquid assets when needed. To manage credit risk, banks calculate credit scores from the financial data of potential borrowers and impose credit limits where necessary, and also use monitoring, collateral, diversification, specialization, insurance, derivative assets and liabilities. To manage market value risk, banks often use insurance, diversification, specialization, and derivative assets and liabilities. To manage settlement risk, banks can rely either on real-time payments or net payments, or both, or use the methods to manage credit risk and market value risk. To manage operational risk, banks often use insurance. To manage capital risk, banks can use the aforementioned methods, and to measure capital risk they often use gap analysis, duration analysis, the risk adjusted rate of return on capital and the value at risk. Each of these methods has shortcomings and involves some subjective decisions about the degree of risk that assets and liabilities have.

Risk management has changed over time. Traditionally, banks did not concern themselves with market value risk because funds were acquired from traditional deposits that paid very stable or fixed interest rates and were used acquire assets with very stable or fixed interest rates. Their principal concern was credit risk. These days, however, a dynamic inter-bank money market, bond market and derivatives market and foreign exchange market make market value risk and possibly other kinds of risk a bigger concern and the management of asset and liabilities a more difficult task. In addition, derivative contracts, involving contingent income and expenses, can add to the complexity when banks both get insured and insure others with these contracts. The expansion of financial activities in foreign countries, as well as the myriad of international regulations, has increased risk for many institutions.

Problems and Applications

<u>Short answer problems</u>

1. Describe the difference between a type I error and a type II error. If a bank refuses to lend to some deserving customers, which type of error will more likely result? If a bank lends easily to any customer, which type of error will more likely result?

2. Explain how the average value from past data can be considered the expected value of potential, uncertain values.

3. Explain how the standard deviation represents risk. What are the shortcomings of using the standard deviation to measure risk?

4. If a bank screens adverse applicants from a pool of loan applicants, what kind of credit risk is it trying to reduce?

5. If a bank tries to monitor and enforce behavior through loan contracts with customers, what kind of credit risk is it trying to reduce?

6. What is duration? How can it be used to measure the present value of assets or liabilities?

7. What are the shortcomings of using the risk adjusted return on capital to measure capital risk?

8. Explain how the value at risk represents risk. What are the shortcomings of using the value at risk to measure risk?

9. Describe 4 strategies to handle the risk of having too few liquid assets at banks. What are the costs of each strategy?

10. Describe how collateral can reduce credit risk. In particular, describe how collateral can reduce adverse selection and moral hazard.

11. If collateral reduces credit risk, why are some forms of credit (loans) *uncollateralized*? And for these uncollateralized forms of credit/loans, should the price of credit, and in particular the risk premium, be higher or lower than collateralized credit/loans?

12. Describe 2 strategies that banks use to manage credit risk. How do these strategies reduce moral hazard and/or adverse selection?

Internet applications

1. Go to http://ecos.bok.or.kr/ to find data for credit risk scores (inversely related to credit scores) under the Survey of Lending Practices. Create a graph of these credit risk scores for large corporations, small and medium corporations, and general households from the earliest available quarter to the latest available quarter. Calculate the average credit risk score during this time. Which institution has the highest credit risk score? Why do you think this is so? Which institution has the lowest credit risk score? Why do you think this is so?

2. Go to http://finance.yahoo.com/q/hp?s=^OEX+Historical+Prices to download daily asset price data for the S&P 100 index and calculate daily returns from the index. (You may ignore dividends in the returns.) Next calculate the mean, standard deviation, median (50th percentile value), 5th percentile value and the 1st percentile value. Based on this historical data, what is the VaR at a 5% probability for the next 100 days? Based on this historical data, what is the VaR at a 1% probability for the next 100 days?

3. Create a histogram (graph) of the historical data from the previous question. A normal distribution predicts than only 1% of observations are more than 3 standard deviations away (in the positive *and* negative directions) from the expected value. Using the average and the standard deviation from the previous question, what percent of observations are more than 3 standard deviations away from the average?

4. Go to http://finance.yahoo.com/q/hp?s=^OEX+Historical+Prices to download daily asset price data for the S&P 100 index and calculate daily returns from the index. (You may ignore dividends in the returns.) Calculate the standard deviation from the historical data, then graph the daily returns. When was the volatility of the daily returns greater than the standard deviation? When was the volatility of the daily return less than the standard deviation?

5. Go to http://finance.yahoo.com/q/hp?s=^OEX+Historical+Prices to download daily asset price data for the S&P 100 index and calculate daily returns from the index. (You may ignore dividends in the returns.) Next calculate the mean, standard deviation, median (50th percentile value), 5th percentile value and the 1st percentile value only from the latest date to 10 years ago. Next, calculate these values only from 20 years to 10 years ago. Next, calculate these values only from 30 years to 20 years ago. Finally, next calculate these values only from 40 years to 30 years ago. By what percent do these values change from decade to decade? Do you think that the values are stable or "stationary" from decade to decade? Why or why not?

6. Go to http://finance.yahoo.com/q/hp?s=^NYA+Historical+Prices to download daily asset price data for the NYSE composite index and calculate daily returns from the index. (You may ignore dividends in the returns.) Next calculate the mean, standard deviation, median (50th percentile value), 5th percentile value and the 1st percentile value. Based on this historical data, what is the VaR at a 5% probability for the next 100 days? Based on this historical data, what is the VaR at a 1% probability for the next 100 days?

7. Create a histogram (graph) of the historical data from the previous question. A normal distribution predicts than only 1% of observations are more than 3 standard deviations away (in the positive *and* negative directions) from the expected value. Using the average and the standard deviation from the previous question, what percent of observations are more than 3 standard deviations away from the average?

8. Go to http://finance.yahoo.com/q/hp?s=^NYA+Historical+Prices to download daily asset price data for the NYSE composite index and calculate daily returns from the index. (You may ignore dividends in the returns.) Calculate the standard deviation from the historical data, then graph the daily returns. When was the volatility of the daily returns greater than the standard deviation? When was the volatility of the daily return less than the standard deviation?

9. Go to http://finance.yahoo.com/q/hp?s=^NYA+Historical+Prices to download daily asset price data for the NYSE composite index and calculate daily returns from the index. (You may ignore dividends in the returns.) Next calculate the mean, standard deviation, median (50th percentile value), 5th percentile value and the 1st percentile value only from the latest date to 10 years ago. Next, calculate these values only from 20 years to 10 years ago. Next, calculate these values only from 30 years to 20 years ago. Finally, next calculate these values only from 40 years to 30 years ago. By what percent do these values change from decade to decade? Do you think that the values are stable or "stationary" from decade to decade? Why or why not?

10. Go to http://finance.yahoo.com/q/hp?s=^N225+Historical+Prices to download daily asset price data for the NIKKEI 225 index and calculate daily returns from the index. (You may ignore dividends in the returns.) Next calculate the mean, standard deviation, median (50th percentile value), 5th percentile value and the 1st percentile value. Based on this historical data, what is the VaR at a 5% probability for the next 100 days? Based on this historical data, what is the VaR at a 1% probability for the next 100 days?

11. Create a histogram (graph) of the historical data from the previous question. A normal distribution predicts than only 1% of observations are more than 3 standard deviations away (in the positive *and* negative directions) from the expected value. Using the average and the standard deviation from the previous question, what percent of observations are more than 3 standard deviations away from the average?

12. Go to http://finance.yahoo.com/q/hp?s=^N225+Historical+Prices to download daily asset price data for the NIKKEI 225 index and calculate daily returns from the index. (You may ignore dividends in the returns.) Calculate the standard deviation from the historical data, then graph the daily returns. When was the volatility of the daily returns greater than the standard deviation? When was the volatility of the daily return less than the standard deviation?

13. Go to http://finance.yahoo.com/q/hp?s=^FVX+Historical+Prices to download changes in daily bond yield rates for 5-year Treasury bonds. (Yield rates are calculated by comparing the future payments of a bond to the current price of the bond and are inversely related to the current price of the bond.) Next calculate the mean, standard deviation, median (50th percentile value), 5th percentile value and the 1st percentile value. Based on this historical data, what is the VaR at a 5% probability for the next 100 days? Based on this historical data, what is the VaR at a 1% probability for the next 100 days?

14. Create a histogram (graph) of the historical data from the previous question. A normal distribution predicts than only 1% of observations are more than 3 standard deviations away (in the positive *and* negative directions) from the expected value. Using the average and the standard deviation from the previous question, what percent of observations are more than 3 standard deviations away from the average?

15. Go to http://finance.yahoo.com/q/hp?s=^FVX+Historical+Prices to download daily bond yield rates for 5-year Treasury bonds. (Yield rates are calculated by comparing the future payments of a bond to the current price of the bond and are inversely related to the current price of the bond.) Calculate changes in these rates and the standard deviation of these changes from the earliest date to the latest date, and then graph the daily yield rates from the earliest date to the latest date. When (or how many days) was the volatility of the daily yield rates greater than the standard deviation? When (or how many days) was the volatility of the daily yield rates less than the standard deviation?

16. Go to http://finance.yahoo.com/q/hp?s=^FVX+Historical+Prices to download daily (opening) bond yield rates for 5-year Treasury bonds. (Yield rates are calculated by comparing the future payments of a bond to the current price of the bond and are inversely related to the current price of the bond.) Calculate changes in these rates and the mean, standard deviation, median (50th percentile value), 5th percentile value and the 1st percentile value of the changes only from the latest date to 10 years ago. Next, calculate these values only from 20 years to 10 years ago. Next, calculate these values only from 30 years to 20 years ago. Next, calculate these values only from 40 years to 30 years ago. Finally, calculate these values only from 50 years to 40 years ago. By what percent do these values change

from decade to decade? Do you think that the values are stable or "stationary" from decade to decade? Why or why not?

10. Bank Regulation

Preview

We learned that risk management is an important part of banking, and that risk represents a quantification of something that is uncertain or unknown. In this chapter, we also consider a particular type of uncertainty or the unknown: when one party in a transaction is less certain than another. As we learned previously, risk management by banks can be used to limit this type of uncertainty or the unknown. In this chapter, we learn that regulation can also be used to limit this type of uncertainty and the unknown, and to limit problems that are associated with it. This regulation is intended to benefit banks, when they are uncertain, as well as bank customers and taxpayers, when they are uncertain about the risky behavior that banks take. And because the risks that banks take sometimes result in bankruptcy and other costly financial problems for bank customers and taxpayers, we learn about regulations intended to handle bankruptcy for the benefit of bank customers, taxpayers and society in general.

Why banks are regulated

As we learned in chapter 6, banks act as intermediaries between savers and borrowers and help funds move through the economy more efficiently. Because of their important role as an intermediary, bankruptcy or bank failure, can cause widespread damage to the economy. **Bank failure** or **bankruptcy** refers to the case where a bank or other financial intermediary is unable to pay for its liabilities. When a bank fails, not only are the employees and owners financially hurt, but so are individuals, commercial enterprises and other businesses that were customers of the bank because they relied on the bank for safe keeping of their deposits, for access to money and credit and for processing payments. In addition, banks are frequently customers of other banks, so that bank failure at one bank may cause financial problems at other banks. Because the financial health of banks is intertwined with the financial health of many individuals and other institutions, governments heavily regulate the banking sector in the US and other countries to avoid bank failure.

But regulation of banks is difficult because information about their financial health and the financial health of their customers is never perfect. As we learned in chapter 9, banks try to limit liquidity risk, credit risk, settlement risk, market value risk and capital risk through various means, but banks can never eliminate risk entirely because information about their customers, investments or the future is never perfect. In particular, parties such as borrowers know more about their current and future financial conditions than the bank knows. In this chapter, I also consider imperfect information in the banking sector from a different perspective: parties such as depositors and other creditors know less about the current and future financial conditions of the bank than the bank itself.

A situation in which one party in a transaction has more information than another is called a situation of **asymmetric information**: there is an asymmetry in the amount of information that parties have. The cause of asymmetric information is an informal or formal barrier (such as a costs of acquiring and processing information, a lack of communication, social norms or laws about privacy) that prevents the less informed party from easily obtaining all of the information that the more informed party has. Individuals and institutions try to reduce asymmetric information by collecting and processing available information about counterparties, but they can never expect to know everything about current and future financial conditions of counterparties.

Furthermore, because barriers to communication prevent the flow of clear information, those who are less informed sometimes rely on *signals*, which are indicators such as past information, non-verbal or non-written cues, hearsay and reputation that help the less informed party learn more information and help them decide whether to enter a transaction with the more informed party.

Figure 10-1 represents the case of asymmetric information when a bank has less information about the financial condition of (potential) customers than the (potential) customers themselves. From this perspective, we say that the bank is the primary party and the (potential) customers are counterparty with more information, and the goal of the bank is to invest its funds in the most profitable way despite its limited information. I considered this situation in chapter 9, when I discussed how banks used past financial information to limit credit risk, market value risk and other forms of risk caused by uncertainty about their (potential) customers.

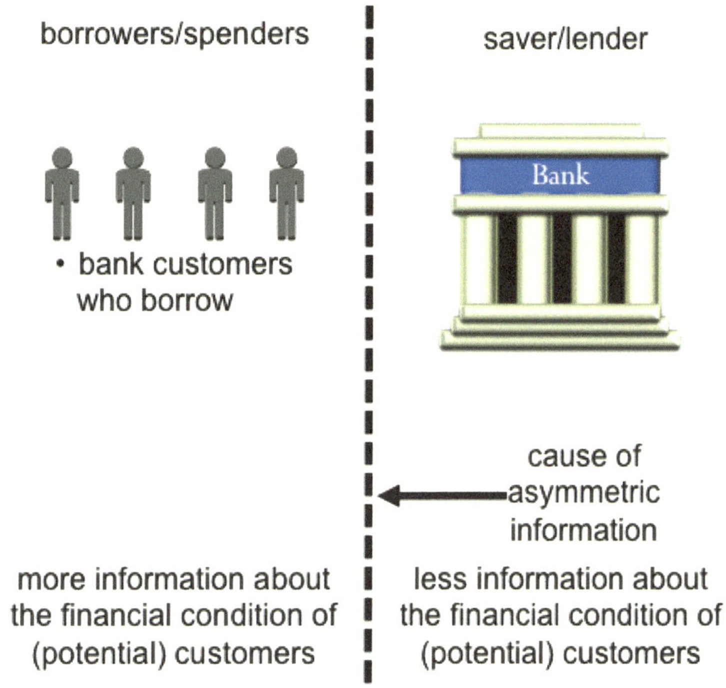

Figure 10-1: A representation of asymmetric information when (potential) customers have more information than a bank

Some regulation is intended to help banks manage this kind of asymmetric information and to manage credit risk, market value risk and other forms of risk because individuals and institutions may be required to report certain information to the bank if they want to become customers.

From another perspective, we can say that potential bank customers are the primary party and the bank is counterparty with more information about its financial condition, and the goal of the potential bank customers is to invest their funds through the bank in the most profitable way despite their limited information.

Figure 10-2 represents the case of asymmetric information when potential bank customers have less information about the financial condition of a bank than the bank itself.

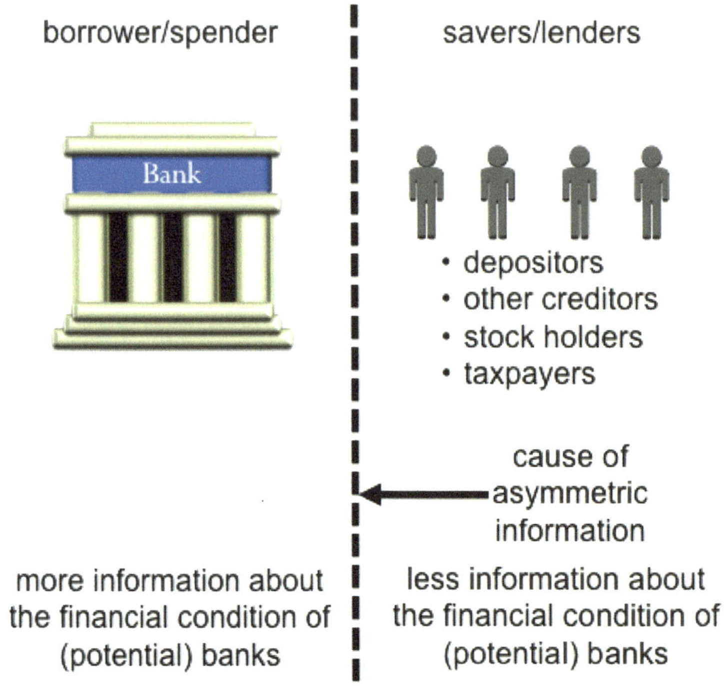

Figure 10-2: A representation of asymmetric information when a bank has more information than its (potential) customers

When asymmetric information exists, special problems may arise which might contribute to financial losses and financial crises, and bank regulation is intended to prevent these problems. These special problems are moral hazard, adverse selection, higher transaction costs, group panic and contagion, each of which I describe below.

Moral hazard is the hazard or chance that those with more information about their actions or intentions will behave inappropriately (or in the extreme, "immorally") from the perspective of the less informed party. Alternatively, we can say that moral hazard is a situation where those with more information about their actions or intentions have an *incentive or tendency* to behave inappropriately from the perspective of the less informed party. The reason that the less informed party would consider the behavior inappropriate is typically because it must bear at least some of the costs from that behavior, while the more informed party does not need to take full responsibility of its behavior. For example, people who rent DVDs from a rental store have more information about their own actions and intentions than the DVD rental store, and the average person has an incentive or tendency not to be careful with DVDs. The DVD rental store would consider the carelessness inappropriate if it were fully informed about the actions of the average renter because it would have to bear at least some of the cost of this carelessness.

Moral hazard ultimately derives from the fact that priorities or interests of parities in a transaction are misaligned when information about those priorities or interests is asymmetric. The first priority or interest of people renting a DVD may be to enjoy movies at the lowest cost; careful attention to and protection of the DVD is likely to be a less important priority for the average renter unless restrictive or punitive policies are enacted by the rental store. The first priority or interest of the DVD rental store is likely to generate revenue from DVD rentals both today and in the future, and protection of DVDs would be necessary to generate revenue in the future. When priorities or interests are believed to be misaligned, the less informed party often tries to realign them by spending time and other resources to prevent the counterparty from neglecting the priorities or interests of the less informed party.

Moral hazard exists in the banking industry when bank managers have an incentive or tendency to undertake an inappropriate amount of risk from the perspective of depositors, other creditors and taxpayers. Because depositors, other creditors and taxpayers often must bear some of the financial losses when bank managers take risks yet will not fully benefit from financial gains from those risks, interests of the two parties are misaligned. Unless regulations are imposed by the government, banks and bank managers may have a tendency to take a lot of risk with the hope that some risks will pay handsomely for them and with the knowledge that other parties will take some responsibility for the risks that turn into financial losses.

Moral hazard in the banking industry can be reduced through regulation. One type of regulation allows government officials and the public to monitor the actions of banks and bank managers, thereby acquiring additional information about the actions of banks and bank managers and reducing asymmetric information. Also, regulation can help align the interests of banks and bank managers on the one hand and depositors, other creditors and taxpayers on the other hand by penalizing banks and bank mangers for behaving in a way that is thought to be inappropriate.

As we learned in chapter 9, we also observe moral hazard when borrowers—who are more informed about their actions, intentions and financial condition than lenders—have an incentive or tendency to spend their funds inappropriately from the perspective of the lender. Because borrowers may not carefully consider the costs and risks of spending their funds once they have acquired a loan, paying back the loan may become more difficult than anticipated, and the lender may likewise have to bear the cost of late payments or default. Lenders try to reduce this type of credit risk by reducing asymmetric information and aligning the interests of the borrower and the lender.

Because the less informed party must spend time and other resources to reduce asymmetric information and to realign interests so that the transaction between two parties becomes acceptable, moral hazard can be considered a special kind of transaction cost. For example, by requiring financial information to calculate credit scores, monitoring, and using covenants in loan contracts and requiring collateral, banks and their customers spend resources to reduce asymmetric information and to better align interests so that the transaction becomes acceptable by both parties. From another perspective, regulators and the public require that banks report certain financial information to them, as I discuss below, and acquiring and processing this information requires time and other resources.

A special case of a moral hazard problem is called the **principal-agent problem**, in which an agent acts on behalf of another party called a principal, an individual or institution with less information about the actions and intentions of the agent than the agent himself. A problem arises when the priorities and interests of the agent and the principal are not aligned, so that the agent has an incentive or tendency to follow his interests rather than the interests of the principal. For example, a bank manager can be considered an agent who acts on behalf of customers or the bank's owners. But sometimes the interests of the bank manager, which might include making the most money for himself through risky investments, are not aligned with the interests of customers or the bank owners, who are not fully informed about the actions and intentions of the bank manager.

A second problem that may arise with asymmetric information is adverse selection. **Adverse selection** is a situation where those that are likely to produce a worse than average outcome from the perspective of the less informed party have a tendency to be selected by the less informed party. The more informed parties have a tendency to be selected because they are naturally attracted to particular transactions with asymmetric information, thereby *self-selecting* by voluntarily choosing to enter markets with less informed parties. For example, those who produce an adverse outcome from the perspective of a DVD rental store would be those who have no intention of returning a DVD if they could rent it. Because they would be very eager to take the DVD from the store and go to the DVD store to do so, the DVD store would have a tendency to select these people in a rental transaction. To protect its interests from these individuals, the DVD store should enact policies like background checks that prevent them from being about to rent DVDs from the store.

Both adverse selection and moral hazard refer to potentially bad behavior or a bad outcome in a transaction from the perspective of the less informed party. But adverse selection refers to potentially bad behavior or a bad outcome because the less informed party may unknowingly select those who have a tendency or incentive to behave badly or cause a bad outcome *before* a transaction has been completed. In contrast, moral hazard refers to potentially bad behavior or a bad outcome because the less informed party is unaware of the behavior *after* a transaction has been completed. Of course, moral hazard and adverse selection can be problems caused by the same institution or individual, but the less informed party would need to enact different policies to protect itself from moral hazard and adverse selection.

Like moral hazard, adverse selection occurs because priorities or interests of parties are misaligned when asymmetric information exists. When priorities or interests are believed to be misaligned, the less informed party often spends time and other resources to prevent those who would neglect its priorities or interests from entering into a transaction. And like moral hazard, adverse selection can be considered a special kind of transaction cost because resources must be spent to reduce asymmetric information and to determine how to exclude those with misaligned priorities and interests from a transaction.

Adverse selection occurs in the banking industry when those who are less careful or knowledgeable about managing liquidity risk, credit risk, market value risk, capital risk or other types of risk than the average person are willing to enter the banking industry. Also, adverse selection occurs when those who are more willing to take advantage of depositors, other creditors and taxpayers than the average person (because of less than average character) are willing to enter the banking industry. Because depositors, other creditors and taxpayers would have to bear some of the financial losses if these people were allowed to enter the banking industry yet would not fully benefit from their financial gains, interests of the two parties are misaligned. Unless the government imposes regulations, those who are less careful, knowledgeable or scrupulous about banking practices may have a tendency to enter the banking industry with the hope that they would be able to profit handsomely and with the knowledge that other parties will take some responsibility for their behavior.

Figure 9-12 represents adverse selection and moral hazard when banks are considered the more informed party about their financial condition and bank customers and taxpayers are considered the less informed party.

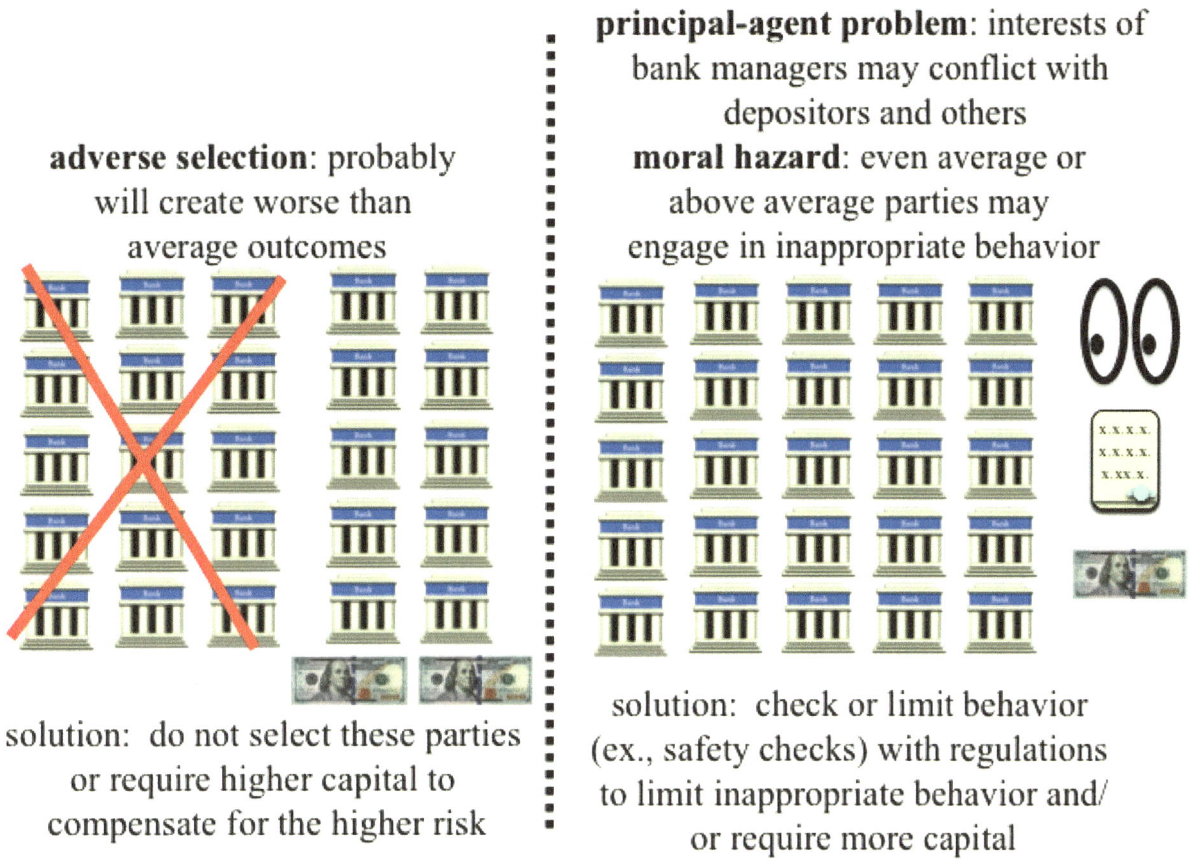

Figure 10-3: A representation of adverse selection and moral hazard (and the principal-agent problem) in the banking sector and policies that are used to limit these risks.

As we learned in chapter 9, we also observe adverse selection when those who have little ability or intention to repay a loan compared to the average loan applicant are willing to borrow from a less informed lender. These risky, careless or unscrupulous individuals and institutions have priorities or interests that are not aligned with potential lenders, and the lender would have to bear higher than average late payments or defaults if credit were extended. Because of the higher than average cost, lenders want to screen these individuals and institutions from the pool of loan applicants, by calculating credit scores and by requiring collateral. But to fully account for adverse selection and potentially bad outcomes, banks must be able to anticipate how potential borrowers would behave in the future if financial conditions for the potential borrowers would deteriorate. During an economic downturn, for example, many people lose their jobs and many borrowers lose their ability to repay loans. Yet, banks are not always good at avoiding adverse selection because they do not always accurately anticipate how the financial conditions of potential borrowers could deteriorate. Alan Greenspan, the former Chairman of the Board of Governors of the US Federal Reserve System, once said that "most bad loans are made in good times".

A third problem caused by asymmetric information arises because one party in a potential transaction is uncertain about the actions or intentions of a counterparty. This uncertainty creates a risk of conducting a transaction, and this risk is a *transaction cost* that risk-averse people must bear and try to avoid. As mentioned previously, institutions and individuals spend resources to reduce this risk and asymmetric information if they want to conduct a transaction. But because the risk causes an added transaction cost, some risk-averse individuals and institutions become unwilling to conduct a transaction when they do not have enough information or resources to acquire information about a counterparty. For example, many people are unwilling to conduct a transaction with a bank by depositing their funds at the bank when they are uncertain about the bank's financial condition, and may simply hold their funds in their homes for safe keeping. As a result, they lose interest that they could have earned by depositing their funds at a bank, and banks lose the use of their funds.

A fourth problem caused by asymmetric information is widespread panic or **group panic**, a situation where less informed members in a group panic because of the expectation that they may experience a loss. This panicky behavior causes the less informed group members to take action to avoid the expected loss, which in turn may cause an actual loss or other problems.

In the banking industry, group panic is called a *banking panic* or a *bank run*, a case in which depositors and other creditors may literally run to their bank to withdraw funds when they expect that the bank may not be able to pay them due to perceived financial problems. Regardless of whether the expectation about the financial situation at the bank is correct, the panicky behavior can cause financial problems even if they did not originally exist. Why?

As we learned in chapter 6, banks typically maintain enough liquid funds to satisfy the needs of only a fraction of depositors, and then lend or invest the rest to make a profit. But if a large number of depositors panic and rush to withdraw their funds at once, banks will not have sufficient funds to pay everyone and may have to close down temporarily or even permanently if it can not acquire funds from elsewhere. Banks could try to sell securities and loans, but securities and loans can usually be liquidated only at a discount or only after paying a substantial transaction cost. Moreover, if large numbers of banks try to sell securities because of widespread group panic (see the next paragraph), the value of securities would fall as the market is flooded with these securities. The bank could also try to borrow funds, but if there is no one to lend to the bank, it may be forced to close due to a lack of liquidity. Even if there is an institution willing to lend to the bank, the bank may have to pay high interest rates if lender believes that the financial condition of the bank is poor. Thus, expectations about financial problems can cause real financial problems.

And the situation could get worse. Group panic by one bank's depositors can cause group panic by depositors at other banks because bank customers believe that banks lend to one another, so that if a bank does not have sufficient funds to pay its depositors then it may not have sufficient funds to pay other banks. Thus, depositors at other banks, without full information about the true financial condition of their banks, may panic and their banks may soon experience a shortage of funds. Group panic may begin to occur throughout the economy. The situation where one bank's financial problems spread to other banks because of group panic or other problems caused by asymmetric information is called **contagion**.

While moral hazard and adverse selection are caused by actions of the more informed party in a transaction, group panic is caused by actions of the less informed party. Group panic may occur regardless of moral hazard problems or adverse selection, although group panic may be more likely if less informed party believes that financial problems caused by moral hazard and adverse selection are widespread. Contagion and high transaction costs may result either from actions of a less informed group of bank customers or from actions of more informed banks and bank managers, whose inappropriate behavior causes a moral hazard or careless, risky, unknowledgeable or unscrupulous behavior would cause adverse selection.

Contagion, group panic, adverse selection and moral hazard can cause or contribute to a **banking crisis**, a situation where large numbers of banks fail or have serious financial problems. Banks may fail because of large withdrawals of deposits (leading to a shortage of reserves), an unexpected increase in interest payments on debt and other liabilities (an increase in the value of liabilities) or an unexpected increase in default rates on loans, bonds or other assets (a decrease in the value of assets).

I consider below the regulations and laws that are intended to avoid the effects of contagion, group panic, high transaction costs, adverse selection and moral hazard. But first, I summarize these problems resulting from asymmetric information in Table 19.

Table 19: Problems caused by asymmetric information

Name of problem	Definition	Party causing the problem	Example
Moral hazard	Those with more information about their actions or intentions have an incentive or tendency to take actions after a transaction has been made that the less informed party would consider inappropriate. The less informed party considers these actions inappropriate because it must bear at least some of the costs when the actions have a bad outcome.	More informed party	Bank managers investing in assets that depositors, other creditors or taxpayers would consider too risky.
Adverse selection	Those that are likely to produce a worse than average outcome from the perspective of the less informed party have a tendency to be selected by the less informed party in a transaction. The more informed parties have a tendency to be selected because they are naturally attracted to particular transactions with asymmetric information, thereby self-selecting by voluntarily choosing to enter markets with less informed parties.	More informed party	People who are careless or risky in finance wanting to get a job in the financial sector and to use funds in a way that depositors, other creditors or taxpayers would consider careless or too risky.
Transaction cost borne by less informed risk averse parties	Some less informed parties are unwilling to conduct risky transactions because they are unwilling to pay the transaction cost of acquiring and processing information to limit risk.	Either party: problem is caused because information is unavailable or difficult to understand	People are unwilling to deposit their funds at banks when they are unable or unwilling to determine their financial health, and hold their funds in their homes for safe keeping.
Group panic	Less informed group members in a transaction panic because they expect that they may experience a loss and therefore take actions to avoid this perceived potential loss.	Less informed party	Depositors running to the bank to withdraw their funds when they suspect that the bank may have problems to pay the full value of the deposits.
Contagion	A situation where one bank's financial problems spread to other banks due to group panic, moral hazard or adverse selection.	Either party: problem is caused because information is	A bank with financial problems is late repaying its borrowed funds from a second bank, causing financial problems for

		unavailable or difficult to understand	the second bank.

Regulations that reduce asymmetric information problems

In this section, I discuss ten regulations that are intended to reduce asymmetric information and the problems that it causes. I discuss charters, capital requirements, asset requirements, requirements for standard accounting and risk management, reserve requirements, debt requirements, examination, disclosure requirements, the lender of last resort policy and deposit insurance.

Charters. Adverse selection in the banking industry occurs when entrepreneurs who are more risky, less careful, less knowledgeable or less scrupulous than average have a tendency to enter the banking industry to start business because depositors, other creditors and taxpayers are not fully aware about the actions and intentions of these entrepreneurs. But this problem can be reduced when regulators require that entrepreneurs who wish to start a bank fulfill certain requirements specified in a legal document, called a **charter**, which limit the risky, careless, unknowledgeable or unscrupulous behavior. A bank's charter is its application to open for business contingent on several requirements, including that:

- bank officers must be able to acquire sufficient capital paid in from investors who buy the stocks/equity/shares.
- bank officers must have policies to protect against liquidity risk, credit risk, market value risk, and capital risk.
- bank board members must have financial experience.
- banks must purchase insurance against negligent or dishonest behavior of employees.

In the US, a bank charter can be for a commercial bank, a savings bank, a savings and loan association or a credit union, and both the national government and the state governments offer each of these charters. Depository institutions that have a charter from the national government are commonly called national banks, while those that have a charter from a state government are commonly called state banks.

A nationally chartered commercial bank obtains its charter from the Office of the Comptroller of the Currency (OCC), an agency within the US Treasury Department. Nationally chartered commercial banks must be members of the Federal Reserve System (FRS) and must have deposit insurance from the Federal Deposit Insurance Corporation (FDIC) (see below). As a result, the OCC, the FRS and the FDIC all regulate nationally chartered commercial banks, although the OCC is primary regulator. There are about 1850 nationally chartered commercial banks.

Almost all state chartered commercial banks purchase FDIC insurance, but most choose not to join the FRS because they do not gain much by joining and they avoid having to deal with FRS regulations by not joining. Of the approximately 5700 state chartered commercial banks, about 4800 are not members of the FRS and only about 900 are members. This minority of state chartered commercial banks that choose to be members of the FRS tend to large banks that can more fully benefit from the FRS payment settlement systems, like Fedwire, and other services by being members. State chartered commercial banks are jointly regulated by either by state banking commissions and the FRS, if they are members of the FRS, or state banking commissions and the FDIC, if they are not members of the FRS. State banking commissions regulate the fewer than 500 state chartered banks that have chosen not to purchase FDIC insurance. These banks usually purchase deposit insurance through the state government.

Commercial banks were traditionally chartered for commercial (business) loans but have expanded into other types of loans and investments. For example, real estate loans now make up the largest share of assets for the average commercial bank.

Other types of banks are called *thrift institutions*, which include savings banks and savings & loan associations. Like commercial banks, each of these financial intermediaries may be chartered by the national government or by state governments.

Savings banks that are chartered by the national government are primarily regulated by the Office of Thrift Supervision (OTS), a branch of the US Treasury Department, whereas those chartered by state governments are regulated by the FDIC and state banking commissions. There are about 500 nationally chartered savings banks and 420 state chartered savings banks in the US. Savings banks are not members of the FRS, but most are members of the Federal Home Loan Bank System (FHLBS), a system that allows the member banks to borrow when liquid funds are needed, especially for purposes of issuing home loans. To qualify for loans from a Federal Home Loan Bank, banks must have at most 20% of their assets as commercial loans at least 65% of their assets as mortgage or consumer loans. In addition, both nationally and state chartered savings banks must have FDIC insurance.

Savings banks were traditionally chartered for household deposits and loans, but today savings banks have expanded into accepting business deposits and providing business loans as well. Like commercial banks, capital of savings banks may be in the form of stock issued by the bank and sold to investors other than depositors. Savings banks that have this type of capital are called stock savings banks. Alternatively, capital may be in the form of "shares" issued by the bank and sold only to depositors. Savings banks that have capital issued only to depositors are called mutual savings banks.

Both nationally chartered and state chartered savings & loan associations are regulated by the Office of Thrift Supervision. Like the savings banks, they are not members of the FRS, but most are part of the FHLBS. In addition, both nationally and state chartered savings & loan associations must have FDIC insurance.

Savings & loan associations are depository institutions that were traditionally chartered for savings deposits and home loans (mortgage loans), but like savings banks and commercial banks they have recently expanded to other borrowing and investing activities. Like savings banks, savings & loan associations generally have a larger percent of their assets in the form of home mortgage loans than do commercial banks. Inter-state branching regulations for savings & loan associations were traditionally less restrictive than for commercial banks, although regulations for inter-state branching of commercial banks have now been relaxed. Unlike commercial banks, savings & loan associations (and savings banks) are generally able to own or be owned by a non-financial business.

Credit unions may also be chartered by the national or state government, and both types are regulated by the regulated by the National Credit Union Administration (NCUA) (and state banking agencies in the case of state chartered credit unions). Nationally chartered credit unions must have insurance from the National Credit Union Share Insurance Fund (NCUSIF). Almost all state chartered credit unions obtain insurance from the NCUSIF as well, although a small number obtain insurance from a state or private insurance agency. The lender of last resort for credit unions can be the Central Liquidity Facility of the NCUA or the FHLBS, depending on which institution a credit union decides to join.

Credit unions were traditionally created to issue non-mortgage consumer loans, although they have expanded into other activities today as well. Credit unions have the distinctive feature of being not-for-profit institutions for which each customer (member) of a credit union has equal ownership (equity) and equal voting power in major decisions. They are also unique in that they may only serve customers who share a "common bond" such as working for the same employer or living in the same area.

		Thrift Institutions		
	Commercial banks	Saving & loan associations	Savings banks	Credit Unions
Regulator for nationally chartered banks	OCC, FRS and FDIC	Office of Thrift Supervision	Office of Thrift Supervision	National Credit Union Administration
Regulator for state charted banks	FRS (members) and FDIC (non-FRS members) and state regulatory agencies	Office of Thrift Supervision	FDIC and state regulatory agencies	National Credit Union Administration and state regulatory agencies
Lender of last resort	FRS	Federal Home Loan Bank System	Federal Home Loan Bank System	National Credit Union Administration or the Federal Home Loan Bank System
Insurer of deposits	FDIC	FDIC	FDIC	National Credit Union Share Insurance Fund

The US Treasury has offered several proposals to create one regulatory agency for all depository institutions, but none has yet been approved by Congress. So regulators currently assign one main supervisor of each type of bank.

Competition between state chartered banks and nationally chartered banks and between the different types of depository institutions has existed throughout US history and has intensified recently as these institutions have begun to encroach on each other's traditional forms of business. As a result of competition, each type of depository institution has often tried to lobby local, state and national government official to create or modify regulations to their benefit and to the detriment of their competitors.

Capital requirements. We learned in chapter 6 that capital serves as an emergency source of funds to protect against an unexpected decrease in the value of assets or an unexpected increase in the value of liabilities. And because of its importance to protect against these risks, regulators will require that financial institutions maintain a certain amount of capital relative to their assets. With a sufficient amount of required capital, the risk of insolvency can be reduced.

Formally, economists say that regulators require capital to reduce adverse selection; because risky, careless, unknowledgeable or unscrupulous entrepreneurs would be unable or unwilling to raise or to maintain the required amount of capital, they choose not to open and operate a bank and instead pursue other opportunities.

Secondly, capital requirements could reduce moral hazard if the bank would be more careful about acquiring assets and liabilities knowing that it would lose the capital of its owners if the value of assets were to decrease or the value of liabilities were to increase. However, for this to occur the managers at the banks who make the investment decisions must have interests that are aligned with the owners and other creditors of the bank, who provide the capital to protect against bad investments. Interests of bank managers are not always aligned with those who provide the bank capital, so that the moral hazard problem may not be reduced by requiring capital. The moral hazard problem in this case is a principal-agent problem: the interests of one party, the bank manager, who acts on behalf of another party might be misaligned with the interests of the other party, those who provide bank capital.

Also, capital requirements can reduce contagion and group panic because when banks have problems or are thought to have problems, contagion and group panic will not occur if capital is sufficient or thought to be sufficient to handle the (perceived) financial problems.

Regulators require a *capital-asset ratio*, in which the values of the assets are adjusted for their risk, of at least 8% for the bank to be considered "well capitalized". When the capital asset ratio falls below 8% more asset restrictions and/or other restrictions are imposed. When the capital asset ratio falls to 2%, the bank is declared *insolvent* and either taken over or closed. (I more fully discuss what happens to insolvent banks in a later section.)

Although there are many kinds of adjustments for the values of assets, the risk-adjusted capital asset ratio looks like:

$$8\% \le \frac{tier\ 1\ capital + tier\ 2\ capital}{w_1(safe\ assets) + w_2(risky\ assets)}$$

where *w*'s represent weights, ranging from 0% to 150% depending on the risk of the assets. The ratio above shows only two weights, one for "safe" and one for "risky" items, but there are actually several weights and degrees of risk used in the calculation. The most risky assets have the highest weights, so that more capital is needed to keep the ratio constant at the level required by regulators. For example, if regulators require that the ratio equal 8%, items with a 150% weight would require 12% of their value in capital; items with a 100% weight would require 8% of their value in capital; items with a 50% weight would require 4% of their value in capital. Very safe items have a 0% weight and would require no additional capital to satisfy the regulation.

US regulations and the Basel Accords state that the risk-based capital ratio must be 8%, 4.5% of which must be in tier 1 capital and 3.5% in tier 2 capital. Note that the definition of capital used in the risk based capital ratio is the economic definition, rather than the accounting definition, which considers only the difference between the book value of assets and the book value of liabilities.

The Basel Accords also specify the following weights for the specified assets, liabilities and off balance sheet items:

- 0% weight: cash assets, gold, loans guaranteed by the US Government, deposits and other claims on government institutions and central banks rated AAA to AA-.

- 20% weight: transaction deposits, cash items in the process of collection, bankers' acceptances, letters of credit and other assets or off-balance sheet activities maturing in one year or less, claims on government institutions and central banks rated A+ to A-.

- 35% weight: mortgage loans secured by homes

- 50% weight: 1-4 person residential mortgages, whether owner occupied or rented; privately issued mortgage backed securities and municipal bonds; claims on government institutions and central banks rated BBB+ to BBB-.

- 75% weight: loans to individuals and small businesses.

- 100% weight: loans to non-citizens, mortgage loans secured by commercial real estate, asset backed securities, collateralized debt obligations, interest rate swaps, currency swaps, other derivative contracts, commercial bonds and loans for joint ventures, claims on government institutions and central banks rated BB+ to B-.

- 150% weight: claims on government institutions and central banks rated below B- .

- claims on depository institutions, investment banks and corporations: risk weights from 20% to 150% depending on ratings by external agencies.

- past due loans: 150% to 100% depending on how much credit has already been secured with specific loss reserves or collateral.

Asset requirements. Regulators will also restrict the types of assets that banks can invest in to limit moral hazard, adverse selection, contagion or group panic. Firstly, banks must invest some in safe assets, like government bonds and secured (collateralized) loans, as part of their total portfolio of assets. Likewise, investments in bonds of new companies, loans for commercial real estate, stocks in other companies are restricted or possibly prohibited to limit the total amount of risky assets in the total portfolio of assets. Thirdly, banks may be required to invest in diverse kinds of assets, since limiting the type of in investment in a single asset can limit losses if a single asset has a poor return. Types of this diversification include limits on the amount of loans in a single sector, such as the housing sector, and limits on the amount of credit to a single borrower. Fourthly, many regulators require that banks limit investment in derivative assets (and liabilities). Although derivative assets can insure market risk, they can also increase risk for other banks that accept that market risk, and therefore cause contagion when many banks use them. Simply put, depending when the underlying assets are bought and sold, derivative assets can be good for the buyer and bad for the seller, or bad for the buyer and good for the seller. Finally, many regulators limit investment in foreign assets (and liabilities) due to (currency) exchange rate risk or because foreign assets and liabilities are deemed as especially risky.

Asset restrictions reduce adverse selection because they prevent entrepreneurs who are more risky, less careful, less knowledgeable or less scrupulous than average from wanting to enter the banking industry to start business. If regulations require that banks must invest principally or exclusively in safe and stable assets, then those with a desire for taking large financial risks will tend not to enter the banking industry and instead pursue another opportunity, perhaps by starting a hedge fund, which would be less regulated than a depository institution. In addition, restrictions on assets reduces moral hazard because they prevent bank managers from being able to invest in assets that regulators (who represent the interests of depositors, other creditors and taxpayers) would consider inappropriate.

Asset restrictions, and particular asset restrictions on inter-bank transactions, reduce contagion and group panic In particular, derivative assets can spread an institution's risk to other institutions, thereby creating contagion (or more systemic risk). In other words, contagion, as well as group panic, can become a bigger problem if systemic risk increases.

As state previously, asset restrictions encourage diversification because they prevent an institution from over-specializing in one or a few types of assets. For example, some depository institutions in the US are required to hold some small business and commercial loans, instead of only house or consumer loans. As we learned in chapter 9, diversification can reduce risk: if one type of asset performs poorly and a bank has a diversified portfolio of assets on its balance sheet, its loss in income could be limited relative to the case where it invested primarily a single asset that could perform poorly.

Requirements for standard accounting and risk management. Regulators require that banks follow standard procedures to record the value of assets, liabilities and off balance sheet activities, as well as require that they measure and manage risk of each of these items well. In particular, regulators require that gap analysis, duration analysis, the risk adjusted return on capital, value at risk or stress testing are "properly" calculated to measure or manage interest rate risk, other market value risk or capital risk. However, "proper" calculation of these measures, as we learned in chapter 9, can be more of an art than a science, so that regulators have some discretion in determining how well banks properly measure and manage risk. And bank managers may know and care more about "proper" risk measurement and management than regulators because bank managers may specialize in risk management and measurement every day at work.

Regulators also require that banks follow standard accounting procedures (those consistent with the Basel Accords and/or with procedures generally accepted by accountants), and require that banks have internal checks of the accounting to correctly determine the value of assets, liabilities, capital and off balance sheet activities. By requiring internal checks, regulators hope to prevent or minimize incorrect and fraudulent accounting. Yet, there can be some discretion in determining the "proper" value of assets, liabilities, capital and off balance sheet activities, so determining if a bank's books follow standard or "proper" procedures can sometimes be difficult and arbitrary.

Like many of the other regulations described above, requirement of standard accounting and risk management are formally said to reduce moral hazard, adverse selection, contagion and group panic.

Reserve requirements. Most central banks require that banks maintain sufficient cash on reserve, or reserves, for normal operations. Reserve requirements were established and traditionally used to ensure that bank customers could redeem the value of their bank notes, checks and deposits, particularly during financial crises. Formally, reserve requirement were established to reduce or avoid moral hazard, adverse selection, group panic, contagion and high transaction costs for depositors. When bank notes were redeemable in gold, silver or another commodity, one bank would agree to redeem another bank's notes as long as the issuing bank held a sufficient amount of the commodity money on reserve so that the redeeming bank could be reimbursed with commodity money. However, periodic financial crises during the 1800s and early 1900s showed that reserve requirements were unable to guarantee full redemption of bank notes, checks and deposits.

But borrowing in today's inter-bank loan market and from the central bank (discussed below) has largely reduced these costs for depositors. Reserve requirements are now enforced to guarantee sufficient funds to settle inter-bank payments (reducing moral hazard, contagion and panic in the inter-bank market) and to maintain a stable amount of reserves to help stabilize interest rates.

Regulators require that banks keep a fraction of transaction deposits as cash on reserve in their vaults or at the central bank, and the reserve requirement is likewise called the **required reserve ratio**. In the US, the Federal Reserve System (FRS) currently sets the required reserve ratio at 10% of transaction deposits larger than $44.4 million. The US central bank is allowed to vary this ratio from 8% to 14% according to the

Monetary Control Act of 1980, although it has not changed the ratio since April 1992. The level of transaction deposits subject to the 10% ratio varies annually according to a formula set by the Garn-St Germain Act of 1982, and has varied from $44 million to $54 million in the last decade. To allow smaller banks to use more of their reserves for investment purposes, values of transactions deposits below this amount require a smaller fraction of reserves, and values currently below $10.3 million do not require any reserves. Values currently between $10.3 million and $44.4 million form a "low reserve tranche" and are subject to a 3% required reserve ratio. Table 20 summarizes the current required reserve ratios for transaction deposits, as well as those for non-transaction deposits and borrowed funds.

Before December 1990, the FRS also imposed a required reserve ratio on non-transaction deposits, but has since lifted this regulation to allow banks to use more of their funds for investment purposes. Savings deposits, time deposits and expatriate currency deposits or borrowed funds have traditionally had reserve requirements, although the current law gives the Board of Governors the power to set a required reserve ratio only on savings deposits, non-personal time deposits, expatriate currency deposits and borrowed funds. The Bank of Korea continues to maintain reserve requirements transaction deposits, savings deposits and time deposits.

Table 20: US required reserve ratios as of January 2009

Type of liability	Required reserve ratio
Transaction deposits	
$0 to $10.3 million	0%
more than $10.3 million to $44.4 million	3%
more than $44.4 million	10%
Non-personal time and savings deposits	0%
Expatriate currency deposits or borrowed funds	0%
Source: Federal Reserve System http://www.federalreserve.gov/monetarypolicy/reservereq.htm	

Reserves earn little or no interest relative to the interest that the funds could earn if they were invested in loans or bonds. Many depository institutions, especially smaller ones, are able to satisfy the required reserve ratio with the cash that they voluntarily hold in their vaults, so that the regulation for these institutions is essentially costless. But larger depository institutions, which have a higher required reserve ratio, have lobbied for the central bank to eliminate the requirement or to pay interest on reserves to eliminate or reduce the opportunity cost of not being able to invest more in loans or bonds. In the US, these banks were partially successful when the FRS began to pay interest on reserve deposits at the district Federal Reserve Banks in 2008. Yet the regulation can continue to be a burden when the amount of reserves that these banks must hold is larger than what they would voluntarily choose to hold. In addition, if banks fail to satisfy the required reserve ratio every two weeks, they must pay penalty fees to the district Federal Reserve Banks.

Despite these burdens, the FRS, or more precisely the Board of Governors of the Federal Reserve System, has maintained this regulation principally to help stabilize its monetary policies and to avoid moral hazard, contagion and group panic in the inter-bank market. When the FRS targeted the growth of M1 in the 1960s, 1970s and early 1980s to influence economic production, reserve requirements helped maintain a stable and predictable link between reserves and M1. Also, as new sources of liquid assets became available through new technologies and financial innovations, the FRS set reserve requirements on these liquid assets to better control their influence on the money supply and economic activity. For example, large denomination negotiable time deposits and expatriate currency borrowed funds became more widely used in the 1960s, and the FRS likewise adjusted reserve requirements on these deposits to better control the money supply and the amount of credit issued by banks.

Because reserve requirements require that banks have at least a fixed ratio of reserves relative to their transaction deposits, they help stabilize the total willingness to hold reserves in the overnight inter-bank loan market. A stable demand of reserves in the overnight inter-bank loan market helps to stabilize the overnight inter-bank loan interest rate, given a quantity of reserves supplied by the central bank. (I discuss how the central bank provides reserves to the overnight inter-bank loan market in a later chapter.) In other words, reserve requirements may reduce the volatility of the overnight inter-bank loan interest rate relative to the case where banks could voluntarily change their reserves to any amount, a result that may stabilize lending and borrowing and broader economic activity.

The overnight inter-bank interest rate can also be stabilized with reserve requirements if the central bank allows banks to take advantage of expected fluctuations in the interest rate. Banks in the US and Korea are not required to meet the required reserve ratio every day, but only to hold an average amount of reserves during a two-week period that satisfies the required reserve ratio. This flexibility allows banks to profit from expected changes in the overnight inter-bank loan interest rate by lending reserves when the interest rate is expected to be high (but not rising) and borrowing reserves to meet the requirement when the interest rate is expected to be low (but not falling). Lending more reserves at a high interest rate tends to decrease the interest rate; borrowing more reserves at a low interest rate tends to increase the interest rate. Thus, this flexibility can help banks stabilize the overnight inter-bank loan interest rate by themselves, as long as expectations are correct on average or as long as banks correct their behavior after making a mistake. When banks can profit from this arbitrage lending and borrowing, central banks have another reason to maintain a required reserve ratio. On the other hand, if the required reserve ratio would be lowered, banks would have less flexibility to adjust their reserves to take advantage of expected fluctuations in the overnight inter-bank interest rate without risking penalty fees.

The reserve requirement is often satisfied in part by deposits at the central bank, and these deposits are used to settle payments and other transactions. As a result, some central banks also want to maintain reserve requirements in order to maintain sufficient deposits to settle payments and to process other transactions if debits to these deposits are larger than expected, so as to avoid overdrawn accounts, penalty fees and delayed transactions.

Thus, because of their stabilizing influence on the overnight inter-bank interest rate and because of their use in settling payments and in processing other transactions, the FRS and other central banks have been hesitant to eliminate reserve requirements. However, central banks in Canada, Australia, the UK, Mexico and Sweden have eliminated the requirement due to the belief that the cost of the requirement for banks exceeds its benefits.

Whatever their relative costs and benefits, reserve requirements have largely outlived their original purpose of guaranteeing the redemption of bank notes, checks and deposits for depositors. The need to satisfy redemption on demand when reserves at banks are insufficient is satisfied today by inter-bank borrowing in today's very efficient money market, and by borrowing from the central bank when inter-bank borrowing and lending is insufficient, particularly during financial crises.

Debt requirements. Regulators may also limit borrowed funds and other forms of debt relative to capital. Borrowed funds and other debt are sometimes called **leverage** because it gives the borrower a greater ability to invest in assets. These regulators now require a *leverage ratio* of at least 3%:

$$3\% \leq \frac{capital}{debt}$$

Because this measure does not use weights, the leverage ratio is easy to calculate and easy to understand. Similar to the capital/asset ratio, the leverage (capital/debt) ratio is intended to limit moral hazard, adverse selection, contagion and group panic by limiting borrowed funds and debt.

Examination. Regulators regularly examine capital ratios, assets and off balance sheet activities, accounting, risk management and other factors to determine the financial health of banks. Regulators will calculate a "CAMELS" rating that summarizes the financial health of the bank and rates a bank's

- Capital adequacy
- Asset quality and asset risk
- Management of risk and accounting
- Earnings or profit (which contributes to capital)
- Liquidity, reserves or cash assets (reserves)
- Sensitivity to market value and capital risks

A CAMELS rating is a number 1-5, with 5 representing the best financial health, and is a weighted average of ratings from each of the individual categories. An individual rating below 4 requires that the bank take corrective actions, such as selling risky assets or acquiring more capital, to limit the problem in that category.

Examination and CAMELS ratings reduce adverse selection, moral hazard and contagion, like many of the other regulations described above. In addition, because the CAMELS rating is disclosed to the public (see below), it can reduce the chance of group panic if ratings remain consistently high. (However, if the ratings are low, they could increase group panic if depositors and other creditors react quickly to the bank's assessment of poor financial health.)

Disclosure requirements. In conjunction with examination, regulators will require that banks disclose the value of assets, liabilities, capital and other financial details to the public using standard accounting. In addition, the CAMELS ratings are made public for depositors and other creditors of banks.

This publicly available information is intended to reduce transaction costs between depositors and other creditors on one hand and the banks on the other hand. With more information, savers can make a better decision about which bank they want to transact with. In addition, publicly available information through the call reports and CAMELS ratings can reduce group panic and contagion if the information shows the public that banks have a financially sound business.

Disclosure requirements also reduce moral hazard and adverse selection. Disclosure requirements reduce the hazard that bank managers will behave inappropriately, because they realize that if they do, their customers will know and can react by withdrawing their funds from the bank to look for alternative investments. Disclosure requirements also prevent risky, careless, unknowledgeable or unscrupulous entrepreneurs from wanting to start a bank, because these individuals may realize that their behavior would be exposed and punished.

In addition to call reports and CAMELS ratings, some regulators recommend that risk management calculations and off balance sheet activities be fully revealed to the public to reduce asymmetric information further. This would give savers better information to decide which bank to transact with and would reduce transaction costs, moral hazard and adverse selection further.

The *Sarbanes-Oxley Act* in the US tries to regulate unfair accounting practices and other problems associated with undisclosed (asymmetric) information. It requires standard and accurate accounting, and holds managers, board managers and external auditors more accountable than previously for the accuracy of financial statements. Formally, it tries to decrease transaction costs/risks, moral hazard and adverse selection.

Other regulations in the US and other countries try to prevent **insider trading**—buying and selling on the basis of confidential information—and **conflicts of interest**—conflicts between the interests of those with more information and those with less information. For example, a conflict of interest arises when a bank underwrites (buys) securities and then recommends to others to buy those securities in the secondary market, because it can profit from selling these securities to its customers. Likewise, when interests of an "agent" who works on behalf of another called a "principal" conflict, a principal-agent problem can arise, which is a special case of a conflict of interest. Regulations that limit insider trading and conflicts of interest also try to limit transaction costs/risks, moral hazard and adverse selection.

Deposit insurance. Deposit insurance insures the value of deposits up to $250,000 at depository institutions in the US and up to 50 million won at depository institutions in Korea. In the US, deposit insurance is provided by the Federal Deposit Insurance Corporation (FDIC), which generally insures checking deposits, savings deposits, money market deposit accounts and time deposits, as well as individual retirement accounts. In Korea, deposit insurance is provided by the Korea Deposit Insurance Corporation (KDIC), which generally insures checking deposits, savings deposits, installment deposits, as well as employment insurance contracts and other insurance contracts.

Deposit insurance reduces transaction costs/risks for savers, making them less reluctant about putting their funds in banks. As a result, deposit insurance increases the incentive to save, which allows lower interest rates on saved and borrowed funds. Lower interest rates on borrowed funds encourages borrowing, in particular borrowing for investment expenditure, such as expenditure on new offices, homes, factories, equipment and roads. And with higher investment expenditure, productivity, production and income from production can increase in the long run.

Deposit insurance also reduces the chance of group panic and contagion because if depositors expect financial problems at their bank, they need not panic if the bank has insurance. And without deposit insurance, group panic can cause financial problems for banks and contagion, even if banks initially had no financial problems. Why? Because banks do not keep all of funds deposited at banks as cash on reserve, if depositors panic and want to withdraw all or most of their funds, they can force the bank into a situation where it depletes its liquid assets and capital and can not pay for its liabilities. And if a bank can not repay borrowed funds from other banks or if other banks' customers also panic, other banks will suffer as well—contagion will result.

Although deposit insurance reduces the chance of group panic and contagion, it can increase moral hazard, since part of the cost of bankruptcy would be borne parties other than the bank that makes risky investments: other banks which pay premiums to the deposit insurance corporation and even taxpayers when insurance funds are insufficient to cover losses. In other words, the bank is no longer fully responsible for the costs of its risky behavior when its deposits are insured, so it has a tendency or incentive to take greater risks than it otherwise would.

In addition, deposit insurance also gives depositors less of an incentive to monitor the investments of banks, because even if the bank engages in risky investments, such as subprime mortgage loans, depositors need not worry as much about losing their deposits. In contrast, depositors who are not covered by insurance may remove their funds from the bank if they think that a bank's investments are too risky.

Finally, deposit insurance creates adverse selection because those who are risky, careless, unknowledgeable or unscrupulous are less deterred from opening a bank with the belief that they would not be fully responsible for bankruptcy if it occurred.

Lender of last resort policy. Central banks may lend emergency reserves and other funds when banks have liquidity problems or other financial problems such as a shortage of capital. Particularly during financial crises, central banks act as a **lender of last resort**—an emergency lender of liquid assets for banks, when reserves have been depleted and inter-bank borrowing and lending can become insufficient. During financial crises, central banks or other government regulators may even take control of the management of banks by buying stock in the bank, thereby giving banks additional capital to cover the larger than expected losses or to pay for the larger than expected expenses.

The Federal Reserve Act of 1913 established the central bank of the US, based on a federal system with a national Board of Governors and 12 regional Federal Reserve Banks that lent to member banks in the region when necessary. Under the act, all national banks were required to become members this system, and thus could have access to loans from the Federal Reserve Banks if necessary. State banks could join the system, but most did not because the new regulations for members were deemed to be burdensome. At the time of creation, only member banks could have access to loans from the central bank, but today all depository institutions, both members and non-members of the system, can have access to the loans from the central bank.

The FRS often promises a readily available source of reserves from discount loans during financial crises. When Russia defaulted on its debt in 1998, investors vastly restricted their buying of many kinds of bonds and other securities as group panic spread due to a fear of contagion. Banks and other financial institutions had trouble obtaining funds by borrowing reserves and by selling bonds and other securities, so the FRS offered to provide discount loans at low rates to those institutions that needed funds. In late 1999, people in financial markets feared that financial institutions would have problems with the computerized payment settlement systems on the first day of the next year, 1 January 2000. The FRS helped financial institutions in a number of ways, including making discount loans at low rates available to institutions that needed them. After 11 September 2001, when payment settlement systems were disrupted due to the attacks in New York and due to the fact that the grounding of airplanes prevented the physical transfer of funds, the FRS made huge quantities of discount loans to financial institutions that were unable to acquire needed reserves.

Although central banks were traditionally created to act as lenders of last resort—as a way to passively react to financial crises by lending reserves during emergencies—they have evolved into institutions that more actively try to manage reserves, banking activity and economic activity, thereby pre-empting financial crises. Regulation of banking activity is part of this pre-emptive role, and we discuss an active role for monetary policy to shape economic activity in chapter 13.

Because the lender of last resort policy provides banks with an emergency source of reserves, it reduces the chance of group panic and contagion. Like deposit insurance and the traditional purpose of reserve requirements, it is intended ensure that depositors will be able to redeem the value of their checks and deposits and that other creditors will be paid on time even if banks temporarily have a low amount of reserves.

And like deposit insurance and the traditional purpose of reserve requirements, the lender of last resort policy reduces transaction costs/risks for savers, making them less reluctant about putting their funds in banks. So the lender of last resort policy can also indirectly increase saving, reduce interest rates, increase investment expenditure, increase productivity, increase production and increase income from production.

But like deposit insurance, the lender of last resort policy can increase moral hazard if the central bank guarantees that all institutions can have access to discount loans, even institutions that are poorly managed. Part of the cost of poor management is borne by the central bank—and by extension taxpayers and anyone who uses money if prices rise due to the additional money that is lent. In other words, banks are no longer fully responsible for the costs of their risky behavior when they have access to loans in an emergency, and therefore have a tendency or incentive to take greater risks than they otherwise would.

In addition, the lender of last resort policy also lowers the need or incentive of depositors and creditors to monitor investments of banks. Even if banks engage in risky investments, such as subprime mortgage loans, depositors and other creditors need not worry as much about losing their funds if banks can receive emergency loans and even capital funds from the central bank. In contrast, depositors and other creditors would tend to remove their funds from banks without access to a lender of last resort if they thought that banks' investments became too risky.

Finally, the lender of last resort policy creates adverse selection because those who are more risky, careless, unknowledgeable or unscrupulous than average are more willing to open a bank or to get a job in the financial sector if they believe that they will always receive financial assistance in an emergency.

How to handle an insolvent bank

Recall that bank failure or bankruptcy refers to the case where a bank or other financial intermediary is unable to pay for its liabilities. **Insolvency** refers to a case where an institution has depleted its capital and is unable to pay for its liabilities. The financial intermediary may then be reorganized, sold to another institution, or shut down. When a financial intermediary is shut down, its assets are sold, or liquidated, so that creditors can be paid. **Illiquidity** refers to a case where an institution has depleted its liquid assets and is unable to pay for its liabilities. Illiquidity can be a temporary problem, and need not lead to bank failure, especially if a lender of last resort is available. But if illiquidity is a persistent problem, it will lead to bank failure. During financial crises, financial institutions often deplete both their liquid assets and their capital, and there is little difference between insolvency and illiquidity.

Regulation of banks is intended to prevent bank failure, resulting from insolvency or persistent illiquidity or both. In the previous section, we discussed how the lender of last resort is intended to limit and reverse the problem of illiquidity. We also discussed several regulations to prevent insolvency, such as capital requirements. But when insolvency occurs, what do regulators do?

The Federal Deposit Insurance Corporation (FDIC) in the US and the Korea Deposit Insurance Corporation (KDIC) in the Korea can use one of three methods to handle an insolvent bank. The first is called **acquisition assistance**, which occurs when the deposit insurance corporation simply advises and assists an institution that wants to acquire and reorganize a failed bank that will continue operate under its current charter—with the hope that the failed bank can soon earn a profit to replenish its capital under new ownership and management. The deposit insurance corporation, and possibly the central bank as well, may provide financial assistance in the form of loans or regulatory advice about how to start managing the failed bank. Deposit insurance funds are not used to pay depositors, and the bank is expected to quickly emerge from insolvency. Figure 10-4 represents the acquisition assistance method.

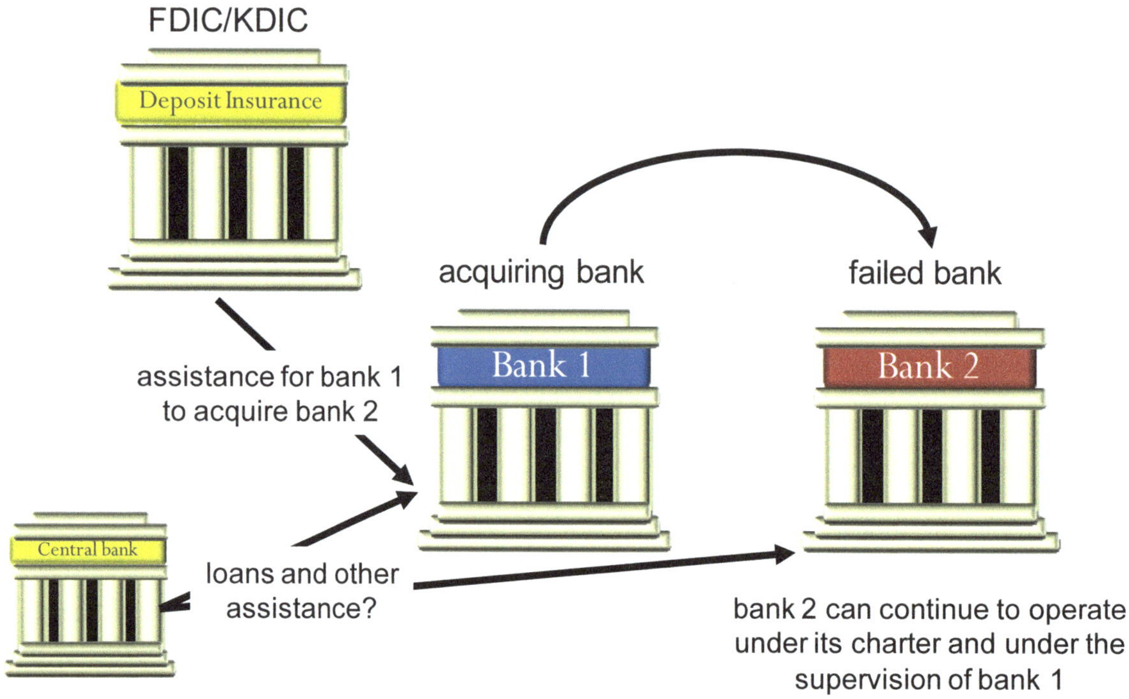

Figure 10-4: The acquisition assistance method

In a second case, however, the bank's charter is terminated by the deposit insurance corporation, which then finds another financial institution to purchase the failed bank's assets and assume its liabilities. This operation is called **the purchase and assumption method**. With this method, the FDIC may provide subsidized loans the purchasing institution for purchasing the failed bank's assets, and the FDIC may buy some bad loans and investments itself if the purchasing institution is unwilling to buy all of them. To the degree that the liabilities of the failed bank's deposits are assumed by another institution, there is no need to pay depositors from the deposit insurance funds. However, some deposits may not be assumed by the other institution, so that the deposits are closed and the depositors are paid with deposit insurance funds, up to $250,000 in the US or 50 million won in Korea. Figure 10-5 represents the purchase and assumption method.

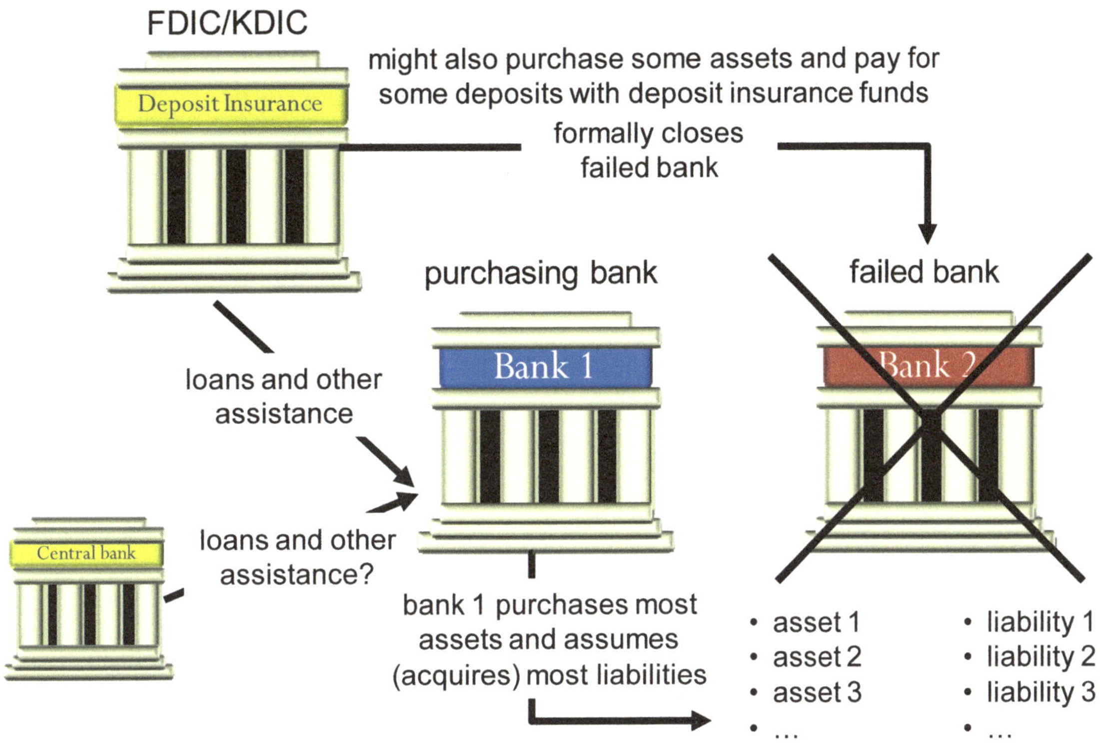

Figure 10-5: The purchase and assumption method

A third method involves terminating the failed bank's charter and operations permanently. In this case, depositors are paid the full value of their deposits from the deposit insurance fund, up to $250,000 in the US or 50 million won in Korea. Then, the assets of the failed bank are sold by the deposit insurance corporation to any willing buyer, and the proceeds of the sale are used to pay other creditors, such as those who lent to the failed bank or bought stock in the failed bank, to the fullest extent possible. This method of handling a failed bank is called the **payoff method**, represented in Figure 10-6.

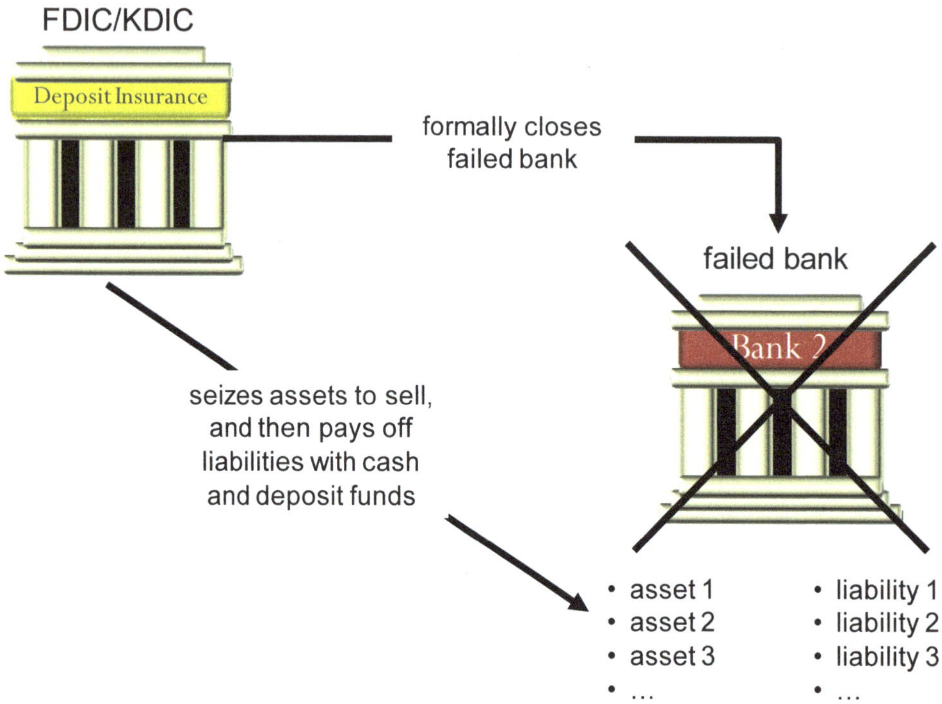

Figure 10-6: The payoff method

In contrast to the payoff method, a general policy of handling an insolvent or illiquid bank is to support them if they fail or are close to failure. The FDIC, the FRS and other regulators have implicitly or explicitly used what is called the **regulatory forbearance** to refrain from closing insolvent banks or from restricting their activity if they become insolvent or are close to becoming insolvent. Under regulatory forbearance, regulators can relax capital requirements, accounting standards, restrictions on assets and off balance sheet activities, and other rules to help a bank continue to operate under its exiting charter, with the hope that the (near) insolvent condition of the banks would improve over time. With regulatory forbearance, the FDIC would use the acquisition assistance method if another institution were interested in acquiring and reorganizing a failed bank or the purchase and assumption method if another institution were interested in purchasing the bank's assets and assuming its liabilities. Also, the FRS or another lender of last resort would readily provide reserves at low interest rates under this policy. Finally, the FDIC or the FRS could even purchase stock in banks, providing them with capital to pay for liabilities or to cover the cost of depreciated assets.

A similar policy of handling insolvent or illiquid banks that are large, called the **too-big-to-fail policy**, is to always support these banks if they experience insolvency or illiquidity. Under this policy, regulators believe that some banks are so big that if they failed, contagion would result: the payment settlement system would be disrupted, many firms that rely on the banks for financing would be negatively impacted, and other banks with financial ties to the large banks could fail as well or at least have liquidity problems. These problems resulting from the bank failure would be unacceptable in the view of regulators. Under the too big to fail policy, the FDIC would use the acquisition assistance method or the purchase and assumption method, and the FRS would always act as a lender of last resort. In addition, the FDIC or the FRS could even purchase stock in the big banks, providing them with capital to pay for liabilities or to cover the cost of depreciated assets.

In 1984, Continental Illinois, the seventh largest bank in the US, became insolvent. About 2300 smaller banks had deposits at Continental Illinois, and most of these deposits were large enough to exceed the insurance limit. As a result, these banks and other uninsured depositors began to withdraw their funds, and others creditors also began to panic. If this group panic had continued, it could have lead to contagion. To stop the group panic and possible contagion, the FDIC used its funds to purchase new stock in Continental Illinois, thereby giving the bank capital to pay for liabilities. The FDIC supported the bank further by purchasing some of its defaulted and delinquent loans, even though it did not purchase the stock from the bank's private share holders and let its value become almost worthless.

The too-big-to-fail policy may prevent group panic and contagion in the short run, but it and regulatory forbearance cause a moral hazard problem in the long run because the costs of risky investment by banks are not fully borne by the banks' managers or owners (and instead are partially borne by many bank creditors, those who contribute to the deposit insurance fund, those who pay taxes to finance government institutions and even those who see the purchasing power of their money fall if additional loans to banks causes inflation) but the benefits are fully reaped by the banks' managers and owners. In other words, banks will not fully pay for the cost of their risky investments when they fail but will fully benefit from their risky investments when they succeed. Furthermore, when bank managers expect the FDIC, the FRS or other regulators to use regulatory forbearance or the too-big-to-fail policy, they have an incentive to take greater risks than they would otherwise, because they expect that the costs of future failures will be partially borne by others. Thus, regulatory forbearance and the too-big-to-fail policy can invite more risky behavior and larger financial problems in the future. And because consolidation of financial institutions has become a trend in the last few decades in the US and around the world, the moral hazard caused by the too-big-to-fail policy has been magnified as more banks become large enough to significantly affect financial activity for the whole economy.

As a result, the FRS and the FDIC do not announce when they will use regulatory forbearance or the too-big-to-fail policy. And in general the FRS may deny insolvent banks discount loans and other forms of credit when it acts as the lender of last resort. The central bank sometimes chooses to let insolvent banks fail, even large ones, rather than lending to an institution whose problems were likely caused by careless, risky or otherwise inappropriate behavior. Furthermore, those banks that are in danger of becoming insolvent because their capital is insufficient to meet capital requirements must pay a higher interest rate on discount loans than healthy banks to compensate the FRS for the higher risk that the bank will not be able to repay the discount loans (on time).

Adverse selection can also result from regulatory forbearance and the too-big-to-fail policy because those who are more risky, careless, unknowledgeable or unscrupulous than average are more willing to open a bank or to get a job in the financial sector if they believe that they will always receive financial assistance in an emergency from the deposit insurance and/or the central bank.

When the FDIC used regulatory forbearance or the too-big-to-fail policy in the past, it often used the acquisition assistance method to keep a failed bank in business. But in 1991 in order to limit the moral hazard caused by regulatory forbearance and the too-big-to-fail policy, Congress required that the FDIC use the least costly method to handle a failed bank and required that an insolvent bank can not be kept open under regulatory forbearance or the acquisition assistance method unless the FDIC, the FRS and the Secretary of the Treasury agree to keep it open. And since 1992, the acquisition assistance method has not been used. The least costly transaction is usually the purchase and assumption method, which has been used by over 90% of bank failures since 1993, with the payoff method used in the remaining cases.

Summary

Asymmetric information causes various types of problems in the bank sector, both for banks themselves and for bank customers and taxpayers who can suffer financially when the bank behaves in a way that is risky, careless, unknowledgeable, unscrupulous or otherwise inappropriate. In particular, when banks have an incentive or tendency to behave in an inappropriate way after bank customers have made a transaction with banks, when the bank customers are not fully informed about this behavior, we say that a moral hazard exists. When those who are more risky, careless unknowledgeable or unscrupulous than average have a tendency to enter the banking industry to take advantage of customers, we say that adverse selection exist. Because of the cost of avoiding these and other problems related to asymmetric information, transaction costs with banks increase, and some risk-adverse people would choose not to deal with banks. And when bank customers are not well informed about the risky behavior of banks, they may panic together as a group and withdraw their funds from banks, which of course, causes problems for the bank. And we one banks problems spread to another, a more likely scenario when, people are uncertain about the true financial health of banks, we say that contagion occurs.

Charters, capital requirements, restrictions on assets and off balance sheet activities, requirements of standard accounting and proper risk management, examination, disclosure requirements, deposit insurance, and the lender of last resort policy are intended to address one or more of the problems associated with asymmetric information. However, when these regulations fail to limit financial problems for banks, and bankruptcy and insolvency results, regulators need to decide how to handle the failed bank. They can assist another institution to use the bank's charter to take over its operations, they can allow another institution to take over its operations after the bank's charter has been terminated, or they can simply close the bank and sell its assets to pay the bank's creditors. Sometimes, regulators are more lenient about failed banks, especially big banks, but this invites problems when banks expect that regulators, as well as bank creditors and taxpayers, can take care of problems that they causes.

Problems and Applications

Short answer problems

1. Describe one situation where a bank has less information about a transaction than a (potential) bank customer. Describe one situation where a (potential) bank customer has less information about a transaction than a bank.

2. How is a principal-agent problem a moral hazard problem?

3. Describe how group panic can also lead to contagion.

4. How do charters reduce adverse selection in the banking sector?

5. How do capital requirements reduce moral hazard in the banking sector?

6. Describe how deposit insurance can reduce group panic and contagion. Describe how this policy can increase moral hazard and possibly adverse selection.

7. Describe how the lender of last resort policy can reduce group panic and contagion. Describe how this policy can increase moral hazard and possibly adverse selection.

8. Describe how the too-big-to-fail can reduce group panic and contagion. Describe how this policy can increase moral hazard and possibly adverse selection.

9. What is regulatory forbearance? How can this policy increase moral hazard?

10. Explain the difference between illiquidity and insolvency.

11. How does the acquisition assistance method differ from the purchase and assumption method?

12. How does the purchase and assumption method differ from the payoff method?

Internet applications

1. Go to http://ecos.bok.or.kr/ to find data for required reserves and excess reserves for Korea's depository institutions, under the "Main Accounts of the Bank of Korea" link from the earliest (half) month to the latest (half) month. Plot the results for both series. What happen in late 2006 and early 2007? (Hint: see the next question.)

2. Go to http://ecos.bok.or.kr/ to find data on the reserve requirements for various kinds of deposits in Korea. Create a table that shows the required reserve ratio for each kind of deposit.

3. Go to https://www.kdic.or.kr/ to find data on the amount of insured deposits in Korea at 1) depository banks, 2) merchant banks, 3) mutual savings banks, 4) dealers, traders, brokers and securities companies, 5) and insurance companies. Create a table with the amount of deposits at each institution. Which institution currently has the largest amount of insured deposits from the KDIC?

11. Purpose and Role of Central Banks

Preview

Central banks control the monetary policy of their respective nation, as well as perform several other functions. In this chapter I describe these functions after considering how central banks were established and after describing the assets and liabilities from specific financial activities central banks undertake. In addition to these assets and liabilities, a balance sheet of a central bank records a central bank's capital, which may be paid by private or public institutions. I discuss which central banks are privately and publicly owned, and discuss the degree of independence from government agencies that central banks have or have gained over time to conduct monetary policy.

A brief history of central banks

In 1668, Sweden was the first country to establish a national bank or "central bank", as an institution to manage the financial affairs of the national government. In 1701, this bank began to issue script, an informal form of currency, on behalf of the government. In 1789, the Swedish government established the National Debt Office, which began to formally issue Swedish government currency. But in 1897, the central bank took over this role and became the only legal issuer of currency in Sweden.

In 1694, British parliament established the Bank of England, also as an institution to manage the financial affairs of the national government. But in addition, the government authorized the Bank at the time to issue currency notes that could be redeemed in silver, even though many other forms of money, from private banks notes to gold and silver coins, existed as well. The primary motivation for founding the Bank of England was to finance a war with France. However, the Bank of England was also given the responsibility of stabilizing the amount of money and credit and to stabilize financial markets.

A national bank was started in the US in 1791, which operated under a 20 year charter. Like the Bank of England, it was also established to manage the financial affairs of the national government, although it did not issue currency notes for general circulation. After this bank's charter expired in 1811, a new central bank with a 20 year charter was established in 1816 with a similar purpose, and in particular to manage the government debt from recent wartime expenditures. But for various political reasons, the charter of the national bank was not renewed in 1836, and the US waited until 1913 to establish its current central bank, the Federal Reserve System. By 1913, a national currency already existed (created in 1863 to finance the war expenditure of the national government), and other currencies issued by private banks had gradually been replaced.

The Bank of France was founded in 1800, with similar responsibilities of those of the Bank of England.

A central bank was first established in Korea in 1909, and it began to issue a national currency, but this currency was soon replaced during the Japanese occupation in 1910. However, in 1946, a newly independent central bank was established to manage the financial affairs of the government and began to issue a new currency. The Bank of Korea with its current charter was established in 1950, although the charter has been amended a several times by Parliament since then.

Even in countries where providing financial services to governments was not the primary reason for establishing a central bank, central banks have begun to do so. The US Treasury quickly began to rely on Federal Reserve banks to secure its deposits and to settle its payments after 1913, even though the primary established to be a lender of last resort for private banks. (I discuss the lender of last resort function below.)

As economies evolved, the role and purpose of central banks evolved and expanded, and the number of central banks likewise expanded throughout the world. Before 1800, only the central banks of Sweden and England existed, and only 18 central banks existed by 1900. But today, there are about 170 central banks worldwide.[43]

Thus, central banks were first established to manage the financial affairs of governments, and then to issue currency on behalf of the government. This currency later became the exclusive form of money in the domestic economy, as the government or central bank eliminated other of forms of money like currency from private banks, silver coins and gold coins. During the late nineteenth century and twentieth century, the role and purpose of central banks began to broaden as economies suffered from periodic financial crises. Central banks started to lend to private banks and other private institutions, which needed reserves to continue normal operations. And then to prevent financial crises and other adverse economic conditions from arising, central banks began to try to control the total quantity of money, credit and spending in general.

I discuss these and other functions of today's central banks below, after first examining how central banks account for financial activities on a balance sheet.

Central bank balance sheets

A central bank's balance sheet records its assets, liabilities and capital at a given point in time. Table 21, Table 22 and Table 23 show balance sheets for central banks in the US, Europe and Japan. We see that central banks of major economies have many similar assets and liabilities, although some differences also exist. I discuss the broad similarities and a few major differences in the text, and leave the reader to look at the notes of each table to find the precise definition of each entry.

Common assets of central banks include government securities and other securities, which include *Bills* (short-term, zero-coupon bonds), *Notes* (medium-term, coupon bonds) and *Bonds* (long-term, coupon-bonds) issued by the treasury/finance departments of the national government. These assets are normally bought and sold in open (secondary) market operations in exchange for money, so that the quantity of money in circulation (money held outside of the central bank) changes when these bonds are exchanged for money. Transactions in the open bond market may be considered permanent (so that securities are held "outright" by the party purchasing them) or they may be temporary, a case in which there is an explicit agreement to repurchase securities in future by the party who originally sells them. These temporary transactions are called **reversible open market transactions**, or more specifically, **repurchase agreements** (a temporary asset for the central bank, in which a counterparty agrees to repurchase the asset after the central bank initially purchases the security) and **reverse repurchase agreements** (a temporary liability for the central bank, in which a counterparty agrees to resell the asset to the central bank after the central bank initially sells the security to the counterparty). A repurchase agreement usually lasts 1 to 15 days and allows private banks to have temporary access to cash. A reverse repurchase agreement also usually lasts 1 to 15 days but allows

[43]Forrest Capie, (1995), "The Evolution of General Banking", World Bank Policy Research Working Paper, 1534.

banks to earn interest income from the securities while money is temporarily moved from circulation by the central bank.

Temporary or permanent open market operations may be conducted only with designated dealers or may occur at public auctions. In either case, the value of the securities purchased or sold is discounted at a certain rate to determine the amount of money to be exchanged for the securities. The open market operations conducted by public auctions are described as "term auction credit" on the Federal Reserve Bank's balance sheet; otherwise open market operations are conducted with designated dealers by the Federal Reserve Bank of New York. The short term and long term reversible open market operations listed on the European System of Central Banks' balance sheet are conducted by public auctions, while securities held outright are purchased by designated dealers. Some of the loans made by the Bank of Japan are made through public auctions where private institutions receive money from the Bank of Japan after they post and discount (pooled) securities.

In addition, central banks make loans directly to private banks and other private financial institutions, loans that are commonly called **discount loans** (although this term is not used on the balance sheets below). For example, the discount loans from the Federal Reserve Banks are listed under the title "other loans" on its balance sheet and those from the European System of Central Banks are listed under the title "loans from the marginal lending facility". Central banks require collateral for the loans, usually in the form of government securities, whose value is discounted at a certain rate called the central bank **discount rate** (to be distinguished from the discount rate determined through open market operations), as represented by. Analogous to open market operations, the discounted value of the securities represents the money that the central bank is willing to lend. Unlike public auctions, the discount rate on these loans is pre-set by the central bank, not determined by competitive bidding.

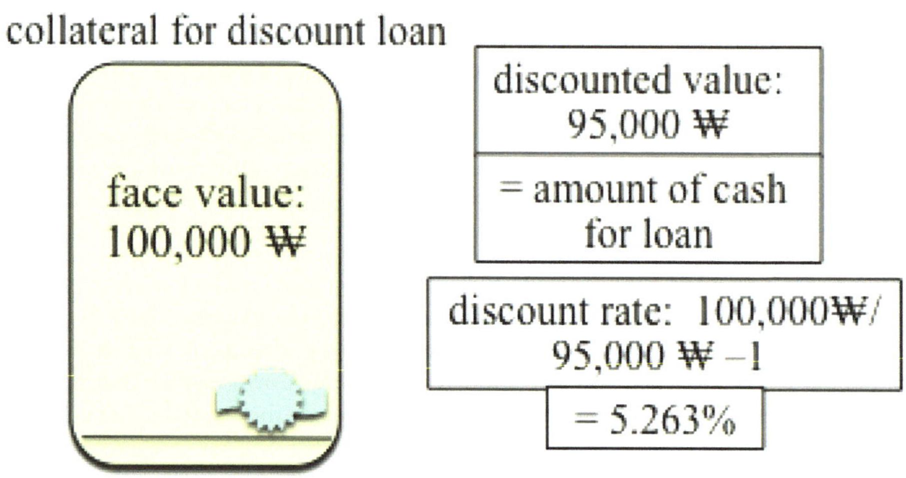

Figure 11-1: A representation of how the discount rate on a discount loan is determined.

Central banks also hold gold and assets denominated in the currencies of other nations (including special drawing right certificates, or SDRs, from the International Monetary Fund), even though these assets are not frequently used in monetary policy operations. The principal reason why central banks hold these assets is to conduct official international transactions and sometimes to influence foreign exchange rates. In addition, the Federal Reserve System recently set up a *central bank liquidity swap* (see entry 12. in Table 21) with other major central banks, in which it exchanged its dollars for other currencies, so central banks could use the foreign currencies, if necessary, to stabilize foreign exchange rates. By setting up this program, central banks tried to reassure investors that central banks had sufficient foreign currency to stabilize foreign exchange rates, and they publicly announced the creation of the program so that individuals and private institutions were aware of the extra foreign currency assets that could be used if necessary.

Finally, Table 21 describes several special programs that the Federal Reserve System started in 2008 during the financial crisis, which added assets and liabilities to the central bank's balance sheet. Other central banks also started special programs, like the central bank liquidity swaps, at this time to manage the financial crisis.

The largest liability of central banks is paper currency, or **currency notes**, circulating outside of the central bank. Currency notes—for example, US dollars, euros or yen—are considered liabilities because central banks are obligated to redeem them with something with value. In today's economies with fiat currency, if individuals or institutions want to redeem currency at a central bank (perhaps because it is worn or torn), then the central bank is obligated to exchange it with newly issued currency. However, before 1933 in the US and before 1931 in Japan and before 1925 in the United Kingdom, central banks promised to redeem the value of currency in gold (or sometimes silver). (In addition, many coins were made of gold or silver, as we discussed in chapter 2). Note that in the US and Japan, the coins in circulation are issued by other institutions and bought by the central banks with their currency notes or electronic deposits of this money, so that the coins are considered assets instead of liabilities after they are purchased by the central banks (and when the central banks pay for the coins with currency notes, both assets and liabilities increase). The central banks then sell the coins to financial institutions in return for currency notes or electronic deposits of this money.

Some central banks record a separate liability for reverse repurchase agreements (described above), but others simply debit the entry for reversible open market operations on the asset side when a reverse repurchase agreement occurs and the central bank is obligated to pay cash in the near future.

Besides currency notes circulating outside of the central bank, another major liability for central banks is the value of *deposits* from private financial institutions, from domestic government institutions and from foreign and international institutions.

Private financial institutions deposit reserves and funds used to settle payments. Most central banks require private banks to hold some reserves, according to a required reserve ratio, as we discussed in chapter 10. In addition, many banks have excess reserves to satisfy the needs of customers or to settle payments through accounts at the central bank, as we discussed in chapter 8. The Federal Reserve System and the European System of Central Banks pay interest on some funds deposited by financial institutions, but other central banks do not.

The treasury/finance department of the domestic government also deposits funds collected from tax receipts, the issuance of bonds and other sources. The US Treasury, Japanese Ministry of Finance and the treasury/finance departments of the governments of the Economic and Monetary Union of the European Union draw on these deposits to purchase goods, to pay government workers and to pay for bonds when they mature and to make tax refunds.

In addition, major central banks accept deposits from foreign central banks and international organizations, especially if foreign central banks need to buy domestic currency in the future to make official international transactions.

Unlike the Federal Reserve Banks and the Bank of Japan, the European System of Central Banks has the ability to issue **debt certificates**, its own discount bond, to influence the amount of liquid and illiquid assets in the financial system in addition to conducting open market operations, holding auctions and issuing discount loans. However, it currently does not have any of these liabilities outstanding. Likewise, the Bank of Korea issues its own bonds to influence the amount of liquid and illiquid assets in the financial system, in addition to buying and selling bonds issued by the Ministry of Strategy and Finance, the government's finance department. The central bank's bonds are called **monetary stabilization bonds** and are considered a liability for the Bank of Korea because the central bank, not the Ministry of Strategy and Finance, is responsible for paying money on the maturity date.

Like corporations, central banks issue ownership shares to investors, their owners, whose value is recorded as capital. The funds that investors pay for the ownership shares are called capital **paid in**. Central banks are often required by law to set aside enough net earnings as another form of capital, called **legal reserves** or **surplus**, to pay an adequate rate of return to these investors/owners and to pay for unexpected losses in the value of assets and unexpected increases in the value of liabilities. The Federal Reserve System issues shares that are privately owned by member banks and pays a 6% semi-annual rate of return to these banks. On the other hand, the most of the shares of the Bank of Japan are owned by the Japanese government. Some central banks in the European System of Central Banks have shares that are privately owned, while others have shares that are owned by their respective governments (see below).

Table 21: Balance sheet of the Federal Reserve Banks on 30 July 2009

Assets	(millions $)	Liabilities	(millions $)
1. Gold certificates	11,037	1. Federal Reserve notes outstanding (net of Federal Reserve Bank holdings)	870,575
2. Special drawing rights certificates	2,200	2. Reverse repurchase agreements	66,010
3. Coin	1,895	3. Deposits	1,007,573
4. Securities, repurchase agreements, term auction credit, and other loans	1,692,070	3.1. Depository institutions	747,124
		3.2. U.S. Treasury, general account	57,825
4.1. Securities held outright	1,344,561	3.3. US Treasury, supplementary financing account	199,936
A. U.S. Treasury securities	695,758	3.4. Foreign official	2,178
a. Bills	18,423	3.5. Other	511
b. Notes and bonds, nominal	627,575	4. Deferred availability cash items	2,602
c. Notes and bonds, inflation-indexed	44,438	5. Other liabilities and accrued dividends	6,725
Inflation compensation	5,323		
B. Federal agency debt securities	105,915	Total liabilities	1,953,486
C. Mortgage-backed securities	542,888		
4.2. Repurchase agreements	0	Capital	
4.3. Term auction credit	237,621	1. Capital paid in	24,522
4.4. Other loans	109,888	2. Capital surplus	21,297
5. Net portfolio holdings of Commercial Paper Funding Facility, LLC	67,300	3. Other capital accounts	3,749
6. Net portfolio holdings of LLCs funded through the Money Market Investor Funding Facility	0	Total capital	49,567
7. Net portfolio holdings of Maiden Lane, LLC	25,870		
8. Net portfolio holdings of Maiden Lane II, LLC	15,144		
9. Net portfolio holdings of Maiden Lane III, LLC	21,137		

10. Items in process of collection	230		
11. Bank premises	2,215		
12. Central bank liquidity swaps	87,738		
13. Other assets	76,218		
Total assets	2,003,053	Total liabilities and capital	2,003,053
Note: Individual elements may not sum to totals because of rounding.			
Source: Federal Reserve System: http://www.federalreserve.gov/releases/h41/current/h41.htm#h41tab9			

Assets of the Federal Reserve System include:

1. Gold certificates: The value of gold held by the Treasury but bought by the Federal Reserve Banks. The Treasury issues receipts to the Federal Reserve Banks for this gold, with a calculated value of $42.22 per troy ounce. The receipts serve as an asset for the FRS, and in return the FRS credit the general account of the Treasury (a liability) by an equal amount of money. Nearly all of the gold previously owned by the Treasury has been monetized in this fashion, and thus the gold certificate account represents the value of government's official gold stock, which can be used as official international reserves.

2. Special drawing right certificates: The value of the means of payment for the International Monetary Fund and a few other international organizations. Special Drawing Rights allow the US and other members of the IMF to obtain loans to make international payments. Thus, they are considered (official) international reserves, like gold. They are purchased by using national currencies such as US dollars, euros, yen and pounds.

3. Coin: Federal Reserve Banks buy US coins at face value from the US Treasury's Bureau of the Mint by crediting the account of the Treasury (a liability) by an equal amount of money at the time of purchase. In other words, although the Federal Reserve System officially issues paper currency (Federal Reserve notes), the Bureau of the Mint officially issues token coin currency, which the Federal Reserve Banks then purchase with its money in paper or electronic form. After purchasing the coins, the Federal Reserve Banks will sell them to depository institutions.

4.1. Securities held outright: The amount of securities held by Federal Reserve Banks from permanent or "outright" open market operations. Section 14 of the Federal Reserve Act defines the securities that the Federal Reserve is authorized to buy and sell in open market operations, which include:

A. US Treasury securities: The face value of U.S. Treasury securities held by the Federal Reserve Banks. Purchases or sales of U.S. Treasury securities by the Federal Reserve Bank of New York (FRBNY) are made only with designated dealers called primary dealers in the secondary market, or with various foreign official or international official organizations that maintain accounts at the Federal Reserve Banks. There are a few different kinds of Treasury securities:

   a. Treasury Bills: discount bonds issued by the US Treasury with a maturity of 52 weeks or less
   b. Treasury Notes and Bonds: coupon bonds issued by the US Treasury with a maturity of 2-10 years (Notes) or more than 10 years (Bonds). Coupon payments, representing interest payments, are paid every six months on both Notes and Bonds.
   c. Inflation-indexed Treasury Notes and Bonds: coupon bonds issued by the US Treasury with a maturity of 2 years or more, whose coupon and face value payments are indexed to inflation.

   Inflation compensation records the compensation for inflation to the principal of inflation-indexed securities.

B. Federal agency debt securities: The face value of debt securities issued by (a direct obligation of) Fannie Mae, Freddie Mac, and the Federal Home Loan Banks.

C. Mortgage-backed securities: The face value of mortgage-backed securities, approximately equal to the principal balance of the underlying mortgage loans, which are guaranteed by (an indirect obligation of) Fannie Mae,

Freddie Mac, or Ginnie Mae.

4.2. Repurchase agreements: The cash value of repurchase agreements, which are open market operations in which US Treasury or federal agency securities are purchased from primary dealers or foreign central banks, in return for cash, with an agreement that the dealer or foreign central bank repurchase the securities at specified date in the future. The Federal Reserve Banks may enter into repurchase agreements for up to 65 business days, but the typical maturity is between one and 14 days. The difference between the purchase price and the repurchase price reflects an interest payment.

4.3. Term auction credit: Under the Term Auction Facility (TAF) program, the Federal Reserve System auctions funds for a specified term to depository institutions eligible to borrow under the primary credit discount window program (see note 4.4.). The auction is settled by the institution that is willing to offer the highest discount rate on (willing to accept the lowest amount of cash in return for) the collateral backing the funds.

4.4. Other loans: Other loans represents the amount of "primary credit", "secondary credit" and "seasonal credit" from the traditional discount loan programs. Under the discount loan program, the Federal Reserve Banks lend funds to depository institutions after requiring collateral and discounting the value of the collateral at a given rate to determine the amount of cash to lend. Primary credit loans refer to loans to depository institutions in good financial condition, and therefore their collateral is discounted at a low rate and they are lent a high amount of cash for a given amount of collateral. Secondary credit loans refer to loans to depository institutions in substandard financial condition, and therefore their collateral is discounted at a high rate and they are lent a low amount of cash for a given amount of collateral. Seasonal credit loans refer to loans to depository institutions that have high seasonal changes in the amount of reserves that they need to operate, such as banks in agricultural regions and tourist areas. The seasonal credit rate is a weighted average of the primary credit rate and a market interest rate such as the interest rate on short-term certificates of deposits that are traded between banks. In addition, Other loans represents loans under non-traditional programs that issue credit to primary dealers and other broker-dealers, the Asset-Backed Commercial Paper Money Market Mutual Fund Liquidity Facility, American International Group, Inc., the Term Asset-Backed Securities Loan Facility and other institutions.

5. Net portfolio holdings of the Commercial Paper Funding Facility (CPPF): The CPPF provides liquidity to US issuers of commercial paper through a limited liability corporation (LLC) special purpose vehicle (SPV), which purchases three-month unsecured and asset-backed commercial paper directly from eligible issuers. Under the CPPF, the Federal Reserve System (or more specifically the Federal Reserve Bank of New York) finances the SPV to purchase this commercial paper and secures its funds through the assets of the SPV and fees or other forms of security paid by the issuers of unsecured commercial paper. The value reported above represents the book value of the commercial paper and other assets of the SPV.

6. Net portfolio holdings of the Money Market Investor Funding Facility (MMIFF): The (MMIFF) provides liquidity to US money market investors through limited liability corporation (LLC) special purpose vehicles (SPVs), which purchase U.S. dollar-denominated certificates of deposit and commercial paper with maturity dates of 90 days or less issued by highly rated financial institutions. Under the MMIFF, the Federal Reserve System finances the SPVs to purchase these money market instruments. The value reported above represents the book value of these money market instruments and other assets of the SPVs.

7. Net portfolio holdings of Maiden Lane, LLC: To facilitate the acquisition of the Bear Stearns Company, Inc. by JPMorgan Chase & Co., the Federal Reserve System created and financed the special purpose vehicle (SPV), Maiden Lane, LLC. Maiden Lane, LLC acquires and manages certain assets of the former Bear Stearns Company to maximize its profit and to minimize disruption in financial markets. The value reported above represents the fair value of the assets of the SPV.

8. Net portfolio holdings of Maiden Lane II, LLC: To provide financial support to the American Insurance Group (AIG), the Federal Reserve System created and financed the special purpose vehicle (SPV), Maiden Lane II, LLC. Maiden Lane II, LLC purchased mortgage backed securities (MBS) from AIG subsidiaries that relied on AIG to insure their values through credit default swaps. The value reported above represents the fair value of the MBS assets of the SPV.

9. Net portfolio holdings of Maiden Lane III, LLC: To provide financial support to the American Insurance Group (AIG),

the Federal Reserve System created and financed the special purpose vehicle (SPV), Maiden Lane III, LLC. Maiden Lane III, LLC purchased collateralized debt obligations (CDOs) from AIG subsidiaries that relied on AIG to insure their values through credit default swaps. The value reported above represents the fair value of the CDO assets of the SPV.

10. Items in process of collection: Items in the process of collection are checks, negotiable orders of withdrawal, matured coupon and face value payments from municipal and corporate bonds, and other items payable on demand that have been presented to the Federal Reserve Banks for payment, which are being processed through the payment settlement system with the institutions on which they are drawn. Other items payable on demand, like US government checks, postal money orders and food coupons and other forms of government assistance, are the responsibility of the US Treasury so are not included in this entry; the value of these cash items are debited from the Treasury's account (a liability for the Federal Reserve System) on the day they are received by the Federal Reserve System to represent a payment by the US Treasury.

11. Bank premises: The initial cost of land, buildings and building-related equipment of the Federal Reserve Banks and their branches, minus depreciation.

12. Central bank liquidity swaps: These represent swaps of currency or other forms of cash with foreign central banks to provide liquidity in foreign exchange markets. With these swaps, a foreign central bank sells a specified amount of its currency to the Federal Reserve System in exchange for dollars at the current (spot) exchange rate. The reported value above represents the dollar value of the foreign currency held by the Federal Reserve System from these swaps. At the same time as the swap, the Federal Reserve System and the foreign central bank make a forward contract in which the foreign central bank will repurchase the foreign currency using US dollars with the same exchange rate at a specified future date, eliminating the chance for profit and losses for both central banks. However, the forward contract specifies that the foreign central bank pay a market interest rate on the US dollars that it acquires, which allows the Federal Reserve Banks to earn interest income on the swaps.

13. Other assets include:

*As-of adjustments to correct accounting errors not related to the payment settlement system (float).

*Assets denominated in foreign currencies other than special drawing right certificates. Since 1963, the Federal Reserve System has occasionally agreed to hold foreign currency for the Treasury in return for US dollars. To avoid the risk of currency fluctuations while it holds the currency, the Federal Reserve System will buy the currency from the Treasury at the spot market rate, and then sell the currency to the Treasury using a forward contract but at the same spot market rate. At the time of the spot market transaction, "Other assets" and "U.S. Treasury, general account" increase. When the forward contract matures or when the Treasury withdraws the foreign currency prior to the maturity of the forward contract, both accounts decrease. In addition, the value of assets denominated in foreign currencies are revalued each day to reflect current (spot market) exchange rates, and changes in the value of these assets represent changes in earnings, which are recorded in "other liabilities and capital" on the other side of the balance sheet.

*Premiums paid on securities bought: If the Federal Reserve System pays more than the face value for securities that it purchased outright, the premiums over the face value are recorded in “Other assets” and “Other liabilities and capital”. In addition, the premiums are amortized daily as the securities mature and the amortized amount is recorded as a reduced premium in "Other assets" and reduced earnings in "Other liabilities and capital".

*Accrued interest and other accounts receivable: This item represents the daily accumulation of interest earned from US government securities, from loans to depository institutions and from foreign currency assets.

Liabilities of the Federal Reserve System include:

1. Federal Reserve notes outstanding: The total value of Federal Reserve notes (paper currency) circulating outside of the central bank (net of the value held by Federal Reserve Banks).

2. Reverse repurchase agreements: Cash value of reverse repurchase agreements, which are open market operations in which US Treasury or federal agency securities are sold to primary dealers or foreign central banks, who pay cash to the Federal Reserve System, with an agreement that the dealer or bank sell the securities back to the Federal Reserve System at specified date in the future. The Federal Reserve Banks may enter into repurchase agreements for up to 65 business days, but the typical maturity is between one and 14 days. The difference between the purchase price and the repurchase price reflects an interest payment.

3.1. Deposits of depository institutions: This reflects the value of accounts of depository institutions at the Federal Reserve Banks, which include reserve accounts and accounts used in processing payments in the various payment settlement systems. The Federal Reserve System recently began paying interest on reserve deposits and deposits used in payment settlement systems to give depository institutions an incentive to increase their cash balances.

3.2. US Treasury, general account: This reflects the value of the primary account of the US Treasury at Federal Reserve Banks. Tax receipts and proceeds from sales of Treasury debt are deposited in this account. Virtually all US government disbursements are made from this account.

3.3. US Treasury, supplementary financing account: This reflects the value of a supplementary account of the US Treasury, created to handle disbursements and deposits from the new liquidity facilities recently created by the Federal Reserve System. The US Treasury has recently borrowed funds from the Federal Reserve Banks and deposited the funds in this account so that the central bank would have enough money to finance its massive purchases of securities.

3.4. Foreign official: This reflects deposits of foreign central banks, foreign governments, and other foreign official institutions at the Federal Reserve System. Unlike deposits of US depository institutions, the Federal Reserve System does not pay interest on these deposits.

3.5. Other deposits: This value includes deposits of international and multilateral organizations, such as the International Monetary Fund, United Nations, International Bank for Reconstruction and Development (World Bank); the deposits used for the exchange stabilization fund, a program designed by the US Treasury to influence foreign exchange rates; and deposits of a few US government sponsored agencies, such as Fannie Mae and Freddie Mac.

4. Deferred availability cash items: Federal Reserve Banks do not always give immediate credit when settling payments with a counterparty, but may defer credit for up to two business days. This deferred credit is a liability and its total value is recorded in this entry. After a previously deferred credit to a depository institution has been settled, this entry is reduced and the depository institution's reserve account (see 3.1.) is increased. The difference between "items in process of collection" on the asset side of the balance sheet and "deferred availability cash items" on the liability side of the balance sheet is called "float" and reflects temporary excess credits or excess debits in the payment settlement system.

5. Other liabilities and accrued dividends: This reflects dividends that have accrued on Federal Reserve Bank capital between the semi-annual payment dates (the last business days of June and December) and liabilities of the SPVs created by the Federal Reserve System—including the Commercial Paper Funding Facility, LLC; the Money Market Investor Funding Facility, LLCs; Maiden Lane, LLC; Maiden Lane II, LLC; and Maiden Lane III, LLC—and in particular, liabilities that accrue when these SPVs lose capital.

Capital of the Federal Reserve System includes:

1. Capital paid in: This reflects the capital investments by member banks of the Federal Reserve System, which own shares of their district Federal Reserve Bank equal to 6% of their own capital. Of this amount, half is paid to the Federal Reserve Banks, while is available for the Board of Governors.

2. Surplus: This reflects net earnings of Federal Reserve Banks after expenses and a 6% dividend on capital paid in have been paid. To provide an adequate return on capital paid in, Federal Reserve Banks should earn enough surplus and other capital to equal capital paid in.

3. Other capital accounts: This represents the unallocated net earnings since the last payment of dividends, the amount necessary to equate surplus to paid in capital at the end of the year, and the interest to be paid to the Treasury on its outstanding Federal Reserve notes.

Table 22: Balance sheet of the European System of Central Banks on 29 January 2010

Assets	(€ millions)	Liabilities	(€ millions)
1. Gold and gold receivables	266,918	1. Bank notes outstanding	783,351
2. Claims on non-euro area residents denominated in foreign currency	195,138	2. Liabilities to euro area financial institutions denominated in euro	387,294
2.1. Claims on the International Monetary Fund	62,822	2.1. Current accounts	244,221
2.2. Claims on external banks and security firms, external loans and other external assets	132,316	2.2. Deposit facility	143,073
3. Claims on euro area residents denominated in foreign currency	27,812	2.3 Fixed-term deposits	0
4. Claims on non-euro area residents denominated in euro	17,395	2.4 Fine-tuning open market operations	0
4.1. Claims on external banks and security firms, and external loans	17,395	2.5. Deposits related to margin calls	0
4.2. Claims from the credit facility of the Exchange Rate Mechanism II	0	2.6. Other liabilities of euro area financial institutions denominated in euro	293
5. Lending to euro area financial institutions	720,920	3. Debt certificates	0
5.1. Short term reversible open market operations	58,629	4. Liabilities to other euro area residents denominated in euro	133,000
5.2. Long term reversible open market operations	662,188	4.1. General government liabilities	124,445
5.3. Fine tuning open market operations	0	4.2. Other liabilities of other euro area residents denominated in euro	8,554
5.4. Structural open market operations	0	5. Liabilities to non-euro area residents denominated in euro	41,016
5.5. Loans from the marginal lending facility	83	6. Liabilities to euro area residents denominated in foreign currency	4,967
5.6. Credits related to margin calls	19	7. Liabilities to non-euro area residents denominated in foreign currency	8,428
6. Other claims on euro area financial institutions denominated in euro	28,468	7.1. Deposits and other liabilities	8,428
7. Securities of euro area residents denominated in euro	328,848	7.2. Liabilities to the credit facility of the Exchange Rate Mechanism II	0
7.1. Securities held for monetary policy purposes	32,054	8. Special drawing rights liabilities	51,249
7.2. Other securities	296,793	9. Other liabilities	166,502
8. Government debt denominated in euro	36,171	10. Revaluation accounts	220,213
9. Other assets	248,673		

		Total liabilities	1,796,314
		Capital	74,028
Total assets	1,870,342	Total liabilities and capital	1,870,342
Note: Individual elements may not sum to totals because of rounding.			
Source: European Central Bank, http://www.ecb.int/press/pr/wfs/2010/html/fs100202.en.html			

Assets of the European System of Central Banks include:

1. Gold and gold receivables: These represent gold and gold deposit accounts, which act as official international reserves of the European System of Central Banks.

2. Claims on non-euro area residents denominated in foreign currency: These also represent official international reserves for the European System of Central Banks, like gold and gold receivables.

2.1. Claims on the International Monetary Fund: These represent special drawing rights certificates, drawing rights (legal ability to draw credit) within a "tranche" assigned by the IMF, loans under other borrowing arrangements such as the General Arrangements to Borrow, or deposits under the Enhanced Structural Adjustment Facility.

2.2. Claims on external banks and security firms, external loans, and other external assets: These represent foreign currency assets from non-euro area residents other than gold, gold receivables and receivables from the IMF. Such assets include foreign currency denominated cash, deposits, loans, commercial paper, bills, notes and bonds owned by the European System of Central Banks.

3. Claims on euro area residents denominated in foreign currency represent foreign currency assets from euro area residents. Such assets include foreign currency denominated cash, deposits, loans, commercial paper, bills, notes and bonds owned by the European System of Central Banks.

4. Claims on non-euro area residents denominated in euro.

4.1. Claims on external banks and security firms, and external loans represent euro denominated cash, deposits, loans, commercial paper, bills, notes, bonds and other assets owned by the European System of Central Banks.

4.2. Claims from the credit facility of the Exchange Rate Mechanism II represent assets of the European System of Central Banks used to stabilize exchange rates with non-euro countries that desire stable exchange rates between their currencies and the euro.

5. Lending to euro area financial institutions.

5.1. Short term refinancing operations represent reversible open market operations—that is, (reverse) repurchase agreements—with a maturity of 2 weeks in which financial institutions offer bids for a discount rate on the value of the collateral through a weekly auction.

5.2. Long term refinancing operations represent reversible open market operations—that is, (reverse) repurchase agreements—with a maturity of 3 months in which financial institutions offer bids for a discount rate on the value of the collateral through a monthly auction.

5.3. Fine tuning open market operations represent *ad hoc* reversible open market purchases of securities—that is, repurchase agreements—without a set maturity designed to manage unexpected changes in reserves.

5.4. Structural open market operations represent transactions in the secondary (open) securities market that are intended to be permanent ("outright") in which financial institutions offer bids for a discount rate on the value of the collateral through an *ad hoc* auction.

5.5. Loans from the marginal lending facility represent overnight loans at a discount rate that is pre-set by the European System of Central Banks.

5.6. Credits related to margin calls represent changes in the value of underlying assets (ex., collateral) used for a loan contract or another contract held by the European System of Central Banks.

6. Other claims on euro area financial institutions denominated in euro represent former foreign currency reserves of financial institutions in the euro area.

7. Securities of euro area residents denominated in euro

7.1. Securities held for monetary policy purposes represent securities bought and sold in the secondary (open) market with designated dealers in transactions that are intended to be permanent ("outright").

7.2. Other securities represent securities that are bought and sold in the secondary (open) market with designated dealers for investment purposes, to finance government spending or for other purposes.

8. Government debt denominated in euro represents non-marketable claims on euro area governments from before 1 January 1994, after which central banks in the euro area could no longer lend to or directly purchase debt securities from governments in the primary market. Nonetheless, euro area governments continue to promise to redeem the debts in euro in due course.

9. Other assets includes cash items in the process of collection (through the payment settlement system), coins of euro area countries and other financial assets, pension funds, severance funds, securities held due to statutory requirements, tangible and intangible fixed assets, revaluations of off balance sheet items, accrued revenue, and deferred expenditure.

Liabilities of the European System of Central Banks include:

1. Bank notes outstanding represents the total value of notes (paper currency) issued by the European System of Central Banks that are circulating outside of the central bank (net of the value held by member national banks).

2. Liabilities to euro area financial institutions that are denominated in euro

2.1. Current accounts represent the value of required reserve deposits of financial institutions and the value of their accounts used to settle payments.

2.2. Deposit facility represents the value of excess reserve deposits of financial institutions. These deposits pay an interest rate that is pre-set by the European System of Central Banks.

2.3. Fixed-term deposits represent excess reserve time deposits of financial institutions. These deposits pay an interest rate for a fixed term that is pre-set by the European System of Central Banks, and they are created to absorb excess reserves at financial institutions for a fixed period of time in order to prevent excess lending and inflation.

2.4. Fine-tuning open market operations represent *ad hoc* reversible open market sales of securities—that is, reverse repurchase agreements—without a set maturity designed to manage unexpected changes in reserves (compare with asset note 5.3. above).

2.5. Deposits related to margin calls represent changes in the value of underlying assets (ex., collateral) used in a contract held by a counterparty that assigns an obligation to the European System of Central Banks (compare with asset note 5.6. above).

2.6. Other liabilities of euro area financial institutions denominated in euro

3. Debt certificates represent the value of unsecured promissory notes issued by the European System of Central Banks, analogous to commercial paper issued by private commercial banks and commercial businesses in the money market.

4. Liabilities to other euro area residents denominated in euro

4.1. General government liabilities include deposits of euro area governments, which come from national tax receipts, are used for various payments to citizens.

4.2. Other liabilities of other euro area residents denominated in euro include deposits by non-financial and non-government institutions and other euro area depositors.

5. Liabilities to non-euro area residents denominated in euro include deposits by foreign central banks, foreign private banks, international institutions and other non-euro area depositors. This value includes balances of the Trans-European Automated Real-time Gross settlement Express Transfer system (TARGET system), the real-time gross settlement payment systems used throughout the euro area and some non-euro area EU member countries.

6. Liabilities to euro area residents denominated in foreign currency include deposits in foreign currency of financial institutions, non-financial institutions, government institutions and non-government institutions. This value includes balances of the TARGET system (see liability note 5. above).

7. Liabilities to non-euro area residents denominated in foreign currency

7.1. Deposits and other liabilities include deposits by foreign central banks, foreign private banks, international institutions and other non-euro area depositors. This value includes balances of the TARGET system (see liability note 5. above).

7.2. Liabilities to the credit facility of the Exchange Rate Mechanism II represent foreign currency liabilities of the European System of Central Banks used to stabilize exchange rates with non-euro countries which desire stable exchange rates between their currencies and the euro. (see also asset note 4.2. above).

8. Special drawing rights liabilities special drawing rights assigned by the IMF with the condition that they are repaid under specific circumstances.

9. Other liabilities include payments due through the payment settlement system, provisions for pensions and severances, provisions for foreign exchange rate and price losses, revaluations of off balance sheet items, accrued expenses, deferred revenue and deferred profit.

10. Revaluation accounts represent unrealized gains that occur when foreign exchange rates and prices change, and unrealized gains of euro area national central banks when they switched to the accounting rules of the European System of Central Banks.

Capital represents capital paid in by private or public sector investors, net earnings (surplus) set aside to offer dividend payments to those investors and other funds like unallocated net earnings since the last payment of dividends.

Table 23: Balance sheet of the Bank of Japan on 31 January 2010

Assets	(billions ¥)	Liabilities	(billions ¥)
1. Gold	441	1. Bank notes outstanding	76,904
2. Coins reserved for circulation	270	2. Current deposits	15,286
3. Receivables under repurchase agreements	6,337	3. Other deposits	36
4. Japanese government securities	73,191	4. Deposits of the government	2,652
4.1. Treasury bonds	49,936	5. Payables under reverse repurchase agreements	20,883
4.2. Treasury discount bills	23,256	6. Other liabilities	785
5. Corporate bonds	197	7. Provisions	3,229
6. Pecuniary trust accounts of stocks	1,342		
6.1. Total value of stocks purchased	214	Capital	
7. Loans	34,629	Capital paid in	0.1
7.1. Loans backed by pooled collateral and loans for corporate financing	34,604	Legal and special reserves	2,660
7.2 Other loans	25		
8. Foreign currency assets	5,446		
9. Deposits with agents	8		
10. Other assets	573		
Total assets	122,434	Total liabilities and capital	122,434

Note: Individual elements may not sum to totals because of rounding.

Source: http://www.boj.or.jp/en/theme/research/stat/boj/ac/index.htm

Assets of the Bank of Japan include:

1. Gold: deposits of gold or gold certificates, which act as official international reserves of the Bank of Japan.

2. Coin reserved for circulation: Like the Federal Reserve Banks in the US, the Bank of Japan buys coins from another institutions with its currency notes and sells the coins to financial institutions.

3. Receivables under repurchase agreements: The face value of repurchase agreements, which are open market operations in which Japanese government securities and commercial paper are purchased from primary dealers or foreign central banks, in return for cash, with an agreement that the dealer or foreign central bank repurchase the securities at specified date in the future.

4. Japanese government securities: The face value of securities issued by the Ministry of Finance ("Treasury") held by the Bank of Japan from permanent or "outright" open market operations, which include:

4.1. Treasury bonds: coupon bonds issued by the Ministry of Finance with a maturity of 2-40 years. Coupon payments, representing interest payments, are paid every six months on both Notes and Bonds. The Ministry of Finance also issues inflation-indexed bonds, but these bonds are not recorded separable on the Bank of Japan's balance sheet.

4.2. Treasury bills: discount bonds issued by the Ministry of Finance with a maturity of 52 weeks or less.

5. Corporate bonds: unlike many other central banks, the Bank of Japan purchases bonds from private corporations.

6. Pecuniary trust accounts of stocks: unlike many other central banks, the Bank of Japan purchases stock of financial institutions. These are purchased through a trust bank or other trusts.

6.1. Total value of stocks purchased in the trusts, valued on the date of delivery.

7. Loans: loans to all eligible banks and non-bank corporations, with the exception of the Deposit Insurance Corporation. This entry includes loans under the Complementary Lending Facility from March 2001.

7.1. Loans backed by pooled collateral and loans for corporate financing: The amount of loans for monetary policy purposes that require pooled assets to back the value of the loans and special loans intended to finance corporate spending. The discount rates on these loans may be determined by either auction bidding or pre-set by the Bank of Japan, although the Bank of Japan has relied only on auction bidding until 2009.

7.2. Other loans: loans that are not backed by pooled collateral and not for financing corporate spending.

8. Foreign currency assets includes loans made by the Bank of Japan in foreign currency, in particular loans in US dollars made since 2008 to influence foreign exchange rates; deposits of the Bank of Japan in foreign currency at foreign central banks and the Bank for International Settlements; as well as foreign currency denominated securities, mutual funds and assets in pecuniary trusts.

9. Deposits with agents: This value represents the value of deposits at institutions that conduct operations with Japanese government securities and treasury funds on behalf of the Bank of Japan.

10. Other assets: This item includes items in the process of collection, tangible (physical) assets, intangible assets, a provision of funds for the New Financial Stabilization Fund, withdrawn cash to be returned to the government, accrued interest and other revenue, and any commercial paper that the Bank of Japan buys from domestic commercial banks, other domestic commercial firms and foreign commercial firms. It also includes the value of capital and other accounts at the Deposit Insurance Corporation, the Agricultural and Fishery Cooperative Savings Insurance Corporation and international financial institutions.

Liabilities of the Bank of Japan include:

1. Bank notes outstanding: The total value of Bank of Japan notes (paper currency) circulating outside of the central bank (net of the value held by the Bank of Japan).

2. Current deposits: This represents the accounts of depository institutions, call loan and discount companies and securities firms at the Bank of Japan, which include reserve accounts and accounts used in processing payments in the various payment settlement systems.

3. Other deposits: This value represents deposits owned by foreign central banks, by international and multilateral organizations, such as the International Monetary Fund, United Nations, International Bank for Reconstruction and

Development (World Bank), and by others.

4. Deposits of the government: This reflects the value of the account of the Ministry of Finance at the Bank of Japan. Tax receipts and proceeds from sales of Treasury debt are deposited in this account, and government disbursements are made from this account.

5. Payables under reverse repurchase agreements: The face value of reverse repurchase agreements, which are open market operations in which Japanese government securities and commercial paper are sold to primary dealers or foreign central banks, in return for cash, with an agreement that the Bank of Japan repurchase the securities at specified date in the future.

6. Other liabilities: Deferred credit in the payment settlement system, dividends that have accrued on Bank of Japan capital, cash submitted to counterparties as collateral when the Bank of Japan borrows Japanese government securities, accrued expenses and deferred revenue.

7. Provisions include provisions for pensions and severances, provisions for foreign exchange rate and price losses, revaluations of off balance sheet items, accrued expenses, deferred revenue and deferred profit.

Capital of the Bank of Japan include:

1. Capital paid in: This reflects the capital investments by private investors and the government of Japan.

2. Legal and special reserves: Legal reserves represent the unallocated net earnings that the Bank of Japan is required by law to set aside as a security again unforeseen decreases in the value of assets and unforeseen increases in the value of liabilities. Special reserves include unallocated net earnings specifically set aside for payment of dividends and other specific purposes.

Functions of central banks

The balance sheets above give specific details about what duties central banks perform as they earn income from assets and pay expenses from liabilities. In this section, I describe the functions of central banks into seven broad categories: as the government's bank, as the institution that issues and primarily influences the quantity of money in circulation and various interest rates, as the lender of last resort, as a regulator of private banks, as an operator in the payment settlement system, as a collector and researcher of economic data, and as the institution that can influence foreign exchange rates.

The government's bank. As described in the previous section, central banks perform banking functions for their nations' governments: they accept deposits from treasury/finance departments of the national government and disburse funds from these accounts.

In addition, central banks will often conduct auctions or perform other operations when government securities are bought and sold in the primary or secondary (open) market. Central banks also usually service and redeem government debt by crediting and debiting the treasury/finance department's accounts and may assist in the primary and secondary market auctions for government by tabulating bids and then issuing the securities to the winning bidder and processing the payment for the treasury/finance department. For example, the Federal Reserve System manages transactions of US Treasury securities through its book-entry security system, which maintains accounts for each individual or institution that buys or sells US Treasury securities. When one party sells a US Treasury security to another, the Federal Reserve System electronically credits the buyer's account and electronically debits the seller's account. In nations with old fashioned financial markets, central banks may act as a broker or dealer of government securities.

Usually, central banks in major economies are prohibited from purchasing bonds directly from treasury/finance departments because such a policy can lead to inflation, by guaranteeing the government a source of money for the bonds that it issues when individuals and private institutions are unwilling to invest their funds. However, some central banks have directly purchased bonds from treasury/finance departments, especially when the government needed or needs to finance a large project and private investors are unwilling to lend their funds to the government. In other cases, the buyers, treasury/finance department requires private banks to purchase government securities, which are then purchased by the central bank if it believes there is a shortage of reserves at banks. In any case, central banks regularly buy the securities in the secondary (open) market, and by doing so they implicitly finance or reduce the cost of government spending.

Monetary policy: the quantity of money and interest rates. Today's central banks are the primary or exclusive issuer of a nation's (fiat) currency: they have the primary or sole power to issue money for the domestic economy and they determine the value of a unit of currency, ultimately by influencing the quantity of money that circulates in the economy.

Central banks primarily control the quantity of money and credit, as well as the cost of credit (interest rates) by buying and selling bonds in the open bond market, by holding auctions and by lending directly to banks, and through a few other monetary policies that I describe in detail in this section. The quantity of money and credit and interest rates affect the amount of spending, which influences economic production, employment and inflation, which I examine in detail in chapter 13.

Open market operations. As the central bank balance sheets above indicate, central banks buy and sell government treasury/finance department bills or other securities either with the intention of holding the bonds until maturity or with the intention of selling or buying the securities in the near future, which causes the money supply to change permanently or temporarily. When the central bank buys government securities or other securities from private financial institutions or individuals, it gives them money in return so that the quantity of money in circulation increases, as represented by Figure 11-2. When central banks sell government or other securities from private financial institutions or individuals, it requires money in return, which it then puts in its vaults or accounts so that the quantity of money in circulation decreases.

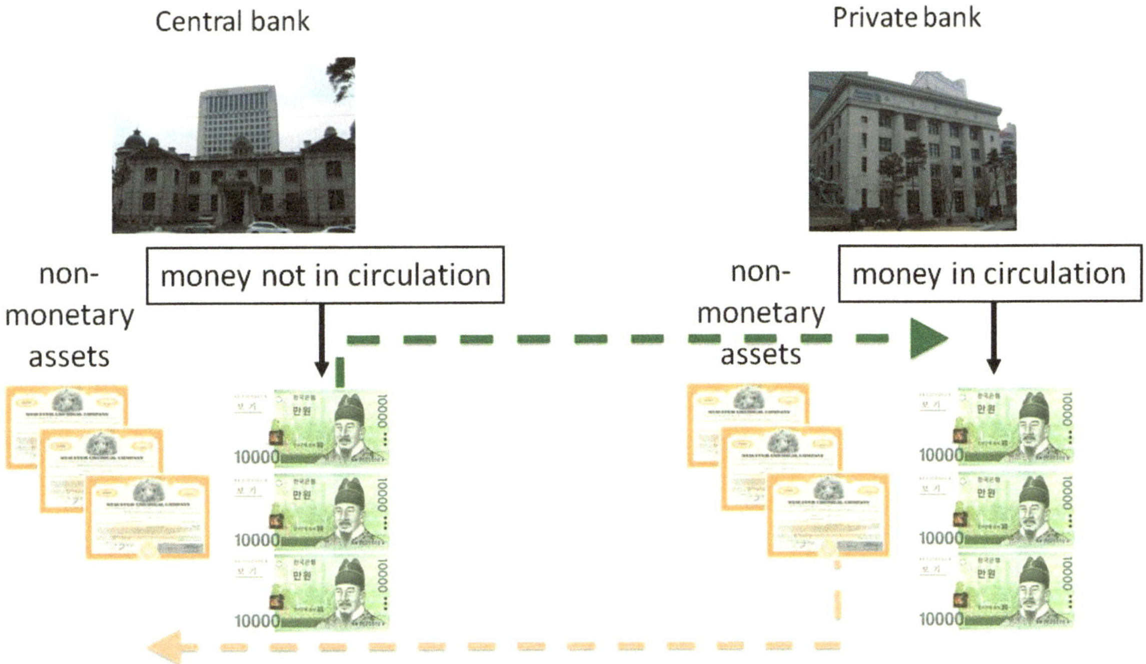

Figure 11-2: When the central bank *buys* government bonds in the open bond market (from a private sector bank) and pays money for the bond, the quantity of money in circulation increases.

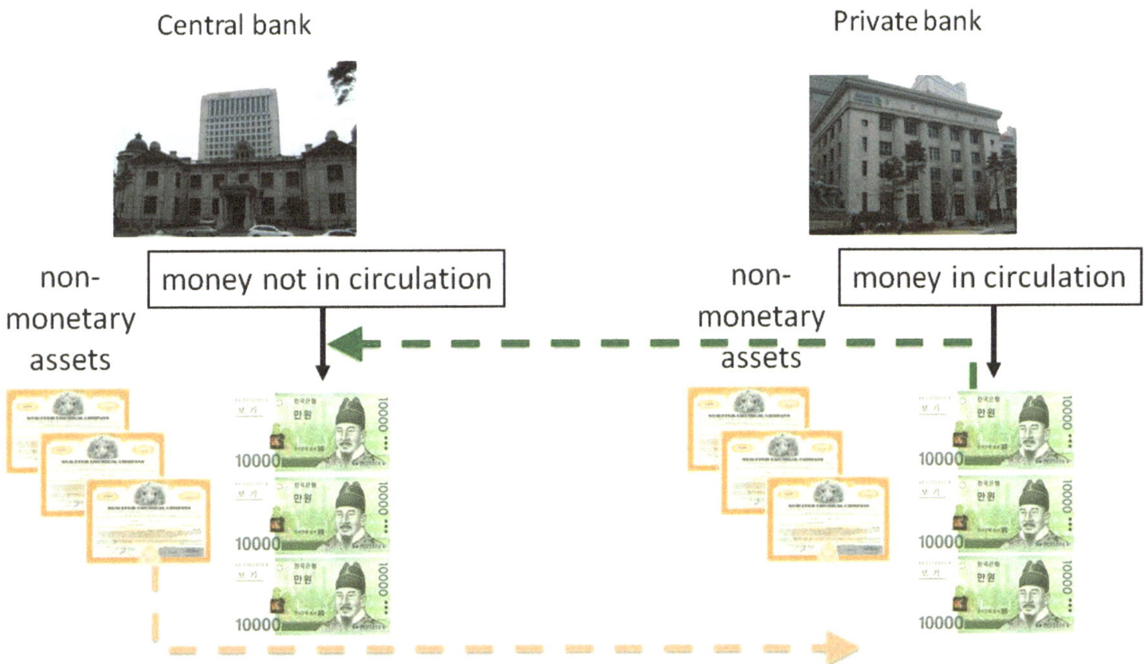

Figure 11-3: When the central bank *sells* government bonds in the open bond market (to a private sector bank) and receives money in return, the quantity of money in circulation decreases.

Open market operations have traditionally been conducted with designated dealers, but central banks now also rely on public auctions to exchange securities for money. Unlike open market operations with designated dealers, public auctions are open to any individual or institution. In public auctions, borrowers post required collateral (usually government securities) for the cash/reserves, and then competitively bid the rate at which they are willing to discount the value of the collateral. As with discount loans and open market operations with designated dealers, the discounted value determines the total amount of cash/reserves that the central bank will lend, and the discounted value relative to the face value determines the auction discount rate. But unlike discount loans and open market operations with designated dealers, auctions held by the central bank allow multiple parties to compete with each other in a single market.

And because the amount of money (or reserves) that banks have changes, banks tend to change their own interest rates on loans and deposits—decreasing interest rates on loans and deposits when they have more money and increasing interest rates on loans and deposits when they have less money. In addition, interest rates on bonds also change when the quantity of money changes. For example, when the central bank purchases more bonds in the open bond market, the demand and price of bonds increases, so that new buyers must pay more for new and existing bonds, which decreases the yield to maturity or interest rate for new buyers (although it will increase the rate of return for existing bond holders).

Within the Federal Reserve System, the Federal Open Market Committee (FOMC) decides how many or when open market operations occur. The voting members of the FOMC are composed of the Board of Governors of the Federal Reserve System and five of the twelve presidents of the Federal Reserve district banks (even though all twelve presidents usually attend the committee meetings, if only as informal participants). When the FOMC meets (usually every 6 weeks), it sets a target for the interest rate in the market for reserves (called the federal funds rate) and creates a summary of its decisions in a document called the FOMC directive. Using the FOMC directive, the Trading Desk at the New York Federal Reserve Bank then targets the interest rate by buying or selling in the open bond market each business morning, either in the form of outright transactions or (reverse) repurchase agreements. When the Trading Desk buys or sells in the open bond market, it will likewise credits or debits the counterparty's account a banking institution, thereby changing the amount of reserves in the banking system and the interest rate in the market for reserves.

Within the European System of Central Banks, open market operations mostly occur at weekly or monthly auctions of reversible open market operations.

The Bank of Canada also conducts similar weekly open market operations once per week to manage reserves. But unlike most other central banks, it participates in the Canadian Treasury's weekly auction of government bills, directly purchasing debt from the government when desired.

At the Bank of Japan, most open market operations involve the purchase or sale of privately issued securities, including commercial paper and bank certificates of deposit.

Open market operations are much less common in poorer economies because the markets for government securities and other securities are often not large enough to find a sufficient number of dealers to trade securities on a daily or weekly basis. Monetary policy in poorer countries relies more on direct lending to financial institutions and direct regulation of interest rates by the central bank. However, central banks in rich countries also lend directly to financial institutions to some degree, which I describe next.

Central bank loans and deposits. Although open market operations are the primary monetary policy tool to influence the quantity of money and interest rates, central banks also influence the quantity of money and interest rates by directly lending to financial institutions, and by changing interest rates on these loans and funds deposited at the central bank.

Central banks have traditionally lent directly to banks when banks had a shortage of cash by requiring collateral for the loan (usually in the form of marketable securities) and then discounting its value to determine the amount of cash in the loan. Central banks have traditionally required either commercial paper or treasury/finance bills as collateral for these loans, but they have also used other securities as well.

Unlike open market operations where the behavior of thousands of buyers and sellers can influence interest rates, the interest rate on this direct lending (the discount rate) is set by the central bank.

Sometimes central banks set the discount rate on their loans slightly below market interest rates, in particular, the interest rate in the overnight inter-bank loan market. This policy is called a **subsidy rate policy** because the central bank subsidizes banks that acquire credit from it. But to keep banks from borrowing unlimited amounts at its subsidy rate, a central bank must ration the quantity of credit to private banks. (I discuss regulation of the quantity of credit below.)

Sometimes central banks set the interest rate on their loans slightly above market interest rates. This policy is called a **penalty rate policy** because the central bank penalizes banks that acquire credit from it. In theory, no bank should want to borrow from the central bank when it can borrow at cheaper market interest rates. Borrowing at the penalty rate is therefore used only in special circumstances, as a last resort, when banks can not get sufficient credit at cheaper market rates.

The Federal Reserve System, the Bank of England and the Bank of Canada each use a penalty rate policy. The Bank of Japan sets a subsidy or penalty rate depending on the term of the loan, which it varies according to its policy goals. Short-term (ex., one day) loans have lower interest rates (subsidy rates) than longer term loans (penalty rates). The Bank of Japan often influences the market interest rate by changing the maturity of loans that it offers, which effectively changes the quantity of funds that banks have and therefore changes the interest rate on inter-bank borrowing and lending.

In addition, some central banks offer interest payments on deposits, usually at interest rates lower than the rate in the overnight interbank loan market. In this case, banks can earn more by lending in the overnight interbank loan market than by depositing the funds at the central bank. Still, banks sometimes want to deposit reserves at the central bank either because they are required to hold a certain fraction of reserves relative to their deposits, or because they want to hold excess reserves available for immediate withdraw, instead of lending them to another institution for a given amount of time.

The market interest rate does not generally rise above a penalty rate and does not fall below a deposit rate, because if it did, banks could make a quick profit by borrowing from the central bank and lending at the market rate or borrowing at the market rate and depositing the funds at the central bank.[44] These actions would change the quantity of funds in the market and the market interest rate until the market interest rate

[44] However, the market interest rate for reserves in the US has recently fallen slightly below the deposit rate at the Federal Reserve System, indicating that banks are more willing to lend to each other than they are willing to deposit their funds at the central bank. Given that many US banks have acquired large amounts of excess reserves, this suggests that the willingness to borrow more reserves from other banks is weak and that the willingness to lend reserves to other banks is stronger than the willingness to deposit funds at the central bank, possibly because transaction costs in the inter-bank loan market are lower than in the newly created deposit policy at the Federal Reserve System.

was no greater than the penalty rate and no less than the deposit rate. Thus, central banks can set an upper bound and a lower bound on the market interest rate by setting a penalty rate and a deposit rate.

When central banks change the interest rates on their loans and deposits, the amount of borrowing from the central bank and depositing at the central bank could change, which would change the quantity of reserves and the quantity of money, as well as market interest rates. Even if market interest rates do not immediately respond to changes in the central bank's interest rates, the upper and lower bound of the market interest rate would change, so that fluctuations of the market interest rate may become smaller over time.

Regulation of interest rates and the quantity of credit. China, Russia and other countries sometimes restrict lending and borrowing in the market for reserves and the money market, or these markets otherwise have few lenders or borrowers so that competitive market interest rates do not exist. Central banks in these countries directly control the amount of credit that banks and other financial institutions may extend to individuals and firms. In addition, central banks in these countries commonly place restrictions on interest rates that private banks offer on loans and deposits. But in countries with large money markets where transactions are free and transaction costs are low, directly controlling interest rates and the amount of credit are viewed as blunt and cumbersome monetary policy tools.

Required reserve ratios. In many countries, including some with a competitive market for reserves and money market, the central bank regulates the reserves that depository institutions must have relative to checking, saving, time and/or other deposits. The central bank can adjust this required reserve ratio, thereby adjusting the amount of cash banks must have on reserve versus investing in bonds, loans or other assets. If the required reserve ratio is increased, banks must hold more reserves and invest/spend/lend less, so that the quantity of credit and money in circulation will be reduced (we discuss why this is true in the next chapter). If the required reserve ratio is decreased, banks can reduce their reserves by lending more, so that the quantity of credit and money in circulation can be increased.

However, because frequent changes in the required reserve ratio would create uncertainty for banks, central banks of major economies rarely change the required reserve ratio these days. In fact, to limit uncertainty and the effects of daily volatility in the quantity of reserves, central banks require that banks meet the requirement only on an average basis during a one-week or two-week period.

Furthermore, central banks in Canada, the UK, New Zealand, Mexico and Sweden have eliminated reserve requirements altogether because they are now viewed as unnecessary and cumbersome. The traditional justification for reserve requirements was to ensure adequate liquid assets for banks and to control the quantity of reserves, but these reasons have been largely obviated through rapid transactions in today's money markets, including those with the central bank.

Even in countries where required reserve ratios are still used, open market operations and modifying the central bank's interest rates are considered more rapid and efficient ways to modify market interest rates and the quantity of reserves in the market for reserves.

Influencing expectations. Central banks also try to influence market interest rates and the quantity of credit by influencing expectations of lenders and borrowers, which in turn influences the amount that they are willing to lend and borrow and the interest rate they are willing to offer or pay. For example, if a central bank announces that inflation is a growing problem, and that high interest rates and a lower growth rate in the quantity of money will likely be needed in the near future to combat it, then the willingness to borrow, lend and spend today could change in anticipation of higher interest rates and a lower growth rate in the money supply in the near future. If the willingness to borrow increases and the willingness to lend decreases in anticipation of higher interest rates in the future, then market interest rates would increase, leading to a self-fulfilling prophesy. On the other hand, if the willingness to borrow for investment expenditure decreases in anticipation of lower aggregate spending, then market interest rates would decrease.

Lender of last resort. A special case of influencing the total quantity of money and interest rates is the function of providing money, or liquidity, during times of financial distress. Traditionally, central banks used their discount window facilities to lend during financial crises, in the last resort when reserves were unavailable or lacking in the market. In fact, after crises had occurred in the late 19th century and early 20th century, many new central banks were created primarily to prevent future crises from occurring.

Although the balance sheets in the previous section show some special lending programs that were created due to the latest financial crisis, the amount of direct lending from central banks is normally insignificant because financial institutions are normally able to acquire sufficient reserves from other private institutions. In other words, the lender of last resort policy is normally not used. Nonetheless, the existence of the lender of last resort policy even when central banks currently do not lend large amounts is still important, and it affects behavior of individuals and institutions in good and bad ways.

First, the knowledge that banks can, if necessary, borrow from the central bank can prevent banks from panicking and refusing to lend to each other and other customers out of fear before and during a financial crisis. If banks believe that they can not rely on loans from the central bank in an emergency, they will want to lend less and hoard more cash to protect themselves. Of course, lending less and hoarding cash will reduce the amount of credit, spending, production and employment. If extreme, this will lead to an economic contraction and a failure in the financial system because individuals and institutions can not earn or borrow enough to pay for outstanding debt and other liabilities. In addition, if bank customers (which often include other banks) believe that banks can not rely on loans from the central bank in an emergency, they will also want to hoard cash because they will lose confidence in the ability of banks to pay for their liabilities (like deposits). They will also want to sell (liquidate) their own assets for cash—driving down the prices of the assets, which reduces the value of the capital for those institutions that continue to hold the assets. The loss in capital precipitates insolvency and both insolvency and illiquidity cause widespread failure in financial markets and financial institutions, or **systemic failure**.

Furthermore, when bank customers lose confidence in the financial health of their banks, this loss of confidence can spread to other financial institutions because many have financial ties to each other and many invest in similar financial assets. This process is called contagion, as we learned in chapter 10.

A central bank can reduce the risk of systemic failure and contagion by promising to lend in the last resort: standing ready to lend to any solvent bank with a temporary shortage of liquid assets when they are unavailable from financial markets or other financial institutions. This will reduce the tendency for private institutions to restrict lending, to hoard cash, to sell assets and thereby decrease the risk of systemic failure and contagion. By lending when access to cash is otherwise impossible, central banks hope to bolster confidence and prevent systemic failure and contagion.

However, a lender of last resort policy has bad effects as well: it creates a tendency to take more risky behavior because the costs when the risk fails are not fully borne by the risk takers while the benefits when the risk succeeds fully accrue to the risk takers. In other words, when risky investments turn out profitable, banks fully enjoy the profits. But risky investments fail, others must pay for the costs as well. This tendency to ignore the consequences of risk when another party will bear at least some to the responsibility of the risk is called *moral hazard*, which we more fully considered in chapter 10. Bank customers or savers who might not enjoy the full returns from bank profits must nonetheless share the burden of the risky behavior when risky investments made by bank managers turn out poorly. Taxpayers must share the burden of the risky behavior when tax revenues are used to buy the bad financial assets of financial institutions or to pay the salaries of government officials who must oversee the financial institutions during bankruptcy proceedings. Money holders must also share the burden of the risky behavior when the central bank increases the money supply through the lender of last resort policy and thereby causes inflation. These bad results that others must share occur because the lender of last resort policy encourages or abets risky behavior.

In addition, the lender of last resort policy creates an adverse selection problem because those who are less careful or prudent than average have a greater incentive to work at financial institutions that will be rescued by the central bank after taking risks that turn out poorly, yet can still enjoy the benefits of taking risks that turn out well.

In general, the lender of last resort policy affects people's expectations about the future, and in particular, whether a financial crisis could occur, and if it does occur, its consequences. Because the lender of last resort policy affects people's expectations, it also affects our behavior at the present time—both in good and bad ways.

But to limit the bad effects of the lender of last resort policy—moral hazard and adverse selection—and to limit other problems of asymmetric information, central banks and government institutions impose various regulations.

Regulation of financial institutions. As I discussed in detail in chapter 10, central banks regulate private banks to promote financially sound banking practices. In particular, central banks sometimes regulate private financial institutions to provide an outside opinion about the risk or safety of their assets and about the adequacy of their capital. In fact, central banks devote most of their resources, including the time and effort of their employees, to regulate and to provide services for banks and government institutions.

Because failure in the banking system disrupts financial intermediation, the provision of liquidity and economic activity more broadly; governments and central banks regulate banks more than commercial firms and providing the lender of last resort almost exclusively to banks. Similar to the lender of last resort policy, these extensive regulations are intended to reduce the concern about the financial health of banks, so that the risks of systematic failure and contagion are decreased. But unlike the lender of last resort policy, many regulations, like asset requirements and capital requirements, are intended to reduce moral hazard and adverse selection.

The United States assigns the responsibility of regulation for depository institutions to several organizations, including the Federal Reserve System, the Comptroller of the Currency, state governments and the Federal Deposit Insurance Corporation.

Payment settlement system. As I discussed in detail in chapter 8, central banks usually provide services in the payment settlement system.

Economic data collector and researcher. Because of its role in monetary policy, central banks need to collect data and to conduct research about the economy, and they can employ thousands of economists and other researchers to do so. Furthermore, central banks often publish this data and research so that individuals and institutions can be better informed about economic activity and make better economic decisions. In fact, the balance sheets in the previous section were published by the central banks themselves and are freely available on their websites.

Foreign exchange rates. Some central banks have a role in fixing or at least temporarily influencing the value of exchange rates, often to promote exports or to reduce volatility in the export and financial markets. Nearly all major central banks sometimes modify the quantity of money and interest rates or try to influence expectations of individuals and institutions with the intent of reducing volatility in foreign exchange markets. We study the relationship between monetary policy and exchange rates in chapter 14.

Types of central banks

Whatever functions central banks currently perform, economists debate about what central banks should do. There are at least three perspectives about the proper role of central banks.

Some argue that central banks should perform multiple functions, like those that we considered in the previous section. A *multi-function central bank* provides services to governments, influences economic activity by influencing interest rates and the quantity of money, acts as a lender of last resort, supervises and regulates private banks, offers services in the payment settlement system, collects and researches economic data, and influences exchange rates. The Federal Reserve System, the European Central Bank and the Bank of Japan are multi-function central banks.

In contrast, some argue that society would benefit if central banks had only a *single function* and one specific goal, such as low and stable inflation. Other functions like bank regulation and services in the payment settlement system, they argue, should be entrusted to other institutions, such as a deposit insurance agency or a special regulatory agency. Likewise, private banks or other institutions should perform the lending and depositing services for governments. Furthermore, some argue that the treasury/finance departments of governments should have the goal of maintaining a steady level of aggregate spending, production and employment instead of the central bank.

Some central banks have fewer roles than multi-function banks, and some central banks have begun to grant functions to other institutions over time, reducing the number of roles that they must perform.

In 1997, the United Kingdom assigned the regulation and supervision of private banks, which previously had been a key duty of the Bank of England, to a separate agency of the British government. The Bank of England, however, retained its role of the fiscal agent for the UK government. In the US, Congress recently has considered creating a single federal regulator to supervise US banks, leaving the Federal Reserve System to concentrate on its other roles. However, other proposals have considered *increasing* the regulatory role of the Federal Reserve System by consolidating agencies like the Office of the Comptroller of the Currency with the Federal Reserve System.

Some economists argue that central banks should be *privatized*—so that all capital paid in comes from private investors and all capital surplus is paid to private investors. (The next section discusses private and government-owned central banks.) These economists argue that private central banks would have a stronger incentive to enforce sound regulations and operate payment settlement systems efficiently because they, not the government, would lose profit if they did not. Private central banks could also act as fiscal agents of governments on a for-profit basis, as they had in the past.

A few even advocate a return to **free banking**, a policy in which the central bank is either eliminated or renounces its power to issue fiat money and to conduct monetary policy, acting only as a fiscal agent of the national government. Under such a policy, private banks would issue their own money and would have to back the money with sound banking practices and gold or silver. Otherwise, depositors and other creditors would lose confidence in the weak banks and force them into bankruptcy. However, the problems with free banking in the past—the loss of confidence in banks and the associated problems from asymmetric information—make it unlikely that free banking will be implemented again in major economies.

Ownership of central banks

The source of the capital paid in determines the ownership of central banks. Central banks may be owned by the national government of their respective countries, they may be privately owned, or they may be owned by both the governments of their countries and by private individuals or institutions. Private commercial banks that are members of the Federal Reserve System pay in all of the capital for the (twelve) Federal Reserve Banks and hence own all of its shares of stock. The Japanese government owns 55% of the shares of stock issued by the Bank of Japan, and individual citizens own the remainder. Some central banks in the European System of Central Banks also have mixed ownership, while others are completely owned by the respective national government. Table 24 shows that most governments have a least partial ownership of the central bank in the country. But regardless of who contributes to the capital paid in, all national governments receive at least a portion of the capital surplus generated by central banks.

Table 24: The ownership of central banks by country

Government ownership	Private ownership	Mixed ownership (% government owned)
Argentina	South Africa	Austria* (50%)
Australia	Switzerland	Belgium* (50%)
Canada	United States	Chile (50%)
China		Greece* (10%)
Denmark*		Japan (55%)
France*		Mexico (51%)
Finland*		Turkey (25%)
Germany*		Italy*§
Ireland*		
India		
Korea		
The Netherlands*		
New Zealand		
Norway		
Russia		
Spain*		
Sweden		
United Kingdom		
*Member of the European System of Central Banks		
§Italy's central bank is 100% owned by government-owned enterprises.		
Source: Forrest Capie, et al., (1994), The Development of Central Banking : The Tercentenary Symposium of the Bank of England, Cambridge University Press, UK		

Central bank independence

Government ownership of central banks is often related to government oversight of central bank operations, since if the government finances the capital (or the operating budget) of the central bank, then it tends to influence the central bank more generally. In this section, I consider the degree of independence that central banks may have.

There are at least two ways to consider the degree of independence that central banks have from government agencies. First, we can consider the freedom to perform specific functions like open market operations, direct lending, regulation of banks, and provision services in the payment settlement system. Government agencies usually do not oversee these specific functions except to ensure that existing laws are not violated. Most central banks have a large amount of independence in this respect, with the possible exception that government regulatory agencies can sometimes override the regulatory decisions of the central bank. More broadly, we can consider the freedom to set and pursue goals like a low and stable inflation rate, steady growth in production, a low unemployment rate, and more strict or more lenient regulatory laws. (I discuss the goals of central banks in greater detail in chapter 13.) Some governments exercise a large amount of control over the goals of central banks, while others do not.

The degree of independence in both senses, but especially the second sense, is related to how governing boards are selected and structured. In the United Kingdom, the prime minister appoints the members of the governing board, and will naturally tend to select people that he or she favors. In Norway, the parliament elects executive officers and directors. In the US, the President nominates the governing board of the central bank, and the Senate must confirm the nominations.

Furthermore, in many countries, governing boards of central banks include representatives of the national government, in particular, representatives of the finance or treasury department. For example, the Australian treasury secretary is a voting member of the board of the Bank of Australia. The Korean Minister of Strategy and Finance appoints a voting member on the board of the Bank of Korea, although the Minister himself does not vote in board meetings. Government ministers or representatives have advisory roles at the Bank of France, the Bank of Denmark and the Bank of Canada: they can make their opinions known at or outside of board meetings, even if they have no formal power in monetary policy or other functions. The US Treasury secretary often consults with the governing board of the Federal Reserve System, although he does not vote in or even attend board meetings. Likewise, the government of Italy has no direct role on the board of the Bank of Italy.

Central banks which have a greater degree of independence from government agencies have a better record of maintaining a low and stable inflation rate. Independent central banks include those from Germany, the EU, the US, Switzerland, Sweden and New Zealand, all of whom have been able to maintain a low and stable inflation rate relative to other central banks.

But when elected government officials can influence monetary policy, they have a tendency to increase the growth rate of the quantity of money during election years to reduce unemployment, which seems more immediately popular than trying to reduce inflation through restrained growth in the quantity of money. But the cost of this policy is that a higher inflation rate will soon result, and then growth rate in the quantity of money will have to be restricted to reduce the high inflation rate. As a result, prices, employment and economic activity in general will tend to fluctuate around political election years rather than being stable over time. In other words, unstable prices and employment result. More generally, politicians who influence monetary policy have a tendency to act in their own interest, in the interest of lobbyists or in the interest of their constituents—rather than in the interests of taxpayers, money holders or citizens in general.

However, independent central banks may cause problems as well. First, a central bank that is completely independent from government agencies may not be held accountable for careless or imprudent monetary policy decisions, or even corrupt behavior. This is yet another example of a moral hazard: an independent central bank, with more information about its potential for careless or imprudent decisions, can cause bad economic results that others (like taxpayers and money holders) must pay for. Thus, independence is never absolute, even in countries where central banks are a large degree of independence. For example, central banks must often report to elected officials about monetary policy and other functions.

In addition, it may be prudent for central banks to coordinate their monetary policy with the policies of government departments, in particular treasury/finance departments, which implement public expenditures and taxation. Because both the central bank and the treasury/finance department can affect the aggregate amount of spending, perhaps the central banks should make its monetary policy consistent with fiscal policies. Otherwise, conflicting economic policies may result. For example, a central bank may want to restrict the quantity of money and restrict spending to reduce the inflation rate. The treasury/finance department may want to increase its spending or the spending of households by cutting taxes to reduce the unemployment rate. In this case, the central bank's policy would thwart the objective of the treasury/finance department and the treasury/finance department's policy would thwart the objective of the central bank.

Throughout history, when countries entered war or experienced other crises, treasury/finance departments often took control of the monetary policy of central banks and began to issue fiat currency and/or bonds to finance the war or to manage the crises. Rapid inflation was generally the result during wars. After wars or crises end, pressure rises for central banks to regain independence. For example, after World War I, many central banks wanted to regain their independence, to reestablish the gold standard and to reestablish price stability, and to some degree they did. After a decade, however, the Great Depression occurred and with it the idea that the government needed to manage the economic policies. That idea, along with World War II that soon followed, greatly limited the independence of central banks throughout the world. The gold standard was abandoned in nearly all major countries by 1933, and was never fully reinstated. Many people regarded the Great Depression as a failure of independent central banking, as well as a failure of commercial banking. As a result, a desire for government intervention in monetary and economic policy increased.

However, during the 1970s and 1980s, when the major economies were relatively peaceful but suffered from high inflation, policies and practices were implemented that increased the independence of central banks. The view developed that if central banks were less susceptible to government influence, they could take the necessary, albeit temporarily politically unpopular, steps to maintain a low and stable inflation rate. Economists have convinced most elected and bureaucratic officials of the legitimacy of this view, independence for a number of central banks has likewise increased during the past few decades.

Under the 1998 Bank of England Act, the Bank of England acquired some degree of independence from the Treasury by creating the Monetary Policy Committee that excluded the Chancellor of the Exchequer (equivalent to a treasury secretary). The Monetary Policy Committee consists only of the Governor of the Bank, two deputies and two senior Bank employees. Yet, the Bank does not enjoy full autonomy because the Treasury appoints four members of the Committee and approves all members of the Monetary Policy Committee. The Treasury also sets the inflation rate target (discussed in chapter 13).

The Bank of Japan Act of 1998 also granted the Bank of Japan some independence. The Policy Board of the Bank can determine monetary policy without being overridden by the Ministry of Finance or other branches of the government. In addition, the Ministry of Finance and the Economic Planning Agency no longer appoint voting members on the Policy Board, even though their representatives can express their views at meetings. Furthermore, the Governor, Vice Governor and members of the Policy Board can not be dismissed by the cabinet, even though they are appointed by the cabinet. Yet, the Bank of Japan still does not enjoy full independence because the Ministry of Finance approves the Bank of Japan's budget and the Bank's semi-annual report. In addition, the Ministry of Finance can require the Bank of Japan to make loans to specific financial institutions.

The Bank of Korea Act of 1997 and 2003 gave the Bank of Korea some independence as well. The Monetary Policy Committee of the Bank can determine monetary policy without being overridden by the Ministry of Strategy and Finance or other branches of the government. In addition, the operating budget of the Bank no longer needs approval from the Ministry of Strategy and Finance. However, each of the seven members of the committee much be approved by the President, and the Ministry of Strategy and Finance is allowed to appoint one member of the Monetary Policy Committee. In addition, the Ministry of Strategy and Finance can require the Bank of Korea to make loans to specific financial institutions under a lending program called the aggregate credit program.

Yet, during the "Great Recession" of 2008-2009, we again saw greater consultation and cooperation between central banks and treasury/finance departments to manage the crisis. Likewise, political pressure for greater oversight of central bank activities increased.

The central bank of Korea

The Bank of Korea (BOK) (한국은행) serves as the Korea's central bank, which is governed by a governor, a senior deputy governor and 5 deputy governors. They manage the head office in 남대문 거리 중구 and 16 branches throughout the country.

Monetary policy of the central bank is conducted by the Monetary Policy Committee (금융 통화 위원회), which is composed of seven members: the Governor, the Senior Deputy Governor, a member recommended by the Governor, a member recommended by the Minister of Strategy and Finance, a member recommended by the Financial Services Commission, a member recommended by the Korea Chamber of Commerce and Industry and a member recommended by the Korea Federation of Banks. The Governor serves as the chairman of the committee.

The President appoints the members of the Monetary Policy Committee for four-year terms except the Deputy Governor whose term is three years. All are eligible for reappointment.

Summary

Central banks of major economies have several functions, as indicated by their balance sheets. They buy and sell government bonds and other securities, which are assets for the central bank, thereby affecting the quantity of money in circulation and interest rates at banks and in the bond market. Central banks also loan to private banks, which can affect the quantity of money in circulation and interest rates as well. This lending is especially significant during financial crises, when policy is called the lender of last resort policy.

Today's central banks are also the sole issuer of fiat currency, which is their primarily liability. As the fiscal agent of national governments, central banks also hold deposits of the national government, as well as deposits of private banks and other institutions. These deposits are also a major liability of central banks. In addition to influencing the quantity of money and interest rates during crises and in general and acting as a fiscal agent of governments, central banks can also regulate private banks, offer services in the payment settlement system, collect and research economic data, and influence foreign exchange rates.

Central banks may be privately owned, when the capital is paid in by private institutions, or publicly owned, when the capital is paid in by the government. Most central banks are at least partially owned by their respective national government. Government ownership of central banks may be related to government influence of monetary policy. Some central banks, however, have a large degree of independence from government agencies, and these central banks tend to have relatively good records in maintaining a low and stable inflation rate.

Problems and Applications

Short answer problems

1. What was the primary role of the first central banks in history? Of the multiple roles of today's central banks, what is/are usually considered the most important?

2. How does a repurchase agreement differ from an "outright" purchase in the open bond market?

3. How does a repurchase agreement differ from a reverse repurchase agreement?

4. How are government treasury/finance bonds accounted for on the central bank balance sheet? How are central bank debt certificates accounted for on the central bank balance sheet?

5. Why is currency in circulation considered a liability for central banks?

6. Why is the interest rate on loans from the central bank called the discount rate?

7. Who may pay in capital to today's central banks? Who pays in capital in your country's central bank?

8. How does a subsidy rate policy differ from a penalty rate policy?

9. Describe why it might be good to have the central bank that is independent from government policy makers. Next describe why it might be good to have the central bank work with government policy makers.

Internet applications

1. Go to http://ecos.bok.or.kr/ to find data for the Bank of Korea's balance sheet for the latest month (under "Main Accounts of the Bank of Korea"). Create a balance sheet analogous to Table 21 for the Bank of Korea. Which asset is the largest? Which liability is the largest? How much capital (or net worth) does the Bank have?

12. Creation of Credit and Money

Preview

In this chapter we study how changes in the monetary base can cause the quantity of money to change through everyday activities of banks and bank customers. Central banks largely control the monetary base; but banks, non-bank institutions and individuals can influence the quantity of money through their lending and borrowing. We first study a few ways how the central bank can change the monetary base, and then we will discover that lending and borrowing allows credit and money to change multiplicatively after the central bank changes the monetary base.

Monetary aggregates and their components

This section reviews the definitions of *monetary aggregates*, the aggregate values of monetary assets or close substitutes for monetary assets, first described in chapter 2.

M0, or the **monetary base**, is defined to be the sum of reserves and currency that circulates outside of private banks (and outside of the central bank), the latter of which is defined as **currency in circulation**. In this chapter, we will see why the monetary base is the base from which other forms of credit and money are created.

Total reserves can be divided into different categories. First, we can divide reserves into money deposited at the central bank and currency deposited in bank vaults. Secondly, many times central banks require depository institutions to hold a certain amount of reserves relative to deposits, but sometimes depository institutions hold excess reserves as well. We can therefore divide total reserves into required reserves and excess reserves. Thirdly, some reserves are acquired from discount loans from the central bank, while others are acquired when private banks and bond dealers sell their bonds and other non-monetary assets to the central bank (or the central bank buys these assets) in return for money through open market operations. We can therefore divide total reserves into borrowed reserves and non-borrowed reserves.

M1 is defined to be the sum of currency in circulation and transaction deposits (checking deposits and other checkable deposits) and traveler's checks.

M2 includes M1 plus savings deposits, money market deposit accounts and retail deposits at money market mutual funds (both of which are deposits that function like savings deposits and checking deposits), certain time deposits. Roughly speaking, M1 equals the value of transaction deposits + currency in circulation and M2 equals the value of M1 + non-transaction deposits.

M1 and M2 can be defined as the *money supply* or *the quantity of money*, monetary assets that are readily available to purchase goods and services or to repay debt. Figure 2-1 shows how the monetary base (M0) relates to other monetary aggregates, M1 or M2. Figure 12-2 shows values of the components of the monetary base, as well as M1, for the US during the last decade and a half. The monetary base is usually smaller than other monetary aggregates, but because of recent measures by the central bank, the monetary base has recently exceeded the value of M1. (However, the monetary base is still smaller than M2, which is not shown in Figure 12-2.)

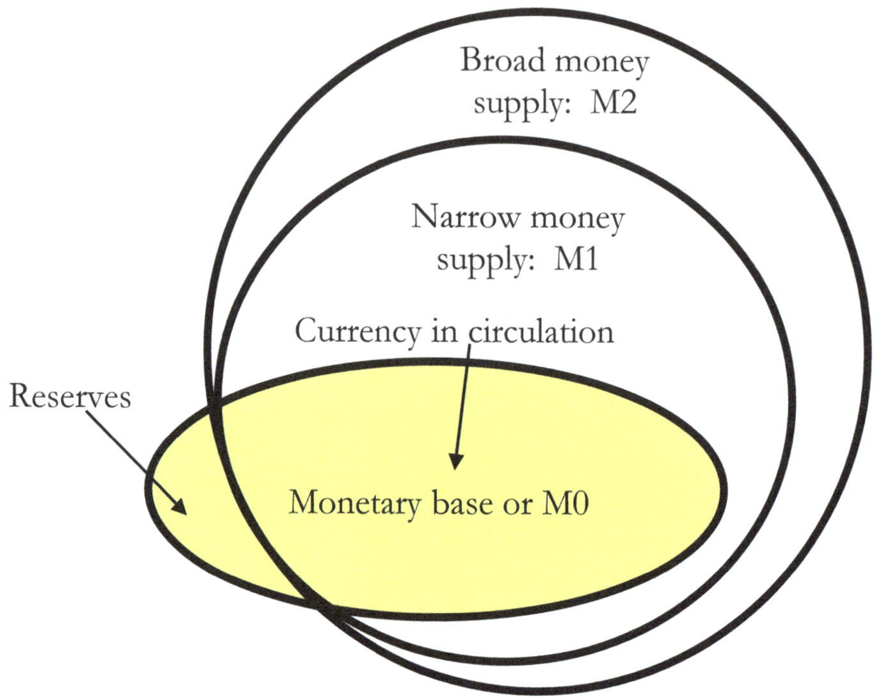

Figure 12-1: A simple representation of monetary aggregates and their components

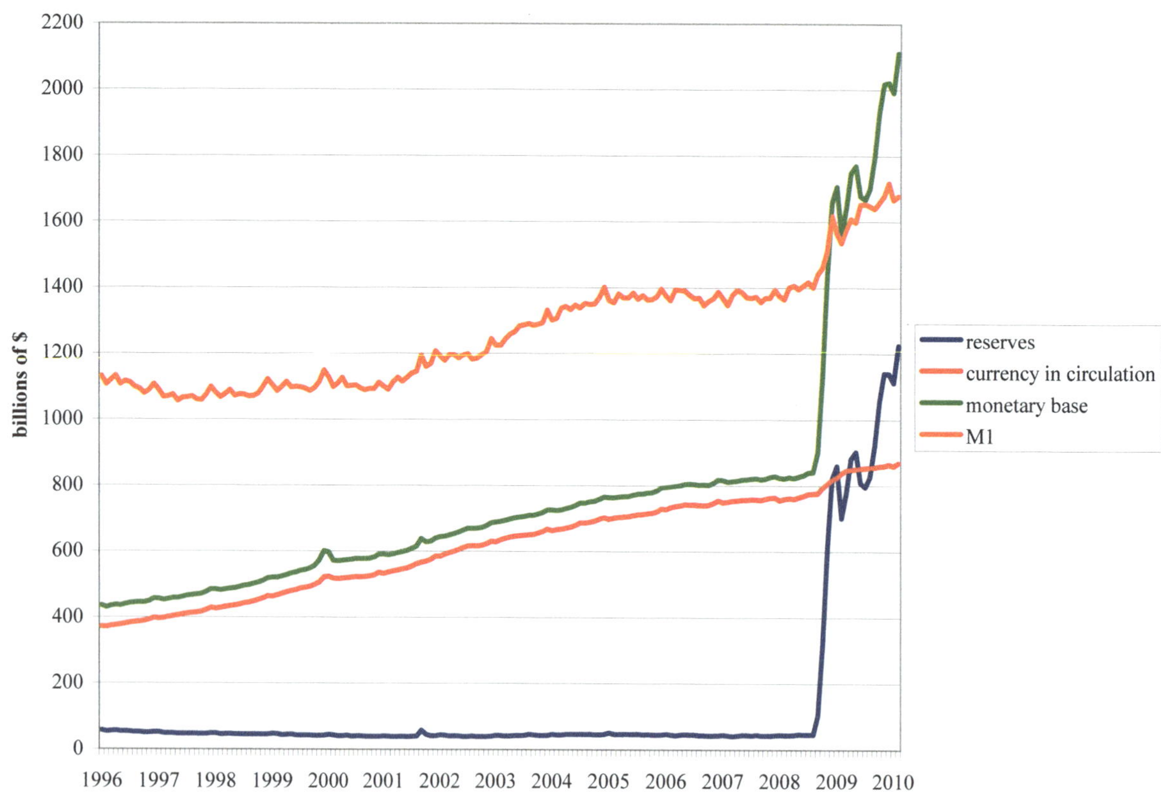

Figure 12-2: M1 and components of the monetary base in the US, 1996-2010

Changes in the monetary base

To determine how the money supply is affected by the monetary base, I first consider how the monetary base is affected by the central bank, depository institutions (private banks), depositors and borrowers. I represent how the monetary base is affected by these parties by representing their actions on simplified balance sheets below.

Recall from the previous chapter that the major assets of central banks are government bonds and other securities, as well as (discount) loans to private banks. Major liabilities are currency outstanding (circulating outside of central banks) and deposits of private banks (reserve deposits) and deposits of other institutions. In addition, central banks may issue their own debt certificates, a simple bond that is a liability for the central bank because the central bank (not the treasury/finance department of the government) is responsible for repaying the debt.[45] I represent these assets and liabilities (and ignore the value of capital, which is relatively small and stable) in a simplified central bank balance sheet below:

Table 25: A simplified central bank balance sheet

Assets	Liabilities
Government bonds	Currency outstanding
Loans to private banks	Reserve deposits of banks
	Central bank debt certificates

Recall also that major assets for private banks are reserves (either in the form of currency in the vault or deposits at the central bank), government bonds and loans to their customers. In some countries, banks will sometimes hold central bank debt certificates as well. Major liabilities are checking, saving and time deposits (invested in money market assets or elsewhere), as well as funds that banks borrow from other financial institutions. I represent these assets and liabilities (and ignore the value of capital, which is relatively small) in a simplified private bank balance sheet below:

Table 26: A simplified private bank balance sheet

Assets	Liabilities
Reserves	Checking deposits
Government bonds	Savings deposits
Loans	Time deposits
Central bank debt certificates	Borrowed funds

Consider how an open market operation between the central bank and either bond dealers who work at private banks or bank representatives at public auctions changes the balance sheet of the central bank and an aggregated balance sheet for the private banking sector. Consider a simple example in which the central

[45] Recall that these debt certificates are called monetary stabilization bonds in Korea.

bank purchases $100 worth of government bonds and deposits funds in exchange for the bonds in the reserve deposit accounts of private banks. The balance sheets of the two parties would change accordingly:

Scenario 1: Central bank purchases government bonds from private banks

Central bank balance sheet

Assets		Liabilities	
Government bonds	+$100	Currency outstanding	
Loans to private banks		Reserve deposits of banks	+$100
		Central bank debt certificates	

Banking sector balance sheet

Assets		Liabilities	
Reserves	+$100	Checking deposits	
Government bonds	-$100	Savings deposits	
Loans		Time deposits	
Central bank debt certificates		Borrowed funds	

Because reserves of the banking sector increase due to this open market operation, the monetary base increases. In subsequent sections, we will study how changes in the monetary base affect the broader monetary aggregates M1 and M2.

Now consider how an open market operation between the central bank and either bond dealers who do not work at banks or a non-bank institution or individual at a public auction changes the balance sheet of the central bank, the counterparties in the open market operation, and the banks of the counterparties. Suppose again that the central bank purchases $100 worth of government bonds and deposits funds in exchange for the bonds in the (checking) deposit accounts of the counterparties at their corresponding banks, which in turn allows the banks to hold more money (reserves). Because reserves of the banking sector increase due to this open market operation, the monetary base increases as well in this case. The balance sheets of the central bank and the counterparties in the open market operation plus the banks of the counterparties would change accordingly:

Scenario 2: Central bank purchases government bonds from non-bank institutions or individuals, who keep the proceeds in their bank deposits.

Central bank balance sheet

Assets		Liabilities	
Government bonds	+$100	Currency outstanding	
Loans to private banks		Reserve deposits of banks	+$100
		Central bank debt certificates	

Non-banking sector balance sheet

Assets		Liabilities	
Checking deposits	+$100		
Government bonds	-$100		

Banking sector balance sheet

Assets		Liabilities	
Reserves	+$100	Checking deposits	+$100
Government bonds		Savings deposits	
Loans		Time deposits	
Central bank debt certificates		Borrowed funds	

Consider again the same open market operation as before, except for the fact that the counterparties with the central bank withdraw the funds from the deposit. In this case, reserves (money held by banks) would not increase, but currency in circulation (currency held by non-bank institutions and individuals) would increase. But because the monetary base includes both reserves and currency in circulation, the monetary base would also increase. The balance sheets of the central bank, the counterparties in the open market operation and the banks of the counterparties would change accordingly:

Scenario 3: Central bank purchases government bonds from non-bank institutions or individuals, who withdraw the proceeds from their bank deposits.

Central bank balance sheet

Assets		Liabilities	
Government bonds	+$100	Currency outstanding	+$100
Loans to private banks		Reserve deposits of banks	
		Central bank debt certificates	

Non-banking sector balance sheet

Assets		Liabilities	
Currency in circulation	+$100		
Government bonds	-$100		

Banking sector balance sheet

Assets		Liabilities	
Reserves	+/-$100	Checking deposits	+/-$100
Government bonds		Savings deposits	
Loans		Time deposits	
Central bank debt certificates		Borrowed funds	

Let's change the previous scenario by considering only a withdrawal of currency from a (checking) deposit account. To make this example analogous the previous example, suppose banks acquire the currency by first debiting the funds from their reserve deposit accounts and then by having currency physically delivered from the central bank. In this case, reserves would decrease, but currency outstanding and currency in circulation would increase. (An alternative scenario is for bank to pay for the withdraw with cash from their vaults, in which case the central bank balance sheet would not change.) Because reserves decrease by the same amount that currency in circulation increases, the monetary base would not change. The balance sheets of the central bank, private banks and non-bank institutions or individuals would change accordingly:

Scenario 4: A withdrawal of currency acquired from reserve deposits.

Central bank balance sheet

Assets		Liabilities	
Government bonds		Currency outstanding	+$100
Loans to private banks		Reserve deposits of banks	-$100
		Central bank debt certificates	

Non-banking sector balance sheet

Assets		Liabilities	
Currency in circulation	+$100		
Checking deposits	-$100		

Banking sector balance sheet

Assets		Liabilities	
Reserves	-$100	Checking deposits	-$100
Government bonds		Savings deposits	
Loans		Time deposits	
Central bank debt certificates		Borrowed funds	

Now let's consider how an open market operation like in Scenario 1, except that the central bank sells $100 worth of government bonds to representatives of private banks and then debits the reserve deposit accounts of private banks accordingly. Because reserves of the banking sector decrease in this transaction, the monetary base decreases. The balance sheets of the two parties would change accordingly:

Scenario 5: Central bank sale of government bonds to private banks

Central bank balance sheet

Assets		Liabilities	
Government bonds	-$100	Currency outstanding	
Loans to private banks		Reserve deposits of banks	-$100
		Central bank debt certificates	

Banking sector balance sheet

Assets		Liabilities	
Reserves	-$100	Checking deposits	
Government bonds	+$100	Savings deposits	
Loans		Time deposits	

Central bank debt certificates		Borrowed funds	

Although most transactions by central banks are open market operations, they also make discount loans to banks. (Some central banks have the authority to lend to non-bank institutions and individuals as well, although they do this less frequently.) When central banks make a discount loan, they typically credit the reserve deposits of banks for the amount of the loan, although they can also physically deliver paper currency to the banks in an armored car as well. Consider how a discount loan of $100 from the central bank to private banks in which the central bank credits the reserve deposit accounts of private banks would change the balance sheets of both parties. A transaction involving the physical delivery of currency is left as an exercise for the reader. Because reserves of the banking sector increase in either type of transaction, the monetary base increases. The balance sheets of the two parties would change accordingly:

Scenario 6: Central bank discount loan to private banks through a credit of reserve deposits

Central bank balance sheet

Assets		Liabilities	
Government bonds		Currency outstanding	
Loans to private banks	+$100	Reserve deposits of banks	+$100
		Central bank debt certificates	

Banking sector balance sheet

Assets		Liabilities	
Reserves	+$100	Checking deposits	
Government bonds		Savings deposits	
Loans		Time deposits	
Central bank debt certificates		Borrowed funds	+$100

Finally, consider an open market operation which involves not government bonds (issued by the treasury/finance department of the government) but debt certificates issued by the central bank. When the central bank sells these debt certificates to private banks, they become assets for the private banks and liabilities for the central bank. In exchange for the debt certificates, private banks must pay cash (usually debited from the reserve deposits) to the central bank. Consider how an open market operation in which the central bank issues and sells $100 worth of its debt certificates to private banks and debits funds to pay for the debt certificates from reserve deposit accounts of the banks. Because reserves of the banking sector decrease in this transaction, the monetary base decreases. The balance sheets of the two parties would change accordingly:

Scenario 7: Central bank sale of central bank debt certificates to a private bank

Central bank balance sheet

Assets		Liabilities	
Government bonds		Currency outstanding	
Loans to private banks		Reserve deposits of banks	-$100
		Central bank debt certificates	+$100

Banking sector balance sheet

Assets		Liabilities	
Reserves	-$100	Checking deposits	
Government bonds		Savings deposits	
Loans		Time deposits	
Central bank debt certificates	+$100	Borrowed funds	

In addition to transactions with the central bank, transactions through payment settlement system can also affect the monetary base, at least temporarily before payments are settled. Recall that when the central bank or an associated institution begins to settle payments, some balances are immediately credited or debited, so that its reserves at some banks immediately increase or decrease. But only after a few hours or days is the value of the payment settled with the counterparty, so that reserves at the corresponding bank(s) will not be immediately adjusted. This processing time temporarily affects total reserves in the banking system and the monetary base. The central bank may therefore need to conduct in reversible open market operations (repurchase agreements and reverse repurchase agreements) each day to stabilize the amount of reserves in the banking system, offsetting these temporary fluctuations in the monetary base.

The creation of credit and money through fractional reserve banking

Now that we understand how the monetary base can change, let's consider how changes in the monetary base lead to changes in the quantity of credit and money by using another simple example. Suppose that the central bank purchases $100 worth of government bonds from a bank, called Bank 1, and credits the reserve deposit account of Bank 1.

Bank 1 now has more reserves, and effectively the central bank has created $100 of additional money for the economy, but even more money can be created by the investment activities of Bank 1. Suppose that Bank 1 invests its additional money by making a loan to a customer or buying a bond from a customer for $100, which allows another institution or individual to spend the money. Suppose Bank 1 makes a loan, and in doing so it would create a transaction deposit for the borrower to place the money before it is spent. As the money is spent, reserves at Bank 1 decline by $100 and the deposit account is depleted, leaving Bank 1 with a $100 loan as an asset (but without $100 worth of government bonds).

After the borrower from Bank 1 spends the money, another institution or individual has access to the money, who then spends or saves the money. If the money is spent, it passes to another institution or individual, who then spends or saves the money. Eventually, an institution or individual saves the money, typically by depositing it at a bank.

When the funds are eventually deposited in a bank, say Bank 2 (or even the same bank as before), this bank will now have more deposits and more reserves, and it will typically invest the money like the previous bank. However, banks typically can not or do not invest all of the money deposited by customers, since they need or want to have reserves to pay their customers whenever they ask for them. But because all customers generally do not withdraw all of their funds at the same time, banks keep only a fraction of their reserves and invest the remainder in loans, bonds or other non-monetary assets. This type of banking is therefore called **fractional reserve banking**. The fraction of reserves that banks hold is influenced by the required reserve ratio and customer needs for cash and on-time payments. But to keep the example simple, I assume for now that the required reserve ratio for the relevant deposits is 10% of deposits and other factors are not important. In this simple case, Bank 2 will be able to lend $90 of the reserves and will maintain $10 as reserves. Like Bank 1, it creates a deposit account for the borrower to place the money before it is spent. As the money is spent, reserves decline by \$90 and the deposit account is depleted. Thereafter, Bank 2 would have a \$90 loan and \$10 reserves as assets and would still maintain the \$100 original deposit as a liability.

Therefore unlike Bank 1, Bank 2 creates \$90 of additional credit and money from the money deposited in its customers' accounts. In other words, Bank 2 creates additional credit and money—in the form of a \$90 loan—not only for its customers but also for the economy as a whole after the central bank created additional money for the economy as a whole through open market operations.

And the process can continue from here. The \$90 of new credit and money is spent by the borrower, but eventually it is saved by another institution or individual, typically at a bank. When it is eventually deposited at a bank, this bank—call it Bank 3—now has \$90 of new deposits and new reserves. From these reserves, it can create a new loan of \$81 when it keeps only 10% of deposits as reserves. Like other banks, this bank creates a deposit account for the loan, which is depleted as the money is spent. Nonetheless, Bank 3 creates \$81 of additional credit and money from the money deposited in its customers' accounts.

This depositing, lending, spending and saving process can continue forever—it happens everyday from the behavior of millions of individuals and institutions—and a large amount of additional credit and money can be created from the original amount created by the central bank. How large? It depends not only on the original amount from the central bank but also on the amount of money that is lent and deposited, which depends on the fraction of reserves. In the simple example above, banks held 10% of their deposits as reserves, implying that they could lend 90% of newly deposited money. If 10% represented the average fraction of reserves that banks maintained, then over time the quantity of credit and money would change by

$$\$100 + \$90 + \$81 + \$72.90 + \$65.61 + \$59.05 + \$53.14 + \ldots. = \Delta M$$

through the depositing, lending, spending and saving process, where ΔM represents the total change in the quantity of money. This infinite sum can be represented as

$$\$100 + l \times \$100 + l^2 \times \$100 + l^3 \times \$100 + l^4 \times \$100 + l^5 \times \$100 + l^6 \times \$100 + \ldots. = \Delta M$$

where l represents the fraction of reserves that are lent = 1 – the required reserve ratio, r. Since \$100 equals the initial change in reserves, ΔR, I write

$$\Delta R + l \times \Delta R + l^2 \times \Delta R + l^3 \times \Delta R + l^4 \times \Delta R + l^5 \times \Delta R + l^6 \times \Delta R + \ldots. = \Delta M$$

$$1 + l + l^2 + l^3 + l^4 + l^5 + l^6 + \ldots. = \Delta M / \Delta R$$

Algebraic manipulation shows that

$$(1 - l)[1 + l + l^2 + l^3 + l^4 + l^5 + l^6 + \ldots.] = [\Delta M / \Delta R](1 - l)$$

$$(1 - l + l - l^2 + l^2 - l^3 + l^3 - l^4 + l^4 - l^5 + l^5 - l^5 + l^6 + \ldots.] = [\Delta M / \Delta R](1 - l)$$

When $l = 1 - r$ is less than 1, the infinite sum will approach the value

$$1 = [\Delta M / \Delta R](1 - l)$$

$$1/(1 - l) = \Delta M / \Delta R$$

$$1/r = \Delta M / \Delta R$$

Therefore,

$$\Delta R \times 1/r = \Delta M$$

In words, this equation means that the initial change in reserves multiplied by the reciprocal of the required reserve ratio equals the eventual change in the quantity of money through the depositing, lending, spending and saving process. Steps in the process take time, but the equation above is a short cut to tell us how much the quantity of money can eventually change when reserves initially change. In the earlier example, when $r = 10\%$ and $\Delta R = \$100$, we predict that \$1000 of new credit and money will eventually be created by the actions of the central bank and through the depositing, lending, spending and saving process, when other factors are not important.

Factors that influence the creation of credit and money

However, other factors sometimes do affect the credit and money creation process. Firstly, when non-bank institutions and individuals choose to hold currency rather than deposits at banks, this reduces the amount of deposits at banks and reduces the amount of credit and money that banks can create. Secondly, banks will sometimes choose to hold excess reserves to settle a large amount of payments or to pay for large withdraws of currency by customers, and therefore do not lend all of the reserves that they could otherwise. This also reduces the amount of credit and money that banks can create. Thirdly, we previously only considered one kind of deposit, transaction deposits, but different kinds of deposits can affect how much banks lend and can affect the aggregate quantities of M1 and M2 differently. Finally, as the previous example indicated, the total amount of credit and money that can be created is affected by the required reserve ratios on deposits, and each kind of deposit may have a unique required reserve ratio.

How important are these other factors, and what are their effects on changes in the quantity of money, both M1 and M2?

To answer these questions, we again rely on algebra to give us specific predictions. First, separate reserves, R, into required reserves, RR, and excess reserves, ER

$$R = RR + ER$$

Required reserves on various deposits are calculated by multiplying the required reserve ratio times the value of the deposits:

$$RR = r_1 \times D_1 + r_2 \times D_2 + r_3 \times D_3 + r_4 \times D_4 + \ldots.$$

for four or more types of deposits and their required reserve ratios (which may be 0%). For the algebra that follows, consider four types of deposits: transaction deposits (D_1), savings deposits (D_2), money market deposit accounts at banks and deposits at money market mutual funds (D_3) and time deposits (D_4) and their respective required reserve ratios, r_1, r_2, r_3, r_4. Thus,

$$R = (r_1 \times D_1 + r_2 \times D_2 + r_3 \times D_3 + r_4 \times D_4) + ER$$

Recall that the monetary base, MB, equals currency in circulation, C, plus reserves, so that

$$MB = C + (r_1 \times D_1 + r_2 \times D_2 + r_3 \times D_3 + r_4 \times D_4) + ER$$

Algebraic manipulation shows that

$$MB = (C/D_1)\times D_1 + (r_1 \times D_1) + (r_2 \times D_2/D_1)\times D_1 + (r_3 \times D_3/D_1)\times D_1 + (r_4 \times D_4/D_1)\times D_1 + (ER/D_1)\times D_1$$

$$MB = [(C/D_1) + r_1 + (r_2 \times D_2/D_1) + (r_3 \times D_3/D_1) + (r_4 \times D_4/D_1) + (ER/D_1)]\times D_1$$

$$MB = [c + r_1 + (r_2 \times d_2) + (r_3 \times d_3) + (r_4 \times d_4) + er]\times D_1$$

where c represents the ratio of currency in circulation to transaction deposits, d_2 represents the ratio of savings deposits to transaction deposits, d_3 represents the ratio of money market deposit accounts at banks and deposits at money market mutual funds to transaction deposits, d_4 represents the ratio of time deposits to transaction deposits and er represents the ratio of excess reserves to transaction deposits.

Because $D_1 = MB/[c + r_1 + (r_2 \times d_2) + (r_3 \times d_3) + (r_4 \times d_4) + er]$, we say that transaction deposits are a function of the monetary base, the required reserve ratio on transaction deposits, the required reserve ratios on other deposits times the ratio of those deposits to transaction deposits, the ratio of currency in circulation to transaction deposits and the ratio of excess reserves to transaction deposits.

From this expression, we can write M1 and M2 as a function of the monetary base. Because M1 equals transaction deposits plus currency in circulation:

$$M1 = C + D_1$$

$$M1 = c \times D_1 + D_1$$

$$M1 = (1 + c) \times D_1$$

$$M1 = \frac{1 + c}{c + r_1 + r_2 d_2 + r_3 d_3 + r_4 d_4 + er} \times MB$$

(19)

Because M2 = $C + D_1 + D_2 + D_3 + D_4$,

$$M2 = c \times D_1 + D_1 + d_2 \times D_1 + d_3 \times D_1 + d_4 \times D_1$$

$$M2 = (1 + c + d_2 + d_3 + d_4) \times D_1$$

$$M2 = \frac{1 + c + d_2 + d_3 + d_4}{c + r_1 + r_2 d_2 + r_3 d_3 + r_4 d_4 + er} \times MB$$

(20)

In words, the quantity of money (either M1 or M2) is a function of

- the monetary base
- required reserve ratios on the different kinds of deposits
- the ratio of other deposits to transaction deposits
- the ratio of currency in circulation to transaction deposits
- the ratio of excess reserves to transaction deposits

The ratio $\frac{1 + c}{c + r_1 + r_2 d_2 + r_3 d_3 + r_4 d_4 + er} \equiv m_1$, which is generally greater than 1, is called the M1 money multiplier and shows how changes in the monetary base have a multiplicative effect on the M1 quantity of money. Likewise, the ratio $\frac{1 + c + d_2 + d_3 + d_4}{c + r_1 + r_2 d_2 + r_3 d_3 + r_4 d_4 + er} \equiv m_2$, which is also generally greater than 1, is called the M2 money multiplier and shows how changes in the monetary base have a multiplicative effect on the M2 quantity of money.

Equations (19) and (20) tell us that when more currency is held by non-bank institutions and individuals relative to transaction deposits, banks can not create new credit and money through loans, so that the M1 and M2 aggregate quantities of money will be smaller than otherwise.[46] Likewise, when banks choose to hold more excess reserves relative to transaction deposits, they do not create as much new credit and money, so that the M1 and M2 aggregate quantities of money will be smaller than otherwise. Individuals and institutions tend to hoard cash as a precaution during these times, represented here as an increase of c and er. As a result, the quantity of money shrinks, which reduces spending, production and employment (further) and exacerbates the financial crisis.

Banks usually hold excess reserves as deposits at the central bank, where they can earn at least a little interest. Although excess reserves in general and deposits at the central bank in particular are usually close to zero, banks in the US have recently acquired huge amounts of excess reserves due to the expansionary policy of the Federal Reserve System. Figure 12-3 shows that the reserve deposits of depository institutions at the Federal Reserve System have were close to zero before 2008 but quickly expanded after 2008 as the central bank provided reserves to the banking system through various means.

[46] We know this because the first derivatives of equations (19) and (20) with respect to c are negative.

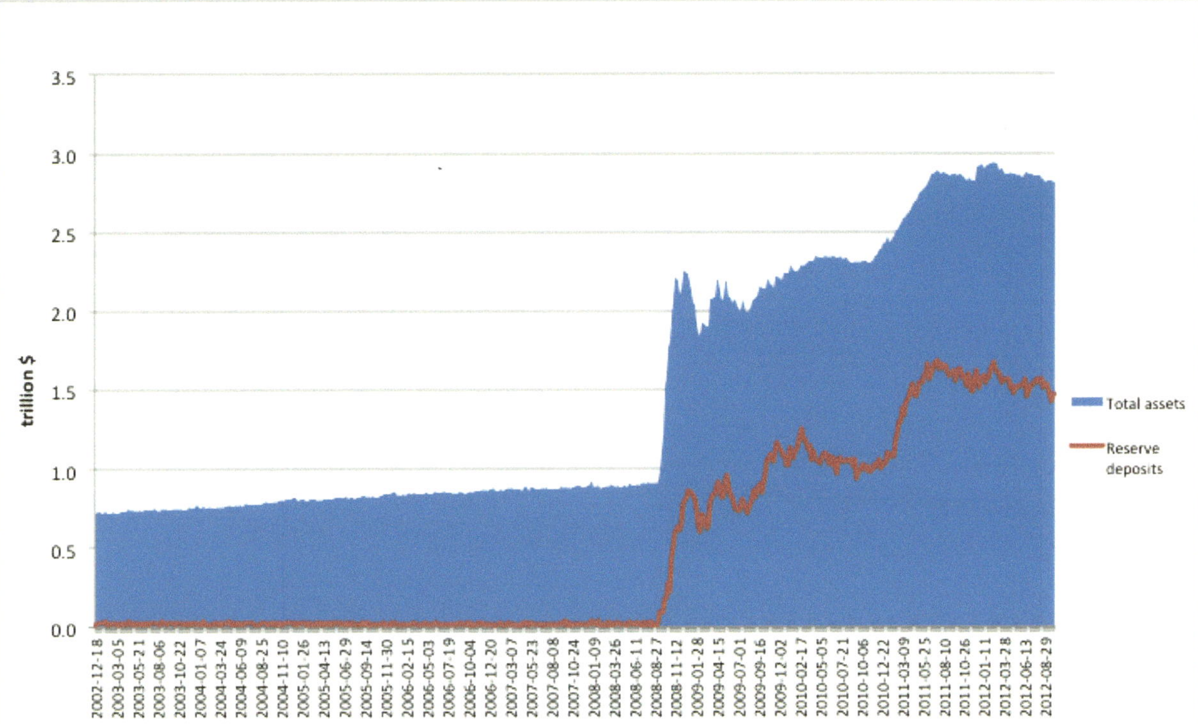

Source: Federal Reserve System, http://www.federalreserve.gov/datadownload/default.htm

Figure 12-3: Reserve deposits of depository institutions relative to total assets at the Federal Reserve System, 2002-2012

Thirdly, when more money is held as non-transaction deposits relative to transaction deposits, M1 will decrease, but the effect on M2 is less clear because the required reserve ratios can be insignificant or not.

Fourthly, if any required reserve ratio increases, banks must hold more reserves relative to deposits and therefore can lend less; the equations likewise predict that both the M1 and M2 aggregate quantities of money will decrease.

Equations (19) and (20) also show us that when the monetary base increases, both M1 and M2 increase multiplicatively. The monetary base usually increases because reserves increase, either as non-borrowed reserves or borrowed reserves. Normally, nearly all reserves in the monetary base are non-borrowed reserves, exchanged for non-monetary assets through open market operations. Figure 12-4 and Figure 12-5 show the value of reserves exchanged for US Treasury securities and other currencies by the Federal Reserve System compared to the value of all assets at the Federal Reserve System. During 2008, the central bank used non-traditional programs like currency swaps to try to increase the amount of reserves in the private sector.

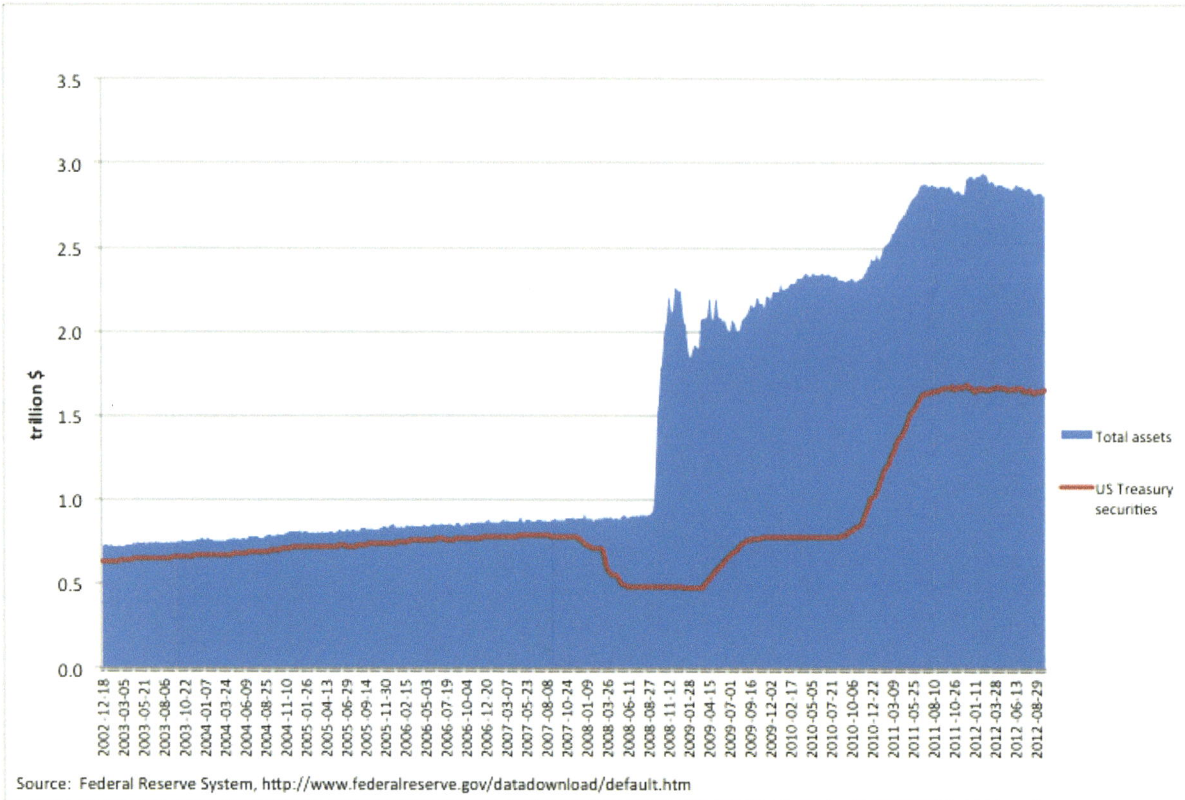

Figure 12-4: Non-borrowed reserves are acquired through purchases of US Treasury securities, which normally make up a large majority of all assets at the Federal Reserve System, 2002-2012

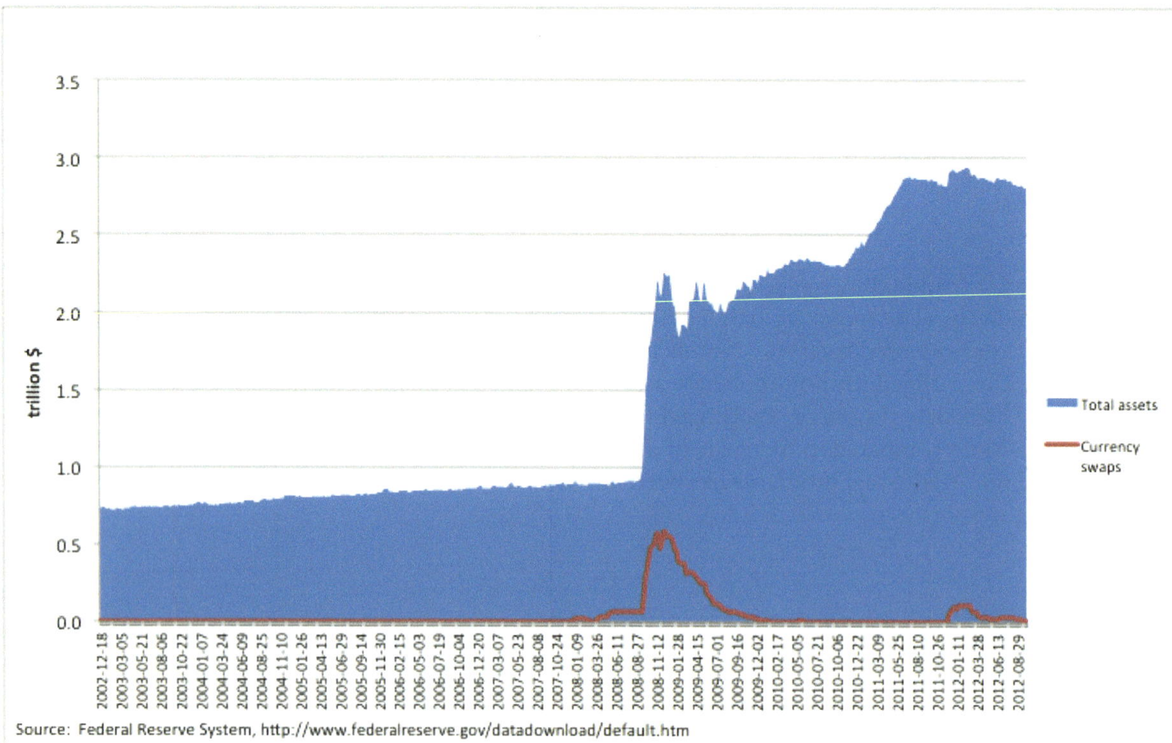

Figure 12-5: Swaps of US dollars for other currencies by the Federal Reserve System, 2002-2012. Currency swaps can also allow the central bank to transfer non-borrowed reserves.

Borrowed reserves through discount loans generally are only a small fraction of the monetary base, although maintaining a lender of last resort policy nonetheless significantly affects financial behavior even when the total amount of discount loans is small. Figure 12-6 shows borrowed reserves acquired from direct (discount) loans from the Federal Reserve System compared to the value of all assets at the Federal Reserve System. Borrowed reserves were close to zero before the financial crisis that began in 2008, although they became significant during the crisis. When banks know that they have the ability to borrow, even when they choose not to borrow, they need not panic and can continue normal operations.

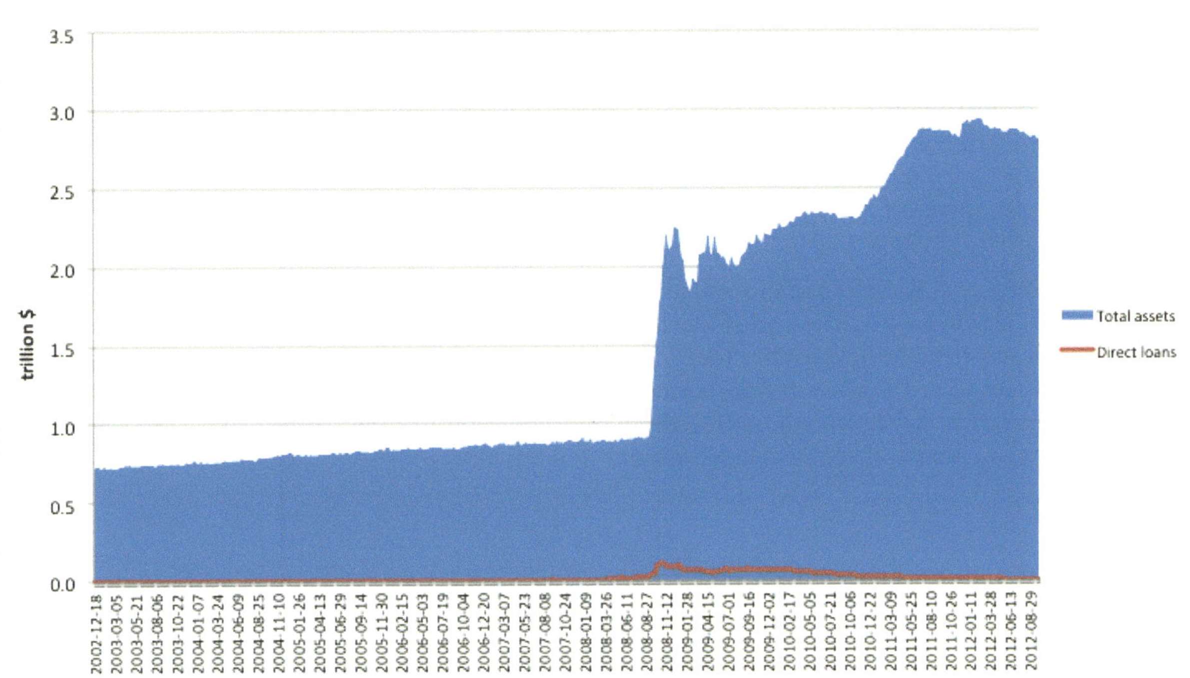

Source: Federal Reserve System, http://www.federalreserve.gov/datadownload/default.htm

Figure 12-6: Borrowed reserves acquired from direct (discount) loans from the Federal Reserve System, 2002-2012. They usually make up a tiny fraction of all reserves and assets of the Federal Reserve System, although they may become important during financial crises.

As the example in a previous section indicated, a change in currency in circulation held by non-bank institutions and individuals usually implies an offsetting change in reserves held by banks, so that the monetary base remains constant. But if the central bank transacts with non-bank institutions or individuals (ex., bond dealers who do not work for banks or non-bank institutions or individuals who use public auctions) and if it pays or requires currency to or from this counterparty, then currency in circulation is affected without an offsetting change in reserves. However, this kind of transaction rarely occurs today because the central banks usually adjust reserve and transaction deposit accounts electronically in open market operations.

Thus, we see that the central bank, private banks, non-bank institutions and individuals can all affect the quantity of money. Through open market operations and by setting interest rates on its deposits, the central bank effectively controls the quantity of non-borrowed reserves and currency in the monetary base. It also determines the required reserve ratios, sometimes by eliminating them entirely. It influences borrowed reserves through the interest rate that it charges on discount loans and the type of collateral that it requires for such loans. Private banks determine the amount of borrowed reserves and their excess reserves, and of course, their lending behavior. Non-bank institutions and individuals determine their borrowing, spending and saving behavior, as well as the amount of currency and non-transaction deposits that they choose to hold relative to transaction deposits.

Summary

The monetary base—reserves and currency in circulation—is the base from which other forms of money—transaction deposits and non-transaction deposits—are created by the everyday lending and borrowing activity of banks and bank customers. The central bank largely controls the monetary base through open market operations and by setting interest rates on its deposits and loans, although private bank ultimately decide how many reserves they choose to borrow from the central bank and deposit at the central bank. Banks, non-bank institutions and individuals significantly influence broader monetary aggregates by depositing this money, lending some of it through a system of fraction reserve banking, borrowing and spending, saving, then re-depositing the money, and so on.... This continual process allows monetary aggregates to grow or contract multiplicatively (although not infinitely) after the monetary base changes largely through the actions of the central bank.

In addition, non-bank institutions and individuals influence this multiplicative change on the money supply through the amount of currency that they hold relative to transaction deposits and the amount of non-transaction deposits that they hold relative to transaction deposits. Banks influence this multiplicative change through the amount of excess reserves that they hold relative to transaction deposits (which is related to the amount of reserves that they borrow from the central bank and deposit at the central bank). The central bank influences this multiplicative change through the required reserve ratios that they set for private banks.

Problems and Applications

Short answer problems

1. List the components in each of the following: M0, M1 and M2.

2. Why is M0 called the monetary base?

3. If bank customers withdraw and hold more currency from their banks, how will the monetary base be affected? How could M1 be affected?

4. If the central bank sells government treasury/finance bonds to a private bank, how would the monetary base be affected? How would the central bank's balance sheet be affected? If the central bank sells its debt certificates to a private bank, how would the monetary base be affected? How would the central bank's balance sheet be affected?

5. Explain why a change in the monetary base has a multiplicative effect on M1.

6. If $r_1 = 5\%$, $r_2 = 5\%$, $r_3 = 2\%$, $r_4 = 2\%$, $C = 400$ billion, $D_1 = 1000$ billion, $D_2 = 2000$ billion, $D_3 = 3000$ billion, $D_4 = 4000$ billion and $ER = 1$ billion, then what is the M1 money multiplier?

7. If $r_1 = 5\%$, $r_2 = 5\%$, $r_3 = 2\%$, $r_4 = 2\%$, $C = 400$ billion, $D_1 = 1000$ billion, $D_2 = 2000$ billion, $D_3 = 3000$ billion, $D_4 = 4000$ billion and $ER = 1$ billion, then what is the M2 money multiplier?

8. If $r_1 = 4\%$, $r_2 = 4\%$, $r_3 = 1\%$, $r_4 = 1\%$, $C = 400$ billion, $D_1 = 500$ billion, $D_2 = 1000$ billion, $D_3 = 1500$ billion, $D_4 = 2000$ billion and $ER = 1$ billion, then what is the M1 money multiplier?

9. If $r_1 = 4\%$, $r_2 = 4\%$, $r_3 = 1\%$, $r_4 = 1\%$, $C = 400$ billion, $D_1 = 500$ billion, $D_2 = 1000$ billion, $D_3 = 1500$ billion, $D_4 = 2000$ billion and $ER = 1$ billion, then what is the M2 money multiplier?

10. If the ratio of non-transaction deposits to transaction deposits increases, what will happen to M1? Explain.

11. If the ratio of non-transaction deposits to transaction deposits increases, what will happen to M2? Explain.

Internet applications

1. Go to http://ecos.bok.or.kr/ to find data for the Korea's monetary base, currency in circulation and reserve deposits at the central bank (under folder 1.2.1) from the earliest month to the latest month. Create a graph similar to Figure 12-2 in the text. Which value is currently the largest: currency in circulation or reserve deposits? (Note currency in circulation according to the BOK includes vault cash.)

2. Go to http://ecos.bok.or.kr/ to find data for Korea's total reserves, vault cash and reserve deposits at the central bank (under folder 2.3) from the earliest month to the latest month. Create a graph similar to Figure 12-2 in the text. Which value is currently the largest: vault cash or deposits at the central bank?

3. Go to http://ecos.bok.or.kr/ to find data for Korea's required reserves and excess reserves (under folder 2.3) from the earliest month to the latest month. Create a graph with required reserves on one axis and excess reserves (a much smaller value) on a second axis. What do you think happened at the end of 1996?

4. Go to http://ecos.bok.or.kr/ to find data for the total amount of discount loans and for the amount of aggregate credit loans (under folder 2.5) from the earliest month to the latest month. Create a graph similar to Figure 12-2 in the text. At what time in the last 5 years was the total amount of discount loans the largest? Why do you think this was true? And why do you think the total amount of discount loans increased rapidly at the end of 1997?

13. Goals and Targets of Monetary Policy

Preview

We learned in chapter 11 that central banks can have several functions, including conducting monetary policy to manage economic activity. But perhaps surprisingly, monetary policy has had to be learned during the past 100 years from trial and error throughout the last century as economies went through evolutionary and sometimes revolutionary changes. In this chapter, I consider the goals that today's central banks try to achieve and targets that they can set through monetary policy to achieve these goals. We will learn that two important goals are low inflation and low unemployment, and to consider how to achieve these goals, I consider the causes and costs of inflation and unemployment. I also discuss how central banks have changed the targets of monetary policy over time as central banks have developed their thinking about how best to manage the economy. And because targets are an indirect and imperfect means to achieve goals, central banks now also try to achieve goals by stabilizing the expectations of producers, sellers and buyers, partially by providing transparent information.

Goals of central banks

Central banks of major economies often have several goals in trying to manage the economy. The most important goals today are a low and stable inflation rate, a low unemployment rate and a stable growth rate in the production of goods and services. Central banks, in conjunction with treasury/finance departments of governments, try to achieve these goals by influencing expenditure (of money) on goods, services and assets. Expenditure can influence to various degrees the production of goods and services; the prices of goods, services and assets; and the employment of people in the labor force and other resources. Central banks are assigned these goals implicitly or explicitly due to the belief among citizens that central banks are responsible for managing the economy, especially when private individuals and institutions are unwilling or unable to do so.

Another common goal is to maintain stability in financial markets, particularly the prices of various non-monetary assets, since the expenditure of money can also affect financial market transactions and the prices of non-monetary assets. Central banks and government regulators may try to decrease instability in the prices of bonds, stocks, houses, currencies and other assets because unstable prices of non-monetary assets, like unstable prices of goods and services, can lead to broader instability in the economy. I consider the costs of unstable prices of goods and services below.

One financial market that central banks may try to stabilize is the market for government bonds, especially when many believe that the government is unwilling or unable to repay the bonds. Even when these beliefs are incorrect, the prices of bonds can plummet as people sell the bonds, preventing the government from acquiring much cash from newly issued bonds. This causes repayment problems on existing debt to develop or makes them worse. To stabilize the price of government bonds, the central bank can buy government bonds in the secondary market, allowing the government to raise more cash in the primary market and giving institutions and individuals more cash to spend and more income from which to pay taxes. As a result, the risk of default can decrease.

Some central banks also try to stabilize the foreign (currency) exchange market. A few large central banks and many small central banks have a goal of fixing or at least temporarily influencing the value of currency exchange rates, often to promote exports or to reduce volatility in export and import markets and international financial markets. Furthermore, nearly all central banks sometimes try to reduce volatility in foreign exchange markets. We study the relationship between monetary policy and currency exchange rates in greater detail in chapter 14.

And as we learned in the chapter on regulation, central banks also try to promote the stability of financial institutions (and financial markets) by enforcing various regulations, by using the lender of last resort policy and by trying to stabilize the expectations of individuals and institutions.

In this chapter, we will focus on the first three goals: a low and stable inflation rate (often called **price stability**), a low unemployment rate, both of which are associated with a stable growth rate of the production of goods and services. To understand the importance of these goals and how monetary policy can achieve them, I first discuss the theoretical causes of inflation, and the theoretical causes of unemployment, and the costs of both inflation and unemployment.

Causes of inflation

Economists say that changes in prices can be caused by two broad factors: one is the willingness to buy (or spend money on) goods and services, often called "demand". Prices tend to increase when there is an increase in the willingness to buy goods and services either because buyers are willing to pay higher prices, or because sellers can raise their prices and continue to sell their products to earn more revenue, or both. In other words, when customers are more willing to buy a given amount of products, prices will tend to rise because those products become more scare or desirable.

And the willingness to buy goods and services is directly related to the quantity of money and credit that we use to buy the goods and services and inversely related to the price of spending, borrowing or saving money—the interest or yield rates on non-monetary assets like deposits, loans and bonds. Of course, monetary policy substantially influences the quantity of money and credit and their prices and therefore can substantially influence the willingness to buy goods and services and the prices of goods and services.

Figure 13-1 represents how an increase in the willingness to buy goods and services (demand), which is influenced by the quantity of money and credit (and their prices), influences the prices of goods and services. As the willingness to buy increases from level 1 to level 2, shortages are predicted to develop when the quantity produced and sold remains at its original amount. Because goods and services are more scarce or desirable, sellers will tend to raise the prices of goods and services to prevent shortages and to earn more revenue, and buyers will tend to bid up prices of goods and services.

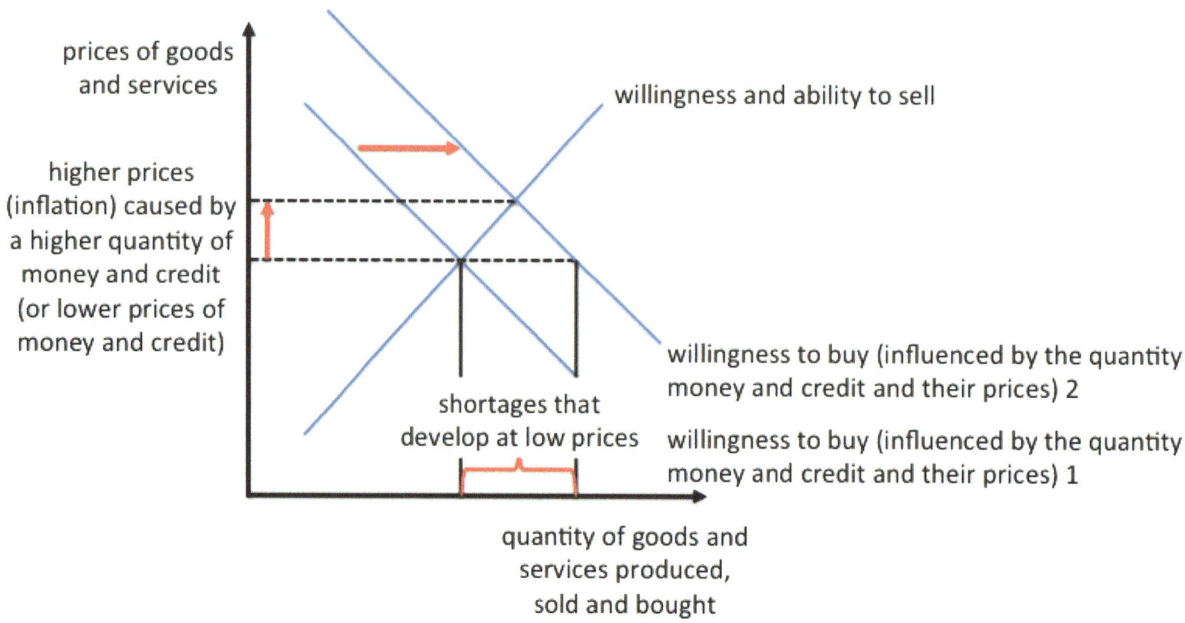

Figure 13-1: An increase in the willingness to buy goods and services (demand)—influenced by the quantity of money and credit and their prices—is predicted to increase the prices of goods and services.

Secondly, prices can change when the willingness and ability to produce and to sell goods and services changes, often called "supply". The willingness and ability to produce is affected by costs of production (which affects profitability) and the productivity of workers. Costs of production and productivity are often influenced by natural (ex., weather), political, legal, foreign (ex., exchange rate), technological or other factors that are hard to measure or to predict. Prices tend to increase when the cost of production increases and profitability decreases, so that the same amount of final products become more expensive to produce, or productivity decreases, so that the same amount of workers and other resources can produce fewer final products. With fewer goods and services, prices tend to rise.

Unlike demand, the central bank has little or no direct control over the willingness and ability of thousands or millions of producers throughout the economy to produce and to sell because they have little or no direct control over natural, political, legal, foreign and technological factors that influence costs of production, profitability and productivity. However, in a later section, I discuss how some central banks try to influence *expectations* of producers and sellers about costs of production, profitability or productivity (as well as the expectations of buyers), thereby indirectly affecting their willingness to produce and to sell.

Figure 13-2 represents how a decrease in the willingness and ability to produce and sell goods and services (supply)—which is influenced by the costs of production, profitability and productivity—influences the prices of goods and services. As the willingness to produce and to sell decreases from level 1 to level 2, shortages are predicted to develop when the quantity that buyers are willing to buy remains at its original amount. Because goods and services are more scarce, sellers will tend to raise the prices of goods and services to prevent shortages and buyers will tend to bid up prices of goods and services.

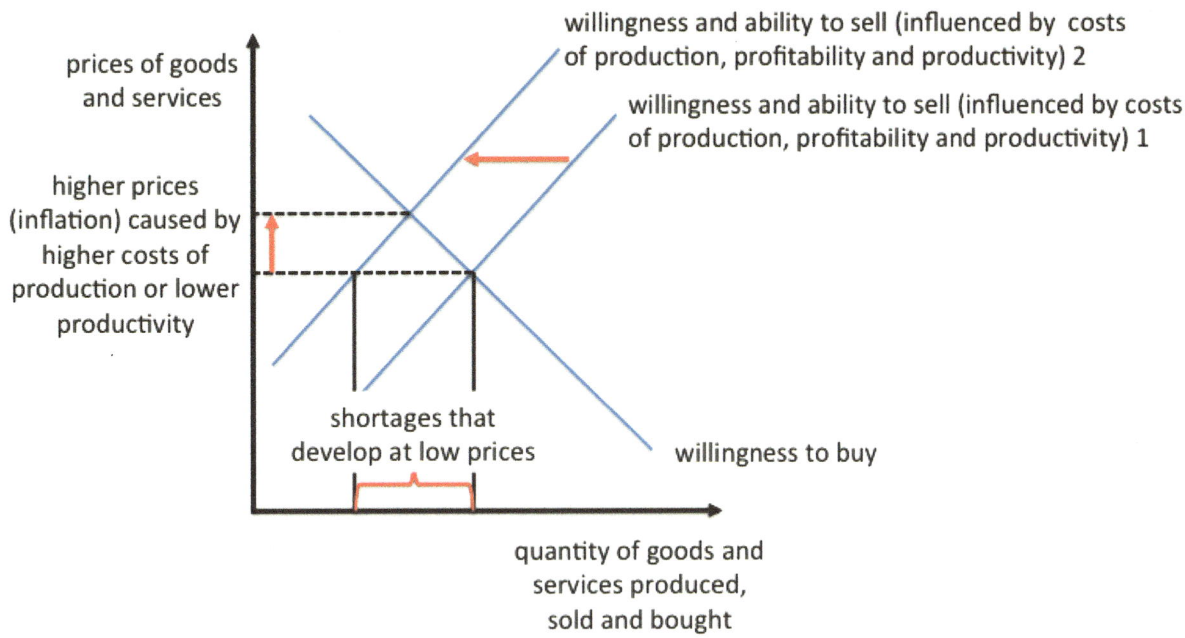

Figure 13-2: A decrease in the willingness and ability to produce and sell (supply)—influenced by costs of production, profitability and productivity—is predicted to increase the prices of goods and services.

In sum, inflation can be caused by 1) a greater willingness to buy goods and services from more money and credit, or 2) a lower willingness and ability to produce and to sell goods and services from higher costs of production, lower profitability or lower productivity.

In contrast, decreasing prices, or **deflation**, can be caused by 1) a lower willingness to buy goods and services and lower willingness to spend money (often because of fear or uncertainty) or 2) a greater willingness and ability to produce and sell goods and services from lower costs of production, higher profitability or higher productivity.

Deflation caused by a lower willingness to buy goods and services and a lower willingness to spend money can be costly for the economy, especially if it involves fear and uncertainty. I discuss the costs of this kind of deflation in a later section, but first I discuss the costs of inflation (caused by either changes in the willingness to buy or the willingness and ability to produce and to sell).

Costs of inflation

Over the past few decades, central banks have become increasingly concerned with keeping inflation at a low and steady rate over time because they have recognized that unstable prices create uncertainty and rapidly rising prices also have costs. Both an unstable and a high inflation rate cause individuals and institutions to spend time and other resources to avoid their effects, which reduces efficiency and productivity throughout the economy. Figure 13-3 shows the inflation rate in Korea over time, which has recently become lower and more stable than in the past.

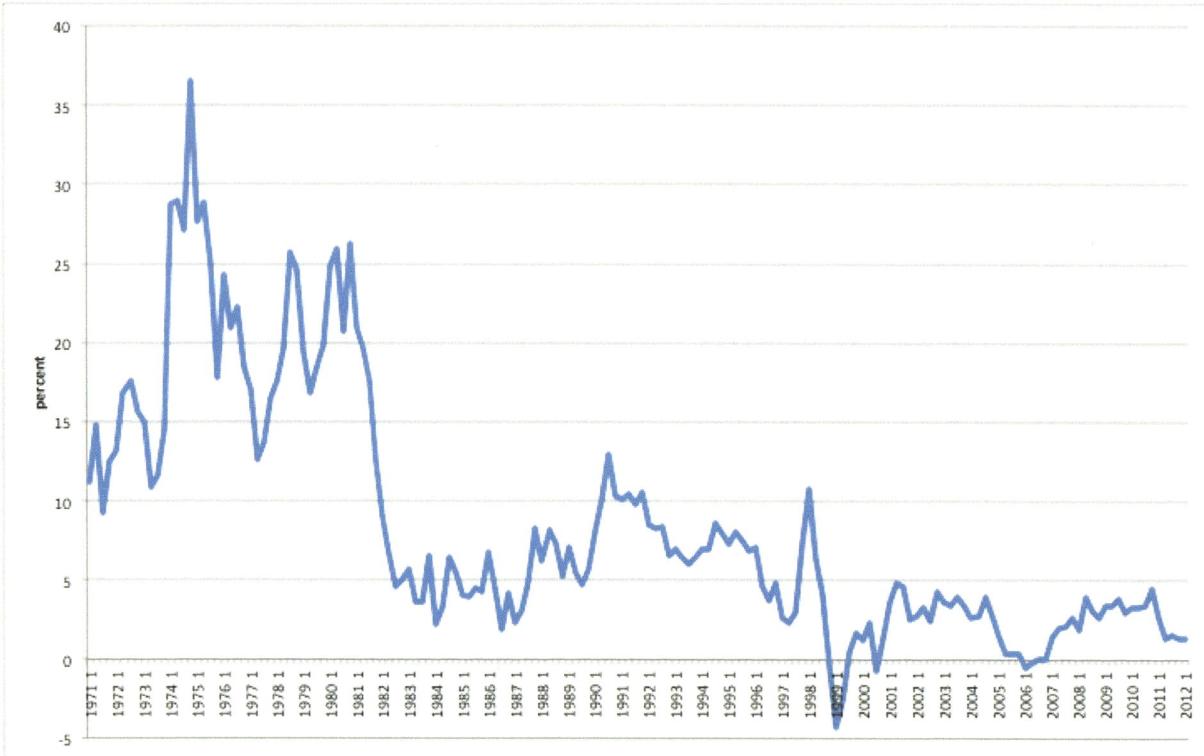

Figure 13-3: The inflation rate of final domestically produced goods and services in Korea, 1971.1-2012.1

We can distinguish between inflation that people *expect* to occur, possibly because of current trends, and inflation that occurs *unexpectedly* as a break from past trends. Expected inflation occurs when people expect that a given inflation rate will occur in the future, perhaps because that inflation rate has regularly occurred in the past. Unexpected inflation occurs when prices increase unexpectedly. Both expected inflation and unexpected inflation have costs for the economy that reduce efficiency and productivity.

When the inflation rate is expected to be high, the purchasing power of money is expected to significantly erode, which is costly for those who must hold money as a store of value. To the degree that some can decrease their holdings of money and can increase their holding of non-monetary assets that compensate for inflation more than others, expected inflation arbitrarily changes the distribution of wealth. It therefore causes groups to compete for resources and can even lead to social unrest. And to the degree that people hold more non-monetary assets to protect themselves against inflation, these methods involve time and other resources that reduce efficiency and productivity. Sellers of goods and services also spend time and other resources to adjust their prices more frequently to compensate for rising costs. In addition, when incomes and revenues rise to compensate for expected inflation, individuals and institutions need to pay higher taxes, which can also erode efficiency. Finally, efficiency decreases because of the time and mental effort needed to adjust monetary values over time to determine real values.

Unexpected inflation has some costs that are similar to, and some that are different from, expected inflation. When prices and the inflation rate are unstable, those who save assets will require higher real interest rates as compensation for the risk of unexpectedly losing purchasing power when prices and the inflation rate are unstable. Higher real interest rates, in turn, will discourage investment expenditure, reducing productivity and production. Unstable prices also make it more difficult to plan how much to save for the future and when to buy goods and services. And because prices of goods and services do not change uniformly over time, the real value of resources relative to other resources can become distorted, causing some individuals and institutions to gain at the expense of others. In addition, unexpected inflation (and unexpected deflation) will unexpectedly and arbitrarily redistribute wealth between those who hold monetary assets or have fixed incomes and those who have assets and incomes that adjust to inflation. Individuals, institutions and social groups would likewise compete for resources, trying to compensate for the higher prices of others by raising their own prices or wages. In an economic sense, this conflict reduces efficiency and productivity. In a political or social sense, this conflict can lead to political or social instability.

In sum, a high and unstable inflation rate decreases efficiency, productivity and production. It also decreases fairness because it redistributes real wealth in an arbitrary manner.

Costs of unemployment

The costs of unemployment should be obvious, but I mention them here to be thorough. Like inflation, unemployment also decreases efficiency, productivity and production because people who want to work and produce something valuable can not. Unemployment may also cause social instability (further decreasing efficiency, productivity and production), especially if it is viewed as unfair.

Causes of unemployment

Economists distinguish between different causes of unemployment, only some of which the central bank can effectively address through monetary policy.

First, unemployment exists due to "frictions" in the labor market caused by the time needed for employees and employers to find a desired match. During the time in which potential employees are searching for suitable employers and potential employers are searching for suitable employees, people who are looking for a job but do not have one are officially classified as unemployed. The unemployment that is results is called **frictional unemployment**.

A second reason why unemployment exists (which could be related to the first) is that some employers are unwilling to hire workers with inadequate skills and low productivity, given the wages that should be paid according to regulations of unions, governments or courts or according to social conventions that are hard to break. This type of unemployment, called **structural unemployment**, exists when labor markets have an inflexible "structure", that is, when available workers have inadequate, hard-to-change skills and/or when wages that need to be paid according to inflexible regulations or conventions are too high.

A third kind of unemployment exists when buyers are unwilling to buy goods and services, so firms are therefore unwilling to hire workers to produce goods and services. This type of unemployment, called **cyclical unemployment**, fluctuates with broader economic conditions or the *business cycle*. When expenditure (demand) and production decrease, this type of unemployment increases; when expenditure (demand) and production increase, this type of unemployment decreases. The central bank can significantly influence this kind of unemployment because if buyers have access to more and cheaper money and credit, then they could be more willing to buy goods and services. As a result, some firms would be more willing to hire workers to produce the additional goods and services because doing so could be more profitable than raising prices.

On the other hand, the central bank has only a limited effect on structural unemployment and frictional unemployment because monetary policy has only a limited effect on the time it takes to match suitable employees with suitable employers, the hard-to-change skills of workers and the inflexible wages that are required by regulations and social conventions.

Natural (rate of) unemployment

Although it may be difficult in practice to classify an unemployed person as "frictionally unemployed", "structurally employed" or "cyclically unemployed", these three theoretical forms of unemployment help us realize that monetary policy is only partially effective in addressing the problems and costs of unemployment.

In theory, central bank should try to reduce cyclical unemployment to zero and can do so without sacrificing price stability. The remaining unemployment—structural unemployment and frictional unemployment, collectively called **natural unemployment**—exists due for reasons outside of monetary policy and to the degree the central bank attempts to decrease it, it can not do so without causing higher inflation and other inefficiencies.

If the central bank increases the quantity of money and credit and decreases their prices, expenditure and demand could increase, and cyclical unemployment could decrease. The other kinds of unemployment could also decrease, at least somewhat, because some firms could mistakenly be more willing to quickly hire (sometimes unsuitable and inadequate) employees. Other firms, however, could respond to the increased demand by raising prices, especially if they are unable to find suitable employees and are unwilling to hire possibly inadequate employees to produce more. And for firms that find out that they have hired unsuitable or inadequate workers, they would find it more profitable to fire these workers or to raise their prices to compensate for the higher costs of production and the lower productivity. Furthermore, if employees know that jobs are plentiful and that firms are willing to hire workers to produce and to sell and that customers are willing to buy, the employees could also request and receive high wages. Employers would compensate by raising their prices, which they could afford to do when expenditure and demand are already high. In sum, a policy of trying to reduce more than cyclical unemployment would result in a higher inflation rate, with its associated costs and inefficiencies, and lower (average) productivity.

Natural unemployment can decrease most effectively through programs that help match employers with suitable employees through job announcements or distribution of resumes (thereby decreasing frictional unemployment), through policies that reduce employment costs or subsidize hiring so that employers can afford to hire unskilled or otherwise unproductive workers (thereby decreasing structural unemployment), or through training and education programs that allow workers to acquire the skills and productivity that employers desire (thereby decreasing structural unemployment).

The *natural unemployment rate* or *natural rate of unemployment* occurs when cyclical unemployment has been eliminated through monetary policy, yet the inflation rate is still as low as possible or at least is not increasing. Some authors call the natural rate of unemployment the *constant-inflation rate of unemployment*, the rate of unemployment consistent with a constant inflation rate. Economists use the average unemployment rate over many periods as a practical measure of the natural rate of unemployment if we assume that the central bank follows a sound monetary policy over time. Figure 13-4 represents the natural rate of unemployment in Korea by using a 12-month moving average unemployment rate. According to this measure, the natural rate of unemployment in Korea was about 3.5% during most of the 2000s.

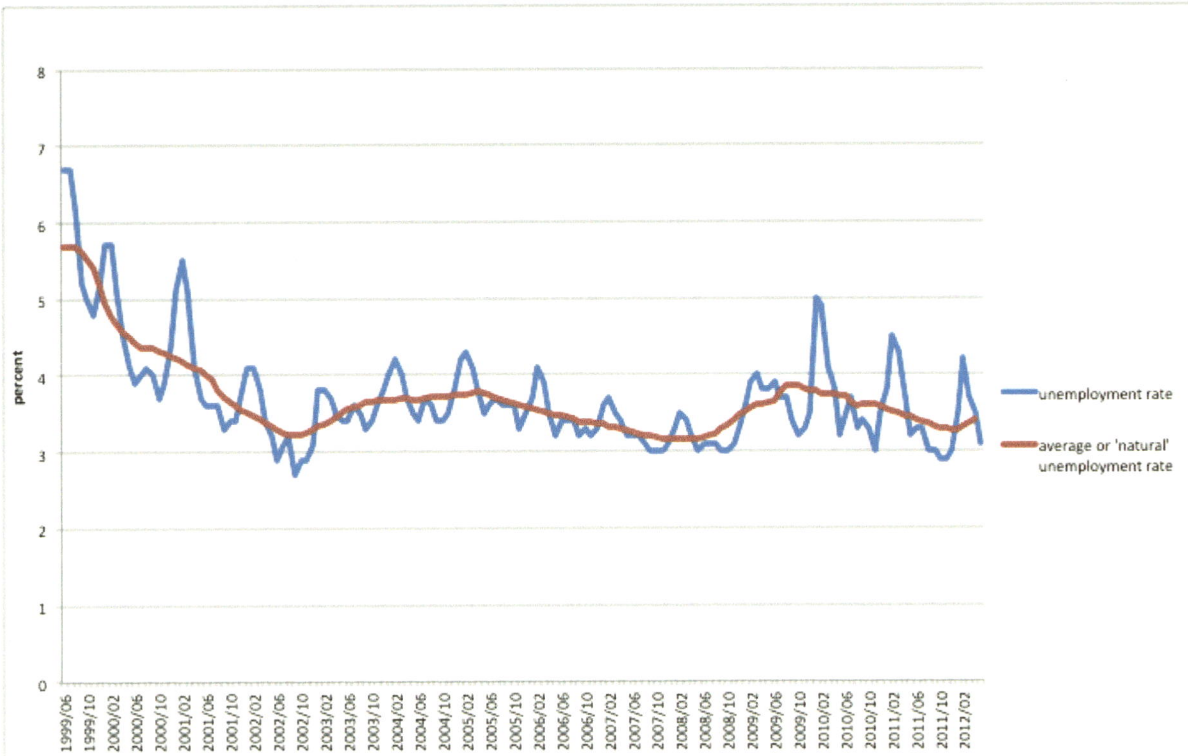

Figure 13-4: The unemployment rate and the average or 'natural' unemployment rate in Korea, 1996.06-2012.03

Potential (growth rate of) production

Related to a low and stable inflation rate and the natural (rate of) unemployment is **potential production** or the **potential growth rate of production**. Like natural unemployment, potential production is a theoretical construction that occurs when the inflation rate is low and stable. We construct it because it helps us realize that monetary policy is only partially effective in encouraging firms to produce and to sell goods and services by giving buyers sufficient money and credit to buy. Potential production refers to the state of the economy when resources or "factors of production", including workers in the labor force, are used to effectively (so that they are not idle or wasted) and sustainably (so that upward pressure on prices or the inflation rate does not occur).

The concept of a "potential" amount or growth rate of production was developed in the 1930s, when many economies were clearly *not* operating at their potential due to the Depression. Economists at the time argued that many resources—including people in the labor force—were wasted or idle, and society was worse than if these resources could be used more effectively.

Of course, the Depression eventually ended, and many economies began producing at a high level. In fact, the opposite problem developed soon after the 1930s. During 1940s, due to the production needs of World War II, many factories and other firms were working overtime to meet production goals and the demand of the government. Many resources, including people in the labor force, were scarce and/or used unsustainably. Although prices were sometimes fixed by government fiat at the time, there was upward pressure on prices of many goods and services. And high inflation occurred after price controls were lifted.

Today, we still use the concepts of ineffective and unsustainable use of resources to describe how the economy can deviate from its potential. Economists say that production is below its potential (growth rate) when resources are idle or wasted: the unemployment rate is high (above its natural rate), employees work relatively few hours, factories are idle, offices are vacant, and the growth rate of expenditure and production are below average—and possibly negative. In this case, workers are unlikely to receive higher wages and may accept lower wages in order to keep their jobs. Producers tend to lower prices or hold them constant if they expect that they will not need to pay more to workers and/or that expenditure will be low. Surpluses from past production may develop in these cases, and prices and/or the inflation rate tend to decrease.

On the other hand, economists say that production "is overheating" or is above its potential (growth rate) when resources are very scarce and/or are used unsustainably: when the unemployment rate is lower than normal, employees work many overtime hours, factories are operating at over-capacity, office space is scarce, and the growth rate of expenditure and production are above average. In this case, workers tend to ask for and receive higher wages if they expect overtime or easy employment. Producers tend to raise prices if they expect that high wages will be needed to attract or keep workers, that newly hired employees will be less suitable, adequate or productive than experienced workers, and/or that expenditure will be high. Shortages may develop in these cases, and prices and the inflation rate tend to increase substantially.

Like the natural rate of unemployment, the potential growth rate of production can be measured in practice by the average growth rate over time or when inflation is said to be low and stable. According to the first measure, production was below its potential during 1997-1998 and again during 2008-2009 when Korea experienced or feared financial crises. Before these periods, production was above its potential, as Figure 13-5 shows.

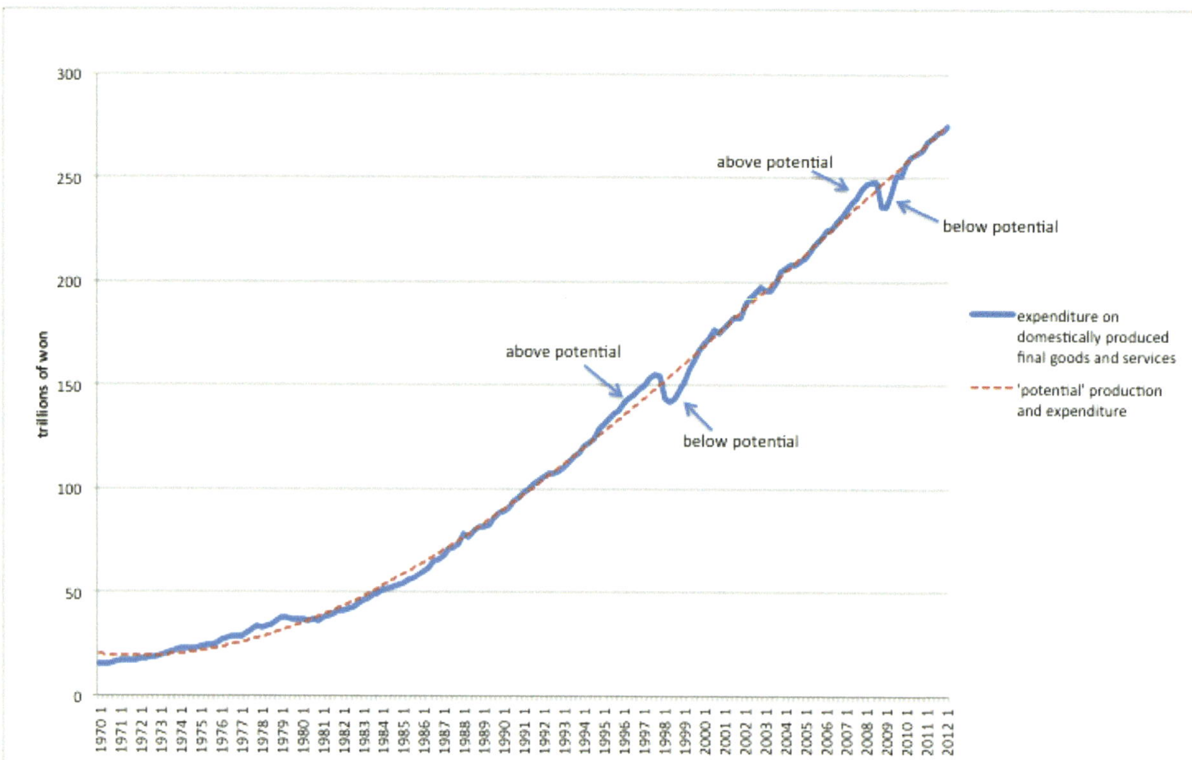

Figure 13-5: Expenditure on domestically produced final goods and services and average or 'potential' production in Korea, 1970.1-2012.1

Thus, because employment, unemployment and inflation are related to production and expenditure, we can say that the central bank also tries to achieve a goal of a potential amount or growth rate of production, which occurs when resources are not idle or wasted and when price stability exists.

Trade offs between goals

To maintain a low and stable inflation rate, central banks generally need to restrict the growth in the quantity of money and credit and to maintain relatively high interest and yield rates, both of which tend to restrict expenditure on (demand of) goods and services. In this case, prices of goods and services on average tend not to increase rapidly (and may even decrease). However, low expenditure on (demand of) goods and services usually causes the growth rate in the production of goods and services to decrease and the unemployment rate to increase because many firms respond to their customers' lower willingness to buy by adjusting production, employment and prices downward to various degrees.

To reverse the effects of this policy, the central bank could increase the growth in the quantity of money and lower interest and yield rates, both of which tend to increase expenditure on (demand of) goods and services. In this case, prices of goods and services on average tend to increase more rapidly than usual because producers feel free or obligated to raise prices as demand and costs of production increase. However, high expenditure on (demand of) goods and services can also cause the growth rate in the production of goods and services to increase and the unemployment rate to decrease because many firms respond to their customers' higher willingness to buy by adjusting production, employment and prices upward to various degrees.

In sum, the quantity of money and credit (directly) and the prices of money and credit (inversely) affect expenditure on goods and services. In turn, expenditure on (demand of) goods and services directly affects the inflation rate and inversely affects the unemployment rate because of how firms tend to adjust employment and prices to the willingness to buy. Central banks generally adjust a quantity of money and credit (like M1) and/or an interest/yield rate (like the overnight inter-bank loan rate) until the unemployment rate reaches its desired (natural) rate or the inflation rate reaches its desired rate. We will consider different quantities of money or interest/yield rates a central bank may choose to adjust in the next section.

As shown in Figure 13-6, because expenditure on goods and services is positively related to the inflation rate and negatively related to the unemployment rate, the central bank should face a trade off in trying to achieve price stability and the natural unemployment rate.

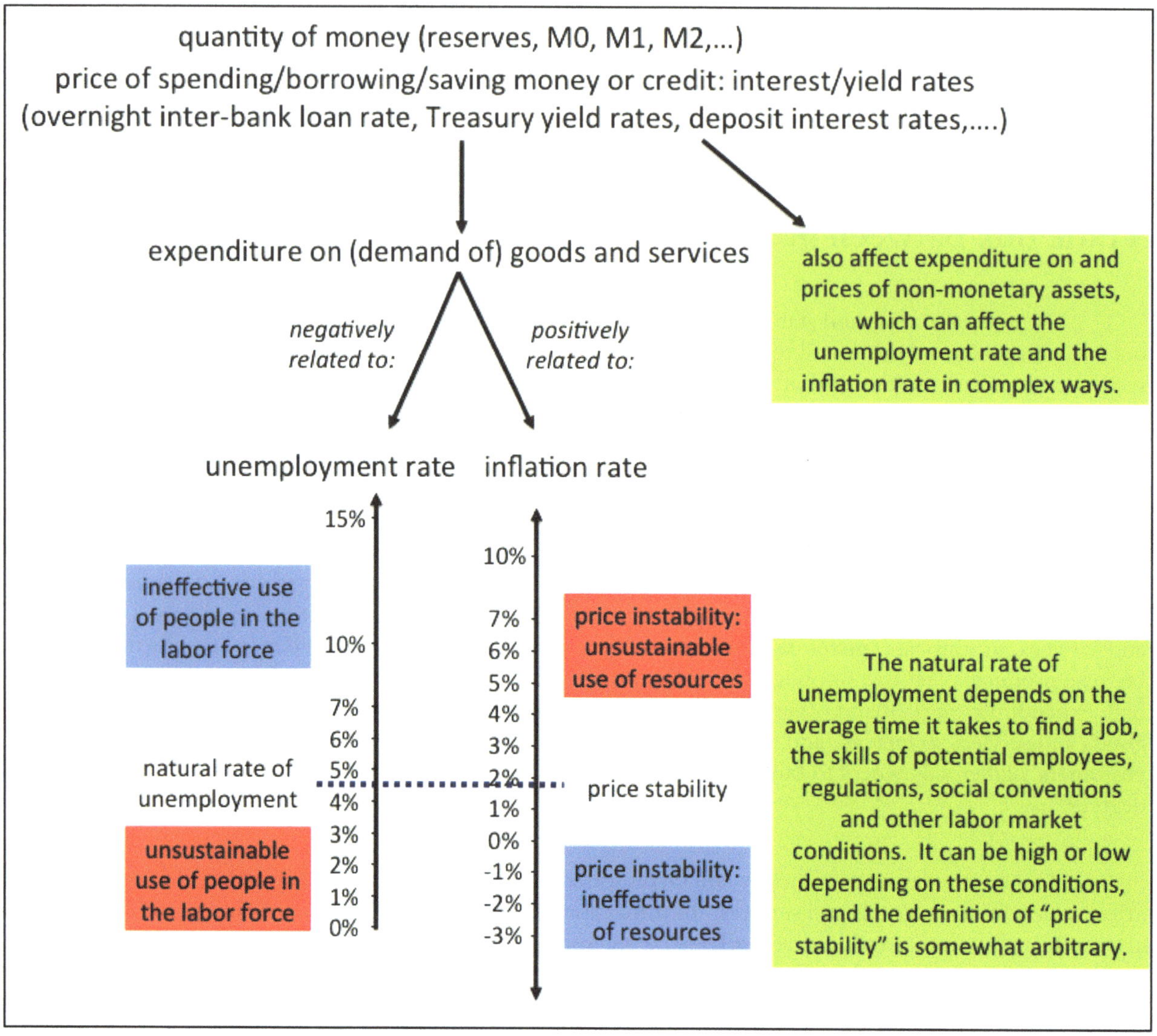

Figure 13-6: Because expenditure on goods and services is supposed to be positively related to the inflation rate and negatively related to the unemployment rate, the central bank may face a trade-off in trying to achieve price stability and the natural rate of unemployment.

Although the inflation rate, the unemployment rate and growth in production are usually the most important goals for central banks; central banks also sometimes consider how monetary policy affects stability in financial markets, investment in financial assets and investment in real assets.

Since banks, other financial institutions and their customers can use money and credit to buy non-monetary assets instead of goods and services, changes in the quantity of money and credit and their prices can affect investment in financial and real assets (some assets more than others). In general, with more money and credit and lower prices of money and credit, institutions and individuals can invest more in non-monetary assets, although they may want to invest less in some assets depending on their expected return rate. In turn, investment in financial and real assets, especially investment in real assets, directly affects the growth in production and employment.

However, if the central bank creates too much money and credit, it might not only create inflation in the prices of goods and services, but it might also create inflation in the prices of assets. When institutions and individuals have additional money to invest in asset markets, they may speculate that they can profit because of increasing demand and prices of the assets. In other words, "over-" investment in some assets and a "bubble" in their asset prices could occur.

To the degree that over-investment occurs, this expenditure and asset prices eventually correct themselves, an adjustment that could be sudden and unexpected. A sudden and unexpected downward adjustment in investment and asset prices is commonly called a "crash", which can cause a more general financial crisis. Because of a financial crisis and ongoing pessimism about the expected return rates on financial and real assets, "under-" investment in assets may persist.

Figure 13-7 shows that expenditure on non-monetary assets is generally positively related to productive investment in financial and real assets, as well as speculation about the return rates on and over-investment in financial and real assets. And investors try to decrease the over-investment (by selling more and buying less), they may overreact, leading to under-investment and a financial crisis. Therefore, the central bank may face a trade-off between creating enough money (and credit) for productive investment and too much money (and credit) that could cause speculation about rising asset prices and over-investment (and a possible sharp decrease in investment later).

However, the distinction between "productive" and "over-" investment is arbitrary and unclear. Likewise, it is unclear when investors are too pessimistic and "under-" invest during a financial crisis. In a private-enterprise, private-property economy; private institutions and individuals ultimately determine whether investment becomes "productive" or "speculative". And it is difficult for anyone, including the central bank, to predict whether the investment will be considered "productive" or "speculative" at the present time.

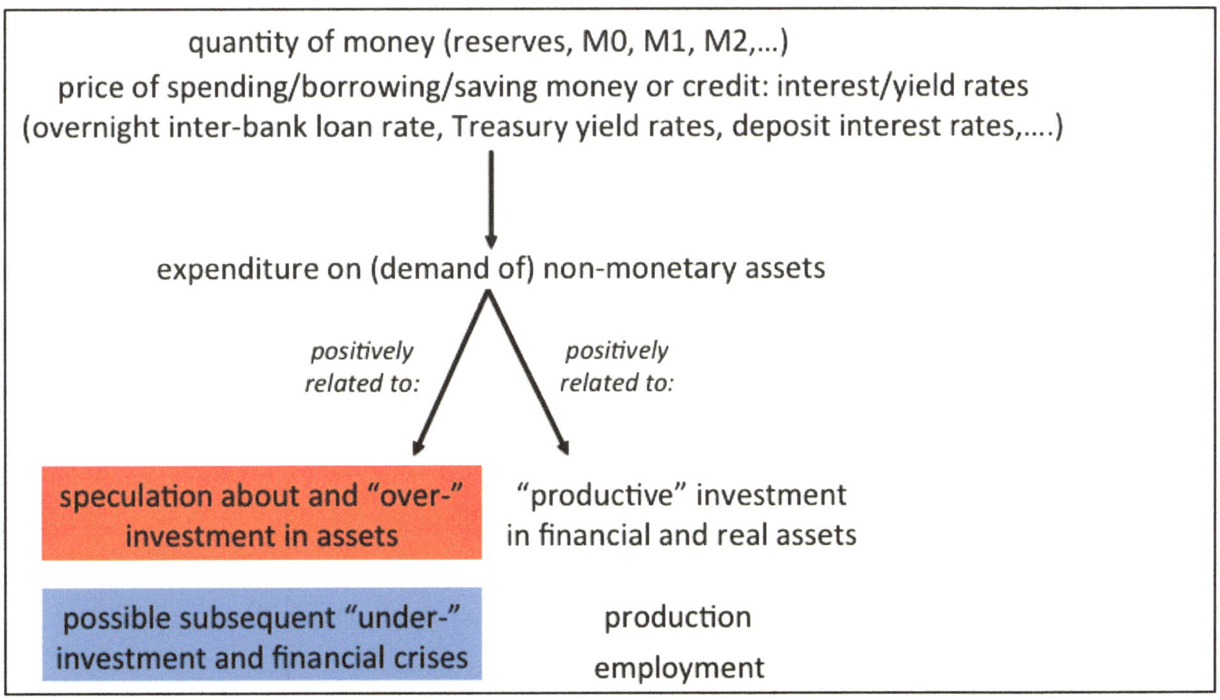

Figure 13-7: The central bank should create enough money for "productive" investment but not too much money to cause "over-" investment. However, the distinction between "productive" and "over-" investment is arbitrary and unclear.

Targets for attaining goals

As Figure 13-6 and Figure 13-7 suggest, central banks have various options, or targets, that they could adjust to try to achieve the goals of price stability, the natural rate of unemployment and stability in financial markets or productive investment. In this section, I describe these various targets, and other targets, in greater detail.

Monetary targets. Monetary targets include growth rates of monetary aggregates like M1 and M2 or growth rates of more narrow measures of the quantity of money like M0, total reserves, non-borrowed reserves (reserves from open market operations and public auctions) and borrowed reserves (reserves borrowed from discount loans). When resources like the number of people in the labor force and (potential) production grow, the quantity of money needs to grow for prices to remain stable for the inflation rate to remain low and stable, when other variables like velocity remain constant. However, growth of money and credit in excess of this amount will generate higher prices and a higher inflation rate. (See chapter 4 for the discussion about the quantity theory of money that supports this claim.)

Given the theory about monetary targets, two ideas have developed concerning the use of monetary targets in practice. First, some economists believe that central banks could adjust the growth rate of the quantity of money actively so that the growth rate of production could match its potential rate. Specifically, central banks could increase the growth rate of the quantity of money when the growth of domestic production is low relative to its potential rate and the inflation rate is lower than average or falling. They could decrease the growth rate of the quantity of money when the growth of domestic production is high relative to its potential and the inflation rate is higher than average or rising.

Other economists believe that passively maintaining a fixed monetary target at about the potential growth rate of production, regardless of short run fluctuations in actual production, is the best strategy to stabilize production, employment and inflation in the long run. Because changes in the quantity of money and credit can take several months or even years to affect aggregate spending (as I discuss in a later section), changes in monetary policy can be too slow to have the desired effect on production, employment and prices. Even worse, because changes in monetary policy are slow, they can aggravate cyclical changes in production, employment and prices—increasing expenditure and demand further after they have already increased for other reasons and decreasing expenditure and demand further after they have already decreased for other reasons. As a result, changes in monetary policy would make expenditure, production, employment and prices more volatile over time. Likewise, changes in monetary policy can make the prices of non-monetary assets more volatile over time as individuals and institutions begin to expect or anticipate changes in the demand and prices of assets due to changes in the quantity of money—buying assets with increasing prices when the quantity of money is expected to increase and selling assets with decreasing prices when the quantity of money is expected to decrease. In contrast, maintaining a fixed monetary target helps to stabilize expectations about expenditure on goods, services and assets, and therefore about production, employment and prices. Finally, these economists argue that trying to adjust the growth rate of the quantity of money to adjust production to its potential rate is simply too difficult in practice, given the multitude of variables that must be accurately measured and the multitude of exogenous changes that can affect the economy.

Economists in the first camp counter that maintaining a fixed growth rate in the quantity of money and credit is too rigid, and that changes in the quantity of money—though a blunt and slow instrument to change expenditure, production, employment and prices—is still better than simply allowing expenditure, production, employment and prices to change through the autonomous decisions of millions of buyers, producers and sellers in the economy. Maintaining a fixed growth rate in the quantity of money and credit can also generate volatility because of volatile decisions of millions of buyers, producers and sellers.

Yet other economists believe that using monetary targets is not the best monetary policy even if the central bank tries to actively manage expenditure, production, employment and prices. Because many hard-to-measure and hard-to-predict economic variables, like velocity, can affect the inflation rate and the unemployment rate, a monetary target—fixed or variable—would soon become outdated or inaccurate. In fact, the growth rates of the aggregate quantities of money have varied considerably as central banks tried to adjust to rapidly changing economic conditions. In addition, it is unclear which monetary target a central bank should use to affect production, employment and prices. Some central banks have used broad measures like M2, while others have used narrow measures like borrowed or non-borrowed reserves, but it is not evident which kind is better.

Despite various objections, central banks relied on different monetary targets for some time and tried to adjust these targets to rapidly changing economic conditions. In 1970, Arthur Burns was appointed as the chairman of the Board of Governors of the Federal Reserve System, and soon thereafter announced that the Federal Reserve System would use monetary targets, and in 1975 it began to publicly announce M1 and non-borrowed reserve targets in response to a Congressional resolution. However, the Federal Reserve System often did not hit the targets, for both M1 and non-borrowed reserves, and as a result, inflation and expectations about inflation became more volatile.

One reason for missing the targets is that banks and bank customers substantially influenced the quantities of money, especially as technical and regulatory changes allowed people to move monetary assets more freely and unpredictably. In addition, the non-borrowed reserves target was based on average lagged reserve requirements, in which required reserves for a given week are calculated according to the average level of transactions during the previous two weeks.[47] In effect, this allows reserve levels (and hence broader measures of the quantity of money) to fluctuate considerably in the short term, even if on average they do not. Because of the ineffectiveness of M1 and non-borrowed reserves targets, the Federal Reserve System stopped using them after 1982 in favor of the overnight inter-bank loan interest rate (called the federal funds rate in the US). The Federal Reserve System continued to implicitly use the growth rate of M2 as a target for some time, but by 1993, it stopped using all monetary targets in favor of interest rate targets.

Similarly, the Bank of Canada and the Bank of England also used various monetary targets during the 1970s and early 1980s, but abandoned them by the 1990s in favor of interest rate targets.

The Bank of Japan also targeted growth rates of different monetary aggregates during the 1970s, and in 1978 it began to target the growth rate of M2 plus large denomination time deposits (used principally by banks and other financial institutions), a much broader measure of monetary assets than either non-borrowed reserves of M1. Unlike in the US and in other countries, the Bank of Japan was able to maintain a relatively stable and modest growth rate in the quantity of money. Likewise, the Japanese inflation rate during 1978-1987 was lower on average and less volatile than in the US. Nonetheless, financial innovation and deregulation in Japan also made this broad monetary target a less reliable guide to influence economic activity

[47] See David Lindsey, "Non-borrowed Reserve Targeting and Monetary Control", in Improving Money Stock Control, ed. Laurence Meyer (Boston: Kluwer-Nijhoff, 1983).

over time, and the Bank of Japan also switched to interest rate targets in the overnight inter-bank loan market by the 1990s.

From the mid-1970s to the mid-1990s, both central banks in both Germany and Switzerland also targeted growth rates of different quantities of money. Germany's central bank, the Bundesbank, first targeted an aggregate quantity of money called *central bank money*, equal to currency in circulation and bank deposits weighted by required reserve ratios. But in 1988, the Bundesbank began to target a very broad aggregate quantity, M3, which equals M2 plus large denomination time deposits, large denomination money market deposit accounts, repurchase agreements and expatriate currency deposits. However, the Bundesbank did not strictly adhere to its targets, because of shifting priorities among goals and because of regulatory and technical changes that made the velocity of money more volatile. Yet, like the Bank of Japan, it did publicly announce this target to provide more information to individuals and institutions that set prices. And like other central banks, the central banks of Germany and Switzerland began to target interest rates by the 1990s, although they continued to set publicly announced targets for the growth rate of M3. They also began to publish reports and speeches by central bank officials to communicate the direction of their monetary policies.

Interest rate targets. Because of the shortcomings of monetary targets, most central banks of major economies now target an interest rate instead. The most common interest rate target is the overnight inter-bank loan rate in the market for reserves. This interest rate is called the *federal funds rate* in the US, the *overnight call rate* in Japan, the *call rate* in Korea, the *London Interbank Offered Rate* (LIBOR) in the UK and the *euro interbank offered rate* in the economic and monetary union of the EU. These interest rates are market interest rates, influenced by lending and borrowing behavior of private financial institutions, although central banks influence these prices of lending and borrowing money also by influencing the quantity of money that banks and others can lend, borrow and save.

In addition to the overnight inter-bank loan rate, central banks will often concurrently target the interest rates on discount loans and on deposits at the central bank. Many central banks set the interest rate on discount loans as an upper bound (under a penalty rate policy) and the interest rate on deposits as a lower bound for the overnight inter-bank loan rate.

Central banks have also targeted yield rates on government bonds, like the US Treasury Bill rate, when they wanted to influence or assist the financing of government expenditures. In the US, the Federal Reserve System implicitly targeted the Treasury Bill rate during the 1940s to allow the national government to borrow to finance war expenditures at low interest rates.

However, central banks can not generally target an interest/yield rate (a price of money and credit) and a quantity of money at the same time.[48] If a central bank wants to stabilize an interest rate, say the interest rate in the overnight inter-bank loan market, then it does so by adjusting the quantity (supply) of money and credit (ex., the quantity of reserves) relative to the willingness to borrow and hold (demand of) money and credit, so that the price of money and credit achieves its target. In other words, the central bank varies a quantity of money and credit to make an interest rate remain stable. On the other hand, if a central bank wants to target a quantity of money, it must let the price of money and credit fluctuates according to the demand of money and credit. In other words, the central bank stabilizes (the growth rate of) the quantity of money and credit at its target, while the interest rate varies according to the willingness to borrow and the save money in the market.

[48] An exception could occur when an interest/yield rate target remains at 0% due to a large quantity of money and credit, and a monetary target that allows the quantity of money and credit to remain large or to grow rapidly.

Inflation rate targets. Instead of or in addition to a publicly announced interest rate or monetary target, some central banks have an implicit or publicly announced inflation rate target. Inflation rate targeting can involve adjusting multiple quantities of money and interest rates, based the ideas illustrated in Figure 13-6, until the central bank achieves its inflation rate target or "price stability".

The most commonly watched inflation rate is the consumer price index (CPI) inflation rate, excluding volatile categories like fuel and food, which is based on a survey about which items consumers typically buy. However, the survey has some measurement problems. One measurement problem is that the survey accounts for only a limited number of items that consumers buy, not all items that consumers or any buyer buys. Another problem is that the limited survey sometimes fails to account for the fact that consumers can sometimes easily switch to relatively less expensive items when inflation occurs, actions that make the measured inflation rate too high to accurately represent the cost of living.

As a result, central banks may instead target an inflation rate based on the implicit price (or GDP) deflator, which accounts for price changes of all final goods and services produced in the domestic economy, not just those purchased by the typical consumer according to CPI surveys. And because the CPI is based on a fairly narrow, but precise, survey of items, central banks also look at a broader measure of consumer prices called the personal consumption expenditure (PCE) inflation, which is based on consumption expenditure data from the national expenditure (GDP) accounts. However, these alternative measures of inflation have their own measurement problems. They are measured only every quarter instead of every month, and the expenditure data is often estimated rather than tabulated from precise surveys.

Although the central bank of the US does not publicly announce an inflation rate target, it has indicated in its speeches or meeting notes an inflation rate that it is "comfortable" with.

In 2012, the Bank of Japan first publicly promised to achieve an inflation rate target of 1% "for the time being" by adjusting the interest rate in the overnight inter-bank loan market or a quantity of money.

The European Central Bank currently has multiple publicly announced targets, including an inflation rate target: the interest rate in the overnight inter-bank loan market, a growth rate of M3, and an inflation rate based on the CPI for the "medium term" that should be "below but close to 2%". To achieve the inflation rate target (and goal), the central bank primarily increases or decreases the interest rate in the overnight inter-bank loan market. The growth rate of M3 is only a publicly announced indicator to estimate current expenditure and is not directly adjusted.

New Zealand was the first country to formally adopt an inflation rate target in 1990, followed by Canada in 1991, the UK in 1992, Sweden and Finland in 1993 and Australia and Spain in 1994. Brazil, Mexico, Chile and Israel have also adopted a form of inflation rate targeting.

In 1989, the New Zealand parliament passed the Reserve Bank of New Zealand Act, which allowed the central bank greater freedom from the Finance Department and stipulated that it and the Minister of Finance set a publicly announced inflation rate target. In addition, the Act stated that if the targets are not attained by the specified dates, the governor of the central bank may be dismissed.

The first inflation rate target set on March 2, 1990 was a 3%-5% target range to be achieved during the subsequent four years. Thereafter, a 0%-2% target range was set in 1994 for the subsequent three years, a 0%-3% target range was set in 1997 for the subsequent 5 years, and a 1%-3% target range was set in 2002 for the indefinite future. The central bank has achieved all of its targets except for brief periods in 1995, 2000 and 2005 when the inflation rate exceed its target by a few tenths of a percentage point. Overall, the policy has been viewed as successful because the inflation rate has generally been contained within its target range, growth in production and employment have been high on average since 1992, and the unemployment rate has been modest since 1994, ranging from about 4%-8%.

On February 26, 1991, the Bank of Canada also established inflation rate targets for the following five and a half years: between 2%-4% until December 1992, between 1.5%-3.5% until June 1994 and between 1%-3% until December 1996. However, in 1993 the central bank decided to lower the target range to 1%-3% from December 1995 to December 1998, and it has been kept at this level since. As in New Zealand, the policy has been viewed as successful because inflation has generally been contained within its target range and growth in production and employment have been high on average since the early 1990s, and the unemployment rate has been modest since 1994.

In October 1992, the Bank of England also established an inflation rate target range of 1%-4% to be achieved by April 1997, with the intent that the inflation rate should generally be below 2.5% during this time. In May 1997, when the inflation rate was already below 2.5%, a new target was set at 2.5% for the indefinite future. But in December 2003, the target was lowered to 2.0% when the central bank started to use an inflation rate based on the CPI. As in other countries, inflation rate targeting in the UK has been viewed as successful because inflation has remained within or below its target, growth in production and employment have been high, and the unemployment rate has been modest until 2008.

Why did these central banks move from or supplement an interest rate target or monetary target to or with an inflation rate target? Some economists believe that the millions of individuals and institutions who set prices, spend money and save money better understand an inflation rate target and therefore are better to make better and more stable decisions about spending, saving, price setting, producing, hiring and working. In brief, these central banks hope to better stabilize economic activity when they use a publicly announced inflation rate target that is better understood than an interest rate or monetary target.

However, other economists argue that when the central bank publicly sets an inflation rate target, the goal of low and stable inflation becomes more important than other goals like a low unemployment rate.[49] In particular, when a high inflation rate is caused by an increase in the costs of production or a decrease in productivity, and if the central bank is serious about achieving a low inflation rate target, it should respond by decreasing the quantity of money and credit (and increasing their prices). In the formal language from Figure 13-2 and Figure 13-1, it should decrease the willingness to buy goods and services after the willingness to produce and sell decreases due to higher costs of production or lower productivity. In theory, this policy would keep prices of goods and services and the inflation rate stable, but it would substantially decrease expenditure, production and employment. And the unemployment rate would substantially increase. As a result, not all central banks use a publicly announced inflation target.

To allow some flexibility, however, most central banks with an inflation rate target set a target range, rather than a specific value, and even the range can be modified over time depending on economic conditions, as described in the cases above. Central banks that have targeted an inflation rate have sometimes gradually set lower target ranges over time so that production and employment could gradually adjust to changes in monetary policy.

[49] In theory, while central banks could explicitly set an unemployment rate target, they do not in practice because achieving and maintaining such a target would be too difficult due to the many factors beyond the influence of monetary policy that can affect unemployment.

Desirable properties of targets

In this section, I discuss desirable properties of any target—monetary, interest rate or inflation rate. After considering these properties, we will continue the discussion about why central banks have largely switched from monetary targets to interest rate or inflation rate targets.

For monetary, interest rate or inflation rate targeting to be as effective as possible, economists argue that a target must be *transparent*, understood by the public, because the public ultimately determines the inflation rate by setting prices, spending money and saving money. Because our price setting is influenced by our expectations about economic activity and because our expectations about economic activity are influenced by what we think about monetary policy, many economists argue that monetary policy, and in particular targets, should be transparent so that we can make decisions that benefit us as individuals or private institutions, thereby benefiting the economy as a whole. For example, if we are fully aware of the targets of monetary policy, we can understand how we should adjust our prices given the expected behavior of buyers that should result from the monetary policy. However, if we are not aware of the targets, it is more difficult to know how we should adjust our prices, and we may increase them too rapidly (causing surpluses) or not increase them enough (causing shortages). In other words, we can lose revenue and profit if we do not adjust prices properly, hurting ourselves and hurting the economy as a whole. Over time, a volatile inflation rate, production and employment will result. And the economy will be less efficient because we will need to spend resources to guess what will happen to monetary policy, expenditure, production, employment and prices.

To increase transparency, central banks now announce their targets to the public and many offer reports and statements about prospective trends in inflation, production and employment. For example, the Federal Reserve System publicizes its targeted federal funds rate immediately after the Federal Open Market Committee decides how to set the target, as well as its intentions about what it plans to do at future meetings. Two weeks after the meetings, it also releases a summary of the committee notes, to provide people with insight about the decision making process. The district Federal Reserve Banks also issue "beige books", which analyze the state of the economy within the district and regional economic issues. In addition, central banks and governments provide a trove of data on the quantity of money, the quantity of credit, interest rates, regulations, expenditure, production, employment and other economic variables through their websites. In sum, the rationale behind providing this information is to give individuals and institutions better information and to make more accurate expectations about future economic activity, so that they can make more efficient economic decisions, and collectively, so that the economy can be made more efficient.

Secondly, a target should be *credible*: individuals and institutions must believe that the central bank will be able and willing to achieve the target. Belief in the central bank's willingness and ability to achieve the target affects expectations about price setting and other economic activity. Credibility of the target, in turn, is influenced by how *accountable* the central bank is for achieving the target. If a central bank is held accountable for achieving a target or if there are consequences for missing a target, the individuals and institutions are likely to see the target as more credible. For example, at some central banks, the chairman of the monetary policy committee (and other members) may lose his job or lose his reputation if the central bank is unable to achieve the target.

To increase credibility and accountability, a central must also announce the *time* during which it plans to achieve the target and an *error band* around a specific target to allow for possible mistakes. For example, a central bank could announce that it will achieve an inflation rate of 2% within the 18 months, plus or minus 0.5 percentage points. In fact, a target does not have much meaning unless it is accompanied with a specific time period. Without a stated time, a central bank could neglect the target and claim that it will achieve the target only in the future. As a result, credibility and accountability would be reduced.

Fourthly, the target must be *effectively measured and controlled.* Central banks can effectively measure aggregate quantities of money after a few days or weeks of collecting and analyzing data from banks, even if they sometimes must revise original measures because of errors and omissions in reporting. While central banks can substantially influence the quantities of money, they can not completely control them because banks, borrowers and savers also affect the quantity of money and credit, as we learned in chapter 12. Formally, we say that while the central bank controls the supply of money and credit; banks, borrowers and savers determine the demand of money and credit, and the quantity of money and credit is determined by the interaction between supply and demand. Moreover, the aggregate quantity of money and credit can be affected by technological changes, regulatory changes, and the velocity of money—factors that the central bank can not directly control.

Central banks can effectively measure interest rates daily or even hourly. Nonetheless, as with the quantity of money and credit, banks, borrowers and savers also influence interest rates because they control the demand of money and credit. Furthermore, borrowing and saving of money are also determined by expectations about inflation, revenue and income, which are more difficult to measure and impossible to directly control. But relative to a targeted quantity of money, targeted nominal interest rates can be more effectively measured and controlled over time. Central banks usually have little difficultly in maintaining an interest rate target through daily open market operations or other policies, although the actual interest rate can vary slightly from its target.

As for transparency, targeted interest rates in the overnight inter-bank loan market (and other interest rates) may be more easily understood and more widely watched than monetary targets by large institutions who set prices, save (lend) money and borrow money, especially internationally. All interest rates are measured in percent, and therefore differences or *interest rate margins* are easy to calculate between lending and borrowing markets. In contrast, quantities of money have units like millions of dollars, billions of dollars and trillions of yen; it is therefore more difficult to determine optimal price setting, lending and borrowing based on a given quantity of money in a particular market. And even though growth rates in quantities of money are also measured in percent, it is still difficult to predict lending and borrowing behavior based on these rates.

For these reasons and the reasons described in the previous section, most central banks no longer publicly set a monetary target and instead publicly set an interest rate target or an inflation rate target.

Several central banks have switched to an inflation rate because they believed that inflation rate targets were more transparent than both interest rate targets and monetary targets, at least for most individuals and institutions in the domestic economy. Economists at these central banks believe that inflation rate targets are understood by more individuals and institutions who set prices, spend money and save money than the price of money and credit represented by the interest rate in the overnight inter-bank loan market—which is mostly watched by large financial institutions—or a quantity of money. With increased transparency of an inflation rate target, they argue, efficiency increases; also expenditure, production, employment and inflation become more stable. Secondly, because the public more easily understands an inflation rate target, it can make the central bank more accountable for sound monetary policy. Missing an inflation rate target would be obvious to more people than missing an interest rate target or a monetary target, so that the central bank may have more pressure to keep inflation under control with inflation rate targeting.

But despite its purported transparency, an inflation rate is very difficult to measure and to control. Central banks try to influence what millions of individuals and institutions expect about prices, but they can not directly control these expectations or price setting itself. And measures of inflation are imperfect and often revised. Central banks and others can measure inflation after a month or more of collecting and analyzing data from sellers and buyers, but they frequently must revise original measures because of errors and omissions in reporting. And as we learned in the previous section, each inflation measure has special measurement problems so that each is a somewhat inaccurate measure of the cost of living.

Because of these reasons and because some believe that inflation rate targeting would neglect the goal of low unemployment (as discussed in the previous section), not all central banks have publicly committed to an inflation rate target. They instead rely on an interest rate target, principally the interest rate in the overnight inter-bank loan market.

A 0% inflation rate target and deflation

While several central banks have set inflation rate targets, no central bank has yet set a target equal to 0% or has centered the target range around 0%. But if price stability is a goal of the central bank, should it not then have a target of 0% or a target range centered around 0%, a situation where prices are not changing on average?

To answer this question, we must first think about what inflation represents. Inflation rates are calculated from consumer expenditure data, national expenditure data or other data that is aggregated and averaged into an index. Thus, a 0% inflation rate would represent a case where *on average* prices are not rising or not falling. However, because individual prices never change uniformly, an average measure of 0% would represent the case where some prices are rising while others are falling.

Also, even though an inflation rate is defined to be the rate of change in prices, changes in prices are associated with changes in revenues for the sellers of the goods and services, changes in wages (a special price) for workers who produce goods and services, and changes in incomes for the workers and firm owners. When prices decrease; revenues, incomes and wages can also decrease. In particular, when demand decreases; price, revenues, incomes and wages should all decrease. (An increase in supply also decreases prices but not necessarily revenues, incomes and wages.)

Thus, a 0% inflation rate from a 0% inflation rate target would likely result from low expenditure and demand and a decrease in prices in some sectors. In addition, lower revenues, incomes and wages would also likely result in some sectors, and this could generate pessimistic expectations and restrict expenditure and demand even further. As a result, a 0% (average) inflation rate with decreasing prices, revenues, incomes and wages in some sectors could result in decreasing expenditure—which would further decrease prices, revenues, incomes and wages. In brief, a 0% inflation rate target could soon result in deflation in particular sectors and on average.

While inflation usually occurs in today's economies, deflation has occurred from time to time in some countries and occurred more frequently in the past when fiat currency was not used. In the US, prices decreased on average during many years of the 1870s, 1880s, 1890s and 1930s. The deflation during the 1870s, 1880s and 1890s is attributed to both an increase in supply (due to increases in productivity from new agricultural, transportation, communication and other technologies) and a decrease in demand (because of periodic financial crises). On the other hand, the deflation during the 1930s is attributed only to a decrease in demand due to pessimistic expectations and other factors during and after the breakdown of the financial markets and institutions.

Deflation more recently occurred in the US and a few other countries during 2008-2009. Japan has also experienced deflation a few years during the 1990s and 2000s, including during the latest financial crisis in 2008. Like the episode in the 1930s, these latest episodes of deflation are attributed to a lack of demand caused by pessimistic expectations.

Once deflation occurs or even once prices start declining in a few sectors, then these changes can set in motion a downward spiral in expenditure, revenue, wages and income. As with inflation, people can expect these changes or they may be surprised. In either case, there can be bad consequences for the economy.

When individuals and institutions expect deflation and expect revenue, income and wages to decrease as well, expenditure will tend to contract for a few reasons. First, when individuals and institutions expect that their income and revenue will shrink, they will tend to borrow and to spend less, which decreases income and revenue for others. Secondly, with less borrowing and spending by firms, investment in productive capacity decreases, further decreasing production, revenue and income. Thirdly, with lower production and lower productive capacity, employment and wage income are likely to fall. In general, if individuals and institutions expect that their revenue, income or wages will decrease while costs from other sectors will remain constant, they will also tend to spend less. Fourthly, workers may also not spend current income as a precaution against job loss and a fall in future income, even if they have not yet or will not lose their job. Finally, individuals and institutions may wait to buy in anticipation of lower future prices.

When deflation unexpectedly occurs and revenues, incomes and wages unexpectedly decrease as well, then expenditure will also tend to decrease. The unexpected decrease in revenues, income and wages may cause borrowers to default on outstanding loans that become too burdensome to pay. A higher default rate hurts banks and other lenders, causing them to lend less at higher interest rates or to go bankrupt. As a result, the total quantity of money and credit will decrease, leading to a decrease in expenditure, production and employment. Furthermore, bankruptcy of banks and other institutions reduces the income and expenditure of their creditors, which reduces expenditure, production and employment further. And after revenues, incomes and wages unexpectedly decrease; people may become pessimistic and *expect* revenues, incomes and wages to decrease, thereby decreasing expenditure for the reasons described in the preceding paragraph.

Thus, when deflation (or even price declines in a few sectors) is associated with a decrease in expenditure (demand), it is associated with a decrease in revenue, income and wages, which can aggravate an economic contraction. And because a 0% inflation rate target can lead to price declines in some sectors or deflation on average and because the cost of a small inflation rate is small (and in fact, maybe beneficial by allowing real costs to adjust to changes in supply and demand when nominal prices/wages do not adjust), central banks are willing to tolerate (and to target) a small rate of inflation.

The role of expectations

We previously discussed how expectations about deflation and inflation can cause changes in economic behavior. In general, changes in expectations can lead to changes in behavior, and in particular changes in the willingness to produce and to sell (supply) and the willingness to spend (demand) to borrow (demand) and to save.

As a result, central banks try to influence what individuals and institutions expect about expenditure, production, inflation, costs of production, profitability and productivity because what we expect about these variables affects our behavior. For example, if individuals and institutions expect a high inflation rate due to monetary policy or due to other factors, they will tend to increase their prices and to ask for more compensation and/or to decrease their willingness to produce and to sell. On the other hand, if individuals and institutions expect a low and stable inflation rate, they will tend not to increase their prices and not to ask for more compensation and/or not to decrease their willingness to produce and to sell.

Central banks are careful about the information that they provide to the public and generally try not to confuse individuals and institutions about the direction of monetary policy so that they do not mistakenly change their behavior, hurting themselves and restricting broader economic activity. In particular, central banks may try to convince individuals and institutions that expenditure, or rather the quantity of money and credit, will grow sufficiently to encourage buyers to buy and producers to produce, to sell and to hire, thereby eliminating cyclical unemployment, but that it will not grow excessively so that high inflation results.

Previously, we discussed how transparency is necessary for a target to be effective. A transparent target is supposedly effective because it affects the expectations of individuals and institutions in a beneficial way, allowing them to take actions that benefit themselves and benefit the broader economy. Central banks have tended to become more transparent and to provide more data to the public for this reason. For example, in 1994, the Federal Reserve System began to announce the target of the federal funds rate to give individuals and institutions a better idea about how to plan for the future, so that uncertainty about prices and production can be lowered. Today most other central banks publicly announce their targets for the same reason. Many central banks also offer their outlook on future economic activity and a projection about their own future monetary policy based on that outlook.

Although monetary policy is supposed to primarily affect expenditure and demand, when central banks try to influence people's expectations, they also try to influence our willingness to produce and to sell by influencing our expectations about the costs of production, profitability and productivity. If we believe that costs of production, profitability and productivity will change as expected, our willingness to produce and sell goods and services (as well as our willingness to buy goods and services) can be more stable and more efficient. Central banks hope that with stable expectations we can continue to produce and to sell as we normally would, and the economy could better achieve its potential. By trying to stabilize (or to increase) our willingness to produce and to sell through transparency and announcements, the central bank can stabilize production (or can increase production to its potential), which tends to stabilize (or to increase) employment, to stabilize (or to decrease) the unemployment rate and to stabilize (or to decrease) the inflation rate. Figure 13-8 represents how expectations about costs of production, profitability and productivity can affect our willingness to produce and sell, which in turn affects production, employment and price setting. Price setting and employment, of course, affect the inflation rate and the unemployment rate.

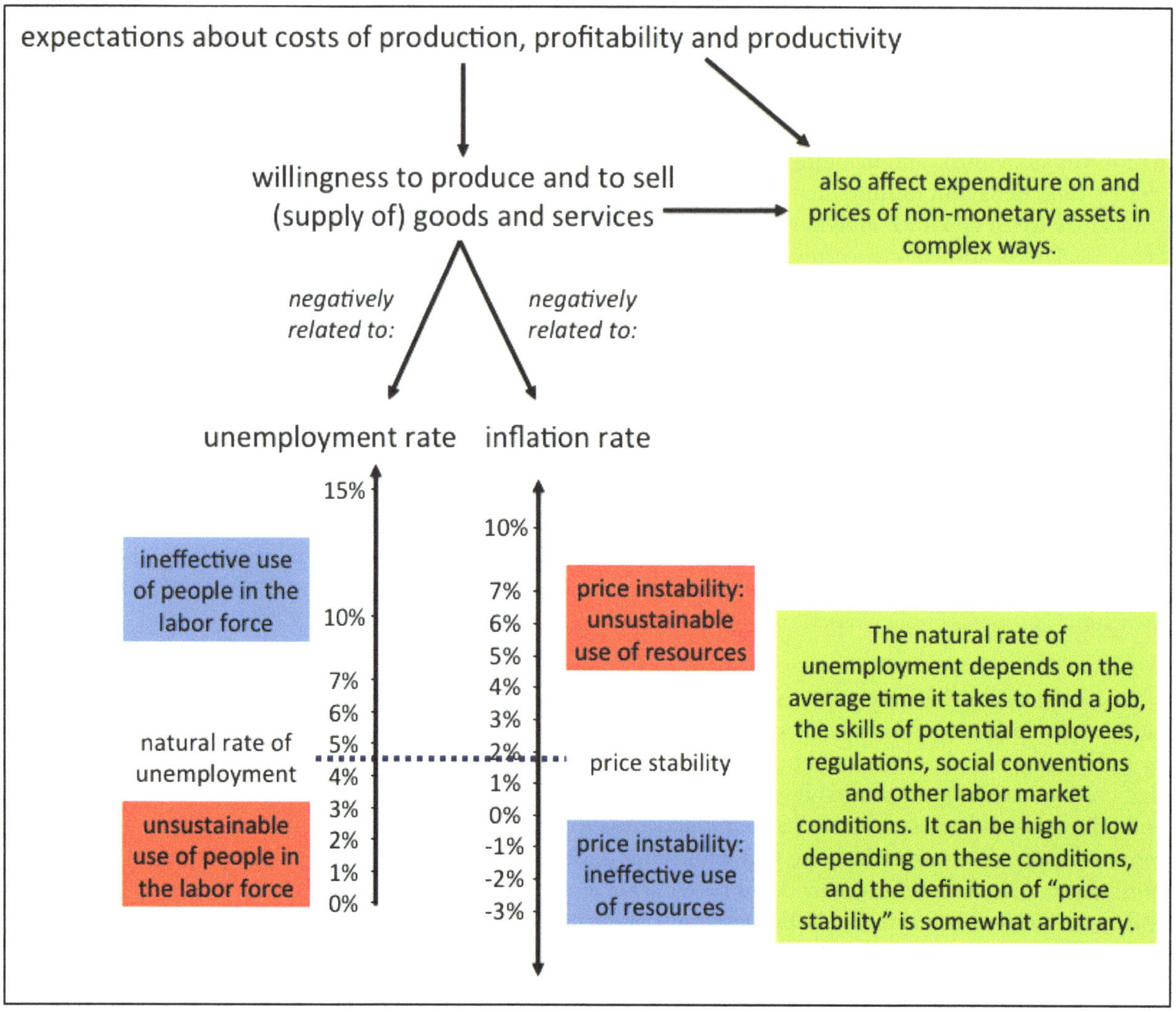

Figure 13-8: The central bank may try to stabilize our willingness to produce and to sell by stabilizing our expectations through transparency and announcements, thereby affecting production, employment, the unemployment rate and the inflation rate.

However, given the inherent uncertainty in trying to manage the economy, central banks may be reluctant to publicly announce changes in a target because such a target might become outdated as economic conditions change. More generally, some economists argue that changes in targets that try to accommodate changes in production, employment and prices will be ineffective and even counter-productive because of the many hard-to-predict factors that can affect production, employment and prices (as I discussed in the section about monetary targets). Also, some economists believe that publicly announcing a target can cause some to try to speculate about changes in asset prices or other economic variables, and can therefore cause volatility in asset prices.

Using transparency and announcements is also difficult task because information can be interpreted in many ways, so the willingness to produce and to sell and the willingness to buy could actually become less stable if information is interpreted incorrectly or if it is interpreted in inconsistent ways. Nonetheless, using secrecy and obfuscation at the central bank would likely cause even less stability in economic behavior and would likely decrease productivity, increase unemployment and increase inflation.

Lagged effects of monetary policy

Central banks also try to affect people's expectations because monetary policy generally has a delayed, or lagged, effect on expenditure, production, employment and prices. Most individuals and institutions do not immediately adjust expenditure, production, employment and prices when monetary policy changes because of institutional or other constraints. In other words, changes in interest rates or the quantity of money today will affect expenditure, production, employment and prices only in the future. Estimates from models of the US economy suggest that changes in monetary policy take over a year to affect production and over two years to have a significant impact on inflation. For countries with frequent and large changes in the money supply, the time lag may be shorter so that inflation is affected sooner, and production is affected less significantly. In any case, to the degree that a lagged effect exists, central banks sometimes try to act pre-emptively to stabilize expenditure, production, employment and prices. For example, the Federal Reserve System tried to act pre-emptively in 2004 by gradually raising its targeted interest rate to reduce expenditure even before the inflation rate began to rise significantly. And acting pre-emptively can influence expectations about expenditure, production, employment and prices, which in turn will influence current expenditure, production, employment and price setting.

Summary

Central banks try to maintain a low and stable inflation rate because by not doing so the economy becomes less efficient and productive, and inequities can result because the costs of inflation are not equally distributed throughout society. Many central banks also try to maintain a low unemployment rate, theoretically described by the natural rate of unemployment. Related to a low and stable inflation rate and the natural rate of unemployment is the theory of potential production. When production grows at its potential rate, resources are supposed to be used effectively (so that they are not wasted or idle) and sustainably (so that prices or the inflation rate do not increase rapidly).

When workers in the labor force can work effectively and sustainably, the unemployment rate is at its natural rate. In this case, there is no upward pressure on prices or the inflation rate, and the only unemployed people are supposed to be those who need more time to find a suitable employer, those who have inadequate skills according to employers and those who are too costly at wages that can not decrease because of rigid regulations or social conventions. To reduce this kind of unemployment, society can try to make the job finding process more efficient, to allow workers to acquire desired skills and to subsidize/reduce the cost of hiring. But monetary policy is not good at reducing this kind of unemployment because it creates inflation and other inefficiencies when central banks try to reduce it. Monetary policy is most effective in reducing the unemployment caused when firms are unwilling to hire workers to produce goods and services because their customers are unwilling to buy goods and services, often because of a lack of money and credit at cheap prices.

To achieve the goals of a low and stable inflation rate, the natural rate of unemployment and the potential growth rate of production; central banks try to adjust, or to target, either monetary values (quantities of money and credit), interest/yield rates (prices of money and credit) or the inflation rate itself. However, because monetary values are not transparent and not easy to measure and to control relative to interest rates, most central banks today target an interest rate instead. Some central banks target an inflation rate instead because they argue that an inflation rate is the most transparent target and can hold a central bank more accountable for conducting sound monetary policy, even though these central banks continue to adjust either a quantity of money or an interest rate to reach this target. On the other hand, an inflation rate is not easily measured and controlled, and some economists argue that inflation rate targeting neglects the goal of low unemployment.

To allow some flexibility in inflation rate targeting, central banks usually set a target range for the inflation rate and do not target a 0% inflation rate, because a 0% inflation rate target can lead to deflation. Deflation is often associated with decreasing revenues, incomes and wages. It can therefore aggravate an economic contraction and precipitate a financial crisis.

Central banks try carefully to influence the expectations of individuals and institutions, because expectations can affect the willingness to produce and to sell, as well as the willingness to buy, both at the present time and in the future. Also, because changes in monetary policy only slowly affect expenditure, production, employment and prices; central banks try to anticipate how individuals and institutions will behave in the future to stabilize expenditure, production, employment and prices.

Problems and Applications

Short answer problems

1. Why is inflation costly for society?

2. Why might deflation be costly for society?

3. What is frictional unemployment? What is structural unemployment? How are they related to the natural rate of unemployment?

4. Explain why central banks face a trade-off in trying to achieve low unemployment on one hand and low and stable inflation on the other hand.

5. Describe how the potential growth rate of production is related to the natural rate of unemployment and price stability.

6. Which kind of target do you think is most transparent? Why?

7. Which kind of target do you think is easiest to measure and to control? Why?

8. How do central banks try to manage the expectations of private institutions and individuals?

Internet applications

1. Go to http://ecos.bok.or.kr/ to find data for the consumer price inflation rate and the unemployment rate. Graph both of these values from the earliest available month to the latest available month. Do you see an inverse relationship between the two values, as predicted by the text? If not, what other factors could affect the inflation rate and the unemployment rate besides monetary policy?

2. Go to http://ecos.bok.or.kr/ to find data for the inflation rate of prices of final domestically produced goods and services (GDP). (See "Deflator" 10.4.3.) Graph the inflation rate from the earliest available quarter to the latest available quarter. Have prices of domestically produced goods ever decreased in Korea? If yes, when did this occur?

3. Go to http://ecos.bok.or.kr/ to find data for the inflation rate of prices of final domestically produced goods and services (GDP). (See "Deflator" 10.4.3.) Calculate the average inflation rate and the standard deviation from the earliest available quarter to the latest available quarter. Do you consider this average inflation rate "low" and suitable for the economy? If not, what would you consider to be a "low" inflation rate that is suitable for the economy? Does the standard deviation indicate a "stable" inflation rate according to your opinion?

4. Go to http://ecos.bok.or.kr/ to find data for the real value of the growth rate of expenditure on domestically produced goods and services (GDP). Calculate the average growth rate from the earliest available quarter to the latest available quarter, and call this average the potential growth rate of production. During which periods was the actual growth rate at least 1 percentage point below average? During which periods was the actual growth rate at least 1 percentage point above average?

5. Collect data from questions 3. and 4. except use annual data instead of quarterly data, from the earliest available year to the latest available year. Graph the inflation rate on the vertical axis from year and the growth rate of expenditure on domestically produced goods and services from each year on the horizontal axis. Do you see a positive relationship between the variables, as the theory illustrated in Figure 13-1 predicts? Do you see a negative relationship between the variables, as the theory illustrated in Figure 13-2 predicts?

6. Go to http://ecos.bok.or.kr/ to find data for the real value of the total value of (expenditure on) domestically produced goods and services (GDP) and the value of expenditure on investment (in goods, real assets and services, not financial assets). Graph the *growth rates* of both values in a single graph from the earliest available quarter to the latest available quarter. Also, calculate the standard deviation of the growth rates. Is investment expenditure more volatile than the total value of expenditure on domestically produced goods and services, indicating periods of "over-" investment and "under-" investment?

7. Do an internet search to find the targeted quantity of money, interest rate and/or inflation rate of your country's central bank at the present time.

14. Exchange Rates and Foreign Exchange

Preview

In this chapter, I discuss characteristics of the foreign exchange market, where traders and dealers exchange foreign currency and other assets for domestic currency, or vice versa. I also discuss characteristics and common observations of the price, cost or value of foreign assets that are exchanged, or exchange rates. Based on these observations, I construct a model using the willingness to buy (demand) and the willingness to sell (supply) foreign exchange that helps us to understand how and why exchange rates can change even though exchange rates are largely unpredictable based on public information.

The foreign exchange market

The foreign exchange market is a set of markets where different currencies and other foreign and domestic assets are exchanged (bought and sold). Recall that a (financial) market is a means by which buyers and sellers of (financial) goods or services conduct a transaction, which could be a location where people meet, a network of telephones, or a network of computers to communicate and to conduct a transaction. The term *foreign exchange* can refer to foreign currencies (a medium of exchange in foreign countries); deposits of foreign currencies (usually short-term, liquid deposits); short-term, liquid bonds denominated in foreign currencies; or even long-term bonds and other assets denominated in foreign currencies. In general, any foreign asset that can be exchanged for a domestic asset can be called foreign exchange.

The foreign exchange market is over-the-counter market, a decentralized network of people, computers and telephones throughout the world, although most trading occurs in major financial cities (where large banks are located) like London, New York, San Francisco, Tokyo, Singapore, Zurich, Hong Kong, Sydney, Paris, Copenhagen and Frankfurt. Figure 14-1 shows transactions in the foreign exchange market by location. Because of London's importance as an international financial center, the UK has the largest fraction of transactions in the foreign exchange market.

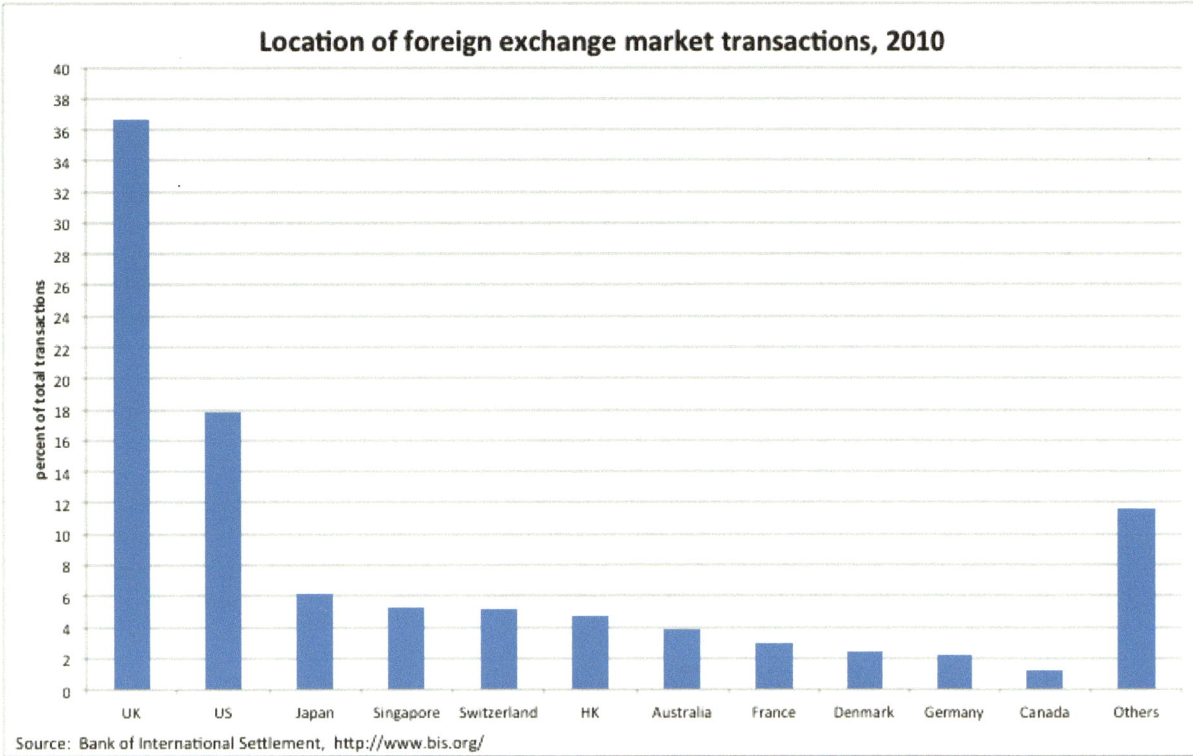

Figure 14-1: Transactions in the foreign exchange market by location

The people who buy and sell in the foreign exchange market include arbitragers, hedgers and speculators. **Arbitragers** are those who try to make a profit by exploiting differences in exchange rates in different locations *today or as soon as transactions can be settled.* (Recall that arbitrage refers to buying at a low price and selling at a high price for a profit.) **Hedgers** are those who try to reduce, or to hedge, exchange rate risk usually with derivative contracts by *promising to buy/sell currencies or other assets in the future but at a price specified today*. **Speculators** speculate that they can make a profit *by buying at a low price and selling at a high price a later date* often with derivative contracts. They often interact with hedgers by buying when the latter wants to sell and selling when the latter wants to buy.

These types of buyers and sellers are dealers or traders. They often work for their customers or work for and with other financial intermediaries.

Other financial intermediaries and other institutions in the foreign exchange market include brokers, who may work for another financial intermediary or may work independently. Also, hedge funds, mutual funds and large commercial firms may buy and sell in the foreign exchange market. Hedge funds often engage in arbitrage or speculate in currency markets with derivative contracts, while commercial firms often want to hedge exchange rate risk with transactions involving foreign customers. Some central banks also buy and sell foreign currencies and other foreign assets on behalf of their governments, and may do so to influence the exchange rate every day or only occasionally.

But the largest transactions and the largest number of transactions occur among commercial banks and investment banks. Commercial banks and investment banks buy and sell for their customers, as well as for themselves in the inter-bank market by speculating and engaging in arbitrage. Many banks reciprocally quote each other's buying and selling prices of foreign exchange to reduce asymmetric information and to facilitate transactions. Figure 14-2 shows that about 39% of transactions occur with dealers, who may work at banks or may work independently, about 48% of transactions occur with other financial intermediaries (such as traders who work at commercial banks or hedge funds) and about 13% of transactions occur with non-financial institutions and individuals.

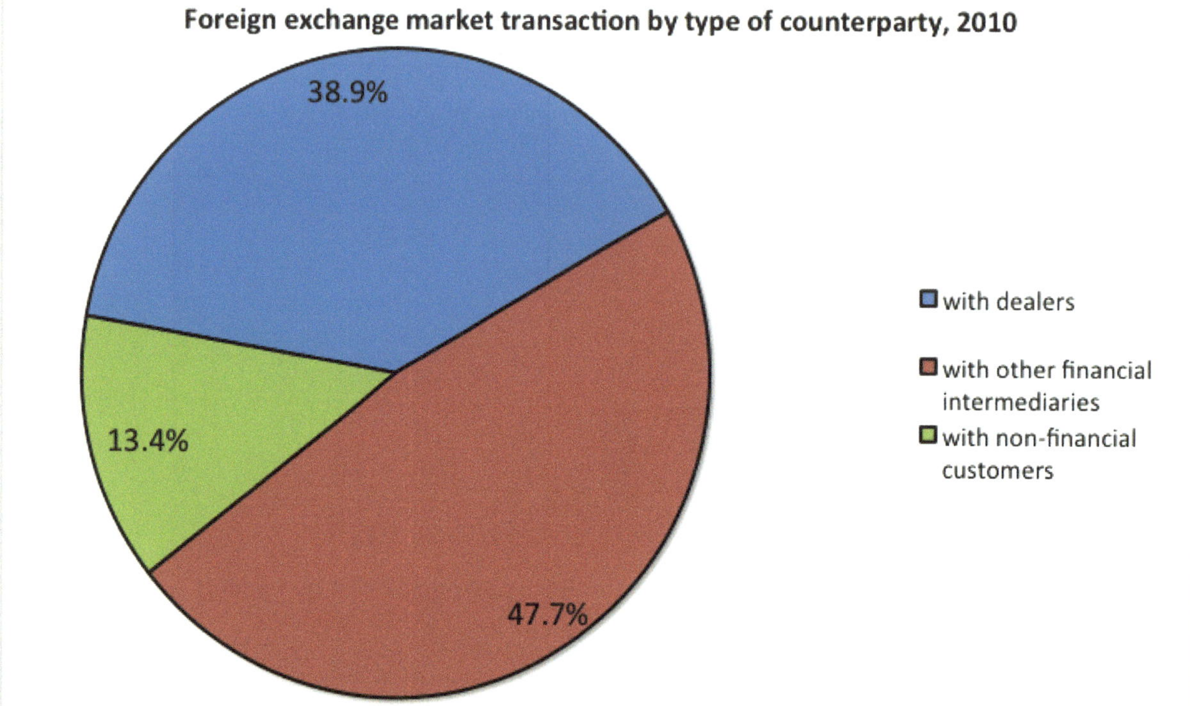

Source: Bank of International Settlement, http://www.bis.org/

Figure 14-2: Transactions in the foreign exchange market by type of counterparty

The *inter-bank* or *wholesale market* involves only large banks that buy and sell large amounts of currency—$1 million or more per transaction. Transactions in the inter-bank market are conducted electronically through the Reuters network or the Electronic Brokering Services. Dealers and traders post buy (bid) and sell (ask or offer) prices through these networks, and when they complete a transaction they make credits or debits to electronic deposits of domestic or foreign currencies. Because major financial cities in the foreign exchange market are located around the world, trading in the inter-bank market occurs 24 hours a day during business days.

The *retail market* involves other institutions and individuals who want to buy or to sell smaller amounts of foreign or domestic currency. But large banks from the wholesale market can also be involved in the retail market, usually by acting as a dealer, trader or broker on behalf of other institutions and individuals.

The average of prices in the inter-bank market can be considered "the market" price or exchange rate, although a range of prices or exchange rates exists. Dealers are free to set prices above or below the average, and do so especially in the retail market, depending on transaction costs. Average or market exchange rates are often freely available from websites of central banks or various private dealers and traders.

The foreign exchange market includes a *spot market*, where transactions are completed at the present time, or as soon as payments can be settled, by using the spot market exchange rate. It also includes a *futures market*, which is where forward (and futures) contracts, foreign exchange swap contracts, currency swap contracts and options contracts are designed so that currencies can be traded in the future by using the forward exchange rate. (We discussed the details of forward contracts, futures contracts, swap contracts and options contractions in chapter 7). In the futures market, buyers and sellers can hedge exchange rate risk and/or speculate. In the spot market, buyers and sellers can engage in arbitrage. Figure 14-3 shows that the average daily volume of transactions in both the spot market and the futures market has grown over time.

Contracts signed/traded in the futures market can hedge or insure exchange rate risk by generating a profit when losses occur elsewhere. For example, a US firm that exports to Europe can lose if the value of the domestic currency appreciates or becomes more expensive, so that its products are more expensive and it sells less to European customers. If this firm agrees to buy US dollars and sell euros at a rate of 0.8€/US$ in 6 months through a forward contract signed today, and if the spot market exchange rate in 6 months is actually 0.9€/US$, then the US$ has appreciated but the firm can profit by buying US$ according to the contract at only 0.8€/US$ and selling them for a profit at 0.9€/US$. This profit of 0.1€/US$ would offset a probable loss in export revenue because European customers could not afford to buy as much of the firm's product. On the other hand, if the spot market exchange rate in 6 months is actually 0.7€/US$, then the US$ has depreciated so that the firm's products are less expensive and it will likely more to European customers. However, the probable increase in export revenue would be offset by a loss from buying US dollars at 0.8€/US$ and selling them for a loss at 0.7€/US$.

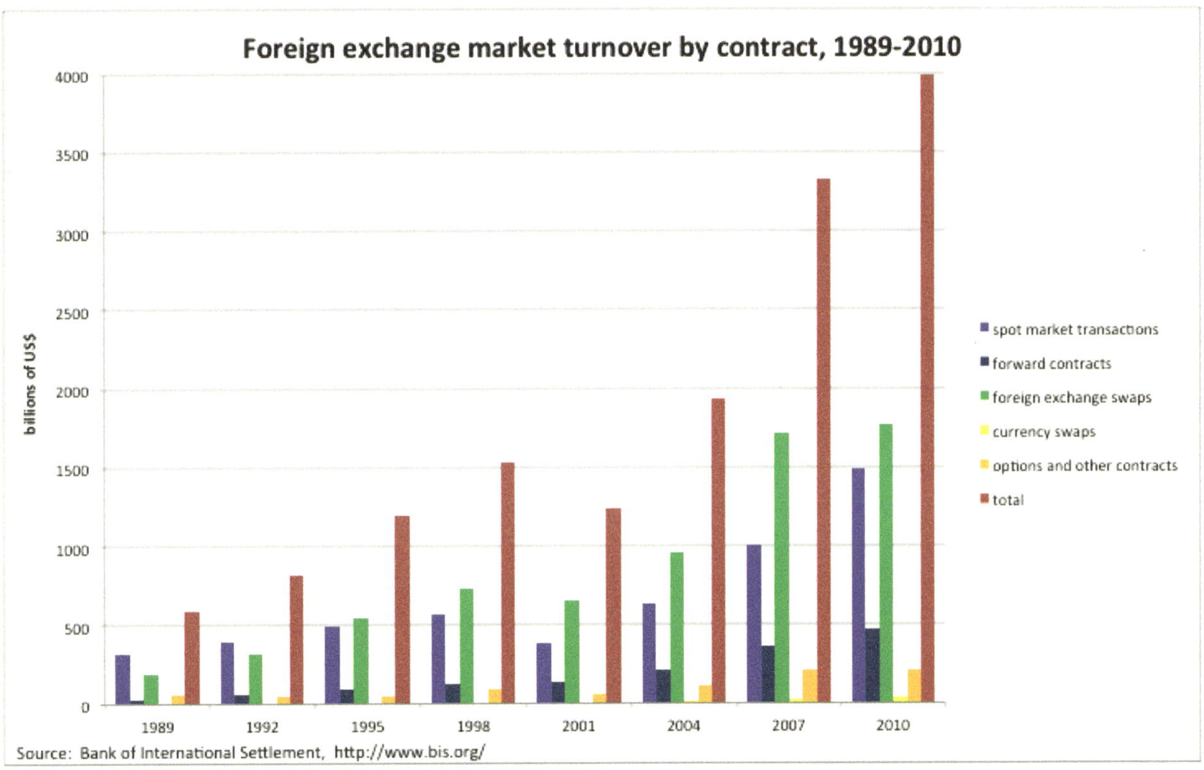

Figure 14-3: Average value of daily transactions in the foreign exchange market by type: spot market transactions and futures market transactions (using forward contracts, foreign exchange swaps, currency swaps or options contracts)

More than 100 currencies are traded in the inter-bank market, but about 85% of transactions involve buying or selling US$, as shown in Figure 14-4 and Figure 14-5. For historical reasons and because the US economy remains so large, the US$ remains the most important single currency in the foreign exchange market. Likewise, because the economic and monetary union of the EU and Japan present large economic blocs, the euro and the yen are also important currencies in the foreign exchange market. About 39% of transactions involve buying or selling the euro, and about 19% of transactions involve buying or selling the yen.

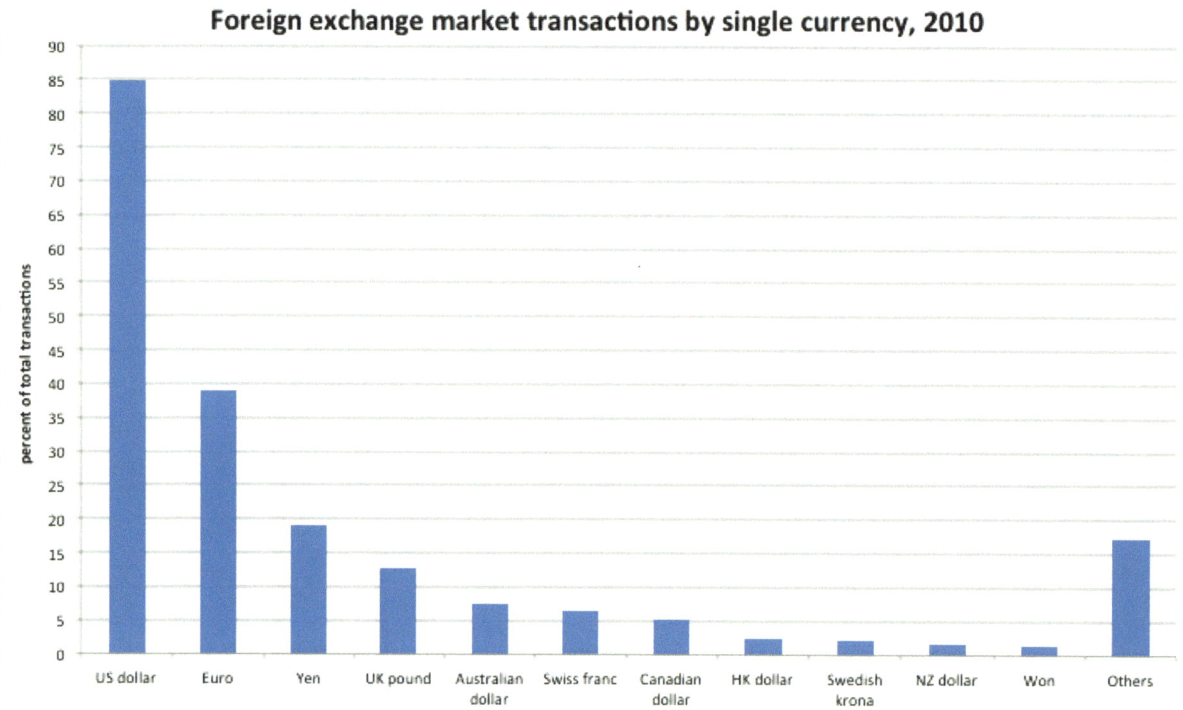

Source: Bank of International Settlement, http://www.bis.org/

Figure 14-4: Transactions in the foreign exchange market by single currency

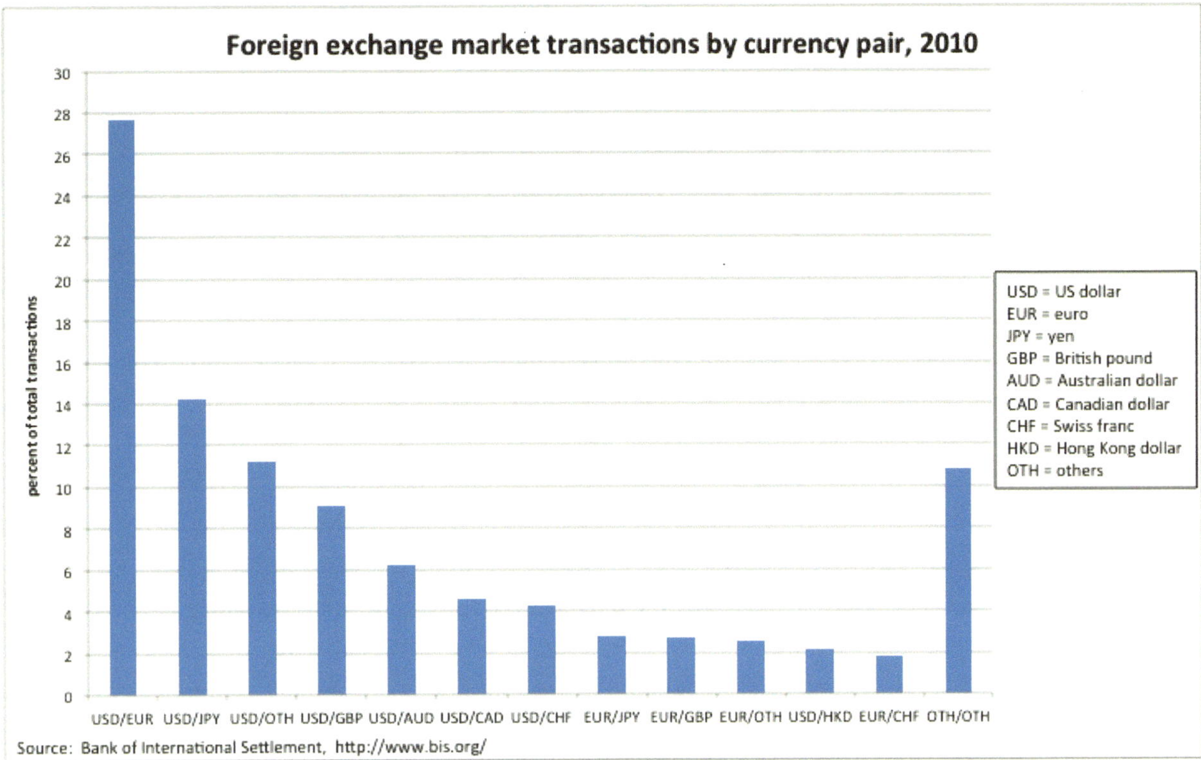

Figure 14-5: Transactions in the foreign exchange market by currency pair

Foreign exchange rates

(Foreign) exchange rates represent the rate of exchange of domestic currency for foreign currency or similar assets. They represent the value, price or cost of foreign currency in terms of domestic currency or vice versa. They are quoted as foreign currency per unit of domestic currency or domestic currency per unit of foreign currency. Figure 14-6 shows the ₩/US$ exchange rate and how it has changed over time. Depending on our perspective, we can treat the US$ as either the domestic currency or the foreign currency.

An **appreciation** of a currency is an increase in its value, price or cost. Each unit of the currency is worth more and costs more in terms of foreign currency. Depending on how we write the exchange rate, appreciation of a currency is represented by a higher or lower exchange rate. A **depreciation** of a currency is a decrease in its value, price or cost. Each unit of the currency is worth less and costs less in terms of foreign currency.

When a currency appreciates or depreciates, some people gain and some people lose depending on their economic position. Let's consider the gains and losses from an appreciating domestic currency. (The gains and losses from a depreciating domestic currency are the converse.) When a domestic currency appreciates:

1. domestic buyers, including tourists in a foreign country, gain because of lower prices of imports. A more valuable domestic currency implies a less costly foreign currency, which means less costly foreign goods and services (denominated in foreign currency). Lower prices of imports contribute to lower consumer inflation.

2. exporters lose because a more costly domestic currency implies more costly domestic goods and services in international markets (exports).
3. import competing firms lose because a less costly foreign currency implies less costly foreign goods and services (imports).
4. However, to the degree that domestic firms *buy* imports, they gain. (see 1.)
5. Domestic holders of foreign assets lose because a more valuable domestic currency implies a less valuable foreign currency, which means less valuable foreign assets in terms of domestic currency.
6. New domestic buyers of foreign assets gain because a more valuable domestic currency implies a less costly foreign currency, which implies less costly foreign assets in terms of domestic currency.

In general, the spot (market) exchange rate can be represented as $S(x/y)$, where y represents one unit of foreign currency and x represents the price (cost) of that unit in terms of domestic currency. Alternatively, $S(y/x)$ represents the quantity of foreign currency y that can be obtained from one unit of domestic currency x. Spot exchange rates are for transactions within 2 days, the normal amount of time to settle payments between banks.

Forward exchange rates, denoted $F(x/y)$, are exchange rates for currency exchanges that will occur at a future ("forward") date—typically 30, 90, 180, or 360 days in the future. Forward exchange rates are negotiated and known in the present, but the exchange occurs in the future.

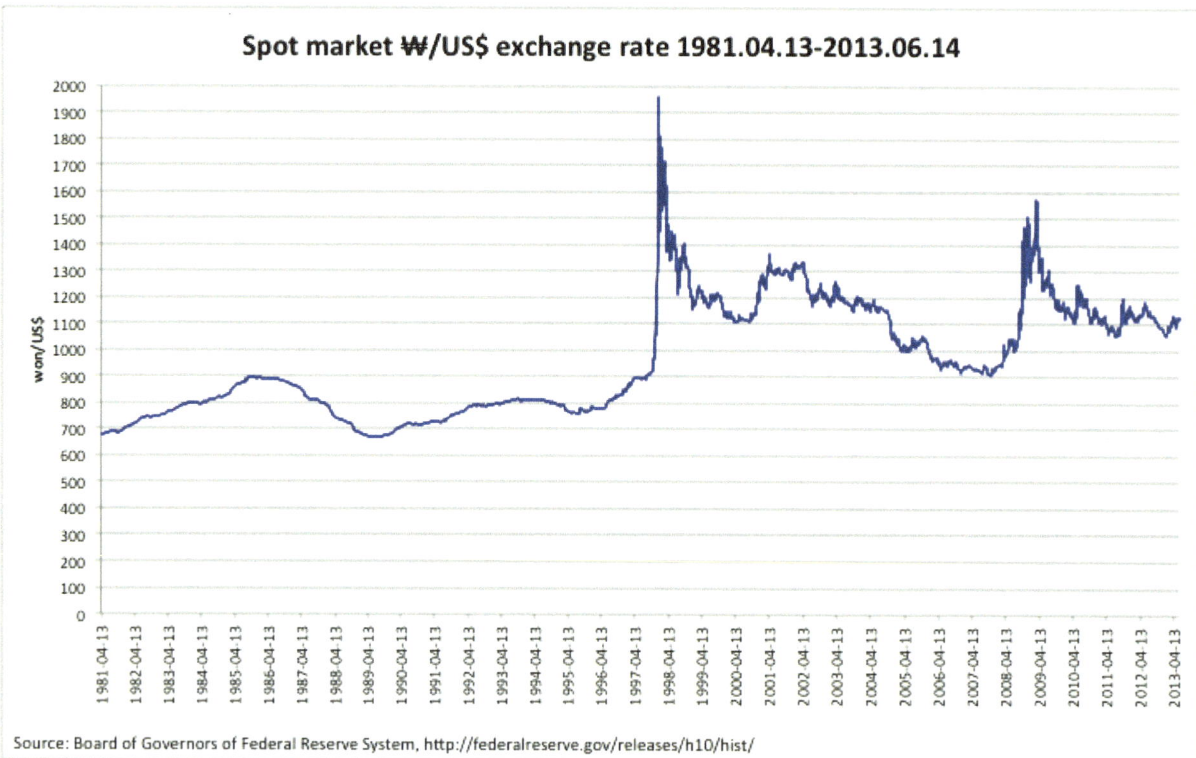

Figure 14-6: The spot market ₩/US$ exchange rate, 1981-2013

In the past generation, computer and telecommunications equipment have been able to transmit information more rapidly and have thus integrated the buyers and sellers in the foreign exchange market. The integration of markets reduces arbitrage opportunities between markets, because if a slight difference in price between locations begins to occur, then dealers and traders can rapidly buy a currency at a low price and sell it for a high price to earn an easy profit. This buying and selling would also rapidly increase the low price and rapidly decrease the high price until the prices in the two locations merge to one price.

But even though rapid communication can eliminate profitable (arbitrage) opportunities quickly, transactions take time and other resources, and banks must earn enough profit to pay their workers. An **exchange rate spread** or **margin** is the difference between the buying price (exchange rate), or **bid price**, and selling price (exchange rate), or **ask/offer price**, of a currency. Figure 14-7 represents an exchange rate spread or margin in which the dealer buys or sells foreign currency (US$) and its customer buys or sells domestic currency (₩). The figure shows that when the dealer buys US$, its customers buys ₩; when the dealer sells US$, its customer sells ₩.

Of course, to make a profit a dealer or trader will want to set a low bid price and a high ask price. And its customers must be willing to pay for this price difference. But competition will tend to keep this margin small; that is, market transactions in which many buyers and sellers exists will tend to have small margins because otherwise dealers or traders will lose customers. For transactions with little competition, low volumes and/or high risk, the margin will tend to be higher to compensate for the higher transaction costs/risks.

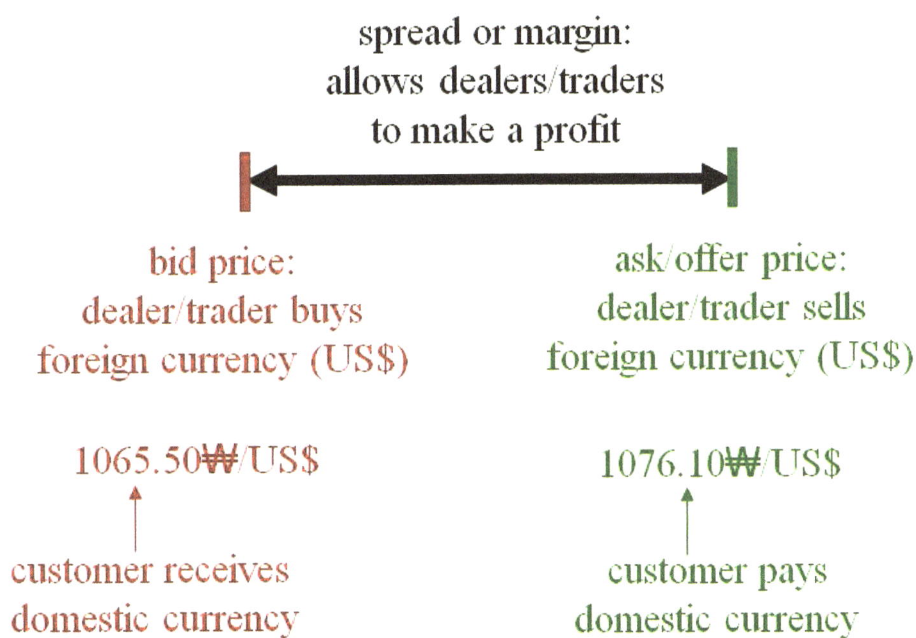

Figure 14-7: An exchange rate spread or margin allows a dealer to buy at a low price and sell at a high price for a profit.

The **forward spread** or **forward margin** is the (annualized percent) difference between the forward exchange rate and the spot exchange rate:

$$\frac{F(x/y)-S(x/y)}{S(x/y)} \times \frac{360}{\text{days until currency is exchanged}}$$

A **forward premium** occurs when the forward exchange rate is greater than the spot exchange rate. More specifically, a forward premium means that $F(x/y) > S(x/y)$ and that currency y is selling at a premium (is expected to appreciate) and currency x is selling at a discount (is expected to depreciate). A **forward discount** occurs when the forward exchange rate is less than the spot exchange rate. More specifically, a forward discount means that $F(x/y) < S(x/y)$ and that currency y is selling at a discount (is expected to depreciate) and currency x is selling at a premium (is expected to appreciate).

When dealers or traders (at banks) deal with large amounts of foreign exchange to buy or to sell, foreign exchange rates are usually quoted with 5 or 6 significant figures. For example, the ₩/US$ exchange rate is quoted as 1065.50 ₩/US$: with 6 significant figures. A **(basis) point** in foreign exchange markets usually equals 1/100 of the smallest currency value in circulation.

For example, a point equals 1/100 of 1 cent and 1/100 of 1 ₩. Thus, exchange rates are often quoted to 1 basis point of accuracy.

Real exchange rates

(Currency) exchange rates in the foreign exchange market are *monetary* or *nominal* exchange rates: they tell us the rate of exchange between domestic currency and foreign currency. However, we might also be interested in the purchasing power of those currencies and the amount of *real* goods and services that those currencies can buy. **Real exchange rates** are price-adjusted exchange rates: they tell us the rate of exchange between real domestic products and real foreign products.

To calculate real exchange rates, let P_x = domestic prices of goods and services produced in the domestic economy, on average, as measured by a price index. And let P_y = foreign prices of goods and services produced in the foreign economy, on average, also as measured by a price index. Alternatively, when prices are measured in monetary units, we must use the same units when we compare prices across countries. For example, we can convert the foreign prices into domestic currency by using the nominal exchange rate: $P_y \times S(x/y)$. If P_y is measured in euros and $S(x/y)$ represents the US$/€ exchange rate, €/units of European products x US$/€ = US$/units of European products.

Thus, real exchange rates compare the price, value and cost of domestic *products* relative to the price, value and cost of foreign *products* when using the same currency units and represent the price-adjusted nominal exchange rate.

The price-adjusted exchange rate for currencies x and y is written as:

$$q(x/y) = \frac{P_y}{P_x} \times S(x/y) \qquad (21)$$

The relative value, price and cost of products is represented as a *quantity* of domestic products that can be exchanged for a *quantity* of foreign products using market prices and (spot) market exchange rates. Because prices represent currency/units of products, we represent the relative quantities of products that are exchanged between the domestic and foreign countries as:

$$q\left(\frac{units\ of\ domestic\ products}{units\ of\ foreign\ products}\right)=\frac{P_y}{P_x}\times S(x/y)$$

(22)

Note that the mathematical formulae of (21) and (22) are equal except for the units. In (21) the units and the interpretation refer to currency units, and prices are measured as indexes. In (22) the units and the interpretation refer to quantities (or units) of products, and prices are measured as currencies/units of products.

Trade-weighted exchange rate index

A trade-weighted exchange rate index represents a weighted average of exchange rates for the currencies of trading partners, with the weights representing relative amounts of trade. In other words, the trade-weighted exchange rate reflects the distribution of trade when averaging bilateral exchange rates. Because bilateral exchange rates are measured in different currencies, we must calculate an index to remove the currency units of each exchange rate in order to average multiple bilateral exchange rates.

For currency x and the currencies of major trading partners (i =1,2,...m), the trade-weighted exchange rate index from time 0 to time t is represented as

$$E_{x,t}=\sum_{i=1}^{m}w_i\frac{S(x/i)_t}{S(x/i)_0}$$

we use a ratio to eliminate currency units in the numerator and denominator

where w_i represents the weight for each trading partner. Weights usually equal the values of both exports (EX_i) and imports (IM_i) with major trading partners relative to the total value of trade:

$$w_i=\frac{EX_i+IM_i}{\sum_{i=1}^{m}EX_i+IM_i}$$

To make the calculations easier, we often use only the "major" trading partners to calculate the index. For example, we often consider only countries with at least 5% or more of total trade and exclude those with only a tiny fraction of total trade. We may also use only the value of exports or only the value of imports in calculating the weights if we are especially concerned about export markets or import markets.

Instead of the arithmetic average used above, we may also use a geometric average if mathematically desired, for example, when exchange rates change exponentially:

$$E_{x,t} = \prod_{i=1}^{m}\left(\frac{S(x/i)_t}{S(x/i)_0}\right)^{w_i}$$

$$= \left(\frac{S(x/1)_t}{S(x/1)_0}\right)^{w_1} \times \left(\frac{S(x/2)_t}{S(x/2)_0}\right)^{w_2} \cdots \left(\frac{S(x/m)_t}{S(x/m)_0}\right)^{w_m}$$

We can also calculate a real (price-adjusted) trade-weighted exchange rate index:

$$Q_{x,t} = \sum_{i=1}^{m} w_i \frac{S(x/i)_t}{S(x/i)_0} \times \frac{\overbrace{P_{i,t}/P_{x,t}}^{\text{foreign prices relative to domestic prices at time } t}}{\underbrace{P_{i,0}/P_{x,0}}_{\text{foreign prices relative to domestic prices at time } 0}}$$

where $P_{i,t}$ represents the prices of goods and services denominated in currency i at time t, $P_{x,t}$ represents the prices of goods and services denominated in currency x at time t, and so on.

In practice, $P_{i,t}$, $P_{x,t}$, $P_{i,0}$ and $P_{x,0}$ are represented by a consumer price index, which measures the prices that the typical consumer pays (some of which are imported); a wholesale price index, which measures the prices that retailers pay to buy intermediate/wholesale products (some of which are imported); the price index (deflator) from the value of gross domestic production (GDP), which measures the prices of all final (retail) goods and services produced and sold in the domestic economy (some of which are exported); or another index.

A rise in $Q_{x,t}$ can result from an appreciation of currency i (and a depreciation of currency x) and/or an increase in the prices of goods and services denominated in currency i relative to the prices of goods and services denominated in currency x.

$$Q_{x,t} = \sum_{i=1}^{m} w_i \frac{S(x/\overset{\uparrow}{i})_t}{S(x/i)_0} \times \frac{\overset{\uparrow}{P}_{i,t}/P_{x,t}}{P_{i,0}/P_{x,0}}$$

Therefore, a rise in $Q_{x,t}$ implies that goods and services denominated in currency i have become more valuable, expensive and/or costly in international markets. In other words, a rise in $Q_{x,t}$ implies that 1) those who use currency i have acquired more purchasing power in international markets (that is, can purchase more goods and services from the country that issues currency x), or 2) those who sell goods and services denominated in currency i have become less "competitive" in the sense that their goods and services have become more expensive relative to the goods and services denominated in currency x, or both 1) and 2).

Common observations of exchange rates

From the perspective of a single dealer or trader among thousands or millions of dealers and traders, exchange rates appear to be unpredictable (and uncontrollable), given publicly available information. In other words, when one tries to predict future exchange rates, they are as likely to be higher as lower than today's exchange rate. In statistics, a **random walk** is a random series of changes or events over time, making the series unpredictable at each point in time. From the perspective of an individual currency trader or dealer with only publicly available information to predict exchange rates, exchange rates over time can appear to be a random walk. After 1997 when the central bank of Korea stopped trying to fully manage the ₩ /US$ exchange rate, Figure 14-6 shows that the exchange rate appears to change somewhat randomly at any point in time.

A second observation about exchange rates is that the spot and forward exchange rate tend to move together, randomly, by the same magnitude and in the same direction over time. This implies that the forward exchange rate is no better than today's spot exchange rate for predicting future exchange rates, even though the forward exchange rate is used for many future transactions. Also, forward exchange rates with different future dates and the values of corresponding forward/futures contracts with different maturity dates also tend to move together by the same magnitude and in the same direction. Buyers and sellers of forward/futures contracts seem to treat "the future" as a uniform concept, rather than distinguishing among different future/maturity dates: 3 months in the future, 6 months in the future, 12 months in the future and other future times. Figure 14-8 shows how forward exchange rates on futures contracts of various maturities relate to the spot market exchange rate (with a maturity date in the present) for the ¥/US$. Each of the values tracks the other values very closely.

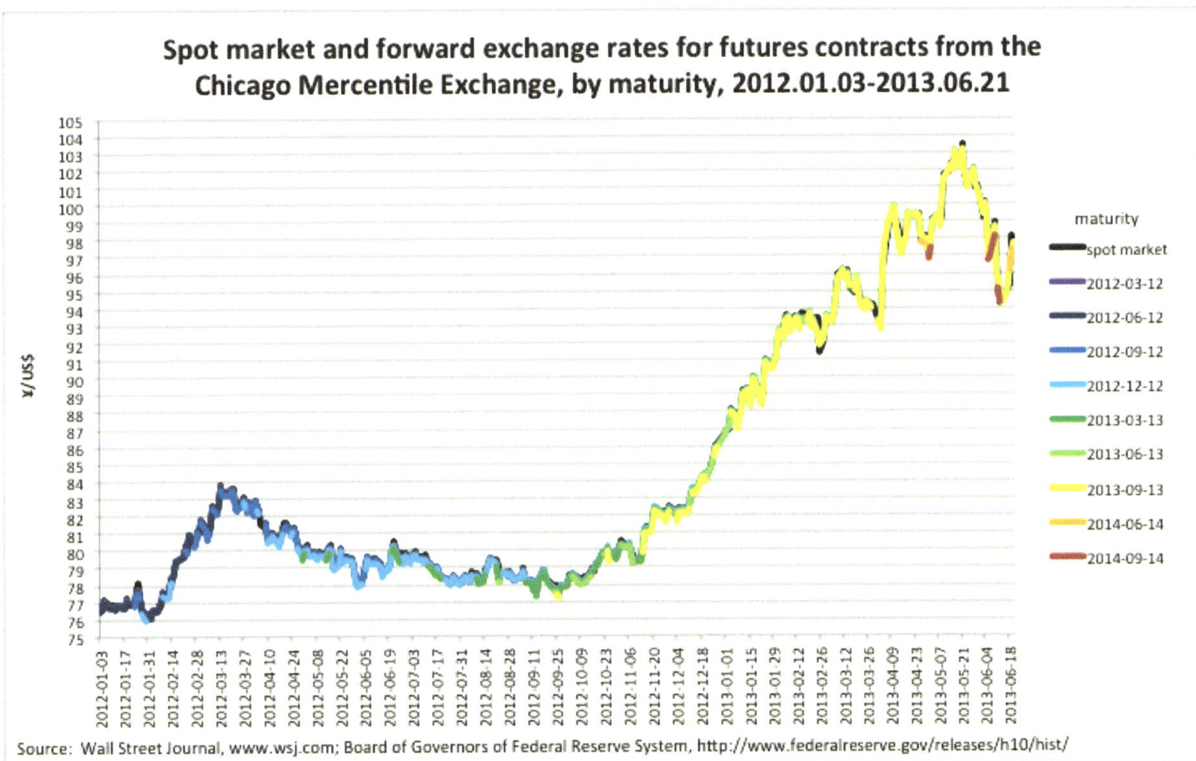

Figure 14-8: Spot market and forward exchange rates for the ¥/US$

Thirdly, volatility or variability in exchange rates tend to be correlated over time. In other words, periods of low volatility tend to occur, and then periods of high volatility tend to occur, rather than having small and large changes occur with the same frequency or probability. Figure 14-9 shows periods of both low volatility and high volatility in the ₩/US$ spot market. However, at any point in time, there is no reference for "low" or "high" volatility except for past values. Similarly, it is unclear when a period of "low volatility" will end or begin and when a period of "high volatility" will begin and end, even when using the past as a guide.

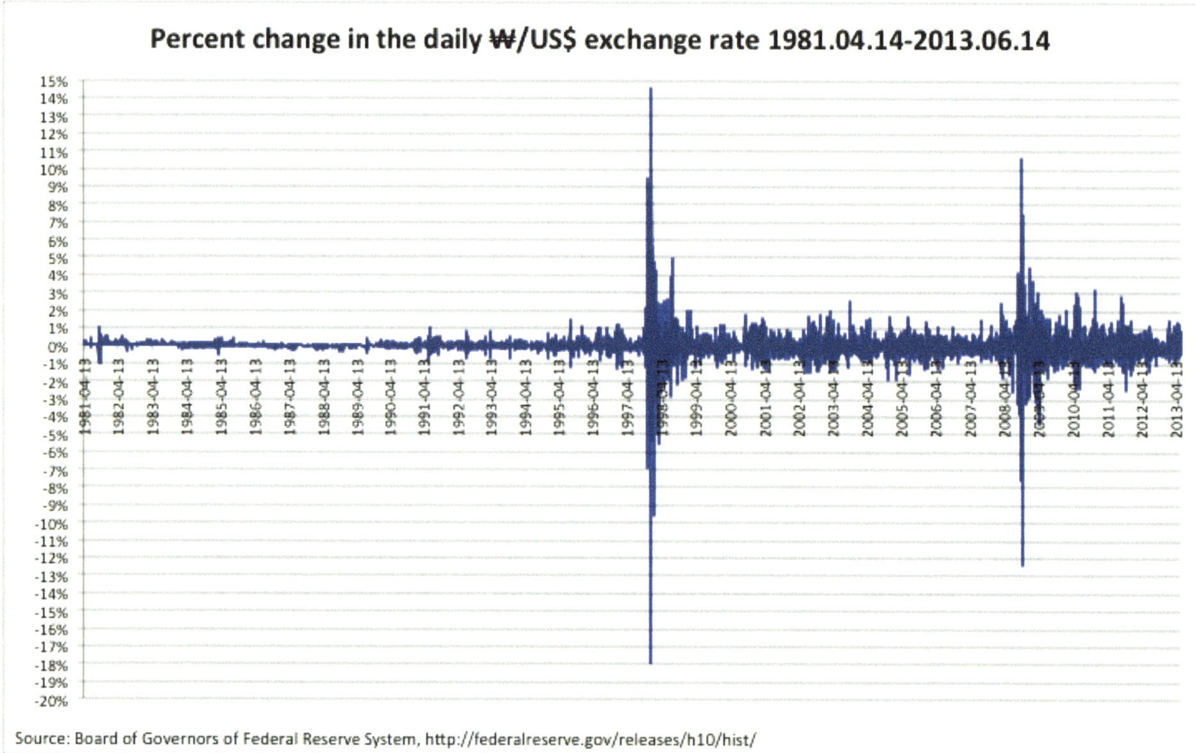

Figure 14-9: Percent changes in the daily ₩/US$ exchange rate, 1981.04.14-2013.06.14

Fourthly, on rare occasions, exchange rates change by huge amounts—due to a devaluation, a financial crisis, government intervention or another unusual event. Figure 14-9 shows large changes in the ₩/US$ spot market in 1997-1998 and in 2008-2009 due to a financial crisis or a perceived financial crisis. The value of the won was effectively devalued in late 1997 after the central bank stopped trying to maintain the value due to the effects of the financial crisis.

Fifthly, an old theory called *purchasing power parity* predicts that prices of goods and services are correlated to exchange rates.[50] This theory claims that the rate of exchange for domestic goods and services relative to foreign goods and services—the real exchange rate—equals one-to-one. Using equation (21), we see that

[50] Purchasing power parity was developed in a time when most foreign exchange was needed to purchase foreign goods, so the prices of those foreign goods relative to prices of domestic goods was viewed as the primary factor influencing the value of foreign exchange or exchange rates. However, in modern economies trade in financial assets can be a more important factor that influences the value and quantity of foreign exchange, especially as credit and capital are able to move quickly and in large quantities from country to country.

$$1 = \frac{P_y}{P_x} \times S(x/y)$$

$$S(x/y) = \frac{P_x}{P_y}$$

$$\%\Delta S(x/y) \approx \%\Delta P_x - \%\Delta P_y$$

In words, the percent change in the (spot market) exchange rate is approximately equal to the inflation rate of the prices of goods and services in the domestic country minus the inflation rate of the prices of goods and services in the foreign country.

When inflation rates vary widely across countries and across time, the purchasing power parity can predict exchange rates relatively well, but largely because of a few extreme cases of high inflation and rapid depreciation. Figure 14-10 shows data from 1971-2012, during which a few countries had extremely high inflation rates and depreciation rates. It was these cases that dominate the analysis. Most countries had values clustered around the origin, even though we can still see a positive relationship in these cases.

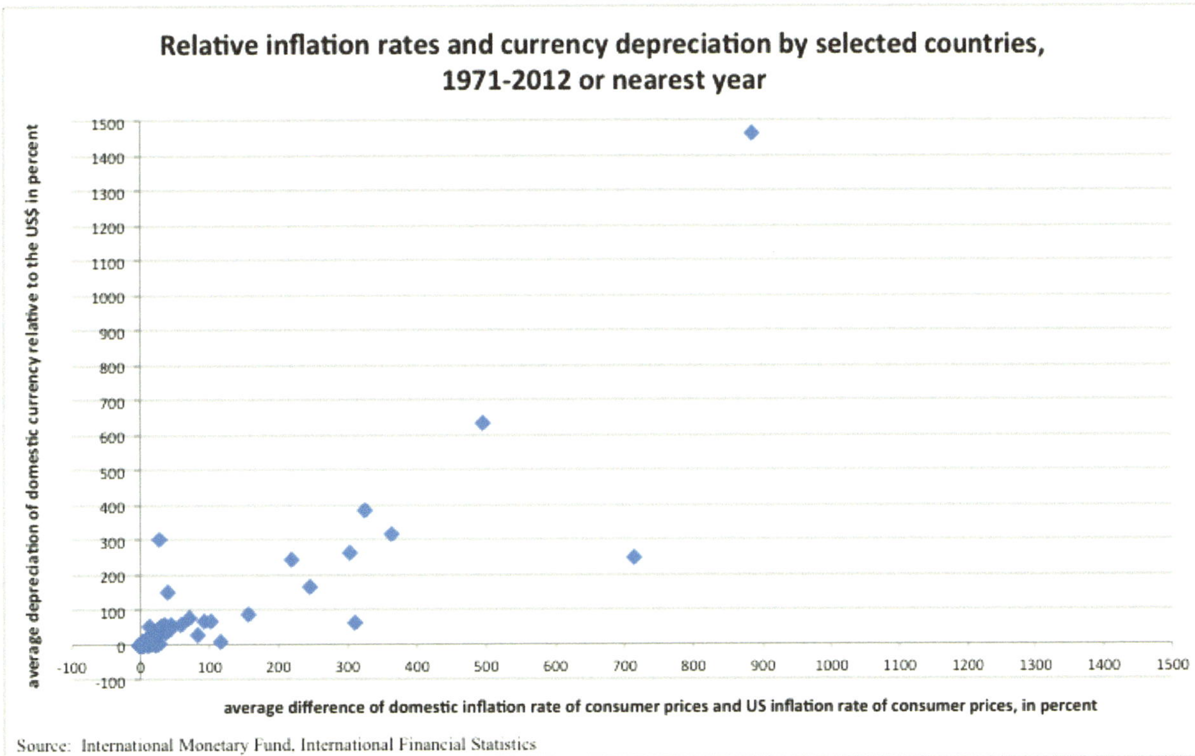

Figure 14-10: Average differences in inflation rates are correlated with average changes in exchange rates when inflation rates vary widely across countries and across time.

When differences in inflation rates are small across countries and when time periods are shorter, the relationship looks less direct. In these cases, other factors like interest, yield and return rates and risk of non-monetary assets might become more important. Figure 14-11 shows the correlation between relative inflation rates and depreciation for countries with modest values for both, 10% or less. Figure 14-12 shows that this correlation for a short time period (1995-2012) for countries with values less than or equal to 10%. A positive relationship between the two variables is still apparent during this short time period, but less so than for longer time periods or for more extreme cases.

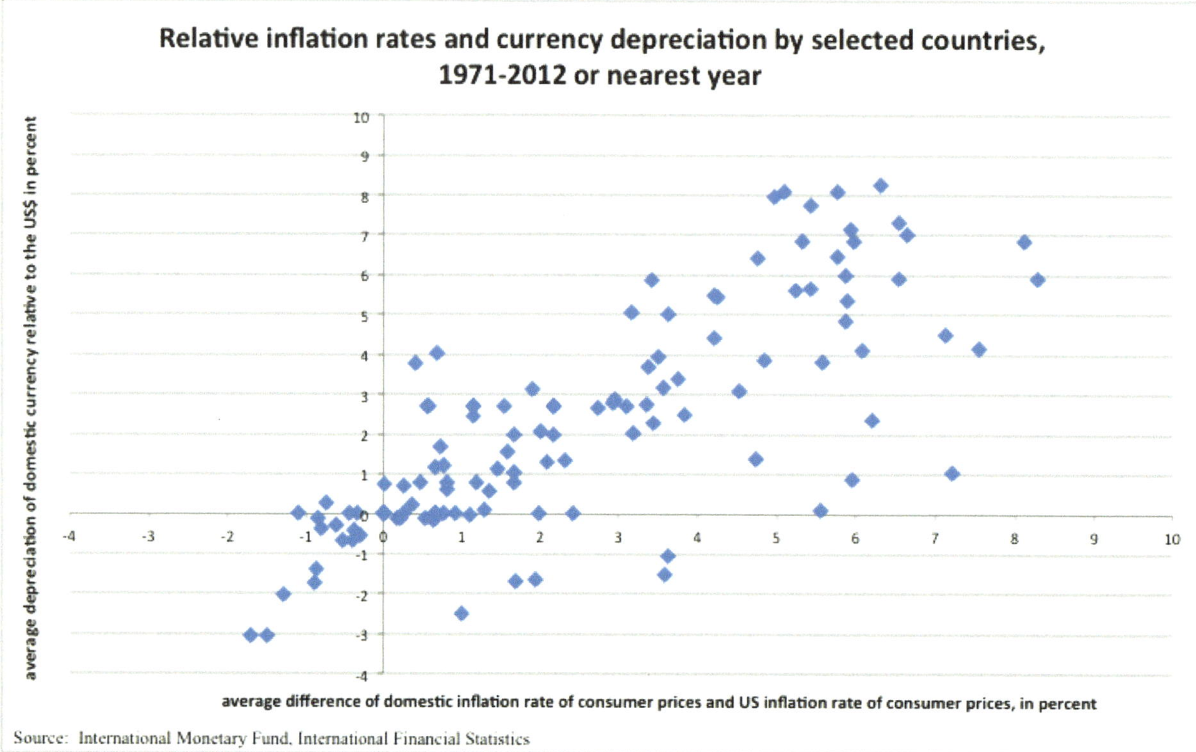

Figure 14-11: Correlation between average differences in inflation rates and average changes in exchange rates when values are modest, at 10% or less.

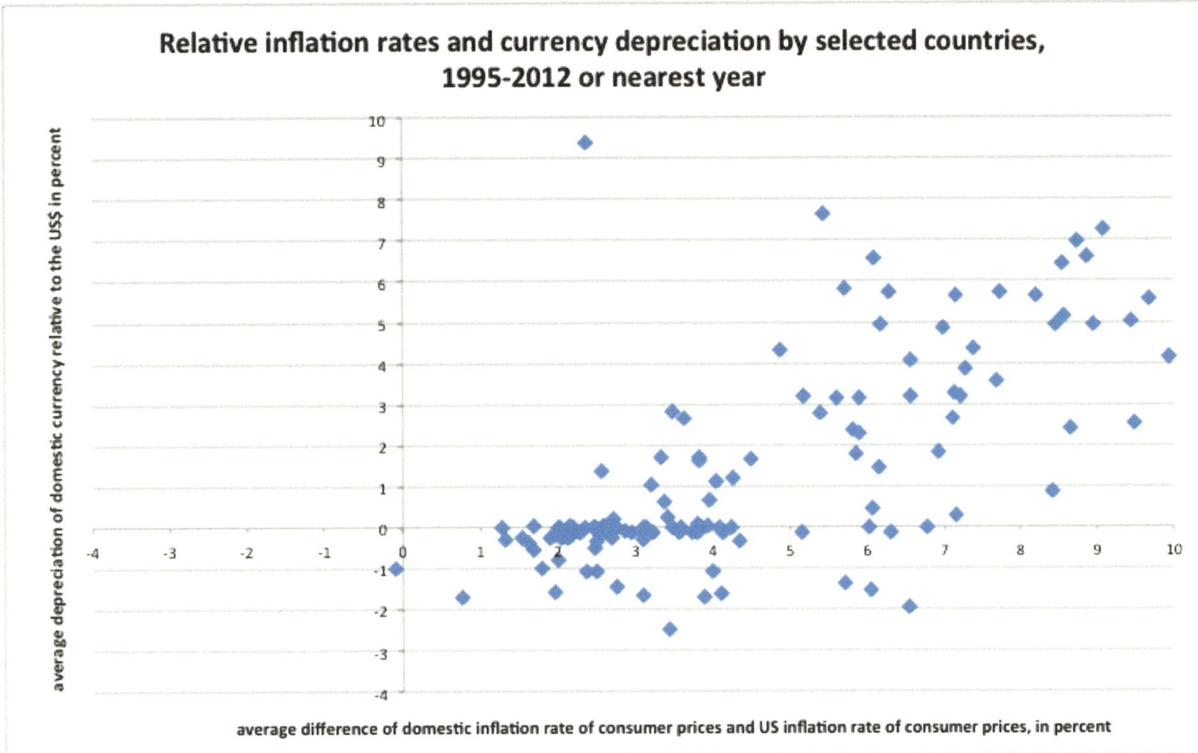

Figure 14-12: Correlation between average differences inflation rates and average changes in exchange rates is less direct when time periods are short.

Instead of considering average values over time and across countries, we can see how well purchasing power parity explains annual (or even quarterly and monthly) values from two countries over a long period of time. When (relative) prices change substantially after several decades, the (relative) value of the currency is supposed to adjust accordingly, at least for countries that trade a large amount with each other. Figure 14-13 shows that consumer prices in Japan have risen less rapidly in Japan relative to consumer prices in the US since about 1978. And since about 1971, the value of the yen relative to the US$ has generally increased, although the trend has not been steady and has not always been in conjunction with the change in relative prices of goods and services.

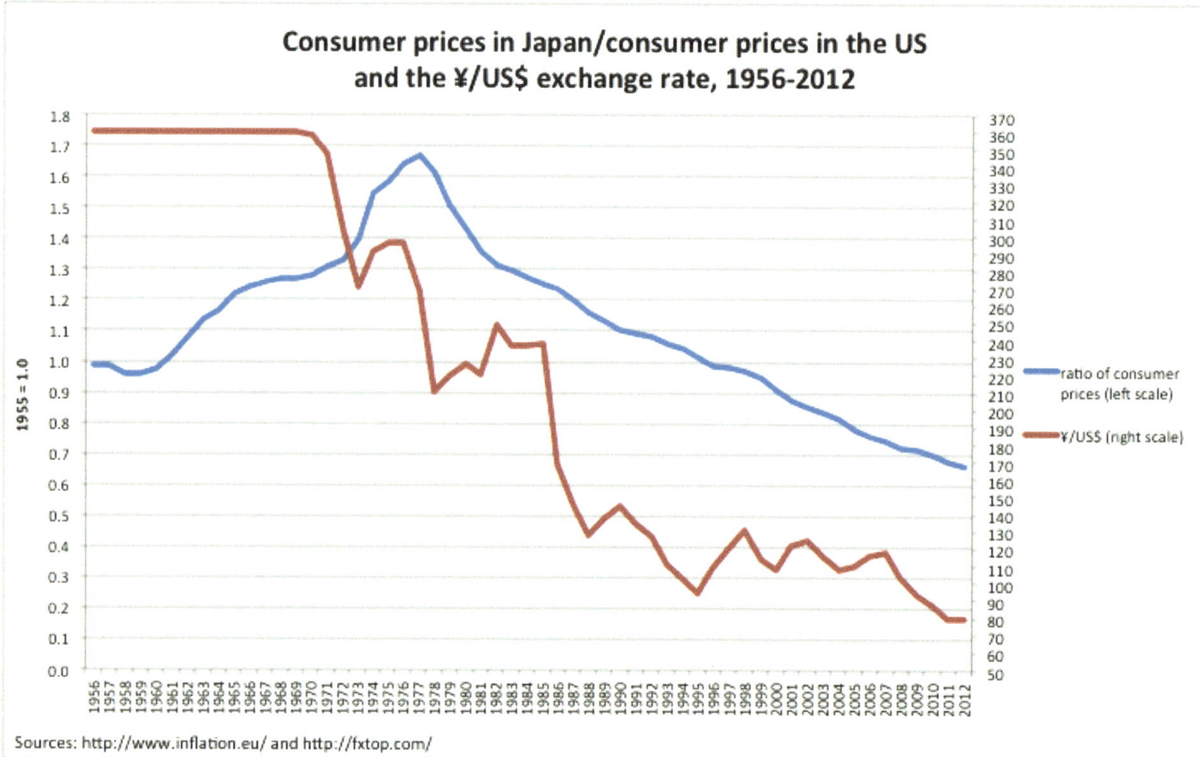

Figure 14-13: Relative consumer prices in Japan and the US and the ¥/US$ exchange rate from 1956-2012

In sum, although exchange rates are largely unpredictable from the view of an individual trader or dealer in the short run when volatility can be especially large, some factors like changes in prices can influence exchange rates over time or once they become publicly known. The next section discusses how changes in prices and other these factors like interest, yield and return rates on assets should affect exchange rates through a formal model.

A model of the foreign exchange market: demand and supply

Before we consider factors that affect exchange rates, we formally represent the foreign exchange market by comparing the willingness to buy foreign exchange at a given price or rate, called the **demand of foreign exchange**, with the willingness to sell foreign exchange at a given price or rate, called the **supply of foreign exchange**. The willingness to buy relative to the willingness to sell is predicted to determine the price or rate at which the foreign exchange is bought and sold. And in particular, if the willingness to buy does not equal the willingness to sell, the price of foreign exchange (the exchange rate) is predicted to change in logical ways.

Even though both foreign citizens and domestic citizens can sell and buy foreign exchange, it is useful to think of sellers of foreign exchange as foreign citizens and buyers of foreign exchange as domestic citizens.

According to the model, the willingness to buy foreign exchange occurs because domestic citizens are willing to buy foreign assets, goods and services. The foreign assets could be short-term, liquid assets including currency or long-term, illiquid assets like long term bonds or direct investments like firms and structures. Alternatively, I write:

demand of foreign exchange = *f*(imports + outflows of funds to buy foreign assets)

As the price, value or cost of foreign exchange increases, domestic citizens are predicted to be less willing to buy foreign assets, goods and services when other factors like expected future exchange rates are constant. Formally, we say that the quantity of foreign exchange that individuals and institutions are willing to buy (the quantity demanded) decreases as the price of foreign exchange increases when other factors remain constant. We represent this formal relationship with a demand function in Figure 14-14.

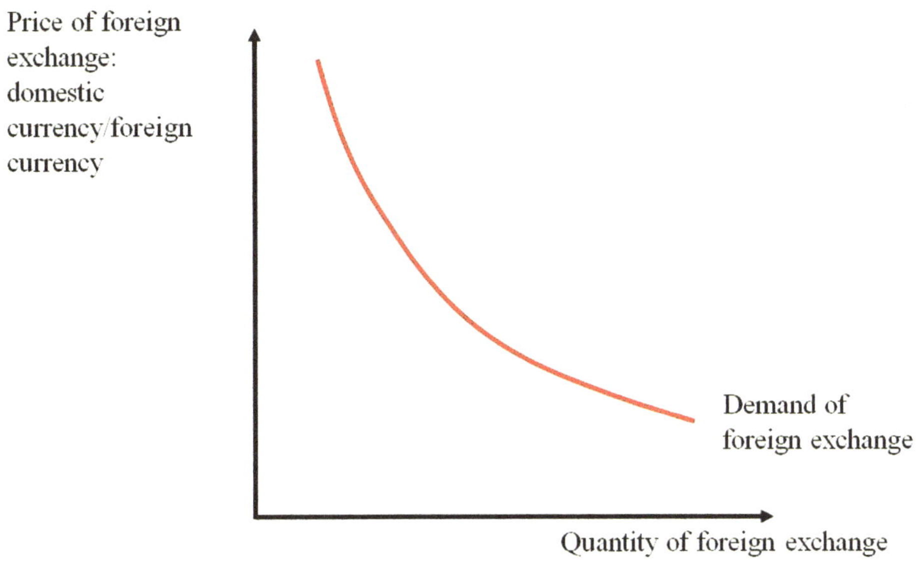

Figure 14-14: A demand function for foreign exchange representing the willing to buy quantities of foreign exchange as a function of the price, cost or value of foreign exchange

According to the model, the willingness to sell foreign exchange occurs because foreign citizens are willing to buy domestic (short-term and long-term) assets, goods and services:

supply of foreign exchange = *f*(exports + inflows of funds to buy domestic assets)

As the price, value or cost of foreign exchange increases, foreign citizens are predicted to be more willing to buy domestic assets, goods and services when other factors like expected future exchange rates are constant. Formally, we say that the quantity of foreign exchange that individuals and institutions are willing to sell (the quantity supplied) increases as the price of foreign exchange increases when other factors remain constant. We represent this formal relationship with a supply function in Figure 14-15.

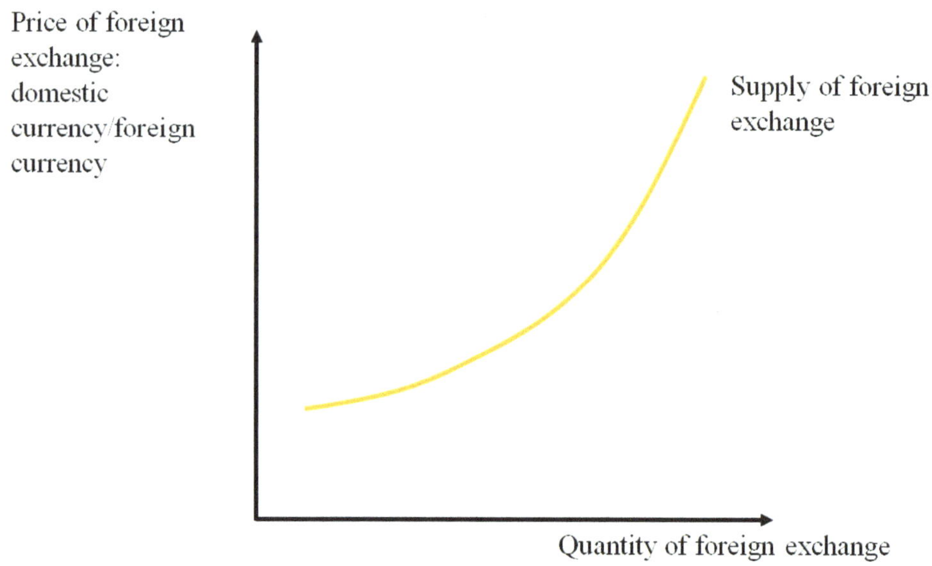

Figure 14-15: A supply function for foreign exchange representing the willingness to sell quantities of foreign exchange as a function of the price, cost or value of foreign exchange

According to the model, net exports (exports – imports) and net funds outflow (funds from domestic residents to buy foreign assets – funds from foreigners to buy domestic assets) determine the demand and supply of foreign exchange, which in turn determine the exchange rate, as well as the quantity of foreign currency exchanged for domestic currency. But in reality, exchange rates can also determine net exports and net funds outflow. For example, a more expensive domestic currency decreases net exports as well as decreases net funds outflow. Thus, causation can occur in both directions, as represented in Figure 14-16.

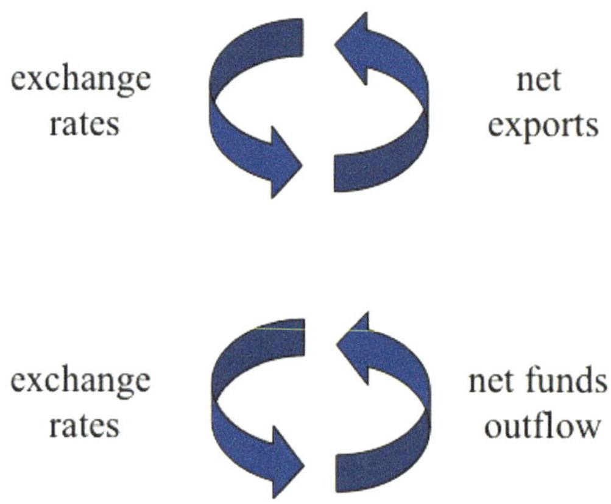

Figure 14-16: Net exports and net funds outflow can affect exchange rates. Exchange rates can affect net exports and net funds outflow.

The model first shows that net exports and net funds outflow determine supply and demand, which determine exchange rates. However, the model also allows for changes in exchange rates to cause changes in the quantity of net exports and the quantity of net funds outflow, or formally, the quantity demanded and quantity supplied.

When there is a difference between the willingness to buy (quantity demanded) and the willingness to sell (quantity supplied), the price, cost or value of foreign exchange is predicted to adjust in ways that seem reasonable. In particular, if the quantity of foreign exchange that dealers and other buyers want to buy is less than the quantity of foreign exchange that dealers and other sellers want to sell, then the domestic currency/foreign currency exchange rate is deemed to be "too" high and is predicted to fall. In this case, dealers and other buyers and sellers will bid down the price, cost or value of foreign exchange because it is deemed to be "overvalued".

We can express this situation from a different perspective: if the price, cost or value or foreign exchange is deemed to be overvalued, then the willingness to buy foreign exchange is predicted to decrease and/or the willingness to sell foreign exchange is predicted to increase. Lower willingness to buy and higher willingness to sell will both tend to decrease the overvalued price, as represented in Figure 14-17.

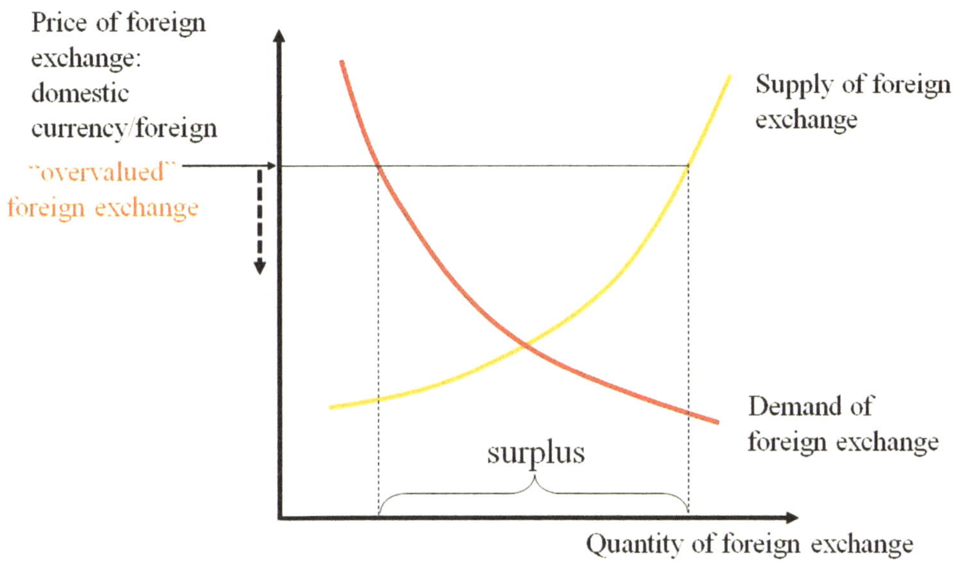

Figure 14-17: Overvalued foreign exchange tends to fall in value when the willingness to buy (quantity demanded) is less than the willingness to sell (quantity supplied).

If the quantity of foreign exchange that dealers and other buyers want to buy is greater than the quantity of foreign exchange that dealers and other sellers want to sell, then the domestic currency/foreign currency exchange rate is deemed to be "too" low and is predicted to rise. In this case, dealers and other buyers and sellers will bid up the price, cost or value of foreign exchange because it is deemed to be "undervalued".

From a different perspective, if the price, cost or value or foreign exchange is deemed to be undervalued, then the willingness to buy foreign exchange is predicted to increase and/or the willingness to sell foreign exchange is predicted to decrease. Higher willingness to buy and lower willingness to sell will both tend to increase the undervalued price, as represented in Figure 14-18.

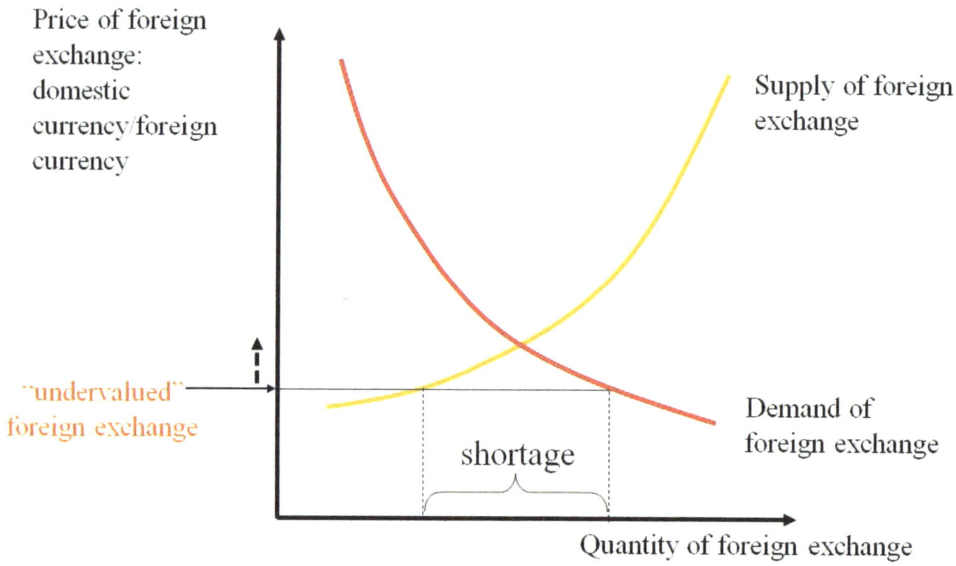

Figure 14-18: Undervalued foreign exchange tends to rise in value when the willingness to buy (quantity demanded) is greater than the willingness to sell (quantity supplied).

In sum, flexible exchange rates will tend to adjust in logical ways when traders believe that foreign exchange is "overvalued" or "undervalued": overvalued rates will tend to fall and undervalued rates will tend to rise. But opinions about the "true" value of foreign exchange vary, so adjustment always occurs, especially after various economic and financial factors change, which we consider next.

Factors affecting exchange rates

Factors that affect the willingness to buy and the willingness to sell foreign exchange are related to foreign and domestic assets, goods and services that we also want to buy and to sell. In particular, these factors represent the (expected) value, price, cost or risk of buying or selling foreign and domestic assets, goods and services. We represent changes in these factors by changing demand of foreign exchange or supply of foreign exchange or both.

Interest, yield and return rates. If domestic interest, yield and return rates increase relative to foreign rates while other factors remain constant, domestic assets become more attractive relative to foreign assets for savers/investors. Domestic and foreign savers and lenders will then want to save and invest in more domestic currency and other domestic assets relative to foreign currency/assets. We can represent this change as a decrease in demand and/or an increase in supply of foreign exchange. When either the willingness to buy foreign exchange decreases or the willingness to sell foreign currency increases, the price and value of foreign exchange is predicted to depreciate and the price and value of domestic currency is predicted to appreciate. We represent these changes in Figure 14-19 and Figure 14-20:

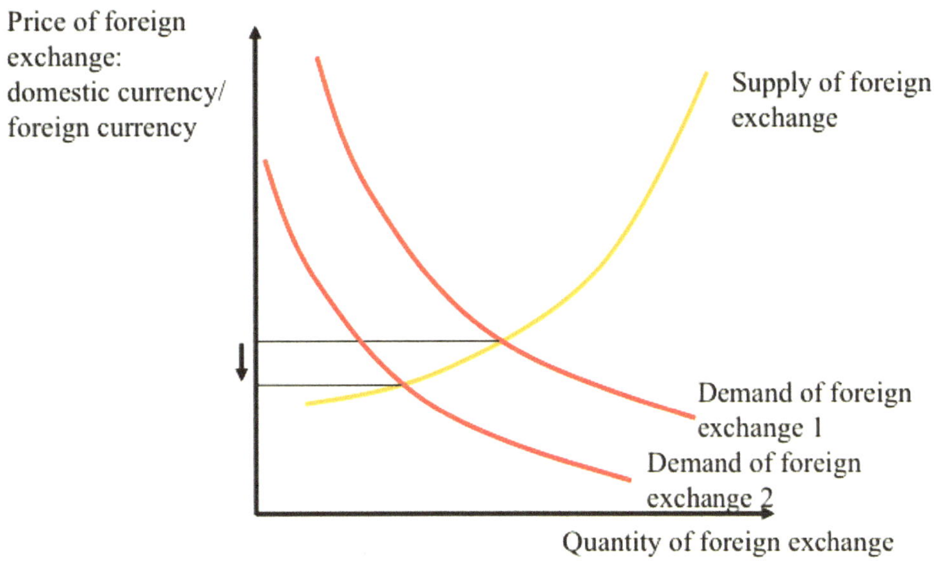

Figure 14-19: When domestic interest, yield and return rates increase relative to foreign rates, the demand of foreign exchange (from domestic citizens) decreases and the value of domestic currency increases (the exchange rate decreases).

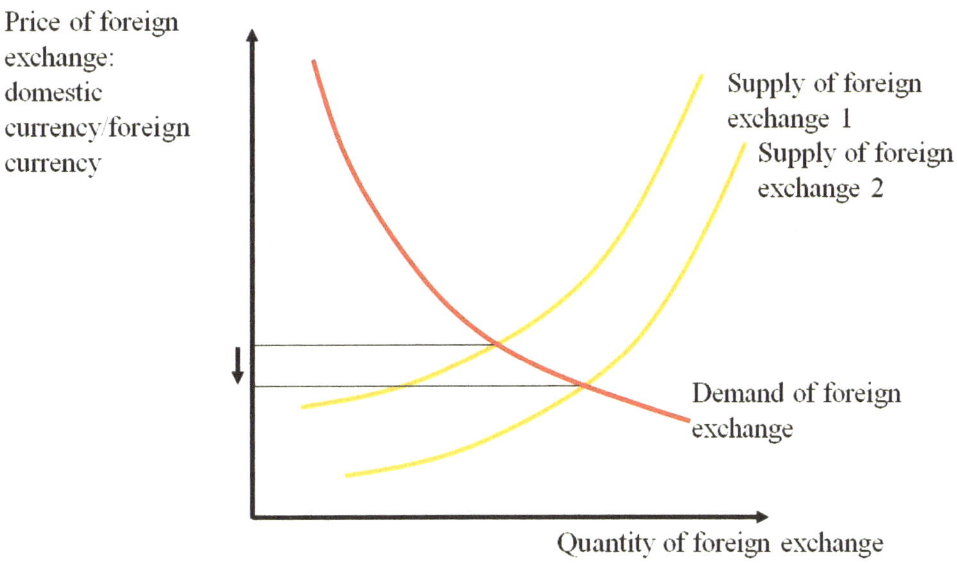

Figure 14-20: When domestic interest, yield and return rates increase relative to foreign rates, the supply of foreign exchange (from foreign citizens) increases and the value of the domestic currency increases (the exchange rate decreases).

However, when other factors like risk and inflation change with interest, yield and return rates, this prediction becomes invalid. In particular, when expected inflation and risk increase, interest and yield rates tend to increase to compensate savers, but the value of the domestic currency tends to depreciate because of the higher expected inflation and risk. Also, when expected inflation and risk increase, expected (real) return rates tend to decrease as market prices decrease to reflect the higher expected inflation and risk. The value of the domestic currency likewise tends to depreciate. The next paragraph considers the effect of risk and a related concept called liquidity:

Risk and liquidity of assets. If domestic assets become more risky and less liquid (less able to be sold for cash) relative to foreign assets, the demand of foreign exchange will increase and/or the supply of foreign exchange will decrease. The domestic currency is then predicted to depreciate, foreign currency is predicted to appreciate, and the exchange rate is predicted to increase. These effects can be shown in Figure 14-21 or Figure 14-22.

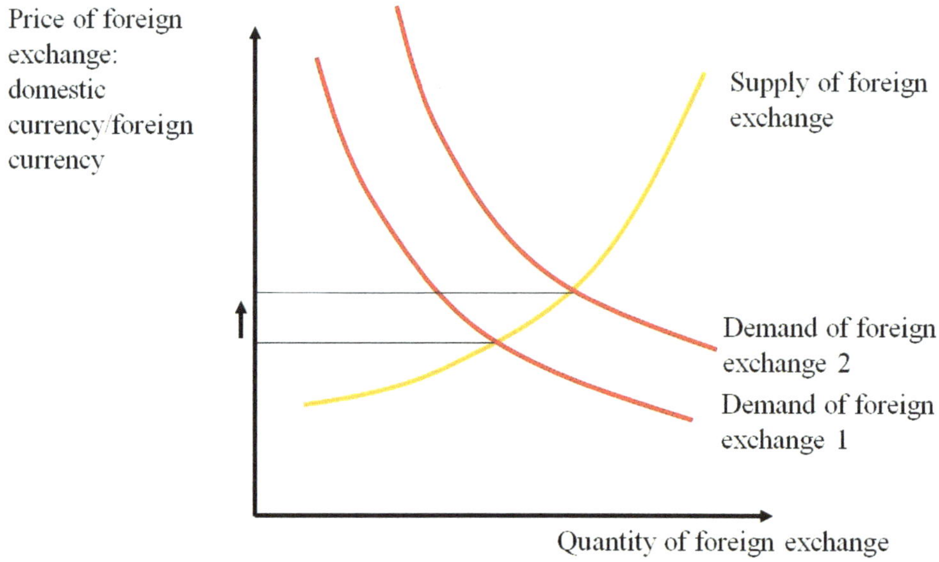

Figure 14-21: When the risk of domestic assets increases and/or their liquidity decreases, the demand of foreign exchange (from domestic citizens) increases and value of the domestic currency decreases (the exchange rate increases).

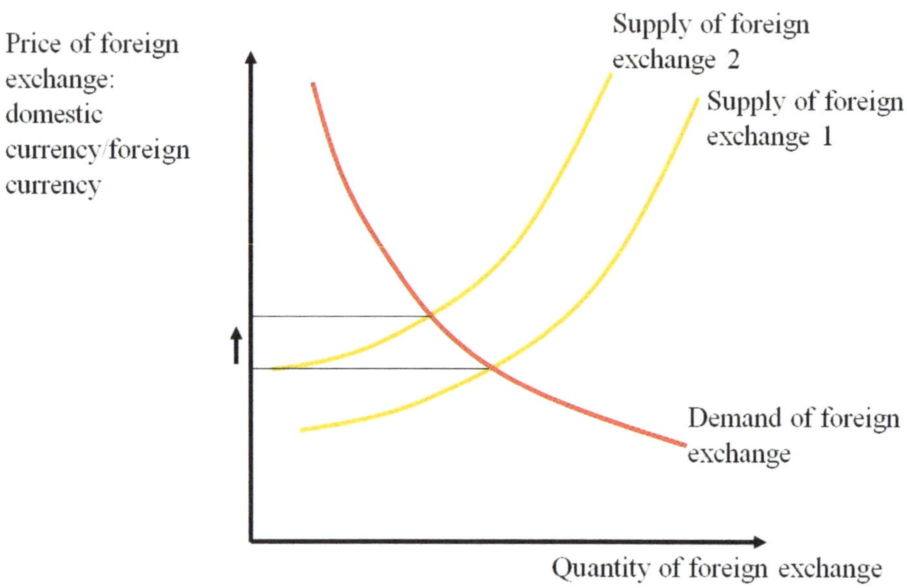

Figure 14-22: When the risk of domestic assets increases and/or their liquidity decreases, the supply of foreign exchange (from foreign citizens) decreases and value of the domestic currency decreases (the exchange rate increases).

Inflation rates. As we learned earlier, prices of goods and services are weakly correlated with exchange rates in the long run. According to the model, if the prices of domestic goods and services rise more quickly than the prices of foreign goods and services and other factors remain constant, the demand of foreign goods, services and currency will increase and the demand of domestic goods, services and currency will decrease. These changes are represented as an increase in demand and/or an decrease in supply of foreign exchange, as shown in Figure 14-21 and Figure 14-22. Likewise, the value of the domestic currency depreciates and the value of the foreign currency appreciates.

Growth rates in production, productivity, income, revenue and expenditure. Domestic or national production, productivity, income, revenue and expenditure are all directly related to each other. And growth rates in these variables affect exchange rates in multiple ways. Firstly, as domestic income increases (relative to foreign income), domestic citizens can afford to spend more on imports, so that the demand of foreign exchange increases, and the domestic currency is predicted to depreciate due to this factor alone. On the other hand, as production and productivity increase, producers can sell more exports more cheaply, so that the supply of foreign exchange (and the demand of domestic currency) can increase and value of the domestic can appreciate. Thirdly, as production, productivity and revenue of domestic firms increase, the stocks, bonds and other securities issued by these firms are expected to earn a higher return rate. Therefore, the desirability of these assets denominated in domestic currency will increase and the willingness to sell foreign exchange to acquire domestic currency will increase. Likewise, the price, cost or value of domestic currency is predicted to appreciate. However, the net effect of all of these effects is unclear, so we can not make a clear prediction how changes in production, productivity, income, revenue and expenditure will affect exchange rates.

Actions of the central bank and the government. The central bank can affect the exchange rate by exchanging its official international reserves for domestic currency. Formally, the willingness to buy foreign exchange or the willingness to sell foreign exchange can change according to the wishes of the central bank.

In the extreme case, the central bank may try to fix the exchange rate by buying and selling official international reserves and domestic currency, as represented in Figure 14-23. In this case, the central bank adjusts the quantity of foreign exchange relative to the quantity of domestic currency by changing its willingness to buy or to sell until the price, value or cost of foreign exchange reaches a targeted (fixed) rate.

The central bank or the government can also affect the exchange rate by affecting net funds outflow or net exports through capital and credit controls, taxes on asset income, tariffs on imports, or quotas on imports and exports. Alternatively, governments can affect net funds outflows net exports through bilateral and multilateral free trade agreements.

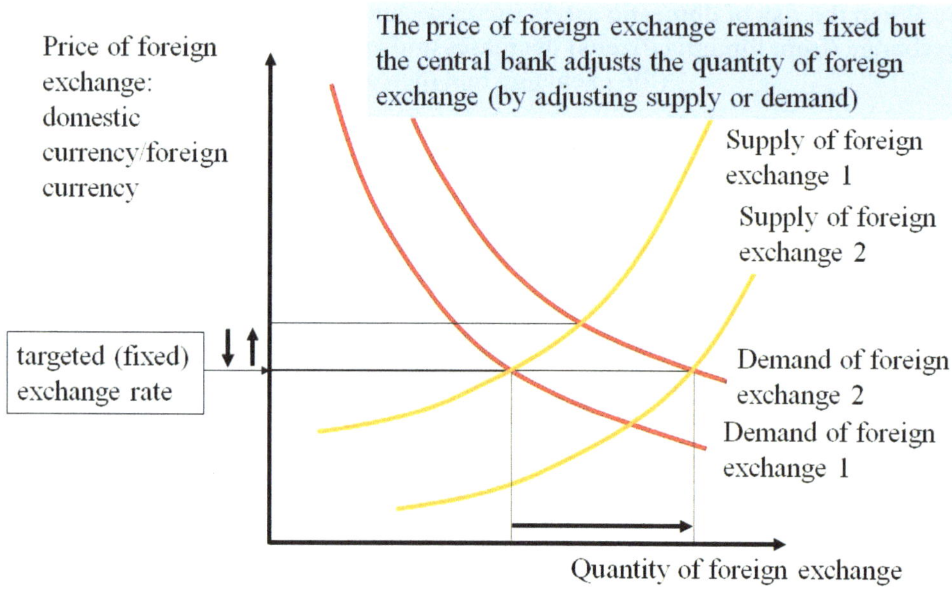

Figure 14-23: The central bank can adjust the supply or demand of foreign exchange, thereby adjusting the quantity of foreign exchange, until the exchange rate reaches a targeted (fixed) rate.

When the central bank buys and sells foreign exchange, it *directly* affects the willingness to buy or the willingness to sell foreign exchange and the exchange rate. It can also *indirectly* affect them through a **signal**, a sign of public information that indicates how the exchange rate should change in the future. In other words, central bank actions may signal information about its future actions and future values of the exchange rate.

For example, if the central bank sells foreign exchange and the domestic currency appreciates, then other buyers and sellers may expect further actions and appreciation. Based on this signal and expectation, individuals and institutions may be more willing to buy domestic currency/assets and more willing to sell foreign exchange, causing the value to the domestic currency to appreciate further. On the other hand, individuals and institutions may expect the opposite, especially when the central bank has limited quantities of official international reserves, and therefore a limited ability to sell official international reserves to influence the exchange rate. (Domestic currency can be freely printed by the central bank if necessary, so it effectively has an unlimited quantity to sell.) If people believe that the central bank does not have sufficient official international reserves to permanently influence the exchange rate, then we can expect/speculate about a devaluation, which influences our willingness to buy and to sell foreign exchange.

Expectations and speculation. In general, if traders/arbitrageurs/speculators expect a currency to appreciate (depreciate), they will want to buy more (less) of that currency and assets denominated with it. Formally, the demand of this currency increases (decreases) and its supply decreases (increases). As a result, the currency actually appreciates (depreciates).

Expectations about the value of a currency may change due to the factors that can actually change its value: changes in interest/yield/return rates, risk and liquidity of assets, prices of goods and services, growth in production/productivity/income/revenue/expenditure and central bank actions.

Due to public information or **common knowledge**—public information that is believed to be commonly known and commonly accepted as true—traders and dealers can have common expectations about future changes in the value of foreign exchange/domestic currency and can therefore adjust their buying and selling behavior in tandem. As a result, the value of a currency can depreciate often suddenly and sharply due to herd-like selling of the currency with common knowledge.

A **speculative attack** refers to widespread selling (short) of a currency because traders/dealers speculate or expect that the value of the currency will depreciate, often because of public information and common knowledge. During 1997, there were speculative attacks against the Thai bhat, Malaysian ringgit, Indonesian rupiah, Philippine peso and the won. Countries with these currencies had fixed exchange rates at the time but persistent negative exports and excessive borrowing in foreign currencies, so central banks had difficulty acquiring foreign exchange and only limited foreign exchange to sell to maintain the fixed exchange rate. This information was public and news reports made it common knowledge. After these attacks, the central banks had to abandon the fixed exchange rates because they had depleted their official international reserves, with the exception of Malaysian central bank, which imposed limits on further buying of foreign exchange (as well as capital and credit controls).

Speculation can more generally create a *bubble* (an overvalued value) or a *crash* (a sudden decline in value to an undervalued value) often because of public information common knowledge. In the case of either a bubble or a crash, market values can deviate from a "fundamental" or "equilibrium" value when repeated or reinforcing changes in buying, selling and prices occur. Widespread and herd-like buying or selling can repeatedly change the demand or supply of foreign exchange and repeatedly change the price, cost or value of foreign exchange. As a result, price, cost or value of foreign exchange can remain overvalued or undervalued or can become overvalued or undervalued slowly or suddenly. Formally, an increase (a decrease) in demand and the value of foreign exchange causes further increases (decreases) in demand and the value of foreign exchange if such changes are expected to continue. These repeated and reinforcing effects are represented in Figure 14-24.

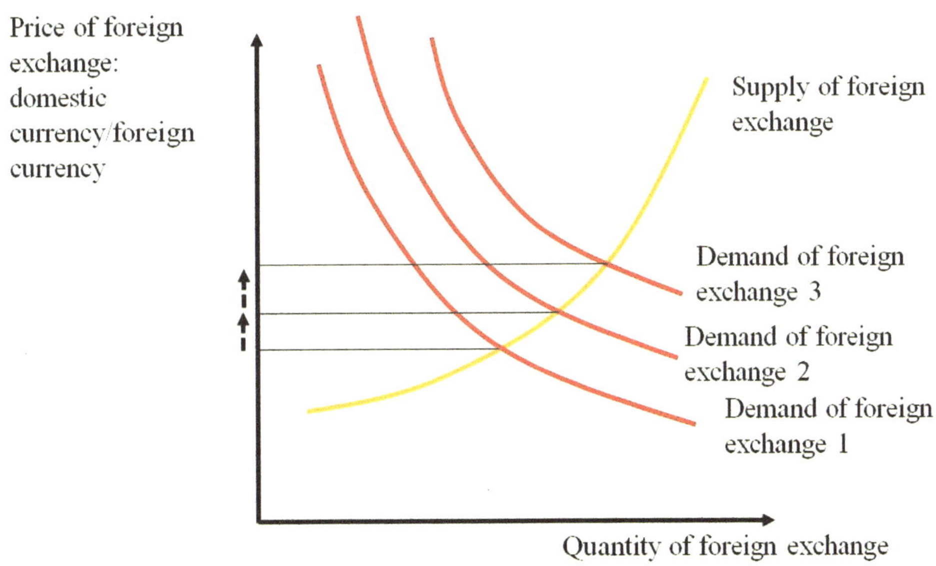

Figure 14-24: An increase in demand increases the value of foreign exchange, which can further increase demand and the value of foreign exchange.

On the other hand, expectations and speculation can also cause exchange rates to revert to an unspecified "fundamental" or "equilibrium" value after changes in demand and supply occur. Formally, an increase (a decrease) in demand increases (decreases) the value/price/cost of foreign exchange, which increases (decreases) the quantity supplied and decreases (increases) the quantity demanded. This stabilizing effect of changes in buying and selling behavior is represented in Figure 14-25.

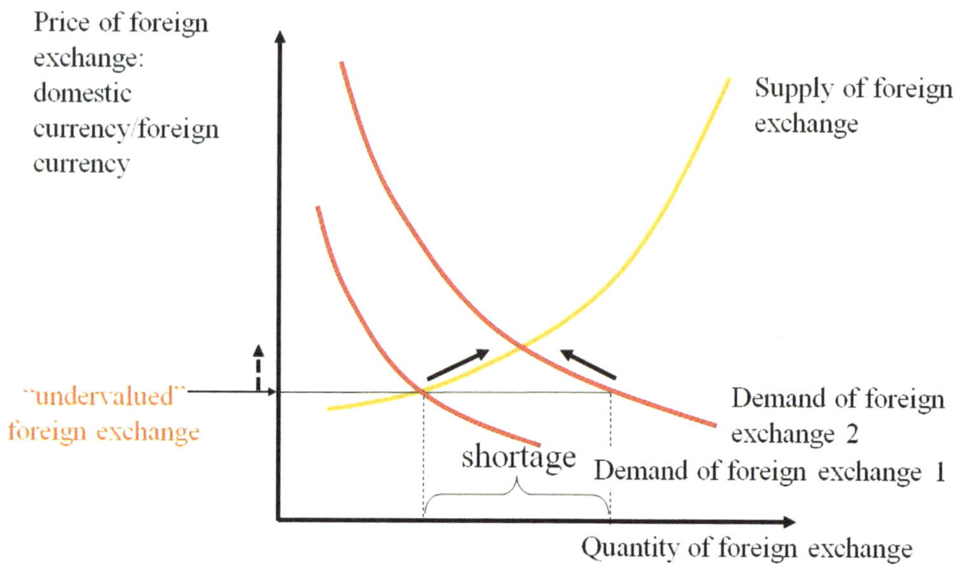

Figure 14-25: Speculation or expectations about undervalued foreign exchange when the demand of foreign exchange increases can eliminate the low value, causing it to increase to its "fundamental" or "equilibrium" value.

In sum, because speculation, expectations and corresponding behavior can create overvalued or undervalued foreign exchange or can eliminate these deviations from a "fundamental" value, it is unclear at a point in time how they will ultimately affect the value of a currency.

Speculation and forecasting exchange rates

Speculators speculate about changes in exchange rates, just as they do for changes in stock and bond prices. And it is easy to speculate these days by using contracts from the futures market, which allow one to bet on a future price relative to the contract price for a small fee.

Speculators might believe that they are smarter than other traders and dealers and can quickly take advantage of a profitable opportunity. When smart people in a market quickly recognize a profitable situation and quickly take advantage of it, the market is said to be **efficient**. The **efficient market hypothesis** says that speculating about changes in asset prices is a waste of time, at best, because the (foreign exchange) market is efficient. This hypothesis claims that if speculating were really profitable over time, some smart people among the thousands or millions of buyers and sellers would have recognized this potentially profitable situation and would have quickly profited from it by quickly buying an undervalued asset and/or by quickly selling an overvalued asset until the undervalued prices rise and/or the overvalued prices fall and the profitable situation disappears. Investors can get lucky occasionally and profit from an undervalued price or overvalued price, but it is hard to consistently out-smart other traders and dealers. (Try it if you like to gamble.)

Speculators might believe that they can beat others in the market, and they therefore try to forecast future exchange rates. Popular methods are macroeconomic analysis, monitoring order flows and imposing upper and lower bounds on exchange rates. However, all of these methods have problems and may be little or no better than guessing, especially if the market is viewed as efficient.

Macroeconomic analysis. Some economists try to forecast exchange rates using the variables that we considered in the model of supply and demand and possibly other macroeconomic variables. Many are interested in forecasting or predicting exchange rates in the "long run" especially if they recognize that short run changes are unpredictable and highly volatile.

However, because many macroeconomic variables can change at the same time, the model of supply and demand and macroeconomic analysis quickly becomes cumbersome and hard-to-follow because it effectively requires that only one variable change at a time. Also, it is difficult to distinguish between a change in demand (or supply) that causes changes in exchange rates and a change in quantity demanded (or quantity supplied) caused by changes in exchange rates. That is, it is difficult to distinguish cause and effect in reality even though the model clearly separates them. Finally, macroeconomic data used for the model is often inaccurate, incomplete and difficult to collect.

Order flow. Some speculators look at the flow of buy and sell orders to determine if demand is greater than supply, or vice versa, and then forecast how exchange rates will change in the immediate future. Based on this immediate forecast, many are interested decision whether to buy or to sell a currency for a profit. The decision rule is simple: if buy orders from various dealers and traders for a currency exceed their sell orders, then the value of the currency is predicted to appreciate in the immediate future (as soon as the orders can be completed). Therefore, the speculator should buy more of the currency because it is expected to appreciate. If buy orders are less than sell orders, then the value of the currency is predicted to depreciate in the immediate future (as soon as the orders can be completed). Therefore, the speculator should sell more of the currency because it is expected to depreciate. Figure 14-26 represents the order flow forecasting method and its supposed relationship to the actual value of a currency.

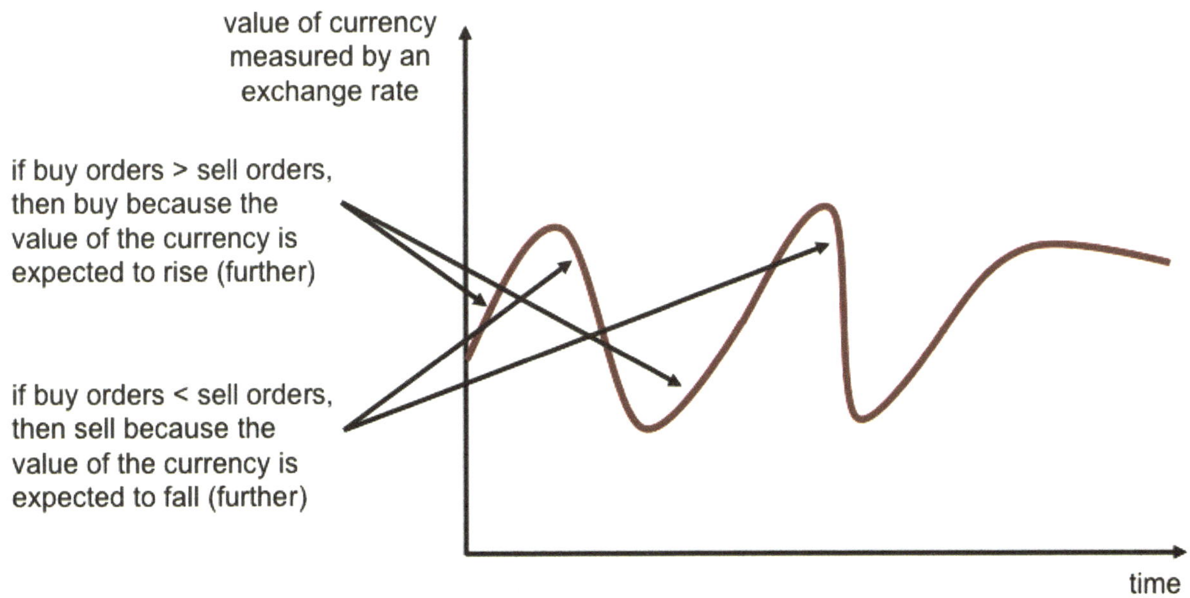

Figure 14-26: Forecasting the value of a currency (exchange rates) and deciding to buy or to sell a currency after comparing buy orders and sell orders from various traders and dealers

While this rule may seem logical, it might be based on limited data, leading to an incorrect prediction. And even if data are complete/correct, tomorrow's data could reverse today's analysis, and it is unclear how long a predicted trend will continue. In other words, it is unclear whether a currency that appreciates today will continue to appreciate tomorrow or will instead depreciate. Likewise, it is unclear whether a currency that depreciates today will continue to depreciate tomorrow or will instead appreciate.

Unlike the order flow method, the next forecasting method assumes appreciation will eventually reverse itself and depreciation will also eventually reverse itself.

Upper and lower bounds. Another prediction or decision rule is based on trends over time and the assumption that the exchange rate or the value of a currency will gravitate towards a median value over time, between an upper bound and a lower bound. One decision rule is that a trader or dealer should sell a currency when its value reaches an upper bound, because above this upper bound the currency is considered "over-valued" and therefore the value is expected to fall. A second decision rule is that a trader or dealer should buy a currency when its value reaches a lower bound, because below this lower bound the currency is considered "under-valued and therefore its value is expected to rise. Figure 14-27 represents the upper and lower bound forecasting method and decision rule.

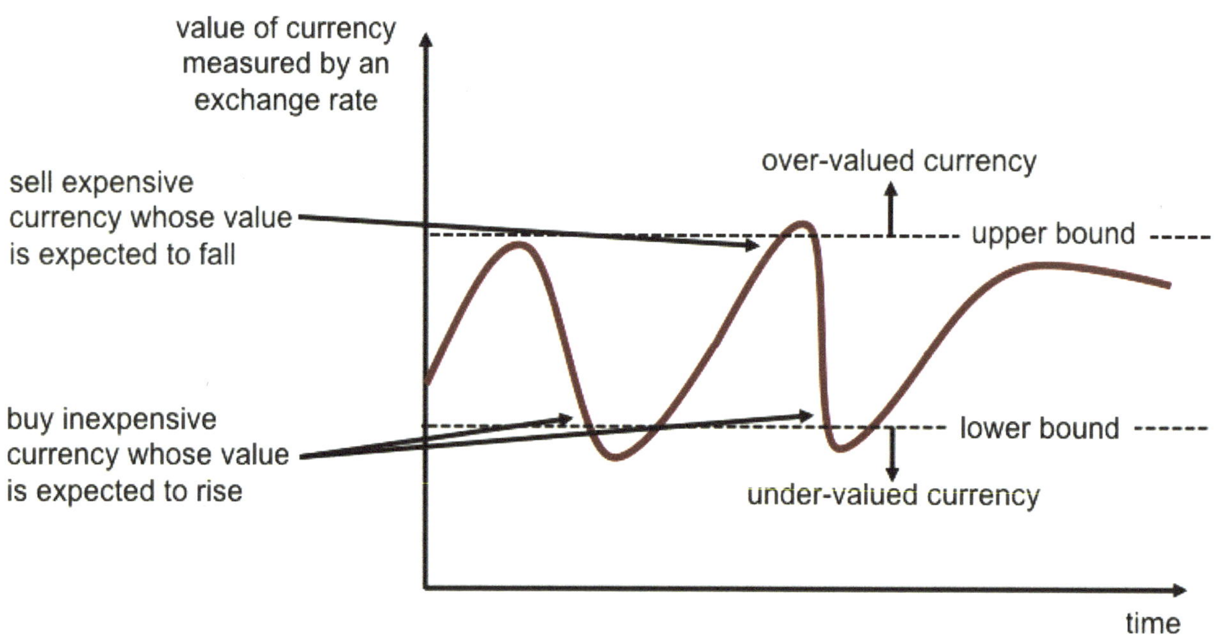

Figure 14-27: Forecasting the value of a currency (exchange rates) and deciding to buy or to sell a currency according to a chosen upper and lower bounds to the value of the currency.

As with forecasting based on macroeconomic analysis and the order flows, forecasting based on upper and lower bounds may seem logical and intuitive, but no one knows how to definitively assign the correct upper and lower bounds for a currency value and when a currency becomes overvalued or undervalued. Likewise, it is difficult to assign a trend to this forecasting method, to account for "fundamentally" rising or falling values over a long or sustained period. On the other hand, if a lower bound and upper bound are common knowledge (and many people therefore use them), then they will be correct because market values will change based on their buying and selling, which are based on the same rule.

Summary

Foreign exchange represents a foreign asset, like foreign currency, than can be exchanged for domestic currency or another domestic asset. The foreign exchange "market" is actually a set of decentralized markets around the world where traders, dealers and other buyers and sellers buy and sell to take advantage of arbitrage, to hedge or insure against possible future changes in the value of foreign exchange by using the forward exchange rate or to speculate about possible future changes.

Spot market exchange rates are largely unpredictable based on public information, although the volatility of changes in exchange rates tends to be correlated over time. Moreover, changes in spot market exchange rates can be huge—possibly resulting in huge losses—because of an unexpected devaluation, financial crisis or government intervention. Also, forward exchange rates, representing one kind of future exchange rate, do not predict future exchange rates well, but instead largely track the unpredictable spot market exchange rates.

Some factors are somewhat related to exchange rates, even if they are also unpredictable: changes in interest, yield and return rates on assets; the risk and liquidity of assets; prices of goods and services; production, productivity, income, revenue and expenditure; central bank actions and speculation. Given changes in these factors, we can predict how exchange rates should change based on the demand and supply of foreign exchange. However, sometimes the demand and supply model gives unclear or ambiguous predictions, which is perhaps good since exchange rates are largely. Nonetheless, speculators might use this model or other methods like order flow and upper/lower bounds to predict and to forecast exchange rates.

Problems and Applications

Short answer problems

1. How does an arbitrager differ from a speculator? How does a speculator differ from a hedger?

2. What is an exchange rate spread or margin?

3. What is forward spread or margin? If currency x is expected to depreciate, should the forward spread or margin be positive or negative, when we use $F(x/y)$ as the forward exchange rate?

4. What is the theory called which predicts that changes in domestic prices are inversely related to changes in the value of the domestic currency, when other factors like foreign prices remain constant?

5. Why is the US$ the most frequently used currency in the foreign exchange market?

6. What are the weights in an exchange rate index?

7. Why must we calculate an index when we want a weighted average exchange rate for a currency?

8. How can expectations and speculation create a bubble or a crash? How can expectations or speculation cause a value to reach its "fundamental" or "equilibrium" value?

9. What is common knowledge and how can it affect buying and selling behavior in the foreign exchange market?

10. How do central banks affect the exchange rates directly? How can they affect exchange rate through a signal?

11. Why do changes production, productivity, income, revenue and expenditure result in ambiguous predictions in the demand and supply model of foreign exchange?

Internet applications

1. Go to http://ecos.bok.or.kr/ and graph the following exchange rates from the earliest month to the latest month: ₩/US$, ¥/US$, 元 (yuan)/US$, £/US$, €/US$ and Taiwan$/US$. Which currency has appreciated the most relative to the US dollar during the last 10 years? Which currency has depreciated the most relative to the US dollar during the last 10 years?

2. Go to http://ecos.bok.or.kr/ and graph the *percent change* in the following exchange rates from the earliest month to the latest month: ₩/US$, ¥/US$, 元 (yuan)/US$, £/US$, €/US$ and Taiwan$/US$. Calculate the standard deviation of these changes for 5-year periods. Which 5-year period had the largest standard deviation (the largest volatility)? Which 5-year period had the smallest standard deviation (the smallest volatility)?

3. Go to http://www.federalreserve.gov/releases/h10/weights/default.htm and create 2 graphs of the total trade weights for the US$ exchange rate index: 1 for the latest year and 1 for the earliest year (1973). How large is Korea's weight currently? Which country/region has the largest weight currently? Which country/region has the largest weight in 1973?

4. Go to http://ecos.bok.or.kr/ and graph the average ₩/US$ exchange rate with Korean consumer prices/US consumer prices from the earliest month to the latest month. Relative consumer prices should have one scale (an index) and the ₩/US$ should have another scale (in monetary units).

5. Go to http://ecos.bok.or.kr/ and graph foreign currency reserves and total (official) international reserves of the Bank of Korea from the earliest date to the latest date.